Date Due

NOV. 30	FEB 1 0 1977	JUN 1 6 1984
APR. 1	APR 1 4 1977	OCT 9
MAR. 15	OCT 1 5 1977	JAN
APR. 23	JUN 1 9 1978	
MAY 18	MAY 1 9 1979	
De 20 73	SEP 1 3 197	
Ja 1974	JAN 2 8	
Oc 1 74	APP	
No 2 74		
Fe 1 '75		
Mr 14 '75		
My 9 '75		
NOV 3		
OCT		

111622

917.1   Putnam, Donald Fulton, 1903–
Put   Canada: a regional analysis [by] Donald
          F. Putnam [and] Robert G. Putnam. Toronto,
          Dent, 1970.
              390 p. illus.

              Includes bibliography.

RELATED   } 1. Canada – Descr. & trav. I. Putnam,
BOOKS IN   Robert G. II. Title.
CATALOG
UNDER   77255

6

CANADA: a regional analysis

Donald F. Putnam, B.S.A., Ph.D.

Robert G. Putnam, B.A., M.A.

J. M. DENT AND SONS (CANADA) LIMITED

ISBN 0-460-90390-x

ACKNOWLEDGEMENTS

Where the drafting of the maps in this book has involved extensive use of information
from existing maps, separate credit lines appear. Likewise, all photographs carry separate
credit lines with the exception of the following:
photo facing page 1, courtesy National Capital Commission
photo facing page 251, courtesy Prairie Farm Rehabilitation Administration

Maps by H. E. Mindak

Cover design by Louise Parks

Printed and bound in Canada

Preface

Canada is a great and changing country and a continuing challenge to further study. Geography, no less than history and economics, must continue to offer new insights into the growth and development of Canada. While retaining many of the features of its predecessors, this study makes use of new techniques and offers new interpretations of Canadian geography. It is hoped that these will prove helpful to both students and teachers as well as seekers of general information about Canada. Particular emphasis has been placed upon the background of human geography, especially on the growth of population and the development of cities and industries in various parts of the country.

In this book, our own field research has been complemented by various papers which have been published by other geographers. Wherever possible, these sources have been footnoted and listed in the bibliography at the end of each chapter. Some of the articles cited have been reprinted in books of readings, such as R. R. Krueger's *Regional and Resource Planning in Canada*, R. L. Gentilcore's *Canada's Changing Geography*, and R. M. Irving's *Readings in Canadian Geography*. The growth of this type of book will serve to augment the materials readily available to students of Canadian geography, and their use is encouraged.

We are grateful to many individuals without whose help and unfailing encouragement this volume would not have been written. Professor D. P. Kerr, chairman of the Department of Geography, University of Toronto, contributed many useful ideas and was especially helpful in the organization of CHAPTER 3.

We would also like to take the opportunity to thank Mrs. D. F. Putnam and Mrs. R. G. Putnam for their assistance in typing manuscript and proof-reading.

D. F. Putnam

R. G. Putnam

Contents

1 Introduction

2 The Physical Resource Base

iv

3 *The Human Geography of Canada*

4 *The Atlantic Provinces*

5

Quebec

6

Ontario

7

The Prairies

8   *British Columbia*

9   *The Canadian Northland*

10 *Transportation*

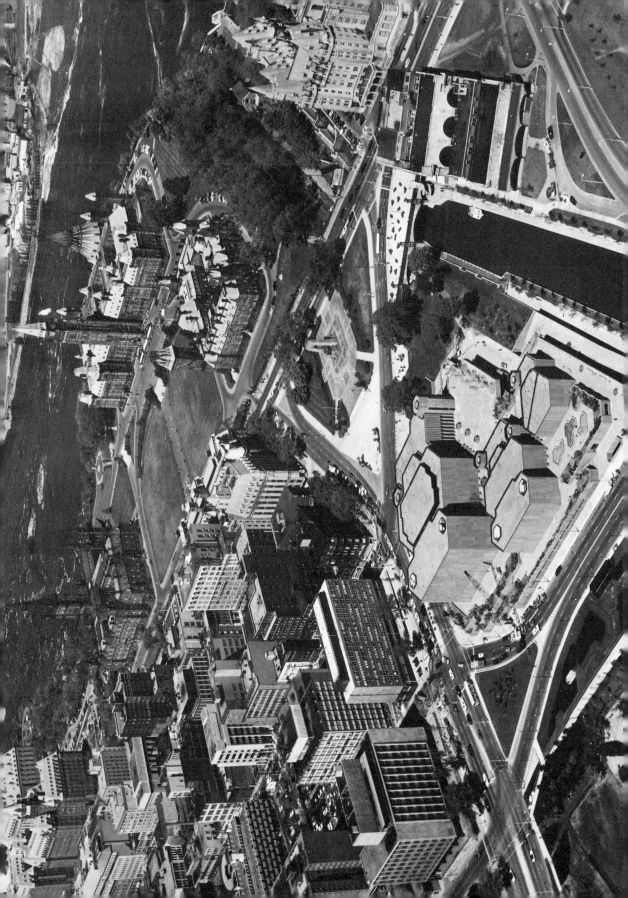

Introduction

1   Canada comprises the northern half of continental North America, with the exception of Alaska, and all of the Arctic archipelago, with the exception of Greenland. It has an area of more than 3,851,000 square miles, including land and fresh-water surfaces, thus forming a national territory more extensive than any other in the world except that of Soviet Russia.

In longitude, Canada extends from Cape Spear, Newfoundland, at 52°32' W, to the Alaskan boundary at 141°00' W, an airline distance of 3,322 miles. The latitude of the most southerly point of land, Middle Island in Lake Erie, is 41°41' N, and that of the most northerly, Cape Columbia on Ellesmere Island, is 83°7' N, while the airline distance between is 2,875 miles. Within an area of such extent and global location, there is obviously room for a great variety of physical environments, while sheer distance will, itself, be a major factor in promoting geographical diversity.

Any atlas or wall map will show that Canada is divided into a number of political units. The larger, southern part of the country is composed of ten provinces, each of which possesses a considerable degree of political autonomy under the provisions of the British North America Act. From west to east the provinces are: British Columbia, Alberta, Saskatchewan, Manitoba, Ontario, Quebec, New Brunswick, Prince Edward Island, Nova Scotia, and Newfoundland. Together they comprise three-fifths of the total area. Yukon Territory and the Northwest Territories make up the remaining two-fifths of the country. The political divisions of Canada exert considerable influence upon the development of its economy and on the differentiation of its geographic regions.

THE THEORY OF REGIONS

What is a region? This question has haunted geographers for a long time. Gordon East has written, "There is only one region — the surface of the earth — on which mankind finds its home."* Yet, certainly, geographical descriptions may be written about areas smaller than the totality of the earth's surface. Many of

these are obvious and easily distinguished from all other constituent areas of the world. Continents such as Africa and Australia come to mind, or countries such as France and Spain. Canada, the subject of the present enquiry, may readily be accepted as an area suitable for special geographical study.

The definition of regions for study in greater detail, however, is fraught with many difficulties. The question is often asked, "Do regions exist? Do they form demonstrable entities on the earth's sur-

---

* Roger Minshull. *Regional Geography — Theory and Practice.* (Editorial Preface by W. G. East). Aldine Publishing Company. Chicago. 1967.

1

Table 1.1   Areas, Populations, and Capitals *

	Area In Sq. Mi.	% of Total Area	Population Census of 1966	Pop. Per Sq. Mi.	% of Total Pop.	Capital City	Pop. Including Suburbs
Provinces							
Newfoundland	156,185	4.1	493,396	3.16	2.5	St. John's	101,161
Prince Edward Island	2,184	0.1	108,535	49.80	0.5	Charlottetown	18,427
Nova Scotia	21,425	0.6	756,039	35.30	3.8	Halifax	198,193
New Brunswick	28,354	0.7	616,788	21.80	3.1	Fredericton	22,460
Quebec	594,860	15.5	5,780,845	9.74	28.9	Quebec	413,397
Ontario	412,582	10.7	6,960,870	16.90	34.8	Toronto	2,158,496
Manitoba	251,000	6.5	963,066	3.83	4.8	Winnipeg	508,759
Saskatchewan	251,700	6.5	955,344	3.80	4.8	Regina	131,127
Alberta	255,285	6.6	1,463,202	5.75	7.3	Edmonton	401,299
British Columbia	366,255	9.5	1,873,674	5.12	9.4	Victoria	173,455
Ten Provinces	2,339,830	60.7	19,971,759	8.53	99.8		
Territories							
Yukon Territory	207,076	5.4	14,382	.07	0.1	Whitehorse	4,771
Northwest Territories	1,304,903	33.9	28,738	.02	0.1	Yellowknife	3,741
Northern Territories	1,511,979	39.3	43,120	.03	0.2		
CANADA	3,851,809	100.0	20,014,879	5.20	100.0	Ottawa	429,761

* Data from D.B.S. Ottawa.

face?" The answer cannot be categorically "yes" or "no". Certainly, some areas are so distinct from their surroundings that they may very easily be recognized. The complex mountain area known as the Alps, the dry plateau of the Spanish Meseta, the desert of the American Southwest, and the Barren Lands of Northern Canada are all strikingly different from adjoining areas. They are also relatively homogeneous in the broad patterns of their landscapes. No one seeing these areas could deny that definite regions do exist.

Many areas of the earth's surface, however, do not exhibit such obvious distinctiveness and homogeneity, while their boundaries are much more difficult to define. Can such areas be called regions, or may they be divided into acceptable regions of lesser extent?

When we look again at the areas that have recognizable identities, we see that they may be defined by use of very few characteristics or factors. The desert lacks vegetation. The mountains are elevated

and rugged; they are defined in terms of relief. Both regions, in fact, may be said to have been segregated because of single dominant characteristics. They may be further subdivided on the basis of the intensity of the occurrence or the degree of influence of such factors.

Canada may be divided into single-factor regions on the basis of such factors as landform, climate, vegetation, and soils. Associations of landforms are quite apparent. The Canadian Shield, the western Cordillera, the Appalachians, and the Interior Plains, all have fairly definite limits, encompassing areas of relatively strong physical homogeneity. Although perhaps less clearly defined, the vegetation pattern of forest, grassland, and tundra may also be used as the basis of a system of visual regions. Behind the pattern of vegetation lies a much more complex system of climatic regions, which is much less obvious and which may only be established through the examination of meteorological statistics. Analysis in terms of single-factor regions is useful for many special purposes, but it does not provide the fundamental pattern necessary for the study of Canadian regional geography.

The alternative to the single-factor region is, of course, a region defined in terms of a number of factors exerting influences simultaneously upon the same area. At one time the most popular attempt of this sort was the development of the concept of the *natural region*.

Natural regions may be defined as areas in which the influences of several dominant factors of the physical environment combine to give a natural unity to the landscape. It is possible to consider the Prairies as a natural region, for relief, climate, vegetation, and soil, together create a natural landscape which is distinctive and recognizable over a wide area. The glaciated plains and deciduous forests of Southern Ontario constitute another recognizable natural region. Peripheral to these recognizable regions, there are transition

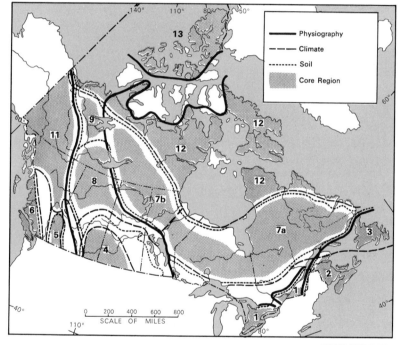

AFTER WATSON

Figure 1.1 Core and Cushion Areas in Canada
The core areas have been defined on the basis of physiography, climate, and soils.
1. Eastern Interior Lowlands; Dfb climate; gray-brown podzols.
2. Appalachians; Dfb climate; eastern podzols.
3. Appalachians; Dfc climate; eastern podzols.
4. Western Interior Lowlands; BSk climate; light brown prairie soils.
5. Intermontane Uplands; BSk climate; brown prairie soils.
6. Pacific Coast; Cfb climate; brown forest soils.
7. Southern Shield; Dfc climate; podzol soils. (*a*) moist; (*b*) dry climate.
8. Western Interior Lowlands — North-central; Dfc climate; gray wooded soils.
9. Western Interior Lowlands — North; Dfc climate; podzol soils.
10. Western Interior Lowlands — Arctic Fringe; ET climate; tundra soils.
11. Northern Cordilleras; Dfc climate; mountain podzols.
12. Northern Shield; ET climate; tundra soils.
13. Innuitias; ET climate; tundra soils.

zones: for example, the aspen groves and forests of Western Canada, and the mixed forests of Ontario and Quebec. Such juxtaposition of definite central areas and indefinite peripheral zones has been aptly designated as the "core" and "cushion" pattern of the natural environment. *

Regions based only upon the factors of the natural environment tend to be arbitrary and semi-geographic at best because they give no consideration to the influence of man who is, himself, often the most important factor in determining regional characteristics and limits. Regions based upon the realities of human, social, and economic patterns are often vastly different from those determined through analysis of natural factors alone. For example, the Great Lakes and St. Lawrence Lowlands possess somewhat similar physical conditions throughout, yet in this area human influences have produced two distinct and recognizable cultural environments. These environments are characterized by differences in language, law, and administration which are reflected in the settlement patterns, agricultural land use practices, and other elements of the cultural landscape. Thus, in terms of human geography two distinct regions have been created in what might otherwise have been regarded as relatively uniform, single, natural environment.

It is obvious that while real regions do exist and may be perceived, they do not neatly cover the whole earth; neither is the natural region, based upon a complex of physical factors, adequate for the purposes of geographic description and analysis. If true *geographic regions* are to be designated, they must be based upon a blending of the influences of both physical and human factors, highlighting the core areas and giving a recognizable unity to each region. The dominating elements in determining regional character may be human factors as in the case of Quebec, or physical factors as in the case of the Arctic regions.

* J. W. Watson. *General Geography*. Copp Clark Publishing Company Limited. Toronto. 1957. p. 267.

The human element contributes much to the structural pattern of the region; but, most importantly, it is human activity that gives function and meaning to the pattern. The layout of a highway net is almost instantly observable from aerial photographs or from maps derived from them, but the function of the highway can only be deduced from the detailed statistical study of series of observations made regularly for a year or for an even longer period of time. The highway net is only one element of the cultural landscape, here chosen to exemplify the functional approach and to emphasize the idea that the human organization of the earth's surface is based upon functional objectives. The same idea, of course, is found in the development of railways and electrical communications.

The functional unity of the region is often provided by the existence of a strong node or center of human population and activity; areas that are dominated by the influence of a centralizing node are classified as *nodal regions*. Thus the social centrality and economic power of Montreal dominate and unify the region of the St. Lawrence Lowland, while the economic domination and numerous central place functions of Toronto provide a similar nodal influence in Southern Ontario. On the other hand, the Canadian Shield and the Arctic, both of which may be recognized on the basis of certain physical characteristics, cannot be said to exhibit any special nodality at all. Moreover, these two regions can and do overlap since they are based on different physical criteria: the Arctic, climatic; the Shield, geological. They, therefore, cannot be grouped as members of the same system of regions.

Given strong similarities of the phenomena in the landscape, undergoing similar or related economic and social experiences, and subjected to centralizing forces emanating from a dominant node, the people of a region may well develop a *regional consciousness* which influences them to identify themselves closely with their region. When this happens, the observer obtains the impression of a *regional per-*

sonality which is very difficult to define but which nevertheless is unmistakably characteristic. The geographic region is therefore an intellectual construct, a mental image or, as Derwent Whittlesey expressed it, "an entity for the purposes of thought, created by the selection of certain features that are relevant to an areal interest or problem and by the disregard of all features that are considered to be irrelevant".* For such a region, the term *compage* was suggested. It is not an all-inclusive term, nor is it completely objective since it implies the use of subjective judgment on the part of the investigator in both the selection and the use of the relevant criteria. This is true even when the criteria are derived from quantified data, analyzed by means of a computer.

---

* Derwent Whittlesey *et al.* "The Regional Concept and the Regional Method." Chapter Two. Preston E. James and Clarence F. Jones (Editors). *American Geography — Inventory and Prospect.* Syracuse University Press. 1954. p. 30.

ECUMENE

Ecumene is the word used by ancient Greek writers to signify the inhabited portion of the earth's surface, thereby setting it apart from the remainder which was uninhabited. Greek geographers spent much of their effort upon the description of the *ecumene.* The term was reintroduced by German geographers early in the nineteenth century and has been subjected to varying interpretations ever since. In recent years the concept has been applied in Canadian geography, specifically by R. Gajda * and L. E. Hamelin. **

Gajda modifies and extends the concept to include work areas as well as living space. Hamelin goes even further and sets up a three-stage classification including

---

* Roman T. Gajda. "The Canadian Ecumene — Inhabited and Uninhabited Areas". *Geographical Bulletin.* No. 15 (1960). pp. 5-18.
** L. E. Hamelin. "Typologie de l'ecoumène canadien." *Mémoires de la Société Royale du Canada.* Section 1, Quatrième série, Tome IV (June, 1966).

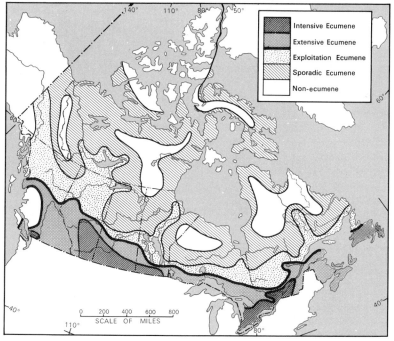

AFTER HAMELIN AND GJADA

Figure 1.2 The Canadian Ecumene
The portion of Canada south of the heavy line can be considered to be *developed.* To the north there are vast portions of Canada which as yet are not effectively utilized by man.

Table 1.2   Zones of the Canadian Ecumene

Zone	Characteristics
Intensive Ecumene	Urban occupancy and industrial patterns, intensive agriculture, services and amenities
Extensive Ecumene	Mainly rural occupancy; extensive types of agriculture; permanent, planned forest production
Exploitation Ecumene	Systematic mining development with permanent transportation facilities and power supplies
Sporadic Ecumene	Very scattered economic activities
Non-ecumene	Empty space with no foreseeable development

functional types, forms of inhabited and exploited area, and schematic zonation of the ecumene. The classification of the ecumene as shown in Figure 1.2 is therefore different from those of both Hamelin and Gajda. In summary form it is presented in Table 1.2. The *intensive* and *extensive* ecumenes together mark out the areas of Canada which have already been appropriately developed by man; they comprise the major urban areas and the important agricultural landscapes. There are four nodes of intensive development, namely, the Fraser Lowland, the Central Prairies, Southern Ontario, and Southern Quebec. On the Prairies agriculture is dominant. In the other three areas, while agriculture is more intensive than on the Prairies, it is overshadowed by the activities of urban residents who far outnumber their rural neighbors.

Beyond the intensive and extensive ecumenes, the pattern of occupancy is strongly influenced by the availability of transportation. This influence may be seen with particular clarity in the exploitation ecumene or resource frontier. For example, in such places as Pine Point, Thompson, Chibougamau, and Schefferville, all economic activity is sustained by mining, while rail connections are necessary to its continued success. Elsewhere there is a vast zone in which little permanent settlement is found and where the main activities are hunting and fishing. The large areas in which man

does not reside are here mapped as *non-ecumene*. The northern Arctic Islands, the interior and more inaccessible areas of the Canadian Shield, and the more rugged portions of the Cordillera fall into this category.

GEOGRAPHICAL REGIONS OF CANADA

Several systems of regions have been proposed in the past to further the study of Canadian geography. In 1947 Griffith Taylor presented a very ingenious system of twenty regions arranged in tiers across the map of Canada.* He used landforms, climatic data, vegetation, history of settlement, population density, and economic development as the basis of description and definition; but the number of regions — twenty — had already been predetermined as a matter of convenience. A rather more elaborate scheme was that of N. L. Nicholson and Z. W. Sametz, who proposed a series of more than sixty units based upon analysis of detailed statistical data.** While this approach may be valid for some purposes, it results in the delineation of numerous micro-regions with very arbitrary and often somewhat unreal

* Griffith Taylor. *Canada.* Methuen & Company. London. 1947.
** N. L. Nicholson and Z. W. Sametz. "Regions of Canada and the Regional Concept". *Resources for Tomorrow Conference. Background Papers.* Vol. I. Ottawa. 1961.

boundaries. It also tends to create some very large and ill-defined regions as well.

Hans Carol has pointed out that the Economic Regions of Ontario, set up according to the system of Nicholson and Sametz, do not conform to the idea of functional, city-based regions.* He states that development in Southern Ontario would be better served by a hierarchical system of regions centered on Toronto, with a second tier of four *high order* regions centered on Toronto, Ottawa, Hamilton, and London, and a third tier of *middle order* regions, centered on these cities and 15 others, having populations of more than 15,000 persons in 1961. Below these, of course, there would be other orders of regions centered on smaller cities and towns. Since Canada has several hundred cities and towns, it is evident that Carol's system could be used to set up a vast and intricate system of functional micro-regions covering the whole country.

It is not the purpose of this book to present a series of micro-regional studies in Canadian geography. Rather, it is the intention to integrate and record the interrelationships and patterns which may be shown to exist for relatively large regions. For such purposes, statistical data from both federal and provincial agencies are available and lend themselves to fairly precise analysis. In each region the approach must vary in accordance with the themes which have been selected for treatment and with the emphasis placed upon each one within the regional framework. However, to permit a country-wide perspective, both physical and human resource bases must be examined. It will thus be possible to make comparisons of the physical resources of various parts of Canada and to allow fundamental differences to become apparent. It will also be possible to compare population densities and other population characteristics, to study the

evolution of settlement forms and the development of economic activities, and thus to effect comparison of the human resource bases. Likewise, the growth, form, and function of the major urban centers contribute much to an understanding of the character of each region.

The major regions which will be described in this book include:

The Atlantic Provinces
Quebec
Ontario
The Prairie Provinces
British Columbia
The Canadian Northland

These regions are delimited in Figure 1.3. It will be admitted at once that as divisions of Canada they are largely traditional. However, while it is recognized that they are defined on the basis of political units, it should be remembered that each region possesses a definite *core* and a *transition zone*. Furthermore, the authors have found in their researches and in their travels throughout Canada that much of the regional differentiation is politically determined at the provincial level. For instance, despite the physical resemblances and, to a considerable degree, the similarities of economic potential in the Shield portions of the provinces of Ontario and Quebec, the patterns of settlement differ widely because of differences in provincial policies for resource development. *

The *Atlantic Provinces* may readily be identified as a unique region in Canada by virtue of their history of development and their present economic traits. Located on the eastern periphery of Canada, the provinces were once one of the focal points of foreign trade. Now they appear to be merely occupying a gateway which funnels trade past them into a much more active economy in Central Canada.

The economic problems facing these provinces and the requirements of any possible solutions seem to the observer to

---

* Hans Carol. The *Geographical Identification of Regional Growth Centers and Development Regions in Southern Ontario*. A Report to the Ontario Department of Economics and Development. Toronto. November, 1966. (Mimeo.)

* G. L. McDermott. "Frontiers of Settlement in the Great Clay Belt, Ontario and Quebec". *Annals, Association of American Geographers*. 51:3 (September, 1961). pp. 261-273.

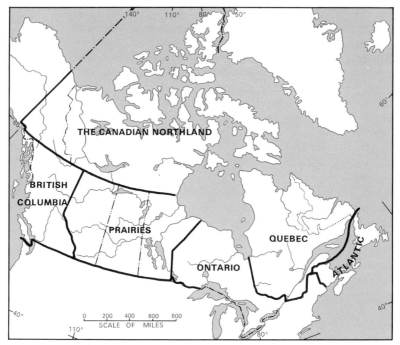

Figure 1.3 Geographical Regions of Canada

provide the Atlantic Provinces with a common objective and a common point of view. However, they have not had sufficient influence to bring about political union.

Quebec, where the major concentration of French culture in Canada is found, is also a unique region in Canada. Despite the variations in both economic development and physical resource base within the region, cultural factors provide a unifying force which results in regional identity. Economic planning and colonization efforts in Northern Quebec are all inextricably linked to Quebec City through control by the provincial government.

Ontario has the largest population and the greatest economic strength of any region in Canada. Yet economic growth in Ontario is not uniformly distributed, and a series of economic regions can be defined. Distance is a factor in promoting diversities and economic disparities within the province. However, even the most remote parts of the Ontario northland are economically linked in some degree with the more densely populated southern core of the province.

The *Prairie Provinces* form a distinct unit in Canada and have a well-developed regional personality. Rolling plains covered with grass and grain combine with subterranean resources of petroleum, natural gas, coal, and potash to give this region potentially great economic strength and, at the same time, the necessity of overcoming special problems of overproduction. The provincial boundaries extend northward beyond the true prairies to include northern fringe areas that do not possess the same physical characteristics as the rest of the region. Despite this, these areas are integral parts of the region of the Prairie Provinces because of political control and other cultural ties centered in southern core areas. Such cultural ties are strong. Agriculture in the "pioneer fringe" suffered the handicap that most settlers from southern regions wished to grow the crop with which they were most familiar even though it was not particularly suited to the new environment.

Transportation links between the fringe areas and the southern cities also provide strong unifying influences. Edmonton considers itself the gateway to the Peace River area and the Mackenzie plain. Saskatchewan has striven to provide both air and surface connections for its northern areas, while the same is true of Manitoba.

British Columbia has its own unique character, imparted on the physical level by seemingly endless mountain ranges with breathtaking scenery. On the level of human and economic geography, however, there are two subdivisions of this region: a *core* which is found in the well-developed Fraser Lowland and the southern part of Vancouver Island, and the less intensive and rather sporadic development of the rest of the region. As in the case of Quebec the provincial government exercises strong control while providing facilities for the exploitation of the resources of the interior. The provincial highways, a provincial railway, and the construction of hydro-electric plants such as the one at Hudson Hope are stages in the plan of provincial development.

The *Canadian Northland* includes the mainland north of latitude 60°N and the Arctic Islands. Politically, it is divided into Yukon Territory and the Northwest Territories. The character of the surface varies from lowland plains almost at sea level to the highest mountains in Canada, while climatically it ranges from the Subarctic with scattered light forest growth to the High Arctic where there is little vegetation except for mosses and lichens. The human population is small and scattered; there are no towns of more than 10,000 people. The economy is based on exploitation; traces of the native exploitation of biological resources still exist, but modern development is almost entirely directed toward making use of mineral resources. The chief sources of employment are found in the exploitive industries, themselves, service industries, and the functions of territorial administration.

Because no strong internal "core" area has yet developed, it is sometimes suggested that the jurisdictions of adjoining provinces should be extended northward to include sectors of the territories. The Yukon seems closely linked to British Columbia because of physical similarities, the Mackenzie Basin depends upon transportation facilities in Alberta, and Manitoba's port of Churchill has long provided access to the central portion of the Northland. However, all northern areas face similar problems of development, and it would seem that in the early stages fewer disparities will develop if a strong oversight by the federal government is maintained.

CONCLUSION

If this system of delineating the regions of Canada appears to be artificial in nature, it is probably because a non-physiographic method of selection has been employed. Regions based strictly on the major physiographic units may appear to be logical, but in the Canada of today they are not justified. Southern Ontario and Southern Quebec are different and the economic activities and regional inter-ties operate in a very different manner.

Throughout this book, an attempt has been made to include for consideration as many factors as are deemed necessary to facilitate regional analysis. Because each region is different, the emphasis in each analysis differs, as do the factors considered. In CHAPTER 2, the elements of the physical resource base are examined with a view to setting the physical stage. Human geography, or the cultural resource base, is defined and studied in CHAPTER 3 where the difficult task of synthesizing the human geography of the past, the evolution of the settlement patterns, and the overwhelmingly urban nature of Canada today has been attempted. The length of CHAPTER 3 alone suggests the importance which the authors attach to the human geography of Canada. The remaining chapters attempt to study in turn each of the regions illustrated in Figure 1.3. The final chapter has been reserved for a study of transportation, the medium which binds Canada together.

BIBLIOGRAPHY

Carol, Hans. *The Geographical Identification of Regional Growth Centers and Development Regions in Southern Ontario*. A Report to the Ontario Department of Economics and Development. Toronto. November, 1966. (Mimeo. 49 pp. 19 exhibits).

Gajda, Roman T. "The Canadian Ecumene — Inhabited and Uninhabited Areas". *Geographical Bulletin*. No. 15 (1960). pp. 5-18.

Hamelin, L. E. "Typologie de l'ecoumène canadien". *Mémoires de la Société Royale du Canada*. Section 1, Quatrième série, Tome IV (June, 1966).

James, Preston E. and Jones, Clarence F. (Editors). *American Geography — Inventory and Prospect*. Syracuse University Press. 1954.

McDermott, G. L. "Frontiers of Settlement in the Great Clay Belt, Ontario and Quebec" *Annals, Association of American Geographers*. 51:3 (September, 1961). pp. 261-273.

Minshull, Roger. *Regional Geography — Theory and Practice*. (Editorial Preface by W. G. East). Aldine Publishing Company. Chicago. 1967.

Nicholson, N. L. and Sametz, Z. W. "Regions of Canada and the Regional Concept". *Resources for Tomorrow Conference. Background Papers*. Vol. 1. Ottawa. 1961.

Taylor, Griffith. *Canada*. Methuen & Company. London. 1947.

Watson, James Wreford. *General Geography*. Copp Clark Publishing Company Limited. Toronto. 1957.

The Physical Resource Base

2 Physical factors set the stage and provide the backdrop for the unfolding of human history. They delimit and describe the space which is divided into regions by the activities of the human population. A knowledge of the ensemble of physical factors enables man, the developer, to judge to some degree at least the possibilities for development. Canada is a large country and most of its extensive area contains a sparsely distributed population. Some areas, however, appear to be already overcrowded. It seems fairly obvious that Canada needs continued population growth, and that for its support there must be continued growth in resource utilization.

In this chapter a brief survey is presented of some of the major environmental factors which must be understood in the formation of any plan of economic development or any understanding of the patterns of settlement. The rigors of climate have often been cited as a major limitation upon the development of the Canadian hinterland; nevertheless, some of the developed areas may be shown to have nearly as harsh a climate as have large undeveloped areas. The climatic pattern is, therefore, to be studied carefully. Rocks, water, vegetation, and soils are all considered as fundamental resource phenomena. The patterns of distribution of these phenomena must be understood if the human occupancy and full development of Canadian space is to be accomplished.

STRUCTURE AND RELIEF

According to geological theory the continents are masses of lighter rock (sial) floating upon a deep-seated layer of the earth's crust composed of heavier rock (sima) which underlies both the continents and the great ocean basins. Geologists have long accepted the fact that continental masses move up and down in equilibrium with isostatic pressure, and thus they are able to explain why many continental surfaces such as those of the Canadian Prairies and Southern Ontario are underlain by rocks which were originally deposited beneath the sea.

More recently it has been suggested that the continents are capable of lateral as well as vertical movement. After studying the similarities of the rocks in Greenland and Northern Canada on both sides of Eureka Sound and making similar studies in other parts of the world, Wegner, a German scientist, became convinced that North America was slowly moving away from Europe and propounded the theory of *continental drift.** Many geologists were reluctant to accept Wegner's theory but J. T.

* Alfred Wegner. *The Origins of Continents and Oceans.* (Translated by John Biram). Dover Publications, Inc. New York. 1966.

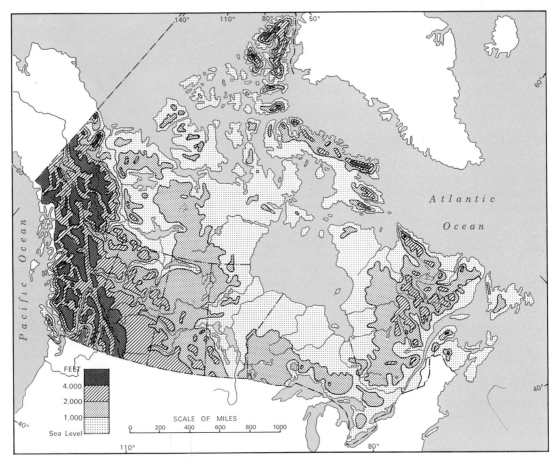

Figure 2.1 Relief Regions of Canada
While the only extensive area of elevated relief exists in the western mountains, the Atlantic coast of Labrador is quite rugged. The southern rim of the Canadian Shield surrounding Hudson Bay has elevations exceeding 4,000 feet in the east, but is more subdued in the west.

Wilson, as well as others, has advanced much evidence in support of continental drift.* This theory helps to explain the general structure pattern of North America. The movement of the continental mass from east to west results in the accumulation of crustal masses on the western margin, the renewal of tectonic activity, and the building of rugged, young mountain ranges. The older structures on the eastern margin of the continent continue to be worn down, resulting in a much more subdued landscape.

Elevation above sea level is the first and most obvious element in regional differen-

tiation. Most of the surface of Canada lies below an elevation of 4,000 feet, the most significant exception being the western mountain belt or Cordilleran region. Mt. Logan in Yukon Territory reaches 19,850 feet above sea level and is the highest peak in Canada, while there are many other peaks above 10,000 feet in the Yukon, British Columbia, and Alberta. In the east the Shickshock Mountains of Gaspé Peninsula have summits above 4,000 feet and the Torngats of Labrador reach elevations of almost 6,000 feet. In the far north the mountains of Ellesmere Island have peaks with elevations of more than 9,500 feet above sea level. A large part of the country, however, is lowland. Hudson Bay lies in a

*J. Tuzo Wilson. "Continental Drift". *Scientific American.* 208, 4 (April, 1963). pp. 86-103.

great geosyncline or structural basin, almost surrounded by an upland rim, while smaller basins contain the Gulf of St. Lawrence and its adjoining coastal plains, the Great Lakes and the surrounding plains, and the lowlands traversed by the Mackenzie River system.

Natural Drainage and Water Supply

Surface drainage and stream patterns are important factors in physical geography. The outlines of the natural drainage basins in Canada are shown in Figure 2.2. Hudson Bay receives the water from the largest drainage basin in Canada — 1,342,000 square miles; but, although it contains two-fifths of Canada's land area, it provides only one-fifth of the total run-off. Within this area the most important river system is that of the Nelson, 1,600 miles in length, which drains an area of 368,000 square miles. Other large rivers flowing into Hudson Bay are the Churchill, the Dubawnt, the Severn, the Albany, the Moose, and the Eastmain.

The Mackenzie, 2,635 miles in length, is in the Arctic drainage area and is the longest river in Canada. Its drainage basin, about 500,000 square miles in area, contains Great Bear Lake, Great Slave Lake, Lake Athabasca, and many smaller lakes, a total fresh-water surface of more than 35,000 square miles. The Mackenzie has long been important for transportation in the north, and its headwaters, notably the Peace, have important hydro-electric power sites.

The Pacific drainage area also contains some very large rivers including the Yukon, the Skeena, the Fraser, and the Columbia. Many power sites have already been developed on the Columbia, and many potential sites exist within the region.

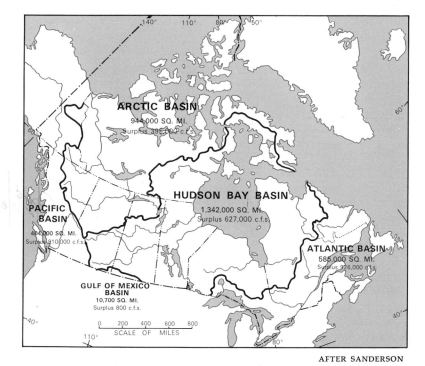

AFTER SANDERSON

Figure 2.2 Major Drainage Basins of Canada
The estimated annual water surplus data is shown in cubic feet per second. Despite the large area drained by the Hudson Bay basin, water surplus is much less there than to the east and west where more precipitation is received.

Table 2.1   Precipitation and Run-off for Settled Areas in Canada *

Region	Area Square Miles (000)	Depth of Precipitation in Inches	Volume of Precipitation in Acre-feet (000,000)	Depth of Run-off in Inches	Volume of Run-off in Acre-feet (000,000)	Run-off as Per cent of Precipitation
Atlantic Provinces	106	41.2	234	25.4	145	62.0
Quebec	216	37.6	433	14.5	167	38.6
Ontario	149	30.3	240	11.2	89	37.1
Prairie Provinces	333	16.6	295	2.8	51	17.3
British Columbia	241	31.3	402	24.4	314	78.1
Canada	1,045	28.7	1,604	13.2	766	47.8

* After D. Cass-Beggs. "Water as a Basic Resource ". *Resources for Tomorrow Conference. Background Papers.* Vol. 1. pp. 173-189. Ottawa. 1961.

Within the Atlantic drainage basin the St. Lawrence system extends 1,900 miles into the interior of the continent. In combination with the Great Lakes and such man-made facilities as the Seaway, Welland, and Sault canals, it provides access for ocean shipping as far west as the Lakehead. A great deal of electricity is generated from the St. Lawrence system and most of its power potential has been realized. Niagara Falls with its spectacular drop of 160 feet has additional importance as a major tourist attraction. Also draining into the Atlantic are numerous rivers from the Labrador Plateau where the enormous potential of the Manicouagan-Outardes and the Churchill river systems are being exploited for the production of hydroelectric power. The Exploits River in Newfoundland and the St. John River in New Brunswick, though much smaller, are of importance in their own regions.

Water is a basic resource for all countries; unfortunately, for Canada it is not evenly distributed within the settled areas of the country (Table 2.1). Nevertheless, most of the settled parts possess a fairly adequate water supply. The exception is the Prairie Region where the low rate of run-off is an indication of the scarcity of surface water during most seasons of the year. British Columbia with its elevated and rugged terrain and abundant annual

precipitation is estimated to provide 32 per cent of the total run-off for Canada.*

Estimates for the unsettled areas of Northern Canada are, of course, less reliable because of the lack of a closely spaced net of weather stations and stream gauging stations. There is less precipitation in the north; but since temperatures are lower, the rates of evapotranspiration are also lower, thus a higher percentage of the precipitation appears as run-off. It should also be noted that in the north a large amount of water remains on the surface of the land in the form of lakes, ponds, and muskeg.

However, water supply is more than just a matter of how great a portion of the precipitation is available as run-off. Quality of water is also important. The problem of pollution is already of considerable magnitude in several parts of Canada.** Pollution is found wherever large quantities of domestic or industrial wastes are discharged into lakes and streams. It is, therefore, bound to occur in the waters adjacent to large cities or large industrial plants unless

* M. E. Sanderson and D. Phillips. *Average Annual Water Surplus in Canada.* Meteorological Branch, Department of Transport. Ottawa. 1967.
** J. R. Menzies. "Water Pollution in Canada by Drainage Basins". *Resources for Tomorrow Conference. Background Papers.* Vol. 1. pp. 353-364. Ottawa. 1961.

great care is taken. The Great Lakes and the Ottawa River and Saskatchewan River Systems provide examples of the serious effects of pollution and the extreme costliness of remedial measures.

Physiographic Regions

Differences in the underlying rock structures and in the patterns of occurrence of surface features make it possible to divide Canada into a number of major physiographic or landform regions (Figure 2.3). Some of these regions are not confined to Canada but extend southward into the United States as well.

The *Canadian Shield* is the physical nucleus of Canada and, probably, that of the continent of North America as well. Composed of ancient Precambrian rocks it is seen in many exposures throughout an area of almost 1,800,000 square miles surrounding the geosyncline or depression which contains Hudson Bay and the ad-

joining Hudson Bay Lowland where Paleozoic rocks are preserved. In addition to the areas in which it is exposed the Precambrian formation underlies the younger geologic formations in the vast interior plains of the continent. Precambrian rocks are exposed in the Ozark Hills and in the lower gorge of the Grand Canyon of the Colorado River in the southwestern States.

Geological evidence indicates that parts of the Canadian Shield were once extremely rugged and mountainous, but during hundreds of millions of years the forces of erosion have reduced its surface almost to a peneplain. However, large areas have been raised and tilted to form such highlands as the Laurentians, the Laurentides, the Torngats, and the mountains of Baffin Island. The surface pattern has been greatly complicated by Pleistocene glaciation. Extensive areas of glacial scour occur in the highlands along the eastern margins, but many areas carry a deep overburden of

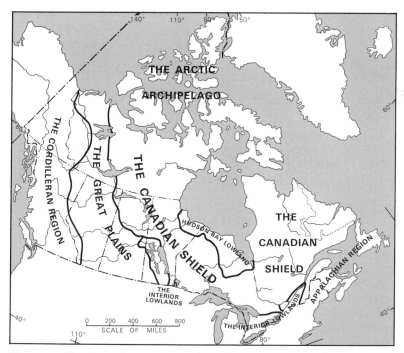

Figure 2.3 Physiographic Regions of Canada
The Canadian Shield forms the core of the country, and on its southern fringe are located the main lowlands of Canada, the Great Plains, and the Interior Lowlands.

Figure 2.4 The Canadian Shield
(a) In the interior of the Shield, the Clay Belt is an area of low relief. Smooth Rock Falls and other communities owe their existence to the pulp and paper industry.
(b) The considerable relief of the southern edge of the Shield makes for scenic beauty near Wawa, Ont.

R. PUTNAM

glacial till and outwash. Great quantities of fine sediment were deposited in proglacial lakes such as Barlow-Ojibway and Agassiz to form the clay plains of Western Quebec, Northern Ontario, and the Manitoba Lowland. Perhaps most typical of much of the Shield is a landscape of low hills and shallow basins containing innumerable lakes. The ancient rocks of the Canadian Shield contain valuable deposits of metallic minerals including gold, silver, iron, nickel, and copper. An important sector of the Canadian economy is based upon the mineral resources of the Shield.

The *Appalachian Region* lies to the southeast of the Canadian Shield. It comprises the hilly part of Quebec to the south of the St. Lawrence River, the island of Newfoundland, and the three Maritime Provinces. It is a northeastern extension of the Appalachian Region of the United States and has a great variety of rock types and landforms. Most of the surface exhibits the marks of continental glaciation. There are four extensive upland areas underlain by hard crystalline rocks: the complex fold mountains of the Gaspé Peninsula with summits about 4,000 feet above sea level, the Central Plateau of New Brunswick with summits above 2,000 feet, the uplands of Newfoundland with large areas above 1,000 feet and some summits above 2,000 feet, and the Atlantic Upland of Nova Scotia.

Underlain by crystalline rocks such as granite, slate, and quartzite, the Atlantic Upland extends the whole length of the Atlantic Coast of Nova Scotia. It has a Shield-like surface of low rock knobs, lakes, and bogs, and the upland at its northern margin varies from 500 to 700 feet above sea level. From this height of land it declines gently toward the ocean with a slope of about two to three feet per mile. The Atlantic Coast is marked by many harbors, coves, and inlets which encour-

Figure 2.5 The Atlantic Coast
At Lunenburg the indented nature of the coast of the Atlantic Upland is apparent. Glaciation has left drumlins on most of the till plains, and very little agricultural settlement occurs inland.

DEPARTMENT OF ENERGY, MINES AND RESOURCES

aged the early European colonists to adopt the fisherman's way of life. The island of Newfoundland has a similar, but somewhat more rugged, topography with fiord-like inlets and rocky knobs in the interior.

Apart from the uplands the Appalachian Region contains extensive lowlands bordering Baie de Chaleur, Northumberland Strait, and the Bay of Fundy. The better parts of the lowlands became the agricultural settlement, but Prince Edward Island was the only area which was uniformly occupied. Coal seams in the lowlands of Cape Breton Island, the northern part of Nova Scotia, and the central part of New Brunswick have been utilized. Extensive deposits of gypsum and salt are also found in the lowlands, while base metals are associated with intrusions and folds in the central plateau regions.

The *Lower Great Lakes and St. Lawrence Lowlands* are underlain by Paleozoic sedimentary rocks which have been only slightly disturbed by tectonic forces. The St. Lawrence Lowland, an area of very low relief, is drained by the St. Lawrence River from the Thousand Islands to Quebec City. Its northern margin is the abrupt scarp of the Laurentians which forms the edge of the Canadian Shield, while on the south the plain is bounded by Logan's Line, a fault zone marking the limit of the Appalachian hilly region. To the southwest in Ontario the boundary for the region lies on the northern flank of the Frontenac Axis, a low extension of the Canadian Shield near the eastern end of Lake Ontario. The flatness of the plain is broken only by a few outliers of the Shield and by the Monteregian Hills, a series of masses of volcanic rock, strongly resistant to the age-long erosion which has planed the surface of the surrounding Paleozoic sedimentary strata. Best known of these hills is Mount Royal, the forested summit overlooking the city of Montreal. During the Pleistocene ice age the plain was heavily glaciated and much boulder clay was deposited. The weight of the ice depressed the surface several hundred feet below sea level, and on deglaciation the lowland was

occupied by salt water. Deposits from this time include the heavy clays of the flat plains, large areas of deltaic sand plains, and numerous gravel ridges marking the old shorelines. The very flat central area, east, south, and west of the city of Montreal, is known as the Montreal Plain. Formerly an area of dense agricultural settlement, it is rapidly undergoing suburban development.

The Lower Great Lakes area is a plain of considerably greater relief than the St. Lawrence Lowland. It is also a roughly triangular tract bordered on the north by the edge of the Shield, on the south by Lake Ontario and Lake Erie and on the west by Lake Huron. It is underlain by almost undisturbed sedimentary rocks, chiefly limestones, dolomites, shales, and sandstones of Paleozoic age. The strongest relief is found along the Niagara Escarpment which stretches from the Niagara River to the Bruce Peninsula and Manitoulin Island. The Escarpment is the steep, eastward face of a cuesta protected by the exposed edge of a resistant Silurian dolomite formation which is part of the Michigan Basin, a great epicontinental geosyncline in which a long series of Paleozoic formations was laid down.* The summit of the cuesta ranges from 600 to 1,600 feet above sea level, its most spectacular promontory, the Blue Mountain, standing 1,000 feet above the shoreline of Georgian Bay. Both the Ontario Plain to the east of the Escarpment and the Huron-Erie Plain to the west of it exhibit a great variety of Pleistocene formations.** Among them are the Horseshoe Moraines, a complex of recessional moraines with associated melt-water channels surrounding "Ontario Island", which is a large upland area just west of the highest part of the cuesta, and the Oak Ridges Interlobate Moraine, with summit elevations of 900 to 1,300 feet above sea level, which forms the divide

---

* J. L. Hough. *The Geology of the Great Lakes.* University of Illinois Press. 1958.
** L. J. Chapman and D. F. Putnam. *The Physiography of Southern Ontario.* University of Toronto Press. 2nd edition. Toronto. 1966.

and the Rocky Mountain Trench which is a remarkably straight and evenly graded fault valley or rift zone separating the main chain of the Rocky Mountains from the Columbia Mountains and extending for hundreds of miles farther to the northwest. The Rocky Mountains are well known for the rugged scenery of Banff and Jasper National Parks.

The Cordilleran Region was heavily glaciated in the Pleistocene Epoch, and even today vast snowfields and many glaciers are to be seen in the St. Elias Mountains, the Coast Mountains, and the higher parts of the Rocky Mountains. Notwithstanding this, however, it appears that extensive areas of the Yukon plateau escaped Pleistocene glaciation. The Cordilleran Region is the source area for a number of Canada's major rivers. The Columbia, Fraser, Peace, Athabasca, and Saskatchewan, all derive their headwaters from the melting glaciers of the Rocky Mountains. Glaciation has been a major factor in the sculpture of landforms, and from the fiorded coast to the Columbia Icefields almost all of this region reflects the influences of glacial scour and deposition.

From the resource point of view the Cordilleran is one of Canada's noted mining regions. Associated with the intrusive and metamorphic rocks are numerous ore bodies yielding gold, silver, iron, copper, lead, and zinc.

The *Hudson Bay Lowland* and the plains of the Arctic Archipelago are floored by Paleozoic sedimentary strata dipping gently northward. In the past extensive areas have been subjected to marine transgression, and the evidence of many recently abandoned shorelines suggests that this region is still actively rebounding after being depressed by Pleistocene glaciation.

In the northern part of the Archipelago is an extensive zone of fold-mountain structures involving rocks of Silurian to Cretaceous age, known as the Innuitian Region. On Ellesmere Island some peaks range between 8,000 and 10,000 feet in elevation. On Ellesmere Island and the neighboring Sverdrup Islands a narrow

coastal plain dips seaward giving an indication of a wide continental shelf beneath the Arctic Ocean. Recent geological exploration suggests that valuable petroleum resources may exist in the Paleozoic rocks of the Arctic Archipelago.

CLIMATE

Because it is such a large country, Canada possesses a great variety of climates and a corresponding variety of vegetation types. Frigid Arctic tundra, hot sun-ripened grain fields, and moist, heavily forested slopes are all part of the Canadian scene. Variations in vegetation type are, in large part, because of climatic influence and reflect the enormous extent of the country. Almost any other large country may be shown to exhibit similarly great climatic variation. It is useful perhaps to draw comparisons between Canadian climates and those of parts of Eurasia. The climate of Vancouver on the coast of British Columbia shows similarities to the climate of Bergen in Norway, particularly in respect to its cool summers and mild, wet winters. In the interior the climate of Calgary, in its annual range of temperature and its summer concentration of rainfall, is comparable to that of Moscow. The climate of Halifax on the east coast of Canada resembles that of Sapporo in Japan in many ways; they have similar temperatures and both have high annual rainfall. However, Halifax gets its maximum precipitation in winter while Sapporo receives its greatest rainfall in the late summer. In these comparisons, and in many others which are possible, the similarities of climate may be matched by similarities in the geographical locations of the cities under review.

Climatic Controls

All differences in climate from place to place on the surface of the earth result from the unequal distribution of the radiant energy of the sun and its subsequent redistribution and loss. Some of these differences are due to variations in the space relations of the sun and the earth, while others are responses to differences in the physical pattern of the surface of the earth itself.

The angle with which the sun's rays strike the land varies with the time of day, the season of the year, and the latitude of the place in question. The heat received by any specified area at any particular instant of time is controlled by the angle of incidence of the sun's rays. The climatic effect depends not only upon the intensity of radiation, but also on the duration of insolation. Thus the length of the day is also important. For example, at Aklavik in the Northwest Territories the daily period of sunlight varies from 0 hours on December 21 to 24 hours on June 21, and the amount of heat received varies accordingly. However, heat received must also be lost; otherwise the surface of the earth would soon become unbearably hot. Heat is received only during the day, but it is lost continuously. In summer the balance is positive and the weather is warm; in winter it is negative and the weather is cold. Taking all factors into consideration, however, it may be said that in all locations poleward of latitude $37\frac{1}{2}°$ there is net deficit of radiant energy. All areas between $37\frac{1}{2}°$ N and $37\frac{1}{2}°$ S receive more heat than they lose.

Canada is located entirely to the north of $37\frac{1}{2}°$ N. Therefore in order to maintain its temperature patterns it must receive a continuous flow of heat from the warmer parts of the earth's surface.

Land areas absorb heat rapidly and warm up quickly; they also cool off rapidly. Water areas warm up slowly and cool off slowly. Consequently, there is nearly always a difference in temperature between land and sea. Climates of large land areas have great variation in temperature and moisture conditions and are known as *continental* climates. Those under the influence of oceanic conditions are known as *marine* climates; they have less variation in both temperature and rainfall. Air which remains for any length of time over any area of the earth's surface takes on the characteristics of that position. Thus the

air over the Gulf of Mexico becomes warm and moist. Air masses, however, do not remain long in the area of origin; they move in response to the influence of the earth's rotation, thus giving rise to atmospheric circulation.

The atmospheric circulation pattern in Canada is primarily from west to east, and westerly winds prevail in almost the whole of the country. As shown in Figure 2.7, Canada is dominated by Polar air masses, both continental and maritime. Only during the summer months and only over a limited area in Southern Canada do tropical air masses have a pronounced effect. The interaction between Polar air masses and Tropical air masses in the zone of meeting along the Polar Front gives rise to the procession of cyclonic storms which characterizes the pattern of Canadian weather. Storms pass from west to east on arcuate courses; and when one is recorded in Western Canada, its arrival in the East may quite safely be predicted. The Polar Front is most important but other fronts may develop whenever two air masses of greatly different conditions meet. In winter a large cold, dry, and fairly stationary air mass (Canadian High) develops over the Northwest Territories. Frontal interaction between it and the sub-polar low pressure cell over the Aleutian Islands may bring winter storms to Western Canada. Similar interaction with the Icelandic Low over the North Atlantic may bring stormy weather to Labrador.

The Cordilleran mountain systems and the Great Plains play significant roles in the climate of Canada. The coastal mountains act as a barrier to marine influences and generate copious orographic precipitation. More moisture is wrung from the Pacific air masses as they pass over the Rocky Mountains. Thus dry areas are found in the interior of British Columbia and on the plains to the east of the Rocky Mountains. On the other hand, the Great Plains do not act as a barrier to air from the Canadian High, and "cold waves" of Polar Continental air may achieve easy access to Eastern Canada.

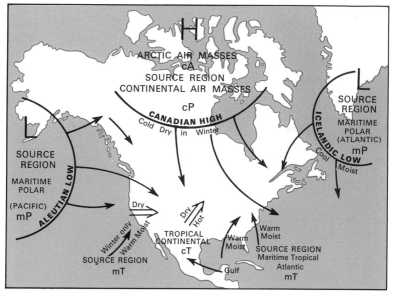

MODIFIED FROM STRAHLER

Figure 2.7 Air Mass Source Regions and Trajectories for North America

Open water surfaces influence the climatic pattern profoundly along the east and west coasts of Canada, but in neither area does the effect extend very far inland. The North Pacific drift helps to create mild winters in coastal British Columbia, while the cold Labrador Current is influential in retarding the advent of spring in the Atlantic Provinces. The Lower Great Lakes have some influence on both the temperature and precipitation patterns of adjoining land areas. Hudson Bay, being largely ice-covered in winter, acts as a smooth, cold continental surface, while in summer the effect of its cold water is to create a much cooler climate along its leeward shores.

The influences of these controls are well illustrated by the isotherm and isohyet patterns of Canada. January isotherms are shown in Figure 2.8. Special mention should be made of the 10°F isotherm in Southern Alberta since its precise positioning is a direct effect of the influence of the Chinook or warm mountain wind. In general, the coastal areas are warmer in winter than the interior, causing the isotherms to dip southward as they pass inland. July isotherms are shown in Figure 2.9. In summer, continental areas are warmer than the oceans; thus the isotherms bend northward over the land. Because of the influence of the long days, average temperatures are higher than might be expected in the north. The circulation of maritime Polar air about the Icelandic Low has a moderating influence on Labrador in both winter and summer.

The isohyetal patterns shown in Figure 2.10 confirm the basic description given earlier. Pacific Coast areas average more than 80 inches of precipitation annually, the Prairie Region about 15 inches, the High Arctic less than 10 inches, and the Atlantic Region more than 40 inches annually. Seasonal distributions vary. The Pacific Coast has a pronounced winter maximum, while the Prairies and the High Arctic have a summer maximum. In Eastern Canada the precipitation regimen is fairly uniform in all seasons although some stations in the Atlantic Provinces experience a slight maximum in autumn and early winter.

It is obvious that agriculture can be successful only when climate and crop plants are fully compatable. However, the rela-

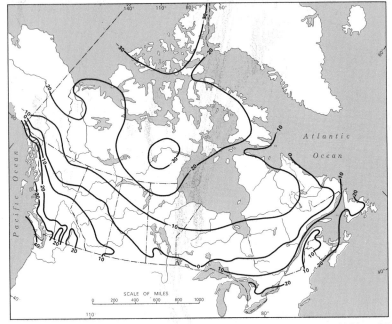

AFTER CANADA YEAR BOOK 1966, P. 26

Figure 2.8 Mean Daily Temperatures in Canada for January
During January the interior of Canada is under the influence of cold Arctic air, and the extreme continentality causes the isotherms to bend considerably towards the equator as they cross the continent.

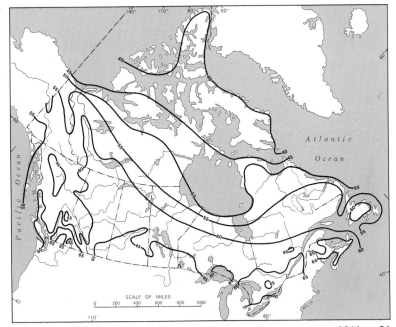

AFTER CANADA YEAR BOOK 1966, P. 26

Figure 2.9 Mean Daily Temperatures in Canada for July
In summer the temperature gradient is not as extreme as in winter.

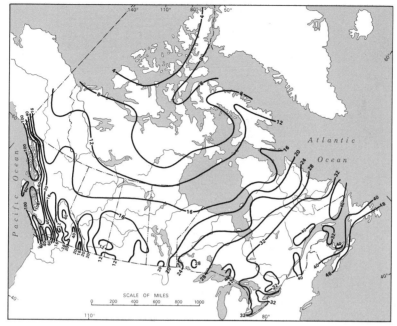

AFTER CANADA YEAR BOOK 1966, P. 26

Figure 2.10 Mean Annual Total Precipitation for Canada
Precipitation is greatest along the Pacific and Atlantic coasts. It is least in
the Arctic where low temperatures inhibit the availability of water vapor
in the air. The effect of relief is illustrated by the striking pattern of the
isohyets along the Coast Range and the Rocky Mountains.

tionship between climatic factors and crop growth is not a simple one. Only occasionally is the farmer free to choose the climate in which to grow a desired crop; rarely indeed is he able to modify a climate in order to make it more favorable. Usually he must choose his crops to fit the climate or modify them to make them more suitable.

For the growth of every plant there are optimal and limiting conditions. Most European wheats will grow where rainfall is adequate (15 to 40 inches per annum) and summer temperatures average between 60°F and 75°F. But wheats are divided into two types: those that are fall sown and those that are spring sown. Fall-sown types begin to grow in the autumn and must withstand low temperatures in order to survive and make a crop the next summer. In Ontario empirical evidence suggests that the lower limit for fall-sown wheat is found where the average January

temperature is about 20°F. At any rate, farmers have found that when they try to grow winter wheat in areas which have colder winters they have little success. If they wish to grow wheat, they must use spring wheat which, of course, does not have to withstand low winter temperatures.

Another well-known case of temperature limitation is that of the peach in Ontario. The peach tree is, of course, perennial and it must be able to withstand winter temperatures. It is well established that a drop in temperature below –20°F is fatal to the peach tree. Consequently, the only place in Ontario where peaches may safely be grown is the Niagara Peninsula where the lowest winter temperature has never been below –15°F. Growers in other areas must expect their orchards to be wiped out every few years.

The most commonly used index of thermal requirements for middle latitude crop plants is the length of the *growing season*.

It has often been noted that pasture grasses and cereals begin to grow when the mean daily temperature,

$$\frac{(\text{maximum} + \text{minimum})}{2}$$

reaches 42°F in the spring and that growth ceases when the mean temperature falls below 42°F in the autumn. The length of the growing season is the number of days between the spring date and the autumn date of the occurrence of the mean of 42°F. It is not an exact index, but it is a simple and useful one.

Another commonly used thermal index is the number of *frost-free days*. This involves finding the average dates of the occurrence of the last killing frost in the spring and the first killing frost in the fall and counting the number of days between. For tender plants such as tomatoes, beans, and squash, this is a more useful index than the growing season above the mean of 42°F.

There are much more sophisticated indices which may be used to achieve a matching of crop and climate. One of these is the index of cumulative degree-days (which may be abbreviated as D-D). The base used is again the date of the occurrence of a daily mean of 42°F. A degree-day is a measurement of one degree over 42°F for one day; a day with a record of 47°F would count as 5 D-D, one with a record of 67°F would count as a 25 D-D. Adding together all the D-D above the base of 42°F gives the total *D-D index*.* As shown in Figure 2.11, this index shows a wide range across Canada, varying from 4,000 D-D in Southwestern Ontario to less than 2,000 in Newfoundland and Central British Columbia. The 4,000 D-D line indicates the northern limit of the area in which intensive specialization in husking corn, sugar beets, and soy beans is thermally possible. In the zone with 3,000 to 3,500 D-D silage corn may be grown but more reliance must be placed on hardier grains and hay crops. In the Prairie Region only the Morden area in Southern Manitoba has a D-D index above 3,000, and it is worth noting that this is a special crop area. In all the rest of the agricultural area of the Prairies the D-D index is between 2,000 and 3,000. This is sufficient for commercial grain and livestock farming.

* L. J. Chapman and D. M. Brown. *The Climates of Canada for Agriculture*. The Canada Land Inventory Report No. 3. 1966. pp. 6-8.

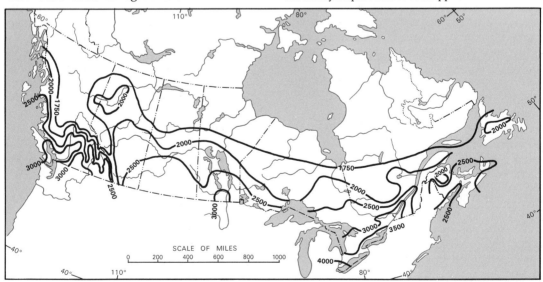

AFTER CHAPMAN AND BROWN

Figure 2.11 Degree-days above 42°F for Canada
Southwestern Ontario receives the greatest amount of heat in Canada.

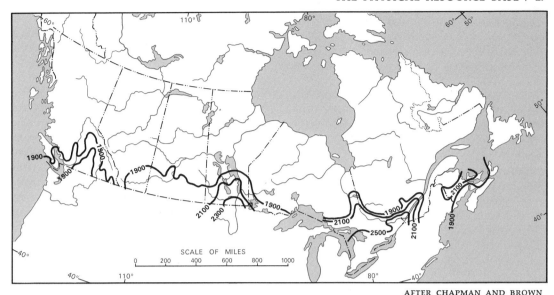

AFTER CHAPMAN AND BROWN

Figure 2.12 Corn Heat Units for Canada
On the basis of this complex measurement, the optimum thermal conditions for grain corn occur only in Southern Ontario and near Montreal.

One of the notable agricultural achievements of this century is the development of hybrid strains of corn (maize). The increasing importance of hybrid corn in Canada is due to the development of strains which have less restrictive thermal limits. Corn has different thermal requirements from those of cereals such as wheat; for instance, it does not germinate well until the soil temperature reaches 55°F and the growing plant is highly susceptible to frost. In order to deal with its thermal requirements research workers have devised another index known as the *Corn Heat Unit* (C.H.U.).* This is a complex measure which makes use of both maximum and minimum temperature values. A Corn Heat Unit map for Canada is shown in Figure 2.12. In Ontario corn is grown for grain in areas defined by a threshold of 2,500 C.H.U. Corn may successfully be grown for silage in areas with a value as low as 2,100 C.H.U. Other areas in Canada with 2,100 C.H.U. or more include the south-central part of Manitoba, the South Saskatchewan River Valley area between Medicine Hat and Taber in Alberta, and

* L. J. Chapman and D. M. Brown. *op. cit.* p. 9.

most of the agricultural lands of Southern British Columbia. In Eastern Canada, the middle St. Lawrence area in Quebec, the lower St. John Valley, the Annapolis Valley, and Prince Edward Island also have indices greater than 2,100 C.H.U. Some corn is grown for silage in all of these areas, but only in Southern Ontario, Southern Quebec, Southern Manitoba, and the Lower Fraser Valley is corn produced as a grain crop. Corn, oats, and barley are used as energy feeds in the livestock industry. If climatic conditions permit its growth, corn is usually the most efficient producer of energy. In the future it is hoped that new hybrids will push the margin of corn production to the threshold of 1,900 C.H.U. Thus corn might become the basis of livestock feeding in large areas in both Eastern and Western Canada.

Moisture supply is of paramount importance to agriculture, and any useful system of agricultural climatology must be based on moisture measurement. However, the conventional measurement of total precipitation is an inadequate index since it fails to take into consideration all of the significant variables such as evaporation, transpiration, run-off, soil storage, and precipitation effectiveness.

A widely accepted method of analysis of moisture data was devised by C. W. Thornthwaite.* Basically, it is simply a comparison of the moisture supply which is actually climatically available (precipitation) and that which would be used by the environment if an adequate supply were made continuously available (potential evapotranspiration, abbreviated to PE). If too much rain falls, there is excess moisture and run-off ensues. If there is not enough rain, moisture is drawn from soil storage (estimated to be equal to a depth of 4 inches of water) until it is all used and a moisture deficiency results. If the state of deficiency is prolonged, the vegetation will wilt and die. Almost any degree of deficiency will retard the rate of growth of crop plants. Within the yearly cycle of climate the same place may experience

both surplus and deficiency of moisture. Normally, in most of Canada spring is the time of surplus and late summer is the time of deficiency.

Through repeated experiments Thornthwaite and his associates were able to accumulate sufficient data under different environmental conditions that they could determine theoretical relationships between water loss on the one hand and temperature and length of day on the other. Thus maps of potential evapotranspiration may be drawn of any area for which sufficient data can be made available. Sanderson has applied the Thornthwaite system of climatic analysis to Canada.* Figure 2.13 is a map of average annual potential evapotranspiration for Canada.

The pattern of mean annual water deficiency is shown in Figure 2.14. Southern Alberta and the interior valleys of British

* C. W. Thornthwaite. "An Approach to a Rational Classification of Climate". *Geographical Review.* XXXVIII, 1 (January, 1948). pp. 55-94.

* Marie Sanderson. "The Climates of Canada According to the New Thornthwaite Classification". *Scientific Agriculture.* Vol. 28 (1948). pp. 501-517.

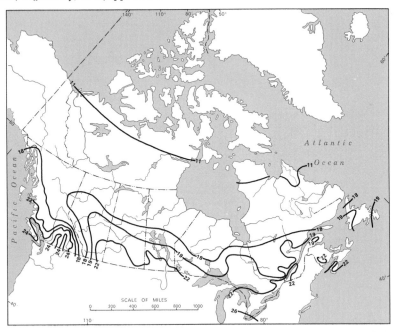

AFTER SANDERSON

Figure 2.13 Average Annual Potential Evapotranspiration for Canada
Potential evapotranspiration is least in the Arctic and greatest in Southwestern Ontario.

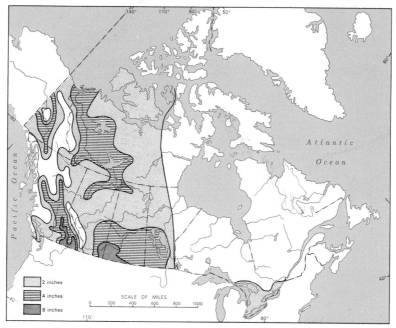

AFTER SANDERSON

Figure 2.14 Mean Annual Water Deficiency for Canada
Note the contrast between this map and Figure 2.15. Some of the areas
have both a surplus and deficiency, but at different times of the year.

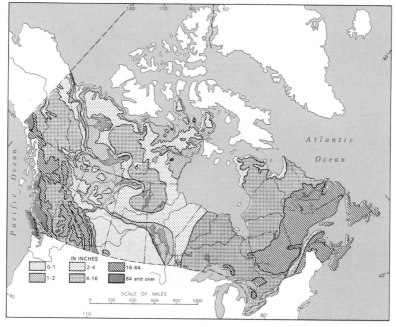

AFTER SANDERSON

Figure 2.15 Mean Annual Water Surplus for Canada
The central and northern areas have little surplus moisture on an annual
basis.

Columbia exhibit the greatest deficiencies. Notwithstanding the very wet winters of the Lower Fraser Valley there is a notable deficiency in the area, which is a reflection of the lack of summer precipitation. Moisture deficiencies in Southern Ontario are comparable with those in Southern Manitoba, but in general moisture deficiencies do not occur in agricultural areas to the east of Trois-Rivières.

Moisture surpluses are shown in Figure 2.15. They are highest on the west coast of Canada and are quite low in the Prairie Provinces. In parts of Ontario surpluses of 4 to 16 inches occur, while in the Atlantic Region a surplus of more than 16 inches is commonplace.

Many areas in Canada may have both a surplus and a deficiency of moisture. The Fraser Valley, already noted, is one such area. It has heavy winter precipitation when temperatures and evaporation are low; but in summer when evaporation is greatest, the rainfall is very light. In some areas the surplus is increased because there is an accumulation of moisture during the winter when the ground is frozen and cannot absorb it. This is carried away in the spring run-off.

The Thornthwaite criteria give quantitative expression to important geographic differences, long appreciated by Canadians. There is an *eastern* climatic zone in which moisture surplus usually outweighs moisture deficiency, and there is an *interior* zone in which moisture deficiency is more important. Prof. Sanderson's studies indicate that this division may well be recognized in the Arctic as well. There is also a narrow, wet zone along the West Coast.

Climate Regions

While the major geographic realities of Canadian climates have never been in doubt, the development of a suitable system of climatic subdivisions has always posed some difficulties. The world-wide system proposed by Köppen years ago and featured in many atlases and textbooks fails to emphasize the geographic differences in the southern parts of Canada.* Numerous other attempts have also been made. A very useful recent analysis of Canadian climates has been issued by the Canadian Department of Transport, but its system of regions is incomplete.**

Based upon criteria derived from the Thornthwaite water balance studies and certain significant ecological criteria such as the temperature limit of forest growth and the growing season above 42°F, a system very similar to the one used in this book was proposed in 1952.***

The outlines of eleven climate regions of Canada are presented in Figure 2.16, while basic thermal and moisture criteria are listed in Table 2.2.

On first approximation a very simple geographic pattern emerges, consisting of four major areas: the Canadian Arctic, Eastern Canada, Interior Canada, and Western Canada. Each of these may be further subdivided by use of further criteria.

The *Arctic* Regions have no monthly mean above 50°F, and they receive most of their meagre precipitation in the warm season. The distinction between the Eastern Arctic and Western Arctic is made on the basis of moisture deficiency, the Western Arctic Region being a relatively drier area. The vegetation of the Arctic is chiefly that of a sparsely distributed, low-growing tundra association, and the region is frequently called a cold desert.

In *Eastern Canada* all regions have adequate moisture supplies although significant differences in moisture need and seasonality may be detected. While precipitation is generally evenly distributed with a slight maximum in summer, the Maritime Cool Summer Region has a slight (but in some places fairly pronounced)

---

* *Goode's World Atlas.* Rand McNally & Company. Chicago. 1964.
** C. C. Boughner and M. K. Thomas. *The Climate of Canada.* Meteorological Branch, Department of Transport. Ottawa. 1967.
*** D. F. Putnam. (Editor). *Canadian Regions.* J. M. Dent and Sons (Canada) Limited. Toronto. 1952.

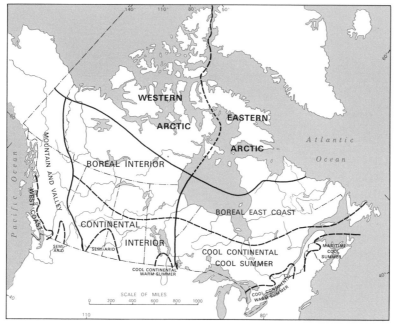

Figure 2.16 Climate Regions for Canada
The climates of Canada have been divided into four major types: the
Arctic, Interior, Eastern, and Western. The limits of these are shown by a
solid line, while the subdivisions of these major regions are indicated by a
broken line.

winter maximum. All the eastern regions
have a cold winter with an average of
more than three and one-half months of
freezing temperatures and more or less
continuous snow cover. Summer thermal
conditions as shown in Table 2.2 are
readily definable in terms of degree-days.
Natural vegetation ranges from open
boreal forest on the northern margin of
the Boreal East Coast Region to the Great
Lakes — St. Lawrence mixed forest of the
Cool Continental Warm Summer Region.

Interior Canada illustrates the full effects
of a continental location. Its winters are
colder than those of Eastern Canada, summers are relatively warm in the south, but
cool in the north; three subdivisions are
readily distinguishable on the basis of
degree-days. In all three subdivisions there
are modest amounts of precipitation with
a pronounced summer concentration. Moisture deficiencies range from two inches in
the Boreal to more than eight inches in the
Semi-arid Region. In the same direction

natural vegetation varies from open boreal
forest to short-grass steppe.

Western Canada has a greater variety of
climate than other parts of Canada because
of the complexities of its relief pattern.
The West Coast has heavy precipitation
with a pronounced winter maximum, but
especially toward the south a pronounced
summer minimum occurs, often causing
drought conditions and high forest fire
hazard. While the West Coast has a low
total of degree-days above 42°F, the
marine influence also affects winter temperatures, making them less severe than
elsewhere in Canada. No station on the
West Coast has a January mean temperature below 32°F, and only toward the
north are freezing conditions occasionally
reported. The climates of the Mountain
and Valley Region are most complex. High
mountains, deep valleys, windward and
leeward slopes of mountain ranges, and
distance from the sea, all have their effects
upon precipitation, and in contrast to the

Table 2.2   Climate Regions of Canada

Category	Region	PE Value in inches	Thermal Conditions	Moisture Conditions
Arctic	Eastern Arctic	11	No monthly mean temperature above 50°F	Moisture deficiency less than 2″
	Western Arctic	11	No monthly mean temperature above 50°F	Moisture deficiency more than 2″
Eastern Canada	Boreal East Coast	18	D-D below 1,750	Moisture deficiency less than 2″
	Cool Continental Cool Summer	19	D-D 1,750-3,000	Moisture deficiency less than 2″
	Cool Continental Warm Summer	22–26	D-D above 3,000	Moisture deficiency from 1″ to 5″
	Maritime Cool Summer	20–22	D-D 2,500-2,750	Moisture deficiency less than 1″
Interior Canada	Boreal Interior	18	D-D below 2,000	Moisture deficiency more than 2″
	Continental Interior	20–22	D-D 2,000-2,750	Moisture deficiency from 4″ to 8″
	Semi-arid	22	D-D above 2,750	Moisture deficiency from 8″ to 10″
Western Canada	West Coast	20–24	D-D above 2,500	Moisture deficiency more than 2″ Summer minimum of precipitation
	Mountain and Valley	16–24	Varies depending on elevation	Variable

PE   Potential Evapotranspiration.
D-D   degree-days above 42°F.

condition on the coast, latitude has a strong influence on the temperature pattern. The region is generally well-forested although open grasslands occur in the southern interior. Agriculture is found in only a few favorable areas of the region.

NATURAL VEGETATION

The control exerted by thermal and moisture relationships on natural vegetation has long been recognized. Forest, grassland, and tundra vegetation zones dominate in Canada. For the regional geog-

rapher, however, the importance of the vegetative regions shown in Figure 2.17 lies not so much in their correlation with definite climates but in the resource base which they indicate.

Various studies of the plant geography of Canada have been made, and valuable summaries have frequently been published in the Canada Year Book. Theoretically, climate favors the selection of certain species which tend to form a stable plant community or association. For example, a maple — beech — basswood hardwood forest is found in a large part of Southern

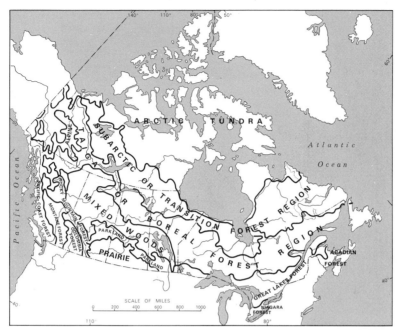

Figure 2.17 Vegetation Regions for Canada

Ontario, while western hemlock and western red cedar dominate the forests of the Pacific Coast.

The forest area of Canada is estimated at 1,710,800 square miles, approximately 57 per cent of which is capable of producing merchantable timber. However, the great areas of forest considered non-productive are significant in the influence they exert on climate, moisture, soil, and wildlife.

The *Arctic Tundra* region is characterized by a dearth of trees. The heath and prairie vegetation found in this region is xerophytic in nature, reflecting the lack of available moisture resulting from low precipitation and permafrost. Four major plant communities are found, namely: rock desert, tundra-heath, strand, and fresh water. Lichen are frequently the best-known plant species. The tundra also impresses the observer, having a variety of Arctic flowers which during their short growing season create a strangely colorful landscape.

Canada's Boreal Forest association can be divided into two main vegetation re-

gions: the *Subarctic* and the *Boreal*. Together they account for 82 per cent of Canada's forest area. White and black spruce are the characteristic species of the Boreal Forest region; balsam fir and jack pine occur in the eastern and central portions, while alpine fir and lodgepole pine are found in the west and northwest. Although there is a preponderance of conifers, white birch and aspen are also found throughout the region. To the north the Boreal Forest displays a transition stage, where open forest and stunted growth create the "land of the little sticks" or the Subarctic region. The eastern half of the Boreal Forest region, from Manitoba to Newfoundland, is the main area of pulpwood exploitation.

In the mild, humid climate of the West Coast, the *Pacific Coast Forest* region is characterized by luxuriant coniferous trees. The principal species are western red cedar and western hemlock, with sitka spruce abundant in the north and Douglas fir abundant in the south. Although this region comprises little more than two per cent of the forest area of Canada, the

Figure 2.18 Arctic Tundra Vegetation

NATIONAL FILM BOARD

(a) Ground View
The view is that of the flat countryside around Pond Inlet settlement on Eclipse Sound, Baffin Island. In the foreground appears a small mound composed of loose rock and fine earth and covered with grass, small bushes, and flowers.

(b) Aerial View
The effect of permafrost on vegetation is readily apparent. The photograph shows the situation on western Baffin Island near Nettilling Lake.

DEPARTMENT OF ENERGY, MINES AND RESOURCES

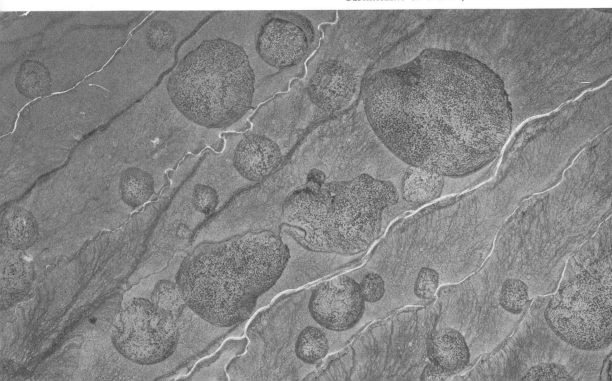

accessibility and quality of its timber resources have encouraged full exploitation by the forest industry.

Inland from the Pacific Coast the forest complex varies greatly, but three regions are distinguishable. The *Columbia Forest* of the Selkirk and Monashee Mountain area is frequently called the "interior wet belt". Here, increased orographic precipitation gives rise to a forest which is found up to an elevation of 4,000 feet and strongly resembles the Pacific Coast Forest. In many of the valleys of the central plateau of British Columbia where drought conditions are prevalent, there occurs an association known as the *Montane Forest*, composed of open grassland and scattered stands of Ponderosa pine.

The *Rocky Mountain Forest* region comprises the Sub-alpine forests of the foothills and the lower mountain slopes. The dominant species are Engelmann spruce and alpine fir. Lodgepole pine and aspen are found as a subclimax association. The forests of both the Columbia and Rocky Mountain regions are now being utilized; several new pulp and paper mills have recently been established in the Prince George area. The *Alpine* vegetation region includes all the mountain areas above the treeline: in general, above 3,000 feet on the

Figure 2.19 Boreal Forest Complex
The black spruce, identifiable by its candelabra shape, dominates the Boreal Forest complex. The aspen is also part of the complex.

Figure 2.20 Pacific Coast Forest
The grandeur of the Douglas fir is particularly striking in the Pacific Coast Forest. The trees shown here are 180 feet in height.

Coast Range and above 5,000-6,000 feet in the Selkirks and the Rockies. A meadow or tundra formation is common although species of plants found only in Alpine situations are present.

The *Mixed Woods* region is found on the southern margin of the interior Boreal region. Here, despite the prevalence of white spruce which is the chief commercial species, there is sufficient admixture of aspen, Balm of Gilead, and white birch to characterize this as a separate vegetation region.

The *Parkland* is a transition area between the forest proper and the prairie grassland. The dominant tree is the aspen which is found in scattered "bluffs" or patches interspersed by open grassland. In many river valleys in this area there are fairly continuous bands of forest. The tall prairie grasses of the region include awned wheat grass, northern wheat grass, and fringed brome grass.

The *Prairies* may be divided into a short-grass zone and a mixed grass zone. The vegetation is largely xerophytic, the distribution of species being largely controlled by the available moisture in the soil. Prairie grasses form a tough sod since they have dense root systems which thoroughly

Figure 2.21 Great Lakes Forest
The mature Great Lakes Forest contains a mixture of both coniferous and deciduous trees.

occupy the soil in search of water. In the driest sections, blue grama grass, common spear grass, western wheat grass, prairie blue grass, and June grass are common. Some of these, for example, June grass, have a shallow widespreading root system which can easily make use of moisture from light summer showers. Sage brush and prickly pear cactus are common. Saline areas contain salt-tolerant plants such as alkali grass, salt grass, and barley grass.

In the mixed grass zone many of the same plants are found along with porcupine grass, green spear grass, rough fescue, and northern wheat grass.

The *Great Lakes—St. Lawrence Forest* is a transition zone to the south of the Boreal Forest in Eastern Canada. It contains a great wealth of species and associations. Both conifers, such as white pine, red pine, and white spruce, and deciduous trees, such as sugar maple, beech, red oak, and red maple, are present. Climatic conditions and accessibility make the forests of this region one of the most valuable timber resources; and while it accounts for only seven per cent of Canada's forest area, it produces more than 50 per cent of the forest wealth.

Between the north shore of Lake Erie and a line drawn from Grand Bend to Toronto, there is a region which Halliday calls the *Niagara* section of the eastern deciduous forest region. Here, in addition to the species typical of the Great Lakes forest, there are many trees such as black walnut, scarlet oak, sassafras, magnolia, tulip tree, sycamore, and Kentucky coffee tree which are characteristic of more southern regions.

The *Acadian Forest* of Nova Scotia, Prince Edward Island, and southern New Brunswick resembles the Great Lakes

Forest and is transitional to the Boreal Forest to the north. White spruce, white pine, red pine, and other conifers are well represented as are deciduous hardwoods such as maple, beech, and birch. The characteristic conifer of the region is the red spruce. Although this forest occupies only two per cent of the forest area of Canada, it has been exploited for a long time and still accounts for eight per cent of the volume of wood cut in Canada each year.

SOILS

The soil is an important part of the resource base. Varying greatly in composition from place to place, soils reflect the characteristics of the rocks and the natural vegetation of the region. The soil zones of Canada shown in Figure 2.22 closely follow those of natural vegetation and to a fair degree those of climate as well.

Fundamentally, there are three major soil divisions in Canada: Tundra, Grassland, and Forest. More importance is attached to the last two because they contain the areas in which agriculture is possible. The

Tundra soils, on the other hand, are economically of little importance. Profile differences between grassland and forest soils are illustrated in the accompanying diagrams, Figure 2.23.

The grassland soils, represented here by *Carrol Silty Clay Loam* from Southern Manitoba, have dark crumbly surface soils, high in organic matter and mineral nutrients. The immediate subsoil is also dark colored and aggregated into columnar clods. Beneath the dark soil there is a whitish zone which is alkaline and high in accumulated calcium carbonate. While this is a typical *Black Soil*, both the *Dark Brown* and the *Brown Soils* resemble it in general characteristics. They are, however, both shallower and less highly developed because of the influence of lower precipitation and scantier growth of vegetation.

Forest Soils are represented by *Londonderry Clay Loam* from Nova Scotia. Developed under a dominantly coniferous forest cover in a humid climate it has a well-marked Podzol profile in which the ashy, white, leached horizon is a prominent

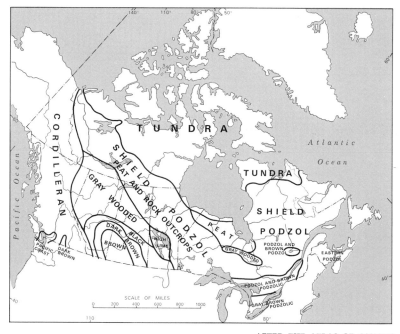

AFTER THE ATLAS OF CANADA

Figure 2.22 Soil Regions for Canada

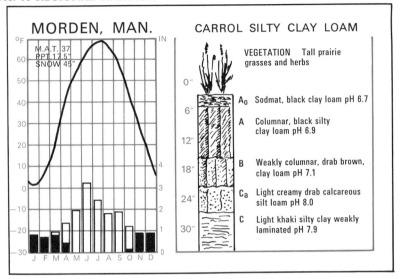

Figure 2.23(a) A Black Soil from Manitoba

feature. The subsoil is nut-structured, rather than columnar-cloddy as in the Black Soil, and there is no sign of lime accumulation. In fact, the profile is acid throughout. The Podzolic soil profiles resemble this in general structure but do not have such an extreme development of the leached horizon. They are also not so highly acid and they usually contain a greater degree of natural fertility in the form of available mineral nutrients. Conse-

quently they have been of more significance in the development of Canadian agriculture than have the soils of the Podzol Zone. Both grassland and forest soils can be divided on the basis of profile development into a number of soil zones. The relative importance of each to the economy of Canada is difficult to gauge, but a first approximation may be obtained by estimating the actual and potential areas of arable land associated with each

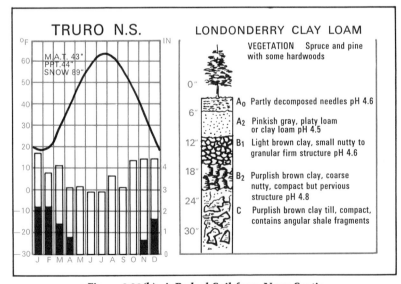

Figure 2.23(b) A Podzol Soil from Nova Scotia

Table 2.3   **Estimates of Arable Land in Canada by Soil Zones ***

Soil Zone	Total Land Area (000 ac.)	Improved Land (1961) (000 ac.)	Additional Potential (000 ac.)	Total Potential Arable Land (000 ac.)
Brown Soil Zone	34,000	10,000	——	10,000
Dark Brown Soil Zone	30,000	25,000	——	25,000
Black Soil Zone	46,000	35,000	6,000	41,000
Gray Wooded Soil Zone **	170,000	10,500	18,000	28,500
Cordilleran Soil Zone	230,000	750	3,000	3,750
Pacific Coast Soil Zone	4,000	250	——	250
Gray Brown Podzolic Soil Zone	25,000	14,500	——	14,500
Eastern Podzol Zone	76,000	5,000	4,500	9,500
Canadian Shield ***	730,000	2,500	10,000	12,500
Ten Provinces	1,345,000	103,500	41,500	145,000

* Sources: Census of Canada; A. Leahey; and map measurement.
** Including the High Lime Soil Area.
*** The Canadian Shield is a physiographic region in which Tundra soils, Podzols, and various Podzolic soils occur.

soil zone. These estimates are shown in Table 2.3 for the area of the ten provinces of Canada. The agricultural potential of the northern territories is extremely limited.

The soil is the basis of agricultural wealth and Canada has long been known as an agricultural country, yet as shown in the accompanying table only a little more than 10 per cent of the land in the 10 provinces may be considered as available for agriculture. Of this more than two-thirds has already been brought under cultivation. A good deal more than this, to a total of 175,000,000 acres, is already owned as farm land in spite of its obvious lack of agricultural capabilities. This, of course, is only a general picture, but it points up the necessity for careful study of the soil within the total framework of Canada's natural resources.

IN SUMMARY

This has been a very brief presentation of a few topics about which a whole series of volumes might be written, as indeed it is to be hoped that some day there will be. The scarcity of definitive pronouncements that it is possible to make on many points indicates the need for further research work in physical geography and the cog-

nate physical sciences, which can make important contributions to a knowledge of the geographic pattern of the country. Only in this way is it possible to formulate an integrated plan for the future development of Canadian resources.

To touch lightly on one particular topic, it seems obvious that Canada is well endowed with water resources. Yet within the more densely settled areas we face the problems of pollution and of impending water shortages. The question has two aspects: should governments plan a system of pipelines, aquaducts, and canals which would bring vast new supplies of water to the settled areas, or should they seek to find a resource base which would permit the development of industrial settlements in some of the areas where water is readily available? The water topic has still a third aspect. Other areas on this continent have even greater water problems than Canada. Is it possible that the use of this resource might be planned in such a way that all forseeable Canadian needs would be met and still provide surplus water that might be sold as a commodity to bring in needed revenue for the development of other resources?

To answer these questions is to bring to the fore not only the problem of the planned development of the water resource but the whole problem of integrated resource planning and national development.

A second topic perhaps should be briefly raised again. Canada has long been known as an agricultural country, and much of its early development was based on agricultural settlement. For decades now it has been known that some sectors of the agricultural economy are in grave difficulty, more so in some years than in others. Those areas in which agriculture is most flexible and amenable to improvement are undoubtedly those with the greatest climatic advantages, but it is in these areas where the competition of other land uses

is most severe. Again, it is not a matter of planning a single resource base but of integrating the use of those resources into a master plan for national development.

The study of physical geography does not give one the solution to these major problems, but it does present and analyze the data which must be used in their solution. In similar vein it may be said that a preliminary study of physical patterns does not provide a complete plan for regional studies of such a large and complex country as Canada, but it does present systematically some very pertinent data which must be kept in mind when reading the regional discussions which follow.

BIBLIOGRAPHY

Boughner, C. C. and Thomas, M. K. *The Climate of Canada.* Meteorological Branch, Department of Transport. Ottawa. 1967.

Cass-Beggs, David. "Water as a Basic Resource". *Resources for Tomorrow Conference. Background Papers.* Vol. 1. pp. 173-189. Ottawa. 1961.

Chapman, L. J. and Brown, D. M. *The Climates of Canada for Agriculture.* The Canada Land Inventory Report No. 3. 1966.

Chapman, L. J. and Putnam, D. F. *The Physiography of Southern Ontario.* University of Toronto Press. 2nd edition. Toronto. 1966.

Espenshade, Edward B. Jr. *Goode's World Atlas.* Twelfth edition. Rand McNally & Company. Chicago. 1964.

Halliday, W. E. D. "A Forest Classification for Canada". *Forest Service Bulletin.* 89 (1937). Ottawa.

Hare, F. K. "Climate and Zonal Divisions of the Forest Formation in Eastern Canada". *Geographical Review.* XL, 4 (October, 1950). pp. 615-635.

Hough, J. L. *The Geology of the Great Lakes.* University of Illinois Press. 1958.

Laycock, A. H. *Water Deficiency and Surplus Patterns in the Prairie Provinces.* Report #13, Compiled for the Prairie Provinces Water Board by the Hydrology Division, Prairie Farm Rehabilitation Administration. Regina. March, 1967.

Leahey, A. "Appraisal of Canada's Land Base for Agriculture". *Resources for Tomorrow Conference. Background Papers.* Vol. 1. pp. 49-54. Ottawa. 1961.

Mayer-Oakes, W. J. *Land, Life and Water: Proceedings of the 1966 Conference on Environmental Studies of the Glacial Lake Agassiz Region.* Winnipeg: University of Manitoba Press. 1967.

Menzies, J. R. "Water Pollution in Canada by Drainage Basins". *Resources for Tomorrow Conference. Background Papers.* Vol. 1. pp. 353-364. Ottawa. 1961.

Putnam, D. F. (Editor). *Canadian Regions.* J. M. Dent and Sons (Canada) Limited. Toronto. 1952.

Rowe, J. S. *Forest Regions of Canada.* Canada, Department of Northern Affairs and Natural Resources, Forestry Branch. Bulletin 123. Ottawa. 1959.

Sanderson, Marie. "The Climate of Canada According to the New Thornthwaite Classification". *Scientific Agriculture.* Vol. 28 (1948). pp. 501-517.

Sanderson, M. E. and Phillips, D. *Average Annual Water Surplus in Canada.* Meteorological Branch, Department of Transport. Ottawa. 1967.

Stockwell, G. H. (Editor). *Geology and Economic Minerals of Canada.* Department of Mines and Technical Surveys. Ottawa. 1957.

Thornthwaite, C. W. "An Approach to a Rational Classification of Climate". *Geographical Review.* XXXVIII, 1 (January, 1948). pp. 55-94.

Wegner, Alfred. *The Origin of Continents and Oceans.* (Translated by John Biram). Dover Publications, Inc. New York. 1966.

Wilson, J. Tuzo. "Continental Drift". *Scientific American.* 208, 4 (April, 1963). pp. 86-103.

The Human Geography of Canada

3 Human geography begins when man moves into a new area and attempts to impose upon wild natural land the patterns which he deems necessary to his continued existence. In this sense the human geography of Canada goes a long way back to the first migrations of the proto-Amerinds into North America in the Pleistocene Epoch. Even though we count some of their descendants among the more than twenty millions of modern Canadians, the effects of their early activities have had little influence upon present patterns of occupance and economic activity. To all intents and purposes the European settler in North America was confronted with wild natural land in which the patterns of the Amerinds, and even the aborigines themselves, were regarded simply as natural phenomena of the land upon which a civilized pattern was to be imposed.

PATTERNS OF SETTLEMENT

One cannot of course, believe that any plan existed about the pattern of the civilization which was to be created. Some colonists had very clear ideas of what they wanted in a New England, a New France, or a copy of some other European region; but many people had become colonists either unwillingly, by force, or because they had wished to get away from old established patterns in order to create something new and different in a climate of greater opportunity. As a result North America, and Canada in particular, bears the unmistakable stamp of western European civilization, but with many of its familiar features considerably modified. Perhaps even more important in determining Canadian settlement patterns is the fact that the whole area was not opened up and occupied at the same time, or even within a few years; instead, the process required generations, even centuries. Changes in technology and economic opportunity, as time went by, have probably had as much to do with creating regional differences, as have the contrasts which the settlers encountered in the physical milieu.

Eastern Canada would be very different country if its settlement could have been postponed until the twentieth century; and a very different pattern would have been imposed upon the Prairies if European settlement had taken place in the seventeenth. A far different occupance pattern would have resulted if Europeans had been able in the early days to discover the mineral wealth of Canada instead of only the coastal fisheries and the furs of the forest. Perhaps one might even speculate upon the pattern that would have evolved had the new waves of population come

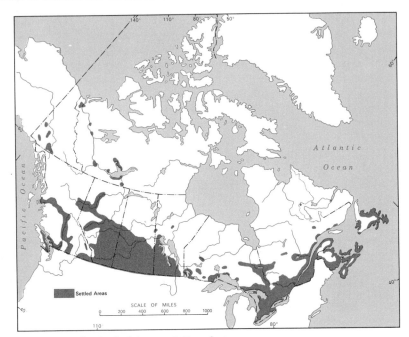

Figure 3.1 The Settled Areas of Canada
As pointed out in CHAPTER 1, only a small portion of Canada is settled.
Compare this map with Figure 1.2.

from Asia and entered by way of the Pacific Coast instead of from Europe by way of the Atlantic.

The regional geographer must take the regions as he finds them. He must describe the patterns which he sees and try to explain their origins and processes of development. Because of the physical pattern of the country and the human reactions to it, Canada has a very clear and distinctive geographic pattern which no amount of heated argument can change. Its foundations are not to be sought in its political boundaries, which are mostly arbitrarily imposed lines, in many cases simply meridians or parallels of latitude. Instead, the pattern is a natural one created by groups of settlers as they sought to exploit the resources of their particular milieu.

For over three centuries European settlements have been associated with the St. Lawrence gateway into North America. As might have been expected, the St. Lawrence Lowland and the plains bordering the Lower Great Lakes became, and remain,

the most heavily populated and highly developed parts of Canada, containing almost two-thirds of the total population and an even greater share of economic activity. The existence of two distinct concentrations of population, one in the Montreal Plain and the other in South-central Ontario, each of them dominated by a different cultural heritage, makes it necessary to treat this strategic and naturally well-endowed lowland as two regions instead of one. Both, undoubtedly, will experience great growth in the immediate future.

The Atlantic Region is quite different. Here, the history of European settlement reaches even farther back than in the hinterland of the St. Lawrence, but the physical milieu was such that there were fewer opportunities for agricultural development. Except on Prince Edward Island, the pattern of settlement was dominantly coastal and peripheral. The interior was rough and inhospitable, providing only logs and furs, rather than extensive areas of potentially arable land. The forest and the sea have been the chief factors in the economy, apart from the mining of coal in Nova Scotia and iron in Newfoundland. Economic growth has been slow and populations have remained relatively stable. New generations have been born, of course, but a constant stream of young people flows outward to seek brighter prospects in other parts of the continent.

Within the span of a half-century an agricultural settlement pattern was imposed upon the prairie plains of Western Canada. Even when the Prairies were fully claimed and occupied, the widely scattered towns and cities of this vast and sparsely settled area functioned only as central places for its wheat farmers. Since 1931 there has been a steady migration from the land. More land is used and more wheat is grown, but changing technology now permits this to be done by fewer people. The central cities have grown and are growing, but the total increase in population has not been great.

West of the Prairies there is another milieu based upon mountains, valleys, rivers, and the sea. Forests, fish, minerals, and waterpower have fed the economy of this region. Starting from a very small coastal nucleus the ecumene has infiltrated more than half the area of the province of British Columbia, but the only large concentrations of population are found in the original centers of colonization. Yet the growth is such that its population now rivals that of the much older Atlantic Region and may perhaps surpass that of the prairie plains in the not very distant future.

The "pioneer fringe", the frontier of agricultural settlement and the subject of almost endless discussions among geographers, is a thing of the past. In only a few places do good land and agricultural opportunities still remain. Instead, a different kind of development, a *resource frontier*, has come into being. Throughout the northern parts of Quebec and Ontario, across the northern spaces of the western provinces, and even in the northern territories, minor changes in population distribution have occurred as mines have been opened and roads and railways built to service them. Most notable in the post-war years have been the iron mines of Quebec and Labrador, uranium and copper in Ontario, nickel in Manitoba, and petroleum and natural gas in Northern Alberta and Northeastern British Columbia. Base metals are being obtained at Pine Point in the Northwest Territories and at various places in the Yukon. But these developments are small specks in an extremely vast area and have very little effect upon the size and shape of the Canadian ecumene established in the decade following World War I. The origins and development of this pattern may now be taken as major themes to provide a basis for later regional discussions.

THE ST. LAWRENCE LOWLAND

The essential facts of early settlement in Canada have been recorded many times. The French held sway over the northeastern and central parts of the continent in the seventeenth and early eighteenth centuries, developing a few small scattered settlements on the tidal lands of the Bay of Fundy, the St. Lawrence Lowland, Detroit, the Illinois country, and the lower Mississippi Valley. It was to the banks of the St. Lawrence, however, that the largest numbers of Frenchmen came and here developed the most stable settlement. Without question the greatest economic opportunity lay in the fur trade. Furs were plentiful, light in weight, and high in value when exported to the European market. The trade was logically centered at Montreal which lay at the head of the easily navigable portion of the St. Lawrence River and which was also the focal point of several inland routes.

In contrast, agricultural propects in the new settlement were not bright. The growing season was too short and too cool for any European crops except for grasses and a few hardy grains. The area of productive land was not extensive, being restricted on the north by the Laurentide Escarpment and on the south by the roughlands of the

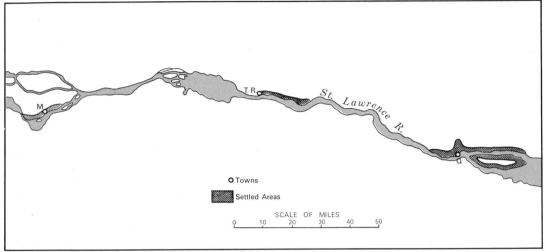

AFTER HARRIS

Figure 3.2 Settled Areas in the Vicinity of Montreal and Quebec in 1667

Appalachians, while within the plain itself swamps and marshes were widespread. The seigneuries were not allowed to spread very far west of Montreal because the officials feared that farming might interfere with their control of the fur trade. Equally discouraging to agriculture was the great distance of the Colony from any overseas market.

From its upstream position Montreal gained control of the fur trade, but Quebec, with its more accessible port, remained the headquarters of the administration and became the dispersal point for the settlement on the land. The second census of the Colony, taken in 1667, recorded a population of about 4,000, of whom 440 lived in Quebec, 400 in Montreal, and 210 in Trois-Rivières. About 2,000 lived on seigneuries within 20 miles of Quebec, 350 on the north bank of the St. Lawrence just to the east of Trois-Rivières, while the remaining 400 were within a few miles of Montreal.

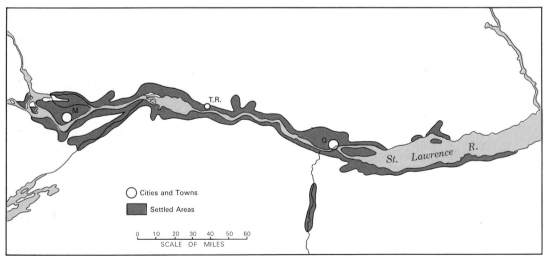

AFTER HARRIS

Figure 3.3 Settled Areas in the Vicinity of Montreal and Quebec in 1760

In a little more than 90 years, at the end of French rule in 1760, the population had increased to about 60,000. Two long ribbons of settlement had formed along the St. Lawrence River: one extended about 150 miles along the north bank of the river between Montreal and Quebec, while the other occupied the south bank for about 200 miles to a point about 50 miles down river from Quebec. There were a few small settlements on some of the tributaries of the St. Lawrence, but even at the time of the British acquisition of Quebec 90 per cent of the French inhabitants lived within a mile of the main river. "The St. Lawrence was an omnipresent element of Canadian life."* The urban component of the population was by no means insignificant for Montreal held 15,200 people, Trois-Rivières 550, and Quebec City 8,000.

A characteristic rural landscape had been developed. Extending inland from the St. Lawrence were long narrow fields on which the farmers grew crops of wheat, oats, barley, and peas. There were scattered apple and plum trees. About half of the cleared land was devoted to pasture, and every farm had a few horses, cattle, pigs, and sheep. The land was not intensively used, and there was no pressure on the forest which lay inland from the settlements along the river. Farming created little wealth, but it did provide a reasonably comfortable standard of living for the "habitant", gave him considerable independence, and inculcated a very strong attachment to the land. Beyond the settlements on the St. Lawrence Canada was a virtual wilderness in which there were only a few forts and trading posts.

As soon as British rule was established, English and Scottish merchants descended on Montreal, recognizing its strategic value for the fur trade and the possibilities for future control of the interior of North America. But there was little immigration of English-speaking people until after the American Revolution when the United Empire Loyalists came to the rolling terrain of the eastern townships and the banks of the St. Lawrence west of Montreal.

During the early part of the nineteenth century the population of the St. Lawrence Lowland continued to grow as French Canadians boasted one of the highest birthrates in the world. The good agricultural lands were rapidly taken up and by the middle of the century the lowland was fully occupied. As population increased and traditional agricultural methods were not updated, per capita yields declined and rural poverty increased. In short, the standard of living which had, in relative terms, been moderately high in the eighteenth century dropped sharply in the nineteenth.

By contrast, Montreal continued to forge ahead as a great commercial entrepôt. Through its control of the Ottawa and St. Lawrence routes Montreal was able to capture much of the fur trade during the eighteenth century and began in the nineteenth to turn its attention to the timber and grain of the Great Lakes region and the American midwest. However, there were difficulties. From the early seventeenth century the Hudson-Mohawk route had been a rival to the St. Lawrence. First under the control of the Dutch and later under the English, the route allowed trade to flourish in New York and Albany. The St. Lawrence and the Hudson-Mohawk are the only continuous low-level corridors between the Laurentians and the Appalachians, and it is no accident that Montreal and New York should have arisen early as rival trading posts, developing subsequently into great cities. The dominance of New York in the nineteenth century may be explained by the political separation of the United States and British North America, which brought about the restriction of the hinterland of Montreal, and by the building of the Erie Canal prior to the canals of the St. Lawrence. New York had a great natural advantage; it was a year-round port on the open Atlantic whereas the approach to Montreal was blocked by ice for at least five months in every year.

* R. C. Harris. *The Seigneurial System in Early Canada: A Geographic Study.* University of Wisconsin Press. Milwaukee. 1966.

With the passage of the Drawback Act in 1846 the trade of Canada West could move freely through the Mohawk route, and Montreal's fortunes reached such a low ebb that its merchants were willing to sign the Annexation Manifesto of 1849.

However, Montreal began to rise again. The St. Lawrence Canals were built during the 1850s and deep water navigation was improved between Montreal and Quebec. The outstanding success of the Bank of Montreal insured the financial supremacy of the city for decades to come, while a vigorous railway building program began to unite the hinterland much more effectively to the port.

UPPER CANADA

Even in the eighteenth century effective human geography in Canada had begun to take shape beyond the confines of Quebec. To be sure, the land was considered part of the province of Quebec until it was renamed Upper Canada under the Constitutional Act of 1791. The fur trade of Montreal held sway and for some time there was little effective settlement on the land. But a rapid change began with the coming of the Loyalists in the early 1780s. Townships were quickly surveyed along the north bank of the St. Lawrence and around the Bay of Quinté near the outlet of Lake Ontario. Far to the west the Niagara Peninsula was occupied as far as Burlington Bay at the head of Lake Ontario. Treaties with the Indians released new lands for settlement, and soon Loyalists, the sons of Loyalists, "late Loyalists", and direct immigrants from Britain created a discontinuous chain of settlement from Montreal to Detroit. In 1793 Lieutenant Governor John Graves Simcoe caused a new town, which he named York, to be laid out on the flat shore of Toronto Bay. It was not the site which he personally would have chosen for the administrative center of Upper Canada; he preferred the forks of the Thames far inland where the city of London now

stands. However, the advantages of the commodious harbor were not to be denied when the transfer of supplies was of such paramount importance. Simcoe, it will be remembered, also had a road cut northward to the Holland River, en route to the Upper Lakes. It can hardly be supposed that Simcoe was consciously attempting to create a serious economic rival to Montreal. York was only an outpost of British rule next door to the wilderness. So rapidly did the settlement develop, however, that only four decades elapsed before "muddy York" became the city of Toronto with a population of 10,000 people.

Upper Canada, or Canada West as it was known after 1841, rapidly became an agricultural region. The early colonists of necessity practiced a high degree of subsistence agriculture, but they had commercial intentions. Their land had a better climate than that of the plain below Montreal. Winter wheat, clovers, and Indian corn could be grown. Wheat quickly became an export crop, a development that stimulated widespread land clearance in the southwest; the other crops helped greatly in establishing a livestock industry. In 1825 the Erie Canal was completed from Buffalo to Albany and its effects began to be felt in the southwestern part of Upper Canada. Also by way of a connection at Oswego, it was possible for goods from Lake Ontario ports to be directed toward New York. Toronto businessmen were thus enabled to bypass the treacherous rapids of the St. Lawrence and to liberate themselves from the hegemony of Montreal. As Lord Durham once remarked, "New York State had made its own St. Lawrence from Lake Erie to the Hudson", and for Upper Canada it became a welcomed route. Not only could it expedite the export of country staples, but it could bring back the much-needed overseas imports as well. The Drawback Act of 1846 permitted free movement of goods by this route into Canada, and in 1854 the Reciprocity Treaty opened markets for Canadian goods and permitted imports from the United States as well.

Railways came in the 1850s and Upper Canada was quick to use them. Naturally they offered quick communication with Montreal, but rail routes were soon opened to the United States as well. Toronto took a strong lead in railway building as rails fanned out in all directions to make connections with the immediate hinterland. Later they were extended north to enter into direct competition with Montreal for the trade of Western Canada.

Apart from the early and rather feeble efforts of Kingston there were no rivals to the dominance of Toronto in Upper Canada, yet the historical geography of the province is far from being that of Toronto alone. Far more than in Lower Canada local centers grew and prospered. Kingston remained a local regional capital although its growth was impeded when it failed to become the capital of the country; the strategic location of Hamilton at the head of the lake made it a natural transportation focus and later it became a center of heavy industry. Local centers began to grow in the Grand River Valley while London, in the railway age, make good the prophetic insight of Simcoe by becoming the local social and commercial capital of the southwest. But many places were refused the boon of growth. The north shore of Lake Ontario and to a lesser degree the shores of the other lakes are dotted with small ports and adjacent small towns. Some of them attempted to capture a hinterland by sprouting railways into the interior but the pull of the main route was too strong. In many cases, the railway station became more important than the port, and many a small town turned its back upon its harbor.

Growth was also denied to those small inland towns missed by the railways. They declined while their rivals "on the line" took over their trading areas. Spur lines were sometimes built but usually to no avail. There is no doubt that the growth pattern of Southern Ontario was almost completely set by the railway builders during a short period around the middle of the nineteenth century.

THE MARITIMES

The peninsula of Nova Scotia is a long wharf extending far out into the Atlantic. In the days of sail this was a great advantage; Nova Scotia and other parts of the Atlantic Region benefited from their coastline and focused much of their economy upon the sea. Every cove along the coast had its strung-out fishing village from which, weather permitting, a fleet of small boats set out daily for nearby fishing grounds. In better harbors where adequate wharfage could be constructed, schooner fleets were based. Their crews came not only from the adjacent small towns but from the coastal settlements as well. In the winter many schooners went into the carrying trade. During the heyday of sail in the nineteenth century many large three- and four-masted ships were built and sailed by men of the Atlantic Provinces. At one time it was claimed that there were more tons of shipping per capita registered in the Maritime Provinces than in any other place in the world. The only commodities available for export were fish and lumber, while much less bulky cargoes were returned. The vessels themselves also became exports, being sold or leased to foreign operators. Their crews often went with them. Once the crews reached foreign ports, many of them signed on other vessels and were dispersed around the world to return to the Maritimes perhaps only after years of wandering. For a time Halifax and Saint John were great ports, but they had no great hinterland and no chance of obtaining any in the face of competition with the strategically placed ports of the east coast of the United States and the St. Lawrence.

The first half of the nineteenth century must be rated as a period of progress in the Atlantic Region. Reliable estimates place the total population at the turn of the century at about 135,000, of which half lived in Nova Scotia, and by the early 1850s it had increased to about 635,000, Nova Scotia containing about 277,000 or 43.5 per cent.

THE GEOGRAPHY OF CONFEDERATION

A reconnaissance of Canada on the eve of Confederation would certainly have emphasized the scattered nature of the settlement pattern. The population was almost entirely rural, and there were only nine cities of any distinction (1861 census): Montreal, 96,000, and Quebec, 51,000, in Lower Canada; Toronto, 47,000, Hamilton, 22,000, Kingston, 15,000, Ottawa, 15,000, and London, 12,000, in Upper Canada; Saint John, 27,000, in New Brunswick; and Halifax, 25,000, in Nova Scotia. Fredericton and Charlottetown, although political capitals, were small towns of 6-7,000 each. The four provinces which entered Confederation in 1867 had approximately 3.3 million people with 46.4 per cent in Ontario, 35.3 per cent in Quebec, 11.1 per cent in Nova Scotia, and 8.2 per cent in New Brunswick. Newfoundland declined to join, and the entry of Prince Edward Island was postponed. The Intercolonial Railway had yet to be completed through the empty lands to link the Maritime settlements with those of Canada. Montreal was clearly the primate city with a population twice as large as that of Quebec or Toronto and almost four times as large as that of Saint John or Halifax. To the north was the almost empty area of the Canadian Shield, but to the south the Appalachian section was being settled rapidly. The growth of the French-Canadian population continued at an extraordinarily high rate and was putting considerable pressure on the land resources. In fact, emigration to New England had begun and was soon to be accelerated. In Quebec the merchant class was almost entirely English speaking, and even many of the seigneuries had fallen into English ownership. The prospects for rural French Canadians on the eve of Confederation were rather gloomy. And Quebec was indeed rural; outside of the two large cities, there were only a few small towns which together contained less than six per cent of the population.

The Upper Canadians had not yet overpopulated their agricultural lands but were within a generation of reaching a maximum rural population in many counties. There

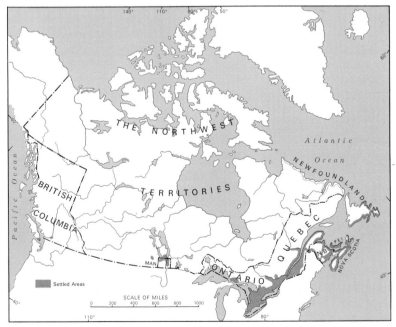

GENERALIZED FROM THE ATLAS OF CANADA

Figure 3.4 Distribution of Population in Canada in 1871

had been little agricultural invasion of the Shield, but all the good land to the south of it had been appropriated. Upper Canada was still not highly urbanized although its five recognizable cities contained eight per cent of its population. It also had a scattering of small towns throughout the province, sufficient to raise the urban population to eighteen per cent of the total.

The differences in provincial development were not, however, the most compelling geographical reasons for recasting the political pattern. Outside influences must also be considered. The rapid territorial consolidation of the United States and its equally rapid growth in population had left the scattered British Provinces in a rather anomalous and dangerous position. For different reasons each was determined not to be engulfed, but it was some time before they adopted the idea of creating another super-state, equal in area at least to the United States, even though it could not hope to be equal in wealth, population, or power.

The mid-nineteenth century was definitely the beginning of a new age in which the old geographical facts were being given new meaning while many new features were being added. The industrial revolution was already giving rise to the factory-town, while steam power on both land and water was causing a re-evaluation of space relations. In 1860 the colonies which now comprise Canada had about 3.2 million people, or about twice the number in the United States at the time of the Revolution. They had a strong nucleus in a fairly compact area adjoining a vast and almost unpeopled land under the same flag. Another, smaller group occupied the Atlantic seaboard, while much smaller groups were to be found in the Red River Colony and in British Columbia. The St. Lawrence River and Great Lakes formed a great, although interrupted, transportation route by which natural products might reach the sea and an overseas market. Unfortunately, a share of this route and a great deal of the tributary area had passed to another

flag, but the remainder was worthy of great effort. Indeed, if the effort were not forthcoming, the whole area might soon be lost.

In the 1860s the long power struggle between the free, northern states with their budding industries, and the slave-holding, cotton-growing, agrarian society of the southern states was finally resolved by force of arms. Undoubtedly the Civil War period bought time for Canada, but it also created political difficulties. Britain had shown considerable sympathy with the South on account of the cotton trade. Southerners had established agencies in Canada which were troublesome to the North. There was, naturally, considerable American resentment. Canada was affected in various ways. The cancelling of the Reciprocity Treaty was a severe blow. The threat of the armed Fenian bands which assembled on the border was a danger of a different sort. The annexation sentiments expressed by many midwestern Americans, also, were not to be taken lightly. There was every reason for the British Provinces to consolidate and strengthen themselves. American feelings soon cooled, however, and Canadians were left to proceed with the solution of their own growth problems. The existence of a strong United States to the south of the unfortified boundary became not a threat but a guarantee of safety to the new country.

It is less than accurate to say that Canada was built in defiance of geography. It is true, of course, that the most productive natural regions of the country are northern extensions of regions in the United States. It is also true that those huge Canadian regions, the Shield and the Northland, are not highly productive. It is even true, in many instances, that north-south communications appear easier than east-west. Yet Canada was consolidated and continues to develop by utilizing the favorable factors in the geographical situation.

The St. Lawrence—Great Lakes waterway, with its navigation and power potential, was a great factor which is now achieving a more complete development.

Certainly it has been one of Canada's strongest geographical assets. Northern rivers are also proving their worth. The Churchill in Labrador, the tributaries of James Bay, the Nelson and Churchill systems in the Prairie Provinces, and the vast Mackenzie and Yukon systems in the Northwest, together with the rivers of the Pacific Coast, will all be utilized eventually. The utilization of a number of them has international complications, but this may be an advantage rather than otherwise.

Neither all the advantages nor all the difficulties were completely foreseen in the bid for continental expansion. But it was clearly seen that agricultural land was running short in the eastern provinces and it was felt that much good land was available on the Prairies. The need, therefore, was to establish a base from which the ambitious project of establishing a country stretching from coast to coast could be mounted; and this was secured under the British North America Act.

PRAIRIE SETTLEMENT

The Canadian Prairie was the last substantial tract of the central North American grassland to be developed. Its occupation, begun in the 1840s in Indiana and Illinois, was completed with the appropriation of the most northerly grassy areas of the Peace River country in the 1920s. Over a period of about 80 years the vast interior plains of this continent had come under the plough to provide agricultural products on an unprecedented scale. The settlement of the Canadian Prairie was no less spectacular than that of the western states, but it was delayed until the closing years of the nineteenth century, the greatest activity taking place in the two decades just before World War I. Until the building of the Canadian Pacific Railway in the 1880s, there were only a few agricultural settlements in Southern Manitoba and some scattered holdings to the west. The total population of the Prairies was only 100,000 in 1881. Without transportation facilities large-scale agriculture was impossible.

Moreover, the rival lands of the American west, reasonably well supplied with railways, were not completely taken up until 1890. At least, until that year, a definite "frontier" line used to appear on the American census maps. Railways were regarded as crucial, but surprisingly there was no great rush to the new lands on the completion of the Canadian Pacific; there were only 200,000 people in the new lands by 1891.

A number of interrelated factors combined to bring about a vigorous growth between 1895 and 1914. Of great importance was the general recovery of world trade and the rising industrialization of Britain and western Europe, causing the price of wheat to rise from the lowest point in 200 years in 1896 to more than $1.00 per bushel in 1897. Further, the Canadian Pacific Railway reduced the rate for grain carriage to the Lakehead and the rate for lake shipment was also reduced, thus making Canadian grain more competitive in the world market. Between 1895 and 1914 over 3,000,000 immigrants came to Canada, mainly from Europe and the United States. Approximately 1,000,000 returned to their homes, about 1,000,000 found employment in other parts of Canada, and about 1,000,000 became farmers on the Prairies. In addition to this stream of immigrants there was a significant internal migration from the Maritime Provinces and from rural Ontario. However, despite the opportunity, relatively few Prairie settlers came from the overcrowded rural areas of the St. Lawrence Lowland. During the height of the activity thousands of miles of new railway were built, especially in Saskatchewan and Alberta. The population of the Prairie Provinces rose from 420,000 in 1901 to 1,328,000 in 1911, and that of Saskatchewan, alone, from 91,000 to 492,000 over the same period.

From the outset wheat assumed the status of a staple commodity, and Prairie farming became almost a monoculture. The economic level thereafter rose and fell in response to two chief variables: the world price of wheat and the vagaries of the

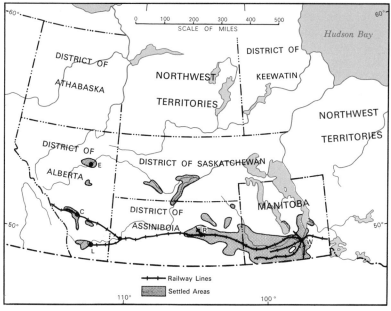

AFTER WARKENTIN

Figure 3.5 Distribution of Population in the Prairies in 1886
For the most part, early settlement followed the railway lines. Warkentin's
map appeared in R. L. Gentilcore's *Canada's Changing Geography*, Prentice-
Hall of Canada Ltd.

Prairie climate. Though basically rural and agricultural the economy supported some nucleated settlement. Hundreds of small towns, villages, and hamlets were strung along the railway lines, their development having a close relationship to the productivity of the land. A few towns and cities also arose, their size and location being determined by the presence of historical fur-trading posts, the density of surrounding population, the requirements of railway administration for divisional headquarters and regional terminals, and the need for higher order service centers for the settlement at large. Winnipeg, on the eastern margin of the Prairies, became the regional capital and major dispersal point. Increasingly, grain flowed eastward through Winnipeg, while goods and services were dispersed westward. Banks, insurance companies, the grain exchange, railway offices, wholesale houses, and manufacturing plants reflected the growing strength and diversification of the city. Its population rose from 30,000 in 1891 to 175,000 in 1914, and many freely predicted

the emergence of a Canadian Chicago. Checked by World War I its growth thereafter has been rather slow and disappointing.

BRITISH COLUMBIA

The building of the Canadian Pacific Railway was as great a stimulus to the far western province as it was to the Prairies. In fact, it was the promise of a railway that induced British Columbia to enter Confederation. Before the railway the census of the province (1881) disclosed the presence of 40,000 people, half of whom were Indians. Settlement was largely centered at Victoria (population about 4,000), the origins of which went back to the Hudson's Bay post founded in 1843. New Westminster near the mouth of the Fraser River was the main distributional point and former capital of the mainland colony, while a few settlements in the interior remained as reminders of the Cariboo gold rush of 1858.

Burrard Inlet was selected as the terminus of the Canadian Pacific instead of

New Westminster, and the new town of Vancouver began to grow rapidly where formerly only a few sawmills had been located. By 1901 its population had risen to 30,000, almost equal to the 31,000 found in the capital, Victoria. The deep, ice-free, well-protected harbor provided a base for modest Asiatic and American trade, as well as a much larger local trade, mainly timber. New Westminster, 15 miles to the southeast on a steep bank of the Fraser River, declined, the river with its relatively shallow water and shifting sandbanks being much less attractive for overseas vessels. Vancouver reached its first growth peak in 1912 with a population of 122,000. World War I brought a sharp drop to 96,000 in 1916. The rapid exploitation of forestry and fishery resources with the accompanying speculative fever in the city had attracted many people, resulting in overexpansion followed by a major setback.

In the interior some farming had begun in the Okanagan, and mining camps were producing intermittently in the Kootenays. Pockets of settlement were founded on small tracts of level land in the valleys traversed by railways. Revelstoke and Kamloops on the Canadian Pacific were the most important. A second Canadian Pacific—the Kettle Valley line—traversed the extreme southerly part of the province from Hope to the Crowsnest Pass. For years vital links in this line of transportation were supplied by steamships on the lakes until the railway was finally completed in 1931. To the north, in the central part of the province, the Grand Trunk Pacific was completed to Prince Rupert where a seaport to rival Vancouver was planned. The growth of the area failed to reach these expectations by a large margin; Prince Rupert had a population of only 6,400 in 1921 while Prince George, the chief divisional point on the railway, had a population of only 2,000.

In British Columbia, as on the Prairies, the pattern of human occupance was fairly well established by the 1920s. The growth rate between 1921 and 1930 was about the same as in the previous decade but much steadier, and during the depression years British Columbia grew at a rate considerably above the national average, providing a haven for many who were forced to leave the depressed areas on the Prairies. During the 1940s the population of the province increased by 30 per cent, and during the 1950s by 40 per cent. The great bulk of this growth, however, has been in the Vancouver and Victoria areas where over 70 per cent of both population and economic activity are now located. North-central and northeastern areas are growing faster at the present time and although they are still underdeveloped, their continued growth will help to provide a much needed geographical balance in the province.

THE CANADIAN SHIELD AND THE NORTHLAND

The largest of Canada's physiographic regions, the Shield, has an enormous influence upon human geographic patterns. Settlement in the St. Lawrence Valley and in Southern Ontario was upon relatively level, fertile plains, restricted to the north by the rough terrain and shallow soil of the Shield. A considerable portion of the Prairie Provinces is also Shield country where the rigor of the terrain is reinforced by the rigor of the subarctic climate. Though it offers very restricted opportunities for agriculture, it was the basis of early wealth from the fur trade and is now the source of wood from which lumber and pulp and paper are manufactured. The abundant rivers and lakes, which offered only routes to the voyageurs in the early days, are now the source of enormous energy harnessed for industrial purposes.

During the early part of Canada's experience as a nation, however, the Shield was, for the most part, a liability — a thousand miles of wasteland which had to be bridged by steel in order that the nation might take form and grow. The work of the railway builders, however, exposed some of its great wealth. The Sudbury Basin was developed after 1885, and silver was discovered at Cobalt in 1904. This was followed by gold discoveries at Porcupine in 1909 and at Kirkland Lake in 1912. Base metals, iron ore, and uranium have since been exploited to provide the support for many small settlements. Modest exploitation of saw-timber on the southern fringes has been followed by the building of a chain of pulp and paper mills. The pattern of forest utilization is now fairly well stabilized and is not likely to result in a much enlarged zone of settlement. There was even some optimism just before World War I concerning the possibilities of agricultural settlement in the various Clay Belts on the Shield, an optimism which evaporated rapidly in the face of post-war agricultural competition. The experiences of Ontario and Quebec in the Clay Belt have shown that the only way to promote farm settlement in such an environment is through complete government supervision and subsidization. Even then it is quite clear that the settlers will have inadequate social and economic opportunities.

The Shield does offer many splendid sites for the development of hydro-electric power which began on a modest scale before World War I, and has continued ever since. Hydro-electric power made possible the development of the other resources of the Shield — its pulp and paper and its minerals. Thus the Shield now contains a number of industrial centers which have or will soon have a population of 50,000 or more. Some very large power schemes are planned such as those of Churchill Falls in Labrador and Nelson River in Manitoba. The outlet for such large supplies of power is usually stated to be industrial development outside the Shield, involving long and costly transmission lines. People can and do live and work in mining settlements and pulp and paper towns on the Shield. Perhaps it would not be too much to expect that other industries could function there also. It would be a partial solution to the evergrowing competition for land in southern urban areas.

THE FOCUS OF CANADIAN DEVELOPMENT

Canada has developed by regions at different times, in different ways, and with dependence upon different resource bases. The account of the developments in the plains of the St. Lawrence Lowland and the interlake region of Southern Ontario was interrupted at the time of Confederation in order to permit some attention to be given to developments in other parts of Canada. It is necessary, now, to review the post-confederation growth of the St. Lawrence — Great Lakes area because, regardless of the growth of other areas, it is evident that this pulsing industrial heartland is the focus of Canadian development.

During the first half-century of Confederation, and particularly in the years 1895-1914 when Western Canada was being opened up and the first settlements were being made on the Shield, the settled parts of Eastern Canada were experiencing significant reorganization. Industrialization and urbanization were accelerating. The urban population of the Montreal area rose from 120,000 in 1871 to 350,000 in 1901, and to 700,000 in 1921. The growth of Toronto was even more rapid; 60,000 in 1871, 220,000 in 1901, and 530,000 in 1921. Increasingly, entrepreneurs in Montreal and Toronto were financing northern and western development and were supplying goods and services to outlying areas.

Shifts in agriculture in Southern Ontario and to a lesser extent in the St. Lawrence Lowland were marked by a reduction in wheat acreage as western grain-growing increased. Commercial dairying, first for cheese and butter and later for fluid milk to supply the growing cities, became significant. Favorable areas such as the Niagara Peninsula, Southwestern Ontario, Georgian Bay, Bay of Quinté, and a few spots in Southern Quebec became horticultural areas. After reaching a peak in the 1880s the rural population of Southern Ontario began to decline, while the economic status of the better farmers began to improve. Even today, however, there are pockets of

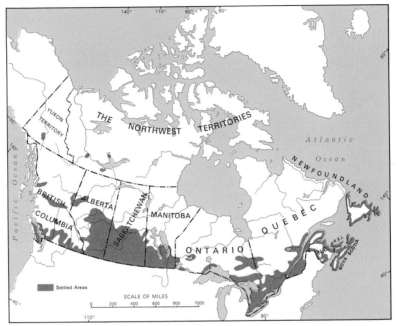

GENERALIZED FROM THE ATLAS OF CANADA

Figure 3.6 Distribution of Population in Canada in 1921
By 1921 the settled areas had expanded westwards from those shown in
Figure 3.4, and the basic pattern was established. It varies only slightly
from that of the present.

rural poverty in Southern Ontario. Similar
stagnation and decline, although often
appearing a few decades later, may be
noted in Quebec. The sponsored settlement of the Shield provided only slight
alleviation. Many who left poor farms
migrated to New England or Quebec's own
growing cities. Many of the surplus farmers of Ontario moved on to farms in
Western Canada, but only a few from Quebec made such a move.

In spite of the availability of capital, a
modest endowment of resources, and an
energetic and enterprising population, the
rate of economic development in the Maritime Region fell behind that of Ontario and
Quebec after 1880 and has remained so to
the present. The abandonment of formerly
cultivated land is particularly notable. The
reasons for growth differentials, however,
are many and complex.

Before Confederation the rural economy
of Southern Ontario supported many small
service centers where some manufacturing

was carried on. Most towns were located
on streams where waterpower could be
harnessed. That some grew into small
cities while others stagnated and declined
may be explained by the adequacy of the
power supply, the location of rail lines, the
productivity of the hinterlands, or the personal initiative of the entrepreneurs. Increasingly, the more successful towns such
as Galt, London, and Hamilton, to mention only three, began to develop a diversified, indigenous industrial structure. In
each town there grew up small pools of
skilled labor and managerial expertise.
Metal working, food processing, and textile
manufacturing had local origins. Developing areas in Western Canada and on the
Shield provided additional markets for
these small centers to encourage industrial
expansion and amalgamation in order to
generate economies of scale. Much of this
growth took place in Southwestern Ontario, reflecting the superiority of its agriculture and its relatively high purchasing

power. It was also the part of Canada most accessible to the developing manufacturing region of the United States, from which new ideas, new techniques and, eventually, new capital originated. The costs of American coal were lower here than any- where else and when hydro-electric power was introduced, the region was rela- tively accessible to power lines from Niagara Falls. Raw materials could be brought cheaply from the West and the Shield to the lakeside ports, particularly Hamilton and Toronto. In short, there was set in motion an early industrial pattern, supported by both physical and economic circumstances, which has grown into the contemporary spatial pattern of economic development.

Southern Quebec also had its pattern of local industries, particularly in the Eastern Townships and along the north bank of the St. Lawrence, and some of these have had a continuous development. The su- periority of Montreal as a port and a mar- ket, however, eliminated the chance of much local expansion.

In the Maritimes many attempts were made to develop local manufacturing in- dustries. It should be recalled, however, that the wealth which accumulated in this region during the first part of the nine- teenth century came from timber, fish, and shipping. The focus was upon commercial activity rather than on industrial growth, and consequently little tradition or exper- tise in manufacturing had a chance to develop. Maritime markets, in any event, were so small that they did not provide a sufficient home base for the economies of scale which were developing in Montreal and Southern Ontario. Thus they were poorly equipped for the nation-wide com- petition which became theoretically pos- sible under the National Policy. Moreover, the factor of distance to the markets of Quebec, Ontario, and, above all, the Prairies always operated against them. As was the case for all of Canada, of course, the market for their primary products was worldwide. They had justification for the contention that the National Policy cut in

on their income by forcing them either to buy in Central Canada or to pay an equiva- lent price for their imported consumer's goods.

The points advanced here to explain the underdevelopment of Maritime Canada are equally valid in the West and indeed in the outlying parts of the central provinces themselves. The economies of scale in secondary manufacturing and most service industries always operate in favor of a central location in or close to a metropolis. The greater the home market, the more cheaply goods may be provided to outside markets. Thus, in Canada the economic focus is always upon its "heartland" which also contains the greatest concentrations of population and the greatest political power.

POPULATION

On the eve of Canada's Centennial Year the census of 1966 recorded a total popu- lation of slightly more than twenty millions occupying a rather narrow band of terri- tory along the southern border with only a few outposts of any importance any- where in its vast hinterland (Figure 3.1). In this respect the picture has changed very little in half a century, the pattern of popu- lation distribution having become rather well fixed by the end of World War I. But, whereas half a century ago less than half the population was found in urban places, today the urban fraction is almost three- quarters. Even more striking is the fact that almost half the total is to be found in twenty metropolitan cities of over 100,000. Montreal, the largest urban grouping, con- tains one-eighth of the whole population, while one-third resides in the five largest cities: Montreal, Toronto, Vancouver, Win- nipeg, and Ottawa (Table 3.1).

To say that Canada has become a nation of cities is an exaggeration perhaps, but clearly the old rural dominance has disap- peared. The census of 1931 showed that even then the expanding cities contained more people than the open countryside. The farm population after reaching a peak of 3.3 million in 1931 began to slowly

Table 3.1   Canada: Metropolitan City Population, 1966 and 1961 *

Census Metropolitan Area	Number	1966 Per Cent of Total	Number	1961 Per Cent of Total	Five-year Increase (Per Cent)
Montreal	2,513,564	12.56	2,183,332	11.97	15.12
Toronto	2,303,919	11.51	1,925,301	10.56	19.66
Vancouver	892,286	4.46	790,165	4.33	12.92
Winnipeg	508,759	2.54	476,543	2.61	6.76
Ottawa	494,535	2.47	429,671	2.36	15.07
Hamilton	449,116	2.24	395,189	2.17	13.64
Quebec	413,397	2.07	357,568	1.96	15.61
Edmonton	401,299	2.00	337,568	1.85	18.87
Calgary	330,575	1.65	279,062	1.53	18.45
Windsor	211,697	1.06	193,365	1.06	9.48
London	207,396	1.04	181,283	.99	14.40
Halifax	198,193	.99	183,946	1.00	7.74
Kitchener	192,275	.96	154,864	.85	24.15
Victoria	173,455	.87	154,152	.85	12.52
Regina	131,127	.66	112,176	.61	16.89
Sudbury	117,075	.58	110,799	.61	5.66
Saskatoon	115,892	.58	95,564	.52	21.27
St. Catharines	109,418	.54	95,577	.52	14.48
Saint John	101,192	.51	95,563	.52	5.89
St. John's	101,161	.50	91,654	.50	10.37
Twenty Metropolitan Areas	9,966,331	49.80	8,643,342	47.39	15.30
Other Urban Areas	4,760,428	23.78	4,056,958	22.25	17.33
Total Urban Population	14,726,759	73.58	12,700,300	69.64	15.95
Rural Non-farm Population	3,374,407	16.86	3,465,072	18.99	−2.68
Rural Farm Population	1,913,714	9.56	2,072,785	11.37	−7.67
Total Rural Population	5,288,121	26.42	5,537,857	30.36	−4.50
Total Population	20,014,880	100.00	18,238,157	100.00	9.74

* Census of Canada.

decline, dropping to 1.9 million in 1966. It may fall still further. The rural non-farm population, however, continued to expand. Newfoundland with a largely rural non-farm population came into Confederation in 1949. Thus, total rural population reached a peak of about 5.7 million in 1956 but had fallen to below 5.3 million by 1966.

On the other hand, urban population continued to expand, even during the depression of the 1930s. Much more rapid expansion, especially of the larger cities, has taken place since World War II. The accession of Newfoundland in 1949 did not change the picture significantly. While few Newfoundlanders were farmers, there were few towns and no cities with more than 100,000 inhabitants at that time. Since then, St. John's has passed 100,000, Corner Brook has become a fair-sized city, and numerous smaller places have been incorporated. However, even without the accession of Newfoundland the population of Canada has more than doubled since the end of World War I. It has increased by 50 per cent since the end of World War II (Figure 3.7).

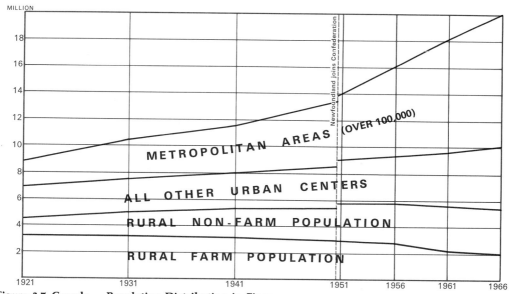

Figure 3.7 Canada — Population Distribution in Figures
Since 1921 the importance of the rural farm population has continued to decrease, while the importance of the population living in *metropolitan areas* has continued to increase.

The discussion of population changes is somewhat handicapped by a series of changes in definition and methods of calculation in the different census years. In earlier years "urban population" included the inhabitants of all incorporated places regardless of size. There are also computations of urban populations based on an urban limit of 500 inhabitants. In 1951 metropolitan areas were recognized and

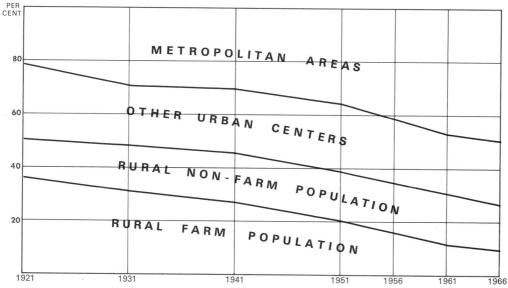

Figure 3.8 Canada — Population Distribution as a Per Cent
Since 1921 the proportion of the population in *metropolitan areas* and in other urban centers has changed dramatically.

"rural-urban fringes" were included in the urban population, while all places with less than 1,000 inhabitants were classed as rural. In 1956 other major urban areas were recognized. Since then numerous adjustments have been made to urban areas. Unofficial estimates of "greater city" populations prior to 1951 also exist. In preparing the data for Figures 3.7 and 3.8, these estimates and minor adjustments in data have been used to obtain a proper geographical perspective.

The change in the character of the population since 1921 is even more dramatically portrayed in Figure 3.8. Rural farm population which was more than 36 per cent in 1921 has declined to less than 10 per cent in 1966. Metropolitan city population has increased from 22 per cent to 50 per cent. Much less change is seen in the population of other urban areas (villages, towns, small and medium-sized cities) which accounts for about 25 per cent, and the rural non-farm category which makes up about 17 per cent.

Several phenomena are involved in the changes in population, some of which show very marked trends while others have varied at random within rather narrow limits. There has been widespread and steady migration of people from farms to urban centers. This has been accompanied by the decline of many of the old rural service centers. Some indeed may completely disappear while others, more strategically located, and well supplied with lines of communication may continue to grow to serve wider areas.* Unfortunately only areas with a dominant agricultural base have yet been examined systematically.

Historically, some areas were endowed with greater numbers of small nucleated settlements. Of more than 8,000 small unincorporated places enumerated in the census of 1966, about 3,750 (almost half)

* Gerald Hodge. "Do Villages Grow?" *Rural Sociology.* Vol. 31 (1966). pp. 183-196.
————. "Urban Systems and Regional Policy". *Canadian Public Administration.* Vol 9, 2 (1966). pp. 181-193.

are to be found in the Atlantic Provinces. In some counties and census divisions, where there is very little agricultural land, almost the entire rural population is found in coastal hamlets. This pattern is particularly characteristic of Nova Scotia and Newfoundland which were settled by people who depended on transportation by water. By contrast, there are relatively few hamlets (775) in the Prairie Provinces and many of them have smaller populations. The focus here is also on transportation: almost all Prairie hamlets and villages are associated with railway lines. Only 19 per cent of the Prairie population is classed as rural non-farm, while the corresponding figure in the Atlantic Provinces is 40 per cent. Ontario has about 1,550 unincorporated places and Quebec has 1,250; in both provinces the rural non-farm population makes up about 13 per cent of the total. In spite of the older settlement experience these figures are proportionately lower than on the Prairies. In British Columbia the rural settlement pattern has some similarity to that of the Atlantic Provinces. There are about 650 unincorporated, nucleated places, and a rural non-farm population of about 20 per cent which is four times as great as its farm population.

In all provinces there are many people who live in scattered non-farm residences. Some of these may have farm jobs or may be associated with other primary resource industries. More generally, they are to be found in areas where good highways provide contact with job opportunities in nearby towns and cities. Table 3.2 compares the population patterns of four census areas in different parts of Canada. None of them represent "average" conditions since their rural and urban populations are nearly equal; instead, they represent inhabited areas lying beyond the "urban shadows" of the great cities — they are the "forgotten lands" of most Canadian geographers who tend to emphasize either the metropolis or the vast and almost uninhabited wilderness.

All provinces but one, however, have their sparsely settled and empty areas,

Table 3.2   Examples of Population Distribution, 1961 and 1966 *

	A		B		C		D	
	1961	1966	1961	1966	1961	1966	1961	1966
Total Population (000)	54.9	60.0	89.4	96.4	61.3	59.5	94.6	105.8
Total Population (per cent)	100.0	100.0	100.0	100.0	100.0	100.0	100.0	100.0
Urban Population (per cent)	65.5	66.8	56.5	59.5	56.0	60.0	52.1	52.9
Rural Population (per cent)	34.5	33.2	43.5	40.5	44.0	40.0	47.9	47.1
(a) Rural Farm Population (per cent)	18.1	14.3	20.8	17.8	24.4	23.0	17.6	16.4
(b) Rural Non-farm Population (per cent)	16.4	18.9	22.7	22.7	19.6	17.0	30.3	30.7
(i) Hamlet and Village Population (per cent)	10.6	8.7	6.2	5.9	13.2	13.3	12.1	11.1
(ii) Dispersed Rural Non-farm population (per cent)	5.8	10.2	16.5	16.8	6.4	3.7	18.2	19.6

* Data from Census of Canada.

NOTES
A. Shefford County, Quebec. The urban centers include the city of Granby and the town of Waterloo. Farm population is slowly declining while urban population and rural non-farm population are rising.
B. Kent County, Ontario. This is a very successful corn-growing and special crop area. Its urban centers include the centrally located city of Chatham and seven towns and villages of 1,000 to 10,000. Population is steadily increasing.
C. Division No. 7, Saskatchewan. This is an extensive, grain-growing region adjacent to the city of Moose Jaw (33,000); Herbert is the only other place with more than 1,000 inhabitants. Population is slowly declining.
D. Division No. 3, British Columbia. Located in the southern interior, Division No. 3 includes the fruit-growing areas of the Okanagan Valley. Three cities, Vernon, Kelowna, and Penticton, each have more than 10,000 inhabitants, while there are half a dozen places with more than 1,000. Urban population is increasing while rural population is stagnant.

while Yukon and the Northwest Territories are almost completely empty. Prince Edward Island was blanketed with a fairly uniform spread of agricultural settlement, but in Newfoundland, Nova Scotia, and New Brunswick settlement is either coastal and peripheral or follows the river valleys into the interior. The other, much larger provinces may all be divided into a southern populated area and a northern wilderness. In this they resemble the country itself.

With only slightly more than five persons per square mile, Canada is one of the least densely peopled countries in the world. However, population is concentrated in certain areas. In Southern Ontario and Southern Quebec, where about three-fifths of all the people live,

population density is approaching 200 per square mile.

Apart from growth and urbanization, the most distinctive characteristic of Canada's population is the presence and persistence of two major culture and language groups — French-speaking and English-speaking. The former group is descended from less than 10,000 original colonists brought to New France in the seventeenth and early eighteenth centuries. At the end of the Seven Year's War they numbered less than 60,000. Though virtually cut off from further streams of migrations from France, Canada has today almost 6,000,000 French Canadians most of whom are found in the province of Quebec.

The English culture and language group is quite mixed. The majority, of course, trace their origins to various parts of the British Isles with rather disproportionate representations from Scotland and Ireland. But even among the early settlers, Loyalists and pre-Loyalists as they are known in history, there were many from other west European countries whose mother tongues were German, Dutch, Flemish, and even French (Huguenots). The English culture group has been reinforced during the past two centuries by waves of migrants from the British Isles and from all parts of Europe, while smaller groups have come from nearly all parts of the world. The settlement of the Prairies in the early part of this century brought many people from central and eastern Europe while one of the dominant streams of post-world War II migration has come from Italy.

Almost completely submerged by the dominant floods of Europeans, the descendants of the original North Americans, the Indian and Eskimo peoples, make up slightly more than one per cent of the population.

Still another characteristic of the Canadian people must be mentioned — its youth. The census of 1966 revealed that almost one-third was under the age of 15 years and almost one-half was under 25. There is, of course, some geographical variation; Newfoundland and New Brunswick have the most children, British Columbia and Ontario the least. The former are among the least urbanized provinces, while the latter are among the most urban-

ized; but there does not seem to be a great degree of correlation between the number of children and the degree of urbanization. On the other hand, there is a fair degree of negative correlation between average per capita income and size of family. This, however, can be overstressed because large families have more people dependent upon a single pay check. Even if wage and employment rates in Atlantic Canada were to be brought into line with those of Ontario and British Columbia, per capita disposable income would still lag until birth rates were also brought into line. Atlantic Canada especially, as well as some other areas, has long served as a reservoir of young people to augment the populations and labor forces of more economically active areas. Unfortunately, because of a lack of advanced education many of the migrants are poorly equipped for any but poorly paid jobs. Even more unfortunate perhaps is the fact that many people in these areas who have been able to obtain a higher education are forced to migrate in order to obtain employment suited to their abilities.

Canada's population is mobile and migratory, but we possess only fragmentary statistics on the matter. Part of the mobility must be laid to the presence of new immigrants at all periods of our history. Often they have not been satisfied with the conditions which they found. Many native-born Canadians also have found conditions to be unsatisfactory and

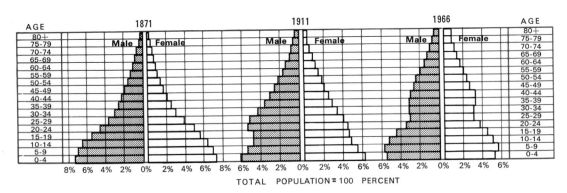

Figure 3.9 Canada — Population Pyramids for 1871, 1911, and 1966

Table 3.3   Elements of Population Growth, 1921-1966 *

	1921-1931	1931-1941	1941-1951	1951-1961	1961-1966	1921-1966
	000	000	000	000	000	000
Natural Increase	1,360	1,174	1,972	3,148	1,522	9,176
Net Migration	229	44	169	1,081	255	1,690
Accession of Newfoundland	——	——	361	——	——	361
Total Increase	1,589	1,218	2,502	4,229	1,777	11,227

† Data from D.B.S. sources.

have left the country, usually to take up residence in the United States. The census of 1961 showed that 15.5 per cent (2.8 million) of the resident population of Canada was foreign born. In retrospect, it should be remembered that in 1911, 1921, and 1931, the census showed that over 22 per cent of Canada's population was foreign born.

While there is no doubt about immigrant origins and no doubt either about the contributions being made by current streams of immigration, the growth of Canada's population depends chiefly upon natural increase (Table 3.3). Since 1921 more than 11,000,000 have been added; the accession of Newfoundland accounted for 3.21 per cent, net migration brought in 15.05 per cent, leaving 81.73 per cent to be attributed to natural increase. The excess of births over deaths during the period of 45 years has not only been much greater than the gain through net migration, but it has also been steadier and more reliable. During the depression of the 1930s Canada suffered a net loss through migration, notwithstanding the fact that more than 75,000 former Canadians returned after periods of residence in the United States. On the other hand, more than one million people were added by migration in the 1950s.

But external or international movement of population is only part of the story. The 1961 census showed that more than 10 per cent of all Canadians were then resident in a province other than that in which they had been born (Table 3.4). Canadian as

Table 3.4   Origin of Population in Provinces, 1961 *

Province	Born in the Province		Born in other Provinces		Foreign Born		Total Population	
	000	%	000	%	000	%	000	%
Newfoundland	442	96.5	10	2.2	6	1.3	458	100.0
Prince Edward Island	94	90.0	8	7.6	3	2.4	105	100.0
Nova Scotia	629	85.5	74	10.0	34	4.5	737	100.0
New Brunswick	518	86.7	56	9.4	23	3.9	597	100.0
Quebec	4,647	88.3	224	4.3	388	7.4	5,259	100.0
Ontario	4,305	69.0	578	9.3	1,353	21.7	6,236	100.0
Manitoba	633	68.6	119	12.9	170	18.5	922	100.0
Saskatchewan	665	71.9	111	12.0	149	16.1	925	100.0
Alberta	788	59.2	255	19.2	289	21.6	1,332	100.0
British Columbia	761	46.7	445	27.3	423	26.0	1,629	100.0
Northern Territories	20	52.6	13	34.2	5	13.2	38	100.0
CANADA	13,502	74.0	1,893	10.4	2,843	15.6	18,238	100.0

* Census of Canada, 1961.

well as foreign-born migrants are found in greatest numbers in Ontario, British Columbia, Alberta, and Quebec. In the province of Quebec, however, migrants do not make up a very large proportion of the population. In fact, Quebec contains more native-born Canadians than any other province. In Quebec and the Atlantic Provinces an average of 88 per cent still lives in the native province, while in Newfoundland the figure rises to more than 96 per cent. On the other hand, Ontario and the western provinces have large numbers of migrants, and less than half the population of British Columbia is native-born.

While most Canadians still reside in their native provinces, they are nevertheless mobile and change places of residence fairly frequently. We have already noted the migration from farm and rural hamlet to the city. But it is city folk who are most mobile.* This mobility is most evident in Quebec and Ontario (Table 3.5). Over 5,000,000 Canadians changed residence between 1956 and 1961, of whom 4,867,000 (92 per cent) were urban; this amounted to roughly 37 per cent of all urban residents. The highest rates of total mobility were found in the largest metropolitan cities: Montreal (57 per cent), Toronto (56 per cent), Vancouver (53 per cent), and Quebec (44 per cent). Total mobility includes movement into a city (*in-migration*) and movement within a city (*internal migration*). Internal migration is usually the greater part of total mobility, as is shown by the following records from the same cities during the same period (1956-

1961): Montreal (45 per cent), Toronto (34 per cent), Vancouver (33 per cent), and Quebec (37 per cent). Toronto and Quebec draw about equally for migrants on the provinces of which they are the capital cities (6.7 per cent and 6.5 per cent respectively), while Toronto has a commanding lead (11.8 per cent) in the proportion of foreign migrants. Inter-provincial migrants are proportionately more prevalent in Vancouver (5.3 per cent) than in either Toronto (2.7 per cent) or Montreal (1.4 per cent). Looking at Canada as a whole, about 52 per cent of the urban population changed residence in the five-year period. Such extreme mobility is an asset to the development of the economy but it does, however, render the gathering and interpretation of other population statistics rather difficult.

CANADIAN CITIES

A discussion of population growth and distribution in such a highly urbanized country as Canada naturally focuses itself upon the cities. Cities, however, are more than mere clusters of dense population haphazardly scattered within a political area. Cities have attributes of site, location, size, and age as well as social, economic, and political functions. These attributes and functions combine to give them personalities of their own and make of them

---

* H. Charbonneau et J. Légaré. "L'extreme mobilité de la population urbaine au Canada, l'exemple de Montréal entre 1956 et 1961". *Revue de Géographie de Montréal.* XXI, 2 (1967).

Table 3.5   Change of Residence, 1956-1961 *

Category of Residence in 1956	Mobile Population							
	Quebec		Ontario		Other Provinces		Canada	
	000	%	000	%	000	%	000	%
Urban	1,499	94.1	1,775	93.9	1,414	87.6	4,687	92.0
Rural	87	5.4	107	5.7	192	11.9	386	7.5
Undetermined	7	0.5	8	0.4	8	0.5	24	0.5
Total	1,593	100.0	1,890	100.0	1,614	100.0	5,097	100.0

* Source: Charbonneau and Légaré.

geographical entities worthy as objects of study, both in themselves and as integral elements of the regions in which they are located.

Cities are defined as political units. A city is an area within clearly defined boundary lines, having a prescribed system of government and a formal administrative organization. Cities may lie side by side along a common boundary as do Kitchener and Waterloo, Winnipeg and St. Boniface, Montreal and Westmount, Outremont and Verdun, or Toronto and the boroughs which encircle it. Such adjacent political units are bound together by all manner of functional ties which make them parts of the same geographical entity. The recognition of the larger geographical unit is coming in the political sphere also, as witness the creation of Metropolitan Toronto and Metropolitan Winnipeg. Fort William and Port Arthur have been united to form the city of Thunder Bay. Other cities such as Regina, Saskatoon, and Calgary have expanded their municipal boundaries to include all their urbanized fringe areas. A somewhat different scheme was adopted by two small towns, Burlington and Oakville, lying on the shore of Lake Ontario between Hamilton and Toronto. In their expansion they included not only their urbanized fringe areas but also the remaining rural areas of the adjoining townships. The neighboring town of Mississauga was created by raising the status of the rural municipality of Toronto Township to that of Town but excluding the long-established enclaves of Port Credit and Streetsville. With populations of 50,000 to 100,000 or more these towns are already of city size, but they are dominated by Metropolitan Toronto and the city of Hamilton. The census considers them as parts of these two metropolitan areas.

"Greater cities" were recognized by the Dominion Bureau of Statistics as early as 1931. In the 1951 census a list of 14 "metropolitan areas" having central cities of 50,000 and over and total populations of more than 100,000 was published along with maps of the census areas. As cities have grown, this list has been enlarged and 19 such metropolitan areas were included in 1966. Since 1951 lists of other "major urban areas", in which the central city had a population of at least 25,000, have also been published. There were 23 such communities listed in 1966. Curious anomalies have always existed in these lists. Regina and Saskatoon were for a time omitted, and it seems hard to justify the exclusion of Lethbridge in 1966. It is even more difficult to deny the metropolitan status of St. Catharines (urban population 109,480, central city 97,101). The Oshawa area and the Brampton area are both, logically, parts of the Toronto Census Metropolitan Area although they are not included with it in the census. With these and other similar minor adjustments one arrives at a list of 20 metropolitan areas (Table 3.1). Incidentally, it is strange that except by footnote the census does not acknowledge the existence of either the Metropolitan Corporation of Greater Winnipeg or the Municipality of Metropolitan Toronto. From the census of 1966 a list of 25 other major urban areas with populations of 30,000-100,000 may also be compiled. Together these 45 large urban areas include about 77.8 per cent of all the urban people in Canada or about 57 per cent of all Canadian residents.

Canada has more than 2,000 incorporated cities, towns, and villages with a population of 12.63 million (63.15 per cent of Canada's total population); however, more than half of these have less than 1,000 inhabitants each (Table 3.6). Thus only 12.18 million (60.85 per cent) are officially counted as urban. To these must be added about 2.55 million who live on the outskirts of towns and cities of over 10,000, making a total of 14.73 million (73.6 per cent) urban folk already noted. Inspection of census data shows that very few of the one thousand small incorporated places are to be found within the fringes of metropolitan and other major urban areas although many larger politically independent units have been absorbed by

Table 3.6   Incorporated Cities, Towns, and Villages, 1966 *

Size Group	Number	Population	Per Cent of Total
500,000 and over	2	1,886,839	14.9
100,000–499,999	12	2,960,793	23.5
50,000– 99,999	26	1,740,466	13.8
30,000– 49,999	22	851,675	6.7
25,000– 29,999	21	586,713	4.6
10,000– 24,999	117	1,800,816	14.3
5,000– 9,999	125	898,136	7.1
2,500– 4,999	237	835,182	6.6
1,000– 2,499	399	619,938	4.9
Less than 1,000	1,057	445,246	3.5
Total	2,018	12,625,784	100.0

* Census of Canada, 1966, Vol. I.

them. The census, however, does not provide complete analyses for all the urban areas in Canada since it lists only those above a population of 30,000. It does, however, note the populations of all municipal units, and it gives data for the urban population of each county, thus including the fringe areas of all small cities.

The occurrence of so many urban centers of such varying size prompts the geographer to investigate the relationship of city to city and of city to the countryside or surrounding region. Many years ago Mark Jefferson said "Cities do not grow up of themselves. Countrysides set them up to do the tasks that must be performed in central places."* But central places are not of the same size throughout a given area, nor do they offer the same set of services. Jefferson also offered the theory of the *primate city*.** In any country or region, he said, one city always tends to surpass all the rest. Thus London in England, Paris in France, and Lisbon in Portugal are clearly primate cities. Some countries, including Canada, are exceptions to this rule. Australia is another, and so is Spain. Another investigator has propounded the rank size rule.* The largest city is twice the size of the second city, three times the size of the third, four times the size of the fourth, and so on. Canada is clearly an exception to this rule also.

The absence of a primate city in Canada is quite striking. The population ratio of Montreal to Toronto is about 25:23 or 1.09 which is about the lowest of any country in the world. Historically Montreal was the primate city, the entrepôt and chief commercial center. Its decline has taken place during the past hundred years. Perhaps it is more accurate to say that Toronto's major advance took place in the latter half of the nineteenth century. Since 1900 the growth rates of the two cities have been relatively uniform. The idea might be advanced that a primate city has great difficulty in establishing its sway over a very large area. The enormous size of Canada necessitates the development of relatively large centers spaced at appropriate distances; thus Winnipeg and Vancouver have grown to be large regional capitals. Toronto is only 350 miles from Montreal, hardly far enough to warrant its substantial growth. However, distance must be judged in relative terms for a century ago Toronto was less accessible to Montreal in traveling time and cost than

* Mark Jefferson. "The Distribution of the World's City Folk". *Geographical Review*. XXI (1931). p. 453.

** ———. "The Law of the Primate City". *Geographical Review*. XXIX (1939). pp. 226-232.

* G. K. Zipf. *National Unity and Disunity*. Bloomington: Principia Press. 1941.

is any western city today. Jefferson suggested that the lack of primate cities in Canada, Australia, and other members of the British Empire was due to the imperial primacy of London. Others have suggested that New York is clearly the primate city of North America and that Montreal and Toronto are no more than ranking American cities.

On the surface it might appear that the answer lies in the ethnic dualism of Canada which made inevitable the emergence of a primate city for both English-speaking and French-speaking sections. Montreal has achieved dominance over the province of Quebec, providing a focus for social and economic aspirations. Rapid urbanization has given it more than 40 per cent of the provincial population and a primacy index of 6:1 over the city of Quebec which is still the political capital. But historically it is difficult to assert that the growth of Montreal can be attributed to the "French fact". Montreal was an entrepôt for a colony; the entrepreneurs were mainly English, Scottish, and American. It was only incidentally important that the available labor force happened to be French speaking.

The merchants of York, which was renamed Toronto in 1834, did not have to strive against French dominance; their resentment was directed against those of their own language in Montreal. The Drawback Act of 1846, which allowed them to trade freely through the port of New York via the Hudson-Mohawk route, was of great value to Toronto, speeding its own development and strengthening its hold on the hinterland where it had to compete with Montreal. The dominance of Toronto in Ontario is almost of the same order as that of Montreal in Quebec; it has one-third of the provincial population and a primacy index of 5:1 over its neighbor, Hamilton. As is the case for Montreal the development of primacy is based upon regional rather than ethnic reasons.

When the concept of primacy is applied to cities in other parts of Canada, great differences are noted. The Atlantic Region has no primate city. Halifax with a population of 200,000 is clearly the largest city, but it has only a modest and relatively recent claim to primacy. Instead each province has its own large city. The Atlantic Region has undoubtedly paid a high price for its continued political partition which has denied it the stimulus of the development of one vibrant, dominant, industrial, and commercial center.

During the period of settlement Winnipeg with 25,000 inhabitants by 1891 had a headstart as the gateway to the West. Its slowdown in growth and relative decline as the regional primate city of the Prairies have been recent. The growth of Calgary and Edmonton and lately of Regina and Saskatoon have done much to undermine the dominance of Winnipeg, while the strong growth of Vancouver has been a constant threat. Winnipeg, however, has never had any rivals within its own province. On the other hand, Calgary and Edmonton in Alberta and Regina and Saskatoon in Saskatchewan have had both geographical position and railway facilities giving them almost equal chances. Thus no primate city has emerged within either province.

By way of contrast, Vancouver holds absolute sway over British Columbia and is also able to make its influence felt in the western margins of the Prairies. On the threshold of becoming a "million city" Vancouver is likely to achieve metropolitan dominance over much of the West and to present increasingly an interesting challenge to the eastern rivals, Montreal and Toronto, on the national scene.

While throughout much of Canada metropolitan and other major urban areas are isolated and for the most part mononucleated, a much more complicated situation occurs in Southern Ontario. Clustered around the western end of Lake Ontario is a densely urbanized region containing five metropolitan areas with over 100,000 population and four other major urban areas of over 50,000 population (Table 3.7). So closely linked have these cities become in recent years that they appear

Table 3.7   Population Changes in Mississaga, 1951-1966 *

	1966	1961	1951
Metropolitan Areas			
Toronto **	2,203,664	1,844,383	1,218,742
(Toronto City)	(664,584)	(672,407)	(675,754)
Hamilton	449,116	395,189	264,568
Kitchener	192,275	154,864	107,474
St. Catharines	109,418	95,577	66,303
Oshawa ***	100,255	80,918	50,200
	3,054,728	2,570,931	1,707,287
Other Major Urban Areas			
Brantford	62,036	56,741	47,064
Niagara Falls	60,768	54,649	42,365
Welland	59,152	54,124	39,620
Guelph	51,377	41,767	30,384
	233,333	207,281	159,436
Metropolitan & Major Cities	3,288,061	2,778,212	1,866,723
Included Rural Population	37,460	45,502	51,291
Metropolitan & Major City Urb. Pop.	3,250,601	2,732,710	1,815,432
Other Urban Areas	91,913	67,180	58,493
Total Urban Population	3,342,514	2,799,890	1,873,925
Total Rural Population	282,525	285,059	235,035
Total Population	3,625,039	3,084,949	2,108,960

* Data from Census of Canada.
** Brampton and Bramalea areas are added to Census Metropolitan Area.
*** The Oshawa urban area includes a small area in Durham county.

almost as a continuous urban development. Variously called Mississaga, Conurbation Canada, the Golden Horseshoe, and the Canadian Megalopolis, this region commands the attention of government at all levels. It contains one metropolitan city and many other local units classified as city, town, village, township, and county. It is difficult to deal with it as a unit. Each municipality is, of course, jealous of its own century-old rights. The Ontario Department of Economics looks upon it as composed of parts of three different economic regions. Federal government agencies are randomly located but seem to be concentrated in Toronto. The provincial Department of Highways has long appreciated the necessity of closer integration and has tried to give it a regional highway network. The Department of Municipal Affairs is currently trying to create a pattern of regional areas of local government to take the place of the inadequate mosaic of authorities that has developed over the years.

Mississaga contains the heavily urbanized parts of ten counties which together have an area of 5,700 square miles. It is also possible that in the near future other nearby counties may have to be included. In 1966 the total population was about 3,625,000 or 52 per cent of the population of Ontario and 18 per cent of that of Canada. The average population density is about 635 per square mile, practically one per acre. The population is overwhelmingly urban (approximately 93 per cent), while 98 per cent of the urban people (91 per cent of the total) is crowded into the five metropolitan and four other major urban areas. During the years 1951-1966 the population of Mississaga increased by 72 per cent, while the urban population grew by 75 per cent. Farm population declined by about 25 per cent, but total rural population increased because of massive rural non-farm settlement of people with jobs in nearby cities. Small centers are also being invaded by commuters, who, at times, often outnumber the local people. Attention is clearly being focused on the expanding nuclei. Even more clearly it is being focused on the Toronto Metropolitan Area which during the same period increased by 81 per cent, thus absorbing 72 per cent of the population growth of Mississaga. But while the metropolitan area has been rapidly gaining population, the central city has been slowly declining (Table 3.7). Such change is, of course, in keeping with the building of large commercial, financial, administrative, and service buildings in the heart of the city, while greater numbers of new residential units are being created on the outskirts. Density differences are well illustrated in Table 3.8.

The focus of population geography in the province of Quebec is quite clearly in the Montreal plain where the Montreal Census Metropolitan Area recorded a population of more than 2.4 million in 1966. Together with the surrounding counties the region had a population of about 3.2 million (Table 3.9). It might be appropriate to name this populous region *Hochelaga*. In contrast to Mississaga it is quite clearly the outgrowth of one dynamic nucleus. Montreal has no large neighbors with their own metropolitan surroundings. The Montreal plain has seven much smaller cities, all of them complex urban areas, but together they add less than 250,000 to the total population.

The total area of the counties involved in this region is more than 12,900 square miles, but about 6,900 square miles belong to the sparsely populated Shield. We can therefore think of Hochelaga as the 6,000 square miles lying on the Montreal Plain. Comprising only one per cent of the area of the province it contains about 55 per cent of the population, with an over-all density of about 525 per square mile. Again, the population is overwhelmingly urban (91 per cent), while the metropolitan area itself houses 85 per cent of the urban people (77 per cent of the total population) in an area of about 490 square miles. The population density of the metropolitan area thus averages about 5,000 per square mile but it rises to four or five times as much in the more crowded parts of Montreal.

During the period 1951-1966 the population of the region increased by 58 per cent, while the actual urban population

Table 3.8   Population Densities in Toronto, 1966 *

	Area in square miles	Population (000)	Density per square mile
Toronto City	35.1	665	19,000
Toronto Metropolitan Municipality (excluding the city)	206.0	1,217	5,900
The Fringe Municipalities of the Metropolitan Planning Area	478.6	219	460
Total Toronto Planning Area	719.7	2,101	2,900
Toronto Census Metropolitan Area	816.0	2,158	2,650

* Population, Census of Canada, 1966. Areas by map measurement.

Table 3.9   Population Changes in Hochelaga, 1951-1966 *

	1966	1961	1951
Metropolitan Area			
Montreal Island	1,923,178	1,747,696	1,320,232
(Montreal City)	(1,222,255)	(1,201,559)	(1,021,520)
Laval (Jesus Island)	196,088	124,741	37,843
Chambly County (part)	173,296	136,640	70,130
Other Areas	144,255	101,602	43,646
Total **	2,436,817	2,110,679	1,471,851
Included Rural Population	3,303	4,633	14,150
Urban Population	2,433,514	2,106,046	1,457,701
Small Cities			
Jolliette	27,446	23,198	18,477
LaChute–Brownsburg	13,811	14,134	10,600
St. Hyacinthe	37,363	33,113	26,708
St. Jean-Iberville	42,627	39,281	27,764
St. Jérôme	33,258	29,195	19,766
Sorel	33,664	28,906	22,157
Valleyfield	34,120	32,372	25,656
	222,289	200,199	151,128
Other Urban Areas	192,441	134,159	31,840
Total Urban Population	2,848,244	2,440,404	1,640,669
Total Rural Population	304,455	316,324	347,712
Total Population	3,152,699	2,756,728	1,988,381

* Data from Census of Canada, 1951, 1961, 1966.
** Includes rural population in Metropolitan Areas.

Table 3.10   Population Densities in the Montreal Area, 1966 *

	Area in square miles	Population (000)	Density per square mile
Montreal City	50.4	1,222	24,000
Montreal and Jesus Is. (less Montreal City)	242.3	897	3,700
Fringe Areas of the Montreal Census Metropolitan Area	197.3	318	1,610
Montreal Census Metropolitan Area (Total)	490.0	2,437	4,975

* Population, Census of Canada, 1966. Areas by map measurement.

grew by 72 per cent. On the other hand, the rural population declined by seven per cent as many people from the farms and hamlets moved into the city. Scattered non-farm residences were built along many rural roads, but apparently not to the extent where this migration outweighed the gradual out-migration of other rural people. The city of Montreal did not lose population since the destruction of residence units during the redevelopment of the central business district was more than matched by the building of multiple-unit housing in other parts of the city. Average densities for the different zones of the metropolitan area are given in Table 3.10.

FUNCTIONS OF THE URBAN CENTER

The functions of the urban area are, of course, those activities which provide goods, services, and employment to the inhabitants. They also provide most of the links whereby the center maintains its close relations with its *umland* or surrounding region. Over the years the organization of the data in Canadian census reports has changed greatly, making it virtually impossible to carry out accurate historical comparisons of city functions in the same way that population changes may be studied. It is well known that Canadian cities all began as small settlements with very simple functions, many of them as ports on the sea coast or on the shores of inland lakes and rivers. In time they began to make useful articles as well as to move and to sell them. Later, waterpower was developed for the purpose of processing lumber and grain, thus laying the foundations of industrial growth. There were also some centers where much of the employment was provided by the activities of government and administration. With the building of railways, terminals and division points became necessary. Some of them provided the stimuli for new urban centers. What-

ever the primary activity may have been, the people thus engaged required services which they had neither the time nor the skill to provide for themselves; and other people moved in to fill the need. Every center of any importance therefore soon became multifunctional, while the original job opportunities were multiplied several times over.

Economic statisticians compile employment data in two different ways. An occupational classification indicates the kinds of jobs which citizens may have, such as carpenter, bricklayer, cab-driver, lathe operator, or mechanic; an industrial classification is based upon the end products of their work, which may be automobiles, newsprint, meat products, clothing, or beer. Those employed in the provision of services may also be classified in two ways: by the nature of their jobs, such as typist, surveyor, advertising executive; and by the industry with which they are associated. For instance, a typist might work for a manufacturer, an advertising agency, or a university; a surveyor might be employed by a government agency, a railway, or a consulting firm. In general, more geographical significance may be attached to the industry as a functioning entity; thus it is the industrial classification which will be stressed in this analysis of Canadian cities.

The student investigating the economy of a city wants to know how many people are employed in each industrial group, and if it is possible, the total economic return to the industrial group. Thus it would be possible to find out how diversified or conversely how specialized the industrial structure is. Such data could then be compared with those from other cities or with average figures for the province or the whole country.

The industrial census of Canada in 1961 listed about 180 different primary and secondary commodity-producing industries and more than 100 different service industries. They may be grouped in various ways for different purposes. For the purpose of the analysis of urban functions the present study will use the following set of industrial groups:

1. Primary Industries: all those which may be classified as agriculture, forestry, hunting, fishing, or mining
2. Manufacturing Industries
3. Construction Industries
4. Transportation, Storage, Communications, and Utilities
5. Wholesale Trade
6. Retail Trade
7. Finance, Insurance, and Real Estate
8. Community Services and Services to Business Management
9. Personal Services
10. Public Administration and National Defense
11. All other Industries

Industrial data for Canada and its six major regions are presented in Table 3.11.

Table 3.12 shows similar data for twenty metropolitan cities. At first glance, Table 3.11 gives the impression of an overwhelming dominance of Ontario in total employment and in all categories except primary industries where the Prairie Provinces take the lead. A similar quick glance at Table 3.12 shows Montreal as the center with the greatest total employment. Its dominance is only partial, however, for it is outranked by Toronto in several categories.

The *location quotient* is a useful device for the measurement of local or regional concentration of industry. From Table 3.11 it is seen that manufacturing employs 8.99 per cent of the total work force of the Prairie Provinces while at the same time giving employment to 21.71 per cent of the total work force of Canada. Comparing the two percentage figures:

$$\frac{\text{Manufacturing as per cent of Total Employment in Prairie Region}}{\text{Manufacturing as per cent of Total Employment in Canada}} = \frac{8.99}{21.71} = .414$$

It might also be shown that the Prairie Region has 7.34 per cent of the manufacturing employment in Canada while at the same time having 17.88 per cent of the total work force in Canada. Comparing these two figures:

$$\frac{\text{Prairie Region Share of Manufacturing Employment}}{\text{Prairie Region Share of Total Employment}} = \frac{7.34}{17.88} = .414$$

Thus the location quotient may be found in two ways.

On the basis of the labor employed, then, it may be concluded that manufacturing is only two-fifths as important in the Prairie Region as it is in Canada as a whole. Similar but slightly different indices would be obtained if *value added by manufacturing processes* were used in the calculation instead of employment figures. However, there is a very strong correlation between value added by manufacture and number of employees engaged in manufacturing. Such analyses tend to raise questions about the balance of economic development within a city or a region. Of course, it cannot be said categorically that the Prairie Region should have as much industrial employment as the average for Canada

any more than it can be said that Prairie wheat or Prairie oil resources should be evenly distributed throughout the rest of the country. But pointed questions may be asked about the possibility of opportunities being missed. From time to time references to location quotients will be made in various sections of this book.

Another approach to the nature of industrial structure is to consider the question of *diversification* versus *specialization*. It is obvious that certain cities have become highly specialized in certain functions; in some cases manufacturing is most important while in other cases more employment will be found in public administration. Some cities have several categories with almost equal employment opportunities. Perhaps the most promising method

Table 3.11 Labor Force by Industrial Divisions in Canada, 1961 *

	Atlantic Provinces		Quebec		Ontario		Prairie Provinces		British Columbia		Yukon and N.W.T.		Canada	
	Number	Per Cent	Number	Per Cent	Number	Per Cent	Number	Per Cent	Number	Per Cent	Number	Per Cent	Number	Per Cent
1.	94,820	16.89	202,508	11.45	231,555	9.68	317,591	27.43	57,015	9.87	3,828	27.95	907,331	14.02
2.	77,771	13.85	466,443	26.38	643,284	26.88	104,107	8.99	113,019	19.57	241	1.76	1,404,865	21.71
3.	38,203	6.80	126,361	7.15	153,866	6.43	75,598	6.53	36,338	6.29	727	5.31	431,093	6.66
4.	64,642	11.50	161,268	9.12	195,223	8.16	117,486	10.15	62,806	10.87	1,871	13.66	603,286	9.32
5.	23,685	4.22	69,334	3.92	102,733	4.29	61,948	5.35	32,074	5.55	110	.80	289,884	4.48
6.	66,012	11.75	178,704	10.11	267,807	11.19	121,097	10.46	67,204	11.63	782	5.71	701,606	10.84
7.	11,515	2.05	62,163	3.52	98,454	4.11	34,037	2.94	22,642	3.92	94	.69	228,905	3.54
8.	35,568	6.33	122,704	6.94	164,053	6.86	71,147	6.15	43,021	7.45	1,025	7.49	437,518	6.76
9.	67,390	12.00	228,160	12.90	303,074	12.66	145,081	12.53	80,761	13.98	1,378	10.06	825,844	12.76
10.	69,841	12.44	99,194	5.61	181,263	7.57	83,409	7.20	46,001	7.97	3,217	23.50	482,925	7.46
11.	12,195	2.17	51,267	2.91	51,703	2.16	26,241	2.27	16,767	2.90	420	3.07	158,593	2.45
Totals	561,632	100.00	1,768,119	100.00	2,393,015	100.00	1,157,742	100.00	577,648	100.00	13,694	100.00	6,471,850	100.00

* Data from Census of Canada, 1961.

Table 3.12 Employment in Canadian Cities, 1961

	Montreal		Toronto		Vancouver		Winnipeg		Ottawa		Hamilton		Quebec	
	Number	Per Cent	Number	Per Cent	Number	Per Cent	Number	Per Cent	Number	Per Cent	Number	Per Cent	Number	Per Cent
1	5,280	.65	8,620	1.09	9,741	3.30	2,094	1.08	1,759	1.05	4,501	2.97	1,842	1.46
2	255,381	31.65	234,511	29.70	57,485	19.50	38,537	19.83	17,766	10.59	61,090	40.29	23,749	18.79
3	56,310	6.98	51,055	6.47	19,897	6.75	12,629	6.50	11,809	7.04	10,585	6.98	9,074	7.18
4	88,634	10.98	68,701	8.70	34,934	11.85	26,812	13.80	11,396	6.80	9,374	6.18	10,976	8.68
5	43,394	5.38	49,594	6.28	22,757	7.72	16,055	8.26	5,993	3.57	6,429	4.24	6,628	5.24
6	85,029	10.54	96,902	12.27	37,142	12.60	25,229	12.98	16,798	10.02	17,599	11.60	15,173	12.00
7	5,467	4.16	5,566	5.09	2,690	3.91	10,252	5.28	7,480	4.46	4,969	3.28	5,127	4.06
8	56,574	7.01	57,868	7.33	22,741	7.72	14,356	7.39	11,152	6.65	9,685	6.39	9,194	7.27
9	110,376	13.68	109,854	13.90	47,639	16.16	27,820	14.32	23,388	13.95	19,145	12.62	23,525	18.61
10	42,050	5.21	42,958	5.44	18,003	6.11	16,156	8.31	55,835	33.29	5,438	3.59	17,819	14.10
11	21,961	2.72	17,250	2.19	8,502	2.89	4,380	2.25	4,336	2.58	2,822	1.86	3,304	2.61
Total	806,973	100.00	789,651	100.00	294,759	100.00	194,320	100.00	167,712	100.00	151,637	100.00	126,411	100.00

Table 3.12 Employment in Canadian Cities, 1961 (cont'd)

	Edmonton		Calgary		Windsor		Halifax		London		Kitchener		Victoria	
	Number	Per Cent	Number	Per Cent	Number	Per Cent	Number	Per Cent	Number	Per Cent	Number	Per Cent	Number	Per Cent
1.	4,337	3.30	8,028	7.35	1,225	1.78	382	.53	1,676	2.27	1,496	2.32	2,037	3.67
2.	17,477	13.28	13,064	11.96	24,602	35.83	7,472	10.24	18,416	24.94	29,294	45.34	5,960	10.75
3.	12,442	9.46	10,613	9.70	4,047	5.89	3,373	4.62	4,383	5.94	4,274	6.61	2,830	5.10
4.	14,649	11.13	12,202	11.17	5,345	7.78	7,667	10.51	5,915	8.01	3,107	4.81	4,272	7.70
5.	10,648	8.09	9,529	8.72	2,501	3.64	4,088	5.60	4,140	5.60	2,360	3.65	1,926	3.47
6.	17,062	12.97	14,317	13.10	8,333	12.14	8,345	11.44	9,094	12.32	7,485	11.58	7,188	12.96
7.	5,467	4.16	5,566	5.09	2,690	3.92	2,988	4.10	4,580	6.20	3,152	4.88	2,244	4.05
8.	9,248	7.03	8,081	7.40	5,666	8.25	4,657	6.38	4,779	6.47	3,661	5.67	4,412	7.96
9.	21,819	16.58	15,373	14.07	9,685	14.11	10,858	14.88	13,275	17.98	6,799	10.52	8,608	15.52
10.	15,211	11.56	9,786	8.96	2,975	4.33	21,981	30.13	6,075	8.23	2,027	3.14	14,316	25.82
11.	3,216	2.44	2,697	2.48	1,590	2.33	1,143	1.57	1,507	2.04	956	1.48	1,657	3.00
Total	131,576	100.00	109,256	100.00	68,659	100.00	72,953	100.00	73,840	100.00	64,611	100.00	55,450	100.00

Table 3.12 Employment in Canadian Cities, 1961 (cont'd)

	Regina		Sudbury		Saint John		Saskatoon		St. Catharines		St. John's	
	Number	Per Cent	Number	Per Cent	Number	Per Cent	Number	Per Cent	Number	Per Cent	Number	Per Cent
1.	816	1.75	12,721	32.73	371	1.11	712	2.00	494	1.41	580	1.98
2.	4,681	10.03	4,998	12.86	6,744	20.19	3,755	10.55	14,895	42.62	2,693	9.17
3.	3,682	7.89	2,317	5.96	2,206	6.60	2,879	8.09	2,225	6.37	2,001	6.81
4.	5,805	12.44	2,488	6.40	4,716	14.12	4,308	12.10	2,376	6.80	4,095	13.94
5.	4,123	8.83	1,185	3.05	2,873	8.60	3,326	9.34	988	2.83	2,218	7.55
6.	6,666	14.28	4,391	11.30	4,317	12.92	4,612	12.96	4,105	11.74	4,817	16.40
7.	2,530	5.42	994	2.56	1,377	4.12	1,471	4.13	1,028	2.94	882	3.00
8.	3,728	7.99	2,451	6.31	2,284	6.84	2,825	7.94	2,321	6.64	1,942	6.61
9.	7,261	15.56	4,678	12.03	5,454	16.32	7,677	21.57	4,558	13.04	5,075	17.28
10.	6,245	13.38	1,657	4.26	2,364	7.08	2,966	8.33	1,273	3.64	4,342	14.80
11.	1,135	2.43	989	2.54	702	2.10	1,062	2.99	690	1.97	721	2.46
Total	46,672	100.00	38,869	100.00	33,408	100.00	35,593	100.00	34,953	100.00	29,366	100.00

of comparison is by use of an index derived from a modified Lorenz curve.* Over the years a number of writers have explored this idea.** The present study acknowledges their work but does not specifically follow them in detail.

The original Lorenz curve plotted per cent of income on the *abscissa* against per cent of population on the *ordinate*, and the curves were thus continuous. In dealing with industrial groups, however, the *abscissa* must be divided into as many equal segments as there are groups, and the individual points must then be plotted. As in the true Lorenz curve, the *ordinate* registers cumulated percentages of the work force. If the points should all fall on the diagonal, it would mean that employ-

ment was equally distributed in all categories. It never does happen, but the assumption is necessary in order to provide a base for comparison.

The procedure begins by arranging the categorical percentages of workers in series according to magnitude. Actually two series are possible: one beginning with the largest group and one with the smallest (Table 3.13). It is not necessary to do both, but it clarifies procedure for it is seen that when the cumulated totals of the two progressive series are added, the final sum equals 100 $(n + 1)$, n being the number of industrial categories. Two curves may also be plotted, one above and one below the diagonal (Figure 3.10). If a series of equidistant points be plotted on the diagonal and summed progressively, the final sum will be seen to be $\dfrac{100 (n + 1)}{2}$. In this example $n = 11$. Therefore the total area of the figure is 1100 units, and the area under the diagonal is 550, whereas the sum of the progressive series is 600. This difference of 50, or one-half of the value of one column, may be seen to obtain in the values of progressive series on all such curves

---

* M. O. Lorenz. "Methods of Measuring the Concentration of Wealth". *American Statistical Association.* Vol. IX (1905). pp. 209-219.
** Edgar G. Conkling. "South Wales: A Study in Industrial Diversification". *Economic Geography.* Vol. 39 (1963). pp. 258-272.
Allan Rodgers. "Some Aspects of Industrial Diversification in the United States". *Economic Geography.* Vol. 33 (1957). pp. 16-30.
R. C. Tress. "Unemployment and Diversification of Industry". *The Manchester School.* Vol. IX (1938). pp. 140-152.

Table 3.13   Analysis of Industrial Structure, Canada 1961 *

Specialization			*Diversification*		
Category	Per Cent	Cum. P.C.	Category	Per Cent	Cum. P.C.
Manufacturing	21.71	21.71	Unspecified or undefined	2.45	2.45
Primary Industries	14.02	35.73	Finance, Insurance, etc.	3.54	5.99
Community and Business Services	12.76	48.49	Wholesale Trade	4.48	10.47
			Construction	6.66	17.13
Retail Trade	10.84	59.33	Personal Services	6.76	23.89
Transportation and Communications, etc.	9.32	68.65	Public Administration and National Defense	7.46	31.35
Public Administration and National Defense	7.46	76.11	Transportation and Communications, etc.	9.32	40.67
Personal Services	6.76	82.87	Retail Trade	10.84	51.51
Construction	6.66	89.53	Community and Business Services	12.76	64.27
Wholesale Trade	4.48	94.01	Primary Industries	14.02	78.29
Finance, Insurance, etc.	3.54	97.55	Manufacturing	21.71	100.00
Unspecified or undefined	2.45	100.00			
	100.00	773.98		100.00	426.02

* Data from Census of Canada, 1961.

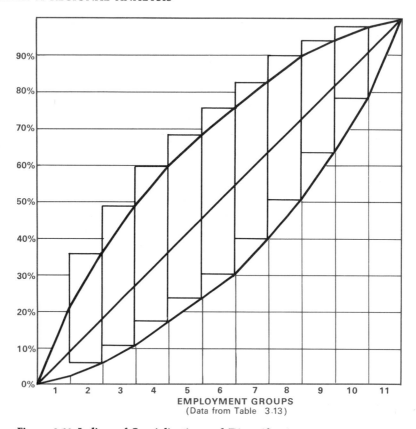

EMPLOYMENT GROUPS
(Data from Table 3.13)

Figure 3.10 Indices of Specialization and Diversification
The employment data for Canada are from Table 3.13. Both the *abscissa*
and the *ordinate* scales represent 100 per cent, but the abscissa is divided
into eleven equal parts representing the eleven employment categories. The
data from Table 3.13 have been rearranged in two ways: (a) (*specialization*), in descending series, with the largest category at the top of the
column; (b) (*diversification*), in ascending series, beginning with the
smallest category. When the curves are plotted, beginning on the left, curve
(a) (*specialization*) will be found to lie above the diagonal, and curve
(b) (*diversification*) will be found to lie below the diagonal.

when compared with the subtended areas.
The sum of the progressive series is usually called the *crude index*, and these
indices may be directly compared with one
another. Most writers feel that these variables should be expressed as abstract numbers such as fractions from 0 to 1, per cent,
or per thousand values. The variables in

question, of course, are the areas enclosed
by the diagonal and the curve, which
theoretically may vary from zero to one-
half the area of the square. The most convenient ratio then is the number obtained
when this area is divided by the area under
the diagonal. In terms of the crude index it
may be expressed thus:

$$\frac{\text{The actual crude index} - \text{the least possible crude index}}{\text{The least possible crude index} - 50}$$

In terms of Canadian industrial structure (Table 3.14):

$$\frac{773.98 - 600}{600 - 50} = \frac{173.98}{550} = .316$$

which may also be expressed as 31.6% or 316/1000.

In the case of the lower curve the area which it subtends may vary from half the square to zero, and the required ratio is the relationship of that area to the area under the diagonal. In terms of the progressive series it is:

$$\frac{\text{The actual crude index} - 50}{\text{The greatest possible crude index} - 50}$$

In terms of the Canadian example it is:

$$\frac{426.02 - 50.00}{600.00 - 50.00} = \frac{376.02}{550.00} = .684$$

which may also be expressed as 68.4% or 684/1000.

It should be noted that the crude indices of the two series as well as the refined indices always add to the highest possible figure $(.316 + .684 = 1.000)$. Moreover, the lowest series may always be derived from the upper, or vice versa, by difference.

Considerable confusion exists in geographical literature because both types of curve are used and both are called indices of *diversification* even when *specialization* is implied. It is proposed therefore to call the upper curve or series the *index of specialization* and the lower one, the *index of diversification*.

Table 3.14 presents the specialization indices for the twenty metropolitan cities of Canada in order beginning with the greatest degree of specialization. It also mentions the major industrial categories. No city in Canada is so specialized that any one category has more than 50 per cent of the employment: those at the top of the list require only two major categories to pass this mark, those in the middle require three categories, and those at the bottom of the list (i.e. those which are least specialized) require four categories in order to surpass the 50 per cent mark. Manufacturing heads the list eleven times; services, five times; administration and defense, three times; and mining, once. The service category is missing only twice from the list, and manufacturing only four times. Retail trade, so often considered to be the keystone of the "central place", never appears in the front-ranking position, takes second or third place in about half the cases, and is of lesser importance in the others. On the other hand, its actual share of the total employment averages just under 12 per cent, and it exhibits less variation from city to city than any other category. The importance of specialization in large cities is seen in the fact that only three categories of employment are necessary to make up 50 per cent of the total, while in Canada as a whole four are required. An interesting geographical contrast is presented in that the four cities with the highest indices are all manufacturing centers in Southern Ontario, while the six with the lowest indices are all located in the western provinces. Notable also are the positions of Ottawa and some of the provincial capitals. Most remarkable of all perhaps is the position of Montreal and Toronto, the only true metropolitan cities in Canada. In spite of the fact that they are clearly the largest manufacturing centers in Canada and manufacturing is their leading industrial category, they are not highly specialized, having important service and retail functions. The fact that Toronto is the capital of Canada's richest and most populous province hardly seems to make any difference in the employment spectrum, while the category of government services remains inconspicuous.

An illustration of the graphic method is shown in Figure 3.11 in which the curves for Calgary and St. Catharines are compared. The curve for Canada is also shown. The area under the curve is seen to depend greatly upon the magnitude of the first and largest category to be plotted.

Tables of data for smaller centers are not presented here. However, it must be pointed out that there are many smaller cities with highly specialized functions; Welland (Ontario), Trail (British Columbia), and Granby (Quebec) might be mentioned. On the other hand, there are many towns and small cities in which there is little intensive specialization. Size alone is seldom a good indicator of industrial structure.

A classification of cities based upon crude industrial structure is far from satisfactory. A large part of the work force of every city is engaged in service industries which have chiefly to do with the maintenance of the city way of life: included here are civic employees, personnel in edu-

Table 3.14   Degree of Industrial Specialization in Canadian Metropolitan Cities, 1961

City	Crude Index	Refined Index	Major Industrial Categories
St. Catharines	887.87	.5234	Manufacturing, Services
Kitchener	885.26	.5186	Manufacturing, Retail Trade
Hamilton	864.64	.4812	Manufacturing, Services
Windsor	845.98	.4471	Manufacturing, Services
Halifax	839.68	.4354	Administration and Defense, Services, Retail Trade
Ottawa	839.25	.4350	Administration and Defense, Services, Manufacturing
Sudbury	833.61	.4247	Mining, Manufacturing, Services
Montreal	828.47	.4154	Manufacturing, Services, Transportation
Toronto	816.08	.3929	Manufacturing, Services, Retail Trade
Victoria	806.43	.3753	Administration and Defense, Services, Retail Trade
London	803.89	.3707	Manufacturing, Services, Retail Trade
Saint John	796.68	.3576	Manufacturing, Services, Transportation
Quebec	795.79	.3560	Manufacturing, Services, Administration and Defense
St. John's	784.68	.3358	Services, Retail Trade, Administration and Defense
Winnipeg	781.47	.3300	Manufacturing, Services, Transportation
Vancouver	768.75	.3068	Manufacturing, Services, Retail Trade
Saskatoon	768.11	.3056	Services, Retail Trade, Transportation, Manufacturing
Regina	751.74	.2758	Services, Retail Trade, Administration, Transportation
Edmonton	749.15	.2712	Services, Manufacturing, Administration, Retail Trade
Calgary	712.34	.2042	Services, Retail Trade, Manufacturing, Transportation
Twenty Metropolitan Cities	793.78	.3523	Manufacturing, Services, Retail Trade
Canada	773.10	.3147	Manufacturing, Primary Industries, Services, Retail Trade

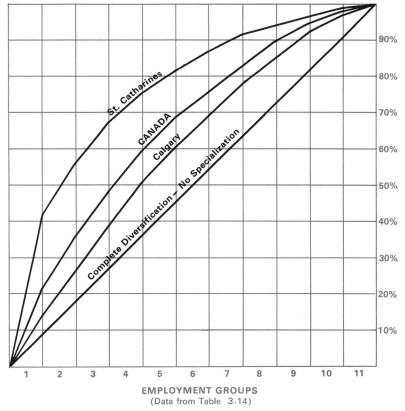

EMPLOYMENT GROUPS
(Data from Table 3·14)

Figure 3.11 Specialization of Employment in Calgary and St. Catharines
The employment data are from Table 3.14. The curve of *specialization* for
Canada is the same as that in the upper part of Figure 3.10. The percentage
data for both Calgary and St. Catharines have been arranged in descending
series and plotted from the left. It is found that the curve for St. Catharines
lies above that for Canada, while the curve for Calgary lies below that for
Canada. Employment in St. Catharines is thus seen to be more specialized
than the average for Canada, while that in Calgary is less specialized or
more diversified.

cation and health services, and, for that
matter, most of those engaged in retail
trade as well as a large share of the manufacturing ensemble. For a long time economic geographers have sought a method
to distinguish the maintenance functions
of a city from those functions which propel its development through exchange of
goods and services with the outside world.*
Official census statistics give little help;
there is nothing to indicate what part of
the work force in retailing is required to

service out-of-town customers or how large
a share of the manufacturing output of
each establishment is actually destined for
use within the city itself. A long process of
interviewing and statistical analysis is
necessary to separate the city work force
into *basic* or *propelling* elements and *non-
basic* or *maintenance* elements. An easier
though somewhat less accurate approach
has been made through the notion of
*minimum requirements.** American cities
were grouped into size-classes, and then

---

* John W. Alexander. "The Basic-non-basic Concept of Urban Economic Functions". *Economic
Geography*. Vol. 30 (1954). pp. 246-261.

* E. L. Ullman and M. F. Dacey. "The Minimum
Requirements Approach to the Urban Economic
Base". *Papers and Proc. of the Regional Science
Association*. Vol. 6 (1960). pp. 175-194.

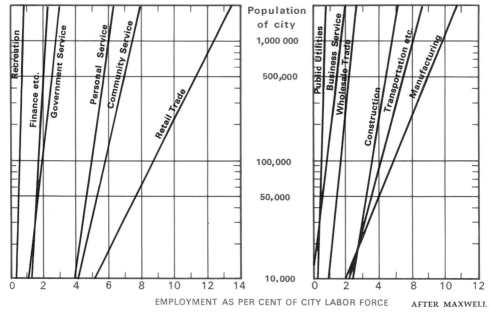

Figure 3.12 Regression Lines for Expected Minimum Requirements for City Functions
All equations are of the form: log y = a + bx; where y is city population and x is the "expected minimum requirement value" The y-intercept and the slope of the equations are:

FUNCTION	y- INTERCEPT(a)	SLOPE(b)	FUNCTION	y- INTERCEPT(a)	SLOPE(b)
Manufacturing[1]	3.2200	0.3526	Finance, etc.[1]	0.8338	2.3162
Public Utilities[2]	1.6145	5.5067	Community Service[2]	1.5092	0.5964
Construction[1]	1.7307	0.8861	Government Service[1]	2.4616	1.2651
Transportation[2]	2.7558	0.5255	Recreation[1]	1.9892	5.0020
Wholesale Trade[1]	2.2731	1.5671	Business Service[2]	3.8772	1.2576
Retail Trade[2]	2.6033	0.2731	Personal Service[2]	0.2929	0.9572

[1] Equation after Ullman and Dacey
[2] Equation based on the "four-class" city-grouping scheme of Canadian cities.

for each size-class the minimum per cent of the work force found in each of the major industrial groups in the U.S. census was determined. When they were plotted it was found that these minima fell almost exactly along straight lines of regression, with small cities having low minimum requirements for maintenance and larger cities proportionately higher ones. Through the use of this device it is possible theoretically to determine what part of the city's work force in each individual category is needed for the service of the city itself and what excess is available to supply the needs of outside markets. Cities may then be classified on the basis of the nature of their *excess* employment.

Through the use of data from the 1951 census this concept was applied in a study

of Canadian cities having populations of 10,000 and over.* Some of the regression lines were adopted without changes from the American study, but special regressions derived from Canadian data were necessary in about half of the categories. The regression lines are shown in Figure 3.12. Those functions which had the greatest excess of employment over the minimum requirements were recognized as *dominant*, while those which had an excess distinctly above that of the average of its category within the same city size-class were termed *distinctive*. It is therefore possible for an industry to be both dominant and distinctive. However, only

* J. W. Maxwell. "The Functional Structure of Canadian Cities: A Classification of Cities". *Geographical Bulletin*. Vol. 7, No. 2 (1965). pp. 79-104.

one function can be dominant, while several may be distinctive within the same city. Finally, the figures for the excess employment in each category within a city may be combined to produce an *index of specialization*. An index of 1.00 indicates that the excess employment is distributed in exactly the same proportions as the minimum requirements for its size-class. Any tendency toward dominance or distinction in any category raises the index of specialization.

As a synthesis of the ideas of *dominance, distinction,* and *specialization,* a *city-type classification* was devised for the eighty cities under study. There are four *major metropolitan centers,* Montreal, Toronto, Vancouver, and Winnipeg; two of these are in the "heartland" of Southern Quebec and Southern Ontario, while the other two are in the "western periphery". There are 31 *specialized manufacturing centers,* all but four of which are in the "heartland". There are 17 *regional capitals* (M.R.U.) or chief central places with moderate specialization in various service categories but with little development of manufacturing. There are 20 *regional capitals* (M.R.I.) or central places in which manufacturing is relatively important. Finally, there is a group of eight *special cities* in which neither manufacturing nor central place functions are important; they are Ottawa, Victoria, Sudbury, Rouyn, Thetford Mines, Timmins, Glace Bay, and New Waterford. Two of these are political capitals and the rest are involved with mining. The five city-type groups are shown in Figure 3.13 reproduced from Maxwell's report.* Many things may be said about this study. It is based on 1951 figures and it is now sadly out of date. Cities have grown and in some cases have changed their structure. The standards of minimum requirements have shifted, some quite markedly. Finally, the index of specialization appears unnecessarily complicated and seems to have no upper limit. Nevertheless, it is a useful study outlining

major city-types and emphasizing the differences between the industrial "heartland" and the far-flung "periphery" of the Canadian ecumene.

An index of specialization, whether derived from crude industrial data or from the theory of minimum requirements, is useful in regional evaluations but it fails to provide precise definitions or indeed adequate descriptions of important centralizing forces. To be specific, no idea is formed concerning the workings of corporation control and financial structure.* The complex of financial institutions, including head offices of industrial, mining, retail, and other corporations, holding companies, chartered accounting, legal and other business-service firms, is highly concentrated in a few metropolitan centers; but apart from data on financial institutions the census of employment does not provide much information about this complex.

Primary functions such as the trade in stocks and bonds and large-scale borrowing and lending are carried out in only a few cities. The overwhelming majority of the financial houses most concerned with the working of the capital market, such as stock and bond exchanges, investment companies, and head offices of banks, tends to locate in Toronto and Montreal. Other financial institutions such as insurance and trust companies are somewhat scattered, but the tendency is for most of them to cluster in or near the financial districts of large metropolitan cities. Head offices of corporations are more widely distributed, but even in this category the majority prefers Montreal or Toronto.

Problems of assembling data to describe the distribution of corporate and financial structure are formidable, hence the following discussion can only be exploratory. On the other hand, the geographical pattern in Canada is relatively simple, and most of the statistical material merely describes something quite obvious to the critical

---

* *op. cit.*

* Donald Kerr. "Some Aspects of the Geography of Finance in Canada". *Canadian Geographer.* IX (1965). pp. 175-192.

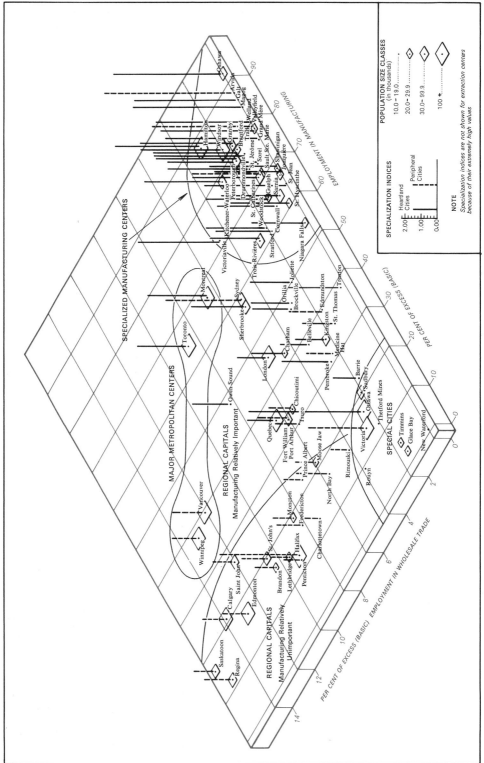

AFTER MAXWELL AND REDRAFTED BY PERMISSION OF THE DEPT. OF ENERGY, MINES AND RESOURCES

Figure 3.13 City-types in Canada — 1951

observer. A recent survey * offers the possibility of defining the status of Canadian cities on the basis of the assets of corporations with head offices located in them. Montreal (38 per cent) and Toronto (37 per cent) clearly dominate; Vancouver (6.5 per cent), Calgary (5.0 per cent), Hamilton (4.0 per cent), Winnipeg (2.0 per cent), and Quebec (1.0 per cent) rank next in order. The status of Montreal is emphasized by the presence of three very large corporations, Bell Canada, Canadian Pacific Railway, and Aluminium Company of Canada. Chemical companies are largely Montreal-oriented, while mining companies are found mainly in Toronto.

Toronto's leading role in retailing is established by the presence of the head offices of Eaton's, Simpson's, Simpsons-Sears, Loblaws, and Dominion Stores. In some other categories including oil refining, tobacco processing, cement, pulp and paper, breweries, and holding companies, little difference can be noted between Toronto and Montreal. Vancouver's large corporations are involved with forest products, pipelines, and utilities; oil and gas companies are the leaders in Calgary; and grain distributors, food and general retailers, and wholesale houses are among the dominant business firms of Winnipeg. The assets of the steel industries, electrical appliance, and farm machinery manufacturers combine to lift Hamilton to fifth place in the business structure of Canada.

Adding the assets of the leading financial houses to those of the industrial corporations and comparing city totals serve to emphasize the dominant roles of Toronto (42 per cent) and Montreal (40 per cent). Vancouver still ranks third with a share of a little over 3.0 per cent. Winnipeg rises to fourth rank (3.0 per cent) followed by London (2.5 per cent), Calgary (2.0 per cent), Kitchener-Waterloo (1.6 per cent), and Hamilton (1.5 per cent). Since the late 1920s all chartered banks maintain their head offices in either Toronto or Montreal. On the basis of total assets less

than 70 per cent of the insurance business is to be found in Toronto and Montreal. London, Winnipeg, and Kitchener-Waterloo have large insurance companies. Trust and Loan companies and other finance companies are also quite widely distributed.

By and large, the activities of what might be called the capital market have centered in Toronto and Montreal. Trade in financial instruments making provision for liquidity of non-monetary financial assets is highly concentrated. No data are available for bond trading, but 95 per cent of all stock transactions go through Toronto (69 per cent) and Montreal (26 per cent). Trade on the Vancouver exchange has grown remarkably to almost 5 per cent of the Canadian total, but on both the Calgary and Winnipeg exchanges it does not exceed 0.1 per cent. In addition to providing facilities for trading, the Toronto and Montreal financial communities have over a long period built the mechanism by which capital is raised. Most new security issues are made in Montreal or Toronto or simultaneously in both markets. Invariably, syndicates comprising investment bankers from both cities are formed to underwrite new issues.

It is abundantly clear that Canadian corporate and financial activity is strikingly concentrated in Montreal and Toronto and that decisions affecting the whole nation emanate chiefly from these two centers. It would be expected then that the greatest representation of what might be called the "corporate elite" would also reside in them. On the basis of a 10% sample * for the five-year period 1957-1962, it was discovered that approximately 30 per cent of Canadian resident directors and managers lived in Toronto and 20 per cent in Montreal. The remainder are scattered, concentrations occurring in Vancouver (6.0 per cent), Ottawa (4.0 per cent), Winnipeg (4.0 per cent), and in Calgary, Hamilton, and Halifax (3.0 per cent each). A comparison of city population with the central place function of the financial insti-

* Financial Post. January 15, 1966.

* Directory of Directors. Maclean-Hunter Publishing Company Ltd. Toronto.

tutions of the metropolitan cities of Canada is offered in Table 3.15. The formula for the calculation of the *index of financial specialization* is explained below.

Table 3.15   The Central Place Functions of Financial Institutions in Twenty Canadian Metropolitan Areas, 1961 *

Metropolitan Areas	A Population 1961 000	P.C. of Canadian Total	B Employees in Financial Institutions	P.C. of Canadian Total	C Value of Checks 1961 $000,000	P.C. of Canadian Total	$\frac{BC}{A^2}$ Index of Financial Specialization
Montreal	2,109.5	11.57	20,067	18.08	78,594	26.75	3.61
Toronto	1,824.5	10.00	23,599	21.26	109,571	37.30	7.93
Vancouver	790.2	4.33	7,103	6.40	17,767	6.05	2.07
Winnipeg	476.5	2.61	4,159	3.75	20,862	7.10	3.91
Ottawa	429.7	2.35	3,602	3.24	5,923	2.02	1.19
Hamilton	395.2	2.16	2,298	2.70	5,988	2.04	1.18
Quebec	357.6	1.96	2,261	2.04	7,913	2.69	1.43
Edmonton	337.6	1.85	2,603	2.35	6,672	2.27	1.56
Calgary	279.1	1.53	2,833	2.55	10,326	3.51	3.82
Windsor	193.4	1.06	1,367	1.23	2,399	.89	.97
Halifax	183.9	1.00	1,539	1.38	2,766	.94	1.30
London	181.3	.99	1,618	1.46	3,729	1.34	2.00
Kitchener	154.9	.84	948	.85	1,322	.45	.54
Victoria	154.2	.84	1,064	.96	2,667	.91	1.24
Regina	112.2	.61	1,106	.99	4,870	1.66	4.42
Sudbury	110.8	.60	539	.48	711	.24	.32
Saskatoon	95.6	.52	627	.56	1,171	.40	.83
St. Catharines	95.6	.52	505	.45	1,110	.38	.63
Saint John	95.6	.52	672	.60	1,282	.44	.98
St. John's	91.6	.50	483	.43	1,103	.34	.54
Twenty Cities	8,469.0	46.44	78,993	77.17	286,746	97.72	3.50
Canada	18,238.2	100.00	110,936	100.00	293,784	100.00	1.00

* Data from Census of Canada, 1961, and Canada Year Book, 1962.

$$S = \frac{BC}{A^2}$$

Where S = index of financial specialization

B = per cent of the Canadian employment in financial institutions

C = per cent of the value of total checks cashed in Canada

A = per cent of Canadian population residing in the city

On the basis of employment and volume of business Toronto is clearly dominant, and it has a very high index. Winnipeg, Calgary, and, rather surprisingly, Regina stand out as regional financial centers. Another feature of this approach is the fact that many smaller metropolitan areas apparently have deficient financial services.

To recapitulate briefly, there are striking concentrations in Montreal and Toronto of diverse economic functions ranging from central place services through manufacturing to the highly specialized activities of the capital market. Vancouver is in a transitional stage, moving gradually from its traditional status as a major regional center to one of greater national significance. Ottawa is clearly national in its function as administrative capital. Hamilton and Windsor are industrial centers of national importance. Winnipeg, Calgary, Edmonton, Quebec, Halifax, and London have diversified functions which set them out as major regional centers.

GEOGRAPHICAL INTERPRETATION

Geography is the study of the surface of the earth and its regions. It is a study of places and at the same time a study of people for many of the characteristics of a place are those which are imparted by the activities of the inhabitants. The purpose of this chapter then has been to review the ways in which people of European culture have modified the original nature of the land to form the resultant landscapes which now characterize the various regions of Canada.

Strong emphasis has been put upon population geography because it is necessary to emphasize that the full geographical pattern of Canada could not have been created without the efforts of an active human population. It is acknowledged that natural forces are responsible for the substance and the major physical lineaments of the land and for the provision of those phenomena which are termed "natural resources". This theme has been discussed briefly in CHAPTER 2. Nature's forces, of course, are still at work, quietly and unobtrusively for the most part, and a continual, slow, natural change is taking place. Natural factors are thus regarded as having a passive role in regional development, while on the other hand the human populations through their cultural activities are regarded as the real creators of the regional landscapes. Like the work of nature, the results of man's activities accumulate through time, although by comparison, much more rapidly. Present Canadian settlement patterns have been developing ever since the first settlers arrived. Settlement studies reveal much concerning the past relations of the Canadian people and the resources of the environment, and to a certain degree settlement patterns may be used to predict future development of the cultural pattern.

At the present stage of Canadian development it is natural to stress the importance of economic geography. Canada is a large country with at present a comparatively small population. This ought to indicate great activity in the primary industries and relatively little in the other sectors, but such is far from being the case. Despite their undoubted importance the primary industries are not the largest employers of labor, nor are they the greatest producers of wealth except within the resource frontier of the ecumene. Agriculture, forestry, and mining lie at the roots of Canadian economic development, but they are greatly overshadowed by manufacturing industries producing consumer's goods, electrical appliances, and industrial equipment. Surprising as it may seem to those whose minds are tuned to the frontier, the secondary industries contribute twice as much to the Canadian economy as do all types of primary production.

The frontier "idea", however, must sustain an even greater shock. When all types of commodity production are considered together, it is found that they do not employ half the people, pay half the wage income, or produce half the new wealth; instead, more than half is provided by the tertiary sector which produces no commodities but only services to the population at large. This third sector of the Canadian economy is an immensely powerful agent in the shaping of the geographical pattern.

The service sector of the economy builds and maintains the metropolitan city, and at the present time there is no doubt about metropolitan dominance in Canada. Some of the facts concerning the influences of metropolitan cities have been presented in this chapter and more will be presented in the chapters which follow. Toronto and Montreal are outstanding centers, but Canada is a large country and some of the dominance must be shared with a number of smaller regional centers, some of which, but not all, are provincial capitals. There is in fact good reason to attempt to formulate the regional geography of Canada in terms of city-centered regions. This prescription for regional definition has, however, been rejected in this book for equally valid reasons. City-regions have tended to become planners' objectives, descriptions of things hoped for, rather than of things as they really are. The point of view is too strictly limited since by definition all city-centered regions are similar: the area over which the socio-economic influences of the central city are paramount. When all the possible city-centered regions have been outlined there will still remain large interstitial gaps, "gray areas" of open countryside, which do not acknowledge the dominance of any particular city. Moreover, extremely large areas, comprising about half of the national territory are beyond the sensible range of any city. Urban influences are increasing, there is no doubt of that. But they have not yet displaced all other criteria of human geography.

The human geography of Canada must be regionalized in order to become amenable to description and analysis. The point of view, however, must be comprehensive enough to include both the city and the countryside or, where cities are lacking altogether, it must be able to deal with the *non-metropolitan region*. It must also be able to deal with regions which have not just one but several cities and be able to integrate them with a non-urban hinterland which to a considerable extent is shared but not divided among them in any rigid fashion.

Regions vary with time both in extent and in development. The reality of Canada West in the middle of the nineteenth century was quite different from that of Upper Canada in an earlier period or that of Ontario immediately after Confederation, and all of them were different from the entity which is recognized as Ontario today. The differences have resulted from the effects of human activities which are recorded on the time-scale of history, but which find their full expression in the qualities and visible characteristics of the present landscape. What is true of Ontario in this regard is surely true in all other parts of Canada as well. Physical factors are not to be neglected by human geographers but interpretations of their effects must also be tempered by the time-scale. Human appreciation of physical phenomena has varied greatly through time. Water bodies were barriers until man learned the arts of navigation; then the barrier became a traveled route. The prairie lands of North America were barriers to settlement because their lack of forest was thought to indicate infertility and because would-be settlers lacked the implements necessary to break up the prairie sod. When these difficulties were overcome, the Prairies were settled by a single wave of land-seekers. The Canadian Shield was thought to be a barrier and a drawback to national development until its wealth of resources was discovered. Facts are important not so much because of what they are but because of what they are thought to be. The landscape has its peculiar qualities because of man's perception of natural possibilities and his technological ability to make desired changes. The study of the regional geography of Canada is essentially the study of its human geography.

BIBLIOGRAPHY

Alexander, John W. "The Basic-non-basic Concept of Urban Economic Functions". *Economic Geography*. Vol. 30 (1954). pp. 246-261.

———. *Economic Geography*. Prentice-Hall Inc. Englewood Cliffs. 1963.

Charbonneau, H. et Légaré, J. "L'extreme mobilité de la population urbaine au Canada, l'exemple de Montréal entre 1956 et 1961". *Revue de Géographie de Montréal*. XXI, 2 (1967).

Conkling, Edgar G. "South Wales: A Study in Industrial Diversification". *Economic Geography*. Vol. 39 (1963). pp. 258-272.

Harris, Richard Colebrook. *The Seigneurial System in Early Canada: A Geographic Study*. University of Wisconsin Press. Milwaukee. 1966.

Hodge, Gerald. "Do Villages Grow?" *Rural Sociology*. Vol. 31 (1966). pp. 183-196.

———. "Urban Systems and Regional Policy". *Canadian Public Administration*. Vol. 9, 2 (1966). pp. 181-193.

Jefferson, Mark. "The Distribution of the World's City Folk". *Geographical Review*. XXI (1931). p. 453.

———. "The Law of the Primate City". *Geographical Review*. XXIX (1939). pp. 226-232.

Kerr, Donald. "Some Aspects of the Geography of Finance in Canada". *Canadian Geographer*. IX (1965). pp. 175-192.

———. "Metropolitan Dominance in Canada". Chapter 16. *Canada — A Geographical Interpretation*. (Edited by J. H. Warkentin). Methuen & Company. Toronto. 1968.

Kerr, Donald and Spelt, Jacob. *The Changing Face of Toronto*. Ottawa. 1965.

Lorenz, M. O. "Methods of Measuring the Concentration of Wealth". *American Statistical Association*. Vol. IX (1905). pp. 209-219.

Maxwell, J. W. "The Functional Structure of Canadian Cities: A Classification of Cities". *Geographical Bulletin*. Vol. 7, No. 2 (1965). pp. 79-104.

Rodgers, Allan. "Some Aspects of Industrial Diversification in the United States". *Economic Geography*. Vol. 33 (1957). pp. 16-30.

Schott, Carl. *Landnahme und Kolonisation in Kanada am Beispiel Sudontarios*. Kiel. 1936.

Tress, R. C. "Unemployment and Diversification of Industry". *The Manchester School*. Vol. IX (1938). pp. 140-152.

Ullman, E. L. and Dacey, M. F. "The Minimum Requirements Approach to the Urban Economic Base". *Papers and Proc. of the Regional Science Association*. Vol. 6 (1960). pp. 175-194.

Yeates, Maurice H. *An Introduction to Quantitative Analysis in Economic Geography*. McGraw-Hill Book Company. Toronto. 1968.

Zipf, G. K. *National Unity and Disunity*. Bloomington: Principia Press. 1941.

The Atlantic Provinces

4 Situated on the Atlantic seaboard of Canada the Atlantic Provinces include the traditional Maritime Provinces of Nova Scotia, New Brunswick, and Prince Edward Island, together with Newfoundland which became a province in 1949. As a region it occupies a little less than six per cent of the area of Canada, but it contains about ten per cent of Canada's population. Indeed, Prince Edward Island, with an average of 50 persons per square mile, is the most densely populated province in Canada.

By virtue of its location this region served as an early gateway to the new continent and was one of the first areas of European transatlantic settlement. Newfoundland was Britain's oldest colony, while the first French settlement in North America was founded at Port Royal in what is now Nova Scotia. Although economic development during the colonial period was oriented toward the sea, the resource base was broadened to include the forests as well as the fisheries. The emphasis was placed on foreign trade, with fish and timber becoming the staple commodities for export. The Atlantic colonies were members of a world trading system in which they were not only producers of staples but were well established in the carrying trade as well.

Confederation was less than completely advantageous to the Maritime Provinces. They thus became members of a political and economic system which on the strength of greater population and superior resources was centered in the regions of the St. Lawrence River and the Great Lakes. The central region itself did not provide much outlet for the staples of the eastern region, and moreover its "National Policy" was designed to protect Canadian markets for its own goods, thus inevitably restricting the scope of the traders in the Atlantic Region.

The manufacturing firms of the Atlantic Region lacked the economies of scale which were possible for the manufacturers of Central Canada and were unable to amass the capital necessary to modernize their methods. As a result the Atlantic Provinces have not experienced growth and prosperity to the same degree as other parts of Canada. In many fields parallels may be drawn between the situation of the Maritime Provinces in Canada and that of their nearest neighbor, the New England Region in the United States.

POPULATION

The population of the Atlantic Provinces was about two million as revealed by the Census of Canada in 1966. The gross population density is about 17 per square mile, but the people are far from evenly distributed. There is a distinctive settlement pattern as shown by Figure 4.1. In all provinces except Prince Edward Island the pattern is peripheral with most of the

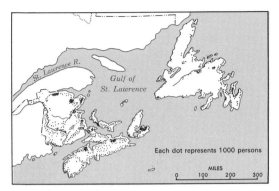

Figure 4.1 Population Distribution in the Atlantic Provinces, 1961
The concentration of population along the coastal peripheries is one of the problems hindering economic development.

people being located in small isolated nodes along the coasts. The densely settled areas in New Brunswick are the northern and eastern coasts, the St. John Valley, and some of the valleys of the smaller rivers in the southern and central parts of the province. Settlement is also distributed along the coastline of Nova Scotia, but there are significant clusters around Halifax and in the eastern part of Cape Breton Island, Pictou county, and the Annapolis Valley. Prince Edward Island has a more even distribution, reflecting its physical uniformity and the dominance of agricultural settlement.

Large areas in Newfoundland are nearly devoid of population, notably the interior, the extreme north, and the southwestern coast. From the central part of the western coast a narrow band of population extends eastward through the interior to the more

extensively settled areas of the Avalon and neighboring peninsulas.

For the most part the empty areas of the Atlantic Region are elevated, rugged, rocky, or otherwise unsuited for agriculture. Thus little settlement occurs on the Atlantic Upland of Nova Scotia or the Central Plateau of New Brunswick, while in Newfoundland only the railway and limited mineral development have encouraged a little interior settlement.

While peripheral settlement was in accord with the fishing and forestry techniques practiced a century ago, this is no longer the case. Technology encourages concentration and many small coastal centers are slowly declining, but their persistence weakens the rate of development in the Atlantic Provinces. Indeed, to achieve a high rate of economic development the region must have "growth centers" with populations of at least 100,000 on which to base its markets, labor force, management and technology, and eventually supporting industry. At present, only St. John's, Saint John, and Halifax qualify, and they account for only 20 per cent of the total population.

The growth of population in the Atlantic Provinces has been about 12.0 per cent over a ten-year period, slightly below that of Canada as a whole. The rate of increase is highest in Newfoundland and lowest in Nova Scotia. Birth rates and rates of natural increase have been higher in the Atlantic Provinces than in other parts of Canada. The low rate of population growth is explained by a very high net loss through migration. Table 4.2 shows that

Table 4.1   Atlantic Provinces — Population Growth *

	1956	1966	Increase number	Increase per cent
Newfoundland	415,074	493,396	78,322	18.8
Prince Edward Island	99,285	108,535	9,250	9.3
Nova Scotia	694,717	756,039	61,322	8.8
New Brunswick	554,616	616,788	62,172	11.2
Atlantic Provinces	1,763,692	1,974,758	211,066	12.0

* Source: Census of Canada.

Table 4.2   Atlantic Provinces — Net Migration *

Province	1951-1956	1956-1961	1961-1966
Newfoundland	+1.7	−16.3	−23.6
Prince Edward Island	−8.1	−3.3	−4.5
Nova Scotia	−10.6	−22.8	−40.3
New Brunswick	−20.7	−16.3	−34.4

* Source: Census of Canada.
Data are expressed in thousands of people.

the negative balance of migration has been steadily increasing for the past fifteen years. It is unfortunate for the region that a significant number of the migrants have been young and well-educated. This benefits Canada but not the Atlantic Provinces.

SETTLEMENT AND ECONOMIC DEVELOPMENT

Pre-Loyalist Period 1497-1783

Fishing, one of the four "cornerstones" of the Atlantic economy, began early in the history of European occupance of North America. Newfoundland, because of its proximity to Europe, was occupied by European people at an early date. By 1600 the English had come to dominate the fishing industry of Newfoundland, and it is reported in that year that 200 English ships and 10,000 fishermen brought in about $500,000 worth of fish. The English required bases in Newfoundland since they engaged in "dry" fishery because of a lack of salt. The fish had to be cleaned, lightly salted, and cured on racks in the sun. The French with abundant supplies of solar salt followed the "wet" fishery method and transported their catch directly to Europe in brine storage. Hence they were not interested in establishing themselves in Newfoundland.

Despite the declaration of formal possession of Newfoundland by Sir Humphrey Gilbert in 1583, it was not until 1610 that the first permanent colony was officially established at Cupid's in Conception Bay. During the first half of the seventeenth century a number of other English settle-ments were founded on the Avalon Peninsula, and by 1650 there were 2,000 permanent inhabitants.

French fishermen also settled in Newfoundland later as foreign trade in fish necessitated a partial use of the "dry" fishery technique. From 1662 to 1713 their chief settlement was at Placentia on the west coast of the Avalon Peninsula. The Treaty of Paris in 1763 guaranteed the possession of St. Pierre and Miquelon for France which still retains these islands today. However, rights to Newfoundland were terminated in 1904; but until these rights ceased, settlement in the northern and western parts of the island was discouraged. Despite the early colonization growth was slow, and by the end of the eighteenth century there were less than 25,000 people residing in Newfoundland. While the policies of France and England were in part responsible, the main factor was the lack of agricultural resources.

Early colonization in the Maritimes followed a different pattern from that of Newfoundland. This was due to a different economic base which recognized not only fisheries but also agriculture, forest exploitation, and foreign trade. In addition, there was the conflict between France and England coupled with the influence of development in New England.

Clark recently examined in detail the role of New England in the underdevelopment of Cape Breton between 1713 and 1758.* Even though Cape Breton was still

* A. H. Clark. "New England's Role in the Underdevelopment of Cape Breton Island during the French Regime, 1713-1758". *Canadian Geographer.* IX, 1 (1965). pp. 1-12.

governed by France, there was little French immigration. Indeed, with the French emphasis on fur trade rather than permanent settlement, it was difficult for immigrants even to enter Quebec. Cape Breton Island did not have land like that of the St. Lawrence Lowland on which a *habitant* type of settlement might take place, and there was no incentive for movement of people from Quebec to that area. Even the Acadians were uninterested, preferring to remain near the Bay of Fundy in spite of the fact that these lands had been ceded to Britain in 1713. A weak agricultural potential did exist, however. Oats, barley, grasses, and clover could have been grown on Cape Breton Island, but the settlers tried unsuccessfully to grow the dietary staples, wheat and peas. The result was a negative assessment of the agricultural potential of the island.

Underdevelopment in Cape Breton was also influenced by dependence upon New England. Louisbourg had been planned not only as a major fortification but also as a key link for an all-French triangular trade network. The failure of the agricultural and forest economy to develop made Louisbourg dependent on other sources for supplies. Limited supplies came from Acadia, but most of the needs were met by New England trade. Cape Breton was attractive to New England shipmasters in that fish could be obtained as well as plentiful supplies of rum and molasses. As a result Cape Breton developments were focused only on the sea and trade.

Similarly, apart from the Acadian settlements in Annapolis Basin, Minas Basin, and Chignecto Bay, little positive development occurred in the areas controlled by France. After the expulsion of the Acadians large portions of the dyked lands reverted to wasteland, and attempts by Britain to develop agriculture elsewhere had only limited success. For example, land clearing was begun near Halifax, but it was soon realized that the soils were too thin, stony, and infertile to be of value. Thus settlement concentrated even more on the sea coast, as shown by Figure 4.2.

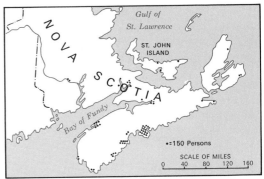

AFTER J. B. BIRD, CANADA YEAR BOOK 1966

Figure 4.2 Population Distribution in the Maritimes, 1767

The peripheral distribution pattern had become a reality, but a number of areas were still not developed. These included northern and eastern New Brunswick, Prince Edward and Cape Breton Islands, and the area now comprising Pictou and Antigonish counties in Nova Scotia.

Loyalist Occupance and Maritime Economic Growth 1783-1876

The outbreak of war in 1775 had immediate repercussions in Maritime Canada, but the civilian population remained fixed in the old settlement pattern and economic activities. However, the truce of 1782 freed the Loyalists and by 1784 more than 25,000 had emigrated to Nova Scotia. The immediate effect was a reinforcement of the Atlantic-shore pattern, and soon this extended into New Brunswick along the

AFTER J. B. BIRD, CANADA YEAR BOOK 1966

Figure 4.3 Population Distribution in the Maritimes, 1786

Bay of Fundy shore, and inland along the St. John Valley. As before, fishing, lumbering, and trade were important, while agriculture continued a minor role. Thus by 1786 the basic elements of present day occupance patterns had been established (Figure 4.3).

The Atlantic economy continued to expand as the growth of its trade by sea exposed new markets in foreign lands. Despite the importance of fishing it was forestry which began to provide impetus for economic expansion. New Brunswick was best endowed with trees, and forestry rapidly evolved from the square timber trade to the export of sawn lumber to England. Concomitant with forestry, shipbuilding grew rapidly with many of the ships being built to carry lumber to England where both cargo and vessel were sold. Atlantic shipbuilding reached a peak in 1864 although in Nova Scotia the high year was later, in 1875. There shipbuilding was oriented not towards ships for export but towards Nova Scotia's extensive fleet of vessels used in the West Indies salt cod and molasses trade. With the exception of Prince Edward Island the agriculture was of little note, and the region imported foodstuffs from Central Canada, Britain, and the West Indies. Thus, during this period a strong economy evolved based primarily on fish, forests, and wooden sailing ships.

Confederation and Economic Change

The "golden age" of the Maritime Provinces had reached its peak with the shipbuilding industry in 1864. With Confederation in 1867 and the completion of the Intercolonial Railway in 1876, maritime economic forces waned and were replaced by those emanating from the interior. Changes in technology, particularly in transportation, required a resource base which the Atlantic Provinces did not possess. Steamships were able to bypass the region easily and to strike deeper into the interior at Quebec and Montreal, for the small maritime ports did not provide sufficient cargoes. Indeed in 1867 Cunard

steamships ceased calling at Halifax because the small cargoes destined there did not justify the extra time and expense.

Shipbuilding declined as wooden sailing vessels were replaced by iron steampowered craft. Immigration had continued after the Loyalists: first the Scottish people who settled in Cape Breton Island, eastern Prince Edward Island, and mainland Nova Scotia, and second the Irish who settled in Newfoundland, Prince Edward Island, and southern New Brunswick. However, after 1876, Central Canada and the West drew most newcomers inland past the Atlantic Provinces. Thus population growth declined, and economic growth stagnated until World War II.

Present Situation

As shown in Table 4.3 the structure of employment in the Atlantic Provinces is quite different from that in Canada as a whole. The structure also varies considerably from province to province. In particular, we should note the importance of mining in Nova Scotia and Newfoundland, forestry in Newfoundland and New Brunswick, and agriculture in Prince Edward Island. In all provinces public administration and defense are much more important than in Canada as a whole, while manufacturing is considerably less important. In the Atlantic Region somewhat more of the labor force is in industries which provide less than the average Canadian income; moreover, the earnings in these categories are far below Canadian standards. The result is a low income area where market potentials usually fail to encourage growth. Personal disposable income per capita ranges from 62 per cent to 78 per cent of the Canadian average in various parts of the area.

Table 4.4 suggests that even today forestry and fishing are significant in the region, but that in terms of net value of production manufacturing and construction are much more important. However, the region does not have the same reliance on manufacturing which is shown by Can-

Table 4.3   Employment in the Atlantic Provinces in 1961 *

Employment Category	Newfound-land	Prince Edward Island	Nova Scotia	New Bruns-wick	Atlantic Prov.	Canada
(a) Earned income per capita above Canadian Average	Per Cent	Per Cent	Per Cent	Per Cent	Per Cent	Per Cent
Mining	3.9	0.0	4.3	0.8	2.8	1.8
Finance, Ins., Real Estate	1.4	1.6	2.4	2.3	2.1	3.6
Public Administration and Defense	11.6	8.7	15.9	10.1	12.4	7.5
Transportation, Communications, and other Utilities	13.6	8.0	10.4	11.8	11.4	9.3
Manufacturing	10.9	8.8	14.2	16.0	13.8	21.7
Construction	7.4	6.1	6.2	5.8	6.8	6.3
(b) Earned income per capita below Canadian Average						
Trade	17.5	14.0	15.6	16.7	16.0	15.4
Community, Business, and Personal Services	16.7	16.7	19.2	20.0	18.4	19.8
Forestry	5.0	0.4	1.7	5.0	3.9	1.5
Agriculture	1.5	27.3	5.2	7.2	6.3	10.2
Fishing and Trapping	7.5	6.2	3.2	2.1	3.8	0.5
Other Employment	3.0	2.2	1.7	2.2	2.3	2.4
Total Employment	100.0	100.0	100.0	100.0	100.0	100.0

* Source: Atlantic Provinces Economic Council. "Productivity, the Use of Resources, and the Income Gap". Pamphlet No. 11 (July, 1967). p. 29.

Table 4.4   Per Cent of Net Value of Production Earned by Selected Industries, 1960-62 *

Industry	Canada	Maritime Provinces
Agriculture	10.4%	8.8%
Forestry	3.4	5.6
Fishing	.6	5.2
Trapping	.1	.1
Mining	8.0	6.6
Electric Power	4.1	6.1
Construction	18.6	25.8
Manufacturing	54.8	41.8
Total	100.0%	100.0%

* Source: Atlantic Provinces Economic Council. "Agriculture and the Atlantic Economy". Pamphlet No. 10 (July, 1966). p. 30.

ada as a whole. It is important to note, however, which of the industries cited in Table 4.4 are important as "propelling" industries. Unfortunately the data suggest a significant role in manufacturing, but it must be remembered that much of the manufacturing in the Atlantic Region is just the processing of primary products. When analyzed in terms of propelling industries, the census figures show that during the recent period the forest product industries have been the most significant, consistently accounting for more than 45 per cent of the value of shipments from the region. Fish and fish products have usually exceeded 18 per cent of the exports. Metallic ores and concentrates were responsible for over 15 per cent and are gaining rapidly. Iron and steel products and agriculture each accounted for only five per cent and are declining. Thus despite the importance of the various industries, when analyzed in terms of total employment and dollar output, the Atlantic Region still relies heavily on wood and fish to pay for most of the goods and services required from outside the region.

URBANIZATION IN THE ATLANTIC PROVINCES

The Atlantic Provinces contain the oldest settled areas in Canada, Europeans having established themselves in both Newfoundland and Nova Scotia before the founding of Quebec. The Atlantic Provinces as a group have the greatest density of population in Canada, the extreme example being Prince Edward Island which has practically no unoccupied area. Yet despite the obvious advantages of an early start and a seaside location the Atlantic Region has no large cities and few of even moderate size,

while the population is almost equally divided between rural and urban residents. However, the farm population is only 6.8 per cent, considerably below the national average. Prince Edward Island, the smallest and most rural province, has only 28.5 per cent of its population on farms, but about 35.0 per cent in rural non-farm locations. Most of the rest of Canada has a much higher proportion of urban people, and the problem is to explain why cities have not arisen to contain a greater share of the population of the Atlantic Region. Probably the chief reason is to be found in the lack of development of secondary industries to provide the propelling power which was instrumental in the growth of so many cities in the region of the St. Lawrence River and the Great Lakes.

While there is no doubt that urban population is generally increasing (Table 4.5), the rate of growth is not equal to that of Canada as a whole and is much behind that of some areas. Halifax, the most vig-

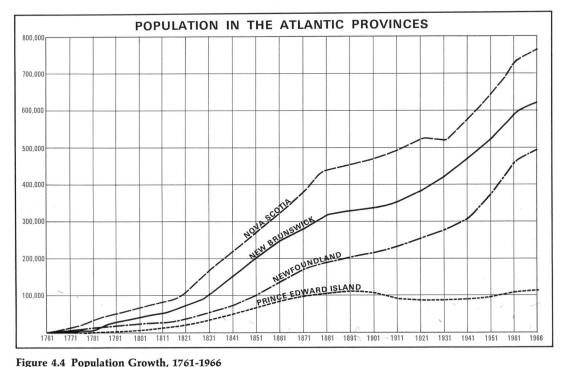

Figure 4.4 Population Growth, 1761-1966
Population has grown slowly in the Atlantic Provinces. There have never been periods of rapid increase such as those experienced in the more recently settled parts of Canada.

Table 4.5   Urbanization of the Atlantic Provinces *

	1951	Per Cent of Population Classified as Urban 1956	1961	1966	Trend
Newfoundland	33.8	44.5	50.6	52.2	+18.4
Prince Edward Island	25.1	30.3	32.4	35.1	+10.0
Nova Scotia	55.3	57.5	54.5	55.0	− 0.3
New Brunswick	42.5	45.8	46.5	49.7	+ 7.2
Atlantic Provinces	46.5	48.8	49.7	51.5	+ 5.0

*Census of Canada.

orously growing urban area in the Atlantic Region, is being rapidly surpassed by cities in Ontario and Alberta. In the past decade Halifax has dropped from tenth to eleventh place among major Canadian cities and will soon be displaced from this position by Kitchener. Statistics for the growth of population of the major urban areas in the Atlantic Provinces are presented in Table 4.6.

Table 4.6   Development of Urban Areas in the Atlantic Provinces *

	1951	1956	1961	1966
HALIFAX	133,931	164,200	183,946	198,193
Halifax	85,589	93,301	92,511	86,792
Dartmouth	23,359	36,235	46,966	58,745
SAINT JOHN	78,337	86,015	95,563	101,192
Saint John	50,779	52,491	55,153	51,567
Lancaster	10,696	12,371	13,848	15,836
ST. JOHN'S	68,620	79,153	90,838	101,161
St. John's	52,873	57,078	63,633	79,884
MONCTON	39,624	48,238	55,768	65,219
Moncton	31,433	38,645	43,840	45,847
SYDNEY-GLACE BAY	100,725	102,928	106,114	100,700
Sydney	31,317	32,162	33,617	32,769
Glace Bay	25,586	24,416	24,186	23,516
CORNER BROOK	13,835	23,225	25,185	27,116
FREDERICTON	16,018	18,303	19,683	22,460
CHARLOTTETOWN	15,887	16,707	18,318	18,427

* Census of Canada.

Halifax, the capital city of Nova Scotia and chief seaport of the Atlantic Provinces, was founded in 1749 by Lord Cornwallis who considered the harbor to be the best on the North Atlantic. Here he established a military and naval station to offset the power of the great French fortress at Louisbourg. Defense functions have been of major importance in Halifax ever since its founding.

Halifax Harbor is a drowned valley, an inlet extending about fourteen miles into the mainland from the Atlantic Ocean. Actually there are two harbors connected by a constricted channel known as The Narrows. The outer harbor, about six miles long and a mile in width, is lined with docks and piers capable of accommodating large ocean-going ships. The inner harbor, known as Bedford Basin, is about four

Figure 4.5 Halifax
Bedford Basin is a natural harbor. George Island to the right is a drumlin. The Angus L. MacDonald bridge in the background connects Halifax with the city of Dartmouth.

miles long and two and one-half miles wide. In this fine shelter many great wartime convoys were assembled.

The city of Halifax is built upon a small peninsula, four and one-half miles long and less than two miles wide, lying between the North West Arm and the harbor, and about midway between the ocean and the head of the inlet. Upon the rock floor of the peninsula are several drumlins, oval hills of glacial drift, one of which is surmounted by the Citadel, which commands a striking view of the whole urban area.

Along the eastern shore of the peninsula are situated shipyards, docks, warehouses, and ocean terminals. There are numerous

Canadian naval facilities in the area. The central business district or "downtown" area is situated on steeply sloping land between the citadel and the harbor. Here are located government buildings, offices, and retail and wholesale facilities. Of interest is Point Pleasant Park covering 200 acres on the extreme southerly tip of the peninsula, while along the North West Arm are a series of wooded lots and the club-houses of many aquatic sporting associations. Near the Arm also lies the campus of Dalhousie University, the outstanding seat of learning in the province.

On the eastern shore of the harbor is the city of Dartmouth. For many years it was a small town connected to the city by

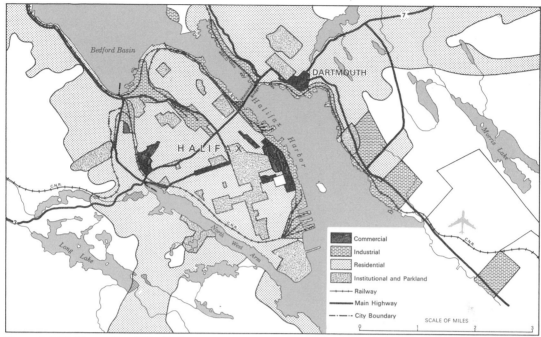

Figure 4.6 Halifax — Land Use Pattern
The land use pattern is further illustrated by the aerial photograph of Halifax at the bottom of the page (Photo by Atlantic Air Survey, Dartmouth, N.S.).

a ferry service. The construction of the Angus L. Macdonald bridge over the harbor brought about an immediate development of Dartmouth which by 1966 (Table 4.6) contained two-thirds as many people as Halifax itself. Oil refineries, factories, military installations, and other facilities line the eastern shore of the harbor. The growth of the city of Dartmouth in recent years has caused the building of a second harbor bridge near Bedford Basin.

In terms of functions the Halifax urban area is highly specialized. Over 60 per cent of its "excess" employment is in government services and defense, while almost 20 per cent is found in transportation. Thus 80 per cent of the propelling force of the Halifax economy seems to be derived from this very narrow base. Wholesale trade, finance, and services having to do with health and education are important. Employment in manufacturing is actually

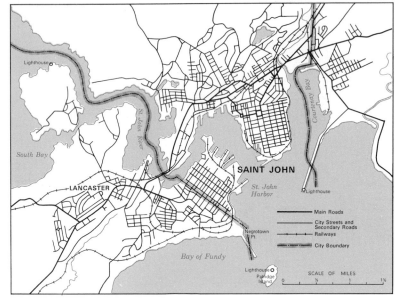

Figure 4.7 Saint John and Vicinity
The city is built on a series of adjacent peninsulas about the harbor at the
mouth of the river. Courtenay Bay acts as a second harbor and has attracted
considerable industry.

considerably below the theoretical minimum requirement for a metropolitan area
of this size.

Saint John is reputed to be the oldest
incorporated city in Canada, having been
granted a Royal Charter in 1785 soon after
the arrival of the United Empire Loyalists.
During the succeeding century it was a
rival of Halifax as an Atlantic seaport and
for a time was actually a more populous
city. In recent years, however, it has grown
somewhat more slowly.

The city occupies a series of peninsulas
abutting on the harbor which is Saint
John's major asset. It is the sheltered estuary of the St. John River which enters
the Bay of Fundy at this point. Piers line
both sides of the harbor with the new
ocean terminals being located on the west
side. The Saint John dry dock is situated in
East Saint John on Courtenay Bay which
forms a second harbor. At the head of the
main harbor are the famous Reversing
Falls. Here the river narrows to a width of
350 feet between rock walls nearly 100
feet high. At low tide the river pours out

in a turbulent flood, falling about fifteen
feet. When the tide comes in, the water
rises more rapidly in the harbor than in
the river above the gorge, and the rapids
are reversed. For a short time at full tide
the gorge is navigable.

Like Halifax, Saint John is a winter port.
It is the eastern terminus of the Canadian
Pacific Railway, and a considerable trade
flows through the port. Shipping, however, is somewhat hampered because there
is a mean tidal range of 28 feet in the
harbor.

Saint John is much less specialized than
Halifax. Transportation, manufacturing,
community services, and trade are about
equally important. Government services
are much less in evidence since Saint John
is not a provincial capital. The manufacturing industries include pulp and paper,
petroleum products, marine construction
and repair, and the processing of overseas
raw materials such as spices and cane
sugar. Saint John is also the focus for the
wholesale and retail trade of southwestern
New Brunswick.

COURTESY C. N. FORWARD AND THE CANADIAN GEOGRAPHER

Figure 4.8 Harbor of St. John's
(a) Aerial view from the northwest. **(b)** Location of harbor installations.

St. John's, the most easterly city in Canada, is located on the eastern tip of the island of Newfoundland. It is the capital and the largest city of that province. Its harbor is a small, pouch-shaped bay, about one and one-quarter miles in length from southwest to northeast, and half a mile in width, with a depth of fifteen fathoms. While it forms a perfect haven for small vessels, it is too restricted for large modern liners. The water's edge is lined by wharves and quays, while the Newfoundland dry-dock and railway terminal occupy the head of the harbor. The old city was

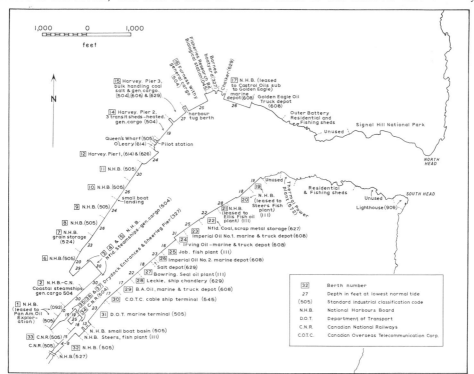

built on the northwestern side of the harbor since the Southside Hills are too precipitous for the construction of urban buildings and streets. Newer sections of the city have spread out widely from the central core just behind the waterfront.

From the earliest days St. John's was primarily a port and fishing station. It is also the administrative center of the province and the chief commercial depot and service center. Like Halifax it is deficient in manufacturing employment but not so highly specialized in government services and national defense.

The Sydney-Glace Bay urban area is found in the coalfield on the eastern shore of Cape Breton Island. It is a multinucleate area with Sydney as the port and heavy manufacturing center and Glace Bay as the chief coal-mining town. Before 1900 Sydney was a rather quiet little seaport of 2,500 people; it rapidly became a city and one of the three primary steel-making centers in Canada. Now, however, both the steel and coal industries are in difficulty, and Sydney has ceased to grow. Other important towns in the area are New Waterford, Sydney Mines, and North Sydney, all of them mining towns. Sydney Harbor is the mainland terminus of the ferry service to Newfoundland.

Moncton is the second-ranking city in New Brunswick. Located at the head of navigation on the Petitcodiac River it was an important shipbuilding center from 1830 to 1870. With the coming of the railway in 1876 Moncton became a major junction. Today it still functions as a transportation node. It is also an important commercial center. Some manufacturing is carried on, especially of food products, wood and metal products, and textiles.

Other towns of more than 10,000 population include Bathurst, Edmundston, and Oromocto in New Brunswick; Amherst, New Glasgow, and Truro in Nova Scotia; and Summerside in Prince Edward Island. Charlottetown is the capital city and chief commercial center of P.E.I. Fredericton, centrally located on the St. John River, is the capital of New Brunswick.

ECONOMIC ACTIVITIES

Agriculture

To the casual traveler in the Atlantic Region, agriculture appears to occupy very little of the land and is far surpassed in area by the ever-present forest. It is with some surprise that one learns that agriculture, despite its narrow base and low income, employs more people and accounts for more of the net value of production than either of the two traditional staples, fish and wood. Nevertheless, agricultural exports are limited to a few specialties, chiefly potatoes and apple products, The region is actually deficient in many foodstuffs and must acquire them from other parts of Canada or other countries.

As shown in Figure 4.10, agriculture in New Brunswick and Nova Scotia is restricted to the coastal lands and the valleys which are tributary to the Bay of Fundy. Most of Prince Edward Island is farm land, while very little of Newfoundland supports any agriculture. It is worth noting the types of commercial farms recorded in the Census of Canada. Although the Maritime Provinces were long known for traditional cash crops such as hay and potatoes, more than 50 per cent of the commercial farmers now receive the bulk of their incomes from the sale of livestock and livestock products. Only in the upper St. John Valley, south of Edmundston, do more than 70 per cent of the commercial farmers rely heavily upon potatoes for cash income. Even in Prince Edward Island, only the southeastern tip can be classified as chiefly a commercial crop area. The Annapolis Valley, so noted in the past for apples and small fruits, has diversified its agricultural program, and today the income derived from livestock is much more significant.

The role of agriculture in the economy of the region has recently been given careful study by R. K. Fletcher.* He suggests that agriculture may play a more signifi-

* R. K. Fletcher. "Agriculture and the Atlantic Economy". *Atlantic Provinces Economic Council Pamphlet.* No. 10 (July, 1966).

Figure 4.9 Annapolis Valley

(a) Ground View

This section of the valley, west of Kentville, has a variety of land uses. The apple orchards and hay give way in the background to a peat bog which is used to supply peat moss for garden enthusiasts in Eastern Canada.

(b) Aerial View

This is the north side of the valley near Sheffield Mills Station. While a significant portion of the area has orchards, grains and hay are also important. Of note is the considerable area in forest.

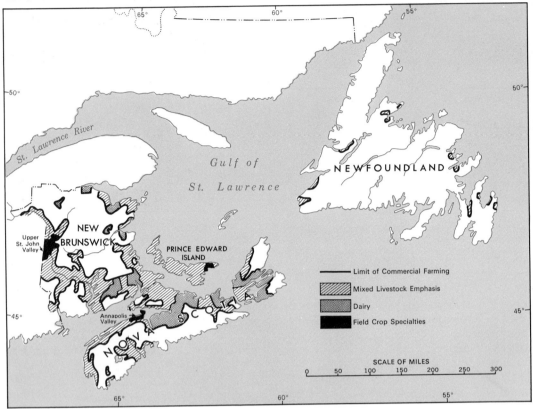

AFTER ECONOMICS BRANCH, CANADA DEPARTMENT OF AGRICULTURE

Figure 4.10 Agricultural Regions in the Atlantic Provinces

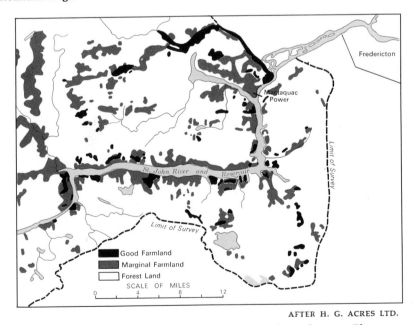

AFTER H. G. ACRES LTD.

Figure 4.11 Land Use Guide — Mactaquac Regional Development Plan

Figure 4.12 Agriculture in Prince Edward Island

cant role in the structure of the total regional economy in the Maritime Provinces than it does in Ontario and Quebec, but that this is really a reflection of the comparative underdevelopment of regional manufacturing. However, agriculture is not as significant an employer in the Maritimes as elsewhere in Canada, and furthermore its importance has been falling at a faster rate. Land abandonment has proceeded rapidly, for the decrease in the percentage of improved land between 1941 and 1961 was about 34 per cent. Of course, many farms are not viable, and it is estimated that more than 30 per cent of the farms in 1961 were operating at a subsistence level. Indeed, more than 50 per cent of the farmers in the Atlantic Provinces reported doing "off-the-farm" work in 1960, and two-thirds of these worked off the farm for periods exceeding four months.

Why have modern techniques, mechanization, and improved crops not produced a better level of agriculture in the Atlantic Provinces? Examination of census data and generalized maps fails to explain this in a satisfactory manner. Figure 4.11 shows the land use pattern for part of the Mactaquac project on the St. John River upstream from Fredericton. This area may be considered typical of agriculture in a considerable part of the Atlantic Provinces. It is apparent from the map that farming is not organized in terms of contiguous blocks but in small patches or clearings and that

forests predominate. For the Mactaquac project area cleared land totalled 91,000 acres of which only 53 per cent was being farmed. The remaining 47 per cent was idle and for the most part was owned by people who resided elsewhere. Full-time farms averaged 318 acres in size including woodlot, with 52 acres being cropland and 26 acres pasture. Between 1959 and 1965 farm sizes increased, with farms working more than 100 acres increasing by 73 per cent. However, the farms in the area are not prosperous. The average net farm income was only $1,650 per year. If it is assumed that a viable farm should have a net income of about $5,000 per year, then only 20 farms in the Mactaquac area were viable. Many of the farmers in the area were more than 55 years of age, and it appears that the prospects for change will be retarded until their farms are offered for sale. In addition, the resource base is limited for only 25 per cent of the cleared area had well-endowed soils suitable for normal agricultural practices. This too is typical of agriculture in the Atlantic Provinces. Under the auspices of A.R.D.A., land capability maps have been published. One of these examines the area around Glace Bay on Cape Breton Island. Fully 90 per cent of the area surveyed was found to have physical characteristics unsuitable for agriculture. Thus to a large extent agriculture in the region reflects the quality of the available resource base.

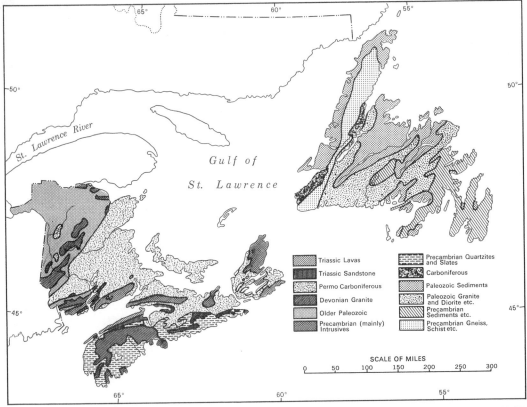

Legend:
- Triassic Lavas
- Triassic Sandstone
- Permo Carboniferous
- Devonian Granite
- Older Paleozoic
- Precambrian (mainly) Intrusives
- Precambrian Quartzites and Slates
- Carboniferous
- Paleozoic Sediments
- Paleozoic Granite and Diorite etc.
- Precambrian Sediments etc.
- Precambrian Gneiss, Schist etc.

SCALE OF MILES
0   50   100   150   200   250   300

AFTER GEOLOGICAL SURVEY OF CANADA

Figure 4.13 Geology of the Atlantic Provinces

Mining

Despite a complex geology the Atlantic Region is not well endowed with economically accessible minerals. Indeed, there has been a tendency to restrict mineral production, and its importance has declined from nearly ten per cent of the net value of production in 1952 to a little more than six per cent in 1962. This decline has been precipitated by changes in the two principal minerals mined, coal in Nova Scotia and iron ore in Newfoundland.

The Carboniferous rocks of the Atlantic Region contain a number of fairly thick seams of bituminous coal, some of which is of coking quality. The Cape Breton coalfield is the most important, accounting for 75 per cent of the total output. The field is located along the Atlantic shoreline and most of the seams extend out under the ocean. Mining is costly. As the workings have progressed, the undersea tunnels have been extended until they are now far beyond the originally proposed limit of two and one-half miles from shore. Glace Bay, New Waterford, North Sydney, and Sydney Mines have been the largest mining towns, but all are now declining. The

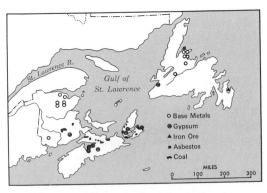

Legend:
- Base Metals
- Gypsum
- Iron Ore
- Asbestos
- Coal

MILES
0   100   200   300

Figure 4.14 Mining in the Atlantic Provinces

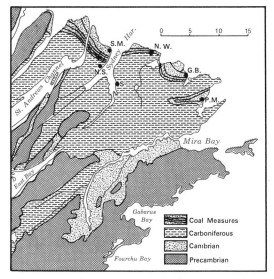

Figure 4.15 The Cape Breton Coalfield
The Cape Breton Lowland is underlain by a tilted basin of Carboniferous rocks, most of which has no coal. The coal measures outcrop just behind the eastern shoreline and most of the coal lies under the Atlantic. Glace Bay (G.B.) and the smaller mining towns are in close proximity to the mines, but the Sydney complex with its huge steel complex is localized by the harbor.

G.B.	Glace Bay	P.M.	Port Morien
N.S.	North Sydney	S	Sydney
N.W.	New Waterford	S.M.	Sydney Mines

coalfields of Pictou and Cumberland in the northern part of mainland Nova Scotia have also been important. However, the Cumberland coalfield virtually ceased production on October 23, 1957 following the mine disaster at Springhill. In Pictou county, Stellarton and Westville are still producing limited amounts of coal.

In contrast to the decline in Nova Scotia the production of the open-pit mines of the Minto field near Fredericton is expanding. The use of coal in nearby thermal electric installations and the relatively low cost of mining have been the major factors in maintaining the industry. The importance of coal mining is greatest in Nova Scotia where, in the past, over 9,000 miners have been employed at one time. The yearly output of coal in Nova Scotia is about 3,500,000 tons and is expected to decline in the near future. The decline of

coal mining, however, is almost universal in North America where heat and power are increasingly being derived from other sources such as petroleum, natural gas, and hydro-electricity. In the near future nuclear energy will probably become fully competitive as a source of power. But even the small market for Maritime coal which might still exist in Central Canada is more easily and cheaply served by mines in the United States, and about 60 per cent of the coal used in Canada is imported. In addition, Canadian production of other fuels is rapidly increasing; coal, which once enjoyed 80 per cent of the market, now supplies less than 18 per cent.[*]

The cost of mining is relatively high in Nova Scotia. Present output is only 2.8 tons per man per day, which may be compared with 4.9 tons per man-day from shaft mines, and 28.2 tons per man-day from surface mines in Alberta. The contrast is startling. In addition, the Nova Scotia mines are distant from the coal-deficient areas of Ontario and Quebec where they must enter into competition with the mines of Pennsylvania and West Virginia which offer better grades of coal at lower prices. Government subventions in aid of transportation of Maritime coal to central Canadian markets amounted to about $12,000,000 in 1964.

As a result of petitions by the Dominion Steel and Coal Company (DOSCO) the government of Canada appointed a royal commission to study the problem. The chairman, J. R. Donald, issued his report in 1966.[**] It recognized that coal mining was a way of life which most coal miners did not wish to change, and in addition many communities depended almost completely upon coal mining as a source of employment. The Donald report contained certain suggestions to ease the situation: the government should set up a Crown Corporation to take over the DOSCO

[*] Benoit Brouillette. "Approvisionnement du Canada en Combustibles". *L'Actualité Economique.* (Jan.-Mar. 1961). p. 576.
[**] J. R. Donald. *The Cape Breton Coal Problem.* The Queen's Printer. Ottawa. October, 1966.

interests and to invest the sum of $45,000,-000; of this amount, $25,000,000 were to be used to rehabilitate certain operating mines, and certain others, being most uneconomic, were to be phased out; the remaining sum of $20,000,000 should be used to generate new industries in the coalfield area. In addition, the province of Nova Scotia should contribute $10,000,000 for the same purpose. It was foreseen that coal production would decline still further but it was hoped that it might be stabilized at about 2,000,000 tons per annum. Older miners were to be urged into early retirement through a generous increase in pensions. All current subvention payments were to cease when the Crown Corporation began operations.

Events moved rather rapidly thereafter. In January, 1968, the management of the coal-mining and steel-making operations of the Cape Breton area were assumed by the Sydney Steel and Coal corporation (SYSCO). Some mines, particularly those at New Waterford, have been phased out, while others continue with a moderate program.

Iron ore has been the chief mineral produced in Newfoundland for many years. The major share of its output went to the steel mills at Sydney although large tonnages were also sold in Europe. The ore

Figure 4.16 Salt Mines at Pugwash
The tiny community of Pugwash relies on its port and the Windsor Salt mine.

could not be used in other North American steel mills because of its high phosphorus content. Under the floor of Conception Bay near the eastern tip of the island of Newfoundland lies an enormous deposit of iron ore which outcrops on Bell Island. Pit heads were located on the island, but the working face was reached by long tunnels extending two to three miles out under the bay, making the operation somewhat expensive.

In June, 1966, after 72 years of activity and a total production of 79,000,000 tons of iron ore, the Bell Island mines were closed, leaving the town of Wabana (10,000) without a major source of employment. The Sydney steel mills now obtain ore from Newfoundland's Labrador mines.

Base metals are beginning to achieve greater importance in the Atlantic Provinces despite their limited contribution in the past. Buchans in Newfoundland has been a producer of long standing, but recently the Notre Dame Bay area has seen the development of three new mines. One at Little Bay has recently reached the capacity of 1,000 tons of ore daily. In New Brunswick base metals are concentrated in the Bathurst-Newcastle area where large mineralized intrusions dominate the York Plateau. Recent estimates suggest that 150 million tons of ore exist in the area. Since 1960 two major mines have been developed, and investment there is now reaching $200,000,000.

Nova Scotia accounts for nearly 80 per cent of the gypsum produced in Canada. Windsor has long been the center of gypsum mining, but newer mines are now in operation at Milford near Halifax. Asbestos is produced in Newfoundland and is currently mined in the Baie Verte area. Newfoundland is also an important producer of fluorspar and talc.

Salt has long been produced in the Atlantic Provinces, and in Nova Scotia new mines at Pugwash have been opened to replace the pits which were closed at Malagash. Salt is also obtained from brine wells near Amherst. However, salt production is geared mainly to local requirements.

Increases in the production of structural materials, particularly cement, have taken place. Since 1960 a new plant producing 15,000,000 bags a year has been opened near Truro, Nova Scotia, the capacity of the cement plant at Havelock, New Brunswick has been doubled, and a cement plant has been built at Corner Brook, Newfoundland.

Forest Industries

Despite European occupance for centuries in the Atlantic Region, 62 per cent of the total area is still in forest. Including Labrador the region accounts for 5.5 per cent of the standing timber in Canada and 7.5 per cent of the productive forest land. The Atlantic Provinces supply an average of 9 per cent by volume of Canada's total cut each year. The most productive forests are found in the northern and central parts of New Brunswick, the north-central part of the island of Newfoundland, and some sections of western Nova Scotia.

In recent years, forest products have supplied an average of 45 per cent of the exports from the Atlantic Region. The forest itself took care of only four per cent of the labor force, but jobs in wood and paper industries provided about 20.5 per cent of the employment. The forest thus contributes substantially to the wealth of the region, particularly in New Brunswick and Newfoundland.

Figure 4.17 Log Storage on the St. John River

It was pointed out that forestry was very early of significance in the Atlantic economy. The "Golden Age" of forestry, however, coincided with the "Age of Wooden Ships", and both declined rapidly in the last quarter of the nineteenth century. Sawmilling acted as a temporary replacement until the pulp and paper industry began to develop strength during the 1920s. Today the production of pulpwood is the dominant aspect of the forest industry, and the annual value of pulp and paper is currently about three times that of all sawmill products.

Figure 4.18 Pulp Logs at Roadside
The photograph was taken near Amherst, Nova Scotia, on Highway 2. The logs are stored by the side of the road and transported by trucks to pulp and paper mills.

R. PUTNAM

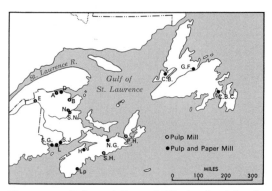

Figure 4.19 Pulp and Paper Mills in the Atlantic Provinces

A	Atholville	H	Hantsport
B	Bathurst	N	Newcastle
C.B.	Corner Brook	N.G.	New Glasgow
C.B.C.	Come-By-Chance	P.H.	Port Hawkesbury
D	Dalhousie	S.G.	St. George
E	Edmundston	S.H.	Sheet Harbor
G.F.	Grand Falls	S.J.	Saint John
L	Lancaster	S.N.	South Nelson
Lp	Liverpool		

Newfoundland and the northern part of New Brunswick contain the chief centers of the pulp and paper industry. All of them, except those at Edmundston, New Brunswick, and Grand Falls, Newfoundland, are located close to the sea coast. This is logical in view of the fact that more than 90 per cent of the product is exported. Supplies of fresh water for industries are readily available even along the coast, and now that logs are widely transported by truck, a riverside location is no longer necessary. Forest cutting in the Atlantic Region is no longer strictly a winter occupation. The gasoline-powered chain saw

and even more sophisticated tree harvesting machines, all weather roads and truck transportation have given the industry year-round stability. The visitor in the forest regions notices immediately the use of road allowances for the storage of pulpwood. The rivers are important, however, as they still provide storage and transportation for logs and, even more significantly, they provide the power to operate the mills.

In Newfoundland two large mills control vast woodlands. Bowater at Corner Brook controls an area of 3,100,000 acres, while the Anglo-Newfoundland complex at Grand Falls has a resource base of 2,100,000 acres of forest. Access to these reserves is provided by both railways and truck roads. New mills are likely to develop in Newfoundland: one is slated to begin production soon at Come-By-Chance, while another has been suggested for Stephenville.

In New Brunswick large plants are located at South Nelson, Newcastle, Bathurst, Dalhousie, and Edmundston, and a new mill has recently been built at Atholville. The timber resources in the north are exceptionally good, combining the attributes of the Great Lakes — St. Lawrence mixed forest and the Boreal forest. Acadian forest resources in southern New Brunswick are utilized by mills close to the St. John River.

During the past decade Nova Scotia has seen the development of new mills to the east which complement the existing ones at Hantsport, Liverpool, and Sheet Harbor. These new mills are located near New

Table 4.7   Forest Resource of the Atlantic Provinces *

Province	Productive Forest Land (thousand sq. mi.)	Estimate of Standing Timber (million cu. ft.)	Annual Cut Five-year Average (million cu. ft.)
Newfoundland — Island	12.9 ⎱	6,964 ⎱	99.0
— Labrador	20.8 ⎰	7,332 ⎰	
Prince Edward Island	.8	250	7.7
Nova Scotia	15.0	9,782	93.6
New Brunswick	23.8	16,871	183.0
Total	73.3	41,199	383.3

* Source: D. B. S.

Glasgow in Pictou county and Port Hawkesbury on the Strait of Canso.

Sawmills are also important in the Atlantic Provinces although the value of sawn lumber is currently equal to only about one-fifth that of pulp and paper production. There are a few large mills such as those at Campbellton, Newcastle, and Minto, but most of the production comes from several hundred small and medium-sized mills. For example, Nova Scotia currently has more than 500 sawmills. Many of these mills are portable and change location to take advantage of variations in the forest resource.

Fisheries

Fishing, the oldest industry in the Atlantic Provinces, has been carried on continuously from the time of the early exploration of the region. The indented coastline is admirably suited for fishing ports, while off-shore lie 200,000 square miles of shallow seas comprising one of the greatest fishing grounds in the world. The shallower areas of these surrounding seas are known as "banks", the largest of which is the Grand Bank to the southeast of Newfoundland with an area of 36,000 square miles. South of Nova Scotia there are several large banks including Banquereau,

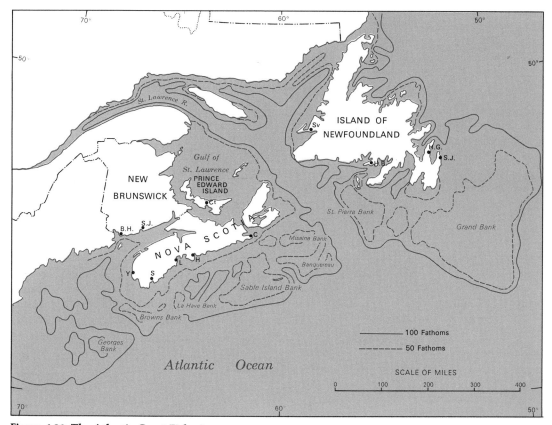

Figure 4.20 The Atlantic Coast Fisheries
The number of active fishing ports has declined in recent years as new techniques make it more efficient to use the major ports such as Halifax, Lunenburg, Saint John, and St. John's.

B.H.	Black's Harbor	H.B.	Harbor Breton	Sv	Stephenville
C	Canso	H.G.	Harbor Grace	S.J.	Saint John
Ct	Charlottetown	L	Lunenburg	S.J.	St. John's
H	Halifax	S	Shelburne	Y	Yarmouth

Sable Island Bank, La Have Bank, and Browns Bank (Figure 4.20). In addition, there are several thousand miles of productive "inshore" fishing grounds within fifteen miles of land.

The shallow waters of the banks are conditioned by the convergence of the warm Gulf Stream drift and the cold water of the Labrador Current, together with the flow of fresh water from the great St. Lawrence River system. During recent decades the warming effect of the Gulf Stream has been expanding northward, and today optimum biological conditions for marine organisms occur to the north of Newfoundland. In these waters the combination of temperature conditions and mineral content appear to be optimum for the growth of myriads of tiny marine plants known collectively as phytoplankton. They furnish the food supply for swarms of tiny marine animals, the zooplankton, which in turn are eaten by teeming schools of fish.

Fisheries are divided into three categories: *groundfish* or bottom feeders, taken on the offshore banks; *pelagic* and *estuarial*, composed chiefly of migratory species; *crustaceans* and *molluscs*, which are not vertebrate fish at all but other forms of animal life which inhabit shallow waters near the shore. The relative importance of these categories in the Atlantic Region is shown in Table 4.8.

The great commercial fish has been the cod which has dominated the North Atlantic fisheries for centuries. As shown in Table 4.8, the cod currently accounts for 37 per cent of the landed weight and 25 per cent of the value of the total catch. Other species of groundfish include flounder and sole, haddock, pollack, halibut, and hake. Large amounts of redfish are taken and processed into fishmeal. The Canadian catch of North Atlantic groundfish amounts to about 500,000 tons annually. A little more than half is taken by Newfoundland fishermen, and most of the remainder is landed in Nova Scotia.

The herring is the most abundant of the pelagic and estuarial species. Sardines are

Table 4.8 Chief Commercial Fisheries of the Atlantic Region *

Category	Per Cent of Total Landed Weight		Per Cent of Total Market Value	
Groundfish	**67**		**47**	
—Cod		37		25
—Flounder and Sole		11		7
—Haddock		7		6
Pelagic and Estuarial	**26**		**12**	
—Herring and Sardines		21		5
Crustaceans and Molluscs	**7**		**41**	
—Lobster		3		28

* Source: Canada Year Book, 1968, pp. 627-628.

most important commercially. Among the crustaceans the lobster is most important; despite the small quantity landed, the quality is high and the market value at times outranks even that of the cod.

Throughout its history the fishing fleet of the Atlantic Region has been subject to great variations in value of production. During the nineteenth century it enjoyed great prosperity with virtually unlimited markets in Europe and Middle America, but by the 1930s foreign competition and worldwide economic depression had dealt severely with the fisheries of Newfoundland and the Maritime Provinces. Several factors contributed to the decline. Among them was the change in the demand for dried fish as standards of living rose in Europe. Other countries developed new and improved methods of catching and processing fish and were thus able to undersell Canadian fishermen.

Only in the last two decades has the Canadian industry begun to modernize and to use new steel-hulled trawlers and diesel-powered draggers. Recently new stern trawlers with fish processing and freezing facilities on board have been acquired by the fishermen of the Atlantic Region. The cost of one of these vessels is more than $500,000 and considerable government aid has been necessary. However, such vessels can spend 82 per cent of their time at sea as opposed to 62 per cent with conventional trawlers.

Today the Atlantic fishing industry is vastly different from that which existed even two decades ago. The traditional "inshore" fishing method which used small boats manned by one or two men has been replaced by the long-liner which carries a crew of six and can take more than ten tons of fish in the course of a day's operation. Likewise, the traditional wooden "deep-sea" fishing schooners, equipped with dories for use in hand-line fishing have been replaced by draggers and more recently by stern trawlers using nylon nets of Danish design. Vessels such as these require fewer men, catch more fish, and market a better quality product. In Newfoundland today, while the "inshore" fishery employs 95 per cent of the fishermen, 25 per cent of the catch is obtained from the new trawlers of the "deep-sea" fishery. As a result the small fishing villages are declining, and the industry is concentrating in the larger urban centers.

Table 4.9   The Atlantic Fishery
in 1965 *

	Employed Total Number	of all Fishery Products Total Value $000
Newfoundland	21,701	52,849
Prince Edward Island	3,566	9,592
Nova Scotia	14,049	91,626
New Brunswick	6,241	46,237
Atlantic Region	45,557	200,304
Canada	62,335	315,745

* Source: Canada Year Book, 1968, p. 629.

As shown by Table 4.9, the number of people involved in the primary fishing industry is quite small, comprising less than four per cent of the regional labor force. Employment has been quite stable and in the last decade has increased by only a few hundred workers. However, with the widespread use of new fish products such as frozen fillets and fish sticks the value of all fish products has nearly doubled during the last decade. As consolidation has proceeded, small ports have ceased operation and the small fish-product establishments have declined. This has been most marked in New Brunswick where 122 such establishments existed in 1957 and only 67 remained in 1961. New developments take place only in the larger centers while "outports" are being abandoned. In Newfoundland, St. John's, Stephenville, Harbor Breton, and Harbor Grace are the most important, while in Nova Scotia, Halifax, Lunenburg, Yarmouth, Lockeport, and Shelburne are the leading fishing ports.

The new strength of the industry can best be shown by considering the case of New Brunswick. In 1966 more than 6,000 fishermen and 2,800 plant workers were involved. The fishing fleet comprised 90 steel draggers, seven steel stern trawlers, 27 Danish seiners, and 35 herring purse-seiners. Developments of a similar nature have taken place in Newfoundland under sponsorship of the provincial government. Since 1950 the province has supplied $1,600,000 to aid in the construction of larger fishing vessels and has loaned $15,800,000 to develop new fish-processing facilities. In addition, since 1963 the province has supplied $1,000,000 to aid in the adoption of new equipment such as synthetic fiber nets and has set up a special training school for fishermen. Thus the old images of the tiny vessels and hand-fishing techniques are no longer true in the new, mechanized Atlantic fishing industry.

Power

The Atlantic Region is not well supplied with waterpower in comparison with Quebec, Ontario, and British Columbia. Despite reliable precipitation and ample run-off, the rivers are often too short and lack sufficient head for waterpower development. But where physical conditions warrant, power sites have been developed. In Newfoundland the largest power plants are those of the large pulp and paper companies on the Humber and Exploits Rivers. Smaller developments supply St. John's, and a new project is under construction in the Baie d'Espoir area. The St. John River is the most important source of power in New Brunswick, large plants being located at Grand Falls, Beechwood, and Mactaquac. Many smaller rivers in New Brunswick and in Nova Scotia are also utilized.

Until recently electric power resources were not well distributed. It was only during the last decade that a Maritime regional power grid was developed so that peak needs could be met satisfactorily. Thermal stations are important since 100 per cent of the power generated in Prince Edward Island, 62 per cent in Nova Scotia, and 44 per cent in New Brunswick come from thermal generators. These are located both near the coalfields of Cape Breton, Pictou, Cumberland, and Minto, and near the large urban centers.

Manufacturing

In comparison with other regions in Canada the Atlantic Region is not an important manufacturing area. Nevertheless, manufacturing is important to the Atlantic economy. It provides nearly 14 per cent of the regional employment and accounts for 41 per cent of the value added by the commodity-producing industries. Manufacturing is the first-ranking industrial division in Nova Scotia and New Brunswick, second-ranking in Newfoundland, and third-ranking in Prince Edward Island.

In terms of major industrial groups the industrial structure of the Atlantic Region is shown in Table 4.10. Primary metallurgy, certainly one of the important groups, cannot be shown because of the provisions of the Statistics Act. Most of the important "propelling" industries, indicated by the location quotients, rely on agriculture, fishing, and forestry for their raw materials. The primary iron and steel industry also relies partly upon local materials. So does the greater part of the transportation equipment industry which is concerned with the building of boats, ships, and railway cars. The major markets for all of these industries lie beyond the confines of the Atlantic Region.

Table 4.10	The Industrial Structure of Manufacturing in the Atlantic Region Compared with That of Canada, 1965 *				
Industry Group **	Industrial Employment in the Atlantic Region (Number)	Industrial Employment in Canada (Number)	Atlantic Region Group Employment as per cent of Canada Group Employment	Atlantic Region Total Employment as per cent of Canada Total Employment	Location Quotient
Food and Beverage	25,114	220,700	11.38	4.45	2.56
Paper and Allied Products	10,251	110,180	9.30	4.45	2.09
Wood Products	6,143	91,589	6.70	4.45	1.51
Transportation Equipment	5,017	135,481	3.71	4.45	0.83
Metal Fabricating	3,518	133,992	2.63	4.45	0.59
Printing and Publishing	2,885	78,737	3.66	4.45	0.82
Electrical Products	1,688	113,463	1.49	4.45	0.33
Non-metallic Mineral Products	1,679	51,218	3.28	4.45	0.74
Others	13,618	634,939	2.14	4.45	0.48
Total	69,913	1,570,299	4.45	4.45	1.00

* Data from Canada Year Book, 1968, pp. 700-708.
** Statistical analysis of several important groups cannot be included because of the withholding of pertinent data under the secrecy provision of the Statistics Act.

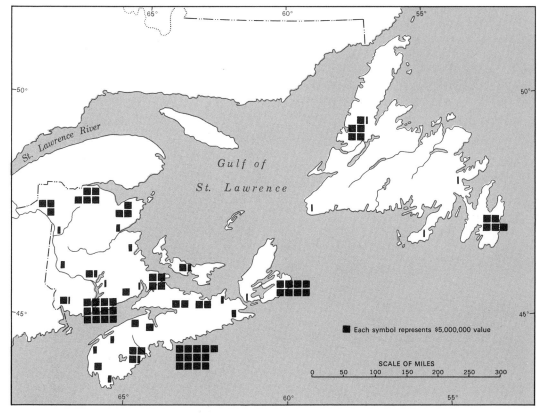

Figure 4.21 Manufacturing in the Atlantic Provinces

Considerable significance may be attached to those industrial groups in which the location quotient is much less than 1.00. The industries making up these groups are not well enough established to meet the needs of the region and imports are necessary. Many of these industries are market-oriented and require skilled labor, and in neither of these requirements is the Atlantic Region well endowed. It is also too far from the markets of Ontario and Quebec to be able to overcome easily the economic barrier of transportation costs on finished goods.

Although in some cases important plants are located in rural areas, the distribution of manufacturing activities corresponds closely with that of urban population. Metropolitan Halifax contains the largest industrial concentration in the region in terms of both employment and value of output. Petroleum refining, fish processing, shipbuilding and repair, electronics, and food and beverage industries are well developed. Metropolitan Saint John (which includes Lancaster and Simonds) is also developing rapidly. Its major industries are shipbuilding and repair, pulp and paper, and sugar refining.

Sydney ranks third in the total output of manufactured products by virtue of its primary iron and steel industry. Coking coal is obtained locally, iron ore is obtained from Labrador, and limestone is brought from Aguathuna, Newfoundland. In the past DOSCO had control of the sources of raw materials, the vessels used for transportation, and also of the market through subsidiary companies in Quebec and Ontario.

There was early specialization in the rolling of steel rails, and when the Cana-

Figure 4.22 Clairtone — Stellarton, Nova Scotia

dian demand for rails declined, large orders were sought abroad and filled. Some steel was used in the Halifax shipyards, some in metal fabrication and rolling stock in the New Glasgow industries, and some in various industries in other Maritime centers. But in order to dispose of its product DOSCO was obliged to acquire a number of subsidiaries in Quebec and Ontario and to compete with the steel industries based in Hamilton. In 1967 DOSCO announced the imminent closure of the Sydney steel works.

Following the suggestions of the Donald report the Nova Scotia Government set up the Sydney Steel and Coal Company (SYSCO) to take over the DOSCO plants in Nova Scotia. The plants in Quebec were taken over by SIDBEC, the agency through which the government of Quebec hopes to establish a primary iron and steel industry in that province. It was announced in 1957 that the steel capacity of the Sydney mills had been raised to 1,000,000 tons per annum. No further expansion has taken place since then although the total steel-making capacity of all Canadian mills has doubled in the meantime. Thus the challenge of the new management is to stimulate new growth.

Corner Brook and St. John's are the chief manufacturing centers in Newfoundland. Long known as the site of a huge pulp and paper mill, Corner Brook also has a cement factory and a plant for the manufacture of gypsum products. St. John's contains many secondary industries which cater to the fishing industries as well as those which make consumer goods for the urban population. Also of economic importance is the pulp and paper center of Grand Falls on the Exploits River.

The Atlantic Region hopes to base its further development on the manufacturing sector of its economy. Despite the problems associated with its coal supply the iron and steel industry at Sydney is able to produce steel of various types to meet the needs of shipbuilding and other industries. Industrial development, outside of the growth in pulp and paper and fish processing, has been nurtured through government aid. In this respect the encouragement given by the province of Nova Scotia via the Industrial Estates and other measures has been responsible for a heavy water plant in Cape Breton, an electronics firm in Pictou county, automobile assembly at Dartmouth and Sydney, and a carpet factory at Truro.

Defense

Defense spending has an important role in the economy of the Atlantic Region in that it involves more than seven per cent of the regional labor force. The region has only 10 per cent of Canada's population but has 24 per cent of all employment in Canadian defense industry. According to a recent study 7.3 per cent of the Atlantic Region's labor force is directly involved in defense services.* Thus more people are employed in the defense industry than in any of the Atlantic Region's primary industries.

Despite its overall importance, the industry is not distributed evenly among the Atlantic Provinces. Nova Scotia and New Brunswick together account for 90 per cent of the Atlantic defense employment. In Nova Scotia defense services employ 11.6 per cent of the labor force. On the other

hand, in Newfoundland only 2.3 per cent of the labor force is employed by defense services.

The impact of defense is best understood in terms of recent growth in employment in the Atlantic Region. Small as the growth is in the region, between 1951 and 1961 defense services accounted for 66 per cent of the labor force growth. Today defense services are not expanding and will no longer propel the Atlantic economy.

The impact of defense spending in the region is hard to assess. In terms of encouraging industry the defense dollar contributes little for only five per cent of the equipment used is manufactured locally. However, the employment offered does have a multiplier effect of about 1.1, and the wage level in defense services is above the average for the region. Thus, defense in reality is responsible for about 80,000 jobs and a raised total consumer demand. Defense services, however, are excessively concentrated and their benefits are very unevenly spread over the region; moreover, the favored areas are exceptionally vulnerable to changes in defense policy. This is particularly true for Halifax, the home base of two-thirds of the Canadian Navy and headquarters of the Atlantic Command. In 1961, 24 per cent of the labor force of Metropolitan Halifax was directly employed by defense services. If one considers the multiplier effect where jobs outside defense services depend on the defense industry, then more than half the labor force in Metropolitan Halifax relies on defense functions. Likewise other centers such as Fredericton and Oromocto rely heavily on defense employment. Similarly the Greenwood air base in the Berwick area and the Cornwallis naval base near Digby have a strong influence on local economic activity. Even though it is localized, defense spending plays a major role in the economic geography of the Atlantic Region.

Recreation

The economic importance of recreation has often been underestimated, and in

* C. R. Marks. "Defense Expenditures and the Economy of the Atlantic Provinces". *Atlantic Provinces Economic Council Pamphlet.* No. 9 (December, 1965). p. 10.

spite of its undoubted influence in many regional landscapes, its geography is usually ignored. For instance, two excellent collections of papers, *Canada's Changing Geography* (R. Louis Gentilcore) and *Readings in Canadian Geography* (Robert M. Irving), contain no article on recreation geography. It is of great importance in the Atlantic Region. In Nova Scotia alone the average gross annual income received from tourism during the past few years is estimated to be in excess of $50,000,000. Tourism encourages employment in the service or tertiary industries; hotels, motels, restaurants, service stations, and summer cottage areas have expanded under its influence. However, despite its apparent importance there is a dearth of statistical information and geographical analysis. Although a summer home is part of the normal way of life for millions of North Americans, only one definitive study of the summer cottage has ever been made in Canada.* One study of New England is particularly pertinent.** Here is a region which is a close neighbor of Atlantic Canada and has suffered a similar lack of growth in comparison with most of the rest of North America. New England has become a mecca for summer vacationers and possesses considerable attraction for winter visitors as well. Since more than 50 per cent of the visitors to the Atlantic Region are from the United States, it is probable that many see it simply as a physical extension of New England and look for many of the same familiar features. It is reasonable to suppose that its drawing power will be enhanced by the development of facilities and land use patterns of the sort which have been successful there. Of course, much has been done. Many old farms, especially in shore locations, have been turned into summer recreation areas, and resorts have been built on both the seaside and on inland

* Roy I. Wolfe. "The Summer Cottage in Ontario". *Economic Geography.* Vol. 27 (1951). pp. 10-32.

** J. F. Hart. "The Three 'R's' of the Rural North East". *Canadian Geographer.* VII, 1 (1963). pp. 7-22.

lakes. Chester has long been a center for yachtsmen. Peggy's Cove preserves the air of an old-time fishing village and relies on tourists as a major source of income. The long sand beaches of the Gulf Coast of Prince Edward Island have been turned into a national park as have the uplands of the northern part of Cape Breton Island, both with the hope of attracting summer visitors. But while highways are generally adequate in all parts of the region and are being constantly improved, there is still a problem of extended delay in the ferry services making connections with both Prince Edward Island and Newfoundland.

PHYSICAL RESOURCE BASE

Thus far the Atlantic Provinces have been analyzed in terms of the human and cultural resource development. It has been apparent that many of the characteristics noted have been due to the physical resource base. Landforms, climate, vegetation, soil, and the sea do much to create the unique geographic character of this region and merit more detailed consideration.

Landforms

Although the Atlantic Region exhibits no great amplitude of relief, there is an infinite variety of landforms. There are no mountains, but there are definite areas of higher and lower relief. In general, the boundary between these natural divisions of the land surface is approximately along for 500-foot contour.

Diversity in landforms can be accounted for in terms of the underlying rock structure. The central Maritime Region is a geosyncline of ancient sedimentary strata, nestled between the Precambrian rocks of the Canadian Shield of Quebec and the Atlantic Upland of southern Nova Scotia and eastern Newfoundland. In this depression are found various systems of Paleozoic rocks including the coal-bearing Carboniferous layers which outcrop in eastern Nova Scotia and New Brunswick.

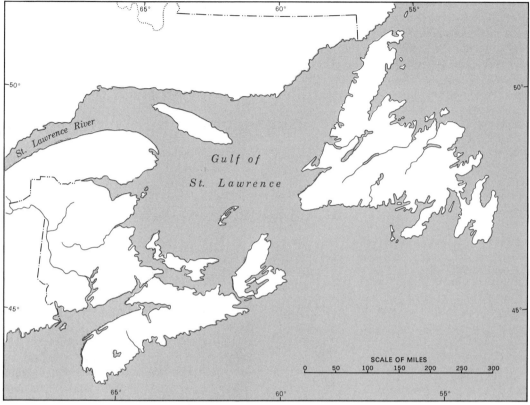

Figure 4.23 Physiographic Features of the Atlantic Provinces

At various times these rocks have been subjected to tectonic forces and the folds have produced a grained topography in which the rocks and relief are oriented in long belts running from northeast to southwest. This orientation is paralleled by the Appalachian fold-mountains in the United States. In addition to the folding there were intrusions of molten magma. The largest exposures of these crystalline rocks are the granites of the Central Highlands of New Brunswick, the Central Uplands of the peninsula of Nova Scotia, and the Central Plateau of Newfoundland. The youngest solid rock formations are the Triassic sandstone and trap of the Bay of Fundy region.

Glaciation has profoundly modified the surface of the Atlantic Region. In many areas the rocky hills were stripped of their soil mantle, while in other areas, often lowlands, a great mixture of unconsolidated debris was left upon the bedrock when the ice melted. Moraines, kames, and eskers occur in abundance, and in particular drumlins form an important part of the landscape in southern Nova Scotia, especially in the vicinity of Lunenburg and Halifax. Stream patterns have been deranged by glacial drift and the countryside is

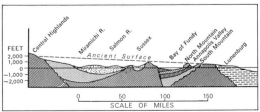

Figure 4.24 Profile and Geological Section across the Maritime Provinces

dotted with lakes and swamps. The rivers, forced by glaciation to carve new courses, experience many interruptions in the form of falls and rapids. Both the Reversing Falls and Grand Falls on the St. John River owe their origin to the effects of glaciation.

The Coast

Easily the most important feature of the physical geography of the Atlantic Region is its sinuous coast which has a length of several thousand miles and exhibits a great variety of landforms. Rectilineal coasts along the northern peninsula of Cape Breton Island and on both sides of the Bay of Fundy are very striking. Related to major fault zones in the earth's crust these coasts are noted for their lineal character. Within the Bay of Fundy the gradual convergence of the shores toward the head of the bay has given rise to some of the most spectacular tides in the world. Variation in water level is greatest in the narrow head waters where the normal daily range is 30 to 40 feet. At spring tide it may increase to more than 50 feet (Figure 4.25). Along the protected parts of the Bay of Fundy shoreline and in river estuaries extensive areas of tidal silt have been deposited. These wide alluvial lowlands have been protected by dykes since the time of the Acadians and form some of the best farmlands of the region.

Figure 4.25 The Tides of the Bay of Fundy
The mean range between high and low tide reaches fifty feet in Cobequid Bay.

The shores of Northumberland Strait and the neighboring shores of the Gulf of St. Lawrence are low and flat. Underlain by almost horizontal rock strata this coast has many deeply-drowned river valleys, while along the shore are long sand bars often crowned by dunes. Good harbors are few, being confined to the larger estuaries. Much of the Atlantic Coast is indented, almost fiord-like in nature, and festooned with small rocky islands. The south shore of Nova Scotia from Canso to Yarmouth and the northeast coast of Newfoundland are good examples. Numerous protected harbors are located here, and from them the fishing fleets set forth. Similarly the deep indentations in the Avalon Peninsula have created good natural harbors such as that of St. John's.

The Lowland

The central feature of the structure of the Maritime Provinces is the broad geosyncline of the Maritime Basin. It underlies the whole southwestern part of the Gulf of St. Lawrence, all of Prince Edward Island, nearly half of New Brunswick, and the Northumberland Coastal Lowlands of Nova Scotia. The basin contains the Maritime coal measures, the workable seams of which are concentrated in the flat central plain of New Brunswick near Minto and the more complex structures of Cumberland and Pictou counties in Nova Scotia. By far the greatest area, however, is underlain by the red beds which characterize the northern parts of the coastal plain of Nova Scotia and all of Prince Edward Island. Boreholes in Prince Edward Island suggest that the red beds are more than 2,000 feet thick. Here the soils are better drained and more productive than in the eastern lowlands of New Brunswick where the most prevalent rock is a rather sterile sandstone called Millstone Grit. Much of the central and eastern lowlands of New Brunswick is flat and swampy, the former drainage having been deranged by glaciation. Deep sandy drift covers most of the plain, but in places the rock lies very close to the surface.

The inland edge of the plain is fringed by rocky limestone hills which reach 500 feet above mean tide. While the Northumberland coastal lowland is the eastward extension of the New Brunswick lowland, it presents a different type of landscape. Modest folding of the strata has created long low sandstone hills which trend slightly north of east, while the coal measures are preserved in the synclines. Surface drainage is fairly good, but the soil is an infertile podzol.

The Annapolis-Cornwallis Valley is the most important and best known of the several scattered lowlands in the northern half of peninsular Nova Scotia. It is carved out of red shale and sandstone which outcrop between the lava sheet of the North Mountain and the granitic escarpment of the South Mountain. Agriculture is well developed in "the Valley" and its mosaic of fields and orchards offers sharp contrast to the adjacent forested uplands.

The wider lowland in the central part of Nova Scotia may be considered as a physiographic extension to the eastward of both the Annapolis-Cornwallis Valley and the Bay of Fundy trench. Important beds of gypsum are found in the Windsor area and farther east near Milford in the Shubenacadie Valley. The lands along Minas Bay, Cobequid Bay, and in the tributary valleys have supported some of the better farm settlements in Nova Scotia.

The Upland

The dominant elements of the physical landscape of the Atlantic Region are the extensive areas of upland. Complex in structure and relief they occur in all provinces except Prince Edward Island and are responsible for the prevailing impression of ruggedness in the landscape.

In New Brunswick there are three main upland areas: the Northwestern Plateau, the Central Highlands, and the Southern Uplands. Developed upon folded calcareous slates, with a general elevation of 1,000 to 1,500 feet above mean tide level, the Northwestern Plateau is an extensive area including adjoining portions of Que-

bec and Maine. Tributaries of the St. John and Restigouche Rivers are deeply incised into the plateau, creating difficulties for overland communication. The Central Highlands comprise a dissected plateau at an elevation of about 2,000 feet above sea level on which erosional remnants or monadnocks such as Mount Carleton (2,600 feet) add to the complexity of the relief.

The underlying rock of the highland is a huge granite batholith surrounded by hardened sedimentary formations. Contact and regional metamorphism have created a "storehouse" of minerals in this area. To the south of the 2,000-foot plateau lies the York Plateau where the summits are approximately 1,000 feet above sea level. The St. John River has cut a rather deep and narrow valley through the complex granite and metamorphosed sedimentaries as it flows toward the Central Lowland. The Southern Uplands of New Brunswick fringe the shore of the Bay of Fundy. East of the St. John River there is a long arched ridge which pitches toward the northeast and is cored by very old volcanic and intrusive rocks. To the north, across the Kennebecasis Valley, the somewhat lower Kingston Hills have a similar anticlinal structure.

The Atlantic Upland, the uplands of northern Nova Scotia, and Cape Breton Island occupy most of Nova Scotia. The Atlantic Upland comprising half the area of the province is the surface of a mass of hard granite and quartzite with belts of somewhat weaker slate. It has an inclined surface rising northward from the Atlantic shore at the rate of fifteen feet per mile to the brow of the South Mountain (600-700 feet A.T.), a northfacing escarpment overlooking the Annapolis Valley. While the surface is extremely irregular, the skyline is flat except for a few residual hills or monadnocks. Glacial action has scattered many erratics over the surface, and the soils are thin, stony, infertile podzols with little potential for agriculture. Drainage is immature and vast peat bogs have developed, a good example of which is to be seen near the new Halifax Airport. Valleys become deeper and drainage is more effective toward the south, but all the river mouths are drowned. Cape Breton Island does not seem quite so inhospitable as the Atlantic Upland; its surface is composed largely of northeast-trending ridges in the south and a huge tableland in the north reaching elevations of 1,500 to 1,700 feet A.T. Limited areas of lowland are found around the Bras d'Or Lakes and in some of the valleys, but they offer rather limited opportunities for agriculture.

There are three outstanding physiographic areas in Newfoundland: the Western Uplands, the Central Plateau, and the Eastern Peninsulas. The Western Uplands include the northern peninsula of the island, the highlands between Bonne Bay and St. George's Bay, and the flat-topped Anguille Mountains. They are underlain by hard Precambrian rocks. The highest points in the Long Range are more than 2,600 feet above sea level. The Central Plateau is underlain by Paleozoic sedimentary and intrusive rocks. Its general level is about 1,000 feet above sea level and its surface is rocky, barren, and marked by innumerable lakes and bogs. The western edge of the upland is a nearly continuous fault-line scarp which overlooks the narrow lowland extending from the Codroy Valley to White Bay. The southern margin is steep and relatively straight, suggesting that it is also a fault zone. The surface declines toward the northeast where it dips below sea level to form a much indented coast with many fringing islands. The Eastern Peninsulas are underlain by Precambrian rocks except for a few areas of Paleozoic remnants preserved in synclines such as Conception Bay. The folded rocks of the region clearly reveal its structural relationship with the Appalachian Region of eastern North America.

Climate

In spite of their maritime location there is a fairly strong continental influence operating in the climate of the Atlantic Provinces. Interior locations exhibit consid-

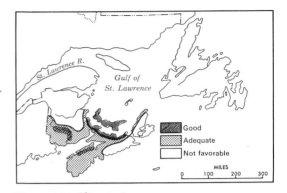

Figure 4.26 Climate Areas
In terms of suitability for agriculture, only a limited portion of the region has climate characteristics which can be considered as *good*.

erable range in seasonal temperatures. Near the Atlantic Coast continental air masses are modified by the ocean so that the summers are slightly cooler and the winters are much milder than they are at inland points. The southern coasts of Nova Scotia and Newfoundland have also much greater precipitation in comparison with the interior.

The general patterns of isotherms and isohyets have been illustrated earlier (Figures 2.8, 2.9, 2.10). Since the Atlantic Region is strongly influenced both by the weather systems from the west and by occasional air masses from the Atlantic Ocean, temperature ranges are greater than on the Pacific Coast. The coastal periphery of the Atlantic Region receives more moisture and has more moderate temperatures than the interior where extreme temperatures are recorded.

It is important to note that while the climate does permit agriculture in the region, areas with optimum conditions are very limited. This is particularly true for specialty crops such as corn which is restricted to the lower St. John Valley, the Annapolis Valley, and Prince Edward Island. At present some degree of success is being enjoyed by tobacco growers on Prince Edward Island and in the Annapolis Valley. However, the upland areas are very restrictive not only in terms of relief but also in their climate. As shown by Table

Table 4.11   Characteristics of the Climate *

Region	Mean Temperatures January °F	Mean Temperatures July °F	Frost-free Period in Days	Degree-days Above 42°F	Potential Evapo-trans-piration	Average Annual Precipi-tation	Per Cent of Precipitation During the Growing Season
S. Newfoundland	4	60	70	1,900	19.5	50	40
S. Shore							
Nova Scotia	25	62	130	2,800	22	55	40
Annapolis Valley	22	66	130	2,950	22	41	39
Middle St.							
John Valley	14	67	120	2,800	22	39	26
New Brunswick							
Uplands	5	63	95	2,000	19	40	45

* After L. J. Chapman and D. M. Brown. *The Climates of Canada for Agriculture.*

4.11, extreme conditions occur in the upland of New Brunswick and in Newfoundland. In such areas agriculture is not really feasible.

Precipitation is also an important factor in the environment, particularly during the winter. Snowfall is relatively heavy and most of Newfoundland and northern New Brunswick receive more than 100 inches of snow per year. Even the southern coasts of Newfoundland and Nova Scotia receive 65 to 75 inches of snow, while freezing rains complicate the situation. Winter conditions are difficult and make normal land transportation very hazardous. This has a strong influence on urban residents and dairy farmers.

The shallow seas along the Atlantic Coast are among the foggiest areas of the globe, and fog often occurs in summer, particularly in July. While the Bay of Fundy is notably affected, Northumberland Strait is comparably fog-free.

Closely allied to the climate are the ice conditions around the coast. The southern shores of Newfoundland and Nova Scotia are never closed in; thus Port aux Basques, Halifax, Liverpool, Yarmouth, and Saint John are always ice-free. St. John's and Sydney are sometimes closed by pack ice in April, while all ports on the northeast coast of Newfoundland and in the Gulf of St. Lawrence are usually ice-bound from late December until April. Because of the cold air from the Atlantic, spring comes later in Newfoundland and Cape Breton than it does in the interior lowlands of Nova Scotia and New Brunswick.

Vegetation and Soils

The natural vegetation of the Atlantic Provinces is forest except for certain elevated, rocky, and exposed areas which have remained treeless. Variations in bedrock, landforms, and climate have resulted in concomitant variations in the forest cover.

The highland of the Gaspé and of northern New Brunswick and most of the forest area of Newfoundland appear to be outliers of the Boreal Forest (Figure 4.27). In the areas of better drainage a valuable timber resource of white spruce and balsam fir is found, while the poorly drained areas contain black spruce and tamarack.

The Restigouche Forest is a mixed forest that is related to the Great Lakes — St. Lawrence forest region. Sugar maple, yellow birch, white cedar, white spruce, and red and white pines are the common species. The pines are abundant and show up prominently in second growth stands which have sprung up following fires.

The Acadian mixed forest covers all of Nova Scotia, Prince Edward Island, and southern New Brunswick. While considerable variations occur, it appears to the

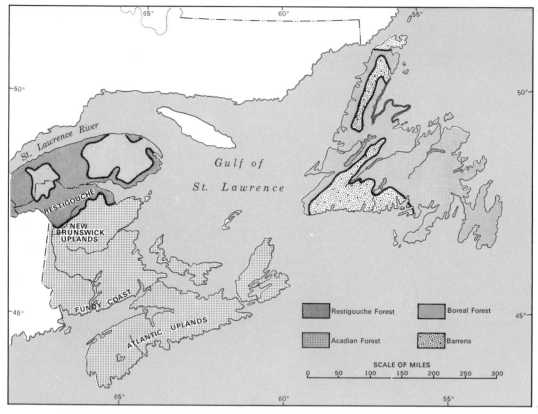

AFTER ATLAS OF CANADA

Figure 4.27 Natural Vegetation of the Atlantic Provinces

observer as largely coniferous with red spruce in abundance. Along the Atlantic Upland there are extensive rocky barrens and black spruce bogs. In the Annapolis Valley the orchard land on the till slopes used to be occupied by stands of hardwoods including red oak and white ash. Hardwoods, including sugar maple, beech, and birch, were commonly found on the uplands of northern Nova Scotia.

On Newfoundland there is an extensive area in the south-central portion which is largely barrens, bogs, and lakes. It is difficult to explain the existence of this area which amounts to nearly half of the island and drastically reduces the forest potential.

In well-drained forest areas the dominant soils are well-developed podzols. In addition, the surface geological deposits of much of the area have been derived from sandstones or acid crystalline rocks such as quartzite and granite. Consequently, the soils tend to be acid, leached, and infertile. This limits their agricultural potential and even affects the rate of forest regeneration.

The soils with the greatest natural fertility have long been recognized and heavily utilized. In most areas they occur in the "intervales" or floodplains along the rivers. The dyked lands bordering the headwaters of the Bay of Fundy are ranked among the most useful agricultural areas in the region. Although they have been misused and depleted, they are now being improved by fertilizers, better drainage, and the erection of new dykes.

REGIONAL DIVISIONS IN THE ATLANTIC PROVINCES

On the basis of variation in physical resource base and economic development, the Atlantic Region can be divided into a series of subregions. Examination of these internal contrasts will enable us to form a clearer picture of the Atlantic Region.

Prince Edward Island is one of the most distinctive subregions. A separate land mass which belongs to the red sandstones of the Maritime geosyncline, it has a gentle relief suited to agriculture. The low rolling hills are covered with large fields of grass, grain, and potatoes; the neatly painted farm buildings, spruce hedgerows, red roads, and winding tidal inlets combine to form an appealing landscape. Agriculture is the largest single source of income for the island although the sand beaches and dunes create a tourist attraction of considerable merit. Urbanization plays a minor role on the island for besides Charlottetown the only other town of note is Summerside. Connected only by ferry to the mainland, Prince Edward Island seems likely to remain isolated from major economic developments and will retain its rural charm for some time to come. The building of a causeway to the mainland would help the economic situation without causing much change in the landscape.

Cape Breton Island is likewise a well-defined subregion which did not have land communication with the mainland until the Canso Causeway was completed in 1955. Settlement has ignored the barren interior, and the people are concentrated in Greater Sydney. The economic difficulties of the coal and steel industries have created problems for the region which have been only slightly alleviated by the encouragement of new industry. The stark ugliness of the coal mining area is in great contrast to the magnificent scenery of the Cabot Trail and Cape Breton National Park. Although Cape Breton Island is culturally distinctive in terms of its Scottish settlement and the memory of the Gaelic tongue, it is a subregion which is still very much a part of the Maritimes.

Within Nova Scotia the Atlantic Upland forms a distinctive subregion in which rough, rocky, forested landscapes predominate. Its influence extends right to the south coast, bringing wild land to the outskirts of the major concentrations of population in Greater Halifax, Yarmouth, Liverpool, Shelburne, and Lunenburg. With the exception of Halifax where defense spending is so important, the whole area relies chiefly on fishing and forestry.

The Bay of Fundy Littoral comprises southern New Brunswick and northern Nova Scotia. Included in this subregion are some of the best and most picturesque agricultural lands of the Atlantic Region. One has only to cross the Cobequid Hills into the Truro basin, traverse Hants county, and then follow the Annapolis Valley from Kentville to Annapolis to appreciate the beauty of upland forests and lowland special crops and livestock farming. Situated in this subregion are a number of urban centers, those of major importance being Saint John and Moncton. Here the economy is well balanced and relies on forestry, manufacturing, fishing, and trade. It is supported by an adequate agricultural base and seems likely to progress in future.

Not physically a part of the basin of the Bay of Fundy and yet having strong connections with it is the Pictou Basin with its industrial and mining towns. Agriculturally it also resembles the area around the headwaters of the Bay.

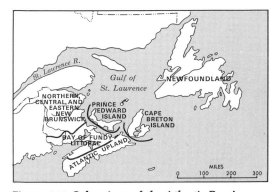

Figure 4.28 Subregions of the Atlantic Provinces

A complete contrast to the prosperity of the Bay of Fundy Littoral is offered by northern, central, and eastern New Brunswick. Largely forest and scrub woodland, it presents a negative image to the tourist. It is one of the areas recorded by A.R.D.A. as suffering economic and social disadvantage.* Here more than 50 per cent of the male rural non-farm wage earners have an annual income of less than $2,000. With the exception of the upper St. John Valley the area has forestry as its main source of income. Recently mining has begun to achieve some importance but as yet has had little effect on the landscape. The population is of mixed origin, with a preponderance of French-speaking people. Such towns as Chatham, Newcastle, and Bathurst have until recently relied upon the forest industry for employment. The situation at Bathurst has been improved

* A. R. D. A. *Economic and Social Disadvantage in Canada.* Canada Department of Forestry. Ottawa. October, 1964. Map 6.

by the development of base metal mines nearby.

Newfoundland is also a distinctive subregion. Despite its isolation from the Maritimes it has developed a similar economy based primarily on fishing and forestry. Large areas are without settlement. The western node, focused on Corner Brook, is connected by the slender link of rail and highway to Grand Falls and the eastern node of settlement on the Avalon Peninsula. Distinctive accents and attitudes occur in this subregion. St. John's, the chief city and capital of the province, is located on a natural harbor on the eastern edge of the Avalon Peninsula.

Labrador, while politically part of Newfoundland, is not really associated in a geographic sense. The major development here is based on mining. The expansion of the iron ore industry coupled with the new Churchill Falls power project give this area a character unlike that of the Atlantic Region proper.

BIBLIOGRAPHY

A. R. D. A. *Economic and Social Disadvantage in Canada.* Canada Department of Forestry. Ottawa. October, 1964.

Brouillette, Benoit. "Approvisionnement du Canada en Combustibles". *L'Actualité Economique.* (Jan.-Mar. 1961).

Chapman, L. J. and Brown, D. M. *The Climates of Canada for Agriculture.* The Canada Land Inventory Report No. 3. 1966.

Clark, A. H. "New England's Role in the Underdevelopment of Cape Breton Island during the French Regime, 1713-1758". *Canadian Geographer.* IX, 1 (1965). pp. 1-12.

Donald, J. R. *The Cape Breton Coal Problem.* The Queen's Printer. Ottawa. October, 1966.

Fletcher, R. K. "Agriculture and the Atlantic Economy". *Atlantic Provinces Economic Council Pamphlet.* No. 10 (July, 1966).

Gentilcore, R. Louis. *Canada's Changing Geography.* Prentice-Hall of Canada Limited. Scarborough, Ontario. 1967.

Goldthwaite, J. W. *Physiography of Nova Scotia.* Canada Department of Mines. Geological Survey Memoir 140. Ottawa. 1924.

Hart, J. F. "The Three 'R's' of the Rural North East". *Canadian Geographer.* VII, 1 (1963). pp. 7-22.

Irving, Robert M. *Readings in Canadian Geography.* Holt, Rinehart and Winston of Canada Limited. Toronto. 1968.

Marks, C. R. "Defense Expenditures and the Economy of the Atlantic Provinces". *Atlantic Provinces Economic Council Pamphlet.* No. 9 (December, 1965).

Putnam, D. F. "The Climate of the Maritime Provinces". *Canadian Geographical Journal.* Vol. 21 (1940). pp. 134-147.

Twenhofel, W. H. and MacClintock, R. "Surface of Newfoundland". *Bulletin Geological Society of America.* Vol. 56 (1940). pp. 1655-1728.

Wolfe, Roy I. "The Summer Cottage in Ontario". *Economic Geography.* Vol. 27 (1951). pp. 10-32.

Parks, A. C. "Productivity, the Use of Resources, and the Income Gap". *Atlantic Provinces Economic Council Pamphlet.* No. 11 (July, 1967).

Quebec

5 Quebec has always been a major factor in Canadian development. Strategically located as a gateway to the continent, it is the second province in total population. With 5,800,000 inhabitants in 1967 it contains 28 per cent of Canada's people. As the province where French culture is dominant, it is a unique region in Canada. Quebec is a diverse region: 84 per cent of its area is found to the north within the Canadian Shield where the environment conspires against a favorable ecumene, while to the south the Appalachians likewise restrict the area suited to man's occupance and industry. Thus only 12 per cent of Quebec can be considered settled country, and this area is concentrated within the St. Lawrence Lowland.

Despite the restricted ecumene, the region is important for the role it plays in the Canadian economy. Montreal is the largest city in Canada and in 1967 gained international reputation as the site of Expo, the most successful World Fair ever held. One-sixth of all Canadian manufacturing is concentrated in the vicinity of Montreal, making it truly one of the primate cities of Canada. Quebec is responsible for about 30 per cent of the manufactured goods produced in Canada and currently has a labor force of slightly more than 2,000,000. Mining makes an important contribution for each year 19 per cent of the mineral wealth of Canada originates in this province. Of note are the copper, gold, and iron mines of the Shield and the non-metallic minerals such as asbestos from the Eastern Townships. Forestry contributes extensively to the economy. In Quebec there exist more than 300,000 square miles of productive forest land. This resource is well exploited, and Quebec accounts for one-third of the value of all the paper and other forest products produced in Canada. Hydro-electric power is abundant and well utilized.

As a region Quebec is not without its difficulties. It is deficient in foodstuffs, for only 20,000 square miles (12,800,000 acres) are utilized as farm land. Manufacturing effort is concentrated in industries which are oriented to raw materials such as pulp and paper or of the power-consuming type such as textiles, while secondary manufacturing has yet to develop satisfactorily. In addition, much of the wealth is poorly distributed being largely concentrated in Montreal. Other areas have experienced very uneven economic growth, and this has created problems of major proportions.

PHYSICAL RESOURCE BASE

Landforms

Quebec falls naturally into three distinct but very unequal physiographic regions: the Canadian Shield, the St. Lawrence Lowland, and the Appalachian Highlands.

The Canadian Shield occupies more than 500,000 square miles in Quebec. Generally referred to as the Laurentian Upland in Quebec, it has a complicated structure which reflects the ancient history of the complex igneous and metamorphic rocks. While the skyline of the Shield is mono-

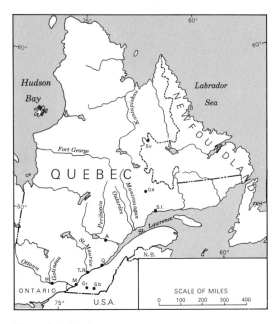

Figure 5.1 Quebec

A	Arvida	Q	Quebec
Ga	Gagnon	Sb	Sherbrooke
Gr	Granby	Sv	Schefferville
H	Hull	S.I.	Sept Iles
M	Montreal	T.R.	Trois-Rivières

Here as in the Shield there have been long cycles of erosion leaving the Appalachian Highlands with varied relief of smooth plateaux and deep valleys with only a few outstanding ridges. To the northeast there is the Gaspé Peninsula where the backbone of this rugged area is formed by the Shickshock range. Along the north shore of the Gaspé there is very little coastal plain, and bold cliffs frequently rise abruptly from the sea to form a stacked coast. In contrast the south shore facing the Baie de Chaleur is much less abrupt, and an uneven coastal plain extends as much as twenty-five miles inland.' Between the valleys of the Matapedia and Chaudière few summits rise above the general plateau level which has an average elevation of about 1,200 feet in this section. Across it the deep valley containing Lac Temiscouata affords easy passage from Rivière-du-Loup on the St. Lawrence to the St. John Valley in New Brunswick.

In the Eastern Townships the relief is more varied. Three parallel ranges trend

tonously even, local relief is considerable; and along the southern edge there is a sharp break from the Shield down to the St. Lawrence Lowland. This break is usually termed the Laurentide Escarpment, and the numerous rivers which tumble down the precipitous slope are very important sources of hydro-electric power. Within the Shield there are various rock structures which contain important concentrations of minerals. In Western Quebec there is the *Greenstone* area where igneous activities millions of years ago created opportunities for the accumulation of copper, gold, lead, and zinc. To the east, in Labrador, a former geosyncline has been filled and has experienced considerable pressure. Known today as the Labrador Trough this geologic feature contains one of the world's largest deposits of iron ore.

In Southeastern Quebec the *Appalachian Highlands* contain Paleozoic sedimentary rocks which have been folded, crushed, broken, and invaded by molten magmas.

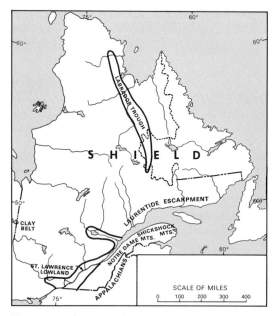

Figure 5.2 Physiographic Regions of Quebec
Very little of Quebec is lowland. The important Labrador Trough has been located within the Shield on the map.

Figure 5.3 Laurentide Escarpment
Downstream from Quebec city the Laurentide Escarpment near Ile-aux-Coudres is still a formidable relief barrier despite the agricultural land along its lower slopes.

Figure 5.4 North Coast of Gaspé
Villages along the Gaspé coast, such as St. Maurice shown here, are located on small inlets where fishing ports are possible.

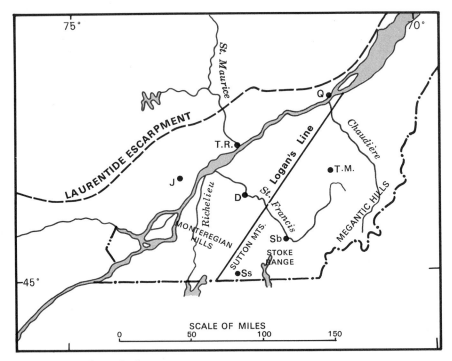

Figure 5.5 Southern Quebec
South of Logan's Line the Appalachians give a distinct grain to the landscape. The
St. Lawrence Lowland extends north from Logan's Line to the Laurentide Escarpment.

D	Drummondville	Sb	Sherbrooke	T.R.	Trois-Rivières
J	Joliette	Ss	Stanstead		
Q	Quebec	T.M.	Thedford Mines		

northeasterly from the southern boundary
and produce a noticeable "grain" to the
landscape. Within the Sutton and Serpentine Ranges vulcanism and regional metamorphism have been responsible for the
formation of asbestos and other minerals.
To the northwest a "fall-line" appears
where the rocks of the Appalachians grade
into the relief and structure of the St. Lawrence Lowland. This structural discontinuity is known in part as Logan's Line,
and along it are located many small towns
such as Victoriaville and Farnham. These
towns are analagous to the "fall-line"
cities of the Appalachian Piedmont in the
United States where readily available waterpower made attractive sites for early settlement.

The *St. Lawrence Lowland* is the smallest
physiographic region in Quebec. It is well
defined by the Laurentian Upland to the
north and the Appalachian Highlands to
the south. The underlying rocks are sandstones, shales, and limestones, similar to
those of the Appalachians, but they have
been relatively little disturbed by mountain-
building processes. In essence the region is
a huge graben in which the relatively
smooth veneer of lacustrine deposits from
the Champlain Sea is only moderately
interrupted by the Monteregian Hills which
extend southeastward from Montreal to
the Appalachians. Composed of igneous
rock and originally buried laccoliths the
hills have been exhumed through differential erosion and now stand well above the
general level of the landscape. Around
their slopes the Champlain Sea cut terraces
and left sand and gravel deposits which
are well suited to specialized agriculture.

The most famous of the Monteregian Hills is Mount Royal which dominates the site of Montreal. Here the terraces control the street pattern as shown by Ste. Catherine and Sherbrooke Streets. On a clear day many of the other Monteregian Hills can be viewed from the high buildings in downtown Montreal.

The landforms of Quebec were considerably modified through the influence of glaciation. On the edge of the Shield the Laurentide Escarpment was made more rugged, while further north, in Labrador, glacial deposits in the form of moraines and eskers further confuse the normal rock knob topography. In the northwest glacial Lake Barlow-Ojibway covered much of the Shield with extensive deposits of clay. The Appalachians were also strongly glaciated providing stony till soils which make agriculture difficult. During the retreat of the ice the St. Lawrence Lowland was inundated by salt water which formed the Champlain Sea. As isostatic rebound progressed after the weight of the ice was removed, the Champlain Sea was drained away leaving behind thick layers of sediments. By and large the sediments were composed of fine particles which formed clay, and it is only along the margins where shorelines and stream deltas prevailed that coarser sand deposits can be found. The result is a generally flat plain on which the clay soils are frequently difficult to drain.

Climate

In Quebec climate is a very important part of the resource base. While the supply of moisture is everywhere adequate, it is strongly influenced by relief and by the funneling of cyclonic storms through the St. Lawrence valley which give rise to periods of severe precipitation. Winter snowfall averages 98.6 inches annually at Montreal, 110.7 inches at Quebec, and 164.3 inches at Sept Iles. This may be advantageous for winter sports such as skiing and snowmobiling, but it poses a major

problem for traffic and the movement of goods within cities. Major snowstorms are expensive in terms of snow removal, and cities in Quebec receive more snow than their counterparts to the west.

Summer heat is also important, particularly for agriculture. Degree-days and Corn Heat Units as heat parameters have been discussed in CHAPTER 2. Applied to Quebec they define very precisely the areas suitable for farming. As shown by Figures 5.6 and 5.7, very little of Quebec is suited to intensive agricultural pursuits. Areas with less than 2,000 degree-days are climatically of little value for agriculture, and even the areas having between 2,000 D-D and 2,500 D-D are seriously limited to the use of grasses and very hardy grains such as barley. As shown by Figure 5.6, the Lake St. John Lowland and Clay Belt are included in this category. The most favored area is the St. Lawrence Lowland upstream from Quebec where more than 3,000 D-D occur.

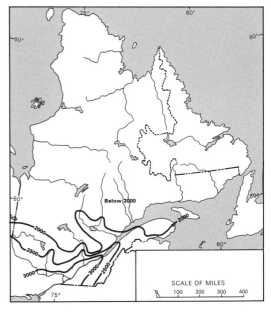

AFTER CHAPMAN AND BROWN

Figure 5.6 Degree-days above 42°F for Quebec
Only in the St. Lawrence Lowland is it warm enough in summer for the 3,000 degree-day index to occur.

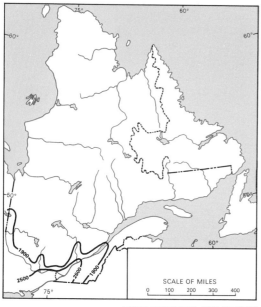

AFTER CHAPMAN AND BROWN

Figure 5.7 Corn Heat Units for Quebec

However, only a small portion, the Montreal Plain, is climatically suited to the growing of corn for grain (Figure 5.7).

Climate graphs constructed from the statistics of six selected stations are shown in Figure 5.8. Particularly noticeable is the variation in precipitation regimes. While precipitation is adequately distributed over the year at all southern stations, there is a tendency in the north for the early spring to have less and the late summer months to have more than the average. This latter characteristic is true for the Clay Belt and often creates poor conditions at the time of harvest. In addition, there is a severe frost hazard during late August which can create hardships for both the farmer and the camper.

Climate, of course, is inextricably linked with the natural vegetation. Various researchers have attempted to define the relationship precisely and have concluded that the northern forests are governed in

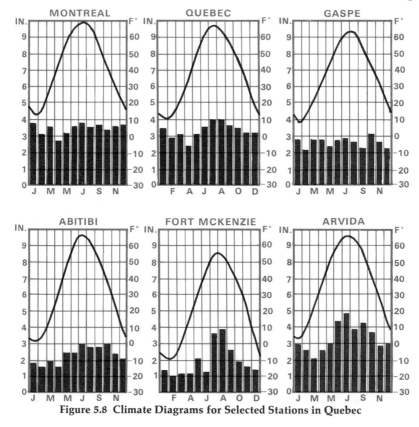

Figure 5.8 Climate Diagrams for Selected Stations in Quebec

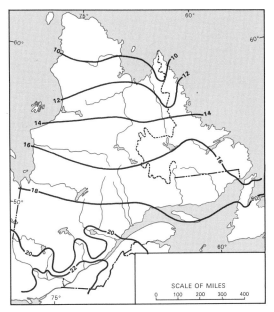

AFTER HARE, AND CHAPMAN AND BROWN

Figure 5.9 Average Annual Potential Evapotranspiration for Quebec

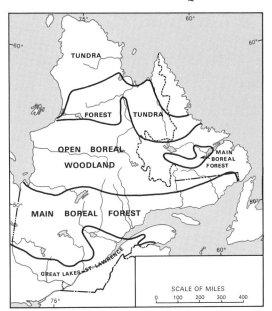

Figure 5.10 Natural Vegetation of Quebec
The Main Boreal Forest and the Great Lakes—St. Lawrence Forest constitute the main forest resource of Quebec.

their growth by temperature. In his study of the Boreal Forest in Eastern Canada, Hare found that zonal forest divisions showed an obvious correlation with thermal efficiency as measured by potential evapotranspiration.* This correlation can be seen by comparing Figures 5.9 and 5.10 and is summarized in Table 5.1. The existence of the Open Boreal Woodland is not well understood. The forest complex is one with widely spaced trees and lichen-covered forest floor, and it does not appear to require a great deal of moisture. Since there is no lack of precipitation, the appearance of drought is probably due to soil conditions. In July the ground is still frozen at very shallow depths. During the most favorable period for growth the trees can derive moisture only from the upper soil horizons and are forced to develop extended lateral roots. Thus competition between root systems for space and water results in the dispersed stand which is characteristic of the Open Boreal Woodland.

* F. K. Hare. "The Boreal Forest in Eastern Canada". *Geographical Review.* XL, 4 (October, 1950). p. 629.

Natural Vegetation

The distribution of natural vegetation is shown by Figure 5.10, and in CHAPTER 2 the various species associated with each region were discussed in some detail. Of note though is the more precise definitions of the vegetation boundaries. In this case there are certain transition areas where two forest divisions overlap. In the botanical sense these are termed "ecotones". Two major ecotones exist in Quebec; the one between the Subarctic and Tundra and that between the Boreal Forest and the Mixed Forest of the St. Lawrence Lowland. The latter, however, is very discontinuous and is not shown on the map.

Of note is the exclave of St. Lawrence mixed forest in the Lake St. John region, an area where the pulp and paper industry has been developed to utilize this timber resource. Here the climate is thermally favorable and tall stands of white pine and red pine are mixed with white spruce and jack pine. Other interesting outliers of vigorous forest growth are found along the Churchill River in Labrador and in the eastern part of Gaspé.

Table 5.1   Forest Divisions and Potential Evapotranspiration in Labrador-Ungava

Forest Division	Typical Value of PE along Boundary in Inches	Dominant Cover Type
Tundra		Tundra
	12.0 – 12.5	
Forest Tundra Ecotone		Tundra and lichen-woodland intermingled
	14.0 – 14.5	
Open Boreal Woodland (Subarctic)		Lichen-woodland
	16.5 – 17.0	
Main Boreal Forest		Close-forest spruce-fir associations
	18.5 – 19.0	
Boreal-Mixed Forest Ecotone		Close-forest with white and red pine and other non-boreal invaders
	20.0	
Great Lakes—St. Lawrence Mixed Forest		Mixed forest

* F. K. Hare. *op. cit.* p. 630.

Soils

Several soil zones cross the province of Quebec. There is a fairly good correlation to be seen between landform region and soil capability. The St. Lawrence Lowland is chiefly characterized by deciduous forest vegetation and normally has Gray-Brown Podzolic soils. Most areas in the Appalachian Highland and the southern part of the Canadian Shield have Podzols, Acid Brown Forest soils, and Regosols. In the far north the Podzols give way to the soils of the Tundra. For a number of years soil surveys have been conducted in Quebec, and field work in most of the settled area has been completed. Detailed soil maps are now available, and recently a more accurate general map of the soils of the province has been compiled.*

* Raymond R. Mailloux and A. Dubé. "Pedologie de la région du Lac St-Jean". *Bulletin No. 11.* Ministre de l'agriculture et de la colonisation. Quebec. 1965.
R. Barile. "Association des séries des sols de la province de Québec". Département d'agronomie, Université Laval. 1967. Mimeographed report.

The *St. Lawrence Lowland* was inundated by the Champlain Sea at the close of the glacial period. Here for the most part there is a covering of sand, silt, and clay through which project occasional hills and ridges of boulder clay. Where drainage is good, zonal types of soil have been developed, but there are large areas of bog and poorly drained soils. When drained, these highly organic soils produce good crops. However, tile drainage is expensive, and the traditional *Richard* system of drainage often fails to lower the water table sufficiently. Thus the flat imperfectly drained clay loams such as those around Lake St. Peter are used chiefly for hay. There are numerous terraces of sand and gravel which are excessively drained and highly leached. These too have been put to special uses. The gravelly soils on the flanks of the Monteregian Hills have been used as orchard sites, while the sand plains of Joliette produce flue-cured cigarette tobacco. On the Island of Orleans the gravelly loams are used for horticultural crops and intensive dairy farming.

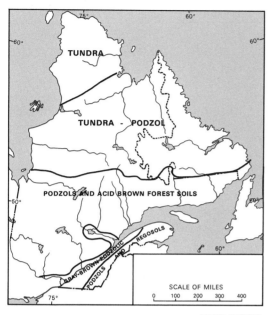

Figure 5.11 Soils of Quebec
The best soils for agriculture are the Gray-Brown Podzolic which are confined to the St. Lawrence Lowland.

The *Appalachian Plateau* has a mixture of soils depending upon the relief and rock structure. On the upland surface the parent material is thin and excessively stony, thus the term regosol is frequently applied. In the valleys terraces, outwash plains, and small patches of old lake bed combine to give soils of varied textures and fertility. These soils generally are classified as Podzols and Acid Brown Forest Soils. The quality is somewhat better in the Eastern Townships, and agriculture is reasonably successful there.

The *Laurentian Plateau* has been incompletely studied, but it is known that the upland soils are stony, often shallow, and excessively leached. It is only in those rare areas where extensive lacustrine deposits occur that agriculture has any possibility of success. There are two such areas: the lacustrine plain around Lake St. John and the Clay Belt of Abitibi county. Although the soils of both these areas are poorly drained, they are more fertile and less stony than the soils of the uplands. The

heavy loams and clays are used for oats, hay, and pasture, while the lighter loams are excellent for potatoes.

The Physical Stage

In spite of the vast area of Quebec physical diversity severely limits the possibilities of human occupance. More than 84 per cent of the surface is underlain by the Canadian Shield and is rugged and rocky and has very little depth of soil. The Appalachian Region also contains much rugged land. Only the St. Lawrence Lowland has the depth of soil and the gentleness of relief to encourage intensive agricultural settlement, and even here the variations in texture and drainage impose serious limitations. Fortunately, the Lowland is also the area having the most favorable climate for agriculture and other human activities, while the St. Lawrence River serves as a corridor into the heart of Quebec and Canada.

Quebec possesses a great wealth of natural resources. Fish, furs, and later, timber were in demand on European markets, and the early colonial trade fixed the patterns of occupance. In the twentieth century a wealth of minerals and abundant waterpower coupled with accessible forest resources encouraged economic growth. Although there is only a limited area of potentially arable land, the people of Quebec have other alternatives to agriculture as a means of making a living. Thus the physical resource base has set the stage for the activities of the residents of Quebec.

THE CULTURAL RESOURCE BASE AND ECONOMIC DEVELOPMENT

The Sequent Occupance of Quebec

Prior to the *French occupance* the Algonquin Indians were tenants of the area now known as Quebec. Primarily hunters, they made little use of the land for agriculture although they had small village settlements along the river. Their prowess in hunting made them desirable allies of the French who were interested in obtaining furs, particularly the pelts of the abundant beaver. Economic considerations made the fur trade very attractive to the early French colonists and their sponsors whereas agriculture seemed difficult and unrewarding. Champlain's efforts to establish a permanent agricultural settlement were not very successful. At the time of his death in 1635 there were 85 adults living in the colony at Quebec, but only 23 of them were actually settlers. Despite this slow start the beginnings of permanent settlement were there, in Quebec, in Beauport, and in the outpost at Trois-Rivières.

By 1665 there was a solid nucleus of settlement. Agricultural pioneers were concentrated in three major nodes: Quebec, Trois-Rivières, and Montreal. As shown by Figure 5.12 the immediate vicinity of Quebec held two-thirds of the 3,315 inhabitants. Under Talon rapid growth commenced and by 1683 the population of New France had tripled. While settlement had continued to accrete around the Quebec nucleus, a significant outpost had developed in the Richelieu Valley as a

result of the Carigan-Salières Regiment taking up land there. Settlement was usually organized in seigneuries with the individual landholdings extending back in long lots from the banks of the rivers. Talon also tried to encourage the development of agricultural villages. Organized as "radial settlements" such as that at Bourg Royal north of Quebec City, this settlement form had little success. Everywhere in New France the long lot system was supreme (Figure 5.13). By the eighteenth century most of the river frontage had been alienated in long lots, and it became necessary to move inland and to establish the second row or *rang*. Now roads were necessary, and no longer was just the width of the lot important for the depth had also to be surveyed. Lots three to four arpents (200 to 250 meters) wide and 30 to 40 arpents deep became standard. While this shape of holding has its disadvantages today, it afforded the early habitant both proximity to neighbors and a relatively large area of land. The narrow lot kept

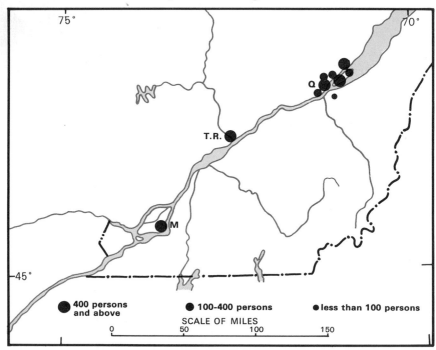

Figure 5.12 Population of Quebec in 1665
The first census recorded only 3,000 people at the colony, and they were clustered close to the river at Quebec, Beauport, Trois-Rivières, and Montreal.

Figure 5.13 The Long Lot System
In Quebec the areas settled by French-speaking people were usually surveyed under the *rang* or long lot system. The long narrow lots stretching back from the river to the forest have produced a unique appearance in Canadian landscapes.

both the responsibilities of road maintenance and rural isolation to a minimum. Thus, by 1765 much of the St. Lawrence Lowland close to the river had been occupied (Figure 5.14).

British rule imposed new conditions upon the expansion of settlement. During the initial stages of *British occupance* very few agricultural immigrants arrived, and most of the English-speaking settlers of the period were merchants and their servants who settled in either Montreal or Quebec. As a result the French inhabitants were little disturbed by British rule and continued to fill in the local lands as population increased. Between 1765 and 1790 the population of Quebec doubled.

After 1790, however, British land alienation began, and the seigneurial survey was replaced by townships in which surveyed lots were provided to the colonists for a minimum fee to cover the costs of surveying and land title registration. The Eastern Townships became the stronghold of the English settlers, while the Irish attempted to settle in the cutover lands bordering the Canadian Shield. By 1831 Missisquoi, Stanstead, Shefford, and Megantic counties together contained 38,650 residents, and of these 95 per cent were Protestants.

Stanstead county to the east of Lake Memphremagog is a good illustration of the English pattern of occupance. Settlement

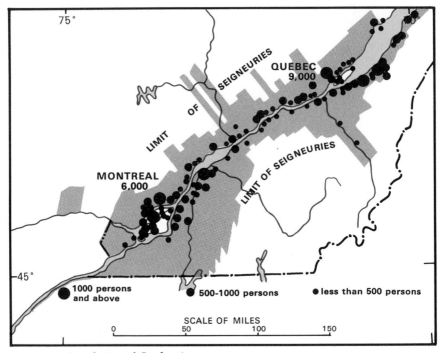

Figure 5.14 Population of Quebec in 1765
At the close of the French regime there were nearly 70,000 people in New France.
The banks of the St. Lawrence were closely settled and colonization was beginning
along the Chaudière and the Richelieu.

was begun in 1793, primarily by squatters
from the United States. Many of these
were allowed to remain or were at least
given the right of obtaining legal title to
the land they occupied. Unlike the French
settlement a pattern of isolated farmsteads
was the rule, and self-sufficiency dominated
the agrarian economy. While roads connected the area with Montreal by 1820,
there was little possibility of normal trade.
Settlers concentrated on growing potatoes
which were fermented and refined into
whiskey. In Stanstead alone there were 26
stills in operation in 1813.* However, only
a small portion of the production found its
way to the Montreal market. Improved
roads soon made other agricultural pursuits more profitable, and general farming
replaced the growing of potatoes. By 1861

the original Eastern Townships were still
inhabited primarily by English-speaking
settlers, but in the surrounding areas
French-speaking settlers predominated.

To the north (the Central Laurentide
area), in the counties of Maskinonge,
Joliette, Berthier, and Montcalm, the Irish
settlers had not fared so well. The poor
quality of the soils in the cutover lands
made agriculture difficult, and most of the
Irish moved on soon after initial settlement. In their place French-Canadian
colonists began to filter in after 1840.*

During this period transportation by
water was steadily improved. The development of steam-powered vessels after 1809
made water transportation more reliable,
and by 1848 a chain of first class canals
connected Lake Erie and Quebec.

* P. J. M. Bailey. "The Geography of Settlement
in Stanstead Township, Province of Quebec".
Geography. XLI, 1 (January, 1956). p. 46.

* P. B. Clibbon. "Utilisation du sol et colonisation de la région des Laurentides Centrales". *Geographical Bulletin*. XXI (1964). pp. 5-20.

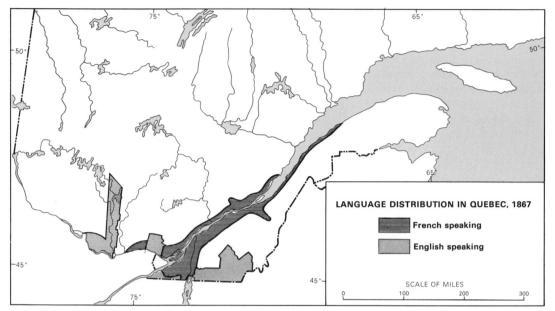

Figure 5.15 Language Distribution in Quebec — 1867
The Eastern Townships and part of the Ottawa Valley were inhabited by English-speaking people at this time.

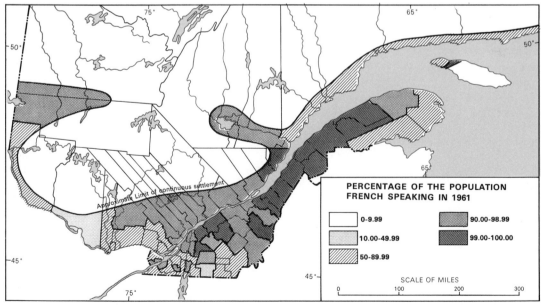

Figure 5.16 Quebec — Percentage of the Population French Speaking in 1961
While most of Quebec is inhabited by people whose mother tongue is French, Brome county in the Eastern Townships still reflects the pattern shown by Figure 5.15.

Under *Canadian occupance* after 1867 Quebec continued to grow and develop. By 1901 there were 1,649,000 inhabitants, and of these more than 60 per cent were rural residents. Population continued to expand towards the peripheries of the province, and by 1901 the character of the Eastern Townships had been modified as the English-speaking inhabitants moved out and French-speaking people moved in. At this time more than two-thirds of the residents were French speaking, and only in Brome and Stanstead were English-speaking residents more numerous. Concomitant with the push southward there was also a movement into the Laurentians. Colonization policies fostered by the Catholic Church with leaders such as Curé Labelle ensured the movement of people up the valley of the Ottawa and its tributaries. The Lake St. John area likewise prospered, and by 1901 had received some 30,000 people who settled along the fertile lowlands traversed by the railroad. It was during this period that primary resources other than agriculture began to receive more

attention. Lumbering became important and the vast resources of the Ottawa Valley and the Lake St. John Lowland were utilized. Waterpower resources began to be developed more fully, and transportation was improved through the construction of railroads which brought the Ottawa Valley and the area south of the St. Lawrence more fully in touch with Montreal.

Since 1901 Quebec has experienced considerable change. The process of creating a French majority in all parts of the region is now complete. The degree to which this has been accomplished is shown by Figures 5.15 and 5.16. Agriculture is now less significant in the economy; it currently supplies employment for less than 10 per cent of the labor force. Also, as is the case for the rest of Canada, the population is no longer dominantly rural-agricultural for nearly 75 per cent of the people now reside in urban centers. The change has been profound, yet the distribution of population is still within the favored ecumene, the St. Lawrence Lowland (Figure 5.17). Manufacturing, forestry, mining, and

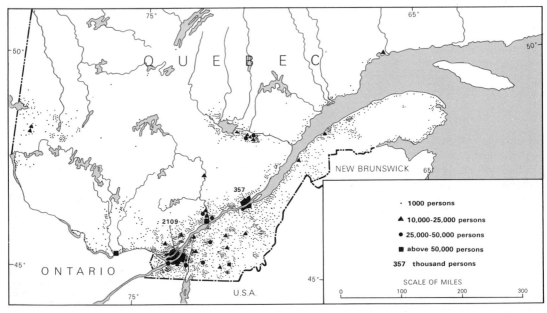

AFTER CANADA YEAR BOOK

Figure 5.17 Distribution of Population in Quebec — 1961

Table 5.2   **Urban Population in 1961 Classified by Type of Residential Change in Per Cent between 1956 and 1961 ***

Category	Canada	Quebec	Ontario	Montreal Metro	Montreal City	Toronto Metro	Toronto City	Vancouver Metro	Vancouver City
Residency unchanged	48.3	48.5	48.5	42.7	42.9	44.3	44.4	47.2	50.1
Residency changed	51.7	51.5	51.5	57.3	57.1	55.7	55.6	52.8	49.9
Within Canada	47.8	49.0	45.9	53.1	52.1	47.1	43.8	47.9	43.8
Within the same city	30.2	32.4	29.9	—	45.3	—	34.2	—	32.9
From one municipality to another	17.6	16.6	16.0	—	6.8	—	9.6	—	10.8
Within the same province	13.5	14.6	12.7	—	5.2	—	6.7	—	5.4
From another province	3.9	1.8	3.1	2.3	1.4	2.7	2.7	6.1	5.3
Change undetermined	0.2	0.2	0.2	0.2	0.2	0.2	0.2	0.1	0.1
From another country	3.9	2.5	5.6	4.2	5.0	8.6	11.8	4.9	6.1
Total per cent of population 5 years of age and over	100	100	100	100	100	100	100	100	100

* H. Charbonneau and J. Légare. *op. cit.* page 239.

abundant electric power, all contribute substantially to the economic vitality.

Today one of the most intriguing characteristics of population is the mobility of urban residents. In a recent study by Charbonneau and Légaré it was determined that 92 per cent of the people in Canada who had changed residency between 1956 and 1961 were urban residents.* Their data for selected regions and cities in Canada is

* H. Charbonneau and J. Légaré. "L'extrême mobilité de la population urbaine au Canada: L'exemple de Montréal entre 1956 et 1961". *Revue de Géographie de Montréal.* XXI, 2 (1967). p. 238.

shown in Table 5.2. In Montreal it is apparent that 53 per cent of the population above the age of five years in 1961 had changed place of residency between 1956 and 1961. Even more astonishing was the degree of mobility within the city for this involved 45 per cent of the population. Moreover the mobility was not proportional throughout Montreal. As shown by Figure 5.18, the change was greatest in Montreal East and in the old city of Montreal. Elsewhere five to ten per cent of the residents had changed their abode between 1956 and 1961.

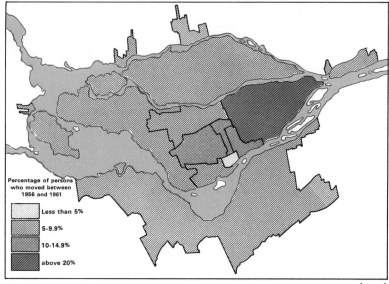

Percentage of persons
who moved between
1956 and 1961

Less than 5%

5-9.9%

10-14.9%

above 20%

AFTER CHARBONNEAU AND LÉGARÉ

**Figure 5.18 Residential Changes in Metropolitan Montreal between 1956
and 1961**
Population mobility for the period was greatest in Montreal East.

Manufacturing in Quebec

Among the Canadian provinces Quebec ranks second in the value of manufacturing output. The annual average of value added by manufacturing during the 1960s has been slightly less than $4,000,000,000 or about one-third of the total Canadian output. At the same time manufacturing accounted for 64 per cent of the value of all commodity production in Quebec although it furnished employment for only a little over 26 per cent of the Quebec labor force.

In the past manufacturing in Quebec has been encouraged by the abundant mineral and forest resources and by readily available hydro-electric power. Traditional industries such as pulp and paper, knit goods, and textiles have been attracted to Quebec because of its available power. Today other industries are achieving importance. Food processing now accounts for one-twelfth of the value added by manufacturing and thus equals the paper industry in value of output. Paper is largely marketed abroad, but food products are usually sold in the home market; thus the growing market of Quebec is becoming a major factor in the industrialization of the province.

One industry which is very sensitive to market is petroleum refining. In Quebec petroleum refineries are concentrated in an area immediately east of the city of Montreal. Here imported crude oil from Southwest Asia and Latin America can be received either by overland pipeline from Portland, Maine, or directly by tanker during the shipping season on the St. Lawrence. With 33 per cent of the Canadian refining capacity concentrated in the Montreal region, the six large and efficient refineries are not only accessible to low cost supplies of crude oil but are also immediately adjacent to the largest market for petroleum products in Quebec.* Petroleum refining would be even more important if the national oil policy did not restrict the market area for Montreal petroleum products to the area east of the Frontenac Axis. Despite the importance of

* Mineral Resources Division. "Petroleum Refineries in Canada — January 1968". Department of Energy, Mines and Resources. Ottawa. 1968.

the industry to the Quebec economy, petroleum refining does not provide a great deal of employment because it is highly automated. Slightly less than 2,500 persons are employed by the industry.

The major manufacturing industries ranked in terms of total employment are listed in Table 5.3. Also shown are the corresponding data for Canada and the location quotient for each category. From the table it is apparent that in only six industrial categories does the index exceed one and indicate a significant concentration. In other words, Quebec does not equal the national average employment in very many industries.

The importance of Quebec in the production of clothing is indicated by the location quotient of 2.0. The clothing industry, particularly women's wear, which is concentrated in Metropolitan Montreal, is nationally famous. Textiles and knit goods are also of significance; indeed, more than 50 per cent of the Canadian textiles industry is located in Quebec. Textile mills are widely distributed within the St. Lawrence Lowland at centers such as Sherbrooke, St. Hyacinthe, Drummondville, Trois-Rivières, and Shawinigan. Leather and paper are also significant as determined by the location quotient. Tobacco processing is of considerable importance for it is a propelling industry which produces a surplus that is marketed outside Quebec. The chemicals industry with a location quotient of 1.1 is closely associated with the fortunes of textiles and paper. Significant concentrations of the industry occur at Valleyfield, Varennes, Montreal East, and Shawinigan. Transportation industries are of note despite the low location quotient. The industry has recently grown beyond the shipbuilding at Lauzon and railway equipment and aircraft

Table 5.3   Manufacturing in Quebec, 1967 *

Industrial Category	Canada Number of Employees	per cent of total	Quebec Number of Employees	per cent of total	Location Quotient**
Foods and Beverages	230,387	13.9	62,877	12.0	0.86
Clothing	97,812	5.9	61,821	11.8	2.00
Textiles	76,706	4.6	45,100	8.6	1.87
Paper and Paper Products	118,552	7.2	42,487	8.1	1.13
Electrical Goods	129,163	7.8	36,201	6.9	0.88
Metal Products	141,948	8.6	35,247	6.7	0.78
Transportation	153,363	9.2	34,296	6.5	0.71
Chemicals	76,061	4.6	26,086	5.0	1.09
Primary Metals	111,762	6.7	25,872	4.9	0.73
Printing and Publishing	84,674	5.1	24,354	4.6	0.90
Wood	87,075	5.2	18,422	3.5	0.67
Furniture	43,360	2.6	17,314	3.3	1.27
Machinery	80,179	4.8	15,189	2.9	0.60
Non-metallic Minerals	50,859	3.1	14,245	2.7	0.87
Leather	31,139	1.9	14,137	2.7	1.42
Knit Goods	23,858	1.4	13,424	2.6	1.86
Tobacco	11,304	0.7	7,268	1.4	2.00
Other Industries	110,960	6.7	30,698	5.8	0.87
Total	1,659,162	100.0	525,038	100.0	—

* Quebec Department of Industry and Commerce, 1967.

** Location Quotient = $\dfrac{\text{Per Cent of Quebec Employment}}{\text{Per Cent of Canadian Employment}}$

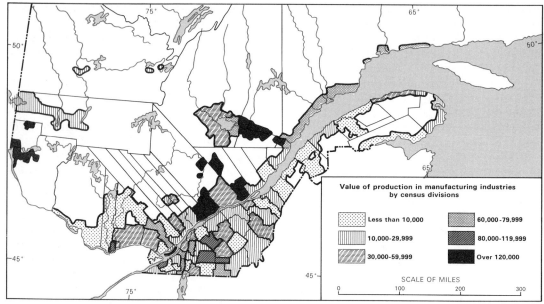

AFTER QUEBEC YEAR BOOK 1965

Figure 5.19 Value of Production in Manufacturing Industries in Quebec — 1960
Plotting by census divisions shows that manufacturing is concentrated in a few isolated locations in Quebec. Most of the manufacturing takes place near Montreal. The figures in the legend are in thousands of dollars, i.e. 10,000 represents $10,000,000.

manufacturing at Montreal to include automobile assembly plants at Ste. Thérèse and St. Bruno.

An interesting interpretation of the distribution of manufacturing is shown in Figure 5.19. Montreal is obviously important, but there are neighboring census divisions where the total value of manufacturing accounts for less than $10,000,-000. Important sectors of manufacturing activity are the almuminum smelting and forest processing of the Saguenay area, pulp and paper industries at Trois-Rivières, smelting in the Clay Belt, and the pulp and paper, cement, and shipbuilding industries of Greater Quebec. Within the Eastern Townships there is also an industrial district extending north from Sherbrooke. However, in much of the settled area of Quebec manufacturing is not very strongly developed. Much of the area between Montreal and Quebec and that of the Gaspé Peninsula contribute little to the manufacturing strength of the province.

Yet continuing development in Quebec means the encouragement of the manufacturing sector of the economy. For Quebec the problem is the primacy of Montreal. Within Montreal there is concentrated 49 per cent of the manufacturing employment and 51 per cent of the value added by all manufacturing in the province of Quebec. Most of the clothing and the food-processing industries and all the petroleum refining and aircraft production are located in Montreal. With the degree of success it has already had in attracting industries, Montreal is likely to draw new industries wishing to locate in the province.

Has industry in Quebec begun to spread into other parts of the province? In a recent study quantitative analysis employing the coefficient of variation was used to determine if Quebec industry was dispersing.* This technique is similar to the one

* J. Davies. "Trends in the Location of Industry in Quebec, 1954-1964". Unpublished paper. Department of Geography, University of Toronto.

utilized by Hays in the study of Ontario.* As recent data are available only on units based on the counties of Quebec, detailed analysis is not possible. However, within the limitations of the data the coefficient of variation showed that while the Montreal area is preeminent, there is a very modest degree of new industry locating, at present, in counties removed from Montreal.

Another means of determining dispersion or growth of manufacturing in Quebec is by considering changes in the number of establishments. Figure 5.20 indicates dramatically that growth in manufacturing has been far from evenly spread throughout Quebec. Terrebonne and Laprairie counties, which are adjacent to Montreal, have shown increases between 1949 and 1960 of more than 20 per cent. The only other areas to record such an increase are Beauce county and the Drummondville

---

* K. A. Hays. "Trends in the Location of Industry in Ontario". *Canadian Journal of Economics and Political Science.* XXXI, 3 (August, 1965).

section of the Eastern Townships. During the same period the Gaspé, Lake St. John, and the Clay Belt have all declined, while only modest increases have been recorded in the vicinity of Quebec City.

The provincial government recognizes the problem and is attempting to encourage manufacturers to locate in areas other than those immediately adjacent to Metropolitan Montreal. In 1968 the Quebec Industrial Credit Bureau was created with a budget of $40,000,000 to be used over the next four years. It replaces the General Investment Corporation as the major lender to small industries.

What has been the effect of provincially sponsored programs to encourage the growth of manufacturing outside Montreal? In the case of the automotive industry government sponsorship resulted in the development of SOMA to assemble Peugeot and Renault automobiles at St. Bruno de Montarville. St. Bruno is not far from Montreal and, in 1966, had a population of 10,712. As a result of industrial

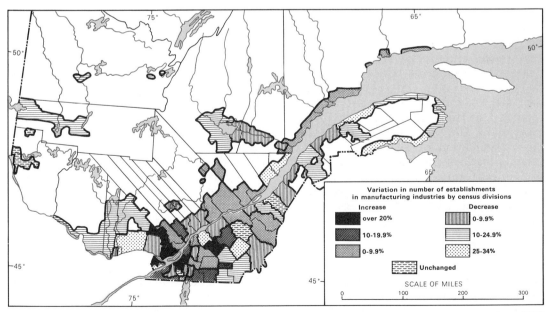

AFTER QUEBEC YEAR BOOK 1965

Figure 5.20 Variation in the Number of Manufacturing Establishments in Quebec between 1949 and 1960
The greatest increase in the number of establishments occurred in the census divisions in the vicinity of Montreal.

development, it is predicted that this small community will attain a population of 35,000 by 1975.* However, in the case of the employees of SOMA, 56 per cent live within 10 miles of St. Bruno, 27 per cent live 10 to 20 miles away, while 11 per cent reside in Metropolitan Montreal. Some communities such as Rimouski are profiting from government encouragement. Long considered an economically depressed area Rimouski is eligible for substantial Federal Grants under the A.R.D.A. program. More than $190,000,000 has been made available to aid industries desirous of locating in the Rimouski area. Linkurt Electric, a producer of micro-wave equipment, began operations in Rimouski in January, 1968 and currently employs 100 people. In addition, a cable factory has been constructed which will add significantly to the employment possibilities in the region. Continued application of these policies may contribute substantially to the dispersion of industrial development in Quebec.

The dominance of Montreal is likely to continue, however, for even government subsidies to outside areas will be unable to counteract the pull of the Montreal market. Moreover, many of the industries which are basic to the strength of Quebec's economy are currently facing serious problems. Textile establishments are plagued with the difficulties of a long-established and over-mature industry and are meeting competition from more efficient foreign companies. The pulp and paper industry faces a condition of overcapacity for its existing markets and is unlikely to expand in the near future. Industrial growth seems possible only in the realm of secondary manufacturing, and it is here that competition with Ontario is very strong.

Forestry in Quebec

Forestry is an important part of the developed resource base. The accessible parts of Quebec's forest domain were early

cut over for square timber, later for lumber, and now sustain a dominant pulpwood production. An average of more than 900 million cubic feet of wood is cut each year; logging alone employs about 21,000 persons and pays about $95,000,000 in wages. The pulp and paper industry began in 1869 when a pulp mill was completed at Valleyfield. Today Quebec is the leading producer of wood pulp in Canada and accounts for 38 per cent of the Canadian production as well as for 44 per cent of the paper and paperboard.

The distribution of forest-processing plants indicates to a large degree the areas where the timber resources of Quebec are being utilized. Quebec has slightly more than 220,000 square miles of productive forest, and of this only 103,000 square miles are presently being utilized. The occupied productive forest is located primarily along the fringes of the Canadian Shield where timber, waterpower, rivers for transportation, and ready access to foreign markets coincide. Quebec pulp and paper mills are markedly concentrated in certain strategic locations. As illustrated by Figure 5.21, the Lake St. John region is one area where forestry is very important; indeed, it usually accounts for about 30 per cent of the value of production of paper in Quebec.* Of the six mills located in the region only four produce paper. The other important focus is along the St. Maurice Valley from La Tuque in the north to Trois-Rivières in the south. Two other nodes occur near St. Jérôme and Hull, while a minor concentration occurs between Drummondville and Sherbrooke in the Eastern Townships. Of note is the mill recently established at Lac Quévillon by Domtar. This establishment has required an investment of over $70,000,000 and was constructed only after labor legislation was finally amended to permit pulp and paper mills in Quebec to operate on a seven-day week basis.

---

* J. B. Racine. "La croissance du Grand-Montréal au sud du Saint-Laurent: le cas de St-Bruno de Montarville". *Revue de Géographie de Montréal.* XXI, 1 (1967). p. 144.

* P. Y. Pepin. "Principaux traits socioéconomiques de la région Saguenay — Lac St-Jean". *Cahiers de Géographie de Québec.* 13 (October, 1962-March, 1963). p. 75.

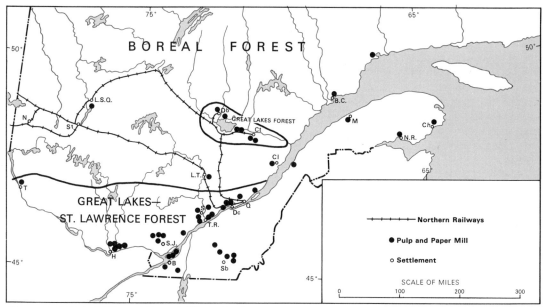

Figure 5.21 Pulp Mills and Paper Mills in Quebec
The greatest concentration of mills is within the Great Lakes—St. Lawrence Forest, close to the Ottawa and St. Lawrence Rivers. Only recently has there been an attempt to establish mills in the Boreal Forest (data from Financial Post, 1968).

B	Beauharnois	H	Hull	Sb	Sherbrooke
B.C.	Baie Comeau	L.S.Q.	Lebel-sur-Quévillon	St	Senneterre
Ch	Chandler	L.T.	La Tuque	S.J.	St. Jérôme
Cl	Clermont	M	Matane	T	Temiscaming
Ct	Chicoutimi	N	Noranda	T.R.	Trois-Rivières
Db	Dolbeau	N.R.	New Richmond		
Dc	Donnacona	S	Shawinigan		

The hardwood forest resources of the Eastern Townships are utilized for furniture and the production of maple syrup. The furniture industry is concentrated in the Victoriaville area, while maple syrup production is relatively ubiquitous throughout the Eastern Townships.

Mining in Quebec

Mining has been important in Quebec for more than half a century, but in terms of value added by production it accounts for only 5.9 per cent of the $5,500,000,000 annually amassed in Quebec. Despite this Quebec contributes nearly 17 per cent of the dollar value of Canadian mineral production and is surpassed only by Ontario and Alberta. In addition, nearly 34,000 persons are employed by the mining industry. Minerals are found in greatest amounts in three areas in Quebec: the Eastern Townships where asbestos has long been important, the Labrador-Ungava Trough where iron ore is abundant, and the Clay Belt where the underlying rock formations contain copper, zinc, gold, and silver in significant amounts.

Mining came of age in Quebec during the 1920s when gold and copper were discovered in the Clay Belt, and thirty years later a second period of growth commenced when the iron ore deposits of Labrador began to be utilized. In 1967 Quebec produced minerals worth slightly more than $736,000,000. Of this total, metallic minerals accounted for 59 per cent, non-metallic minerals 24 per cent, and structural materials 17 per cent. Quebec produces little in the way of mineral fuels for in 1967 the total production

Table 5.4   Minerals of Quebec, 1967 *

Mineral	$ Value in Millions	Major Mining Areas
Copper	151	Murdochville, Chibougamau, Noranda
Asbestos	138	Eastern Townships — Asbestos, Thetford Mines, Black Lake
Iron Ore	135	Labrador Trough — Gagnon to Schefferville
Zinc	70	Clay Belt — Val d'Or, Mattagami Lake
Stone	53	St. Lawrence Lowland
Cement	41	Montreal, Trois-Rivières
Gold	31	Clay Belt
Titanium Dioxide	23	Lake Allard, St. Urbain
Sand and Gravel	21	St. Lawrence Lowland
Silver	8	Clay Belt

* Source: Canada, Dominion Bureau of Statistics. *Preliminary Report of Mineral Production — 1967.* Queen's Printer. Ottawa (July, 1968).

amounted to only $8,000 worth of natural gas from the Trois-Rivières area.

The Clay Belt in Western Quebec has long been a major mineral region (Figure 5.22). The Greenstone formation which surrounds Ontario mining centers such as Timmins and Kirkland Lake is also found in Quebec. Mining began here in 1923, and by 1927 there was a smelter at Noranda. Soon other mining centers, Rouyn, Malartic, and Val d'Or, sprang up along the C.N.R. branch line through the mineralized zone, and gold and base metals became the main source of economic life for the region. Then in 1947 renewed interest in the copper deposits of Chibougamau developed in response to the construction of a new road from Lake St. John into the Chibougamau area. By 1960 a C.N.R. branch line from Barrante to St. Félicien had been constructed at a cost of $33,000,000. Power needs were met by a new transmission line from St. Félicien in the Lake St. John region. Chibougamau, a new mining community, came into being and by 1966 contained more than 8,900 persons. Copper ore is mined and sent by rail for smelting at Noranda. It appears likely that Chibou-

gamau will be the scene for further activity as copper mines begin production at Lake Mistassini.

While Western Quebec is not noted for iron ore, there is the Hilton iron ore mine near Shawville. Here open pit mining exposes magnetite ore which is mined, concentrated, and pelletized prior to shipment.

In the Eastern Townships asbestos has been mined since 1877 in the central portion of the *serpentine belt* between the St. Francis and Chaudière Rivers. In this eighty mile section there are ten active mining companies, employing a total of about 6,200 workers, and three sizable mining towns: Black Lake, Thetford Mines, and Asbestos.* These and some outlying, smaller settlements have a total population of over 50,000. From this region comes 85 per cent of the asbestos produced in Canada.

Both open pit and shaft mining techniques are utilized in asbestos mining, but it is the open pit technique which has the

* W. G. Ross. "Encroachment of the Jeffrey Mine on the Town of Asbestos, Quebec". *Geographical Review.* LVII, 4 (October, 1967). p. 523.

greatest impact on the landscape. The town of Asbestos has gradually been encroached upon by the expanding open pit operation of the Jeffrey Mine. Of the original village area in 1905, nearly 54 per cent has been engulfed. The people of Asbestos accept the encroachment for "they know that the big crater at their back door is their livelihood".* Still, it is disconcerting to return to Asbestos after several years and discover that certain streets now end abruptly and that a huge hole has replaced the houses. This and other modifications of the landscape such as the mountains of waste rock are biproducts of mining that are often overlooked in considering the minerals industry. Similar phenomena may be encountered in and around Thetford Mines.

Asbestos is not the only mineral obtained in the Eastern Townships; copper has been mined for a number of years near Sherbrooke. In the last two decades Murdochville in the Gaspé Peninsula has become a major copper mining center. There mine and smelter both operate and contribute substantially to the local economy.

In the last two decades Quebec mining has had its greatest growth in the production of iron ore in the northeast. More than 400 miles long and 40 miles wide, the

* B. Swarbrick. "The Hole That's Eating a Town". *Canadian Weekly.* (5 March, 1965). p. 12.

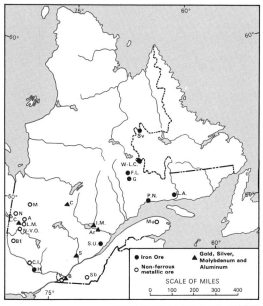

AFTER CANADA YEAR BOOK 1967

Figure 5.22 Mining in Quebec

A	Amos	M	Mattagami
Ar	Arvida	Mu	Murdochville
B	Beauharnois	N	Normetal
Bt	Belleterre	N-V.O.	Noranda—
C	Chibougamau		Val d'Or
C.I.	Calumet Island	P.N.	Pointe Noire
F.L.	Frye Lake	S	Shawinigan
G	Gagnon	Sb	Sherbrooke
H	Hilton	Sv	Schefferville
I.M.	Isle Maligne	S.U.	St. Urbain
L.A.	Lake Allard	V	Valleyfield
L.C.	Lacorne Cadillac	W-L.C.	Wabush—
L.M.	La Motte		Labrador City

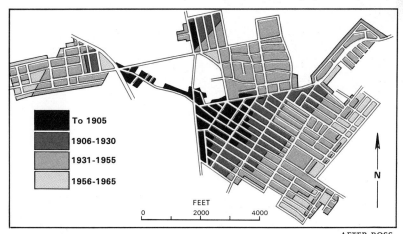

AFTER ROSS

Figure 5.23 The Growth of Asbestos
The development of Asbestos is indicated in terms of municipal subdivisions.

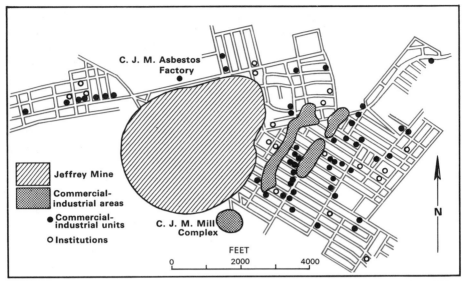

Figure 5.24 Land Use in Asbestos in 1965
The Jeffrey Mine plays a dominant role in the land use pattern.

Figure 5.25 Asbestos, Quebec
Directly adjacent to the town of Asbestos is the open pit mine and an enormous mound of waste material.

COURTESY CANADIAN JOHNS-MANVILLE CO., LIMITED

Labrador Trough extends in an open arc south from Ungava Bay to the Lakes Plateau. It contains many of the richest deposits of iron ore in Canada. Since the ore deposits straddle the provincial boundary between Quebec and Newfoundland, some of the mines do likewise, thus profoundly influencing the economics of both provinces. Only the southern portion of the trough has yet been developed although some preliminary work has been done farther north.

The first step towards exploitation of the ores was taken by the Iron Ore Company of Canada in 1949.* This company was formed by a consortium of American iron and steel producers: Armco, Republic, National, Wheeling Steel Corporations, the Youngstown Sheet and Tube Company, and the Hanna Coal and Ore Corporation. With them were associated the Hollinger interests that controlled the Labrador and Quebec concessions. By and large, the American corporations involved were interior iron and steel producers whose plants were concentrated in the Lake Erie-Ohio Valley portion of the "steel triangle". The ore resource was a high grade hematite, 55 per cent iron, which was low enough in phosphorus to permit direct use by Bessemer furnaces. The ore could be mined by the open pit method and shipped direct to the consumer (Figure 5.26).

The construction of the town of Schefferville, the 357 mile railway to the port site of Sept Iles, and the necessary terminal and processing facilities began shortly after the incorporation of the Iron Ore Company of Canada in Delaware in 1949, and operations commenced in 1954. Since this early beginning the markets for direct shipping ores have decreased as new steel technology requires that iron ore between 60 and 70 per cent iron be supplied. Labrador ores thus need to be beneficiated and pelletized to meet these new demands. Despite the added investment required for pelletization facilities, the processing is an

* F. K. Hare. "The Labrador Frontier". *Geographical Review*. XLII, 3 (July, 1952). pp. 405-424.

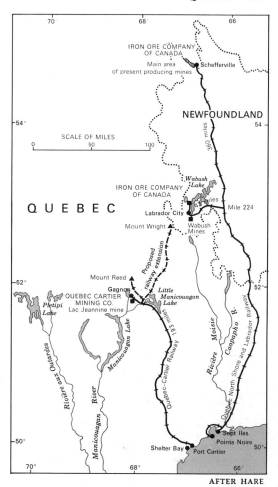

Figure 5.26 The Iron Ore District in Labrador and Quebec
The map is redrafted, by permission, from the *Annals of the Association of American Geographers*, Volume 54, 1964.

advantage in that pelletized ores can be shipped year-round as the pellets do not freeze in the stockpile or on board ore cars.

In response to this new demand the Iron Ore Company of Canada has developed a major mining operation at Carol Lake, about 40 miles west of mile 224 on the Quebec North Shore and Labrador Railway. As in the case of Schefferville a new town, Labrador City, was constructed to house the miners. Through co-operation with the Iron Ore Company of Canada a Canadian consortium of producers developed Wabush Lake, and as in the case of Carol Lake mine, concentration and pelletization facilities were constructed. Wabush Mines share the railroad with Carol Lake and Schefferville but have developed a separate terminal at Pointe Noire near Sept Iles. As shown by Table 5.5, there is a unique subdivision between mining and concentration facilities, and frequently the concentration is done at the port site rather than at the mine.

An iron ore mine entirely within Quebec, near Gagnon, has been made operative by the Quebec Cartier Mining Company, a subsidiary of the United States Steel Corporation. Their Lac Jeannine mine is connected by private railway with Port Cartier,

a new all-season port about thirty miles west of Pointe Noire.* In addition, there is the Quebec Iron and Titanium Corporation which mines an ilmenite deposit at Lake Allard near Havre St. Pierre. The titanium and iron ore is shipped by water to Sorel for smelting into titanium oxide and pig iron.

Expansion of processing capacities has continued. In 1968 the Carol Pellet Company had a capacity of 10,000,000 tons and the Wabash Mines Pelletizer at Pointe Noire had a capacity of 6,000,000 tons. The iron ore produced in Labrador —

* F. K. Hare. "New Light from Labrador-Ungava". Annals, *Association of American Geographers.* Vol. 54, 4 (December, 1964). pp. 459-476.

Figure 5.27 Sept Iles Ore Docks
At the Sept Iles port automated transfer of ore from the stockpiles to the ore carriers is accomplished by a complicated system of conveyors.

COURTESY IRON ORE COMPANY OF CANADA

Table 5.5   Iron Ore Producers in Labrador — Ungava *

Company	Property Location	Type of Ore Obtained	Product Shipped	Shipments 1966 (000 long tons)
Iron Ore Company of Canada (IOC)	Schefferville	Geothite Limonite 53.6% Fe	Direct Shipping Ore 54.3% Fe	6,653
	Labrador City	Specular Hematite 38.4% Fe	Concentrate 62.7% Fe	2,017
	Carol Pellet Co. Adjacent to Labrador City Concentrator	Process IOC Concentrate	Pellets 64.2% Fe	5,214
Wabush Mines	Wabush	Specular Hematite-Magnetite 33.9% Fe	Concentrate 64.2% Fe	136
	Pointe Noire	Process Wabush Concentrate	Pellets 65% Fe	3,702
Quebec Cartier Mining Company	Gagnon	Specular Hematite-Magnetite 33.9% Fe	Concentrate 64.7% Fe	8,319

Ungava is destined largely for export markets; of the entire production less than 2,000,000 tons is utilized in Canada. Future growth will depend upon world competition and the strength of the iron and steel industry in the United States.

The St. Lawrence Lowland possesses a small portion of the mineral wealth of Quebec. Construction materials dominate: cement in the Montreal region and dimension stone quarries on Montreal Island, Jesus Island, and at Joliette, Trois-Rivières, and St. Marc. In addition, there are brickworks at Laprairie and St. Jean and the mining of columbium at Oka. However, this region is not as important in the mining industry as are the hinterland regions of Quebec.

Table 5.6   Crude Ore Mined in Labrador — Ungava *

Company	Property Location	Total tonnage mined
Iron Ore Company of Canada	Schefferville Carol Lake	6,653,299 16,970,600
Wabush Mines	Wabush	10,744,507
Quebec Cartier Mining Company	Gagnon	17,643,618

* V. B. Schneider. "Canadian Iron Ore Industry in 1966". Mineral Resources Division, Department of Energy, Mines and Resources. *Information Bulletin MR 89.* (1968). Tables 15, 17.

Figure 5.28
The aluminum smelter at Baie Comeau is a good example of a modern industrial complex situated within the Canadian Shield.

Mineral Industries

Quebec contributes a major share towards Canada's role as the third most important producer of aluminum in the world. Raw materials, bauxite, alumina, and cryollite do not occur here, but the aluminum smelting industry is attracted to Quebec by the abundant resource of cheap hydroelectric power. Currently Quebec produces more than 700,000 tons of aluminum annually.

In 1904, ALCOA established the first electrolytic reduction smelter at Shawinigan Falls on the St. Maurice River. The success of this site led to the development of Arvida on the Saguenay River in 1926. Increased market demands during and after World War II created the need for expansion, and smelters were built at Isle Maligne near Lake St. John and at Beauharnois on the St. Lawrence River west of Montreal. Then in 1960 Canadian British Aluminium commenced operations at Baie Commeau on the North Shore of the St. Lawrence estuary. This smelter has been very successful, and existing facilities now produce 115,000 tons annually. If market conditions continue to improve Baie Commeau will, by 1971, have a capacity of 175,000 tons. This continued development is unusual, for aluminum smelting today tends to locate closer to markets and sources of thermal electricity. Increased efficiency in thermal generation has lowered the cost differential between hydro-electric and thermal electric power. During the last decade aluminum smelting has developed in the Ohio Valley near thermal stations using local low-cost coal.*

* J. F. Lounsbury. "Recent Developments in the Aluminum Industry in the United States". *Journal of Geography.* LXI, 3 (March, 1962). pp. 97-103.

Copper smelting is concentrated near the mines in preliminary operations such as those at Murdochville and Noranda. For final processing to create pure copper a large refinery is located in Montreal. There is a smelter at Valleyfield to treat the zinc mined at Mattagami and elsewhere in the Clay Belt mineral region. Sorel as mentioned previously is the site for the electrolytic reduction of the ilmenite ores from Lake Allard. These smelter operations, together with the numerous pulp and paper operations along the southern fringe of the Shield, create an enormous need for electric power.

Power

Abundant hydro-electric power is one of the principal stimulants to the industrializ-ation of both Quebec and Ontario and is especially important in that neither province possesses significant amounts of mineral fuels. In Quebec, electric power accounts for slightly less than five per cent of the value added for all commodity-producing industries. However, this does not truly indicate the importance of hydro-electric power in Quebec for within the province there is 48 per cent of the developed waterpower for all Canada, and the undeveloped potential amounts to 45 per cent of the Canadian potential. The Canadian Shield with its precipitous southern edge, the Laurentide Escarpment, and the high amount of run-off from the 35 to 40 inches of annual precipitation combine to ensure a waterpower resource of superb quality.

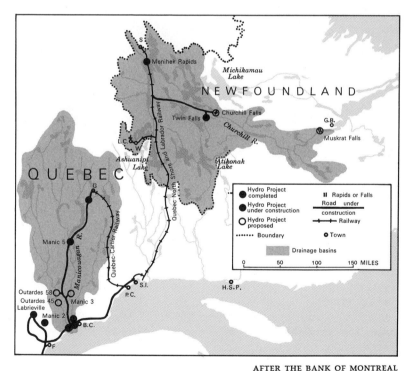

AFTER THE BANK OF MONTREAL

Figure 5.29 Power Developments in Eastern Quebec and Labrador

B.C.	Baie Comeau		L.C.	Labrador City
F	Forestville		P.C.	Port Cartier
G	Gagnon		S	Schefferville
G.B.	Goose Bay		S.I.	Sept Iles
H.S.P.	Havre St. Pierre		W	Wabush

Figure 5.30 Daniel Johnson Dam
The dam, formerly Manic 5, is the heart of the huge Hydro-Quebec Manicouagan Power Project in the northeastern part of the province and is the largest concrete structure of its type in the world. A multiple arch dam, it rises 703 feet and stretches 4,310 feet from end to end.

Until recently electric power generation in Quebec was controlled by a series of private power companies, but in May, 1963, the Quebec Hydro-Electric Power Corporation acquired control of eight private companies and brought almost all electric power production for domestic purposes under one single authority. The only power generation not controlled by Hydro-Quebec is that generated by certain industrial concerns for use in their own manufacturing plants.

The Ottawa and St. Lawrence Rivers have been fully utilized in terms of hydro-electric power potential: the completion of the Beauharnois plant on the St. Lawrence in 1961 and the Carillon project on the Ottawa in 1966 as well as the Quinze Rapids development on the upper reaches of the Ottawa River has forced Hydro-Quebec to search elsewhere for electric power. A thermal power station is in operation at Tracy near Sorel, but this power station produces only 300,000 kilowatts. Recently two power projects were also put into operation on the Bersimis River with total installed capacity of 2,100,000 horsepower.

Currently Hydro-Quebec is harnessing the power potential of the Manicouagan and Outardes Rivers. The project involves the construction of seven new generating stations on two rivers and the installation of additional capacity at an existing station. When the project is completed, generating capacity in excess of 7,500,000 horsepower will be available. Manic 2, eleven miles upstream from the mouth of the Manicouagan River, commenced operation in 1965 with five units, and in 1967 all eight units were on stream. Similarly Manic 1 went on the line shortly after the completion of Manic 2. The Daniel Johnson Dam is the largest station in the complex for it is designed for a total capacity of 1,800,000 horsepower. Investment has been considerable: the dam is 4,310 feet long and towers 703 feet above the bedrock. It is expected to be in operation by 1972. Two years later Manic 3 with a capacity of 1,505,000 horsepower will also be providing electricity. In addition, there are power stations on the Outardes River. Power generated by the Manicouagan — Outardes complex is remote from the main market area. To achieve transmission efficiency electricity at 735,000 volts is sent along hollow aluminum cables mounted on special insulators and hydro pylons. In this manner the old economic limit for power transmission has been extended.

Although it is outside the borders of Quebec, the development of hydro power at Churchill Falls in Labrador is inextricably linked with Quebec. Now under construction the Churchill Falls project is a mammoth power scheme which will make available 6,000,000 horsepower. When completed in the mid-70s electric energy will be available using extra high voltage transmission techniques for markets in Quebec and in New York State.

Agriculture

For over two centuries agriculture was the traditional way of life for most of Quebec's inhabitants. Now less than 500,000 people live on farms, and farming has become a minor source of employment.

There were only 80,000 farmers in Quebec in 1966, of which 27,000 were only part-time operators. Quebec agriculture is no longer merely self-sufficient and non-commercial for in 1965 more than $360,000,000 worth of farm products were marketed. However, the disparity of the agricultural resources base and the encouragement of pioneer farming by the provincial government are both responsible for the existence of agricultural areas of low economic return.

In 1966 the farms of Quebec occupied 12,886,000 acres of land, only 7,629,000 acres of which were classified as improved. Farm land is concentrated in the St. Lawrence Lowland and the Eastern Townships; elsewhere there are small areas in the Saguenay — Lake St. John graben and the Clay Belt of Western Quebec, and limited pockets along the Gaspé coast. In the latter areas many farmers rely heavily on the forest resource for supplementary income. Farm woodlots occupy 3,777,000 acres in Quebec and more than 14,000 farms provide pulpwood for cash sale. Maple syrup is important in the Eastern Townships where 13,000 farms reported tapping maple trees in 1966.

Mixed crop and livestock farming is characteristic of most of rural Quebec. However, as shown by Figure 5.31, a majority of the farmers derive the bulk of their income from the sale of dairy products. This is true even in the Clay Belt and the Lake St. John Lowland where conditions are far from ideal for this type of farming. General livestock operations occur in the counties along the Lower St. Lawrence both north and south of Quebec City and in the isolated pockets along the Gaspé coast. Specialty crops are confined to the Montreal Plain (Figure 5.32). Of note are the vegetable growing areas of Jesus Island, and Châteauguay, Napierville, Bagot, St. Hyacinthe, and Rouville counties. Orcharding is most important near the confluence of the Ottawa and St. Lawrence Rivers in Deux Montagnes and Huntingdon counties and on the slopes of the Monteregian Hills. Tobacco is an impor-

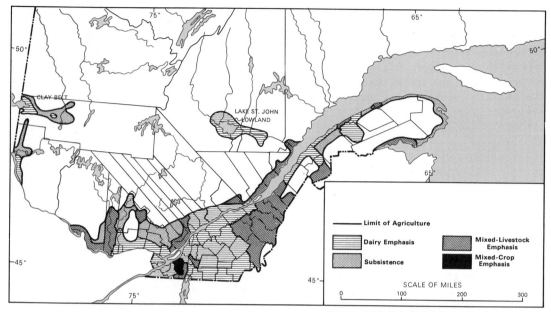

AFTER CANADA DEPARTMENT OF AGRICULTURE

Figure 5.31 Types of Farming in Quebec
Dairy farming is widespread, but it is most concentrated in the vicinity of Montreal.

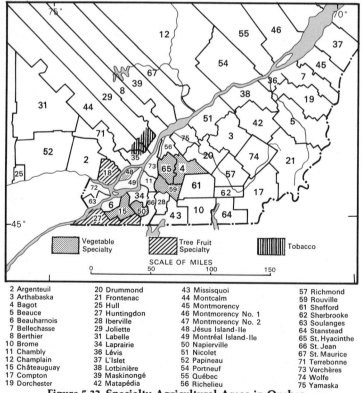

2 Argenteuil	20 Drummond	43 Missisquoi	57 Richmond
3 Arthabaska	21 Frontenac	44 Montcalm	59 Rouville
4 Bagot	25 Hull	45 Montmorency	61 Shefford
5 Beauce	27 Huntingdon	46 Montmorency No. 1	62 Sherbrooke
6 Beauharnois	28 Iberville	47 Montmorency No. 2	63 Soulanges
7 Bellechasse	29 Joliette	48 Jésus Island-Ile	64 Stanstead
8 Berthier	31 Labelle	49 Montréal Island-Ile	65 St. Hyacinthe
10 Brome	34 Laprairie	50 Napierville	66 St. Jean
11 Chambly	36 Lévis	51 Nicolet	67 St. Maurice
12 Champlain	37 L'Islet	52 Papineau	71 Terrebonne
15 Châteauguay	38 Lotbinière	54 Portneuf	73 Verchères
17 Compton	39 Maskinongé	55 Québec	74 Wolfe
19 Dorchester	42 Matapédia	56 Richelieu	75 Yamaska

Figure 5.32 Specialty Agricultural Areas in Quebec

tant specialty on the sandy soils near Joliette (Figure 5.33).

Dairy farming is the most important sector of agriculture; over 60 per cent of all commercial farms in Quebec are dairy farms. Metropolitan Montreal is, of course, the major market for fluid milk, consuming more than 186,000 gallons every day.* As shown in Figure 5.34, Montreal obtains

* M. J. Scarlett. "Milk Market of Montreal". *Revue de Géographie de Montréal.* XXI, 2 (1967). p. 343.

its supply from a wide "milk shed" extending from Brownsburg and St. Hyacinthe in the north to the United States border on the south. About 70 per cent of the farms shipping milk to Montreal are located south of the St. Lawrence River. However, two counties in this area, Granby and Drummondville, do not participate in the Montreal trade because the demands of their own urban areas for fluid and industrial milk are great enough to absorb the supply. In general, very little of the

Figure 5.33 Tobacco Growing
The tobacco farms situated on the sandy soils near Joliette have become an important specialty crop area in Quebec. To the right there is an area where wind erosion of an old shoreline is being stabilized by trees.

QUEBEC DEPARTMENT OF LANDS AND FORESTS

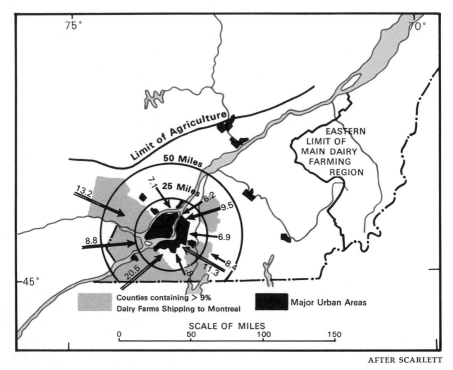

AFTER SCARLETT

Figure 5.34 The Montreal Milk Shed

Montreal milk supply is produced within 25 miles of downtown Montreal, nor is much of it obtained from more than 50 miles distant. Beyond this limit the cost of transportation is usually disadvantageous to the Montreal fluid milk trade as opposed to the local demands for fluid and industrial classes of milk. It is also important to note that farmers who supply milk for manufacturing purposes have not had to install facilities for bulk cooling.

The agricultural frontier is of interest in Quebec, especially since the provincial government has actively encouraged land settlement on the Canadian Shield. Since 1913 the Quebec Department of Colonization has implemented settlement programs in the Clay Belt and other forested areas. In Abitibi county 27 parishes have been surveyed, mapped, and planned. Lots of 100 acres are sold to prospective settlers at a price of 30 cents an acre, payable in five interest-free instalments. The settler must agree to clear 30 per cent of the lot within

five years and build a habitable house at least 20 by 24 feet in size and a barn 32 by 34 feet. If necessary, the payments may be deducted from the government grants. These grants under arrangements in effect since 1947 involve a maximum of $4,345 payable to each settler who fulfills the requirements of the Quebec Department of Colonization.*

In his study of marginal agriculture in Eastern Canada, Biays suggests that there are significant differences between successful farming areas and those where agriculture is a marginal economic activity.** As shown by Table 5.7, the county unit is used as a means of comparison. The marginal counties selected illustrate conditions

* G. L. McDermott. "Frontiers of Settlement in the Great Clay Belt, Ontario and Quebec". *Annals, Association of American Geographers.* Vol. 51, 3 (September, 1961). pp. 261-273.
** P. Biays. "Problèmes de l'agriculture marginale dans la zone pionnière de l'Est du Canada". *Cahiers de Géographie de Québec.* 16 (April-September, 1964). p. 220.

in the Clay Belt, Lake St. John Lowland, Gaspé, and the fringe of the Shield north of Montreal. It is apparent that the agricultural fringe counties have changed markedly between 1961 and 1966 in terms of the total area of farm land. Moreover, part-time farming is much more important than in the older agricultural counties. It should be noted that the term *part-time* refers to farm operators who earned more than $750 from off-farm employment or worked more than 75 days off the farm during the year.* In terms of economic strength most of the farms in the agricultural fringe

* Canada, Dominion Bureau of Statistics. "Census of Agriculture — 1966 Quebec". Ottawa. June, 1968. p. ix.

areas are small-scale farms which earn less than $2,500 annually. However, the possibilities for off-farm employment are not evenly distributed throughout Quebec. The Shield fringe as exemplified by Terrebonne county is close to urban influence and is rapidly developing as a major recreation area for Montreal. Abitibi county has a well-developed mining economy which is supplemented by forestry. The Lake St. John Lowland has both aluminum smelting and pulp and paper as alternate employment possibilities. The Gaspé Peninsula offers few opportunities for off-farm work; forestry and fishing are both rather marginal and the one large mine of the area is in the rather remote interior.

Figure 5.35 Land Abandonment in the Laurentides
Areas in the Laurentides were settled early, but abandonment of the farms had begun to take place by the turn of the century because the soils were too stony and very infertile.

QUEBEC DEPARTMENT OF LANDS AND FORESTS

Table 5.7   Characteristics of Agriculture for Selected Counties, 1966 *

County	Area of Farm Land 1966 Acres	Per Cent Change in Area of Farm Land 1961-1966	Part-time Farmers as Per Cent of All Farmers	Small-scale Farms as Per Cent of All Farms
Agricultural Fringe				
Abitibi	516,218	−11	57	74
Chicoutimi	254,299	− 5	42	61
Matane	164,951	−14	41	67
Terrebonne	88,708	−22	42	55
Agricultural Counties				
Châteauguay	129,205	− 5	25	33
St. Hyacinthe	140,937	− 7	27	21

* Census of Canada — Agriculture 1961, 1966.

Agriculture in Quebec therefore is really successful only in the St. Lawrence Lowland. Despite official encouragement the rigors of climate and topography strongly limit its distribution elsewhere. While agriculture is most successful on the Montreal Plain, certain choice areas are being threatened by urbanization. As shown by Figure 5.36, urbanization is affecting the vegetable growers on Jesus Island. This situation is repeated in many other areas as Metropolitan Montreal expands ever outwards.

Figure 5.36 Urban Growth and Agriculture
On Jesus Island the original landscape of long lot farms is rapidly being obliterated by urban expansion from Montreal.

QUEBEC DEPARTMENT OF LANDS AND FORESTS

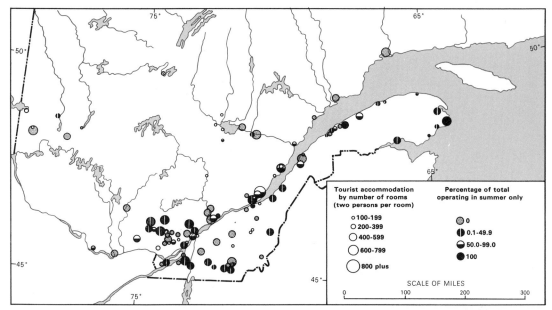

Figure 5.37 Local Motel and Hotel Capacities
This map excludes the capacity of Montreal but shows the degree to which tourist accommodation has developed elsewhere.

AFTER LUNDGREN

Recreation and Tourism

As the one area in Canada where significant cultural variations are apparent, Quebec has long been an important tourist area. Even in 1958, 5,000,000 persons visited Quebec, and by 1963 more than 7,500,000 were attracted to the region. It is estimated that in 1963 these visitors spent about $264,000,000 while they were in Quebec. Expo in 1967 attracted millions of people, and it is likely that many of them will make repeat visits to Quebec in the future.

Why do tourists visit Quebec? The Laurentian Plateau has long been an attraction not only in terms of rugged grandeur but also as a sportsman's paradise for hunting and fishing. In the winter the Shield has abundant snow cover and the relief necessary to create challenging skiing conditions. Likewise, the Gaspé has been a tourist attraction, and countless tourists have tasted the bread baked in outdoor ovens and bought small hand-carved boats sold by children in every hamlet. Montreal and Quebec City are both important tourist attractions.

Tourism and recreation are intertwined, and in a recent study an attempt was made to determine the strength of these two activities by analyzing accommodation capacities.* Montreal and Quebec City contain 57 per cent of the accommodation in Quebec. For the rest of the province the distribution of facilities is far from uniform. Figure 5.37 illustrates the distribution of motel and hotel capacities in areas other than Montreal and Quebec City. Two main areas stand out: the Laurentian region north of Montreal and the St. Anne de Beaupré district on the north shore of the St. Lawrence. In addition, there is a continuous line of coastal villages of the Gaspé, while at Percé more than 1,200 persons can be accommodated during the summer season. Seasonality in tourism is also apparent along the north shore of the St. Lawrence where up to 50 per cent of

* J. O. Lundgren. "Tourism in Quebec". *Revue de Géographie de Montréal.* XX, 1 (1966). pp. 59-74.

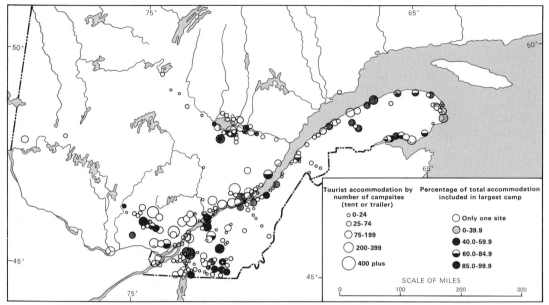

Tourist accommodation by number of campsites (tent or trailer)	Percentage of total accommodation included in largest camp
○ 0-24	○ Only one site
○ 25-74	◐ 0-39.9
○ 75-199	● 40.0-59.9
○ 200-399	◓ 60.0-84.9
○ 400 plus	● 85.0-99.9

SCALE OF MILES
0   100   200   300

AFTER LUNDGREN

Figure 5.38 Local Capacities of Camps and Campsites
With the increase in popularity of camping this tourist facility is becoming much more important. There are very few camps which have more than 400 campsites, and in many areas only one camp exists. The size of the camp is indicated by the graduated circles, while the dominance of the largest camp in an area is indicated by the pattern shown within the circles.

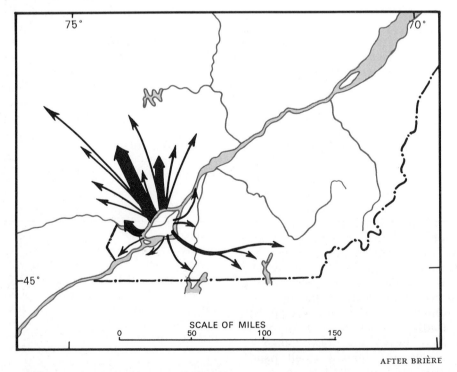

SCALE OF MILES
0   50   100   150

AFTER BRIÈRE

Figure 5.39 The Cottage Hinterland of Montreal

the accommodation is available only during the summer. In the case of the Laurentians most of the facilities are run on a year-round basis.

Camping has become more important during the last decade. Figure 5.38 shows the distribution of camping facilities in Quebec. These are best developed along the Shield fringe between Montreal and Quebec City and in the Lake St. John and Upper Saguenay regions. Camping facilities are largely provided by independent operators, and it is only in isolated areas such as the Laurentides Provincial Park that the provincial government has become involved.

Montreal is obviously a major influence on recreation in Quebec. Traversing the Laurentian Autoroute during the peak traffic periods of "le weekend" can be a most gruelling experience as thousands head north in the Laurentides. As shown by Figure 5.39, most cottagers head northwards to what Brière terms "Les Laurentides Montréalaises".* As more and more people desire summer cottages, the pressure for cottage sites increases, and inevitably cottage subdivisions develop. Figure 5.40 illustrates how St. Adolphe de Howard has been influenced by recreation. Once a marginal agricultural area, the abandoned farmland was allowed to once more become forested, and now recreation has taken over.

---

* R. Brière. "Les cadres d'une géographie touristique du Québec". *Cahiers de Géographie de Québec*. 11 (October, 1961-March, 1962). p. 61.

Figure 5.40 Recreation Land Uses
The residents of Montreal are seeking rural retreats in the Laurentides, north of the city. The shores of the lake in the photograph have been alienated and a cottage subdivision has developed to the west.

QUEBEC DEPARTMENT OF LANDS AND FORESTS

THE CITIES OF QUEBEC

Urban development has been proceeding at a rapid rate in the province of Quebec. The census of 1966 showed that 78 per cent of the population lived in an urban environment (Table 5.8). In this respect Quebec is slightly behind Ontario and slightly ahead of British Columbia.

Urbanization began fairly early in Quebec. Pioneer census-taking during the French regime recorded respectable towns at both Montreal and Quebec, and village nuclei at Trois-Rivières and several other places. In general it is to be supposed that urban centers arose in response to the requirements of administration and defense and the needs of the fur trade which was the propelling industry of the colony. The self-sufficiency of the *habitants* living on the land afforded very little support for villages and small towns in the early days.

Urban populations began to grow more rapidly during the first century of the British regime. Particular emphasis must be placed upon Montreal which, because of its position at the head of navigation, gained an early lead over Quebec. This lead was maintained and increased in the

railway building age when Montreal became the railway center not only for the St. Lawrence Lowland but for all of Canada. Quebec was bypassed by the railways. For a long time the only access to rail transportation was by way of Lévis on the south bank of the St. Lawrence. Eventually, however, a Canadian Pacific Railway line along the north bank made connections with Trois-Rivières and Montreal.

Forest exploitation, particularly the saw-milling phase which sought out good waterpower sites on medium-sized streams provided the impetus for many small towns. Small industries (usually wood-working, flour-milling, and woolen manufacturing) were attracted to such sites also, thus adding to the urban economic base. The three historic colonial towns, Montreal, Quebec, and Trois-Rivières, were all incorporated in 1792; so also was the much smaller village of Sorel at the mouth of the Richelieu River. Fifty or more additional places were incorporated as villages or towns between 1792 and 1867. Many of them had an extremely restricted resource base or trading area as is attested by the fact that they remain as villages even today. Others, such as Sherbrooke (1823),

Table 5.8   Changing Population in Quebec, 1871-1966 *

		Total Population	Urban Population	Rural Population	Rural Non-farm Population	Farm Population
1966	Number	5,780,845	4,525,114	1,255,731	762,168	493,563
	Per Cent	100.00	78.27	21.73	13.18	8.55
1961	Number	5,259,211	3,906,404	1,352,807	787,981	564,826
	Per Cent	100.00	74.28	25.72	14.98	10.74
1951	Number	4,055,681	2,715,341	1,340,340	760,905	579,435
	Per Cent	100.00	66.93	33.07	18.79	14.28
1941	Number	3,331,882	2,109,694	1,222,188	429,432	792,756
	Per Cent	100.00	63.32	36.68	12.89	23.79
1931	Number	2,874,255	1,683,400	1,190,855	447,257	743,598
	Per Cent	100.00	58.58	41.42	15.55	25.87
1901	Number	1,648,898	654,065	994,833		
	Per Cent	100.00	39.66	60.34		
1871	Number	1,191,516	271,851	919,665		
	Per Cent	100.00	22.80	77.20		

* Data from Census of Canada, 1931, 1941, 1951, 1961, 1966.

QUEBEC / 163

Joliette (1845), St. Jean (1848), St. Hyacinthe (1849), Granby (1858), Chicoutimi (1863), have all become regional cities. Hull is a rather peculiar case; actually settled in 1800 and long associated with the timber industry, it was apparently not incorporated until it became a full-fledged city in 1875.

Many of today's cities, however, date only from the twentieth century. Among such are the pulp and paper centers of Grand'Mère, Shawinigan, Jonquière, Kenogami, and Port Cartier; so also are centers of mineral industry such as Arvida, Sept Iles, Gagnon, Schefferville, Rouyn, Noranda, Val d'Or, and Chibougamau. The resource frontier of Quebec has been remarkably active.

The changing nature of the Quebec population and economic base is suggested in Table 5.9. During the century since Confederation the composition has changed from four-fifths rural and one-fifth urban to one-fifth rural and four-fifths urban. The rural population in 1871 undoubtedly contained numerous tradesmen and artisans, but the great majority of the rural folk were *habitants* living on the land. Today only 8.5 per cent is found on the farms, while a much larger percentage lives in rural villages and along the highways, finding work in industries other than agriculture. Up until World War II, however, it seems safe to say that the rural non-farm group was considerably the smaller. Since the beginning of the depres-

Table 5.9   The Growth of Urban Population in Quebec, 1961-1966 *

Greater Cities	1966		1961		Five-year Increase
	number	per cent	number	per cent	per cent
Montreal	2,436,817	42.15	2,110,679	40.13	11.45
Quebec	413,397	7.15	357,568	6.80	15.91
Hull	110,138	1.90	96,862	1.84	13.70
Chicoutimi-Jonquière	109,142	1.89	105,393	2.00	3.65
Trois-Rivières	94,476	1.64	88,350	1.68	6.93
Sherbrooke	79,667	1.38	70,253	1.33	13.40
Shawinigan	65,098	1.14	66,077	1.26	−1.48
Drummondville	42,855	.74	39,307	.75	9.03
St. Jean	42,627	.74	39,281	.75	8.51
Granby	34,349	.59	31,463	.60	10.91
Valleyfield	34,120	.59	32,372	.61	5.40
Sorel	33,360	.58	28,906	.55	15.41
St. Jérôme	33,258	.56	29,195	.56	13.91
Large Cities	3,529,304	61.05	3,095,706	58.86	16.72
Other Urban Areas	995,810	17.23	810,698	15.42	22.82
Total Urban Pop.	4,525,114	78.28	3,906,404	74.28	15.82
Rural Non-farm Pop.	762,168	13.18	787,981	14.98	−3.27
Rural Farm Pop.	493,563	8.54	564,826	10.74	−12.61
Total Rural Pop.	1,255,731	21.72	1,352,807	25.72	−7.19
Total Population	5,780,845	100.00	5,259,211	100.00	9.91

* Data from Census of Canada, 1961, 1966.

sion (1931 census) agricultural population has almost been cut in two, while total rural population has been slightly increased. Because of the great growth of the cities, however, the proportion of farm dwellers has declined to less than 9 per cent. It is notable too that despite its burgeoning suburbs Montreal is not the fastest growing urban area in the province; Hull, Sherbrooke, Sorel, and in fact a great many cities of less than 30,000 are growing at faster rates. But because of its great bulk the Montreal metropolitan area does account for more than half of the total growth.

There is a striking phenomenon of "filling in" of roadsides in the vicinity of large cities (Table 5.10). The Quebec landscape is notable for its wealth of parish nuclei, many of which have become urban centers.

But even in an almost purely rural county such as Bellechasse in the uplands south of the St. Lawrence, the non-nucleated rural non-farm people make up one-fifth of the rural population; in Hull and Gatineau, and St. Jean and Iberville, which are on the outskirts of large metropolitan areas, the proportion rises to almost 40 per cent, while in the isolated but highly urbanized county of Sherbrooke, scattered population comprises 55 per cent of all rural folk. Such areas are striking examples of "urban shadow". However, not only are the front roads filled in by residences, but much land is also appropriated for business and industrial purposes. The process of urbanization, especially in the Montreal Plain, threatens to engulf the countryside. The final stages of such a process are, to say the least, difficult to imagine.

Table 5.10 Selected Examples of Location of Residence *

	Hull County		Sherbrooke County		St. Jean and Iberville		Bellechasse	
	number	per cent	number	per cent	number	per cent	number	per cent
Total Population	129,111	100.0	80,490	100.0	56,550	100.0	26,054	100.0
Urban Population	100,796	78.1	70,253	87.3	35,763	63.3	2,530	9.7
Rural Population	28,315	21.9	10,237	12.7	20,787	36.7	23,524	90.3
Rural Population	28,315	100.0	10,237	100.0	20,787	100.0	23,524	100.0
Farm Population	8,191	29.0	2,810	27.4	8,181	39.3	13,075	55.6
Non-Farm Pop.	20,124	71.0	7,427	72.6	12,606	60.7	10,449	44.4
Village Population	9,708	34.1	1,720	16.9	4,343	21.4	5,468	23.2
Scattered Population	10,416	36.9	5,707	55.7	8,263	39.3	4,981	21.2

* Data from Census of Canada, 1961.

Montreal

Montreal is an interesting and in fact unique city. It is at once picturesque, old, historic, and traditional, and at the same time, striking, modern, cosmopolitan, and vibrant. It is the outstanding example of a provincial *primate city*; and although it is not the political capital, it is the cultural, social, and commercial focus and the site of the most productive enterprises. That it is not the undisputed *primate city* of all Canada is due first of all to the existence and growth of the city of Toronto and

secondly to the fact that its major culture and language group is French. In order to have retained undisputed primacy Montreal would have had to retain a much higher degree of biculturism than it now possesses.

Montreal is an old city. It was founded by Maisonneuve in 1640 in a strategic location for the fur trade. At the head of the easily navigable channel of the St. Lawrence it is the natural crossing-place of land routes and water routes to the interior. The improvement of its access to the sea and the development of its land routes into the hinterland have been of major concern ever since it was founded.

The building of the railways in the middle of the nineteenth century, an effort in which Montreal took a leading role, naturally focused on the same strategic area as the earlier routes. This delayed the improvement of upstream navigation since capital used for railways could not also be used to build canals. At the same time, however, Montreal insisted on dredging downstream on the St. Lawrence so that newer and larger ships might reach its harbor. Ports in the hinterland were not developed and even Quebec, though more accessible, was left behind.

Maisonneuve selected a site for the new settlement on the river bank with a splendid view of the mountain to the rear. Apparently much the same site had been selected by Champlain years before when he named the eminence Mount Royal. The new settlement was christened *Ville Marie de Montréal*. During its early years it was surrounded by a wooden stockade for defense against the Iroquois. Later a more substantial wall was built. Still later the wall was demolished and replaced by streets. The outline of the old city is roughly that of McGill Street, Craig Street, and Place Viger.

Settlement progressed outside the city. Roads were built east and west along the shore and farm settlements were established at Lachine, Ste. Anne, Rivières-des-Prairies and Point-aux-Trembles. The land was divided into lots 6 arpents wide along the front and 50 arpents deep running back up the slope. The road along the shore was called "la côte" and the row of lots constituted "le rang". Eventually, when the front row was fully occupied, another row of lots was laid out behind it; and when it in turn was filled, still another one was opened. Thus in many Quebec settlements there are several "rangs" numbered I, II, III, and so on. These early holdings stamped a pattern on Montreal Island as well as on other areas. Somehow, the back concessions on Montreal Island also became known as "côtes". The narrow farm lanes leading back up the slopes were known as "montées", and these became some of Montreal's old narrow streets.

There does not seem to have been any great influx of colonists to Montreal, but the early settlers had a high birth rate and the population increased rapidly. Soon new parishes were founded in various parts of the island. Some of the early ones were: Point-aux-Trembles (1674), Rivière-des-Prairies (1687), Ste. Anne (1672), Lachine (1675), Pointe Claire (1717), and St. Laurent (1720). Others followed until within 100 years, the forests of Montreal Island had been reduced almost to their present extent. Some steep slopes and rock outcrops resisted the farmers' efforts. Mount Royal with its three summits, 750', 600', and 600' above sea level, stands out even today as an island of forest although urban development is nibbling at its slopes more energetically than rural settlement ever did.

The city soon filled the rectangle within the old walls and began to extend along the roads outside. By 1761 there were already four fairly important suburban settlements. Beyond the old city and its adjacent slopes the builders found good natural sites — the flat terraces of the Pleistocene shorelines, often with sandy or gravelly soils.

The old city was densely populated. People walked to work; in fact, many of them lived in dwellings adjoining their shops. Of course, the docks, some early factories, mills, and shipyards were somewhat removed from the residential areas, but they were still within walking distance. There were some coach routes to outlying settlements, but they were hardly modern commuting facilities. However, some well-to-do citizens began to build suburban estates in Westmount, Outremont, and other places. They could afford horse-drawn carriages.

The city began to take on the shape of an inverted T, with the horizontal member along the river and the shaft extending up-slope. From 1847 onward the Montreal and Lachine Railway provided a commuter service of sorts, and in 1861 the Montreal City Passenger Railway, a horse-car service, was established. The city began to spread out rapidly to newly-built residential areas even though most of its activities continued to be concentrated in the "downtown" area.

As Montreal grew, it annexed the adjoining suburban parishes. In the half-century after Confederation it spread over an area ten times as great as the original city although its population became only six times as large (1871, 107,000; 1921, 618,000). Many municipalities, however, such as Westmount, Outremont, and Verdun, remained independent. Even today Montreal Island contains more than thirty independent towns and cities. A similar swarm of fifteen independent municipalities on Jesus Island recently became the city of Laval with close to 200,000 inhabitants. But Montreal is not contained by the islands. In all directions suburban development has invaded the mainland and parts of seven other counties are included in the census definition of the Montreal metropolitan area containing 2.5 million people (Table 5.11).

What is the total measure of this enormous city? Is there a *Hochelaga*? Does the Montreal Plain support a conurbation of the same size and growth potential as that described for the Mississaga area around the western end of Lake Ontario? It would seem that there is little difference. The Quebec economic planning bureau recognizes a Montreal region composed of 14 counties including the two islands. However, a slightly different Hochelaga in the Montreal Plain is envisioned by the authors: besides Montreal and Jesus Islands, it includes 15 counties with an area of 3,500 square miles. Its population at the 1966 census was almost 2.8 million of whom 2.6 million could be counted as urban. Its rate of growth is seemingly slightly slower than that of the Ontario conurbation, but it already has a higher population density (790 compared with 635 persons per square mile) and it is more strongly concentrated in a single nucleus, the city of Montreal.

Montreal is a city of many facets, only a few of which may be considered here. Certainly it shows some elements of the concentric system of urban growth, spreading more and more as bridges are built, but its fringe zone has many complexities. Valleyfield, St. Jean-Iberville, and St. Hyacinthe must be classified as satellite communities. Others may develop to the west and north, and each will add its quota to the commuter traffic of Montreal.

Placing industries in the suburbs may not always solve the problem. For instance,

Table 5.11   **Populations of the Major Municipalities of Greater Montreal, 1966 ***

Municipality	Population	Municipality	Population
Montreal	1,222,255	Longueuil	25,593
Laval	196,088	St. Leonard	25,328
Verdun	76,832	Westmount	24,100
St. Michel	71,446	Anjou	22,477
Montreal N.	67,806	Mount Royal	21,840
St. Laurent	59,479	Dorval	20,905
Jacques Cartier	52,527	Côte St. Luc	20,546
LaSalle	48,322	St. Hubert	17,215
Lachine	43,155	St. Lambert	16,003
Outremont	30,881	Beaconsfield	15,702
Point-Aux-Trembles	29,888	Ste. Thérèse	15,628
Pierrefonds	27,924	Boucherville	15,338
Pointe Claire	26,784	Repentigny	14,976

* Data from Census of Canada, 1966.

the industrial park at Pointe Claire was meant to alter the purely dormitory function which formerly characterized this west-end community.* Pointe Claire was formerly a white-collar residential area with workers commuting to the city. However, the new factories in the industrial park have created jobs for the blue-collar workers who reside in Montreal's eastern suburbs. Thus the Trans-Canada Highway has become a two-way commuter route and traffic problems have been increased.

The case of the General Motors plant at Ste. Thérèse is slightly different; it will supply work for local residents. However, many of the workers will come inevitably from the densely packed wards of Montreal.

Throughout Canada's century the port of Montreal has been Canada's chief trade outlet to the world as well as the key to a considerable internal development of water transportation. An authoritative study of this port's activity has recently appeared.** The early growth of its commerce can be seen from the fact that in 1867 the port was visited by 464 vessels from the high seas with 200,000 tons of cargo, and 5,428 river boats transporting 745,000 tons. In other words, almost 5,900 vessels and one million tons of cargo passed through the port. In 1966 there was almost the same number of boats, but the flow of cargo had increased to more than 12 million tons. Montreal, however, is not a one-way port. While incoming cargo totalled 12 million tons, 9 million tons were dispatched. In recent years Canada's Pacific gateway, Vancouver, has been a close rival with more than 20 million tons, but more than two-thirds is outgoing cargo while less than one-third is unloaded.

The flow of goods through the port is a double blessing. Transportation itself is an important employer of labor, while the service industries attracted by the activities of the port and the processing and manufacturing which must be done near the port employ a great many more. Another function of great importance a century ago and becoming much greater during the following half-century was the service to passengers. Much of the flow of immigration during Canada's most expansive years came through the port of Montreal. However, the passenger business has now been largely transferred to the airport.

The modern port is extensive and complex. Officially it extends from Victoria Bridge to Sorel, a distance of 35 miles and includes both banks of the river. The channel has been dredged to a minimum depth of 35 feet. There are 135 piers, wharves, and jetties with berthing spaces totalling 74,000 feet. There is an area of 3,750,000 square feet of transit shed space; the harbor elevators can hold more than 22,000,000 bushels of grain; and oil storage can be provided for more than 1,250,000,000 gallons. The immensity of the installations is strikingly apparent from the view afforded by Montreal's new buildings. The port of Montreal is not only an immense terminal itself, but it is also the entrance to the St. Lawrence Seaway giving access to Toronto, Chicago, and all other Great Lakes ports.

In earlier years the smaller port was obviously of much greater importance to the smaller city. Waterfront lands, even if rather restricted, were undoubtedly the favored sites for most of the propelling industries. Railways, of course, made possible the spread of industry into other locations, while modern truck transportation has increased the spread. Now only those industries which have a compelling connection with water transportation find it necessary to seek waterfront sites. Such industries are ship-building and repair, sugar refining, petroleum refining, and flour milling. But even though a waterfront site is not always possible, many industries still locate somewhere in Montreal because its port facilities enable them to assemble

---

* Frank C. Innes. "Concepts in Urban Geography in Relation to the Local Milieu — Montreal". Revue de Géographie de Montréal. XXI, 1 (1967). pp. 165-168.
** Benoit Brouillette. "Le port de Montréal, hier et aujourd'hui". Revue de Géographie de Montréal. XXI, 2 (1967). pp. 195-223.

Figure 5.41 Montreal Harbor, 1893
The layout of the port of Montreal is largely the same as that at Confederation. To the right can be seen the Notre Dame de Bonsecours church. The harbour to the left was still basically simple in design and did not have any high-level piers.

Figure 5.42 Montreal Harbor, 1967
The photograph illustrates the considerable development of the port. New high-level piers have been constructed. The Expo pavilions on Ste. Hélène Island can also be seen.

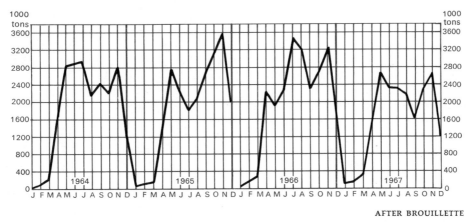

AFTER BROUILLETTE

Figure 5.43 Fluctuations in Cargo Tonnage Handled by the Port of Montreal

materials easily from many parts of the world.

A few geographical points about the port, not all of which are favorable, may be recorded. Lying a thousand miles from the open sea it is tideless, requiring no docks and basins such as are needed by many other world ports. The approach through the St. Lawrence channel is comparatively narrow and must be dredged continuously. Many other navigation aids are needed. Finally, it is not yet a real winter port for freezing conditions prevail for at least five months. The consequent seasonality of the port activity is shown in the accompanying graph (Figure 5.43). Long ago Canada accepted this as one of the facts of life. In 1853 a railway was built connecting Montreal with Portland, Maine. Later the Intercolonial Railway and the Canadian Pacific Railway made possible the winter use of Halifax and Saint John. During World War II pipelines were laid to Portland to insure a supply of petroleum at all times. Montreal was not very receptive to the idea of the improved St. Lawrence Seaway, yet events have shown it to be a blessing; certainly the port activity has grown since it was opened. Icebreakers and other means have been used, but the most fervent hope of the port of Montreal still is that the problem of winter navigation may be solved in such a way that shipmasters and insurance firms may come to regard the St. Lawrence as a normal winter route, thus eliminating the peaks and valleys of its activity graph.

The World Fair, Expo 67, was not a normal port activity, yet it took place within the port locality and port facilities were sometimes used. Because of its location on the harbor and beside the St. Lawrence Seaway, one of the strongest impressions obtained by the 60,000,000 visitors to Canada's Centennial Showplace must have been a sense of the greatness of the port of Montreal.

Montreal is and for long has been an outstanding manufacturing center. In the 1860s its industrial structure was dominated by huge flour mills which supplied almost one-quarter of the value of its total industrial output. Sugar refining was a strong second. Other industries included breweries and distilleries, tanneries, soap factories, sawmills, paper mills, and numerous establishments making rubber articles, machinery, and metal products. Tobacco processing was also an early industry. Later, although flour milling and sugar refining remained strong, the leadership in industry passed to clothing, shoes, and textiles; while for many years the manufacture of railway equipment was very important.

The record of a modern year is given in Table 5.12 for the census year of 1961. Because of the grouping we cannot easily identify the industries. Beverage and food industries head the list, including large brewing, milling, and sugar-refining plants. Meat packing is a large industry. The clothing industry, taking the hundreds of small firms as a group, is the largest both in value added and in number employed. Petroleum refining with six large refineries in Montreal East is very important. Transportation equipment includes railway rolling stock which has been important for over a century. The modern giant in this group is the aircraft industry which of necessity is located outside the old city. There are many metal fabrication plants and chemical product plants. Finally, it must be mentioned that Montreal is the site of the major printing and publishing activities of French Canada and of a considerable volume of English publishing.

Only about 30 per cent of the economic activity of Montreal is based on manufacturing. Transportation, retail trade, financial matters, and a great number of service industries provide the metropolitan area with a highly diversified economy. However, upon analysis it is found that the propelling force appears to come largely from manufacturing, transportation, and service industries (Tables 3.12 and 3.14).

The well-known and easily recognized "city" of Montreal occupies an area of about two square miles between the harbor and the mountain. This must be divided into two areas: a "fringe" in which are clustered activities which like to be close to the business center but not part of it and the Central Business District itself which occupies an area of about 500 acres. The fringe area contains many small manu-

Table 5.12   Manufacturing in Montreal *

Industrial Category	Number of Establishments	Employees number	per cent	Value Added $000	per cent
Foods and Beverages	506	28,328	11.96	322,721	17.75
Tobacco Products	10	5,161	2.18	61,014	3.35
Rubber Products	18	2,124	.90	13,595	.75
Leather Products	171	8,872	3.75	38,396	2.11
Textiles	256	12,226	5.18	63,076	3.47
Knitting Mills	134	6,294	2.66	28,740	1.58
Clothing	1,255	42,178	17.85	194,481	10.70
Wood Products	99	1,976	.83	10,927	.60
Furniture and Fixtures	366	7,582	3.21	40,682	2.25
Paper and its Products	97	7,789	3.30	47,655	2.62
Printing and Publishing	576	15,243	6.45	139,872	7.70
Primary Metals	43	5,358	2.27	31,730	1.75
Metal Fabrication	449	13,284	5.63	162,331	8.92
Machinery	48	4,802	2.04	35,887	1.97
Transportation Equipment	55	26,076	11.03	155,398	8.55
Electrical Products	83	18,004	7.62	128,957	7.10
Non-metallic Mineral Products	116	7,519	3.18	67,407	3.70
Petroleum and Coal Products	13	2,932	1.24	81,509	4.48
Chemical and Chem. Products	249	10,844	4.60	136,091	7.42
Miscellaneous	511	9,650	4.09	58,841	3.23
Total	5,055	236,242	100.00	1,819,310	100.00

* D. B. S. Industry Division, Catalogue No. 31-209, Ottawa, 1964.

Figure 5.44 Montreal
The view of Montreal is that afforded by Mount Royal in June, 1969. The downtown area or CBD is one of tall buildings. Dominating the skyline is Place Ville Marie and the CIL building.

facturing and service industries, schools, hospitals, and McGill University.

The Central Business District has taken shape around two distinct nuclei which may be called the "Financial Core" and the "Commercial Core". The financial core is a compact area of about 30 acres characterized by heavy, old-fashioned buildings, centered on St. James Street. Over 80 per cent of its space is occupied by business offices. Centered on Dominion Square from which Peel Street leads to Ste. Catherine Street is the commercial core containing an area of about 100 acres. It gives the impression of being new, exciting, and expansive. This development dates from the location of several large retailing houses in the early part of the twentieth century. Roughly 30 per cent of the space is currently devoted to retailing, but the building of new skyscrapers is rapidly adding to the available office space. This is the area of Place Ville Marie, the Queen

Elizabeth and other large hotels, Dominion Square and the Cathedral, and both the Canadian National and Canadian Pacific Railway terminals. Insuring the continuance of the focus on this area is the new Montreal "Métro" or subway rapid transit system which gives improved access to this central area. Within a decade this area has experienced a growth of about 71 per cent compared to 12 per cent for the older core. However, it will not be long until expansion brings about the coalescence of the two cores, for new buildings are already being erected in the intervening space. To one who remembers the Montreal of pre-war years the developments are dynamic and startling.

To look into the future of Montreal is to visualize many problems. The trend to suburban industry and suburban living is naturally concomitant with the development of office towers in the Central Business District. While there will be even

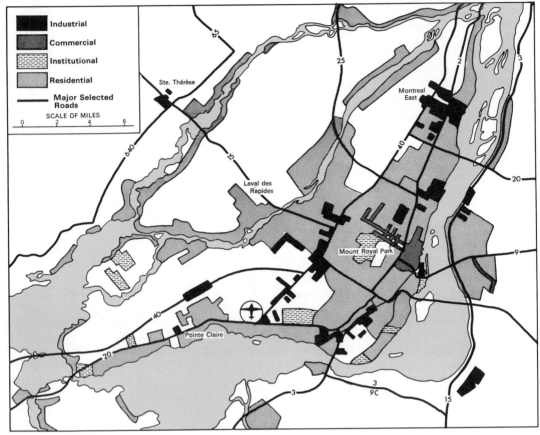

Figure 5.45 Montreal Land Use

more high-rise apartment buildings providing accommodation within the city, many families will continue to move to the periphery, and the development of transportation facilities will become more and more important. Although the "Métro" and the surface bus lines will take care of thousands who live within a radius of about eight miles from the core, the road and street system must continue to provide for at least one-third of all those who move in and out of the central business area, and parking space will be in even shorter supply.

Montreal is a strong city and worthy of its place in the urban world of North America. In spite of the fact that its problems do exist or perhaps because they will inevitably be solved, Montreal will con-

tinue to develop. Its function as the chief "central place" of French Canada is assured, but it should not be forgotten that it is also a Canadian city with a major role to play in the economy of the whole country.

Quebec

Founded by Champlain in 1608 Quebec is older than Montreal. Throughout the years Quebec has retained the eminence of the political capital, yet rather early in its history it lost out to Montreal in terms of population, transportation, and most economic functions. Today with a fairly well-filled metropolitan area of about 135 square miles and a population of 415,000 people greater Quebec is the largest urban complex in Canada, east of Montreal. Its economic influence extends over the eastern part of the province of Quebec and to some extent over parts of the Maritime Provinces as well.

· The old city of Quebec enjoys one of the finest urban sites on the continent. In the Algonquin language its name signifies "where the river narrows". Below this constriction between high banks the river expands rapidly into a great estuary. Its strategic position at this entrance to the interior of the continent earned for Quebec the title of "Gibraltar of North America".

The old city was built on two levels. The upper town is perched on the eastern end of "la colline de Québec", an isolated fragment of the widespread Quebec platform which underlies the St. Lawrence Lowland. The Citadel and the old walled city, protected by steep cliffs, are accessible by steep tortuous streets, ascenseurs, and flights of stairs. On the upper surface are found the Parliament Buildings, government offices, large commercial buildings, the old complex of Laval University, and the older hotels, chief of which is the immense Château Frontenac. The old Lower Town with its narrow streets is crowded between the cliff and the river but has found room for expansion north and west on the flat floor of the valley of the St. Charles. Railway yards, commercial streets, industrial sites, and the homes of industrial workers occupy most of this plain. There are two areas of port facilities: the older one occupies the mouth of the St. Charles River, while the newer wharves have been built in the St. Lawrence below the heights of Battlefield Park. South of the river are the twin cities of Lauzon and Lévis, directly connected with downtown Quebec by a ferry service. Highway linkage by way of the Quebec Bridge lies about ten miles upstream. These long-established and rather well-known features of Quebec City, however, constitute only a small part of the modern metropolis which in 1966 included ten cities, eleven towns, one village, and eight other municipal divisions.

In recent studies the widespread landscape of the metropolitan area has been divided into three zones: central, peripheral, and suburban.*

The central zone consists of the city of Quebec (excluding only the most northerly part), the eastern part of the adjoining city of Sillery and the older, central portion of the city of Lévis. It has many old buildings, historical monuments, churches, parks, and office buildings. It includes the port facilities and many industrial establishments. In addition, within its six square miles of area it houses over 150,000 persons giving the area a density of more than 25,000 per square mile. Recent redevelopment has reduced the total somewhat. There are few single-family houses; about 75 per cent of the population lives in apartments and flats.

The peripheral zone includes the northern part of Quebec City, Beauport, Gifford, Charlesbourg, Vanier, Duberger, Ste. Foy, the western part of Sillery, and Lauzon and Lévis on the south bank. In an area of 30 square miles live approximately 180,000 persons giving the area a density of 6,000 per square mile. Almost half of them live in single-family dwellings, 30 per cent in apartments and 15 per cent in duplexes.

Beyond the peripheral zone to the north, northwest, and southwest lie the suburbs covering an area at least three times as large as the contiguous city but containing a population of about 90,000. The population is very unevenly distributed; there are urban nuclei such as Loretteville, L'Ancienne Lorette, Neufchâtel, and St. Romuald d'Etchemin; but much of the landscape is still rural, and the average population is about 800 per square mile. Housing conditions vary greatly: 63 per cent of the units are single family dwellings, 19 per cent apartments, and 13 per cent duplexes. The airport, various institutions, and other establishments requiring large land areas are found in this zone. Year by year, however, open land is being taken over by subdivisions.

* Louis Trottier. "Transformations récentes de l'agglomération Québecoise: fonctions, population et organisation de l'espace". Cahiers de Géographie de Québec. 13 (October, 1962-March, 1963).

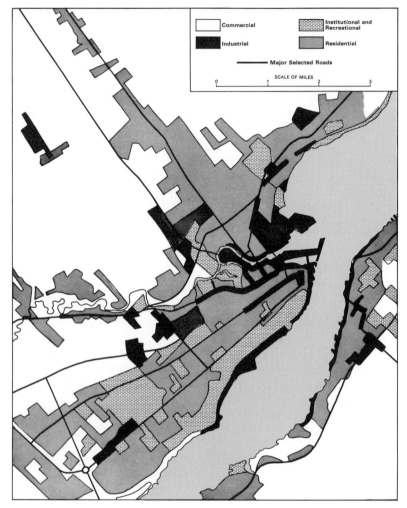

Figure 5.46 Quebec Land Use

Quebec is and always has been a city with dominant tertiary or service functions. According to the census of 1961 only 28 per cent of the labor force was employed in primary and secondary commodity-producing industries (Table 3.12). Quebec has a large number of manufacturing establishments; most of them are small industries engaged in the production of non-durable goods. The largest establishments include pulp and paper mills, textile mills, meat-packing plants, shipyards, and a cement plant. Because Quebec is a provincial capital, the printing and publishing

industries employ a large number of workers. It is useful to compare Quebec and Montreal in terms of their central place functions (Table 5.13). Neither is an outstanding retail center. Montreal is dominant in wholesaling, finance, insurance, and services to business management. Quebec stands out in health and welfare services, religious organizations, national defense, federal government services, and above all provincial administration.

Apart from its function as the provincial capital and the minor roles played by manufacturing and the port function, Que-

Table 5.13   Tertiary Employment in Montreal and Quebec, 1961 *

Category	Province of Quebec number	per cent	Montreal number	per cent	L.Q. **	Quebec number	per cent	L.Q. **
Transportation	107,690	11.7	60,811	13.0	1.11	7,476	8.4	.72
Storage	1,398	0.2	846	0.2	1.00	117	0.1	.50
Communications	34,654	3.8	20,107	4.3	1.13	2,338	2.6	.68
Electric Power, Gas, and Water	17,526	1.9	6,870	1.5	.79	1,045	1.2	.63
Wholesale Trade	69,334	7.5	43,394	9.3	1.24	6,628	7.5	1.00
Retail Trade	178,704	19.4	85,029	18.2	.94	15,173	17.2	.89
Financial Institutions	30,698	3.3	20,067	4.3	1.30	2,261	2.6	.79
Insurance and Real Estate	31,465	3.4	21,917	4.7	1.38	2,866	3.3	.97
Education	79,539	8.6	29,992	6.4	.74	6,486	7.3	.85
Health and Welfare	75,049	8.1	39,007	8.3	1.02	9,223	10.5	1.30
Religious Organizations	23,699	2.6	7,940	1.7	.65	3,958	4.5	1.73
Motion Pictures	9,944	1.1	5,837	1.2	1.09	642	0.7	.64
Services to Bus. Management	25,601	2.8	18,324	3.9	1.39	1,987	2.3	.82
Personal Services	122,704	13.3	56,574	12.1	.91	9,194	10.4	.78
Misc. Services	14,324	1.6	9,276	2.0	1.25	1,229	1.4	.88
National Defense	24,417	2.6	8,582	1.8	.69	4,076	4.6	1.77
Federal Administration	19,545	2.1	7,967	1.7	.81	2,037	2.3	1.10
Provincial Administration	20,971	2.3	5,355	1.1	.48	9,026	10.1	4.39
Local Administration	33,747	3.6	19,692	4.2	1.17	2,663	3.0	.83
Other	514	0.1	454	0.1	1.00	17	0.0	.00
Total	921,523	100.0	468,041	100.0		88,442	100.0	

* Data from Census of Canada. Vol. III, Part 2 — 2. 1961.

** Location Quotient = $\dfrac{\text{Per Cent of City Workers in Category}}{\text{Per Cent of Provincial Workers in Category}}$

bec does not have strong support for economic growth. It is central to a group of counties in which population is either stagnant or declining.* The Quebec metropolitan area itself has more than half the population of the region. It is the center of attraction of a strong tourist movement because of its historical and cultural significance. It is also the gateway to *Les Laurentides* and other hilly areas of the Canadian Shield which offer attractions for vacationers in both summer and winter. Quebec's own Winter Carnival draws thousands to the city. However, the opinion is often expressed that Quebec needs greater development of secondary industry.

* Fernand Grenier. "La région de Québec: peuplement et problèmes de population". *Cahiers de Géographie de Québec*. 13 (October, 1962-March, 1963). pp. 37-56.

Sherbrooke

Sherbrooke, "Queen of the Eastern Townships", is located in the valley of the St. Francis River, about 100 miles east of Montreal. Sherbrooke and the adjoining town of Lennoxville have a combined urban population of about 80,000; thus they form the largest city in the area to the southeast of Montreal. Founded in 1794 at the confluence of the St. Francis and Magog Rivers, Sherbrooke was from the beginning an industrial town based upon the development of waterpower. Today, its chief manufacturing industries produce textiles, knitted goods, clothing, rubber goods, and leather goods, all of which are sold in a fairly wide market; and food products, beverages, and builders' supplies of various kinds, most of which are sold in local outlets. But it is as the chief "central place" in its region that Sherbrooke plays its greatest role. Health and educational services are important. The University of Sherbrooke is the only French language university outside of Montreal and Quebec. There is also Bishop's University giving instruction in the English language located in adjoining Lennoxville. Commerce, finance, and professional services are also important.

The Trois-Rivières Region

The Trois-Rivières region in Central Quebec is a rather large area of the Laurentian Plateau drained by the St. Maurice River. Most of it is forested and very sparsely populated. The economic activities are centered in four cities: Trois-Rivières, Cap de la Madeleine, Shawinigan, and Grand'Mère, located in the lower reaches of the valley and at the confluence of the St. Maurice and St. Lawrence Rivers. These cities and some adjoining suburbs constitute an urban community of about 160,000 people. More than 40 per cent of the labor force is employed in manufacturing, the largest industries being those concerned with pulp and paper, chemicals and chemical products, textiles and clothing, and aluminum smelting and refining. Most of these industries are large users of electric power obtained by harnessing the St. Maurice River. The river also serves to transport pulpwood from the forests of the watershed, while the port at Trois-Rivières facilitates the importation of ores and the shipment of manufactured goods.

The Saguenay Valley

Agricultural settlement in the Saguenay-Lake St. John Lowland began in 1849, an event which was soon followed by exploitation of the surrounding forest, first for lumber and later for pulpwood. Readily available waterpower and the accessibility of the Saguenay to ocean shipping led in the 1920s to the establishment of one of the largest aluminum industries in the world. These industries provide the economic base for an urban complex of more than 100,000 in the contiguous conurba-

tion of Chicoutimi-Jonquière or about 150,000 if two outlying cities, Alma and Port Alfred—Bagotville are included.

Chicoutimi (33,000) is located on the south bank of the Saguenay River at the head of navigation. An early lumbering center and the gateway to pioneer agricultural settlement, it is now the commercial, service, and administrative center of the region. Arvida (15,000) is the site of the great aluminum smelter and refinery. Kenogami (12,000) and Jonquière (30,000) both have large pulp and paper mills and some smaller manufacturing plants. Chicoutimi North (13,000) is a residential suburb across the Saguenay River from the central city of Chicoutimi; it has grown very rapidly. Rivière-du-Moulin (4,500) and St. Jean-Eudes (2,700), although somewhat isolated and semi-rural, must also be considered as parts of the urban complex. Alma (22,000) is a collection of formerly independent nuclei near the outlet of Lake St. John and has important pulp and paper and aluminum plants. Port Alfred—Bagotville, a few miles downstream from Chicoutimi, is located on one of the finest natural harbors in Canada. It has extensive docking facilities which serve the whole industrial complex of the Saguenay. Large amounts of bauxite are unloaded here to be transported to the smelter at Arvida; large amounts of pulp and paper and aluminum ingots are loaded for export. Port Alfred also has a pulp mill, and just outside Bagotville there is a large airport.

Hull and North of the Ottawa

Greater Hull with a population of more than 110,000 in 1966 ranks as the third city of Quebec. However, it may also be considered as part of the Ottawa urban area, more than half of which is located in the province of Ontario. Hull is an older settlement than Ottawa. It was founded by Philemon Wright, an early "timber king", and was an important center of the square timber trade before Ottawa had any settlement. Later it became important for its sawmills, and in this century much of its industrial strength has been based in its pulp and paper mills. Other industries producing meat products, cement, and outdoor clothing are also important.

Facing Ottawa from the north bank, Hull is connected with it by bridges and has offered "close in" sites for the erection of a number of government buildings and laboratories, while its residential areas have become the homes of numerous federal civil servants.

Hull may also be considered as the gateway to the recreation areas of the Gatineau Valley and the western region of the Laurentians famed for both summer and winter activities. Hull is also the chief central place of the Quebec portion of the Ottawa Valley, a diversified area of farms and forests extending for a hundred miles along the Ottawa River.

An Urban Summary

Despite its seeming complexity the pattern of urbanization in Quebec is relatively simple. The two older and larger cities, Quebec and Montreal, had a long headstart over subsequent urban developments. Through its location in closer proximity to the open sea and because of its function as the provincial capital, Quebec has been able to grow even though it is greatly overshadowed by Montreal which has the better location with respect to continental transportation. Modern Montreal is definitely part of the national scene, in fact a part of the world scene, whereas Quebec is simply the capital of the province of the same name and a noted historic site.

The province of Quebec has a few middle-sized cities and a considerable number of small ones. They have some significance as regional and subregional central places. Most of them, however, are resource oriented, water sites having much to do with their locations and functions.

REGIONAL ENTITIES IN QUEBEC

Quebec is not a very uniform region. Once the curtain of its French culture has been penetrated, Quebec is found to have as much diversity as might be expected in any large area. Its physical pattern has

already been discussed and it has been noted that geology, landform, and climate have marked out a rather limited area in which conditions were favorable for dense human settlement. This does not mean that the resources of other areas are beyond economic utilization. Far from it, for the industrial strength of Quebec has up to now been based largely upon the development of the forests, mines, and waterpower of the empty or only sparsely inhabited regions.

Attempts have been made in the past to describe a system of city-centered regions for Quebec. It functions very well for the area in which large cities occur. It may be demonstrated that there is a Montreal Region, a Quebec Region, and to a somewhat lesser degree a Trois-Rivières Region, a Sherbrooke Region, and a Hull or Ottawa Region. Perhaps, to stretch a point, there is also a Chicoutimi Region; it is based not on the pull of a single city but on the economic power of a group of great industries within a limited geographical area. But any formal scheme of recognizable city-centered regions stops there, hampered by the lack of cities in over 90 per cent of Quebec's provincial domain. There are, of course, some inhabited areas beyond the range of any city-centered region, but the plain fact is that there, as in so much of Canada, the regional personality is based primarily upon the sparseness of human population.

Some of the areas which possess considerable regional identity may be mentioned briefly.

The Laurentian Upland, that massive plateau which presents such a solid front against both agricultural and urban settlement, has an impressive personality compounded of rocks, lakes, and forests. Yet there is a strong tendency to think of it in four parts: "les Laurentides de Québec", "la Maurice", "les Laurentides Montréalaises", and the Gatineau Valley. Two of these subregions emphasize the relationship with the cities from which most of their visitors come, while the other two are focused on the great rivers which have in large part given them their industrial strength. How far north one might extend the boundaries of the Laurentians or the Laurentian Upland is a moot point. Traditionally it has been the height of land or the water divide between the drainage of the St. Lawrence Basin and that of Hudson Bay.

Beyond the Laurentians lie the mining areas and the agricultural settlements of Western Quebec. The mines of the Greenstone Area have for half a century produced the gold and base metals that were the symbols of Quebec's mineral wealth. Now they are overshadowed by the iron mines of New Quebec. The farms of the Clay Belt were to have become another base of habitant culture like that of the St. Lawrence Lowland but have become instead a problem area of marginal agriculture and social disadvantage.

Older areas of disadvantage also exist. The south shore of the St. Lawrence Estuary and the Gaspé coast were always recognized as marginal for agriculture but they were settled in the hope that the other resources of the area, fish and timber, would help to support an economy. Also, an even more disadvantaged area of settlement is strung along the north shore although no possibilities for a viable agriculture have ever existed. Thus the problem area of what might be called Quebec Gulf Shore extends for a weary length of nearly 1,000 miles broken only by a few settlements which have an aura of prosperity.

Quebec also has an Arctic coast stretching from the southern end of James Bay to Cape Chidley at the entrance of Hudson Strait. Here again is a disadvantaged area, but the population of the area is not French Canadian but is mostly Eskimo in the north and Indian in the south.

The great resource frontier of New Quebec must be mentioned as well. The Plateau of the Lakes of Ungava or New Quebec is shared with Newfoundland's Labrador through the award of the Privy Council in 1927. Here in less than two decades has arisen a mining region which provides three-fourths of all the iron ore produced in Canada. The average annual production in recent years has been about 30,000,000 tons, about half from Quebec and half from Newfoundland. However, it is all shipped through the Quebec North Shore ports of Sept Iles, Pointe Noire, and Port Cartier, making these new port settlements functioning members of the Northeastern Frontier Mining Region.

Finally there is the vast interior in which no mines or towns exist and in which there are hardly any people at all. This is just as distinctive a region as any of the others, and it covers at least half the area of the province.

Of what use are regions in the study of the geography of Quebec? Do they exist? One can only answer that "la région Saguenay—Lac St-Jean" or "la région Québecoise" or "la région Montréalaise" and some of the others certainly have meaning and existence for a number of people. There are several regions in Quebec as in other provinces that are ill-defined or defined arbitrarily as groups of counties but which bring to mind no definite regional personality and hence no areal reality. However, they are useful insofar as they may serve to focus attention on the problems to be studied.

BIBLIOGRAPHY

Bailey, P. J. M. "The Geography of Settlement in Stanstead Township, Province of Quebec". *Geography*. XLI, 1 (January, 1956). pp. 39-48.

Beauregard, L. "Population nocturne et diurne à Montréal". *Revue Géographie de Montréal*. XVIII, 2 (1964). pp. 292-293.

Biays, Pierre. "Problèmes de l'agriculture marginale dans la zone pionnière de L'Est du Canada". *Cahiers de Géographie de Québec*. 16 (April-September, 1964). pp. 219-230.

———. "The Agricultural Ecumene of Lake St. John". *Cahiers de Géographie de Québec*. 13

(October, 1962-March, 1963). pp. 101-110.

———. "Les marges de l'oekoumène dans L'Est du Canada". *Les Presses de L'Université Laval.* Quebec, 1964. 760 pp. + maps.

Blanchard, Raoul. "Le Canada Français". *Artheme Fayard.* Paris. 1960.

Brière, R. "Les cadres d'une géographie touristique du Québec". *Cahiers de Géographie de Québec.* 11 (October, 1961-March, 1962). pp. 29-64.

Brouillette, B. "Le port de Montréal, hier et aujourd'hui". *Revue de Géographie de Montréal.* XXI, 2 (1967). pp. 195-223.

———. "Les régions géographiques et economiques de la provence de Québec" *Cahiers de Géographie de Québec.* 6 (April-September, 1959). pp. 65-83.

Bussières, B. and Trottier, L. "Une carte de l'utilisation du sol de Rimouski". *Cahiers de Géographie de Québec.* 19 (October, 1965-March, 1966). pp. 122-128.

Camu, Pierre. "Types de maisons dans la région suburbaine de Montréal". *Canadian Geographer,* 9 (1957).

Cazalais, P. "Le Saint-Laurent: facteur de localisation industrielle". *Cahiers de Géographie de Québec.* 23 (April-September, 1967). pp. 327-342.

———. "Sherbrooke: sa place dans la vie de relations des Cantons de l'Est". *Cahiers de Géographie de Québec.* 16 (April-September, 1964). pp. 165-198.

Charbonneau, H. and Légaré, J. "L'extrême mobilité de la population urbaine au Canada: L'exemple de Montréal entre 1956 et 1961". *Revue de Géographie de Montréal.* XXI, 2 (1967). pp. 234-265.

Clibbon, P. B. "Changing Land Use in Terrebonne County". *Cahiers de Géographie de Québec.* 15 (October, 1963-March, 1964). pp. 5-40.

Clibbon, P. B. and Gagnon, J. "L'évolution récente de l'utilisation du sol sur la rive nord du Saint-Laurent entre Québec et Montréal". *Cahiers de Géographie de Québec.* 19 (October, 1965-March, 1966). pp. 55-72.

Dagenais, P. "Le mythe de la vocation agricole du Québec". *Cahiers de Géographie de Québec.* 6 (April-September, 1959). pp. 193-201.

Denis, P. Y. "Conditions géographiques et postulants démographiques d'une rénovation urbaine à Montréal". *Revue de Géographie de Montréal.* XXI, 1 (1967). pp. 149-164.

Grenier, F. "La région de Québec: peuplement et problèmes de population". *Cahier de Géographie de Québec.* 13 (October, 1962-March, 1963). pp. 37-56.

Hamelin, L. E., Cayouette, G. and DeKoninck, R. "Un indice de primatie appliqué à la concurrence entre Montréal et Toronto". *Revue de Géographie de Montréal.* XXI, 2 (1967). pp. 389-396.

Hare, F. K. "The Boreal Forest in Eastern Canada". *Geographical Review.* XL, 4 (October, 1950). pp. 615-635.

———. "The Labrador Frontier". *Geographical Review.* XLII, 3 (July, 1952). pp. 405-424.

———. "New Light from Labrador-Ungava". *Annals, Association of American Geographers.* Vol. 54, 4 (December, 1964). pp. 459-476.

Harris, R. C. *The Seigneurial System in Early Canada: A Geographical Study.* University of Wisconsin Press. 1966.

Innes, F. C. "Concepts in Urban Geography in Relation to the Local Milieu — Montreal". *Revue de Géographie de Montréal.* XXI, 1 (1967). pp. 165-168.

Langois, C. "Problems of Urban Growth in Greater Montreal". *Canadian Geographer.* V, 1 (1961). pp. 1-11.

Lundgren, J. O. "Tourism in Quebec". *Revue de Géographie de Montréal.* XX, 1 (1966). pp. 59-74.

Pépin, P. Y. "Principaux traits socioéconomiques de la région Saguenay—Lac St-Jean". *Cahiers de Géographie de Québec.* 13 (October, 1962-March, 1963). pp. 57-80.

Racine, J. B. "Exurbanisation et metamorphisme peri-urbain: introduction à l'étude de la croissance du Grand-Montréal". *Revue de Géographie de Montréal.* XXI, 2 (1967). pp. 313-341.

Racine, J. B. "La croissance du Grand-Montréal au sud du Saint-Laurent: le cas de St-Bruno de Montarville". *Revue de Géographie de Montréal.* XXI, 1 (1967). 111-148.

Ross, W. G. "Encroachment of the Jeffrey Mine on the Town of Asbestos, Quebec". *Geographical Review.* LVII, 4 (October, 1967). pp. 523-537.

Scarlett, M. J. "Milk Market of Montreal". *Revue de Géographie de Montréal.* XXI, 2 (1967). pp. 343-360.

Trottier, L. "Les sites industriels dans l'agglomération Québecoise". *Cahiers de Géographie de Québec.* 10 (April-September, 1961). pp. 245-356.

Ontario

6 One of every three Canadians is a resident of Ontario. In 1968 the population of the province was estimated to be 7,200,000, an increase of almost 17 per cent since the census of 1961. Even more significant has been the process of urbanization. During the fifteen-year period from 1951 to 1966, the total population of Ontario increased by 51 per cent. Practically all of this was added to towns and cities for the rural population increased by a meagre 1.5 per cent in the same period. By 1966 more than 80 per cent of the people of Ontario were urban residents.

The economic strength of Ontario is outstanding. Its industries account for more than 40 per cent of the value of all the commodities produced in Canada. Ontario also has one-third of Canada's employment in tertiary or service industries. It is the leading province in manufacturing, being responsible for 52.8 per cent of value added annually by manufacturing processes. Agriculture is surprisingly strong; during the three-year period, 1965-7 inclusive, the annual farm net income averaged about $400,000,000, a provincial record exceeded only by that of Saskatchewan. Mineral production in 1967 was in excess of $1,150,000,000, accounting for 27 per cent of the Canadian total. Power supplies are important in an industrial society, and Ontario has more than one-third of the Canadian generating capacity.

This apparent well-being poses certain questions for geographical analysis. First, what aspects of the physical resource base have encouraged economic growth to this degree? Is it simply that Ontario possesses the best of everything, or are the developmental factors more complex? Second, is this economic strength well distributed, or is it concentrated in specific areas? If regional disparities in economic growth are present, how great are they, how are they distributed, and why do they occur?

Of geographical importance also is the variety of regional landscapes occurring in Ontario. As in Quebec, there is a well-defined urban-industrial core in the south, surrounded by relatively prosperous agricultural environs. Much of the north is occupied by the Canadian Shield which serves as a major source of primary materials. However, there are some differences from the situation in Quebec. The agricultural areas are more extensive and more prosperous, and development is not so completely centered in one vast urban area, but rather in a series of urban cores. In the east there is the Ottawa node, which is somewhat isolated from the rest of Southern Ontario by the Frontenac Axis. The Mississaga complex is the core of Central Ontario, while to the west are the London, Windsor, and Sarnia nodes. Southern Ontario is effectively tied together by "Mainstreet Ontario", Highway 401, permitting rapid communication between the urban core areas. The Canadian Shield, despite its isolation from the main forces of urbanization, is tied to the south by economic policies generated in the core. Mining developments in Timmins, Sudbury, and Wawa, forest-processing industries in Sault Ste. Marie, Terrace Bay, Dryden, and Iroquois Falls, all operate in conjunction with the economic demands of governmental policies emanating from the southern core. Despite the regional disparities, economic ties are such that Ontario functions to a great degree as an economic and regional unit in Canada.

PHYSICAL RESOURCE BASE

The boundaries of Ontario enclose an area of 412,582 square miles or 10.7 per cent of the surface of Canada. Fresh water is abundant: lakes occupy more than 68,000 square miles, and there are numerous rivers. The vast size of Ontario may be appreciated by considering that its greatest extent, both from north to south and from east to west, is approximately 1,000 miles.

Ontario is often considered to be two regions, separated by a line drawn along the Mattawa River, Lake Nipissing, and French River. To the south lies Southern Ontario where agriculture, manufacturing, and urban activities are concentrated; to the north lies Northern Ontario, a vast area comprising 88 per cent of the province. Only sparsely settled, the latter reflects a very different milieu where economic development is sustained by primary industries such as forestry and mining. While this division is valid, it is only a generalization for there are large areas south of the line which are also sparsely settled.

Geology, physiography, climate, natural vegetation, and soils all combine to produce a series of environments in Ontario. As the matrix of factors varies from area to area, it should be examined carefully before regional analysis is attempted.

The Land

As shown by Figure 6.1, the Precambrian rocks of the Canadian Shield occupy more than two-thirds of the area of Ontario. The Hudson Bay Lowland on the southwest shores of James Bay and Hudson Bay consists of low-lying Paleozoic sedimentary rocks. To the south of the

Shield, the Great Lakes—St. Lawrence Lowland is floored by Paleozoic rocks which are likewise of sedimentary origin.

The ancient crystalline rocks of the *Canadian Shield* have been peneplaned and relief rarely exceeds 1,000 feet, with the exception of the Superior Highlands, north of Sault Ste. Marie, where elevations approach 2,200 feet above sea level. Highlands also occur in Algonquin Park and in the vicinity of Thunder Bay where Thunder Cape has an elevation of 1,850 feet. Fault lines are prevalent along the flanks of the Ottawa-Bonnechère graben in Renfrew county where the Mount St. Patrick Scarp has a local relief of more than 1,000 feet. A similar downfaulted graben structure may exist in the Lake Timiskaming Basin where an outlier of Paleozoic rocks is preserved. Faulting is also found near the western end of Lake Superior. Areas in the Canadian Shield which contain volcanic and intrusive rocks are of extreme significance to the mining industry for within these areas are located the gold, silver, nickel, copper, and iron deposits which are part of the mineral heritage of Ontario. Basic volcanic rocks of the Keewatin series (Greenstone layer) are important hosts for the gold and base metal deposits of the Clay Belt area. Ultra-basic rocks of intrusive origin in the Matheson area contain asbestos, while the gold deposits of Porcupine and Kirkland Lake are associated with acid intrusives which have cut into the Timiskaming series of sedimentary rocks.

The complex nature of the geology of the Canadian Shield and the intricate interrelationships which exist between geology and mining can best be illustrated in the

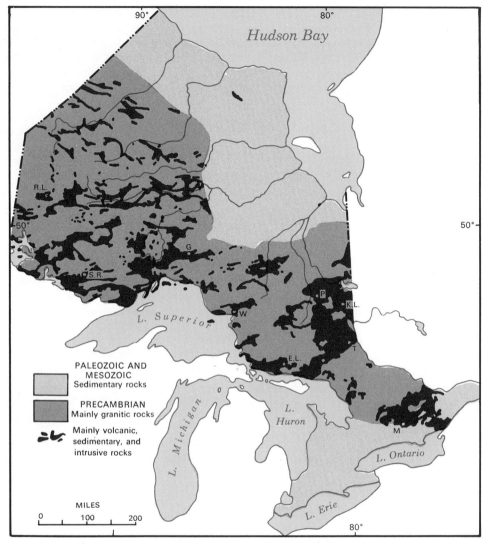

Figure 6.1 Geological Map of Ontario
Precambrian rocks occupy more than two-thirds of Ontario. Within the Precambrian division,
the volcanic, sedimentary, and intrusive areas are shown. It is within these areas that most
of the mineral finds are located.

E.L.	Elliot Lake	P	Porcupine	T	Timagami
G	Geraldton	R.L.	Red Lake	W	Wawa
K.L.	Kirkland Lake	S	Sudbury		
M	Marmora	S.R.	Steep Rock		

Sudbury Basin (Figure 6.2). The nickel-copper sulphide ore bodies are closely associated in age and location with the Norite layer, an irruptive rock of Keweenewan age. The nickel irruptive is an elongate, basin-shaped feature some 37 miles long and 17 miles wide. The width of the out-crop varies from 1.0 to 3.5 miles. Nickel-copper sulphide ore bodies are found along the outwall contact of the Norite layer in mineralized shear zones or in mineralized embayments of quartz diorite. Creighton, Falconbridge, Levack, Murray, and Garson mines are located in these contact deposits.

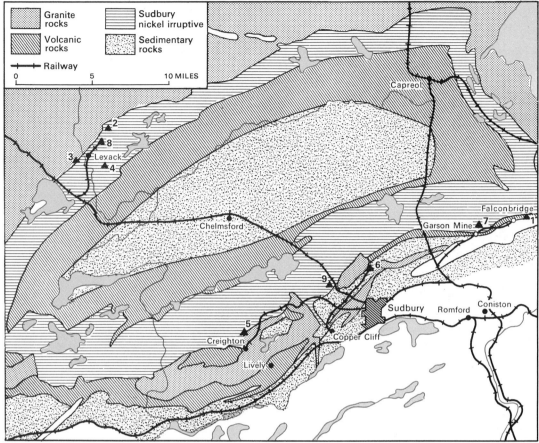

AFTER ONTARIO DEPT. OF MINES, G.C. 13

Figure 6.2 Geology of the Sudbury Basin
The Sudbury nickel irruptive goes around the perimeter of the Sudbury Basin. Levack, Creighton, Garson Mine, Falconbridge, and the area north of Sudbury are all major mining sites.

Falconbridge Nickel Mines Ltd.
1. Falconbridge mine.
2. Fecunis Lake mine.
3. Hardy mine.
4. Onaping mine.

The International Nickel Co. of Canada Ltd.
5. Creighton mine.
6. Frood-Stobie mine.
7. Garson mine.
8. Levack mine.
9. Murray mine.

Both Creighton and Falconbridge mines have been developed to depths greater than 6,500 feet. Ore bodies are also found in quartz-diorite offshoots, and mines utilizing this type of deposit include Frood-Stobie and Copper Cliff. As shown by Figure 6.2, the placing of the mines follows the outcropping of the nickel irruptive, and the city of Sudbury has no mines within its corporate limits.

Although the Canadian Shield in Ontario is generally considered to be an area of comparatively low relief, it is sufficiently rugged, locally, to make overland travel difficult. While such areas as Muskoka, Kenora, and Algonquin Park exhibit landforms due to glacial scour, these are only isolated instances. In reality, landforms resulting from glacial deposition are usually dominant. The extensive lacustrine plain created by glacial Lake Barlow-Ojibway dominates the Timmins-Cochrane region, while in the northwest extensive lacustrine deposits from Dryden west are

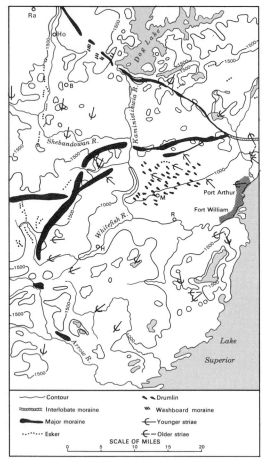

AFTER ZOLTAI

Figure 6.3 Glacial Features of the Lakehead Area

B Buda	Ho Horne	R Rosslyn
H Hymer	M Murillo	Ra Raith

believed to have originated in glacial Lake Agassiz. Analysis of all the landforms in the Shield has not been completed, but the results of some research in the area from Lake of the Woods to Terrace Bay have been published.* As shown by Figure 6.3,

* S. C. Zoltai. "Glacial History of Part of Northwestern Ontario". *Proceedings of Geological Association of Canada*. XIII (1961). pp. 61-83.
———. "Glacial Features of the Canadian Lakehead Area". *Canadian Geographer*. VII, 3 (1963). pp. 101-115.
———. "Glacial Features of the Quetico-Nipigon Area, Ontario". *Canadian Journal of Earth Sciences*. II (1965). pp. 247-269.
———. "Glacial Features of the North-central Lake Superior Region, Ontario". *Canadian Journal of Earth Sciences*. IV (1967). pp. 515-528.

a variety of glacial features including ground moraine, drumlins, eskers, kames, and outwash occurs in the Thunder Bay area. The deposits vary greatly in depth, but in some areas a till cover of nearly 250 feet was observed. Much of the till has a very coarse texture, while in the vicinity of Murillo drumlins composed of a stony, silty, sand till are found. These drumlins are long and narrow and rarely exceed 30 feet in height. Thus, in the Thunder Bay area certain lands have sufficient soil cover to make agricultural settlement possible. Similar traits have been noted in the Clay Belt area of Northeastern Ontario where a study by Dean indicates that there are extensive areas of drumlinoid features, numerous eskers, and old shorelines in the area between Hearst and Cochrane.*

As a result of the bedrock and surficial geology, the drainage pattern on the Canadian Shield is rather aimless, and numerous small lakes are present. In areas where relief is flat, as in lacustrine plains, drainage is frequently very poor. In the Clay Belt normal podzolic soils are found in well-drained areas, but most soils are severely affected by poor drainage and are frequently covered with peat. As shown by Figure 6.4, the most fertile lands lie close to the major streams where drainage is best and the thickness of the peat is least. Other areas which appear to be good for agriculture are the fringes of the sandy hillocks where the coarse nature of the soil makes for improved drainage. The biggest

* W. G. Dean. "Glacial Features of the Hearst-Cochrane Map Sheet Area". *Canadian Geographer*. 8 (1956). pp. 35-45.

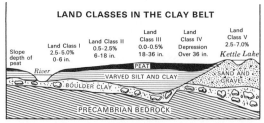

AFTER HILLS

Figure 6.4 Physical Land Classes in the Clay Belt

drawback, however, is the discontinuity of the land suitable for agriculture. These sections are often small and scattered in such a way that effective utilization is almost impossible.

The *Hudson Bay Lowland* is an area of low relief. Drainage is poor and permafrost lenses are present.* The area has not been as completely surveyed as other areas in the Ontario northland. The mineral potential has not been fully explored although deposits of gypsum of high purity are known to exist. During the summer of 1968 preliminary soil surveys were made along certain river valleys, and some of the prominent physiographic features appear to be raised beaches marking previous levels of Hudson Bay. This area can be considered to have a low potential for most land uses.

---

* R. J. E. Brown. *Permafrost Investigations in Northern Ontario and Northeastern Manitoba.* Technical Paper No. 291. Division of Building Research. National Research Council of Canada. Ottawa. November, 1968.

The *Great Lakes—St. Lawrence Lowland* is underlain by Paleozoic limestones, shales, and sandstones. It is separated into two portions by a southward extension of the Shield in the form of a Precambrian arch known as the Frontenac Axis. To the northeast the Ottawa Valley portion is occupied by Cambrian sandstones and Ordovician limestones and shales. Some of this limestone is soluble and karstic features occur in the Ottawa Valley near Renfrew.* Minerals are not abundant, the most important being the Black River—Trenton limestones which are quarried in the Ottawa and Cornwall areas as a source of crushed stone and concrete aggregate.

Southwest of the Frontenac Axis there is an extensive area of Paleozoic rocks. As shown by Figure 6.5, there are numerous strata which outcrop at the surface. The southern flank of the Frontenac Axis is

---

* D. C. Ford. "The Bonnechère Caves, Renfrew Ontario: A Note". *Canadian Geographer.* V, 3 (1961). pp. 22-25.

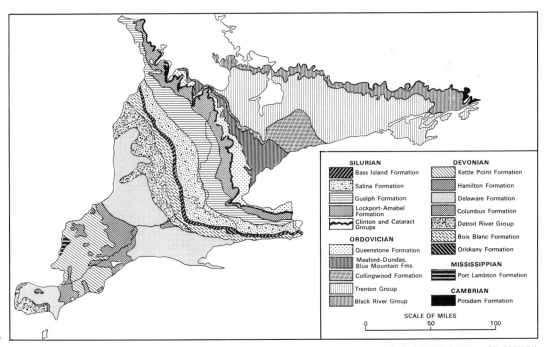

AFTER GEOLOGICAL SURVEY OF CANADA

Figure 6.5 Regional Geology of Southwestern Ontario

covered by Black River—Trenton limestones which have been quarried extensively; the stone is used in cement manufacture and as a flux in metallurgical industries. Crushed stone is used as road metal and as concrete aggregate in many types of construction. West of these there is a series of Ordovician shales: Collingwood, Meaford-Dundas, and Queenston. In the Toronto area the Dundas and Queenston shales are used for the manufacture of brick and tile. The Silurian rocks occupy a wide band stretching from Niagara Falls and Fort Erie north to the Bruce Peninsula and Manitoulin Island. The Niagara Escarpment marks their eastern limit. It is the steep face of a cuesta and is one of the most prominent landforms in Southern Ontario. It is capped by

resistant dolomitic limestones of the Guelph-Lockport series and underlain by softer shales and sandstones. As the strata dip gently toward the west, the scarp faces toward the east, overlooking Georgian Bay and the Lake Ontario plain. The cuesta is the result of differential erosion. The Medina sandstone of the lower part of the Niagara Escarpment is quarried for building stone and was used in the construction of the old Toronto City Hall and in the main edifice of the Ontario Parliament Buildings. The Guelph-Lockport dolomites are quarried extensively for use as crushed stone and as flux in the steel mills at Hamilton.

West of the Guelph dolomite the Salina dolomite and shale formation contains commercially important deposits of gypsum

Figure 6.6 The Niagara Escarpment
The natural beauty of this landform is steadily being defaced by man's activities. Stone quarried here near Milton is crushed and trucked as far as Metropolitan Toronto.

R. PUTNAM

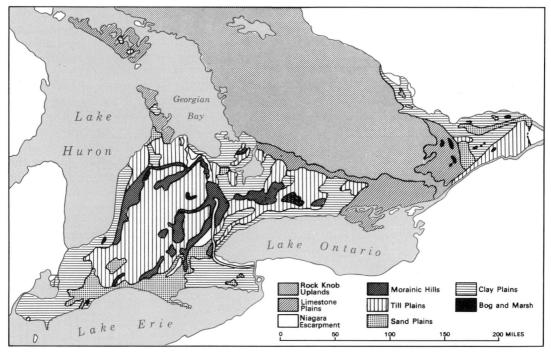

Figure 6.7 Physiography of Southern Ontario

Legend:
- Rock Knob Uplands
- Limestone Plains
- Niagara Escarpment
- Morainic Hills
- Till Plains
- Sand Plains
- Clay Plains
- Bog and Marsh

0   50   100   150   200 MILES

and salt. The former is quarried near Hagersville, while the latter is mined near Windsor and Goderich. Devonian rocks occupy most of Southwestern Ontario, overlying the Silurian formations. Here again limestones are quarried for construction purposes. The Devonian rocks of Southwestern Ontario also yield small quantities of petroleum and natural gas.

The pattern of landforms in Southern Ontario is a complex mosaic of surface features, only partially controlled by the nature of the bedrock. Surface formations are largely the consequences of Pleistocene glaciation and the former high water levels of the basin of the Great Lakes. Moraines, drumlins, and till, sand, clay, and limestone plains combine to produce the varied pattern shown in Figure 6.7. This area has been the subject of much research for many years and a fairly complete summary of its physiography is available.*

Agriculture in Ontario is concentrated in this region, but obviously it operates under greatly varied conditions. Matthews lists ten major land use hazards which severely limit the use of the agricultural land resources of Southern Ontario.* The extensive distribution of these hazards is shown in Figure 6.8 and should be compared with the map of physiographic regions.

The limestone plains occupy both flanks of the Frontenac Axis and also occur in areas adjacent to the Niagara Escarpment north of Hamilton, in the Bruce Peninsula, and on Manitoulin Island. Glacial scour removed much of the regolith, and the remaining materials are excessively stony and very shallow. Fields in Flamborough Township north of Hamilton have less than three inches of soil before limestone bedrock is reached. Because of these characteristics, the limestone plains are of limited value for agriculture.

* L. J. Chapman and D. F. Putnam. *The Physiography of Southern Ontario.* University of Toronto Press. 2nd edition. Toronto. 1966.

* B. C. Matthews. "Soil Resources and Land Use Hazards in Southern Ontario". *Canadian Geographer.* 8 (1956). pp. 55-62.

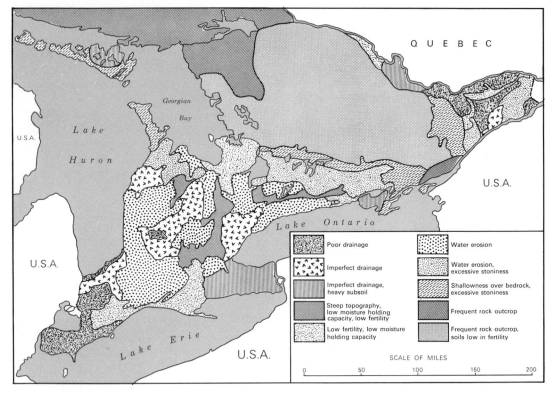

Figure 6.8 Major Land Use Hazards in Southern Ontario
Areas having steep topography as a land use hazard occur primarily in the moraine landscapes of Southern Ontario. The Canadian Shield and flanks of the Frontenac Axis suffer from shallow soils and frequent rock outcrops.

Clay plains result from the deposition of finely divided rock material in fairly deep water in either lakes or seas. The chief areas of lacustrine clay are in the Kent-Essex plain near Windsor, the Haldimand plain in the Niagara Peninsula, the Georgian Bay—Lake Simcoe region, and the northern shore of Lake Ontario. Clay plains in the Ottawa Valley are thought to be of marine origin. While the soils in the clay plains are as rich as any in Southern Ontario, they often suffer the disadvantage of poor drainage. However, tiles and drainage ditches can overcome this problem.

The sand plains are also of marine or lacustrine origin. In Southwestern Ontario the Kent and Cardoc sand plains were deposited in the deltas of the Thames River, and the Norfolk sand plain resulted from

the delta of the Grand River. There are also limited sand plains resulting from the shorelines of old glacial lakes. In Eastern Ontario the Petawawa and Plantagenet sand plains were deltas of the ancient Ottawa River, built into the Champlain Sea. In many cases the sand plains suffer from low fertility levels. The sterile sands are often excessively droughty, and the only crops which can be grown successfully are those which require an easily tilled soil and yield a sufficiently high cash return per acre to sustain the costs of commercial fertilizers and supplemental irrigation. More than 12 per cent of the area of Southern Ontario has deltaic sands of this sort.

Till plains make up about 40 per cent of the land surface of Southern Ontario. Till plains may be fairly smooth, but frequently they have been considerably modified. In some places deep valleys were cut by glacial melt-water streams; other places exhibit the results of strong bevelling by the waves of temporary lakes. Most striking of all, however, are the concentrations of oval "whaleback hills" or drumlins (Figure 6.9). The largest drumlin field in Southern Ontario is found in the vicinity of Peterborough and Rice Lake. Drumlin fields pose problems for agriculture. Drainage is usually poor in the inter-drumlin areas, while the drumlin slopes are susceptible to soil erosion and present difficulties in the operation of farm implements.

Moraines often impose fairly severe limitations on land use. The chief moraine systems, as shown in Figure 6.10, are the Dummer Moraine, the Oak Ridges Moraine, and the Horseshoe Moraines. While each of these three systems evolved in response to rather different glacial processes, the effects on land use potential have been remarkably similar. In each in-

stance, uneven slopes, susceptibility to erosion, excessive stoniness, and low fertility have combined to give the morainic areas an exceedingly limited usefulness for agriculture.

The Niagara Escarpment, already mentioned, is likewise of limited potential for agriculture. However, the till-mantled scarp face presents very challenging slopes which attract thousands of skiing enthusiasts every winter. The Escarpment has had an important influence on the pattern of transportation routes in Ontario as it forms a barrier which may be overcome easily in only a few selected places.

From this analysis it is apparent that land conditions in the Great Lakes—St. Lawrence Lowland are far from ideal. At present only 8,000,000 acres or about 25 per cent of Southern Ontario is used as crop land, and according to Matthews it is possible to add only about 2,000,000 acres to this area. Thus the crop land potential is less than 30 per cent of the total land area. In terms of mineral wealth also, the Low-

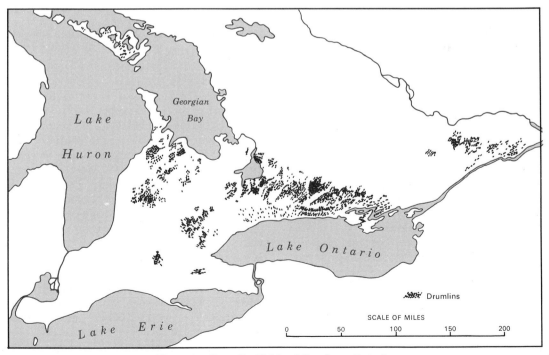

Figure 6.9 Drumlin Fields of Southern Ontario

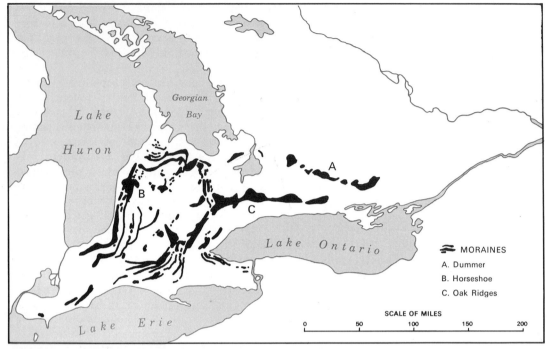

Figure 6.10 Moraine Systems of Southern Ontario

land has a rather limited potential, while the Shield is endowed with numerous rich deposits.

Climate

Ontario has a wide range of climates. Conditions are most favorable in Southwestern Ontario, but a bitter subarctic climate prevails along the shore of Hudson Bay. Directly in the path of the westerly winds, Ontario is particularly stormy in winter. Differences in relief, though not great, are significant. In the south two important upland regions, the Grey County hills and the Algonquin Park area, and in the north the Superior Highlands have a definite influence on temperature and precipitation. The waters of the Great Lakes to the south and west and Hudson Bay and James Bay to the north all influence the climate profoundly.

In thermal terms the basic differences are illustrated by the January and July isotherm patterns (Figures 6.11 and 6.12).

Winter temperatures are highest along the Great Lakes in Southwestern Ontario and below the Niagara Escarpment in the Niagara Peninsula. Even in Northern Ontario the Great Lakes act as a modifying influence during the winter months, and it is not until the 49th parallel is reached that the monthly mean decreases to 0°F. Unlike Lakes Superior and Huron, Hudson Bay freezes over and serves only to make the winter temperatures more extreme in the far north.

In July the area between Chatham and Windsor is the warmest, while most of Southern Ontario is uniformly warm. The Grey County hills and the Algonquin area are both conspicuously colder, as are the Superior Highlands in the north. Were it not for the cooling effect of Lake Superior, the July temperature over Northern Ontario would be remarkably uniform, varying only from 62° to 66°F. However, the overall temperature gradient from north to south is still much less in summer than during the winter months.

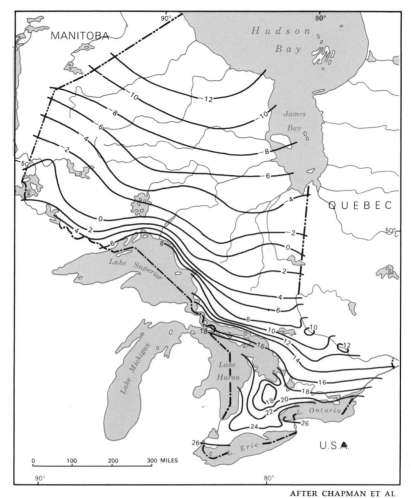

AFTER CHAPMAN ET AL

Figure 6.11 Mean Daily Temperatures (°F) for January
January is bitterly cold in Northern Ontario but moderates to the south.
The temperature gradient from north to south is 38°F.

Table 6.1   Critical Thermal Parameters *

Daily Maximum Temperature	below	32°F — no plant growth
Daily Maximum Temperature	below	50°F — corn growth unlikely
Daily Maximum Temperature	at	86°F — optimum corn growth
Daily Minimum Temperature	below	32°F — tender plants freeze
Daily Minimum Temperature	below	−12°F — peach bud survival unlikely
Daily Minimum Temperature	below	−21°F — peach trees are killed

* After L. J. Chapman and D. B. Brown. "Climates of Southern Ontario".

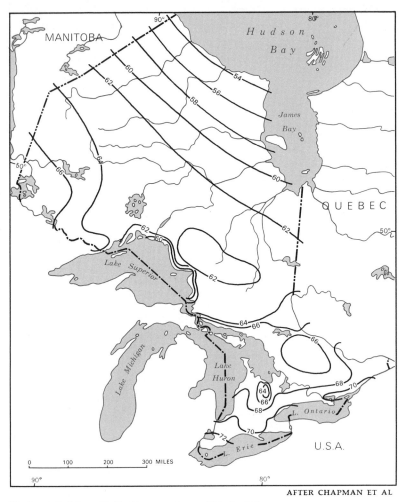

Figure 6.12 Mean Daily Temperatures (°F) for July

AFTER CHAPMAN ET AL

As was discussed in CHAPTER 2, monthly mean temperatures are not sufficiently precise criteria for determining the needs for various crops. While certain general critical values are shown in Table 6.1, the most precise thermal parameters involve both the degree-days above 42°F and Corn Heat Units. The variation of mean annual accumulation of growing degree-days is shown in Figure 6.13. The basic pattern is closely allied with that shown by the isotherms, with the highest values being found over southwestern Ontario and the lowest in the far north, near Hudson Bay. The 4,000 D-D line serves nicely as the northern boundary of the area

where specialized crops such as grain corn, soy beans, sugar beets, and other cash crops are concentrated in southwestern Ontario. Between the 3,000 and 4,000 D-D lines most of the areas of agricultural significance occur. In the north the Clay Belt area generally has more than 2,700 D-D, while the north shore of Lake Superior is distinctly colder than either the Clay Belt or the Kenora areas. As shown previously in CHAPTER 2, the distribution for Corn Heat Units closely parallels that of degree-days, with values below 2,100 C.H.U. being normal for Algonquin Park and areas north of North Bay and Sault Ste. Marie. To the south the 2,900 C.H.U. line

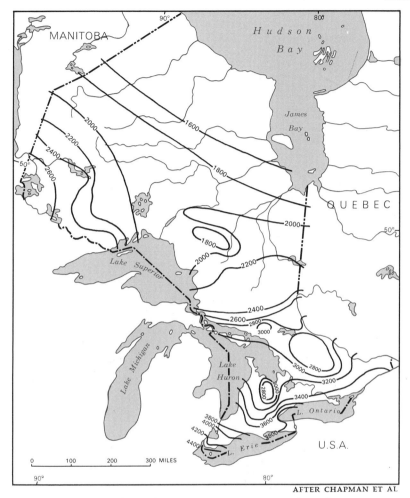

Figure 6.13 Mean Annual Number of Growing Degree-days above 42°F

AFTER CHAPMAN ET AL

stretches from Belleville along the Lake Ontario shore and west to London and Goderich. Most shelled corn is grown south of the 2,900 C.H.U. line, while *some* corn is grown for grain in areas having C.H.U. values as low as 2,500.

However, for tender tree fruit crops such as peaches, winter temperatures are just as critical as those of spring and summer. In a study by Mercier and Chapman, the peach climate of Southern Ontario was determined using the occurrence of the two critical temperatures −12°F and −20°F.*

* R. G. Mercier and L. J. Chapman. "Peach Climate in Ontario". *1955-56 Report. Horticultural Experiment Station and Products Laboratory.* Vineland, Ontario.

Figure 6.14 Winter Damage to Peach Trees

COURTESY HORTICULTURAL RESEARCH INSTITUTE OF ONTARIO

Climatically, only two areas in Ontario have a sufficiently low probability of bud damage to make peaches commercially feasible, namely, the area below the Niagara Escarpment in the Niagara Peninsula, and that in the extreme southwestern part of Ontario. Elsewhere, only in special micro-climatological situations is peach growing likely to be successful.

Moisture supply is not a major problem for agriculture in Ontario, as most areas where temperatures are suitable receive more than 23 inches of precipitation. However, the pattern of isohyets illustrated in Figure 6.15 is of interest as it shows the range in precipitation received over Ontario. Of particular note are the areas receiving westerly winds off the Great Lakes, for these areas are often designated as the Snow Belt during the winter months. South of Owen Sound, in the vicinity of Parry Sound, and west of Sault Ste. Marie, the annual snowfall exceeds 100 inches. The Toronto-Hamilton area, being in the partial rainshadow of the Niagara Escarpment, receives much less snow, usually less than 60 inches annually. This, of course, is a considerable advantage in terms of the cost of snow removal in this highly urbanized area.

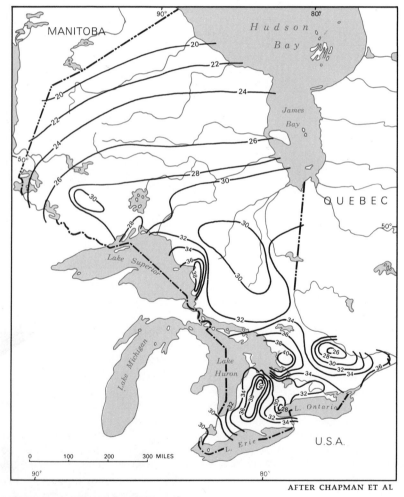

AFTER CHAPMAN ET AL

Figure 6.15 Mean Annual Precipitation
Precipitation (given in inches) is greatest to the lee of the Great Lakes where areas of high relief are found.

Figure 6.16 **Forest Divisions of Ontario**

Natural Vegetation

Much of the original forest vegetative cover of Ontario has been removed or greatly modified by the operations of the farm-clearing pioneers or lumbermen. Large uncleared areas are still present in the Shield of Northern Ontario, but in the south the wooded area has been reduced to about 10 per cent of the total. As was shown in CHAPTER 2, the boundaries of the forest regions correspond rather well with those of the major climatic divisions. However, landform and soil differences give rise to rather varied distribution of tree types within regions.

The Niagara section is part of the great deciduous forest region of eastern North America and is the only part of Canada in which Carolinian vegetation is found. Chestunt, tulip-tree, magnolia, paw-paw, and sassafras are some of the southern types which occur. The chief species of the forest vary depending upon the texture of the soil. On well-drained till plains, sugar maple, beech, basswood, walnut, and oak are common, while on clay plains, silver maple, ash, hickory, and, until recently, elm were all found. The drier sand plains originally had stands of white pine; red cedar and sumac occupied the droughty sites.

The Great Lakes—St. Lawrence Forest can be climatically defined as lying between the isolines of 2,400 and 3,600 degree-days. As subdivided by Halliday, it includes the Huron-Ontario section in peninsular Ontario, the Upper St. Lawrence section in the Ottawa Valley, the Algonquin-Laurentides section, and the Superior section known as the Great Lakes Mixed Forest.* In all cases it is a mixed forest which in its northward portions is dominated by conifers such as the white pine and white spruce. The Great Lakes—St. Lawrence Forest has always been the most important source of timber in Ontario and has been well worked by lumber and pulp and paper interests. The proportion of area in forest varies, however, from 15 per cent in Southern Ontario to over 90 per cent in the Superior and Algonquin districts.

North of the Great Lakes Forest there is the Boreal Forest which can be subdivided into the Patricia area on the west and the Central Coniferous Forest on the east. For both these areas the predominant species is black spruce although in drier areas tamarack, white spruce, balsam fir, and jackpine also occur. The Patricia Forest contains the same species, but the drier climate has caused a somewhat lesser degree of growth than is found to the east. The Central Coniferous Forest constitutes the most important source of pulpwood in Northern Ontario today.

The Subarctic Forest complex is characterized by extremely poor drainage, and few large dense stands of trees occur. While thermal conditions are adequate for tree growth, the lack of adequate drainage results in the dominance of vast open marshes and muskegs. These, together with a narrow zone of tundra along the shore of Hudson Bay, contribute little to the vegetative resources of Ontario.

All in all, Ontario does have an impressive forest resource base, for an area of more than 164,000 square miles is consid-

* W. E. D. Halliday. "A Forest Classification for Canada". *Forest Service Bulletin.* 89 (1937). Ottawa.

ered to be productive forest land. It is estimated that the coniferous trees alone constitute a resource of merchantable timber in excess of 66,654 million cubic feet. This timber resource is exceeded in Canada only by those of Quebec and British Columbia.

Soils

The mature soils of Ontario are typical of those developed under forest vegetation in a humid, temperate climate. They are all podzolic in nature although only in the north are there podzols with the typical ashy gray upper horizon. In general, there are three major soil zones: the Gray-Brown Podzolic soils of Southern Ontario, the Brown Podzol of the Shield fringe, and the true Podzol of Northern Ontario (Figure 6.18). These range in fertility and natural productivity, but for the most part the Podzol soils of Northern Ontario are inferior to those in the south.

It is important to remember that local variations in relief can cause differences in drainage which affect soil profile development and soil fertility. Figure 6.19 illustrates the way in which soil profile development may be affected by conditions of slope and drainage. Under normal conditions of good drainage the soil profile will show the well-developed, characteristic horizons, but if an area is excessively flat or the soil material is clayey in nature, rusty red and yellow streaks in the B horizon indicate imperfect drainage. Under

Figure 6.17 Trenching for Tile Drains
Many areas in the Shield which possess fertile soil are poorly drained. This photograph taken near Earlton shows the installation of tile drains to improve the productivity of the land.

R. PUTNAM

AFTER HILLS AND ONTARIO SOILS SURVEY

Figure 6.18 Soil Regions of Ontario

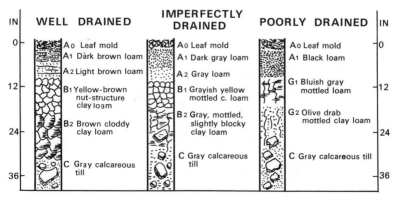

Figure 6.19 Profiles of a Representative Soil Catena in Southern Ontario

poor drainage, oxidation is even more imperfect, the degree of mottling increases, and a sticky clay-like layer known as *glei* is formed. As shown previously by Figure 6.8, poor drainage is one land use hazard which affects significant portions of Southern Ontario, particularly in areas of clay plains. Extensive drainage schemes have been installed. In Northern Ontario the high water table is a major hazard and tile drainage is frequently required before successful agriculture can be achieved.

The Physical Stage

From a resource base point of view, Ontario is unusually well endowed. Climate, soils, and landforms combine to make agriculture possible in Southern Ontario. To the north the Canadian Shield has a considerable resource potential in terms of minerals and forests. Moreover, the accessibility provided by the Great Lakes and St. Lawrence water route has provided Ontario with a unique opportunity to make full use of these resources. However, there are regional disparities in economic development which are of geographic importance.

ECONOMIC DEVELOPMENT

Manufacturing in Ontario

For many years Ontario has ranked as the outstanding industrial province of Canada. Her manufacturing plants are many and varied; some of them are very large and employ thousands of production workers.

Table 6.2 shows that Ontario has slightly more than half the value of Canada's manufacturing output, while employing slightly less than half the workers. Thus it might be argued that the average Ontario industry is somewhat more efficient than the average Canadian industry. Wage rates are also relatively high.

Many influences may be seen behind the patterns of composition and distribution of Ontario industry as a glance at Table 6.3 will show. Despite its dominance in manufacturing as indicated by the location quotient for overall employment in such industries, Ontario is not dominant in all. In fact, in 11 out of 20 general categories of manufacturing Ontario has less than its share of the national employment. This, however, is more than balanced by the concentration in the other nine categories. Particularly noticeable is the concentration in transportation equipment (especially motor vehicles), machinery, electrical products, and rubber (tires).

The listing of the twenty categories of industry in Table 6.3 does not indicate the importance of the individual type of industry. Consequently, the Bureau of Statistics makes another set of figures available based upon more specific categories. Selected data from this source are shown in Table 6.4.

The first three groups of leading industries, motor vehicles, iron and steel, and pulp and paper, with only 65 plants in all, furnish 12 per cent of the employment and account for 17 per cent of the value added by manufacture. On the other hand, two other important groups, commercial print-

Table 6.2   Manufacturing in Ontario, 1965 *

Category	Number	Per Cent of Canadian Total	Location Quotient **
Establishments	12,766	39.2	1.11
Employees	774,428	49.4	1.43
Salaries and Wages	$4,100,212,000	52.3	1.52
Total Value Added	$8,421,760,000	53.7	1.56
Total Value of Shipments	$17,675,864,000	52.1	1.51

* Data from Canada Year Book, 1968.
** Location quotient based on total population.

Table 6.3   Manufacturing in Ontario, 1965 *

Industrial Group	Employees in Canada Number	Per Cent	Employees in Ontario Number	Per Cent	Location Quotient
Food and Beverage Ind.	220,700	14.06	88,994	11.48	0.82
Tobacco Products Ind.	10,253	0.65	3,147	0.41	0.63
Rubber Ind.	26,206	1.67	17,657	2.28	1.37
Leather Ind.	32,585	2.08	14,711	1.90	0.91
Textile Ind.	76,676	4.88	27,698	3.58	0.73
Knitting Mills	24,070	1.53	9,260	1.20	0.78
Clothing Ind.	98,659	6.28	23,877	3.08	0.49
Wood Ind.	91,589	5.83	17,671	2.28	0.39
Furniture and Fixture Ind.	40,374	2.57	18,861	2.44	0.95
Paper and Allied Ind.	110,180	7.02	42,020	5.43	0.77
Printing, Publishing, and Allied Ind.	78,737	5.01	40,354	5.21	1.04
Primary Metal Ind.	107,504	6.85	66,323	8.56	1.25
Metal Fabricating Ind.	133,992	8.53	76,651	9.90	1.16
Machinery Ind.	70,683	4.50	47,922	6.19	1.38
Transportation Equipment Ind.	135,481	8.63	92,325	11.92	1.38
Electrical Products Ind.	113,463	7.23	75,498	9.75	1.35
Non-metallic Mineral Products Ind.	51,218	3.26	24,701	3.19	0.98
Petroleum and Coal Products Ind.	14,330	0.91	6,887	0.89	0.98
Chemical and Chemical Products Ind.	70,975	4.52	37,795	4.88	1.08
Miscellaneous Manufacturing Ind.	62,624	3.99	42,076	5.43	1.36
Totals	1,570,299	100.00	774,428	100.00	1.00

* Data from Canada Year Book, 1968.

ing and dairy products plants with a total of 1,479 establishments, employ only 4.5 per cent of the workers and account for only 3.7 per cent of the value added. The former groups count their employees in hundreds and even thousands, while the latter groups average about 20 persons per plant. An important third group includes miscellaneous machinery, metal stampings, publishing and printing, and miscellaneous metal fabricating. These industries include 1,168 separate plants, employ 9 per cent of the industrial workers, and supply 9 per cent of the value added. The average plant employs about 60 workers.

The first three groups are quite obviously part of the highly capitalized, highly auto-mated, highly specialized, industrial system of the twentieth century. The plants are large, their sites have been chosen with great care, attention being given to suit-ability for plant layout, water supply, and transportation facilities. The general plant location must also consider sources of raw materials, areas of greatest market poten-tial, and, in the case of very large plants, the availability of a suitable labor force.

Pulp and paper mills make an interesting study. Most of the very large ones are in Northern Ontario and are situated on lake-shore sites, as at Thunder Bay, Terrace Bay, and Marathon, or on river sites, as at Sturgeon Falls, Espanola, Kapuskasing, and Iroquois Falls. In the beginning the river supplied water, power, and transportation for logs. Nowadays power is not such a locative factor because of the development of the Ontario hydro-power grid. Trans-portation of logs may also, in large part, be land based; but water supply and waste disposal still depend upon the river. All sites must, of course, be given railway access for purposes of supply and trans-portation of the product to market. While

Table 6.4   Leading Industries in Ontario, Ranked in Order of Value Added, 1964 *

Industry	Establish-ments	Employees	Earnings $000	Value Added $000
1. Motor Vehicle Manufacturers	8	32,709	216,438	531,649
2. Iron and Steel Mills	18	32,332	199,317	478,664
3. Pulp and Paper Mills	39	20,637	117,349	282,383
4. Motor Vehicle Parts and Accessories	123	28,392	163,959	278,909
5. Miscellaneous Machinery	314	25,098	133,323	261,355
6. Industrial Chemicals	37	10,830	67,170	205,720
7. Electrical Industrial Equipment	84	17,903	100,053	186,837
8. Rubber Industries	52	16,457	85,966	169,421
9. Commercial Printing	861	18,788	98,968	161,327
10. Communications Equipment	97	17,893	81,130	158,818
11. Metal Stampings and Allied Industries	341	14,949	75,380	150,486
12. Publishing and Printing	272	14,834	81,643	148,249
13. Office and Store Machinery	18	6,112	38,319	145,331
14. Miscellaneous Metal Fabricating	241	12,468	60,923	121,432
15. Dairy Products	618	14,011	61,997	113,899
16. Miscellaneous Food Products	104	6,589	32,420	111,496
17. Agricultural Implements	38	10,096	58,268	102,040
18. Breweries	15	3,181	20,592	98,978
19. Aircraft and Parts	35	12,508	69,654	96,121
20. Major Appliances	24	9,131	44,769	94,520
Twenty Leading Industries	3,339	324,918	1,807,638	3,897,635
Total—All Industries in Ontario	12,781	728,936	3,666,810	7,489,116

* Data from D. B. S. Manufacturing Industries of Canada. Section D. 1964. Catalogue No. 31-206.

some plants have been established near already existing towns, many were placed in sparsely settled areas; and as a result new towns had to be built, either through the efforts of the company concerned or the provincial government. Examples of such one-industry towns include Kapuskasing, Iroquois Falls, Marathon, and Terrace Bay. Pulp and paper plants also exist in Southern Ontario. Usually they are older and smaller and were located with water supply, power, and transportation facilities in mind. Their raw materials come from a distance and their continuation on their present sites is perhaps largely a matter of industrial inertia.

Primary iron and steel has long been a leading industry in Ontario. It is a highly centralized industry with the greatest activity being found in Hamilton where two huge metallurgical complexes, STELCO and DOFASCO, are located. Here they are close to the industrial heart of Ontario and within easy reach of a multitude of steel-using secondary manufacturing industries. The ALGOMA mill is a third steel-making complex, located at Sault Ste. Marie in Northern Ontario. A blast furnace is located at Port Colborne while special purpose steels are made in the ATLAS plant at Welland where there is also a very large pipe mill. Large rolling and fabricating mills are found in the Hamilton and Toronto metropolitan areas and near Oshawa. In one form or another the Mississaga urban complex has the capacity for the primary production of almost 7,000,000 tons of steel annually, while the capacity of ALGOMA is approximately 2,500,000 tons. Strong links exist between these mills

Figure 6.20 STELCO, Hamilton

and the mining areas. STELCO has long had interests in the Mesabi area west of Lake Superior and is now receiving pellets from its new Griffith mine near Red Lake in Ontario. STELCO also has links with the Hilton mine north of Ottawa and with the Wabush area in Labrador. DOFASCO, after years of buying ore on the open market, has opened the Sherman mine near Timagami, from which it will receive 1,000,000 tons of pellets per year. ALGOMA has links with Wawa in the Michipicoten area, including its own Algoma Central Railway, and with the Steep Rock area west of Lake Superior. One more facet of the steel industry in Ontario is the building of a new and extensive steel complex at Nanticoke on the shore of Lake Erie. Here STELCO will have another plant that will eventually produce as much

steel as the older Hilton works in Hamilton. Steel is not only a commodity to be sold to pay wages and dividends, but it is also a basic requirement for a multitude of other industries as well.

The motor vehicle industry for two decades has been at or near the top of the industrial categories of Ontario in terms of employment, wages paid, net value of production, and gross value of sales. Ontario, of course, has had almost a monopoly of the motor vehicle trade in Canada, but at the same time it provides a large part of the market. Of the more than 7,000,000 motor vehicles registered in Canada, Ontario has 57 per cent.

The real beginning of the automobile industry in Canada was the establishment of the Ford Motor Company of Canada at Windsor in 1904. It was thus located very close to its parent firm in Detroit. In 1907 the McLaughlin Motor Car Company Limited was organized in Oshawa, becoming General Motors of Canada in 1918. Studebaker entered the Canadian market in 1910 with an assembly plant in Windsor. After World War I other companies followed including those that eventually amalgamated to form the Chrysler Corporation. During the depression many motor car companies failed, leaving Chrysler, Ford, and General Motors as the "Big Three" in control of the market. For some years during World War II, the manufacture of passenger cars was discontinued and all efforts went into the production of military vehicles. The post-war years have been marked chiefly by the expansion of the "Big Three" and by the elimination or consolidation of all others until only one, American Motors, is left in the passenger car business. A few other companies produce trucks, buses, and special purpose vehicles. The motor vehicle industry, however, must also be taken to include the manufacturers of parts and accessories in more than 120 small plants. Thus the total employment is more than 60,000, or about 8.5 per cent of the total gainfully employed in all manufacturing industries in the province. The market, however, is not exclusive; many foreign cars have been imported, especially economical compacts from Europe and lately from Japan as well. To offset the effect of this, an agreement has been made with the United States whereby much freer movement of cars across the border is possible.

The geographical distribution of this industry may be stated fairly simply. Passenger cars are assembled by Chrysler at Windsor, General Motors at Oshawa, Ford at Oakville and St. Thomas, and American Motors at Brampton. Ford operates a foundry, an engine plant, and machining and stamping facilities in Windsor. Until 1953 its assembly plant was located there also; since 1954 cars and trucks have been assembled in Oakville, and in 1967 an assembly plant was also opened near St. Thomas. The huge General Motors car and truck assembly plants are located at Oshawa. For years all engines were made in Windsor. In recent years the McKinnon Industries plant at St. Catharines has become the largest manufacturer of automotive parts in Ontario. It is a General Motors subsidiary making engines, transmissions, differentials, and a great range of other equipment.

The assembly plants, variously located on the periphery of Metropolitan Toronto, bring together component parts from Windsor and St. Catharines and from American parent plants as well as accessories from dozens of small plants in Ontario and Quebec. In addition to being located close to Canada's largest car market, that of Central Ontario, they are well placed to ship finished cars to the Montreal area as well.

The automobile is one of the most significant phenomena of modern life. The car, itself, no longer a status symbol since most people have one or perhaps two, is simply regarded as a necessity. Ordinary living and the use of space are predicated on the availability of personal transportation. There are enough cars in Ontario to put the province's entire population in motion simultaneously. Trucks are now extensively used in the transportation of goods. The pattern of the motor vehicle industry might therefore be regarded as geographically mature. Further adjustment will undoubtedly take place, but the chief effort of expansion will simply be a matter of keeping up with the population.

In contrast to the centralized pattern displayed by those industries previously discussed, there are some types that are widely disseminated in very small units. Such a condition is found in the dairy industry. Dairy plants carry on fluid milk processing, butter making, cheese making, and the making of minor dairy products. Two strong locational factors are involved: one, the nearness of the source of supply and the other, the proximity of the customer. Both of these factors are largely due to historical inertia, and we may expect considerable adjustment in the light of advancements in modern technology. Traditionally, milk was produced by farmers near towns and cities and peddled by them from door to door. The quality of the milk depended upon the speed with which it reached the customer. Even when bottling works took over the distribution, distance remained an important factor until the modern technology of pasteurization and homogenization, rapid cooling, and bulk hauling was developed. Cheese and butter factories tended to be dispersed through rural areas, located as close as possible to their patrons, the dairy farmers. Freshness here was also necessary. Transportation was slow and distances from the customer had to be short. Each day's milk was processed as soon as it was received. However, the final products, cheese and butter, could be transported long distances. Dairy plants are now larger and modern techniques are used, yet hundreds of small ones still exist.

The baking industry is also highly dispersed. Despite the existence of enormous bread factories, much baking is done in very small plants within easy reach of the consumers who demand that baked goods be fresh.

Another dispersed, highly customer-oriented industry is commercial printing. Orders are often small, specifications unique, and satisfaction depends upon prompt delivery. A small production unit located within the district to be served is usually indicated, but it must be admitted that fairly large commercial printing shops also exist.

The great concentration of manufacturing activities is to be found in Mississaga, the highly urbanized region located in ten counties around the western end of Lake Ontario, including the Niagara Peninsula, the Grand River Valley, and the north shore of Lake Ontario (Table 6.5). Here is found 63 per cent of all the manufacturing

Table 6.5   Location of Manufacturing Activity in Ontario, 1964 *

	Establish-ments	No. of Employees	Earnings $000	Value Added $000	Value of Shipments $000
Metropolitan Toronto	4,853	235,197	1,145,278	2,351,150	5,123,346
Toronto Census Metropolitan Area	5,352	263,325	1,296,452	2,734,704	6,291,309
Mississaga (Ten County Area)	8,010	470,369	2,539,604	4,989,170	11,485,816
Province of Ontario	12,781	728,936	3,666,810	7,489,116	17,431,963
As Per Cent of Ontario Activity					
Metropolitan Toronto	38.9	32.3	31.2	31.4	29.4
Toronto C. M. A.	41.9	36.1	35.4	36.5	36.1
Mississaga	62.7	64.6	69.3	66.6	65.9
Province of Ontario	100.0	100.0	100.0	100.0	100.0
Location Quotients **					
Metropolitan Toronto	1.46	1.24	1.20	1.21	1.13
Toronto C. M. A.	1.43	1.23	1.21	1.25	1.23
Mississaga	1.27	1.30	1.40	1.35	1.33
Province of Ontario	1.00	1.00	1.00	1.00	1.00

* Dominion Bureau of Statistics. #31-209. Manufacturing Industries of Canada. Section G. Table 6. Ottawa. 1968.
** Location quotients based on population census, 1961.

establishments, 65 per cent of all manufacturing employees, 69 per cent of all wage payments in manufacturing, 67 per cent of all value added by manufacturing industries, and 66 per cent of all shipments of manufactured goods in the province. Perhaps even more noteworthy is the fact that the municipality of Metropolitan Toronto itself employs about one-third of all the manufacturing workers in the province. It has a greater ratio of small plants and its share of the total returns and its wage rates lag behind those of peripheral areas. Much of the manufacturing is geared to the daily needs of the vast metropolitan population. Such industries are highly competitive. A great many kinds of goods are made in small quantities and overhead costs are high. The demands for articles of clothing and for many food products are highly seasonal and surplus goods must be disposed of cheaply. Material costs are high because a great deal of labor has already been put into them. For these and other reasons the small plant in the metropolitan area often has difficulty in maintaining production. Nevertheless, because of its great volume and its great variety the metropolitan area must be regarded as the workshop of Ontario. It is also the great market of Ontario, for much of the production from the peripheral areas is finally sold and used in the metropolitan area.

Centered on Toronto, the Mississaga urban complex has a number of smaller cities which have considerable functional similarity as components of the larger region. It is notable that Maxwell classed them all as Manufacturing I, that is, as having dominance in the field of manufacturing.* In most cases also, manufacturing was indicated as a distinctive function. In Toronto itself manufacturing is dominant but not distinctive; Toronto's distinctiveness is in central place functions: wholesale trade, finance, insurance, and real estate.

Carrying the enquiry into other parts of the province, it is found that Sarnia,

* J. W. Maxwell. "The Functional Structure of Canadian Cities: A Classification of Cities". *Geographical Bulletin.* Vol. 7, No. 2 (1965). pp. 79-104.

Windsor, and London all have a dominant function in manufacturing, but in London as in Toronto other central place functions are distinctive. Manufacturing is dominant in Sault Ste. Marie but places well back of mining in the Sudbury area and transportation in Thunder Bay. In two large cities in Eastern Ontario, Ottawa and Kingston, manufacturing is overshadowed by other central place functions.

This study of industrial location might be carried out in much more detail on more specific industrial groupings. The evidence is so far reasonably clear, however. The dominance of manufacturing in all the Mississaga centers, together with the vast bulk of manufacturing in the Toronto Census Metropolitan Area have over the years been sufficient to establish the importance of the Mississaga conurbation, not only in Ontario, but to a large extent in the rest of Canada. And along with manufacturing there has been a great development of most other central place functions.

Agriculture

A century ago agriculture was the major commodity-producing industry in Ontario and the basis of both economic and social life of most parts of the province. Now, however, less than half a million people (1966 census) live on farms and their contribution to the provincial commodity production is less than six per cent.

Ontario has a vast area of more than 220,000,000 acres, but because of climate, landform, and soils, only a small part of its total area has ever been developed as farmland. Most of this is in Southern Ontario where Gray-Brown forest soils and warm summer growing seasons are favorable for most middle latitude crops of European origin. Thus Ontario agriculture has very definite resemblances to that of Northwestern Europe. Dairying, livestock raising, and the growing of fruits and vegetables are the dominant agricultural activities. The livestock industry is supported by the growth of grain and fodder crops, most of which are also of European origin. The European tradition is broken, however, by the adoption of maize or Indian corn which is of North American origin and is now so important that the word "corn" is no longer used to include all cereals as it was originally.

In the early years of colonization in Upper Canada, farming was largely of a subsistence nature. Patches of cereals, potatoes, and other garden vegetables constituted the main crops. The log cabin in each clearing was soon joined by other small shacks to house a few hens, pigs, sheep, and a cow or two. There were no large nearby markets nor transportation facilities to reach more distant ones. Therefore commercial specialization was at first out of the question.

However, the sale of wheat developed rapidly in Upper Canada. To begin with, any surplus occurring in the early colony could be sold to British garrisons. As early as 1794 some wheat moved down river to Montreal, and by 1812 wheat had become a staple commodity. The revision of the British Corn Law in 1825 permitted the sale of Canadian wheat in Britain and the building of canals facilitated its export. By 1850 half the crop acreage in South-central and Southwestern Ontario was devoted to wheat. Wheat farming remained the order of the day until the 1880s when the area under wheat surpassed 2,000,000 acres. In the 1890s wheat growing rapidly fell off to 1,500,000 acres in 1901; its fall continued to 600,000 acres in 1931 and to less than 400,000 acres in the 1960s. But during the same period the yield per acre has about doubled. Wheat remains today as a specialty on farms in Southwestern Ontario where conditions are nearly ideal for its growth.

The loss of the wheat industry turned the attention of Ontario farmers to dairy and livestock farming. During the "wheat era" butter and cheese were imported into Canada. Many areas were often short of a milk supply. There were few cattle and most of them were not of dairy quality anyway. The first development of commercial dairying was the opening of a cheese factory in Oxford county in 1864. The first creamery was established in Bruce county in 1874. Farmers in Oxford and neighboring areas began to import dairy stock from the United States and from Europe. The subsequent growth of dairy herds cannot be traced through the census records, however, for no attempt was made to keep separate returns of dairy cattle. Anyway, in the welter of cross-breeding that went on in most areas, a statistical analysis would have been impossible. Estimates of milk production were given, and they show consistent intercensal increases. By 1931, the average production per cow had reached 4,500 pounds per annum, and by 1961 it had passed 7,000 pounds. During the first half of the twentieth century, dairying came to be regarded as one of the most progressive types of farming in Ontario.

An outstanding example of dairy farm development is the area in Southern Ontario which supplies milk to Toronto, Hamilton, and other nearby cities. Approximately 3,400 farmers supply 200,000 gallons of milk per day or 6,200,000 gallons per month to city dairies. Most of this comes from a compact area of 20 counties, having an area of 15,700 square miles and a population of about 4,000,000 people, half of whom live in Metropolitan Toronto. In 1961 these counties had about 43,000 commercial farmers, 15,000 (35 per cent) of whom reported monthly sales of 20,-400,000 gallons of milk or approximately 1,360 gallons each. The average for fluid milk shippers on contract, however, was about 1,800 gallons each. The three counties nearest Toronto were the biggest suppliers, with 38 per cent of the shippers, while the three counties nearest Hamilton had 23 per cent. The six counties have only 21.5 per cent of the area of the "milk shed". Twenty-five years ago these six counties had more than 80 per cent of the fluid milk shippers.

Urban expansion has taken some of the land formerly used for dairy farming, but it has greatly increased the market. New shippers have been found in outlying areas.

The new techniques of bulk cooling and shipment in glass-lined tanks have forced dairy farmers into heavy new capital expenses. Many small dairy herds have been forced out and their contracts have been awarded to the operators of larger farms. In only a few townships do dairy farms amount to half the total number of farms, and in no county do they account for more than half the total value of farm products. In Oxford county where two-thirds of the commercial farmers sell milk, less than half the commercial farms qualify as "dairy farms". Even in Peel, York, and Ontario counties on the doorstep of Metropolitan Toronto, other livestock (cattle, sheep, and hog) farms outnumber dairy farms about three to two. In spite of the fact that these counties still constitute an outstanding area of milk production, it can no longer be regarded as predominantly a dairy region.

The other bastion of the dairy industry is the triangle of Eastern Ontario, lying between the Ottawa and the St. Lawrence Rivers. Lacking many large urban areas to stimulate the fluid milk trade or many other specialties and the climatic advantages that stimulated wheat growing in Southwestern Ontario, the eastern area became a producer of "industrial milk". At first the only outlet was through cheese factories. The system was known as summer dairying. Cows were bred to freshen in the spring. This produced the greatest flow of milk from lush pastures in the early summer, and production tapered off in the fall. Cattle were wintered on hay and straw with very little else in the way of supplement. The price paid for "cheese milk" was very low, but the farmers were put to little expense in maintaining producing standards normally required for the fluid milk trade. The countryside had hundreds of small cheese factories to which the farmers delivered daily the milk produced by their herds. Like the farmers, themselves, the cheese factories were restricted to summer production. Canadian cheddar cheese, however, had a reputation for quality, which it still enjoys, and thus became a staple export to British markets.

Other manufacturers producing evaporated, condensed, and powdered milk, and other types of milk products are now found in the region. The cheese industry itself has changed. No longer dispersed in hundreds of small units, it has large centrally located plants which are operated throughout the year. This has resulted in a change in farm methods also, and dairy farmers are now producing milk in the winter as well as maintaining an improved forage crop program in the summer season. The good dairymen have increased the intensity of their operations, while many smaller operators have sold out. Thus it is that many dairy farms in Eastern Ontario are comprised of two or more farm lots, sometimes some distance apart. In twelve counties in Eastern Ontario, more than 50 per cent of the commercial farms are classified as dairy farms and, in five of them, this density surpasses 85 per cent. Many small, part-time operators also produce milk. This is truly a dairy area where other types of farming occupy only a minor portion of the land.

The majority of Ontario farmers were not fond of dairying. In fact, during the late nineteenth century more purebred beef cattle were brought into the province than those of the dairy breeds. Up until 1911 the Shorthorn breed had a clear majority over all other breeds in Ontario. During those years, also, the Ontario farmer was establishing a record as a cattle feeder. Certain areas in the province also became established as grazing areas. Thus, even though succeeding decades saw a great rise in dairying, certain areas in Central and Western Ontario maintained a beef-raising tradition. In the post-war years the raising of beef has been gaining over dairying. This is true particularly in the counties bordering Lake Huron, but also in interior counties as well. The northwestern part of peninsular Ontario has maintained its interest in grazing, whereas cattle feeding has increased in those areas which have found it possible to grow more corn. Because of high prices and rising demands for beef during the late 1950s and the

1960s, steer feeders, as a group, seem to have been making the highest farm incomes, and fairly large feeding lots have become common. To maintain these feed lots, herds of replacement cattle have been increasing in the grazing areas, while many feeder cattle have also been brought annually from Western Canada.

The third element in livestock farming which must be mentioned is hog raising. A swine map of the province shows a rather peculiar distribution with the greatest concentration in Waterloo and adjoining counties. On the other hand, Eastern Ontario raises few hogs. This is partly to be explained by historical preferences and partly by the availability of feed. Not only do farmers in Southwestern Ontario grow more feed grains but, since Goderich is the port through which most Western feed grain supplies enter Southern Ontario, they may also obtain extra feed grains more cheaply than farmers elsewhere. The addition of hog raising to the cattle industry of this area makes it the prime meat-producing area in Canada. It is particularly noticeable that Essex county, in the extreme southwest, once an area of hog raising on the basis of its corn supplies, has become a minor pork producer.

In the post-war period Ontario farms have undergone vast changes. While it must be admitted that some of them may be more apparent than real because of improvements in statistical methods, they may certainly be taken as indications of the trends. Table 6.6 presents the cash values of Ontario farm products as given in the census reports for 1966 and 1941. The dollar volume in 1965 was 4.77 times that of 1940, but only about half of this is due to increased production, the other half being due to rise in prices through the twenty-five year period. There have been some extraordinary developments. Corn grown for grain has increased nearly four times in acreage and has doubled in yield per acre. Corn for ensilage has also increased greatly. Both of these are reflected in the great increase in livestock production, but considerable corn also enters the cash market.

Tobacco growing has spread to many new areas, while better growing methods have greatly increased the yields per acre and the final gross return. Horticultural methods have improved, and while many old areas have gone out of production, particularly in rapidly urbanizing areas, new enterprises have been initiated, and the total share of horticulture has increased.

The growth of the livestock industry has been spectacular. In 1940 it was already the most important type of farming, providing almost one-third of all the farm cash income. Volume of production and

Table 6.6   Farm Production in Ontario: A Comparison of Cash Values of Farm Sales, 1940 and 1965 *

| | 1965 | | 1940 | | |
	Value $000	Per Cent	Value $000	Per Cent	Index of Change **
Field Crops	208,483	20.13	28,002	12.89	+7.24
Horticultural Crops	102,596	9.91	16,604	7.64	+2.27
Livestock	406,487	39.29	71,646	33.04	+6.25
Poultry and Poultry Products	105,757	10.21	19,038	8.77	+1.44
Dairy Products	196,258	18.96	52,069	23.98	−5.02
Forest Products	2,964	.28	4,392	2.02	−1.74
Other Products	12,792	1.22	25,329	11.66	−10.44
Totals	1,035,337	100.00	217,080	100.00	0.00

* Data from Census of Canada, 1966 and 1941.
** Per cent share of 1965 compared with per cent share of 1940.

market price have both risen to the point where livestock industries now provide about two-fifths of the total cash sales in agriculture. The numbers of beef cattle in the province more than doubled in the twenty-five year period. While much of this increase has been in feeder cattle, it is notable that the breeding herd is now four times as large. Improved methods of feeding and handling the larger numbers has also contributed to the rise in value of production. Pork production has fluctuated widely but its over-all trend has not increased significantly. On the other hand, the sheep flocks of the province have decreased almost to the vanishing point.

The share of the total agricultural production attributable to dairying has fallen. While the efficiency of the industry has undoubtedly risen and the average number of dairy cows per operator has increased from eight to seventeen, there are still many marginal and submarginal dairy farmers.

The share of cash income attributable to forest products, honey, and other specialties has fallen greatly; in fact, there has been an absolute reduction in dollar value and many small specialty farms have gone out of business.

The change in total numbers and in type of farm for the same period is equally striking although not necessarily similar in all respects (Table 6.7). The total number of farms has fallen by 38 per cent but the decrease is not the same in all categories. Strangely enough non-commercial farms have been reduced only slightly in total numbers and now comprise 12 per cent more of the total than they did 25 years ago. It must be pointed out also that the criteria for differentiation have changed considerably. The most obvious change, however, is the virtual disappearance of the old "mixed" or general farm, on which the farmer has not specialized to the extent of putting 50 per cent of his activities in any one enterprise. The loss in this category more than balances any gains and results in a proportional shrinkage of the number of commercial farms amounting to nearly seven per cent. It is to be noted that both dairy farms and other livestock farms made relative gains, but the gain in dairy farms was greater. This is in sharp contrast to the loss in relative returns, which is shown in Table 6.6. This may mean either that many of the old "mixed" farmers were dairymen at heart and began to specialize in dairying as a matter of choice,

Table 6.7 Change in Type of Farm, 1940-1965 *

Type of Farm	1965		1940		Index of Change **
	Number	Per Cent	Number	Per Cent	
Dairy	21,159	19.25	21,479	12.05	+7.20
Cattle, Hogs, and Sheep	28,809	26.21	35,563	19.95	+6.26
Poultry	2,179	2.00	3,258	1.83	+ .17
Small Grains (incl. Wheat)	4,999	4.55	6,701	3.75	+ .80
Other Field Crops	4,488	4.08	3,971	2.23	+1.85
Fruits and Vegetables	3,920	3.57	7,380	4.14	− .57
Forest and Miscellaneous	1,517	1.38	2,543	1.43	− .05
Mixed	3,653	3.32	46,111	25.87	−22.55
Commercial Farms	70,724	64.36	127,006	71.25	−6.89
Non-commercial Farms	39,163	35.64	41,917	23.47	+12.17
Unclassified	—	—	9,281	5.28	−5.28
Totals	109,887	100.00	178,204	100.00	0.00

* Data from Census of Canada, 1941 and 1966.
** Per cent in each category in 1966 compared with that in 1941.

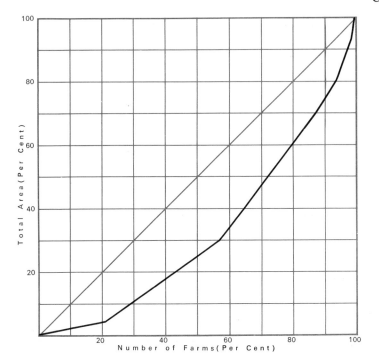

Figure 6.21 (a) & (b) Number and Area of Farms, 1940 and 1965
The Lorenz curves illustrate the division of land into farms. It
can be seen clearly that the land occupied by small farms has
decreased while that occupied by large farms has increased.

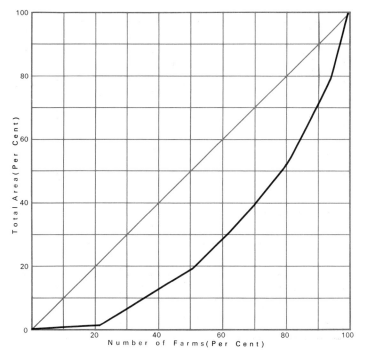

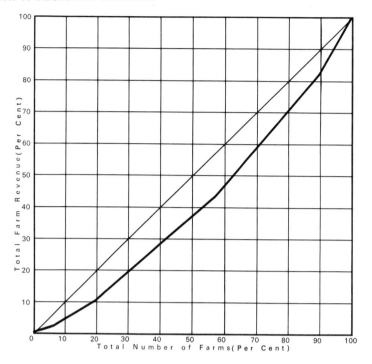

Figure 6.22 (a) & (b) Farms and Production, 1940 and 1965
The Lorenz curves illustrate the change in distribution of farm
revenue on Ontario farms. Ontario farms are being separated
into those that are economically viable and those which are not.

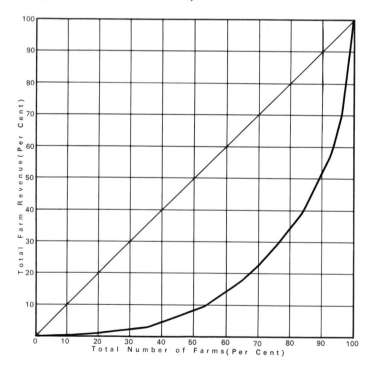

or that the agricultural industry, as a whole, misjudged the economic climate, and expected the consumption of dairy products to keep pace with the growth of population. This it did not do. Whereas in the immediate post-war years Canadians annually consumed an average of 71 pounds of milk solids per capita, this had dropped to less than 61 pounds per capita in the middle 1960s. On the other hand, the consumption of red meats rose from about 130 pounds to 148 pounds, and poultry from 24 pounds to 36 pounds. Thus, it is relatively easy to see why the dairy industry has been accumulating unsalable surplus stocks, while dairy farmers complain of low returns.

Total area of land in farms in 1941 amounted to 22,387,981 acres, having decreased slightly from the peak registered in 1931. There were 178,204 occupied farms, representing a 16 per cent decrease from the peak of 212,108 recorded in 1911. The average size of farm in 1941 was 125 acres. By 1966 the total area in farms had fallen to 17,826,045 acres, a decrease of over 20 per cent in 25 years, while the average area of farm had risen to 162 acres. The change to larger farm size is graphically illustrated in the diagrams on page 209 (Figure 6.21 (a) & (b)).

A drastic change has been taking place in the distribution of returns to farm enterprises. This is illustrated in Figure 6.22 (a) & (b), drawn from data derived from the Census of Canada, 1941 and 1966, and representing the years 1940 and 1965. Although there were disparities in the year 1940 (when 21 per cent of the farms received only 11 per cent of the revenue and 57 per cent received only 43 per cent of the revenue), in the year 1965 the disparities were much more marked: 53 per cent of the farms had only 10 per cent of the production, and it required 84 per cent of all the farms to reach 40 per cent of the production. Stated in another way, 90 per cent of Ontario's farm production is obtained on 47 per cent of the farms and it would perhaps not require much extra effort to produce the other 10 per cent. The disparities may be stated in still another way by reference to specific localities. Four counties in the Grand River watershed and adjacent parts of Southwestern Ontario have 9.45 per cent of the farms, 7.00 per cent of the farm land, and 16.9 per cent of the value of farm production. In contrast, six counties astride the Frontenac Axis in Eastern Ontario have 8.70 per cent of the farms and 12.30 per cent of the farm land, but yield only 4.26 per cent of the value of Ontario's farm products. To emphasize the problem it is only necessary to state that the former area produces at the rate of 140 dollars per acre, the latter area barely averages 20 dollars per acre.

Some years ago, on the basis of the 1941 census report and much field observation, a map of agricultural regions of Southern Ontario was prepared (Figure 6.23).* The general features of that map are preserved in Figure 6.24, but some changes must be noted. First, there is a shrinking of the Eastern Dairy Belt as the outlying areas have shifted toward general livestock farming. Second, the Western Dairy Belt is now to be regarded as part of the Field Crop and Livestock Region, but it is still recognizable because more than 25 per cent (although in no county is there more than 50 per cent) of the farms supply milk to the large cities of the region. Other livestock and crop specialties are numerous, tending to submerge the dairy industry in some areas. The tobacco belt has expanded somewhat.

Changes in the last twenty-five years are such that it seems logical to think of the whole of Southwestern Ontario as a single Crop and Livestock Region in which it is possible to distinguish subregions. The Dairy subregion has already been pointed out. The old Corn Belt has expanded so greatly, while soy beans and other cash crops have also come in to such an extent, that none of the counties of the Lake Erie region has a 50 per cent livestock farming base. Cash sales of field crop commodities comprise from 20 to 50 per cent of the

* D. F. Putnam. (Editor). *Canadian Regions*. J. M. Dent and Sons (Canada) Limited. Toronto. 1952.

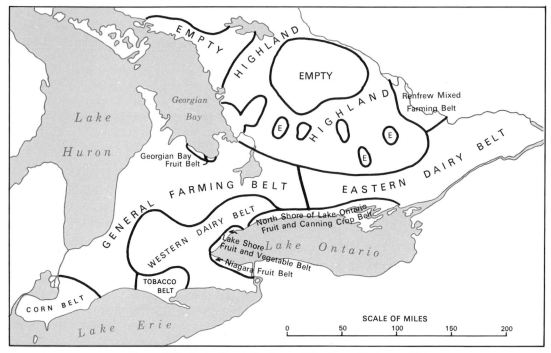

Figure 6.23 Agricultural Regions of Southern Ontario, 1940

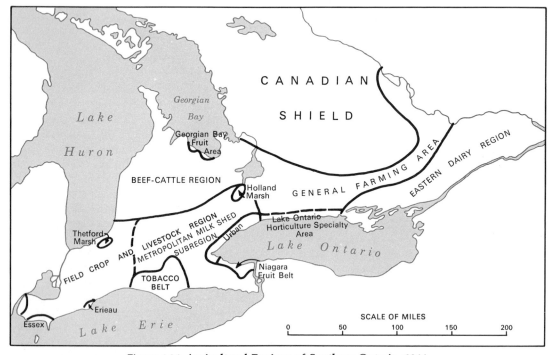

Figure 6.24 Agricultural Regions of Southern Ontario, 1966

total farm returns. The northern part of the Interlake peninsula, however, does have a livestock base, all counties getting more than 60 per cent and some more than 75 per cent of their farm revenue from cattle, hogs, and sheep.

Eastward from Lake Simcoe to the Ottawa Valley there is a belt in which crop land is not uniform and there is a good deal of rough grassland. This area borders on the southern margin of the Canadian Shield; thus many farms have much bare rock, shallow soil, moraine, and many large erratics. There are many lakes and swamps, and large areas of land are poorly drained. Most of the farms in this belt receive over half of their total revenues from livestock sales although some dairying is also carried on.

As pointed out previously there has been considerable concern over marginal agriculture in Eastern Ontario, and a number of studies have been sponsored by A.R.D.A. One study of 299 farms in 1963 presents some interesting findings.* All participants in the survey were farmers as defined in the census even though about 14 per cent used the farm as a rural residence only, while an additional 25 per cent secured most of their income from off-farm employment or from other sources. Only 22 per cent of the farms surveyed were capable of producing a family living income from the farm alone, while for nearly 80 per cent of the farmers some off-farm income was necessary to supplement the low farm income. To what degree can this be ascribed to lack of personal initiative? Noble found that the use of commercial fertilizer was *not* a regular practice on nearly 50 per cent of the farms and that the majority of the full-time farmers had not availed themselves of assistance from the local Department of Agriculture representative nor had they attended agriculture meetings. Educational levels were low; 69

* H. F. Noble. *Socio-economic Problems and Adjustment Needs of the Farm Family in Eastern Ontario.* Farm Economics, Co-operatives and Statistics Branch, Ontario Department of Agriculture. Toronto. January, 1967.

per cent of the operators had not gone beyond the Grade VIII level. Age levels were high; 61 per cent of the part-time farmers and 57 per cent of the full-time farmers were over 50 years of age. Many of the farm operators expressed no desire to change their plan of operation within the next five years. Yet the average age of farmers in Eastern Ontario does not differ significantly from that in the rest of Ontario. Personal initiative would seem to be an important factor. Agriculture in Eastern Ontario certainly has its problems, but many of them are common to agriculture in other parts of Ontario. All areas have problems: the size of operating unit, the cost of mechanization, and low economic return despite great investments in land, buildings, equipment, and livestock.

It remains to point out the small, scattered, special agricultural areas which mean a great deal in the total pattern. The Niagara Fruit Belt, between the Niagara Escarpment and Lake Ontario, has been famous for its peaches and grapes for nearly a century. Vegetables and small fruits are also grown. Since World War II this area has been invaded by industry and urban development to the point that many believe that fruit-growing will soon disappear. A similar belt on the north shore of Lake Ontario, between Toronto and Hamilton, has already been fully urbanized. A number of marshy areas have been drained and devoted to vegetable growing. The largest of these is the Holland Marsh at the south end of Lake Simcoe, which profits from its close proximity to the Toronto market. Others are the Thetford, Erieau, and Pelee marshes in Southwestern Ontario. The southern part of Essex county is noted for its culture of early vegetables and canning tomatoes. A small area on Georgian Bay and a number of areas along the shores of Lake Erie and Lake Ontario have long been noted for their apple orchards.

In Northern Ontario agriculture is a minor industry; only a few people live on farms and only a small proportion of them are full-time farmers. In most cases dairying is the dominant enterprise but some beef cattle are raised on Manitoulin Island, and in Timiskaming, and Rainy River.

Southern Ontario is the most intensively developed agricultural area in Canada. In recent years an annual average cash income of more than $1,000,000,000 has been obtained from less than 18,000,000 acres of land in farms, an agricultural return considerably exceeding that of Saskatchewan which has a farm area more than three times as large. Ontario does not attempt to compete in wheat and other small grains. The value of farm animals, milk, poultry, eggs, fruits, vegetables, and tobacco is much greater than that of grains. Ontario farms are highly specialized and are becoming more so every year. Specialization in animals or in crops of high unit value invariably involves the farmer in higher production costs. Thus in some years the net income of the Ontario farmer may be lower than that of the Saskatchewan farmer. On the other hand, over a long period of years the prosperity of the Ontario farmer appears to be more secure.

Intensification of agricultural practices is particularly noticeable in the more favorably endowed areas of Ontario, while in areas which are less well-endowed or those which are more remote from city markets, many farms are going out of production. Good land is being removed from agricultural use near the expanding cities of the Mississaga urban belt and other urban centers. On the whole, farm population in Ontario is declining, while the farms are becoming fewer, larger, more highly mechanized, more efficient, and capable of greater production.

Forestry

While forestry accounts for just less than one per cent of the census value added for commodity-producing industries, it still contributes $97,000,000 annually to the economy of Ontario. This was more than that of the Atlantic Provinces and places Ontario as the third-ranking forestry province of Canada. Forest lands comprise 75 per cent of the total land area; however, only 164,000 square miles are considered to be productive. The Crown owns almost all of the productive forest land, and administration is accomplished by the Ontario Department of Lands and Forests. Under long term plans, 155,000 square miles of forest land are regulated so that the volume and location of cuttings are such that optimal yields will be sustained.

However, the forest industry is basically under private enterprise, and currently 26 pulp and paper mills are operating. In addition, there are 28 veneer and plywood mills and 890 sawmills which are licensed by the province. The industry is experiencing rising cost structures, and despite increasing production, profit margins have lessened. In an effort to overcome this problem the industry is undergoing mechanization and has introduced new methods of logging and product transfer. In some instances unprofitable operations such as the Domtar lumber mill at Blind River are being closed.

The pulp and paper industry has been established in Ontario since the turn of the century. The first sulphite paper was produced in 1887 at Cornwall, but it was not until the first decade of the twentieth century that mills began to operate at Thorold, Trenton, and Sault Ste. Marie. Soon afterward larger mills began to develop in Northern Ontario, and today 17 mills are found within the Shield. As shown by Figure 6.25, these mills are concentrated close to the shores of Lakes Superior, Huron, and Nipissing, and at favorable locations along large rivers.

Geographical location is an important factor in deciding the site of a large pulp and paper mill. In addition to a plentiful supply of timber, power and transportation facilities are vital. There is considerable advantage in placing the mill where a main railway crosses a large river. While rivers are still used for transportation of the pulpwood, trucks are becoming increasingly important as the distance of the timber source from the mill increases.

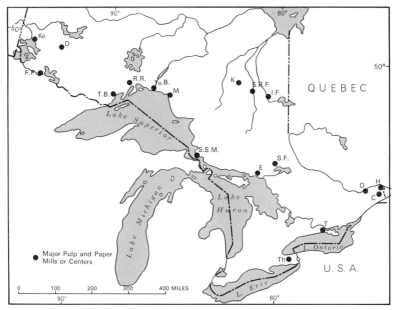

Figure 6.25 Pulp and Paper Mills in Ontario

C	Cornwall	O	Ottawa
D	Dryden	R.R	Red Rock
E	Espanola	S.F.	Sturgeon Falls
F.F.	Fort Frances	S.R.F.	Smooth Rock Falls
H	Hawkesbury	S.S.M.	Sault Ste. Marie
I.F.	Iroquois Falls	T	Trenton
K	Kapuskasing	Th	Thorold
Ke	Kenora	T.B.	Thunder Bay
M	Marathon	Te.B.	Terrace Bay

However, there is more to the forestry industry than pulp and paper, for sawmilling, veneer, and plywood are also of significance. As shown by Figure 6.26, the forest industry in Northeastern Ontario is strongly influenced by the location factors mentioned previously. Centers such as Sault Ste. Marie rely on coastal transport of timber. Espanola, Sturgeon Falls, and Kapuskasing depend upon river and truck transportation of their timber. The pattern of large timber license blocks is rather striking. Almost all the area is under Crown management, but certain companies control impressively large areas. Forestry is important in Northern Ontario, and it is estimated that annually the industry generates more than $60,000,000 in wages. However, the number of sawmills is steadily declining. The plywood and veneer industry is a relatively recent addition. In

the southern margin of the forest region, firms at Sault Ste. Marie and Thessalon primarily produce furniture grades of veneer from yellow birch and hard maple, while northern mills located at Hearst and Cochrane primarily produce construction grades of plywood from poplar and white birch. Poplar provides the bulk of the raw material for particle board produced in mills located at Kirkland Lake, New Liskeard, and Sturgeon Falls.

The older pulp and paper mills located in Southern Ontario were attracted to their sites primarily by low power costs. Most of them obtain pulpwood from distant areas. The Ontario Paper Company plant at Thorold, for instance, obtains its wood from places as far away as Baie Comeau and markets its newsprint in the United States. Some companies are still using very old mills, and with the economic advantage

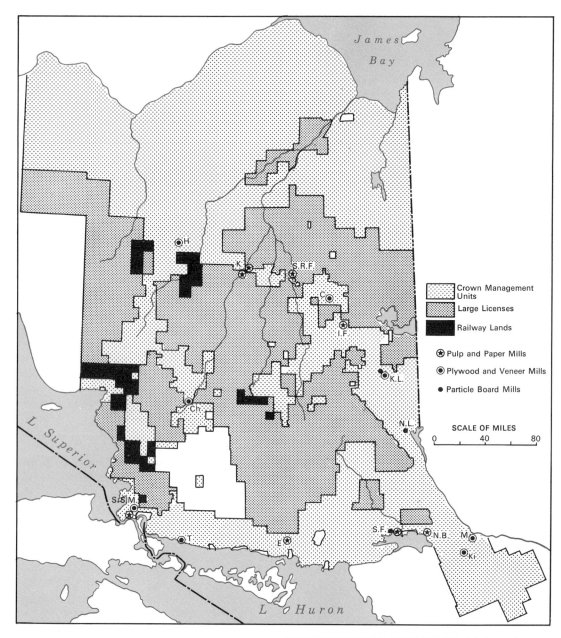

AFTER ONTARIO DEPT. OF ECONOMICS AND DEVELOPMENT

Figure 6.26 Forest Concessions and Activities in Northeastern Ontario
The linear pattern of forest-processing plants along the shoreline and the C.N.R. line is quite striking.

C	Cochrane	M	Mattawa
Ch	Chapleau	N.B.	North Bay
E	Espanola	N.L.	New Liskeard
H	Hearst	S.F.	Sturgeon Falls
I.F.	Iroquois Falls	S.R.F.	Smooth Rock Falls
K	Kapuskasing	S.S.M.	Sault Ste. Marie
Ki	Kiosk	T	Thessalon
K.L.	Kirkland Lake		

the antiquated machinery in some mills and the up-to-date methods used in many woods operations.

Mining

Ontario's mineral production reached almost 1.2 billion dollars in 1967, setting a new record. Ontario still has the highest minerals output of any province in Canada, yet mining contributes only five per cent to the net value of production in Ontario. Mining is important to the economy of many parts of Ontario, but it is overwhelmed by enormous concentration of manufacturing in the province. A major part of the mineral production (80 per cent) comes from the metallic group, in which nickel and copper are most significant. Structural materials, such as sand and gravel, cement and stone, contribute 16 per cent to the provincial production total. Non-metallic minerals account for about three per cent, while fuels provide less than one per cent.

As shown by Table 6.8, much of the production is in the metallic minerals category. The metallic minerals, for the most part, are mined in the Shield area of Ontario. It is apparent that certain geographical factors have influenced the location of mineral developments in Ontario. Obviously the developed deposits are those which have sufficient quality and ease of mining to make for profitable operation.

COURTESY ONTARIO DEPT. TOURISM & INFORMATION

Figure 6.27 A Mechanical Tree Harvester
Forestry operations in the Shield have become far more sophisticated during the last decade. Shown here is a mechanical tree harvester in operation near Thunder Bay.

of cheap power long since dissipated, they are continuing to operate only as a consequence of industrial inertia. Naturally a company wishes to get as much use as possible of its capital equipment. Nevertheless, there is a striking contrast between

Table 6.8   Minerals Industry of Ontario *

Leading Minerals	Production	Value in $000,000
Nickel	190,684 tons	354.9
Copper	269,855 tons	256.7
Iron Ore	8,401,000 tons	95.1
Zinc	272,738 tons	79.0
Sand and Gravel	98,760,000 tons	70.6
Gold	1,492,620 ounces	56.3
Cement	3,243,000 tons	48.1
Uranium	5,448,471 pounds	39.2
Stone	25,036,351 tons	36.6
Silver	15,582,832 ounces	27.0
Salt	4,580,000 tons	20.2

* Dominion Bureau of Statistics. *Preliminary Report of Mineral Production, 1967.* Ottawa. July, 1968.

But other factors are significant also. Accessibility is very important and in most cases the mines operating in Ontario are close to major rail lines and highways. Only in instances where a mineral deposit of exceptional quality has been discovered, as at Steep Rock, have the necessary transportation facilities had to be constructed. Improved methods of prospecting with magnetometers, geiger counters, and air reconnaissance have resulted in new mineral discoveries being made in areas already noted for mining. The now famous Kidd Creek copper deposit near Timmins has

been developed in an area where obviously gold mining was the main economic activity.

Nickel and copper are the two leading minerals produced in Ontario. Sudbury Basin with its unique geological structure is noted for massive ore bodies containing both metals. Although discovered in the early 1880s and worked continuously ever since, it is still Canada's foremost mining area. Two of the world's largest producers, International Nickel and Falconbridge, operate more than 20 mines which are grouped along the edges of the structural

Figure 6.28 Mining in the Shield Area of Ontario
Mining is one of the major extractive industries in the north. The photograph is of the Lowphos Moose Mountain Mine near Capreol and shows some of the varied machinery which is utilized.

COURTESY ONTARIO DEPT. TOURISM & INFORMATION

Figure 6.29 Denison Quirke Mine — Elliot Lake
The stark nature of a mining complex is often in complete contrast to its sylvan setting.

basin. Both companies conduct primary smelting operations within the area, but the nickel is sent elsewhere for refining. International Nickel operates a nickel refinery at Port Colborne in the Niagara Peninsula, while Falconbridge ships nickel-copper matte to its refinery in Kristiansand, Norway. International Nickel has a copper refinery at Copper Cliff near Sudbury. Because world markets for copper and nickel are well established and the ore bodies of the area are so large, a stable and prosperous community of more than 100,000 people has been established in the greater city of Sudbury.

Copper and nickel or copper and zinc mines have been established at Manitowadge, Matheson, Timmins, and several other Northern Ontario points. Zinc stands fourth in value among the minerals produced in Ontario.

Iron ore has become a mineral of some significance in Ontario. While the developments have not been as spectacular as those in Ungava-Labrador, nevertheless, ore shipments reached a level of 8.4 million tons in 1967. Iron ore is now obtained in seven widely separated areas. Steep Rock Lake near Atikokan is the most pro-

ductive area, two companies together having a capacity of about 7,000 tons of iron ore pellets per day. Mining began at Steep Rock in 1943. In order to reach the ore the lake was drained and the course of a river diverted. The exposed lake bottom was then cleared of silt and mined as an open pit. A large ore dock was built at Port Arthur, and the ore shipped by lake carriers to points in Canada and the United States. Recently underground mining has been started and new pelletizing plants built; production is expected to reach 3,000,000 tons per year, about double the previous output.

Two new mining sites developed by Canadian steel companies have recently commenced production. The Sherman mine near Timagami produces concentrates in the form of pellets for use by DOFASCO in Hamilton. Special rail cars are used by the company to transport the ore to Hamilton. In 1968 the Griffith mine near Red Lake began production and now ships concentrated pellets to STELCO in Hamilton. Open pit mining at Marmora has been in operation since 1955, and the concentrates are shipped by rail to Picton and then by boat to Buffalo. Iron ore is also recovered as a bi-product from the copper-nickel tailings from the concentrators at Copper Cliff and Falconbridge. It finds a ready market at Sault Ste. Marie and in the United States.

Uranium has had a rather checkered history of development in Ontario. Between 1955 and 1959, the uranium boom sparked the development of Elliot Lake from a wilderness area into a modern fully serviced community of 29,000. The cancellation of contracts to the United States in 1960 resulted in a severe economic setback. Elliot Lake became almost a modern ghost town.* However, in recent years, new demands for uranium as a source of energy for electric power generation have occurred, and markets have improved. Elliot Lake has responded and has now regained a part of its former glory. All the houses previously abandoned are now occupied and the town has about 10,000 inhabitants. However, like most mining communities, it is still totally reliant on the fortunes of the neighboring mines. Another important source of uranium is found near Bancroft in Eastern Ontario.

Gold was once the most important mineral in Northern Ontario, but in recent years production has seen a steady decline as mines are becoming exhausted. Timmins, Kirkland Lake, and Red Lake are the most productive areas. Silver and cobalt are produced near Cobalt. Salt is obtained at Goderich and Windsor, while gypsum is found near Hagersville and Caledonia. Cement is produced from limestones in Southern Ontario. Plants are operated at Belleville, Clarkson, Picton, St. Marys, and Woodstock. Sand and gravel are obtained in many parts of Ontario, while large quantities of limestone are taken from pits along the Niagara Escarpment. Bricks are made from the shales found at the base of the Escarpment; large plants are found near Milton, Streetsville, Cooksville, and Hamilton. Elsewhere limited supplies of suitable Pleistocene clay have been

* R. G. Bucksar. "Elliot Lake, Ontario: Problems of a Modern Boom Town". *Journal of Geography.* LXI, 3 (March, 1962). pp. 119-124.

made the resource base for local brick and tile factories. The first petroleum production in Canada came from Lambton county in Southwestern Ontario around 1860. The field still produces small quantities of crude oil. Gas wells are found in Southern Ontario from the Niagara River to the Detroit River, and some wells have recently been brought into production on the bed of Lake Erie.

Power

Ontario is the most highly industrialized part of Canada. The basic need of an industrialized society is for a supply of energy to motivate its production and transportation facilities and to provide light and heat for the functions of modern life. The pioneers harnessed the energy of the streams and the winds and that of domestic animals to operate crude machinery. A much more elaborate industry was founded on steam power in the second half of the nineteenth century, with large mills, factories, and steam railways for the transportation of goods. The internal combustion engine has found many uses but has been especially valuable in the field of transportation. All these uses of energy are still with us, but within this century so great an impact has been made by the use of electricity that the word *power* has come almost to mean *electric* power.

Ontario has long been in the front rank of electric power users and was a leader in the development of waterpowered generating stations. Because of the development of a great publicly owned generating and distributing system operated by the Hydro-Electric Power Commission of Ontario, the word *hydro* has come to be synonomous with *electric power* in all parts of the province even though much of the supply is now derived from thermal sources instead of waterpower. A small part of Ontario's power requirement is available from other sources, located chiefly in the province of Quebec, but most of the power supply, both *hydro* and *thermal*, is provided by the generating stations of the HEPCO. At the end of 1968 Ontario

Hydro had a peak generating capacity of slightly more than 10,300,000 kilowatts and was scheduled to add 1,200,000 kw of new generating capacity during 1969.

The largest hydro-electric generating station in Ontario is the Sir Adam Beck complex at Queenston on the Niagara River which has a capacity of 1,800,000 kw. Other smaller stations in the area may be added to reach a total capacity of 2,235,000 kw obtained by the use of water from the Niagara River. The Robert H. Saunders—St. Lawrence generating station near Cornwall has a peak capacity of 845,000 kw. It must not be forgotten that both the Niagara and the St. Lawrence are international rivers and an equal power capacity is developed in the state of New York. The Ottawa River and its largest tributary, the Madawaska, provide a capacity of about 1,245,000 kw. Ottawa power is also used by Quebec. The largest hydro-electric stations in Northern Ontario are at Abitibi Canyon (226,000 kw) and Otter Rapids (177,000 kw), both on the Abitibi River in the James Bay watershed. Stations on the Mattagami River have a capacity of about 500,000 kw.

New hydro-electric generating capacity totalling 1,030,000 kw is scheduled to be added to the Ontario Hydro-Electric System during the period from 1966-1971 (Table 6.9). These new stations are all on the forested Canadian Shield, and some of them are rather remote from the centers where power is required. New high voltage transmission lines have been constructed to carry the current from the James Bay watershed to the large industrial centers with little loss of power. There are now no very large power sites left to be developed in Ontario, and future capacity will have to be developed in large conventional thermal stations or in nuclear power stations.

Among the large coal-fired stations are the Richard L. Hearn plant on the Toronto waterfront (capacity 1,190,000 kw), Lakeview Generating Station in Mississauga, which reached its full capacity of 2,400,000 kw in 1968, and the J. Clark Keith Station (225,000 kw) in Windsor. Large new thermal plants are under construction at Nanticoke on Lake Erie (2,000,000 kw), Sarnia (2,000,000 kw), and Bath (2,000,000 kw) near the eastern end of Lake Ontario. Large nuclear power stations are under construction near Douglas Point (3,000,000 kw) on Lake Huron, and at Pickering (2,160,000 kw) just to the east of Metropolitan Toronto. Shortly after 1975 more than 50 per cent of Ontario's power needs will be supplied by conventional thermal and nuclear power stations.

The distribution of large electric generating stations was once an important factor in industrial location but the development of the Ontario power grid now gives all locations an almost equal opportunity for power supply (Figure 6.30). On-

Table 6.9   Ontario Hydro Power Development Program *

Site	River	Date of Completion	Generating Capacity in Kilowatts
Kipling	Mattagami	1966	125,400
Mountain Chute	Madawaska	1967	139,500
Barrett Chute	Madawaska	1968	111,600
Stewartville	Madawaska	1969	91,800
Aubrey Falls	Mississagi	1969	130,200
Wells	Mississagi	1970	203,300
Lower Notch	Montreal	1971	228,000
Total			1,029,800

* Data from the annual reports of the Hydro-Electric Power Commission of Ontario.

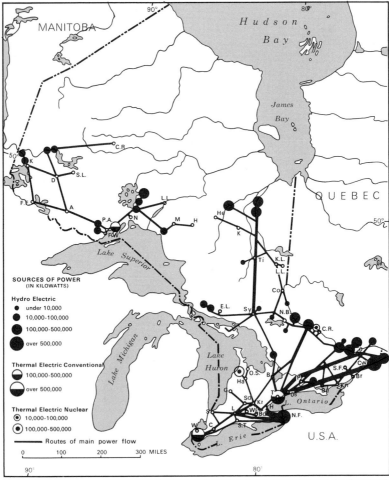

AFTER THE HYDRO-ELECTRIC POWER COMMISSION OF ONTARIO

Figure 6.30 Ontario Power Grid, 1967
Increased needs for power in Southern Ontario are being met with conventional and atomic thermal power stations.

Main Utilization Centers

(a) Key to electrical network in Northwestern Ontario:

A	Atikokan	F.W.	Fort William	M	Manitowadge
C.R.	Crow River	H	Hornepayne	N	Nipigon
D	Dryden	K	Kenora	P.A.	Port Arthur
F.F.	Fort Frances	L.L.	Long Lac	S.L.	Sioux Lookout

(b) Key to electrical network in the remainder of Ontario:

B	Barrie	He	Hearst	P	Peterborough
Bd	Brantford	K	Kapuskasing	S	Sarnia
Be	Belleville	Kn	Kingston	Sd	Stratford
Br	Brockville	Kr	Kitchener	Sy	Sudbury
C	Chatham	K.L.	Kirkland Lake	S.F.	Smith Falls
Co	Cobalt	L	London	S.T.	St. Thomas
Cw	Cornwall	L.L.	Larder Lake	T	Toronto
C.R.	Chalk River	N.B.	North Bay	Ti	Timmins
E.L.	Elliot Lake	N.F.	Niagara Falls	W	Windsor
G	Goderich	O	Ottawa	Ws	Woodstock
H	Hamilton	Os	Oshawa		
Ha	Hanover	O.S.	Owen Sound		

tario has for many years obtained power from Beauharnois and other stations in Quebec; it has connections with New York State at Niagara Falls and at Cornwall, and with Michigan at Windsor and Sarnia. The power system in Northwestern Ontario is connected with power developments in Minnesota and Manitoba. A 230 kilovolt transmission line was completed in 1969 along the north shore of Lake Superior to connect the eastern and western power systems of Ontario. Sometime in the future Ontario will probably be the market for much of the power to be produced by the development of the Nelson River system in Northern Manitoba.

THE CITIES OF ONTARIO

Ontario is the most highly urbanized province in Canada, the census of 1966 revealing the fact that more than 80 per cent of the population is to be found in urban places. Urbanization has been going on almost continuously since the early days of colonization and its tempo has increased fantastically since the end of World War II (Table 6.10). In a period of twenty-five years the urban population of

Ontario has more than doubled. Ontario is slightly more urbanized than Quebec and its urban growth has been somewhat more widely distributed. Its primate city, Metropolitan Toronto, has a smaller share of the provincial population than Montreal has in Quebec, and there are several large cities in other parts of the province.

European settlement in Upper Canada (as Ontario was first called) came in response to an entirely new conception of the political geography of North America, following the Revolutionary War in which the United States became independent of the British Empire. Previously, Canada had seemed to be only a fringing wilderness; suddenly, it became the only basis for the continuation of British development on the continent. Even more important it presented the nearest opportunity for the resettlement of the Loyalists displaced from their homes and properties in the former colonies.

The new colony was conceived as a rural, agricultural settlement, of course. The settlers were already pioneers, or the sons of pioneers, forced to begin again on isolated sites beyond the margins of civilization. The land was laid out in townships,

Table 6.10   The Growth of Population in Ontario, 1871-1966 *

		Total Population	Urban Population	Rural Population	Rural Non-farm Population	Rural Farm Population
1966	Number	6,960,870	5,593,440	1,367,430	885,735	481,695
	Per Cent	100.00	80.36	19.64	12.72	6.92
1961	Number	6,236,092	4,823,529	1,412,563	906,864	505,699
	Per Cent	100.00	77.35	22.65	14.54	8.11
1951	Number	4,597,542	3,132,711	1,464,831	786,397	678,434
	Per Cent	100.00	68.14	31.86	17.10	14.76
1941	Number	3,787,655	2,491,094	1,296,561	605,495	691,066
	Per Cent	100.00	65.77	34.23	15.98	18.25
1931	Number	3,431,683	2,186,579	1,245,104	361,127	783,977
	Per Cent	100.00	63.72	36.28	13.44	22.84
1901	Number	2,182,947	935,978	1,246,969	n.a.**	n.a
	Per Cent	100.00	42.87	57.13		
1871	Number	1,620,851	355,997	1,264,854	n.a.	n.a.
	Per Cent	100.00	21.96	78.04		

* Data from Census of Canada, 1931, 1941, 1951, 1961, 1966.
** n.a.—not available.

concessions, and lots to facilitate agricultural occupancy. The lots were usually 100 acres in area, supposedly the right size for a family farm; the townships covered from 80 to 100 square miles, which was thought to be a convenient size for a community. Original plans show that service centers were envisioned, sometimes in the center of the township to minimize the effects of distance, sometimes on the waterfront because most of the early transportation was by water. Many, in fact most, of the projected towns never materialized. Instead, natural power-sites, river crossings, small harbors, and strategic road junctions spawned most of the early nucleated settlements. Some of these were deliberately founded and planned in an embryo fashion, but many grew spontaneously in very dis-

orderly patterns. It would not be correct to say that no one foresaw the need of a regional center or a political capital. The need was foreseen but there was no agreement concerning the site. In the early days, the Governor's seat was at Quebec, Montreal became the entrepôt of trade, while all places in Upper Canada were simply somewhere in the backwoods and eventually they would somehow sort themselves out.

Local government developed slowly. The first village was Toronto (1793), but only nine more incorporated places (5 villages and 4 towns) were set up before the separation of Canada West in 1841. Toronto (1834) was the only municipality ever given city status in Upper Canada. Four more cities: Hamilton (1846), Kingston (1846), Ottawa (1854), and London (1855)

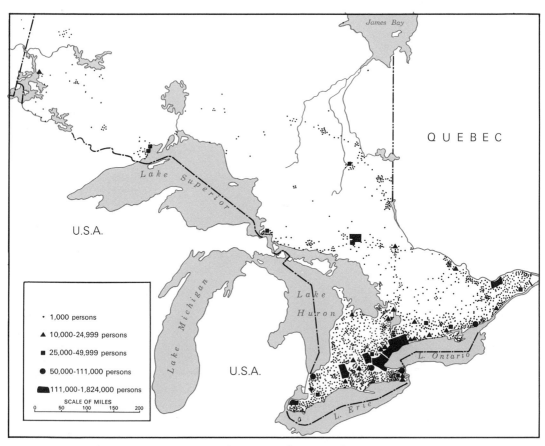

Figure 6.31 Population Distribution in Ontario, 1961

Table 6.11   The Growth of Urban Population in Ontario, 1961-1966 *

Greater Cities	1966 Number	1966 Per Cent	1961 Number	1961 Per Cent	Five-year Increase Per Cent
Toronto	2,158,496	31.01	1,824,589	29.26	18.30
Hamilton	449,116	6.45	395,189	6.34	13.64
Ottawa **	384,397	5.52	322,899	5.18	19.04
Windsor	211,697	3.04	193,365	3.10	9.48
London	207,396	2.98	181,283	2.91	14.40
Kitchener	192,275	2.76	154,864	2.48	24.15
Sudbury	117,075	1.68	110,799	1.77	5.66
St. Catharines	109,418	1.57	95,577	1.53	14.48
Oshawa	100,255	1.44	80,918	1.30	23.89
Fort William-Port Arthur	97,770	1.41	91,625	1.47	6.70
Sault Ste. Marie	74,594	1.07	64,963	1.04	14.82
Kingston	71,540	1.03	63,419	1.02	12.80
Sarnia	66,713	.96	61,293	.98	8.84
Brantford	62,036	.89	56,301	.91	10.18
Niagara Falls	60,768	.87	56,621	.90	7.32
Welland	59,152	.85	54,124	.87	9.28
Peterborough	56,177	.81	51,982	.83	8.07
Guelph	51,377	.74	44,232	.71	16.15
Cornwall	45,766	.66	43,639	.70	4.87
Brampton	45,168	.65	19,794	.32	128.19
North Bay	45,076	.65	40,892	.66	10.23
Timmins	39,806	.57	40,121	.64	− .79
Belleville	32,782	.47	30,655	.49	6.93
Chatham	32,424	.47	29,826	.47	8.71
Large Cities (24)	4,771,274	68.54	4,108,970	65.89	16.12
Other Urban Areas	822,166	11.82	714,559	11.46	15.06
Total Urban Population	5,593,440	80.36	4,823,529	77.35	15.96
Rural Farm Population	481,695	6.92	505,699	8.11	−4.75
Rural Non-farm Population	885,735	12.72	906,864	14.54	−2.33
Total Rural Population	1,367,430	19.64	1,412,563	22.65	−3.20
Total Population	6,960,870	100.00	6,236,092	100.00	11.62

* Data from Census of Canada, 1961, 1966.
** Ottawa includes only that part of the C.M.A. lying within the province of Ontario.

were incorporated in Canada West before Confederation. Before Confederation also, approximately 50 other towns and villages were set up, about 15 of which have since become cities. At some point in the 1840s, Upper Canada passed Lower Canada in total population and early in the 1850s in terms of urban population as well.

The first census after Confederation was taken in 1871 and showed that 22 per cent of Ontario's population dwelt in incorporated urban places, while 78 per cent was classed as rural. Unfortunately, we do not have data to tell how many actually lived on farms. Nor do we know how many lived in rural hamlets and small unincorporated villages although we know that the latter were numerous in many counties.

By 1901 Ontario's population was 43 per cent urban. There were 13 cities with a total population of 466,000, more than half of whom were found in Toronto and Hamilton. Outside the cities 255 towns and villages held about 470,000 to bring the total urban population to 936,000. However, since 82 of these incorporated places held less than 1,000 each, the threshold for an urban place according to the Census of Canada in recent years, about 56,000 might be subtracted from this total.

During the next thirty years rural population remained static, while more than one million people were added to Ontario's cities. The number of cities also increased from 13 to 27. Again, Toronto and Hamilton together held more than half the city population which then amounted to more than 1,516,000, while about 160 towns and villages of more than 1,000 held more than 770,000 to bring the urban population to 2,286,000 or about two-thirds of the total for the province.

During the depression population expanded very little and the rural population grew as fast as the urban, in fact, slightly faster. Since the war the urban population of Ontario has doubled while rural population has hardly grown at all. Indeed, rural population in Ontario has remained remarkably steady for the past 100 years! Practically the total population growth during the whole century has taken place in urban centers.

The growth of urban population in Ontario during the 1960s is shown in Table 6.11. Here we see that 24 large cities now hold two-thirds of Ontario's population. They are growing slightly faster than other urban areas while rural population continues to lose ground, not only in proportion but in actual numerical count. Outside the large cities, about 180 other urban areas with more than 1,000 inhabitants each have a population of almost 900,000. Thus the total urban population in Ontario is almost 5.6 million people or more than 80 per cent of the total.

Distribution of Urban Development

Although the population of Ontario is strongly concentrated, a degree of disper-

sion in the locational pattern of large cities must be noted. No less than five of the "greater cities", Sudbury, Thunder Bay (Fort William and Port Arthur), Sault Ste. Marie, North Bay, and Timmins are in Northern Ontario where the combined "greater city" populations make up more than 50 per cent of the total, and "other urban centers" contain another 20 per cent. Northern Ontario cities, however, are not growing as fast as those of Southern Ontario. Windsor, London, Sarnia, and Chatham are the largest cities in Southwestern Ontario, while Peterborough, Belleville, Kingston, Cornwall, and Ottawa are the largest in the southeastern part of the province.

The outstanding feature of the population pattern of Ontario, however, is the Mississaga conurbation around the western end of Lake Ontario. Here are to be found five census metropolitan areas with populations of more than 100,000 each and four other major cities of over 50,000 each (Table 3.8), together with a large number of smaller urban centers. Mississaga contains more than 3,600,000 people, 92 per cent of whom live in environments that are definitely urban in character. Mississaga also contains some of the best farms and some of the best agricultural land in Ontario. In the fifteen-year period from 1951 to 1966, the urban population of Mississaga increased by 84 per cent from 1,806,000 to 3,335,000 (Table 6.12). During the same period 7,700 farms disappeared and farm population decreased by 29 per cent from 147,000 to 104,000. Land in farms decreased from 2,995,000 acres to 2,515,000 acres, a loss of 16 per cent, mostly in improved land. Some years ago, it was shown that for every thousand persons added to the population of the Toronto-Hamilton urban region, an area of 382 acres was withdrawn from agricultural use.* Over the fifteen-year period the ten counties of Mississaga have lost 479,000

* A. D. Crerar. "The Loss of Farmland in the Growth of the Metropolitan Regions of Canada". *Resources for Tomorrow Conference. Background Papers.* Supplementary Volume. Ottawa. 1962.

Table 6.12 — Distribution of Population in Mississaga, 1951-1966 *

(a) Classification of Total Population	1966 Number	Per Cent	1951 Number	Per Cent
Total Population	3,623,024	100.00	2,107,978	100.00
Urban Population	3,334,477	92.04	1,805,628	85.66
Rural Population	288,547	7.96	302,350	14.34
Farm Population	104,269	2.82	146,645	6.96
Rural Non-farm Population	184,278	5.14	155,705	7.38
Hamlet and Village Population	57,695	1.59	41,000	1.94
Dispersed Rural Non-farm Population	126,583	3.55	114,705	5.44
(b) Classification of Rural Population				
Rural Population	288,547	100.00	302,350	100.00
Farm Population	104,269	34.68	146,645	48.51
Rural Non-farm Population	184,278	65.32	155,705	51.49
Hamlet and Village Population	57,695	20.01	41,000	13.55
Dispersed Rural Non-farm Population	126,583	45.31	114,705	37.94
(c) Classification of Rural Non-farm Population				
Rural Non-farm Population	184,278	100.00	155,705	100.00
Hamlet and Village Population	57,695	31.30	41,000	26.27
Dispersed Rural Non-farm Population	126,583	68.70	114,705	73.73

* Data from Census of Canada, 1951, 1956, 1961, 1966.

acres while adding 1,529,000 persons to the urban population. Thus, for each thousand persons added, about 315 acres were withdrawn from agriculture. As might be expected, the largest withdrawals were near the large cities of Toronto and Hamilton, but very large withdrawals also took place between Toronto and Hamilton and in the Niagara frontier. On the other hand, the land losses to agriculture in the counties along the Grand River were relatively small considering the rapid growth of their urban populations.

While withdrawal of land from agriculture is most striking in areas closely adjacent to the built-up urban areas, it also takes place at some distance as well. This is reflected in the classification of residential location shown in Table 6.12 which indicates that despite the pronounced loss of farm people there has been a considerable increase in rural non-farm population. Part of this is attributable to the expansion of old rural nuclei and to the formation of new ones and part to the ever-growing

distribution of scattered rural residences. Many areas now considered urban have become so during the period under study, by the filling-in of areas already well invaded by rural non-farm residences. In some townships the scattered rural population is considerably greater than the remaining farm population.

Residential developments, nucleated and scattered, are not the only encroachments in agricultural areas. Manufacturers and service industries of all sorts find it convenient to occupy open land, often themselves assisting in the formation of new zones of nucleation as well as providing employment for many of the dispersed population.

Distribution of Economic Activities

With about 55 per cent of the gainfully employed people of the province, the Mississaga conurbation will serve us well for the examination of the spectrum of economic activities (Table 6.13). In view of the fact that Toronto is the largest urban

Table 6.13 Differentiation of Activities in Mississaga as Indicated by Location Quotient *

	Mississaga	Toronto	Remainder of Mississaga	Guelph	Hamilton	Oshawa	St. Catharines	Welland
1. Primary Industries	0.32	0.11	0.68	0.93	0.30	0.02	0.14	0.89
2. Manufacturing	1.23	1.10	1.44	1.38	1.49	1.84	1.58	1.85
3. Construction	1.00	1.10	1.01	0.92	1.08	0.60	0.78	0.96
4. Transportation, Communication, and Utilities	0.95	1.06	0.78	0.64	0.75	0.70	0.83	0.74
5. Wholesale Trade	1.28	1.46	1.00	0.77	0.98	0.55	0.65	0.43
6. Retail Trade	1.05	1.09	0.98	0.97	1.03	1.01	1.04	1.00
7. Finance, Insurance, and Real Estate	1.28	1.61	0.76	0.71	0.79	0.60	0.71	0.46
8. Personal Services	1.00	1.06	0.90	0.85	0.93	0.74	0.96	0.81
9. Community and Business Services	1.03	1.09	0.93	1.59	0.99	0.98	1.03	0.88
10. Public Administration and National Defense	0.63	0.71	0.50	0.76	0.47	0.51	0.48	0.44
11. Unspecified or Undefined	0.93	1.01	0.79	0.98	0.86	0.87	0.91	1.01

* Data from Census of Canada, 1961.

Table 6.14 Differentiation of Activities in Outlying Ontario Cities as Indicated by Location Quotient *

	London	Sarnia	Windsor	Ottawa	Kingston	Thunder Bay	Sault Ste. Marie	Sudbury
1. Primary Industries	0.24	0.09	0.18	0.12	0.05	0.47	0.15	3.38
2. Manufacturing	0.93	1.35	1.34	0.36	0.75	0.65	1.49	0.44
3. Construction	0.92	1.36	0.92	1.09	0.84	1.32	1.18	0.93
4. Transportation, Communication, and Utilities	0.98	1.03	0.95	0.84	0.65	2.30	0.98	0.78
5. Wholesale Trade	1.30	0.55	0.84	0.84	0.59	1.20	0.79	0.70
6. Retail Trade	1.10	1.08	1.08	0.89	0.94	1.09	1.04	1.01
7. Finance, Insurance, and Real Estate	1.26	0.76	0.95	1.12	0.75	0.64	0.63	0.63
8. Personal Services	0.95	1.02	1.21	0.97	0.95	1.11	1.04	0.92
9. Community and Business Services	1.42	1.08	1.11	1.08	1.79	1.20	0.89	0.95
10. Public Administration and National Defense	1.08	0.53	0.54	4.42	2.99	0.70	0.59	0.57
11. Unspecified or Undefined	0.92	0.92	1.07	1.20	1.30	1.32	1.12	1.16

* Data from Census of Canada, 1961.

center in the complex and presumably is also the chief central place, it is convenient to compare it with the remainder or peripheral area. This is done by working out the location index of each major census industrial group, using Ontario per cent values as the base. We note that in only three cases are the Mississaga values significantly higher than those of the province, namely, in manufacturing, wholesale trade, and finance, insurance, and real estate. When we look at the Toronto Census Metropolitan Area, there are only two categories, wholesale trade and financial activities, in which there is significant centrality. On the other hand, the peripheral area is not an area of concentration of any major economic activity except manufacturing, with a highly significant location quotient of 1.44.

The table also contains location quotients for five individual cities in the complex. All are notably higher in their concentration of manufacturing than is Toronto; Oshawa and Welland are very high indeed. Guelph is the only city that departs radically from the general pattern, being lowest in the manufacturing sector and having a very high community service sector because of its institutions. It is noticeable also that retail trade, which is supposed to be one of the best indicators of centrality, nowhere varies as much as ten per cent from the normal and shows its greatest concentration in Toronto.

Metropolitan Toronto

Toronto as a name stands for a number of geographical concepts. In popular parlance it stands for the second-most populous city in Canada, acknowledging that Montreal has a larger official population. But Toronto is also a metropolitan municipality with a much larger population than the city of Montreal, while the fact that it contains a city and five boroughs seems of less and less importance as time goes by. Toronto stands as well for a Census Metropolitan Area only slightly less populous than that of Montreal. The statistical record of the various parts of the Toronto

metropolitan area are given in Table 6.15, and the space relations are shown in the accompanying sketch map (Figure 6.32).

Toronto was founded by Lieutenant-Governor John Graves Simcoe who in 1793 fixed upon a small area on the shore of Toronto Bay as a site for a new town to be named York. He regarded the bay as the best harbor on Lake Ontario, suitable for all military, naval, and commercial activities. Since the American occupation of Detroit might create difficulty in maintaining communications with the Upper Lakes, Simcoe set great store by the development of the Toronto passage and in 1796 had Yonge Street cut through the bush to Holland Landing. Simcoe did not wish the government to have its seat at York, but this was decided by the Governor, Lord Dorchester.

York was captured and burned by American forces in the War of 1812. It was rebuilt and gradually assumed status as the focus of settlement in Upper Canada. Though trade was limited and communications with the Upper Lakes failed to develop rapidly, the fact that it was the center of administration fostered some growth. In 1834 with a population approaching 10,000, York was incorporated as a city and the historic name of Toronto was restored. The built-up area of the time included Simcoe's original town at the eastern end of the harbor and the newer developments west of Yonge Street. The new city extended from the shore to Bloor Street and from the Don River, west to Dufferin Street. Included also was the area east of the Don River, lying between Queen Street and the lake. The built-up area was less than 400 acres in extent, while the city boundaries encompassed an area of eight and one-half square miles, enough, as it turned out, to contain the expansive growth of almost fifty years. In the 1850s Toronto was caught up in the railway age, not only through the building of the Grand Trunk from Montreal to Chicago, but by the building of its own Northern Railway to Collingwood on Georgian Bay. Later several lines fanned out to give

Table 6.15   Toronto Census Metropolitan Area—
Populations of Constituent Municipalities *

	Area	Population		Five-year Growth Rate Per Cent
	Sq. Mi.	1966	1961	
City of Toronto	37.7	697,422	702,524	0.00
Borough of East York	8.3	95,450	90,988	+ 4.90
Borough of Etobicoke	47.9	265,187	198,670	+33.43
Borough of North York	68.1	399,534	269,959	+48.00
Borough of Scarborough	70.1	278,377	217,286	+28.12
Borough of York	9.0	145,721	139,360	+ 4.56
Metropolitan Toronto	241.0	1,881,691	1,618,787	+16.24
Markham (Township)	—	17,386	13,320	
Markham (Village)	—	7,769	4,294	
Richmond Hill (Town)	—	19,773	16,446	
Stouffville (Village)	—	3,883	3,402	
Vaughan (Township)	—	19,022	16,701	
Woodbridge (Village)	—	2,473	2,315	
York County (Part)	221.0	70,306	56,478	+24.48
Milton (Town)	—	6,601	5,629	
Oakville (Town)	—	52,793	42,109	
Halton County (Part)	111.0	59,394	47,738	+24.42
Mississauga (Town)	—	93,492	62,616	
Port Credit (Town)	—	8,475	7,203	
Streetsville (Town)	—	5,884	5,056	
Peel County (Part)	132.0	107,851	74,875	+44.04
Ajax (Town)	—	9,412	7,755	
Pickering (Township)	—	27,851	17,201	
Pickering (Village)	—	1,991	1,755	
Ontario County (Part)	115.0	39,254	26,711	+46.96
Toronto Census Metropolitan Area	820.0	2,158,496	1,824,589	+18.30

* Data from Census of Canada, 1966.

Toronto a sure grip on its hinterland. By the 1870s Toronto had a population of 60,000 and had become the capital of Ontario. By 1881 it had 86,000 people. Toronto lost out to Montreal through the building of the Canadian Pacific Railway from that port to the West and thus did not participate in the western grain trade. Nevertheless, its manufactures expanded under the National Policy of the Macdonald government and it found markets in the West. At the close of the nineteenth century Toronto had reached a population of 200,000. Beginning in the 1880s and continuing until 1921, Toronto continued to enlarge its area and population through annexation of developing suburban areas, becoming a city of more than half a mil-

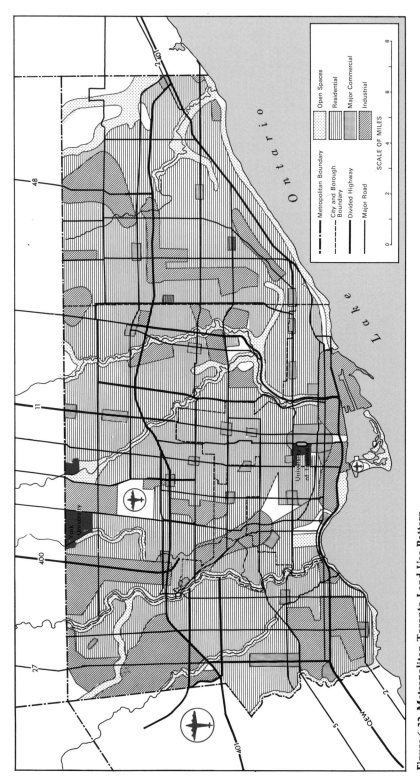

Figure 6.32 Metropolitan Toronto Land Use Pattern
Although the map is based on a development plan published in 1968, the land use pattern illustrated is fairly accurate. Of note is the intention to preserve the river valleys as open space and the distinct clustering of industrial-use land close to the major roads.

lion people with an area of 35 square miles. During World War II it was crowded with more than 700,000 inhabitants.

Though suburban areas continued to expand, no more annexations of adjacent areas took place. By 1951 the "greater city" had a population of more than 1,100,000 in thirteen separate municipalities. Transportation, water, and sewers, as well as other services, were badly in need of co-ordination. In 1953 the Municipality of Metropolitan Toronto was incorporated to include the city and twelve surrounding municipalities with an area of 241 square miles. The metropolitan government was reorganized in 1967 to include the city and five boroughs; thus seven of the former small divisions have been absorbed by their larger neighbors.

There is, of course, still much that is controversial about the metropolitan organization. Many argue that it would be more efficient at this stage when the whole area is almost completely built-up to have

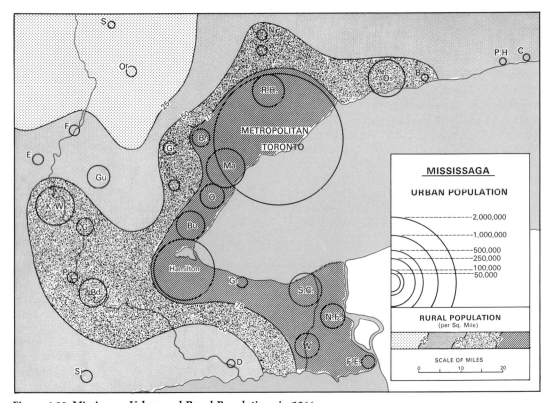

Figure 6.33 Mississaga Urban and Rural Populations in 1966
As shown by the map, a rural population density of over 50 per square mile extends from Bowmanville to the east, west to Georgetown and Kitchener-Waterloo and from Newmarket to the north, south to the Lake Erie shoreline near Dunnville.

A	Aurora	G	Galt	P.H.	Port Hope
B	Bowmanville	Ge	Georgetown	O	Oakville
Bd	Brantford	Gr	Grimsby	Or	Orangeville
Br	Brampton	Gu	Guelph	Os	Oshawa
Bu	Burlington	K-W.	Kitchener-Waterloo	R.H.	Richmond Hill
C	Cobourg	M	Milton	S	Shelburne
D	Dunnville	Ma	Mississauga	Si	Simcoe
E	Elmira	N	Newmarket	S.C.	St. Catharines
F	Fergus	N.F.	Niagara Falls	W	Welland
F.E.	Fort Erie	P	Paris		

a single large city and thus to co-ordinate all urban services. There is also the question of further expansion since already more than half a million urban people are to be found in the fringe municipalities surrounding the metropolitan area. The Census Bureau recognizes the existence of a larger geographical unit, including parts of York, Peel, Halton, and Ontario counties, with a total of 2,158,000 inhabitants in the Census Metropolitan Area. However, even this is not the complete measure of the metropolis which should include further areas in both Ontario and Peel counties which would add at least 145,000 to the total. Reorganization of governmental areas must take place. The old dichotomized rural-urban make-up of the counties is obsolescent. Towns continue to expand into rural areas. Two enormous towns, Oakville and Mississauga (formerly Toronto Township) with populations of 53,000 and 93,000 respectively in 1966, are already of city size. The Ontario Government has proposed a pattern of regional governments to supercede the old system of counties and rural municipalities. Thus the area between Toronto and Hamilton would be occupied by a buffer region with its own center. Another proposal is that a system of satellite cities be created, focused on existing cores, such as Guelph, Orangeville, Alliston, and Barrie, to take the pressure from the center of the metropolis. The metropolitan population has doubled in two decades, and its rate of growth shows little signs of slackening.

Morphology and Function

Morphology and function are closely interlocked in urban development. The user tends to arrange the space and to erect structures suitable to the purpose in hand. However, structures become obsolete, and functions tend to change; thus any developed area will carry the signs of its origin while desperate attempts are made to adapt to new functions. Toronto shows many signs of change.

The Toronto site was chosen because of the harbor, and after many vicissitudes the harbor is still the focus of attention. The port function was very important in the early years but became strictly secondary during the railway era. In fact, it would not be too much to say that by preempting The Esplanade, the railways effectively isolated the city from its waterfront, while the old port facilities fell into neglect. In the early years of this century new facilities were created on extensive land-fill which added approximately two square miles of new land along the waterfront. Since the opening of the St. Lawrence Seaway in 1959 Toronto has become a world port and its facilities are being used almost to capacity. During the 1960s a new land-fill project was begun which will add another harbor in an area reclaimed from Lake Ontario. The port function is again important. In recent years the port has handled about 6,000,000 tons of cargo annually, about 25 per cent of which should be credited to the opportunity for direct overseas shipping.

Behind the waterfront and its flanking barricade of land transportation facilities lies the downtown area of the city of Toronto, an area of about 1,600 acres stretching northward to Bloor Street, the ancient limits of the corporation. It has several well-developed axial routes, two of them, Yonge Street and University Avenue having recently been emphasized by a subterranean rapid transit system. Bloor Street is also paralleled by a subway line from one city limit to the other. But these and all the surface grid of improved traffic ways simply emphasize and reaffirm a century-old pattern whereby thousands of people each morning funnel into the working city and disperse again toward their homes in the evening.

Downtown Toronto is a composite area containing many special areas. There is a *central business district* (C.B.D.) or downtown core, about half a square mile in area, including the financial district of Bay Street, the department stores and other shops along Yonge Street, large hotels, office towers and, most outstanding, the Toronto-Dominion Center. The adminis-

Figure 6.34 Skyline, Toronto

trative function is served by the City Hall, an Ontario Government Building, and a Federal Government Building. But the C.B.D. is only part of the central city. Much of the northwestern quarter is taken up by the University of Toronto complex which itself is nearly as large as the C.B.D.; while in close proximity there are Queen's Park, the Ontario Legislative Building, and the main group of Ontario Government office buildings. Between these and the C.B.D. is a zone in which there are several large hospitals. Other institutions in the downtown area are Ryerson Polytechnic Institute, Ontario College of Art, the community colleges, the art gallery, and the museum. Already mentioned as the northern boundary of the downtown area, Bloor Street has many specialty shops and professional and finan-

cial offices and may be expected to draw more because of its transportation facilities. All in all, downtown Toronto is an impressive display of the results of capital investment. It is somewhat raw and unfinished yet, and it has surprising gaps. Its worst deficiency, undoubtedly, is the failure to solve the parking problem. The city already has remarkably good automobile access routes in the Gardiner Expressway and the Don Valley Parkway and, eventually, it will have completed the Spadina Expressway as well. The city has about 700,000 registered motor vehicles, about 400,000 of which make daily trips to the downtown area; the need for parking is intense.

The Yonge Street—University Avenue, and Bloor-Danforth subway systems serve those areas admirably, and undoubtedly take much pressure from the surface circulation. However, so far, they are only an indication of the kind of service needed by such a large center.

Downtown Toronto even has an airport. It is located on Toronto Island and is reached by a ferry across the western entrance to the harbor. It has facilities for planes equipped with either wheels or pontoons and is extremely busy, being used by many small private planes and by chartering firms as well. Another small airport is found about eight miles to the north, in Downsview. Toronto International Airport, Canada's busiest air terminal, lies approximately 12 miles northwest of the city center, in the northeastern part of the Town of Mississauga. Airports are extremely important to the activities of central business districts but the matter of surface transportation to and from them has not been satisfactorily solved.

The importance of moving people into and out of the downtown area has been highlighted by the GO train, the experimental service instituted by the Ontario Government. Using the C.N.R. tracks this service extends from Dunbarton in the east to Hamilton in the west, giving the whole lakeshore area fast service to the Union Station where connections can be made with the subway system. GO trains are twenty minutes apart in rush hours and hourly during the rest of the day.

Although Toronto is involved in a multiplicity of economic activities, it has been shown that manufacturing is the dominant function of the city.* Much has already been written in this chapter about the concentration of manufacturing industries in the Toronto area, but a few important facts remain to be emphasized. The Toronto Census Metropolitan Area ranks first among all Canadian metropolitan areas in total value of shipments of manufactured goods and in value added by the manufacturing process. It is a close rival of Montreal in number of manufacturing establishments and number of production workers. However it has a substantial mar-

gin in total disbursements for wages and salaries.

Table 6.16 gives an analysis of the manufacturing industries of Toronto in terms of the grouping used by the Bureau of Statistics. The outstanding groups are: foods and beverages, metal fabrication, and electrical products. Clothing industries, which are so important in Montreal, are well down the list. Machinery, chemical products, transportation equipment, and printing and publishing are four groups comprising the second rank and standing not far below the first three. Some industries such as meat packing, brewing, distilling, and metal fabrication were already present in the days before Confederation. With the building of railways and the opening up of western markets Toronto was the logical site for the establishment of new industries. One such industry was the manufacture of farm implements, serving both the well-established farms of Southern Ontario and the new grain farms of Western Canada.

Manufacturing facilities are well scattered throughout metropolitan Toronto and the suburban municipalities.* More than 1,000 establishments with over 40,000 employees are located in the downtown area. Most important are the clothing industries, publishing, printing, lithography, jewelry, and other specialties. The downtown area in the past has served as an incubator from which many industries have moved to new, larger quarters elsewhere as their business expanded. The harbor area has a few large industries including grain milling, sugar refining, brewing, metal working, and chemical processing. The location of many industries has been strongly influenced by the railway pattern of the city since most raw materials were received and most finished goods were shipped by rail. The agricultural implement industry and the meat-packing industry are two outstanding examples of this trend. In recent

* J. W. Maxwell. op. cit.

* D. P. Kerr and J. Spelt. The Changing Face of Toronto. Canada Department of Mines and Technical Surveys. Geographical Branch. Memoir II. Ottawa. 1965.

Table 6.16   Industries of the Toronto Census Metropolitan Area, 1964 *

Industrial Group	Establish- ments	Employees Number	Per Cent	Value Added $000	Per Cent
Wood Ind.	121	2,963	1.13	21,498	0.78
Furniture and Fixture Ind.	436	8,096	3.07	58,133	2.13
Primary Metal Ind.	59	4,638	1.76	50,712	1.85
Metal Fabrication Ind.	806	28,910	10.98	284,612	10.40
Machinery Ind.	169	15,154	5.75	246,427	9.00
Transportation Equipment Ind.	93	22,056	8.38	256,484	9.38
Electrical Products Ind.	221	29,932	11.36	282,727	10.34
Non-metallic Mineral Products Ind.	156	7,959	3.02	92,285	3.36
Food and Beverage Ind.	549	30,638	11.64	368,213	13.45
Leather Ind.	99	3,969	1.51	19,601	0.71
Textile Ind.	196	6,735	2.56	46,968	1.72
Knitting Mills	61	3,230	1.23	18,282	0.67
Clothing Ind.	460	16,779	6.37	89,631	3.28
Paper and Allied Ind.	142	12,237	4.65	107,112	3.92
Printing, Publishing, and Allied Ind.	751	24,225	9.20	237,171	8.75
Chemical and Chem. Products Ind.	300	15,879	6.03	240,506	8.78
Miscellaneous Ind.	695	22,975	8.72	206,947	7.56
Other Major Groups **	38	6,950	2.64	107,395	3.92
Totals	5,352	263,325	100.00	2,734,704	100.00

* Dominion Bureau of Statistics. *Manufacturing Industries of Canada. Section G. Geographical Distribution* 1964. Queen's Printer and Controller of Stationery. 1968. Catalogue No. 31-209. Ottawa. 1968.
** Includes Tobacco Products, Rubber Industries, and Petroleum and Coal Products Industries.

decades the development of truck transportation has freed many industries from their dependence on the railways, allowing new suburban industrial areas to develop along the main highways leading from the city. Petroleum refining has sought suburban sites along the lake where both rail and highway facilities are within easy reach; so also have cement and clay products establishments. Practically all plants requiring large areas of land must now seek locations outside of the metropolitan municipality where space for employees' parking lots as well as large building sites may be secured. The establishment of large manufacturing plants tends to encourage residential and commercial development in nearby areas, thus further complicating the pattern of an already complex city.

Other Cities

Hamilton is the second city in Ontario in terms of population and value of economic activity. Located at the western end

of Lake Ontario its center is less than 45 miles from that of Toronto, and the two cities are connected by an almost continuous built-up urban area. Metropolitan Hamilton with a population of 450,000 (300,000 in the central city) is a very strong sector of the Mississaga urban complex. Though ranked sixth in Canada in terms of total population, the Hamilton C. M. A. ranks third in the development of manufacturing industries. This is in large measure due to the waterfront location of two large primary iron and steel plants which turn out about three-fourths of all the steel produced in Canada. The industry is well located for not only is there a large steel market in Hamilton itself, but there are many steel-using industries in nearby cities. Hamilton has important port facilities, handling around 10,000,000 tons of cargo per year, much of it being iron ore and coal for the steel industry.

The shoreline of Hamilton Harbor is occupied by heavy industry, while other zones with light industrial, commercial, and residential land uses lie between this and the precipitous face of the Niagara Escarpment, which is here known as "the mountain". On the flat land above the Escarpment widespreading new suburbs have been built. McMaster University occupies a large site in the western part of Hamilton.

The Niagara Frontier comprises three large cities: St. Catharines (115,000), Niagara Falls (64,000), and Welland (60,000). Power from the Niagara River and from lesser sites along the Niagara Escarpment has focused industry in this area for a long time. The canal has provided essential transportation for materials used in some industries, particularly pulp and paper. St. Catharines was particularly noted as a center of the fruit-growing and processing industries. At the present time its major industries are concerned with motor vehicle parts, shipbuilding, metal fabricating, and pulp and paper. Brock University has recently been established on the brow of the Niagara Escarpment.

Niagara Falls was at one time a relatively small tourist resort town beside the famous cataract. Today it is also a bustling industrial center. Just north of the city are to be found the great Sir Adam Beck generating stations of the Ontario Hydro-Electric System. Manufactured products of the city include chemicals, fertilizers, wines, cereal products, and silverware.

Welland, together with Port Colborne, is a large industrial center along the Welland Canal. Among its industries are large nickel refineries, steel plants, pipe mills, and textile factories.

The problems of growth in these centers have caused the province to consolidate them under a Niagara regional government.

The Kitchener C. M. A. (200,000) comprises the cities of Kitchener, Waterloo, and Galt, together with several small centers in the Grand River Valley. Meat products, beverages, tires, metal products, textiles, and electrical appliances are produced in large quantities in this complex industrial area. Two universities are located in Waterloo. The nearby city of Guelph (56,000) is the site of a noted university.

London (220,000), situated half way between Toronto and Windsor, functions as the chief central place in Southwestern Ontario. Long a noted railway center, it became the center of a highway network as well. Prepared cereals, beverages, electrical appliances, and locomotives are important products. London is the site of one of the major universities of the province.

Windsor (220,000) in the extreme southwestern part of the province is the original home of the automobile industry in Canada. Chemicals, pharmaceuticals, beverages, and metal products are also important products of the city. Geographically Windsor is part of the great Detroit urban complex comprising several million inhabitants and is joined to it by a highway bridge and tunnel and railway services. Windsor also has a university.

The eastern part of the province has few large cities. Ottawa (385,000) is the capital of Canada. The largest sector of its working force is engaged in the public service. Ottawa is the site of two universities and many government research institutions.

Kingston (75,000) at the eastern end of Lake Ontario has two universities and large government defence centers. Its chief industries produce textiles and aluminum goods.

The cities of Northern Ontario include North Bay (45,000), noted as a transportation and defense center; Sudbury (120,000), center of the largest mining district in Canada; Sault Ste. Marie (77,000), Canada's second-ranking steel-making center; and Thunder Bay. Recently consolidated into a single municipality with more than 100,000 inhabitants, Thunder Bay comprises the former cities of Fort William and Port Arthur, together with adjoining urban areas. With an annual transshipment of about 20,000,000 tons of cargo it ranks with Montreal and Vancouver as one of Canada's greatest ports. Among its industrial products may be listed pulp and paper, wood products, grain products, and transportation equipment. Universities are found in both Sudbury and Thunder Bay.

REGIONAL DIFFERENCES
IN ONTARIO

Despite its enormous resource base and high degree of industrialization, Ontario suffers from regional disparities in economic development. All peripheral areas feel that they are experiencing discrimination because of the concentration of industry in the major urban centers, Metropolitan Toronto in particular. Ontario does not face this problem alone. All the provinces in Canada suffer from uneven development, but in Ontario the range of per capita wealth is wider and the regional pattern is more complicated. Agriculturists, foresters, economists, geographers, and others have long been trying to establish a set of regions in Ontario that would be a suitable base for statistical comparisons. All efforts have been disappointing because of the hard fact that all statistics are collected and compiled on the basis of the mosaic of political units which includes counties, townships, cities, towns, and villages of extremely varied populations, areas, and other characteristics.

Economic Regions

In recent years a determined effort has been made to analyze the economy of Ontario on the basis of ten economic areas or regions, each of which comprises a group of contiguous counties and districts. Cities and separated towns, although politically independent, are included with the surrounding areas and in most cases provide the economic focus of the region. The regions were officially presented as described in the *Ontario Economic and Social Aspects Survey* prepared by the Ontario Department of Economics and published in 1961. Since then, special detailed reports have been published for each of the ten regions.

The scheme was drafted at the end of World War II by the Canada Department of Defense Production in order to facilitate the changeover to peacetime conditions.*

An outline of the scheme and its philosophy was given by Nicholson and Sametz at the Montreal Convention.* Later a full description of the methodology of the scheme was incorporated as Part III of the volume by Camu, Weeks, and Sametz.** This regional scheme is based on "the *S F P M* formula". *S* connotes basic "structural" factors such as physiography, population, and capital; *F* refers to functional factors such as transportation and communications networks and other service industries; *P*, the productive factor, includes natural resources and commodity-producing industries and their interrelationships; and *M* denotes markets and consuming areas. The ten "economic regions" of Ontario may be accurately described using these factors, and so may all smaller statistical units within them.

Hans Carol has launched a full-scale attack on the system.*** The economic regions are purely arbitrary groupings of political statistical units, completely lacking any analytic foundation. Carol would replace it with a hierarchy of city-centered regions on the basic hypothesis that certain cities do now in fact serve as regional centers. Carol's scheme has its attractive points but translated into an administrative system it might eventually become an administrative straight jacket and an impediment to rational future growth under changed conditions.

The Ontario Department of Municipal Affairs is revamping local government by creating new regional units including an Ottawa Metropolitan Region, a Niagara Region to include the former counties of

* Economics and Statistics Branch. *Economic Zoning of Canada and the D.D.P. Geographic Code.* Department of Defense Production. Ottawa. August, 1953.

* N. L. Nicholson and Z. W. Sametz. "Regions of Canada and the Regional Concept". *Resources for Tomorrow Conference. Background Papers.* Vol. 1. Ottawa. 1961. pp. 367-383.
** P. Camu, E. P. Weeks, and Z. W. Sametz. *Economic Geography of Canada, with an Introduction to a 68-Region System.* Macmillan of Canada. Toronto. 1964.
*** Hans Carol. *The Geographical Identification of Regional Growth Centers and Development Regions in Southern Ontario.* A Report to the Regional Development Branch of the Department of Economics and Development, Province of Ontario. Toronto. November, 1966.

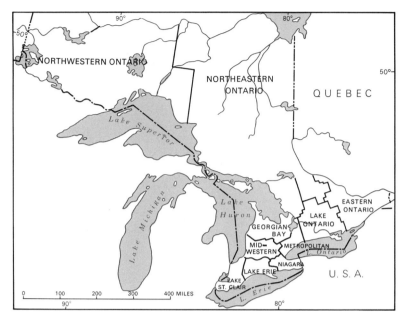

AFTER DEPT. OF ECONOMICS AND DEVELOPMENT

Figure 6.35 Economic Regions of Ontario

Lincoln and Welland, and a unit amalgamating Port Arthur, Fort William, and adjoining areas to form a new city of Thunder Bay. There is, however, no clear evidence that economic and political planning are being used as complementary procedures.

Economic Health

Although admittedly imperfect, the Economic Regions of Ontario may be used to study conditions of economic health. Bell and Stevenson selected 16 variables and then ranked the 53 counties and districts of Ontario for each of the variables and subjected the data to statistical analysis in order to determine an economic health component.* Table 6.17 shows data for ten counties and districts in Ontario, selected to represent conditions in the ten Economic Regions of the Province. The "Health Index" derived from the statistical

* W. H. Bell and D. W. Stevenson. "An Index of Economic Health for Ontario Counties and Districts". *Ontario Economic Review.* II, 5 (September, 1964).

procedures is shown in the last line of the table. Because of the way in which it was derived, a high number indicates poor economic health while a low or even a minus index indicates good economic health. This will be understood from a study of the rankings shown in Table 6.18. Those counties which rank high in a large number of variables, naturally rank low in the summation of rankings and, eventually, in the ranking of the "Health Index". The calculation of the "Health Index" involves a much more sophisticated procedure than is shown here, yet it obviously indicates little more than may be seen from the totals of the rankings.

However, one must be careful not to place too much emphasis on such exercises. In the total context of geographical reality these are only sample data from (hopefully) representative units at a definite point in their economic development. To be specific, Glengarry county which represents Eastern Ontario is one of the most rural and resource-poor areas in the province and it has very little urban and indus-

Table 6.17   Economic Data for Ten Selected Ontario Counties and Districts

Variable	Unit	Thunder Bay	Sudbury	Glengarry	Hastings	Peel	Lincoln	Perth	Elgin	Essex	Grey
1. Value Added in Manufacturing 1951-61	Percentage Change	8.5	61.7	374.7	66.9	83.9	15.0	78.7	27.1	13.9	39.0
2. Population with a University Education	Percentage of Population over 5 Years of Age	3.8	3.9	2.7	4.1	8.4	5.6	3.1	3.7	5.3	2.8
3. Retail Sales 1951-61	Percentage Change	56.3	75.6	20.7	45.1	218.7	45.7	12.4	26.1	19.1	17.8
4. Agricultural Employment 1961	Percentage of Industrial Employment	1.9	1.4	40.9	8.3	6.9	9.5	25.7	25.5	8.5	30.7
5. Total Population 1961	Thousands	138.5	165.9	19.2	93.4	111.6	126.7	57.5	62.9	285.2	62.0
6. Population 1951-61	Percentage Change	31.5	51.4	8.6	25.7	100.4	41.8	9.6	13.2	18.9	5.2
7. Average Family Income 1961	Dollars	5,480	5,973	3,814	5,211	6,834	5,681	4,969	4,920	5,311	4,563
8. Persons 20 to 49 Years of Age 1961	Percentage of Population	40.2	41.0	30.9	38.0	42.0	39.1	35.1	36.2	37.2	33.6
9. Wage Earners Making More than $6,000 a Year 1961	Percentage of Total Wage Earners	9.8	10.5	2.8	8.1	18.4	9.4	4.8	6.3	9.3	4.0
10. Wage Earners Making Less than $1,000 a Year 1961	Percentage of Total Wage Earners	11.8	9.9	24.1	14.0	11.7	14.3	16.7	19.4	14.5	18.0
11. Average Income of Employees in Manufacturing 1961	Dollars	4,903	4,952	2,873	3,633	4,572	4,422	3,410	3,711	4,955	3,080
12. Immigrant Population 1961	Percentage of Total Population	24.2	14.1	4.7	9.6	22.7	26.4	10.8	18.6	22.1	7.2
13. Value Added in Manufacturing Per Employee 1961	Dollars	11,393	23,713	7,616	7,838	9,496	7,619	6,915	6,163	9,964	5,224
14. King's Highways 1961	Miles	652	324	59	238	125	79	131	116	216	144
15. Motor Vehicle Registrations 1951-61	Percentage Change	97.8	118.9	34.2	57.1	181.8	86.0	30.1	51.8	52.3	25.3
16. Homes in Need of Major Repairs 1961	Percentage of Total Homes	6.0	6.8	13.5	7.2	2.5	3.6	3.8	7.6	5.1	5.2
Health Index		20.5	-8.2	431.3	150.8	-16.7	59.2	295.9	258.5	102.1	375.8

Table 6.18 Ranking Among Selected Ontario Counties and Districts by Variables

	Thunder Bay	Sudbury	Glengarry	Hastings	Peel	Lincoln	Perth	Elgin	Essex	Grey
1. Value Added in Manufacturing 1951-61	9	5	1	4	2	8	3	7	10	6
2. Population with a University Education	6	5	10	4	1	2	8	7	3	9
3. Retail Sales 1951-61	3	2	7	5	1	4	10	6	8	9
4. Agricultural Employment 1961	2	1	10	4	3	6	8	7	5	9
5. Total Population 1961	3	2	10	6	5	4	9	7	1	8
6. Population 1951-61	4	2	9	5	1	3	8	7	6	10
7. Average Family Income 1961	4	2	10	6	1	3	7	8	5	9
8. Persons 20 to 49 Years of Age 1961	3	2	10	5	1	4	8	7	6	9
9. Wage Earners Making More Than $6,000 a Year 1961	3	2	10	6	1	4	8	7	5	9
10. Wage Earners Making Less Than $1,000 a Year 1961	3	1	10	4	2	5	7	9	6	8
11. Average Income of Employees in Manufacturing 1961	3	2	10	7	4	5	8	6	1	9
12. Immigrant Population 1961	2	6	10	8	3	1	7	5	4	9
13. Value Added in Manufacturing Per Employee 1961	2	1	7	5	4	6	8	9	3	10
14. King's Highways 1961	1	2	10	3	7	9	6	8	4	5
15. Motor Vehicle Registrations 1951-61	3	2	8	5	1	4	9	7	6	10
16. Homes in Need of Major Repairs 1961	6	7	10	8	1	2	3	9	4	5
Total of Rankings	57	44	142	85	38	70	117	116	77	134
Ranking of Totals	3	2	10	6	1	4	8	7	5	9
Ranking of Health Index	3	2	10	6	1	4	8	7	5	9

trial development. Eastern Ontario also contains the cities of Cornwall, Kingston, and Ottawa, which present a quite different picture. Rural and urban areas in other economic regions of the province also present considerable contrast.

The problem of *rural poverty* has been given considerable study by the A.R.D.A. researchers of the Canada Department of Forestry.* They considered "low income farms", "low rural non-farm wages", "low urban wages", "low non-farm family incomes", "registration for employment", "education levels", and "infant mortality". Each of the factors was defined and mapped for all of Canada and each has some significance in the differentiation of regions. Two of these maps have been selected for discussion.

The distribution of *low income farms* is shown in Figure 6.36. To be classed as such, a farm must have a capital value of less than $24,950, the value of its gross

* A.R.D.A. *Economic and Social Disadvantage in Canada — Some Graphic Indicators of Location and Degree.* Canada Department of Forestry. Ottawa. 1964.

sales of agricultural products must be less than $2,500, and the operator must have had off-farm work for less than one month in the year. This definition eliminated many of the part-time farms on the Shield where the operator usually has off-farm employment for more than a month. However, based on the other criteria, these are also "low income farms". The Georgian Bay Economic Region has from 20 to 40 per cent of its census farms in the low income category; Northeastern Ontario and Eastern Ontario both have from 20 to 30 per cent. Northwestern Ontario has surprisingly few low income farms, presumably because of the small number of farm operators who spend only one month or less at off-farm work. Low income farms occur least frequently in the rural areas located in close proximity to the Mississaga urban complex.

The distribution of *low income non-farm families* is shown in Figure 6.37. In this case the A.R.D.A. researchers excluded all families in urban centers having populations of 10,000 and over. The incomes of all family members 15 years of age and

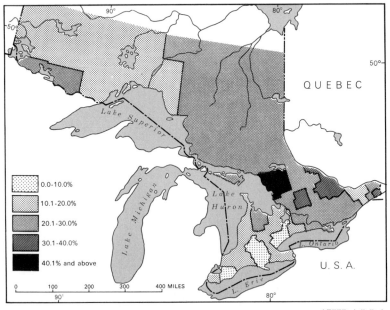

AFTER A.R.D.A.

Figure 6.36 Low Income Farms in Ontario

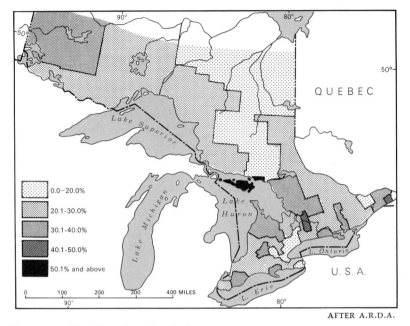

Figure 6.37 Low Non-farm Family Incomes
The data are based on the twelve month period prior to the 1961 census
and plotted by counties or census divisions.

over were counted, and a family was considered to have a low income if the total amount was less than $3,000 per annum. As in the previous map both the Georgian Bay and Eastern Ontario regions fared badly, 30 to 40 per cent of the non-farm families reporting incomes below $3,000. However, other groups of families with low incomes were shown to exist in the Lake St. Clair, Midwestern, Lake Ontario, and Northwestern regions.

The Problems of Differential Economic Growth

There are many problems underlying regional differences in economic growth. One major problem already discussed is that of marginal agriculture. In this Ontario is not unique for marginal farming poses an economic threat to many areas in Quebec and the Atlantic Provinces and even in certain parts of Western Canada. In Ontario it is particularly prevalent along the borders of the Canadian Shield and in pockets within the Shield. Moon has termed the Shield

fringes in Frontenac, Lanark, and Renfrew counties, the "Ozarks of Ontario".* Small farms based on rocky pastures and miniscule bush clearings are typical of this area in Eastern Ontario.

However, similar patterns occur in the Clay Belt, on the fringes of the Algonquin Lake plain near Sault Ste. Marie and in the vicinity of Thunder Bay. Marginal agriculture is widespread and is not necessarily to be blamed on the natural environment. Many of the original 100-acre farms in Southern Ontario can no longer be operated profitably simply because they are too small for general crop and livestock agriculture. Unless they can find a profitable specialty, they will be forced to cease operations and their land will be sold to more prosperous neighbors.

Marginal agriculture is not the only cause of regional weakness. Many communities which formerly depended upon small local industries have been equally

* Barbara Moon. "Ontario's Rural Slum". *Toronto Globe and Mail.* January 11-15, 1965.

hard hit. Small sawmills and woodworking plants, and small woolen mills and grist mills might be mentioned. In pioneer times these were signs of growing economic strength in a new settlement. Now they are apt to be regarded as signs of backwardness.

Within regions small areas of retarded growth may be balanced by expanding cities. A good example of this is found in Eastern Ontario where Bell and Stevenson chose Glengarry county as a representative study area. However, if all eleven counties are studied in the same way this region may be seen to fall into three zones: (a) Carleton county, which contains Metropolitan Ottawa; (b) the St. Lawrence "Front" with the cities of Kingston, Brockville, and Cornwall; (c) the counties of the Ottawa Valley (except for Carleton). If indices of economic health are calculated, they are found to rank in the same order. When an economic health index for the whole region is calculated, Eastern Ontario is by no means the poorest region in Ontario. That dubious honor seems to be in dispute between the Georgian Bay region and Northwestern Ontario.

This criticism does not mean that the worth of such studies is doubted, only that there is a necessity to carry them on to more definitive conclusions. What it does mean, probably, is that the ten Economic Regions are not tailored to the realities of Ontario geography and that Carol is right to insist on the importance of city development. It also means that the student dare not take for granted *any* series of economic health indices; he must know how they were constructed. Quite obviously, population growth is the best indicator of economic activity in the present and the immediate past, but what is wanted is a prognosis for the future. How can economic growth be initiated in areas now stagnant?

Industrial Concentration

One of the problems in Ontario arises from the fact that industrial development has accelerated and concentrated in a few favored areas. Large areas in Ontario, especially the Eastern Ontario, Lake Ontario, Georgian Bay, and Northern Ontario regions have *not* developed manufacturing and tertiary services to the extent that is locally desirable. For the most part, this can be shown to be a response to basic location factors. Kerr and Spelt found that market potential, transport costs, labor stability, and personal initiative were most important in explaining the concentration of manufacturing in the Mississaga region.* They also suggested that once a manufacturer elected not to locate in either Metropolitan Toronto or Montreal, then on the basis of market access and transport costs the industry was relatively "footloose" to locate almost anywhere in Southern Ontario. However, this does not explain the relatively slow growth of manufacturing in the Eastern Ontario and Georgian Bay economic regions.

Michael Ray studied the location of Ontario branch plants of American companies and found an interesting pattern based on "desire lines" from the parent company.** Eastern Ontario was seen to be in the zone of "economic shadow" of Metropolitan Toronto because the major market center was the focal point for many of the American branch plants (Figure 6.38). The Georgian Bay region is under the same shadow. To what degree has this been true in the past? Blackbourn has studied the problem intensively and concludes that "although Ontario's share of the American-owned plants in Canada had changed little since the nineteenth century, considerable changes had taken place in the locations of American-owned plants within Ontario".*** In 1913 the percentage of such

* D. P. Kerr and J. Spelt. "Some Aspects of Industrial Location in Southern Ontario". *Canadian Geographer*. 15 (1960). pp. 12-25.
** D. Michael Ray. *Market Potential and Economic Shadow*. Department of Geography Research Series. No. 101. University of Chicago. Chicago. 1965.
*** A. Blackbourn. *Locational Patterns of American-owned Industry in Southern Ontario*. Ph.D. Thesis. University of Toronto. Department of Geography. 1968. p. 10.

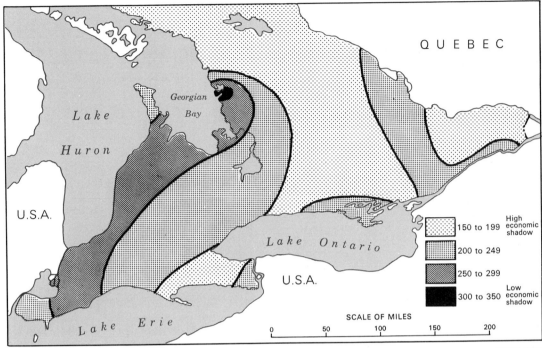

AFTER RAY

Figure 6.38 Economic Shadow in Southern Ontario

plants located in border cities such as Windsor was relatively high, while the comparative percentages for Toronto and other non-border regions were low. Since that time the percentage in the Toronto area has increased markedly. Because many of the manufacturing establishments in Ontario are American owned, the disparity in industrial development throughout Ontario will be difficult to modify even with governmental aid.

Urban Centers Dominated by a Single Function

For many cities in Ontario this is not a problem, but severe instability may result where the economic life depends almost completely upon a single industry. Even in a large city such as Oshawa, the overwhelming influence of General Motors on the community poses certain problems. If a strike ensues, the local economy stagnates until it is settled. Even a large center such as Metropolitan Toronto can be affected by the closing of a large factory. Considerable problems were created in 1959 when A. V. Roe closed its doors and 10,000 men were suddenly without employment.

However, the problem is much more severe in smaller communities, particularly those in Northern Ontario. The problems faced by Elliot Lake when the uranium mines were closed illustrate just how slender the thread of economic life is for communities dominated by a single industry. When the mine shafts were being sunk in 1955, a new town became necessary. Between 1955 and 1958 the provincial government invested $19,000,000 in a new approach highway and municipal services. At the same time the federal government, through Central Mortgage and Housing Corporation, advanced $40,000,-000 in first mortgages to permit the construction of 1,800 single family homes and

R. PUTNAM

500 city-type apartment units. By 1959 there were more than 25,000 people in Elliot Lake. However, in November, 1959, it was announced that the U.S. Atomic Energy Commission would not take up its post-1962 Canadian uranium option. Elliot Lake, a model community in the north, was suddenly without a future. The miners by and large lost little for their investment in housing was protected through their "buy-back" agreements with the mining companies. The entrepreneurs faced the greatest loss. While Elliot Lake did not completely vanish, its population dwindled to almost one-fifth of its previous size. New homes and stores were vacated and boarded up, and evidence of neglect became widespread by 1962. However, since 1967 some new uranium contracts have been secured, and certain mines have been reactivated. At the beginning of 1969 a housing shortage loomed again as the population passed the level of 10,000. Still, the future of the town is tied inextricably to that of the uranium market.

Figure 6.39 Elliot Lake, Ontario
As a modern planned mining community, Elliot Lake has all the necessary amenities for urban life. Even the trailer parks are well maintained and have water, sewage, and hydro facilities. These photographs illustrate the situation in January, 1969.

Similar problems face most of the towns in Northern Ontario. Dryden, Marathon, Terrace Bay, Sturgeon Falls, and Espanola, all depend on the fortunes of the pulp and paper industry, while Timmins, Kirkland Lake, Wawa, Atikokan, and Red Lake rely on mining. All are based on the use of natural resources which may easily be affected by changing market conditions outside of Canada. In the case of mining towns, the problem is worse for they are based on non-renewable resources which inevitably will become exhausted. The declining "railway town" is also an important phenomenon. In the days of coal-burning locomotives a large number of divisional points were established across Ontario. The adoption of diesel power has caused many of them to be phased out as maintenance work is centralized in fewer shops. This forced mobility has produced a peculiar philosophy among the people for they are really within the "frontier" and normally expect that any Northern Ontario community may at best be home for no more than five years. The basic problem for the region is to find industries to replace those which have been phased out and to locate them in communities which have the potential to become future growth points.

REGIONAL DEVELOPMENT

Ontario is a land of regional contrasts. Some of these contrasts are physical, such as those between the climates of northern and southern regions, or between the landforms and soils of the Canadian Shield and those which are based on the overlying Paleozoic rocks. Other contrasts are the results of long-continued human activity such as the development of agriculture in Southern Ontario and the extraction of wealth from the forests and mines of the northern regions. Both the physical and the human factors interact to produce a pattern of extreme contrast in population distribution. Northern Ontario, with more than seven-eighths of the area of the province,

has less than one-eighth of the total population and about one-ninth of the annual production of wealth. One must point out, however, that some parts of Southern Ontario are also less productive than other parts.

The outstanding feature of the development of Ontario is the phenomenon of urbanization, and the outstanding contrast is that which exists between the highly urbanized areas, with active growth centers, and those in which the cities are either small or widely scattered, or perhaps both. Ontario cities have now developed to the point that more than 80 per cent of the population now lives in an urban environment. More than 50 per cent lives in one rather restricted area around the western end of Lake Ontario, and about 25 per cent in the single urban municipality of Metropolitan Toronto. Wealth is similarly concentrated; some of the more highly urbanized counties have personal disposable incomes ranging close to $3,000.00 per capita per annum, while in the less urbanized counties the average is about $2,000.00. The centralization of economic power and political influence which these contrasts imply creates considerable stress and resentment in peripheral areas. At times there have even been suggestions that new and smaller political units ought to be created, especially in Northern Ontario. It must be remembered, of course, that the citizens of the cities of Northern Ontario also have high incomes and that the contrast between the cities and their surroundings are even greater than in Southern Ontario. How may these contrasts be reduced?

Unfortunately, the usual approach to this question is couched in negative terms. Cities must *not* be allowed to grow so fast; they must *not* be permitted to proliferate and sprawl over the countryside; wealth must *not* be so completely concentrated in the cities. Much more thought is given over to the purpose of controlling and restricting the phenomenon of urban growth than to the purpose of solving the real problems of economic disparity.

The positive approach to regional development requires much more thought and some real attention to the planning process. There are statistical procedures that show fairly conclusively that economic health is strongly correlated with urbanization. It is also known that many secondary industries and some kinds of service industries are relatively footloose. It is known too that either private or public enterprise can successfully launch an urban center on the basis of a single strong enterprise. It should be possible to create a regional city by taking a "single enterprise" center and deliberately adding other functions. In a sense this is what has happened to North Bay to transform it from a stagnant "railway town" of less than 20,000 inhabitants to an urban complex of more than 50,000 within a quarter of a century. North Bay has a good geographical location, and perhaps its modern prosperity would have happened anyway; but it certainly has been promoted by a number of positive decisions. Similar positive decisions might well activate growth centers elsewhere. Carefully selected and purposefully encouraged growth centers appear to offer much in the creation of a balanced regional development.

BIBLIOGRAPHY

A.R.D.A. *Economic and Social Disadvantage in Canada — Some Graphic Indicators of Location and Degree*. Canada Department of Forestry. Ottawa. 1964.

Bell, W. H. and Stevenson, D. W. "An Index of Economic Health for Ontario Counties and Districts". *Ontario Economic Review*. II, 5 (September, 1964).

Blackbourn, A. *Locational Patterns of American-owned Industry in Southern Ontario*. Ph.D. Thesis. University of Toronto. Department of Geography. 1968.

Brown, D. M. *The Climate of Southern Ontario*. Canada Department of Transport Meteorological Branch Study No. 5. Ottawa. 1968.

Brown, R. J. E. *Permafrost Investigations in Northern Ontario and Northeastern Manitoba*. Technical Paper No. 291. Division of Building Research. National Research Council of Canada. Ottawa. November, 1968.

Bucksar, R. G. "Elliot Lake, Ontario: Problems of a Modern Boom Town". *Journal of Geography*. LXI, 3 (March, 1962). pp. 119-124.

Camu, P.; Weeks, E. P.; and Sametz, Z. W. *Economic Geography of Canada, with an Introduction to a 68-Region System*. Macmillan of Canada. Toronto. 1964.

Carol, Hans. *The Geographical Identification of Regional Growth Centers and Development Regions in Southern Ontario*. A Report to the Regional Development Branch of the Department of Economics and Development, Province of Ontario. Toronto. November, 1966.

Chapman, L. J. and Putnam, D. F. *The Physiography of Southern Ontario*. University of Toronto Press. 2nd edition. Toronto. 1966.

Chapman, L. J. and Thomas, M. K. *The Climate of Northern Ontario*. Canada Department of Transport. Meteorological Branch Study No. 6. Ottawa. 1968.

Crerar, A. D. "The Loss of Farmland in the Growth of the Metropolitan Regions of Canada". *Resources for Tomorrow Conference. Background Papers*. Supplementary Volume. Ottawa. 1962.

Dean, W. G. "Glacial Features of the Hearst-Cochrane Map Sheet Area". *Canadian Geographer*. 8 (1956). pp. 33-45.

Economics and Statistics Branch. *Economic Zoning of Canada and the D.D.P. Geographic Code*. Department of Defense Production. Ottawa. August, 1953.

Ford, D. C. "The Bonnechère Caves, Renfrew County, Ontario: A Note". *Canadian Geographer*. V, 3 (1961). pp. 22-25.

Halliday, W. E. D. "A Forest Classification for Canada". *Forest Service Bulletin*. 89 (1937). Ottawa.

Hewitt, D. F. "Rocks and Minerals of Ontario". *Ontario Department of Mines*. Circular No. 13. Toronto. 1965.

Kerr, D. P. and Spelt, J. "Some Aspects of Industrial Location in Southern Ontario". *Canadian Geographer*. 15 (1960). pp. 12-25.

———. *The Changing Face of Toronto*. Canada Department of Mines and Technical Surveys. Geographical Branch. Memoir II. Ottawa. 1965.

Krueger, R. R. "The Niagara Fruitlands". *Royal Canadian Institute Proceedings*. Vol. XXXII part 2 (October, 1959).

Matthews, B. C. "Soil Resources and Land Use

Hazards in Southern Ontario". *Canadian Geographer*. 8 (1956). pp. 55-62.

Maxwell, J. W. "The Functional Structure of Canadian Cities: A classification of cities". *Geographical Bulletin*. Vol. 7, No. 2 (1965). pp. 79-104.

McDermott, G. L. "Frontiers of Settlement in the Great Clay Belt, Ontario and Quebec". *Annals, Association of American Geographers*. 51: 3 (September, 1961). pp. 261-273.

Mercier, R. G. and Chapman, L. J. "Peach Climate in Ontario". *1955-56 Report. Horticultural Experiment Station and Products Laboratory*. Vineland, Ontario.

Moon, Barbara. "Ontario's Rural Slum". *Toronto Globe and Mail*. January 11-15, 1965.

Nicholson, N. L. and Sametz, Z. W. "Regions of Canada and the Regional Concept". *Resources for Tomorrow Conference. Background Papers*. Vol. 1. Ottawa. 1961. pp. 367-383.

Noble, H. F. *Socio-economic Problems and Adjustment Needs of the Farm Family in Eastern Ontario*. Farm Economics, Co-operatives and Statistics Branch, Ontario Department of Agriculture. Toronto. January, 1967.

Putnam, D. F. (Editor). *Canadian Regions*. J. M. Dent and Sons (Canada) Limited. Toronto. 1952.

Putnam, R. G. "Changes in Rural Land Use Patterns on the Central Lake Ontario Plain". *Canadian Geographer*. VI, 2 (1962). pp. 60-68.

Ray, D. Michael. *Market Potential and Economic Shadow*. Department of Geography Research Series. No. 101. University of Chicago. Chicago. 1965.

Spelt, J. "Downtown Toronto: A Look at an Air Photo". *Canadian Geographer*. X, 3 (1966). pp. 184-189.

Tovell, W. M. "The Niagara Escarpment". *Royal Ontario Museum*. Toronto. 1967.

Warkentin, John. "Southern Ontario: A View from the West". *Canadian Geographer*. X, 3 (1966). pp. 157-171.

Zoltai, S. C. "Glacial History of Part of Northwestern Ontario". *Proceedings of the Geological Association of Canada*. XIII (1961). pp. 61-83.

——— . "Glacial Features of the Canadian Lakehead Area". *Canadian Geographer*. VII, 3 (1963). pp. 101-115.

——— . "Glacial Features of the Quetico-Nipig area, Ontario". *Canadian Journal of E... Sciences*. II (1965). pp. 247-269.

——— . "Glacial Features of the North-central Lake Superior Region, Ontario". *Canadian Journal of Earth Sciences*. IV (1967). pp. 515-528.

The Prairies

7 Manitoba, Saskatchewan, and Alberta include the Canadian portion of the vast grass-covered interior plains of North America. Traditionally, these Prairie Provinces have been considered the agrarian heart of Canada, and with wheat production capacity now exceeding 830,000,000 bushels per annum, the concept of this region as one vast grain field is still basically correct. However, petroleum, natural gas, and potash are also significant, and during the past two decades these resources coupled with the development of metallic minerals, forestry, and hydro-electric power in the Shield portion have resulted in a level of economic activity which now involves much more than agriculture alone. Moreover, migration of population from the rural scene to the Prairie cities has also produced great changes in regional character.

Since this region comprises 751,985 square miles, variety in natural scenery and human activities is to be expected. From Ontario on the east to the Rocky Mountains on the west the average distance is about 1,000 miles, while the north-south distance between 49°N and 60°N is about 760 miles. The three provinces divide this expanse about evenly, but significant variations in economic activities and landscapes occur. Water resources are important, particularly the Nelson River System, and future developments depend on the wise use of this river and its tributaries. The major fresh-water lakes occupy about nine per cent of the surface area of the region, but are all located on or close to the Canadian Shield and are of minor importance. Despite the interior position of the region direct access to the sea is possible via Churchill on Hudson Bay.

THE PHYSICAL RESOURCE BASE

Landform and Geology

Several of the great physiographic divisions of North America are represented in the Prairie Provinces.* As shown in Figure

* Geological Survey of Canada. *A Provisional Physiographic Map of Canada*. Paper 64-65. Geological Survey of Canada. Ottawa. 1964.
G. H. Stockwell. (Editor). *Geology and Economic Minerals of Canada*. Department of Mines and Technical Surveys. Ottawa. 1957.
W. A. Mackintosh. *Prairie Provinces: The Geographic Setting*. The Macmillan Company of Canada Limited. Toronto. 1934.
M. Y. Williams. "The Physiography of the Southern Plain of Canada". *Transactions, Royal Society of Canada*. 3rd Series. Vol. 23, Section 4 (1929). pp. 61-79.

7.1, the main physiographic divisions are, from east to west, the Hudson Bay Lowland, the Canadian Shield, the Interior Plains, the Foothills, and the Rocky Mountains.

The lowlands adjoining Hudson Bay are underlain by limestones and dolomites of the Silurian and Ordovician Periods. On the flat, muskeg-covered plain the most notable relief features are the abandoned shorelines of the former higher levels of Hudson Bay.

The Canadian Shield is generally composed of gneisses, granites, and other acidic metamorphic rocks. There are also belts of mineralized greenstones and other basic intrusives in which rich mineral de-

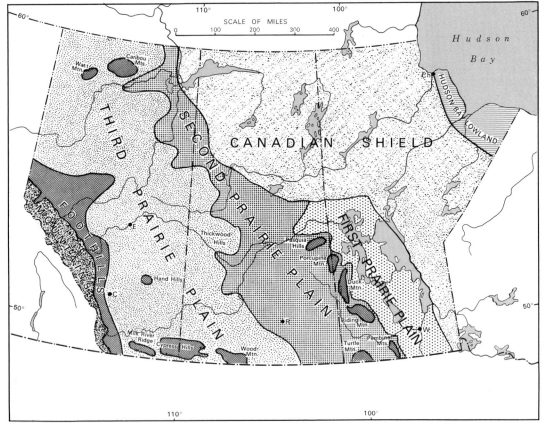

Figure 7.1 Physiographic Regions of the Prairies
From east to west, the Prairies rise in step-like fashion until the Rocky Mountains are reached near the western border of Alberta.

| C | Calgary | E | Edmonton | W | Winnipeg |
| Ch | Churchill | R | Regina | | |

posits occur. Despite the low overall relief the area is difficult to traverse for the rough surface is poorly drained and is dotted with lakes and muskeg areas. As a result only a few of the mineral deposits, such as the nickel formation at Thompson, Manitoba, have been actively exploited.

As shown by Figure 7.2, the Interior Plains are structurally a broad geosyncline in which the Palaeozoic and Mesozoic sedimentary rocks have been eroded by running water and continental glaciation into three broad levels of varying altitudes which are separated by two narrow hilly belts. From east to west the general relief increases in complexity and elevation from the broad, flat lacustrine plain of glacial

Lake Agassiz of the First Prairie Plain to the rolling plain dissected by the Saskatchewan River System of the Third Prairie Plain. Hilly lands along the Manitoba Escarpment and the Missouri Coteau have been profoundly influenced by morainic deposits.

The First Prairie Plain or Manitoba Lowland is underlain by horizontal bedded Ordovician, Silurian, and Devonian rocks. Lying between the Shield and the Manitoba Escarpment it forms a great natural basin the lower areas of which are occupied by large natural fresh-water lakes. In Pleistocene times the whole basin was flooded by glacial Lake Agassiz. The southern part of the basin known as the Red River Valley contains fertile black soils developed upon the silt and clay deposits of the old lake floor. The Interlake area between Lake Winnipeg and Lake Manitoba is not as well endowed for here the soils are shallow and are interrupted by rock outcrops and depressions filled with peat and muck. However, Ordovician rocks may yield good building materials, as evidenced by the Tyndall limestone. The lower slopes of the escarpment are marked by sand and gravel beaches of the old lake. Water is readily available, for in the Red River Valley artesian water is obtained beneath the heavy capping of lacustrine clay. However, the general lack of relief does pose problems,

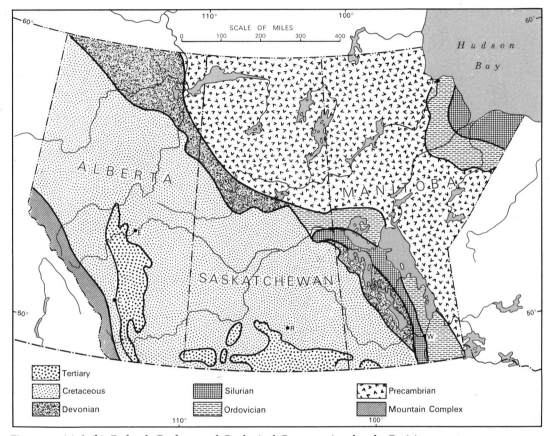

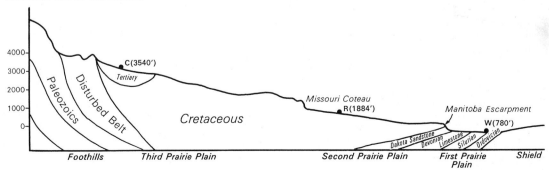

Figure 7.2 (a) & (b) Bedrock Geology and Geological Cross-section for the Prairies
As shown by the cross-section, the Prairies are really underlain by a geosyncline in which the Cretaceous materials are at the center.

Figure 7.3 The Red River Plain
The flatness of the Red River Plain is apparent in this photograph taken in the 1940s prior to the urbanization of the Winnipeg area. Of interest is the contrast in survey patterns. Close to the Red River there is the long lot pattern of the early Métis settlement, while in the foreground the large square fields of the township and range system can be seen.

Figure 7.4 The Qu'Appelle Valley, Saskatchewan
The broad spillway is occupied by a small meandering stream which at Lumsden is only eight feet wide. The southern slopes of the valley support a fair growth of trees, while the northern slopes, because of exposure to the sun's rays and consequent drier conditions, are much less forested.

and each year the Red River may swell beyond its banks and cause serious flooding.

The Manitoba Escarpment is the hilly eastern edge of the Cretaceous formation which underlies the Second and Third Prairie Plains. Caused initially by a resistant layer of sandstone at the base of the escarpment, it has been cut by wide river gaps into distinct hilly areas. The tops of these isolated uplands are remnants of a widespread Tertiary erosion surface which extended westward to the Rocky Mountains. Upon them the continental ice sheets deposited rough moraine. Riding Mountain and Duck Mountain have numerous small lakes contained in morainal depressions, and both are important recreation areas.

The Second Prairie Plain is much more extensive than the Manitoba Lowland. Often referred to as the Saskatchewan Plain it comprises the dip slope of the great Cretaceous formation. During the past two decades the underlying rocks have yielded important quantities of petroleum and potash. For the most part it is an area of gentle relief, the surface being composed of glacial boulder clay or ground moraine interspersed with wide flat areas of clay plain representing the floors of glacial lakes.* The Souris Basin in Southwestern Manitoba, the Regina Plains from Regina to Weyburn, the clay plains from Yorkton Lake to Quill Lake, and the plains of the Carrot River and Saskatchewan River Valleys, were all laid down in post-glacial lakes. Prominent belts of moraine occur along Moose Mountain and in the Touchwood Hills farther north. Some of these deposits are very stony and present a rugged relief as can be seen about twenty miles east of Saskatoon. Other major relief features are the large deep valleys occupied by misfit streams such as the Qu'Appelle, the Pembina, and the Assiniboine which are trenches scoured out of the flat Cretaceous sediments by old glacial melt-water streams.

The Missouri Coteau is a hilly zone separating the second from the third

* F. H. Edmunds. "Recession of the Wisconsin Glacier from Central Saskatchewan". *Saskatchewan Geological Survey Report*. No. 67 (1962).

prairie level. It is neither as high nor as abrupt as the Manitoba Escarpment, but it represents a similar break between old erosion levels. A barrier to the continental ice sheet, the Coteau is paralleled by two belts of moraine, one along the crest and one a few miles to the west. The result is a wide band of strongly rolling topography for which grazing is the most frequent land use.

The Third Prairie Plain or the Alberta Plain rises gradually from about 2,500 feet above sea level at the crest of the Coteau to nearly 4,000 feet at the Foothills of the Rocky Mountains. Because of the greater elevation greater relief occurs as the various tributaries of the Saskatchewan River System flow in valleys which have been deeply cut into the plain. Frequently the degree of entrenchment is such that portions of the region might better be classified as plateau. Additional relief is provided by remnants of an earlier Tertiary erosion surface. Included in this category are uplands such as Wood Mountain, Cypress Hills, Milk River Ridge, and, far to the north, Watt Mountain and the Caribou Mountains. Near Drumheller extensive badlands have developed in which are exposed fossil beds containing the skeletons of dinosaurs and other extinct animals. In the complex structure wnich underlies the region petroleum and natural gas deposits abound. In addition, coal occurs, and at Drumheller and Lethbridge seams of coal are exposed by the deeply cut river valleys.

Viewed from the plains, the Rocky Mountains appear as an immense, abrupt, snow-capped wall to the west. Closer approach reveals that between the plains and mountains there is a rough foothill region which, though fairly narrow in the south, widens considerably in the north. The Rocky Mountains are young high mountains produced by intense folding and faulting in Tertiary times. The abrupt Front Range is the edge of a huge fault block of older rock thrust over the Cretaceous shales of the Prairie Plains. The rocks of the Foothills have been more

Figure 7.5 Third Prairie Plain and Foothills
This photograph, taken near Pincher Creek, shows the pattern of land use for the Third Prairie Plain and the Foothills. The industry in the foreground is a natural gas processing plant which produces sulfur.

gently folded, but some of the ridges exceed an elevation of 5,000 feet above sealevel. During the Pleistocene Epoch glaciation was widespread, but only the highest parts of the Rocky Mountains are now snow covered. Cirques, serrate ridges, horned peaks, hanging valleys, and U-shaped valleys are examples of the diversity of alpine landforms.

Climate

By virtue of location the Prairie Provinces have a continental climate. The data for selected stations shown in Table 7.1 illustrate certain regional characteristics.

Generally, extreme seasonal ranges in *temperature* occur. Thus Winnipeg on the east experiences a 67F° range, while Calgary on the west records only a 46F° range on the average. The severity of the winter season is shown by the total of degree-days below 65°F, particularly when these are compared with the 5,390 value recorded for Vancouver and 7,008 for Toronto. Temperature is also significant in terms of frost-free days. Calgary and Regina both illustrate the limitations imposed by temperature alone on crops which cannot withstand a light frost.

Precipitation reflects the continental regime, for not only is the annual average

Table 7.1   **Climatic Comparison of Some Prairie Cities ***

	Elev.	Jan. Mean Temp.	Jul. Mean Temp.	Ann. Mean Temp.	Frost-free Period (days)	Degree-days below 65°F	Total Ppt.	Total Ann. Snowfall	Percentage Ppt. during Growing Season
The Pas	890'	− 6°F	65°F	31°F	102	12,460	16.98"	53.2"	61
Winnipeg	786'	− 1°F	68°F	37°F	111	10,658	19.72"	49.4"	62
Regina	1884'	− 2°F	67°F	36°F	93	10,770	15.09"	40.1"	66
Calgary	3540'	−16°F	62°F	39°F	92	9,520	17.47"	57.0"	66
Medicine Hat	2365'	−14°F	70°F	42°F	126	8,650	13.55"	41.6"	72

* After Meteorological Branch, Dept. of Transport.

less than 20 inches but there is a distinct concentration during the high sun period. Snowfall is limited in amount. However, the low winter temperatures make possible considerable accumulation during this season.

While the climate is strongly continental and under the influence of Polar Continental air during most of the year, certain variations occur. One of the major controls is that of the Rocky Mountains which are instrumental in blocking out the influence of moist mP air from the Pacific and in providing the physical conditions necessary for the Chinook winds which have their greatest effect during late winter. Another influence is that of the Skeena Saddle which permits some mP air to enter the Peace River country. The Hudson Bay region exhibits dual characteristics: strongly continental when ice-covered in winter, and marine in summer when ice-free.

Mean annual temperatures (Figure 7.6) vary from about 18°F in Northern Mani-

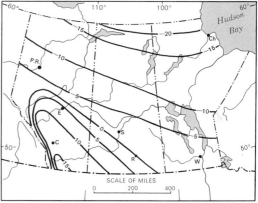

Figure 7.7 Mean Daily Temperatures for January
Winter is cold. Only the southwestern section has a January mean temperature above 0°F.

toba to 42°F in Southern Alberta. In general, the isotherms trend from northwest to southeast across the plains though, of course, the elevated ranges of the Rocky Mountains also have low temperatures.

Winter temperatures as shown by the January isotherms (Figure 7.7) vary from 20°F below zero in the northeast to 15°F above zero in the southwest. The high plains of Southern Alberta owe their advantage to the effects of the Chinook winds which, from time to time, sweep down from the mountains raising the temperature 20° to 40° in a few hours. The summer temperatures show much less variation (Figure 7.9). The 60°F isotherm bends far to the northwest to enclose most of the area. Only the coasts of Hudson Bay and the elevated stations in the Rocky Mountains have July mean temperatures of 55°F. The southern parts of the plains have over

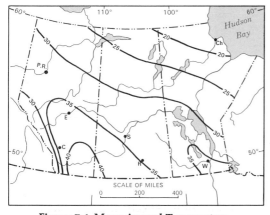

Figure 7.6 Mean Annual Temperature

COURTESY ALLAN F. MCQUARRIE, METEOROLOGICAL SERVICE OF CANADA

Figure 7.8 The Chinook Arch
The photograph was taken looking west-southwest from Calgary, Alberta. The dark part of the arch in the upper half of the picture is heavy Altostratus and Altocumulus cloud. The light area in the center actually shows clear sky or high thin cloud. The Rocky Mountains can be seen on the distant horizon and over them some Stratocumulus or rotor clouds can also be seen. The cloud stretches from far south to far north and, because of perspective, appears as an arch.

65°F, with a few stations in Southern Alberta reaching 68°F and 69°F. Note that the 65°F isotherm forms a "cold loop" on the crest of the Manitoba Cuesta, and a corresponding "warm loop" in the adjoining lowland.

Figure 7.10 shows the length of the frost-free period. This varies from more than 110 days in the southern parts to about 80 days in the Peace River area. There is very little variation throughout a large part of

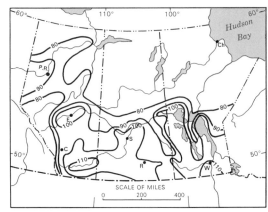

Figure 7.10 Mean Annual Length of Frost-free Period
The map shows the length of the frost-free period in days for most of the settled area of the Prairies. Below 80 frost-free days there is little chance for successful commercial agriculture.

Central Alberta. This is perhaps of less importance in the Prairie Provinces than in Eastern Canada. Cereals and forage crops are less affected by late spring frost than tender fruits and vegetables such as are grown in Southern Ontario.

The degree-days over 42°F are particularly important in explaining the distribu-

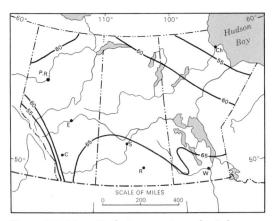

Figure 7.9 Mean Daily Temperatures for July

tion of grains. This temperature has been generally accepted as the base point at which effective cereal growth is possible. In general, 2,200 degree-days are necessary for optimum yield. However, in the Peace River country the added length of day makes wheat-growing successful where degree-days exceed 2,000.

Figure 7.12 is a map of isohyets of mean annual precipitation. It reveals that the moisture supply of the Prairie Provinces varies from less than 12 inches to more than 20 inches of rainfall per year. The least precipitation is experienced in the far

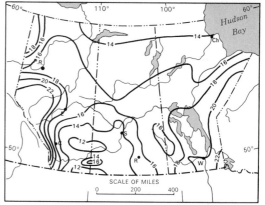

Figure 7.12 Mean Annual Precipitation
Precipitation in the Prairies varies from 12 to 22 inches annually.

northwest and in the "dry belt" of Southern Saskatchewan and Southern Alberta. The Foothills of the Rocky Mountains have about 20 inches per year, while Southeastern Manitoba gets slightly more. The effect of elevation is seen in the increased precipitation of the Cypress Hills area in Southwestern Saskatchewan. The general pattern, however, seems to show a crescent-shaped area of higher precipitation extending from Southeastern Manitoba to Central Alberta, with areas of lesser precipitation both north and south.

Temperature and precipitation are important but so is evaporation which, being the result of the application of heat, is closely tied to temperature. In some cli-

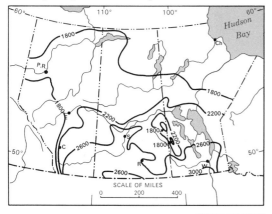

AFTER MACKAY

Figure 7.11 Mean Annual Number of Growing Degree-days above 42°F
Based on data from May 1 to September 30, this map defines the heat available for the growth of cereal crops. Southeast Manitoba is the warmest area in the Prairies. Elsewhere most of the agricultural area is within the 2200 D-D limit.

mates there is more moisture than the
atmosphere can absorb, while in others
there is less. This is the case in the Prairie
Provinces where\there is a definite water
deficiency. Figure 7.13, adapted from a
map by Sanderson, shows that this deficiency varies from more than ten inches
per year in Southern Alberta to less than
two inches in Northeastern Manitoba and
in the Foothills of the Rocky Mountains.*
This lack of moisture is experienced in the
summer season since the winter, even
though it has low precipitation, has very
little evaporation.

---

* Marie Sanderson. "The Climates of Canada
According to the New Thornthwaite Classification". *Scientific Agriculture*. Vol. 28 (1948). pp.
501-507.

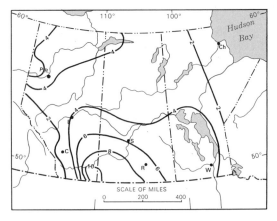

AFTER SANDERSON

Figure 7.13 Mean Annual Water Deficiency
All places in the Prairie Region experience a water
deficiency which varies from two to more than ten
inches.

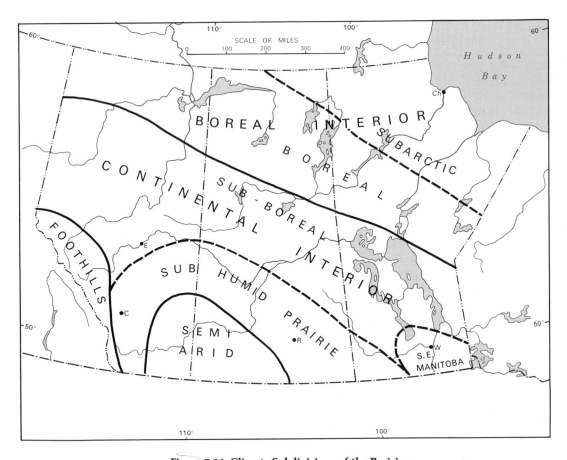

Figure 7.14 Climate Subdivisions of the Prairies

Climatic Divisions *

Despite the very obvious differences in climate from place to place in the Prairie Provinces, it is not easy to make exact subdivisions. The pattern is simplest in Saskatchewan, where our various climatic maps and, as shall be shown later, vegetation and soils, all suggest a five-fold division (Figure 7.14). These might, for convenience, be labelled: The Semi-arid or Dry Belt, the Sub-humid Prairie, the Subboreal, the Boreal, and the Subarctic. In the west where the pattern is interrupted by elevation, the Foothill and Mountain Region has a series of climates all its own. In Southeastern Manitoba greater availability of moisture and higher summer temperatures suggest that a small area with a humid climate should be recognized.

While a number of the boundaries depend upon moisture relationships, especially in the south, those in the north depend very largely on temperature. Several of the maps show important temperature lines running from Central Manitoba to the northwest corner of Alberta, suggesting a division in the broad Boreal Zone. When we see that this boundary is also recognized by foresters, we can have little doubt about it. Minor subregions may be recognized on minor criteria. The Edmonton district, for instance, has a higher summer rainfall than the Peace River area. Swan River and Prince Albert have much the same climates, but they are separated by a hilly and somewhat cooler belt. The Athabasca River area has distinctly more rain in the summer than the Peace River area but a little less snow in winter. However, for the purposes of broad-scale regional geography such minor divisions are unnecessary.

Vegetation and Soils **

While the Prairie Provinces take their well-known name from the great area of grassland which they contain, this in actu-

---

* L. J. Chapman and D. M. Brown. *The Climates of Canada for Agriculture*. The Canada Land Inventory Report No. 3. Ottawa. 1966.
** D. F. Putnam. "Pedogeography of Canada". *Geographical Bulletin*. No. 1 (1951). pp. 57-85.

ality comprises only about one-third of the total area. To the north and northeast of this somewhat triangular tract are found several zones of forest and in the far northeast even treeless tundra. The forests then form a transition zone between the regions that are too dry and those which are too cold for forest growth. Both forest and grassland regions, however, can be further subdivided as shown in Figure 7.15.

While soil geography is a scientific discipline of relatively recent development, considerable research into Prairie soils has been carried out since the initial surveys which began in 1921 in Alberta and Saskatchewan. From the accurate picture which is now available, the pattern of zonal soils in the Prairie Provinces is shown by Figure 7.16. Comparison between the distributions of vegetation and soil types shows a fair degree of similarity. Both, in effect, are the result of climatic influences, particularly temperature extremes, frost-free days, precipitation, and moisture differences. For each of the grassland soil zones a typical soil profile has been selected, and the characteristics of each are shown in the accompanying illustrations. Combined with the diagrams are climatic graphs which show the seasonal ranges of temperature and monthly precipitation. In addition, the principal vegetative species associated with each soil zone are indicated.

The gradation in soil characteristics is significant. Comparison of the pedocal soil profiles of the Prairies suggests that the major differences are those of amount of organic matter present and the depth at which the calcium layer occurs. Both of these characteristics are directly related to moisture supply. Therefore, the greater the precipitation, the greater the accumulation of soil organic material and the greater the depth at which the calcium layer is found.

The Brown Soil Zone comprises Southwestern Saskatchewan and Southeastern Alberta and is also represented in the interior valleys of British Columbia. It occurs in the driest part of the treeless prairie, where the vegetation cover is a

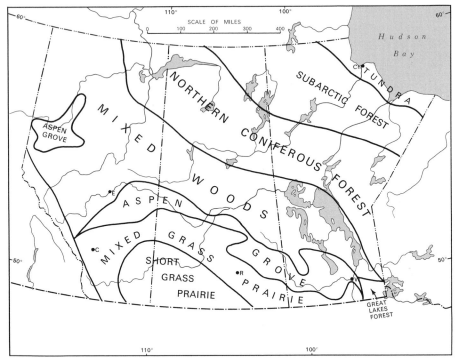

Figure 7.15 Vegetation Zones of the Prairies

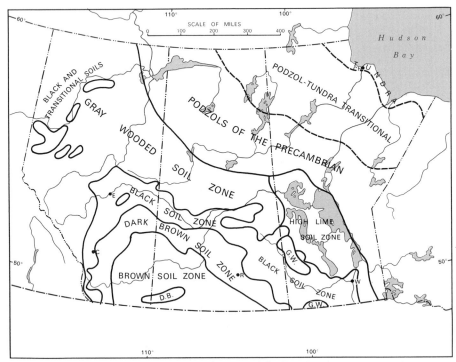

Figure 7.16 Soil Zones of the Prairies

short grass steppe. The characteristic species of the short grass association are June grass, blue grama grass, common spear grass, western wheat grass, Sandberg's blue grass, nigger wool, pasture sage, and prickly pear cactus. In addition to being short, the vegetation is sparse, and considerably bare soil is exposed between the plants. However, the extensive root systems invade the soil mass and provide some degree of cohesion against erosion.

The center of this zone is found in the Medicine Hat area where precipitation is less than 14 inches and the moisture deficiency exceeds eight inches. The precipitation received here is less effective than elsewhere in the Prairie Provinces for more than 110 frost-free days occur and higher April temperatures are recorded. Thus, of the 32,500,000 acres estimated to be in this zone, only 25 per cent is considered arable land.

As shown in Figure 7.17, the Brown Soils have the shallowest profiles of the grassland soils. The accumulation of lime and other salts is closer to the surface, and the concentration of these substances is greater. Frequently, a hardpan of these substances will occur within eight inches of the surface, with a deleterious effect on

agricultural crops. Because the organic matter content is low, the surface soil is light in color, sometimes almost gray rather than light brown. Cultivation of these soils causes a rapid breakdown in structure as the organic material is depleted, and severe erosion by wind and water often results.

The natural fertility of the Brown Soils is adequate, and when sufficient precipitation occurs, wheat of high quality may be produced. However, the cyclical nature of yearly precipitation on the Prairies often produces a series of good years followed by a prolonged drought. Thus, much of this area should be left in grazing land or range, as excellent pasture results from proper management of the grassland.

It is significant that this is the region where large irrigation projects have been developed. Of note are the intensively irrigated areas near Lethbridge, Taber, and the new South Saskatchewan project between Elbow and Outlook.

The Dark Brown Soil Zone is also found under open grassland but possesses better climate and vegetation. This zone follows a crescentic pattern and stretches from south of Calgary north and east to the Regina Plain and southeast to the Manitoba border. Of the 35,000,000 acres in-

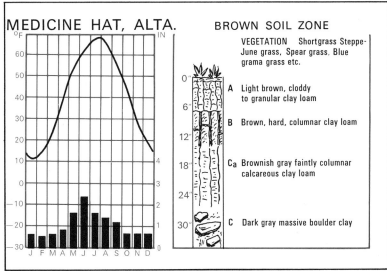

Figure 7.17 Environment of the Brown Soil Zone

volved more than 60 per cent is considered to be arable.

Within this area there occurs the mixed grass prairie where species similar to those mentioned previously are found in association with taller grasses such as northern wheat grass, green spear grass, rough fescue, and side-oats grama grass. In some of the natural depressions and stream valleys small groves of poplar, willow, and various shrubs appear. Precipitation is between 14 and 16 inches in this area, and the moisture deficiency is from six to eight inches. The moisture received is more effective, for lower April temperatures result in a slower melting of the snow cover and less uncontrolled run-off.

As shown by Figure 7.18, the surface is somewhat darker and deeper than that of the Brown Soil, for more organic material is present. Natural fertility, moisture holding capacity, and resistance to erosion are higher than in the Brown Soil, and consequently the productivity of the Dark Brown Soil is much greater. The most notable of the Dark Brown soils are those of the Regina Plains where clays and silts were deposited in a pro-glacial lake. Because of the smooth, level topography and lack of stones, the well-drained Regina heavy clays are suited to mechanized farm-

ing and are rated as the best wheat lands in Saskatchewan. It is significant that both the Brown and Dark Brown Soil Zones were included within Palliser's Triangle.

The Black Soils are found beneath the tall grass cover of the Park Belt which lies between the open prairie and forest vegetative realms in all three Prairie Provinces. The area of the Black Soil Zone is estimated to be 42,000,000 acres of which 78 per cent is potentially arable. This zone stretches in a crescentic band from Winnipeg north to Prince Albert, west to Edmonton, and then south to Calgary.

Developed under the influence of tall grass vegetation interspersed with small "bluffs" or groves of trees, the soils of this region possess a better moisture supply. Precipitation exceeds 16 inches annually, and to the east in Manitoba more than 20 inches is received. Moisture deficiency is still present but is generally less than six inches per annum, while the frost-free period exceeds 100 days.

In keeping with their more favorable moisture supply these soils are characterized by a darker color and higher content of organic matter and nitrogen in the surface horizon. The soil profile is of greater depth (Figure 7.19) and the horizon of lime accumulation lies 15 to 30 inches below the

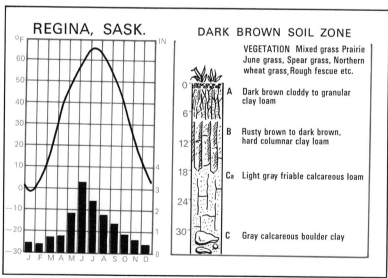

Figure 7.18 Environment of the Dark Brown Soil Zone

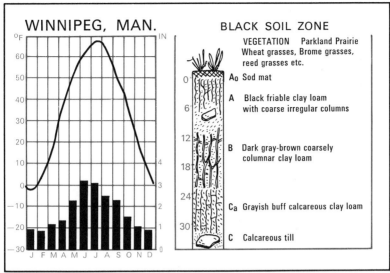

Figure 7.19 Environment of the Black Soil Zone

surface. However, within the Black Soil Zone there is considerable variation in profile types, and while the **A** horizon is usually 12 to 15 inches in depth, many "Shallow Black" profiles are described in which the **A** horizon is less than four inches thick.

The Black Soils are regarded as the most fertile soils in Canada. Wheat yields are better and more reliable in this soil zone than in the other grassland regions, but the improved conditions encourage more diversification in farm operation. Hence, in many places other grains and forage crops are grown in support of a livestock economy, and farm incomes are more often derived from the sale of cattle, hogs, and dairy products than from cash grains.

The Gray Wooded Soil Zone comprises some 150,000,000 acres, but less than 20 per cent is considered to be arable land. It is derived from the Mixed Wood Belt which occupies the southern portion of the forested zone. This woodland consists of a mixture of deciduous, broad-leafed trees and evergreen coniferous types. Poplar, white spruce, and jack pine are typical species.

The climate of this zone is colder in winter and cooler in summer than that of the adjoining Black Soil Zone, and the frost-free period is less than 80 days. Precipitation is about 16 inches per annum along the southern margin but decreases northward as temperature falls. Although the climate is more humid than that to the south, its lower temperatures do restrict agriculture.

The Gray Wooded Soil profile exhibits both pedocal and pedalfer characteristics (Figure 7.20). Developed under forest vegetation it has the traditional gray leached A_2 horizon of the Podzolic Soils of Eastern Canada. However, there occurs at the base of the profile a zone of lime accumulation which is typical of grassland soils. Gray Wooded Soils are considerably lower in natural fertility than the soils to the south, and mixed farming with reliance on livestock, clover, and coarse grains seems necessary for their advantageous agricultural use.

The High Lime Soils are intrazonal in type, not having developed normally because of the great amount of limestone in the parent material. They occur in the Mixed Wood Belt north of Winnipeg. The soil profile is very shallow, and drainage is often poor; excessive stoniness also creates problems for agriculture. These soils, therefore, are considered of little value for future agricultural use.

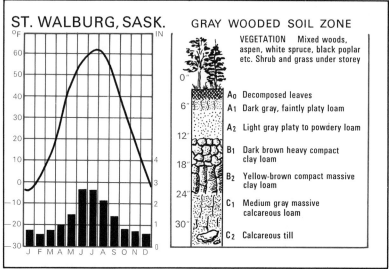

Figure 7.20 Environment of the Gray Wooded Soil Zone

The Podzol and Podzol-Tundra Soils of the Shield and Hudson Bay Lowland have evolved under Boreal Forest and Tundra vegetation. They are strongly leached, lack adequate drainage, and are found in a climatic situation which is unfavorable for most agricultural crops. They, therefore, do not constitute a valuable soil resource for the Prairie Provinces.

POPULATION

The population of the Prairie Provinces was about 3,500,000 according to the census of 1966. Nearly all the people live in the southern area where the population density is about 9 per square mile.

During the first three decades of this century population of the Prairie Provinces increased rapidly from 420,000 in 1901 to 2,354,000 in 1931. From 1931 growth remained gradual until the last decade when the rate increased considerably. However, rural farm population between 1951 and 1961 declined by almost 200,000. This was due to increased opportunities for employment in non-farm occupations and to a marked rate of migration from small farm operations as farm consolidation proceeded. The chief casualty was the small commercial farm where the operator did not participate in off-the-farm employment to alleviate the economic stress.*

Concomitant with the rural depopulation has been the growth of the larger urban centers. Calgary between 1951 and 1966 increased in population by 130 per cent and was the fastest-growing city in Canada. Edmonton during the same interval enjoyed a 120 per cent increase in population. Winnipeg, however, still retained the leading position on the Prairies, and in 1966 finally achieved a population of 500,000. In addition, certain well-established smaller cities of the Prairie Provinces such as Brandon, Moose Jaw, and Lethbridge grew by an average of 50 per cent during the 15 year period. Small centers dependent on agriculture have not experienced the same growth, and many have declined.

As shown by Figure 7.21, population is not evenly distributed in the Prairie Provinces. Despite recent economic developments north of the limit of agricultural settlement, the northern area, with the exception of a few communities such as Thompson, Churchill, and Lac La Ronge, is

---

* Michael L. Szabo. "Depopulation of Farms in Relation to the Economic Conditions of Agriculture on the Canadian Prairies". *Geographical Bulletin.* Vol. 8, No. 3-4 (1965). pp. 187-202.

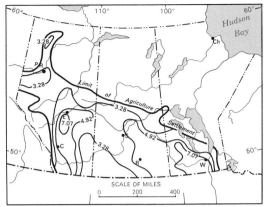

Figure 7.21 Rural Population Density — 1961
Isoline values are at quartile intervals for the distribution. Rural population densities vary from a little over seven persons per square mile near Winnipeg and Edmonton to less than three in the Dry Belt and Peace River area.

virtually devoid of people. In the south significant differences can be noted, for two distinct nodes of high density rural population occur: one in Central Alberta, the other in the Lake Agassiz Plain of Southern Manitoba. The Dry Belt is well defined by the isoline of 3.28 per square mile, and most of the census subdivisions there recorded less than three persons per square mile in 1961.

If gross population density is considered, as illustrated by Figure 7.22, the influence

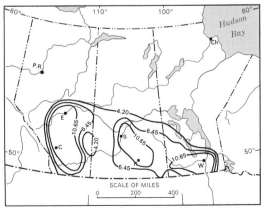

Figure 7.22 Gross Population Densities — 1961
As shown by the isoline of 10.56 persons per square mile, the influence of the major cities in the Prairies is quite marked. Isoline values are in persons per square mile and are determined by median and quartile points in the distribution.

of the main urban centers is apparent. In this instance three distinct nodes of high population density occur as defined by the 10.65 isoline, namely: Calgary-Edmonton, Saskatoon-Regina, and Metropolitan Winnipeg. This pattern clearly reflects the concentrations of economic activity in the Prairie Provinces.

SETTLEMENT PATTERNS

Indian Settlement

The aborigines can hardly be said to have had any true settlements before the white men came. In both the forest and the grassland environments they lived by hunting, and they were forced to be as migratory as the game animals which they followed. There were, of course, many favorite camping sites, situated at river crossings or on portages, and to these the tribes might return with great regularity year after year. They did not build permanent villages in the same way as the agricultural Indian tribes of the Great Lakes region.

With the coming of the white fur traders the pattern changed. At first, the Indians set up temporary encampments at the traders' forts for a short period during the summer when they brought in their winter catch of furs. Gradually the settlements became more permanent. Then too, many of the voyageurs in the employ of the fur-trading companies married native women, and the Métis race was founded. These people usually regarded the settlement as home rather than the tribal lands of their mothers' kinfolk. Many, though not all, of the voyageurs were French Canadians, and the little settlements along the Red and Saskatchewan Rivers resembled those along the St. Lawrence.

Fur Trade

For almost two centuries the fur trade was the chief and almost the only economic activity of the Prairie Provinces. Part of Rupert's Land, the area was administered by the Hudson's Bay Company, which was founded in 1670. Many settlements began as Hudson's Bay Posts.

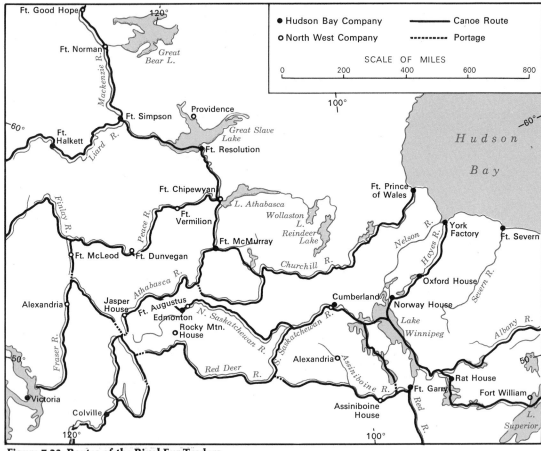

Figure 7.23 Routes of the Rival Fur Traders
Competition between the Hudson's Bay Company and the North West Company resulted in duplication of trading posts and in use of most of the rivers.

The French in Canada were also interested in the fur trade of the west. The La Vérendrye's, from 1731 to 1743, were the pioneers of the plains and the first white men to reach the Rocky Mountains. Thus, Montreal, the greatest fur-trading center on the North American continent, began to extend its influence into Rupert's Land. After 1763 English as well as French-Canadian traders worked out of Montreal. In 1784 the North West Company was organized.

The best beaver land was in the far northwest. Drained by the Athabasca River towards the Arctic, and not to Hudson Bay, this was not part of Rupert's Land. The routes to Montreal, however, had to make use of the Saskatchewan and Red River Systems. Within a few years the rival companies covered the disputed territory with a network of forts. Sometimes, as at Winnipeg, Fort Qu'Appelle, Cumberland Lake, and Edmonton, the forts of the two companies were quite close together, and the rivalry was intense. In the far northwest and in British Columbia the Hudson's Bay Company had few outposts, while the North West traders did not attempt to establish themselves close to the Bay.

With their North American headquarters at York Factory the Hudson's Bay Company enjoyed a great geographical advantage over their rivals in Montreal. To offset this the latter established an intermediate headquarters at Fort William on Lake Superior. Brigades of voyageurs, or canoemen, came from Montreal each summer, bringing supplies, and taking back the furs brought in by brigades from the outposts. The latter returned home with the goods from Montreal. The men were thus not required to be away from home over winter, as they certainly would have been had they made the complete journey from Montreal to Lake Athabasca.

In 1821 the Hudson's Bay Company absorbed its rival. The development of routes was continued; York boats were used on the rivers, while overland trails were established, along which the fur brigades traveled by ox-drawn Red River carts. Thus the outlying points on the Saskatchewan River were directly connected with Fort Garry and with the east. With the building of the Canadian Pacific Railway the overland brigades came to an end.

The fur trade is still of importance to the Indians and Métis of the north, and the Hudson's Bay Company is still in business, not only in its scattered outposts, but also in its large department stores in Winnipeg, Calgary, and other Prairie cities.

The Selkirk Settlement

The first agricultural settlement in the Prairie Provinces was founded along the Red River by Thomas Douglas, third Earl of Selkirk, on land purchased from the Hudson's Bay Company.

The first colonists arrived at York Factory late in the summer of 1811, reaching the Red River the next summer. Others came out during the following years. They had a hard time at first. Food was scarce, and their first crops, being unsuited to the environment, resulted in failure. Plagues of grasshoppers attacked their crops. The Red River also overflowed its banks, flooding their farms.

The colonists suffered greatly during the hostilities between the rival fur traders, and many of them were killed. After the amalgamation of the fur-trading companies in 1821, the colony had peace in which to develop.

The settlement was laid out along the river, the farms being long, narrow strips. Only a small amount of land was cropped, and each family tried to grow everything they needed for themselves. They also had to make everything they used, including furniture, clothing, household utensils, and farm implements since they were completely isolated from the markets of the world. Not for many years could wheat from the Red River Valley be transported to European markets in exchange for manufactured goods.

In spite of all hardships, however, the population of the colony continued to increase. In 1870 the descendants of the Red River settlers, the fur traders, and the Métis numbered 12,000, and the district which Lord Selkirk had purchased became the province of Manitoba.

Exploring the Agricultural Resources *

As the population of the eastern part of Canada continued to grow and to press upon the limits of its agricultural land, there were many people who felt that the western lands should belong to Canada and be opened to agricultural settlement.

In 1857 the British Colonial Office sent Captain John Palliser to examine and report upon the area. During the years 1857 to 1860 he traveled from Lake Superior to beyond the Rocky Mountains. As a result of his explorations he divided the plains into two parts, a "fertile belt" and the "true prairie", which he regarded as a semi-arid desert. The latter area, according to him, embraced most of what is now the southern part of both Saskatchewan and Alberta. In spite of the fact that it is an irregular, five-sided area, it is often referred to as Palliser's Triangle.

During the same years, the Government of Canada also dispatched explorers to the west. Professor H. Y. Hind was commissioned to report on the country of the Assiniboine and the Saskatchewan Rivers. In general, he agreed with Palliser, stating

* John Warkentin. *The Western Interior of Canada*. Part VI. The Carleton Library, No. 15. McClelland and Stewart Limited. Toronto. 1964.

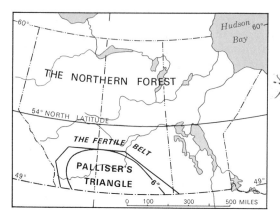

Figure 7.24 Palliser's Triangle and the Fertile Belt
Palliser's Triangle includes most of the open prairie and falls largely within the area having more than six inches of moisture deficiency per year.

that the treeless prairie was unsuitable for settlement, but that millions of acres of arable land were available in the wooded area, as he termed the Park Belt.

Later, Professor John Macoun accompanied the engineers of the Canadian Pacific Railway across the Prairies. He disagreed with Palliser and Hind, allowing only 20,000 square miles for the arid country of Palliser's Triangle. He was the first to point out that most of the rainfall came during the summer months and also that

warm summer conditions extended to the 60th parallel in the northwest.

The System of Land Survey

With the exception of a few early settled areas such as the Red River and Saskatchewan River settlements, the land of the Prairie Provinces is divided into practically square townships, each containing thirty-six sections of as nearly one mile square as is permitted by the convergence of the meridians.

For convenience in surveying, certain meridians were designated principal meridians. The first of these is located a few miles west of Winnipeg, at longitude 97° 27' 30" W. The second, at 102° W, forms part of the Manitoba-Saskatchewan boundary; the third, at 106° W, is approximately in the middle of Saskatchewan; and the fourth, at 110° W, forms the boundary between Saskatchewan and Alberta. The fifth principal meridian, at 114° W, passes through the eastern outskirts of Calgary; and the sixth, at 118° W, bisects the Peace River district.

Base lines are surveyed east and west, the first base line being the 49th parallel of latitude, which is also the southern boundary of this part of Canada. Base lines are

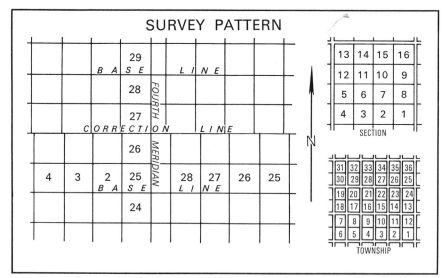

Figure 7.25 The Pattern of Land Survey in Western Canada

numbered consecutively from south to north and are twenty-four miles apart.

Along each base line points are established at six-mile intervals, and from them lines are surveyed twelve miles due north and twelve miles due south. These lines, twenty-four miles in length, are true meridians and converge towards the north; consequently, they are not directly in line with corresponding off-sets from the next base line. Thus all north-south lines have a jog every twenty-four miles. The line along which these jogs occur, lying midway between the base lines, is known as the "correction line". Townships are numbered from south to north beginning at the International Boundary. Each meridional row of townships is called a "range", and these are numbered from east to west, beginning at each principal meridian.

Each township is divided into sections of 640 acres, or one square mile. Road allowances are provided every mile, east and west, and every second mile from north to south (Figure 7.25). Each section is divided into quarter sections of 160 acres each, and into 16 legal subdivisions of 40 acres each. Both sections and subdivisions are numbered, beginning in the southeast corner. From these references exact locations may be given. Thus Catherwood Station is in legal subdivision 4, section 6, township 35, range 11, west of the third meridian, which places it thirty-eight miles west, and eleven miles south, of the center of the city of Saskatoon.

TRANSPORTATION

The Railway Pattern

The settlement and economic development of the Prairie Provinces might almost be said to have been under complete control of the railways. It is important therefore to make a careful study of the railway pattern.

At the time of Confederation British North America consisted of a series of small disconnected, settled areas along the southern border of a great wilderness. Any one of them might have and did have more dealings with its neighbor on the south than with its fellows. The first railroad reached Winnipeg in 1878, providing connections with St. Paul and Chicago. The Canadian Pacific Railway was completed across the Prairies in 1885. It was built to hold the new nation together, as well as to provide a route for settlement.[*]

In spite of the adverse reports of Palliser and Hind upon the character of the country, the railway was built along the shortest route and directly across the semi-arid grasslands. Much of the land received as subsidy by the Canadian Pacfic Railway Company, however, was located farther north in the fertile belt.

Within a few years, branch lines were built from Regina to Saskatoon and Prince Albert and from Calgary to Edmonton. Southern Manitoba also saw a number of short lines built in its settled territory.

Aided by these railways settlers poured north into the fertile crescent, while relatively few located in the semi-arid south. A close net of railways, however, began to appear in Manitoba and eastern Assiniboia. After the formation of the provinces of Saskatchewan and Alberta two more trans-prairie lines were completed. These were the Canadian Northern and the Grand Trunk Pacific, both traversing the fertile crescent to the north of the open grassland. At the same time most of the prairie was occupied, save for small scattered areas in the most difficult parts of the dry south.

During the period of World War I both railway building and land settlement were less rapid but during the 1920s further expansion took place. By 1931 there was very little of the settled area which was not within ten miles of a railway.

Under the conditions of early settlement, with horse-drawn vehicles and poor prairie trails, the distance from the railway was highly important. While, of necessity, hauls of fifty miles might be undertaken, studies have shown that it was not economical to

* John Warkentin. "Western Canada in 1886". *Transactions, Historical and Scientific Society of Manitoba.* Series III, No. 20 (1963-64). pp. 85-116.

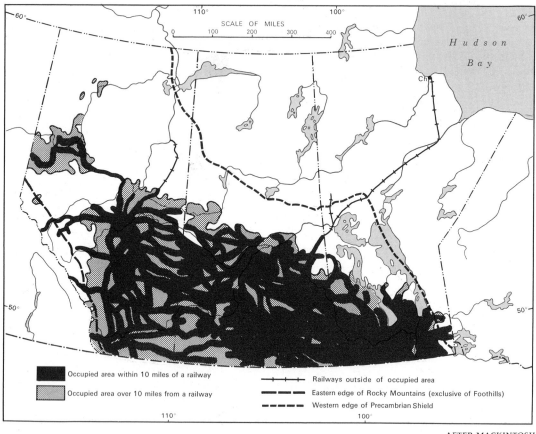

AFTER MACKINTOSH

Figure 7.26 Accessibility to Railways — 1931

haul grain more than twelve ⌐ fifteen miles. Thus the railways needed to be about twenty miles apart with sta⌐ns or sidings every seven to ten miles.

The Role of Transportation

In no other part of Canada does transportation play a more important role in the regional geography than in the Prairie Provinces. The Prairies remained empty as long as they lacked transportation facilities; they were settled quickly once they were given railways to the outside world.

Over 19,000 miles of railway lines are in operation in the Prairie Provinces. Included are such important transportation links as the main lines of the Canadian Pacific and Canadian National Railways,

with many passenger and freight trains per day, strategic links with the north such as the Hudson Bay line and the Alberta and Great Waterways, and many small Prairie lines whose only function is to haul wheat in the fall. Saskatchewan with nearly 9,000 miles of line stands second to Ontario in total mileage and is well ahead in mileage per capita.

Most of the railway mileage belongs to either the Canadian National Railway or the Canadian Pacific Railway system. The Northern Alberta Railway serving the Peace River district is jointly operated by the two systems. The Great Slave Lake Railway was completed in 1966, and the Alberta Resources Railway in 1968. Short branches of American railways enter the southern sections.

Local railway services are declining and, as everywhere else in Canada, are being replaced by improved highway services. The total length of highway and road systems in the Prairie Provinces in 1966 was about 243,000 miles. About 15,000 miles of main highways are paved, and there are about 133,000 miles which have gravel surface. About 40 per cent remain unsurfaced.

The extensive road net is a great problem for the sparsely-populated Prairie Provinces. Prairie roads are impassable in spring and fall, but the provincial governments cannot hope to put a hard surface on any but the main roads to connect the larger cities. The railway retains much of its prestige, for it is still the most economical way to move bulk commodities long distances.

Water transportation was important in earlier times, and it is still necessary to carry heavy freight into the north. There is commercial navigation also on Lake Winnipeg, between Selkirk and Norway House.

High hopes for ocean transportation led to the building of the Hudson Bay Railway and the port of Churchill with its large grain elevator. Several million bushels of wheat are exported each year, but the season of navigation is short. Churchill also serves as a gateway to the central section of the Canadian Arctic.

The great distances of the Prairie Provinces make their people naturally air-minded. Air Canada and Canadian Pacific Airlines serve the larger cities on cross-country runs, while Transair and Pacific Western airlines provide regional services.

Agriculture, forestry, mining, and manufacturing form the basis of the economy of the Prairie Provinces, but the dominant factor in each case is facility of transportation.

AGRICULTURE

In spite of the increasing importance of secondary industries and the discovery and development of new primary resources, agriculture continues to provide about 25 per cent of the annual net income of the people of the Prairie Provinces. Farm enterprises have become quite diversified in some areas, but commercial grain farming is still the dominant type, especially on the extensive plains of Saskatchewan. The varying demands of the world wheat markets as well as the competition for land by other agricultural commodities may, from time to time, result in fluctuation of the acreage sown to wheat. During the 1960s, trends, however, were fairly steady, rising to a peak of 29,000,000 acres sown in 1966, with a harvest of about 830,000,000 bushels. Other cereal grains are grown on ten to twelve million acres of land every year. Prairie agriculture certainly produces wheat, but increasingly it is becoming the source of the meat which is being demanded by Canada's growing population. About 6,000,000 cattle are found on the farms and ranches of the Prairie Provinces, while about 2,300,000 animals are marketed each year. Approximately 2,300,000 hogs and 270,000 sheep and lambs are also sold. Thus large areas, particularly in Alberta and Manitoba, may be termed mixed-farming districts.

Agricultural settlement may be said to have begun with Selkirk's Red River Settlement in 1811, but it cannot be said to have been a very successful introduction to grain growing.* Neither the settlers themselves nor their introduced crops were very well adjusted to the environment. Moreover, the fur traders of the Hudson's Bay Company had no wish to see their realm invaded by farmers. Nevertheless, there were many people in the "province of Canada" who felt that the Northwest should be settled. Both the British and the Canadian governments sent expeditions to report upon the suitability of the Prairies for agricultural settlement. Although they differed markedly in their estimates of the area of available land, all agreed that there was much land which could support the same kind of agriculture expanding at the time

* John Warkentin. "Manitoba Settlement Patterns". *Transactions, Historical and Scientific Society of Manitoba.* Series III, No. 16 (1961). pp. 62-77.

across the "American West". Almost immediately after Confederation the Hudson's Bay lands became the Northwest Territories of Canada, railways were projected, and the first phases of settlement began.

Among the first real grain farmers were the Mennonites who settled in the southern part of the Manitoba Lowland in 1876. Coming from the steppes of southern Russia they understood the environment. The completion of the Canadian Pacific Railway in the 1880s, however, signalled the beginning of a flood of settlers which during the next forty years occupied practically all of the grasslands and much of the adjoining "park" and bush land on its borders.

The wheat farmer had many problems. Some of the hazards were insects, late summer frosts, and black stem rust. All of these indicated a need for earlier maturing varieties of wheat. Among the most successful of these was Red Fife developed by an Ontario farmer from a few seeds originating somewhere in Eastern Europe. With Red Fife the plains of Southern Manitoba soon gained a reputation for fine bread wheat.

The rising price of wheat after 1900 served as an incentive to settlement, and soon the limits of the old variety were reached. Plant breeders introduced new varieties which matured in a shorter season and enabled the wheat frontier to be expanded. Beyond the wheat belt an agriculture based on other crops such as oats, barley, and rye was possible. Much of the credit for extending Canadian wheat production must go to the Saunders, father and son, who developed "Marquis", a hard red wheat of excellent quality, which matured six to ten days earlier than Red Fife and was also more resistant to stem rust. The first widespread distribution of Marquis seed was made in 1909, and by 1912 it had become the dominant wheat on the Canadian prairie. It also became the most important variety in the northern grain-growing region of the United States.

During the period 1900-1930 the area sown to wheat in the Prairie Provinces increased from 1,500,000 to 25,000,000 acres, while the harvest grew from 23,000,000 to 353,000,000 bushels. During the first decade of the twentieth century the population of Canada grew at an unprecedented rate as the prairie was brought under cultivation. Then came World War I which gave an advantage to North American producers over those of Argentina and Australia. Much of Europe's best wheatland was put out of production by the hostilities, and it was some years after the war before it recovered productivity.

Wartime expansion carried certain seeds of weakness. High prices stimulated the breaking of submarginal land, both in the "dry belt" and on the colder margins of the agricultural realm. Much capital was invested in equipment, and despite the efficiency of the new power-driven machinery the costs of production were high. European wheat fields began to recover their productivity and, furthermore, European governments were prepared to protect and assist their farmers in competition with Canadian wheat growers. Nevertheless, Prairie farmers continued to specialize in wheat production which reached a peak in 1932.

Wheat prices fell after the "crash" of 1929. Wheat markets vanished, and Canada became the holder of an uncomfortable wheat surplus which mounted to more than 200,000,000 bushels in 1935-6. Then came the drought, and two very poor crops in 1936 and 1937 reduced the carry-over to 24,000,000 bushels in 1937-8. The low prices and the poor crops of the 1930s placed many farmers in an almost hopeless position, requiring large-scale government aid. The Prairie Farm Rehabilitation Act of 1935 provided technical and financial assistance in overcoming the effects of drought. In the same year the Canadian Wheat Board was set up to provide for the orderly marketing of wheat and the carry-over of surplus. The Prairie Farm Assistance Act of 1939 provided for relief payments in low-crop areas.

World War II disrupted world trade patterns and brought back wheat surpluses at

Figure 7.27 Pense, Saskatchewan
The community of Pense is on the C.P.R. main line just west of Regina. As in most small communities, grain elevators and a curling rink are integral parts of the urban landscape.

an even higher level. The average annual carry-over for 1940-4 was 431,000,000 bushels; for 1945-9, 120,000,000 bushels; for 1950-4, 304,000,000 bushels; 1955-9, 607,000,000 bushels. Even after the poor crop year of 1961 there was still a carry-over of 391,000,000 bushels, while the average for 1960-4 was 515,000,000 bushels. In 1963 a record crop of 703,000,000 bushels was harvested, and this was surpassed by 830,000,000 bushels in 1966. In spite of record harvests, however, the carry-over had begun to decline in the face of large, long-term sales contracts with the U.S.S.R. and China. Larger amounts were also sold to traditional customers such as Britain and Japan, bringing the total clearances for the 1965-6 crop year to about 600,000,000 bushels. How long such markets may remain open is a question that cannot be answered, but wide fluctuations in demand may be expected. However, the day of grain growing is far from an end.

As populations increase around the world, there is no doubt that markets will open for all the grain that can be produced. There must also be developed efficient distribution systems and methods of economic exchange so that those who need food may obtain it readily from those who produce a surplus.

We have reviewed the background of a major industry during its developmental period; let us now look briefly at the operation of the grain farm itself. The pioneer settler arrived on his quarter-section with a team of horses, a wagon, a plough, a harrow, and a grain drill. He had a few tools and household equipment. By harvest time he would also have acquired a grain binder. Gradually increasing his enterprise, within a few years he might have 160 acres in operation with 80 to 100 acres in crop, 40 acres in fallow, and the rest in pasture. At this point he would probably be able to buy an adjoining quarter-section from a land company or from a fellow pioneer who had decided to pull out. Some of course would not, but others would buy more. At any rate, the census of 1931 reported 288,000 farms and more than 110,-000,000 acres of occupied land, an average of 380 acres per farm. Also reported were 18,300 vacant and abandoned farms and 3,600,000 acres of vacated land.

Since then the area in farms has slowly and steadily increased, reaching a total of 133,000,000 acres in 1966 while the number of farms has steadily decreased dropping to 195,000 in the same year, with an average area of 685 acres. However, only 75 per cent of the farms are classified as "commercial".

It is perhaps of interest to inquire more closely into the details of the changes in land use on the farms of the Prairie Provinces. Some of these are shown in the adjoining table which has been derived from the results of the agricultural censuses taken in 1931 and 1961. It is most noticeable that the area of improved land has increased by more than one-third while that of wheat and other grains and seeds has not increased at all. On the other hand, the area of summer fallow has increased substantially while the area of sod (pasture and hay crops) has more than tripled. Fallow, however, is three times as prevalent as sod.

Fallow, of course, is the basic practice of dry farming found in many parts of the world. Its objective is to enable the farmer to conserve as much as possible of one season's rainfall for the use of the next season's crop. To do this he systematically cultivates a field to destroy all weeds that might extract the moisture from the soil while it remains uncropped. Fallow was introduced into Western Canada by Angus MacKay of Indian Head in the 1880s. It resulted in increased yields and was quickly and widely adopted. Census statistics show that the practice of fallowing has increased steadily ever since. A certain amount of fallow seems to be necessary, but agricultural scientists believe that it is being overdone by many farmers. C. F. Bentley states that the grain economy and summer fallowing have adversely affected much of the originally fertile grassland soil.* Records over 50 years show that the grain-fallow combination results in gradually declining yields and lowered soil fertility. On the other hand, where sod, forages, and other crops have been used in rotation with grain, soil organic matter and mineral nutrient levels have been maintained and larger wheat yields have been harvested. A swing to forages and sod implies the raising of more cattle and sheep in order to make profitable disposal of the products resulting from land use change. It will also contribute to the disappearance of the surplus of small grains other than

* C. F. Bentley. "Soil Management and Fertility — Western Canada". *Resources for Tomorrow Conference. Background Papers.* Vol. 1. Ottawa. 1961. pp. 67-73.

Table 7.2   Changes in Land Use on Prairie Farms *

		Improved land (000 ac.)	Wheat (000 ac.)	Other Grains (000 ac.)	Fallow (000 ac.)	Sod (000 ac.)
Manitoba	1931	8,522	2,150	3,316	2,070	687
	1961	11,964	2,914	2,678	3,230	1,799
Saskatchewan	1931	33,549	14,714	6,980	9,941	914
	1961	43,118	16,082	4,892	17,180	2,877
Alberta	1931	17,749	7,943	3,114	4,547	813
	1961	25,289	5,633	4,858	7,450	4,655
Totals	1931	59,820	24,807	13,410	16,558	2,414
	1961	80,371	24,629	12,428	27,860	9,331

* Derived from Census of Canada, 1931 and 1961.

Figure 7.28 Combine in Operation
As is typical in most grain harvesting in the Prairies, the wheat is not directly combined. Instead, the crop is first swathed into long rows and then after drying is picked up by the combine.

wheat although this is perhaps equally the function of hog and poultry production.

Farm operations have changed greatly since the days of the pioneers and even since the post-war days of the 1920s. Farms are now much larger and more highly mechanized. Large tractors drawing several large machines at once prepare the seedbed and sow the grain in a single operation. The land which a man can now work in a day would have required weeks in the days of horse-drawn implements. Harvesting with the swather and the combine, or under ideal conditions with the combine alone, either tractor-drawn or self-propelled, is now a simple and rapid operation. From the combines the grain is run into the bodies of large trucks which haul it to the elevator or to storage facilities in the farmyard when elevator space is temporarily lacking. Loading and unloading are almost automatically per-

formed. The great gangs of men, formerly characteristic of the Prairie harvest scene, are no longer needed. Nor are the numerous teams of horses which drew the wagon loads of sheaves from the fields to the threshing rigs. No longer are straw mountains built to be later set on fire as the only way of getting rid of them. Scattered behind the combine, the straw remains on the field and may be incorporated with the soil on which it grew. Haymaking too is greatly simplified by use of the swather and the baler. Straw may also be saved for farm use, or perhaps for sale, by use of the baler after the grain has been combined. It has been estimated that each tractor in use on Prairie farms has replaced ten or more horses that formerly were used. Each horse required at least ten acres of land for its support so, in effect, each tractor has released 100 acres to be used for cash crop or for the support of other animal units in

Table 7.3   Major Types of Commercial Farms in the Prairie Provinces, 1966 *

		Commercial Farms	Grain Farms	Livestock Farms	Mixed Farms	Dairy Farms	Poultry and other Specialty Farms
Manitoba	No.	27,372	16,505	5,488	2,969	1,240	1,170
	P.C.	100.0	60.3	20.0	10.8	4.5	4.3
Saskatchewan	No.	69,962	59,396	6,605	2,995	592	374
	P.C.	100.0	84.9	9.4	4.3	0.9	0.5
Alberta	No.	48,971	19,488	20,418	5,287	2,089	1,689
	P.C.	100.0	39.8	41.7	10.8	4.3	3.4
Prairie Provinces	No.	146,305	95,389	32,511	11,251	3,921	3,233
	P.C.	100.0	65.2	22.2	7.7	2.7	2.2

* Derived from the Census of Canada, 1966.

the farm economy. More than 230,000 tractors are found on Prairie farms. Not only is crop land released, but there has been a great release of the farmer's time enabling him to work more land or to look after more productive animal units. It is estimated that each man on the average can handle about 350 acres of crop. The farmer and one hired man, the farmer and one son or, often enough, the farmer and his wife take the harvest from more than a square mile of land.

It has already been pointed out that animal husbandry is important in the Prairie farm economy. For the most part, this means the raising of cattle and hogs; sheep have long been in decline despite what may seem obvious advantages for such a close-grazing animal. Chickens and turkeys have increased; but although the necessary feed is grown nearby, the economic advantage seems to lie with the producers in Eastern Canada who are located near their markets.

Dairy farming constitutes a minor part of the animal industry of Western Canada. It is most prevalent in Manitoba and Alberta where there are large cities to be supplied with fluid milk. In addition, there are also extensive areas in Southern Manitoba and Central Alberta where creameries are in operation. Ice cream and a certain amount of cheddar cheese are also produced.

The raising of beef cattle is much more important than dairying. Although present to a minor degree in Saskatchewan and relatively important in Manitoba, it is dominant in large areas of Alberta. Cattle raising may be carried on in several different ways. Many farms have always had a small beef herd after the fashion of the general farms of Eastern Canada. Sometimes the cows were milked, but often they were not. The small calf-crop was carried through winter-feeding and summer pasture until at 2½ to 3 years they had grown large enough to send to the stockyards. Cattle are also raised under ranch conditions, especially in the Dry Belt and the Rocky Mountain Foothills. It is not always easy to say what is a farm and what is a ranch, but two facts seem significant. The rancher usually states his area in thousands of acres whereas the farmer talks of quarter-sections or perhaps hundreds of acres. Most of the ranch area is devoted to grazing while only a minor area is used for crops; on the other hand, crop growing is usually the major enterprise on a farm. However, there are many small ranches, and there are also some very large farms where 50 per cent or more of the land is used for pasture.

The raising of beef cattle tends to be specialized. There are cow-calf enterprises in which a breeding herd is kept, and the calf-crop marketed at the end of each graz-

Figure 7.29 Range Area
Water and grass are necessary prerequisites for the range cattle industry. This land is too rolling and too dry to permit successful crop farming.

ing season, the calves weighing perhaps an average of 400 pounds. The calves may be purchased by farmers or feeders who have supplies of forage for wintering them over until they may go on grass again for another summer season. Finally they go to a feedlot where they may require from three to six months to be finished to slaughter grade. Each stage of the beef animal's life may involve a journey from one place to another as well as a change in ownership. On the other hand, there are ranchers with winter feed available who raise steers to the stage at which they are ready for the finishing lot. There are feeders with plenty of land who buy calves off the range and then carry them through to market grade, and there are feeders who handle only short-keep cattle that require only three months of intensive feeding to produce

prime beef animals with a live weight of 1,050 to 1,200 pounds.

Formerly, many calves and feeder cattle raised on western farms and ranches were shipped to Ontario to be finished for market. Many are still handled in this way, but there is a growing tendency for western cattle to be fed and marketed in the West. Winnipeg, Calgary, and Edmonton have large meat-packing industries which serve the local region and ship finished meat products to other parts of Canada. These industries are increasing in size and production as the increase in the population and buying power of these cities creates a demand for more and more beef.

In general, the most notable areas of livestock farming are in Alberta. The cattle and hog populations there are only slightly below those of Ontario, while the sheep population, although not great, is considerably above that of Ontario. Dairying is important in Central Alberta, in a broad belt extending from Olds, Red Deer, and Lacombe north to Barrhead and Athabasca and east to St. Paul and Bonnyville with special concentration in the Edmonton area. Livestock farming with emphasis on various phases of beef cattle production is widespread. Areas in which the calf-crop is significantly larger than the herd of yearlings occur in the Dry Belt of Southeastern Alberta. Lethbridge, Calgary, and Red Deer appear to be centers of steer-feeding regions. Hog raising is most concentrated in the central part of the province, especially around and for some distance east of Edmonton. The Black Soil Belt in Saskatchewan is also an area of mixed farming where dairying, steer feeding, and hog raising are carried· on, though not to the same degree as in Alberta. Mixed farming is fairly generally distributed in many parts of Manitoba as well. However, since over half of the commercial farms of Manitoba and four-fifths of those in Saskatchewan are designated as grain farms, it is obvious that much of the livestock raising is to be considered a subsidiary enterprise conducted on grain farms. There are large areas in Southern Alberta and Southwestern Saskatchewan which have a semi-arid climate and often a rough surface and are dominated by large land holdings and a grazing economy. Here the calf-crop is significantly large in comparison with the total herd, thus providing a source of replacement cattle for the growers and feeders of the mixed farming districts as well as a source for shipment to other parts of Canada and to the United States.

Cattle ranching on the Prairies dates from 1874 when range cattle were brought into the Wood Mountain area from Montana. In 1882 the Government of Canada set up regulations permitting the leasing of tracts up to 100,000 acres in area, and for some years the industry expanded rapidly. After 1900, however, the rapid increase in agricultural settlement forced the breaking up of most of the very large ranches. Ranching dominates in those areas generally unsuitable for crop farming in the Short-grass Plains or Brown Soil Zone, the Cypress Hills, the Rocky Mountain Foothills, and in the Northern Prairie Area near Wainwright. Census returns show these areas still to have many large operational units, about 1,500 having areas over 3,000 acres each. Of these it is estimated that 200 are ranches of 10,000 acres or more. About 2,000 acres on the average are owned by the rancher and constitute his headquarters area. The remainder of the range is under lease and consists mainly of provincial lands. Herds range from 200 to 500 head in various districts. Herefords are preferred by most ranchers as they seem more able than other breeds to take care of themselves on the open range. Water supplies are limited, and range animals must often travel one to two miles or more between watering places and grazing grounds. The climate of the southern plains permits a long grazing season, winter feeding being required for less than 100 days. The Foothills and the Northern Prairie area, however, have a shorter grazing season.

Irrigation

Throughout Southern Alberta and Southwestern Saskatchewan the mean annual precipitation is less than 14 inches, of which only half falls in the months of May, June, and July, the critical season for crop growth. Irrigation is thus advisable wherever water can be provided for suitable land. Since early settlement days, various attempts have been made. The first irrigation ditch was constructed in 1879 near Calgary. In 1894 the Northwest Irrigation Act was passed, and by 1896 the area "under ditch" was 79,000 acres. The Canadian Pacific Railway was the most active promoter of irrigation, nearly one-half of the existing irrigated land in Alberta having been developed on land which was granted by the Crown to assist in building the railway. Other land companies also set up irrigation schemes. More recently, all of these lands have been organized into about

Figure 7.30 Irrigation
If the land is flat and water available, irrigation is possible. The picture shows potatoes being successfully grown with the aid of irrigation water, northeast of Vauxhall, on the Bow River Project.

Figure 7.31 Sugar Refinery
Sugar beets provide high yields when grown under irrigation in Southern Alberta. This processing plant near Taber converts the sugar beet into sugar. The beet residue is then fed to livestock.

a dozen irrigation districts under the auspices of the Alberta government. The census of 1961 reported 4,200 farms with an irrigated area of over 540,000 acres in Alberta. Saskatchewan had only 760 farms with 49,000 irrigated acres.

About one-third of the irrigated land of the Prairie Provinces is devoted to wheat production. Next, in order of area, are hay, oats, barley, sugar beets, pasture, potatoes, vegetables, and peas. The sugar beet is a good example of an irrigated crop with a high value per acre. Canadian Sugar Factories operates a factory in Southern Alberta, making contracts with about 1,500 growers to produce 35,000 acres of sugar beets per year. The area produces about eight per cent of the total sugar consumed in Canada or about the equivalent of the amount needed to supply the population of Alberta where, indeed, most of it is sold. Potatoes and vegetables from the irrigated farms are sold throughout Alberta and to some extent in Saskatchewan and British Columbia as well. As the cities of Western Canada grow, so also in all probability will both the extent and the intensity of irrigated farming. In the meantime the greater part of this intensive facility will be used to produce field crops in competition with surrounding dry-land farms.

For the sake of the future, however, it is worthwhile to inquire into the possible extent of irrigation potential. Agricultural scientists estimate that the core of the Dry Belt contains 15,000,000 acres of land which conceivably might benefit from irrigation. On the other hand, hydrologists estimate that the water available in the South Saskatchewan River System and all that might be diverted from the North Saskatchewan would barely be adequate to service 3,000,000 acres. Already a small potential in the Missouri basin is also being partially utilized. The total facilities now existing are capable of supplying water to about 850,000 acres of irrigable land while further facilities are being built or projected.

In support of continuing investment in irrigation, agriculturists point out that

although the irrigated area is only about four per cent of the improved land of Alberta, it produces about 20 per cent of the gross farm revenue.

Further development of irrigation is under the auspices of the Prairie Farm Rehabilitation Authority. The Prairie Farm Rehabilitation Act which was passed in 1935 authorized the federal government to appropriate funds "to provide for the rehabilitation of drought and soil drifting areas in the provinces of Manitoba, Saskatchewan, and Alberta". Later the scope of the Act was broadened to include all problems of land utilization and land settlement. The head offices of the Authority are in Regina. The program was designed to improve farm practices so as to conserve soil moisture and to control soil drifting, to aid in building irrigation projects as well as smaller water-conservation dams and dugouts, and to transform worn-out crop land into useful pastures for livestock. Millions of acres of community pastures have been set up under this program, but its most spectacular efforts seem to be directed toward the building of irrigation works.

Among the major projects are: the St. Mary River Project and the Bow River Project (both in Alberta) and the South Saskatchewan River Project.

The St. Mary Irrigation Project was undertaken jointly by the government of Alberta and the federal government in 1946. The St. Mary Dam and storage facilities were completed in 1951; the diversion of the Belly River was completed in 1958 and that of the Waterton River in 1965, thus greatly increasing the water supply of the St. Mary Reservoir. This makes possible the addition of 240,000 acres to the 296,000 acres already under irrigation between Lethbridge and Medicine Hat. The Bow River Irrigation Project was taken over from the Canada Land and Irrigation Company in 1951. About 240,-000 acres are potentially irrigable, of which 60,000 acres are already in use.

The South Saskatchewan River Project has been the subject of much political and technical attention for many years. Geographically and economically it is an attempt by the province of Saskatchewan to extract some benefit from the 5,000,000 acre-feet of water which constitute the average annual flow of the South Saskatchewan River. In 1958 an agreement between the Saskatchewan government and the federal government was signed to undertake a multiple purpose project including irrigation, power development, municipal water supply, control of river flow, and development of recreational facilities. Two dams had to be constructed, one on the main river between Elbow and Outlook and the other across the Qu'Appelle Valley, an ancient outlet of the Saskatchewan to the east. The main dam has a total length of 16,700 feet and a height of 210 feet; it is the largest rolled-earth dam in Canada and one of the largest in the world. Its cost is estimated at $100,-000,000. Behind it lies a reservoir 140

miles long with a capacity of 8,000,000 acre-feet of water, of which 2,750,000 acre-feet will be usable. Power potential at the dam site is 475,000 kwh, while water will eventually be made available to irrigate 500,000 acres. The soils of this area are of lower fertility than those of the irrigated lands of Southern Alberta, and the growing season is shorter; thus the choice of crops for this area is likely to be fairly closely restricted to those already produced by dry-land farmers. The provision of power and water supply for cities and industries in Central Saskatchewan will be an important factor in regional development.

Other P.F.R.A. projects include the drainage and flood control of large tracts of alluvial land along the lower reaches of the Saskatchewan River, 100,000 acres lying near The Pas in Manitoba. Major flood control measures on the Assiniboine River, with a diversion canal near Portage la Prairie to carry excess water to Lake

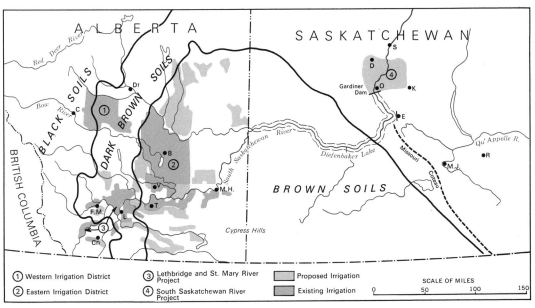

Figure 7.32 Irrigation Areas — the Saskatchewan River System

B	Brooks	F.M.	Fort Macleod	R	Regina
C	Calgary	K	Kenaston	S	Saskatoon
Cn	Cardsten	L	Lethbridge	T	Taber
D	Delisle	M.H.	Medicine Hat	V	Vauxhall
Dr	Drumheller	M.J.	Moose Jaw		
E	Elbow	O	Outlook		

Figure 7.33 Gardiner Dam, South Saskatchewan River Project
The recently completed Gardiner Dam holds back the waters of the South Saskatchewan River to form Lake Diefenbaker. The water is used for irrigation and is diverted into the Qu'Appelle River for use by industry and cities such as Regina.

Manitoba, are also being constructed. Since 1937, 75 community pastures have been developed in the Dry Belt. They contain an area of 2,250,000 acres and provide summer grazing for 150,000 head of cattle.

Agricultural Gradients

An analysis of the distribution of the various elements of the geographical pattern of the Prairies and an understanding of the pattern itself are only possible through the use of statistical maps. The following series of isoline maps has been constructed, using data from the agricultural census of 1961, the spacing of the isolines being based on quartile intervals. The outline of the area of agricultural settlement has been generalized from a study and comparison of census outlines and topographical maps of Western Canada.

Somewhat less than one-third of the total area of the Prairie Provinces is occupied by farms, large areas in the north, particularly in Manitoba and Saskatchewan being entirely without agricultural settlement. The pattern of density of agricultural occupancy is shown in Figure 7.34. Large parts of Southern Saskatchewan and Southern Alberta have more than 90 per

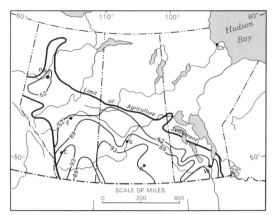

Figure 7.34 Total Farm Land as Per Cent of Total Area — 1961

Isolines are plotted on the basis of data for census divisions. Isoline intervals are based on median and quartile divisions of the distribution. The areas west of Regina and south of Calgary have the greatest proportion of their total area in farm land.

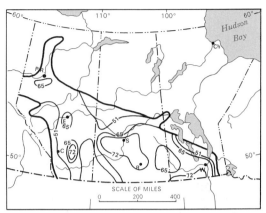

Figure 7.35 Improved Land as Per Cent of Total Farm Land — 1961

cent of the land in agriculture. These are the areas which are topographically and climatically most favorable for commercial grain growing. On the other hand, a variable northern margin extending from eastern Manitoba to the northern part of the Peace River country has only 50 per cent or less of its land in farms. This used to be designated as the Pioneer Fringe when settlement within it was fairly new. Now the wave of settlement is no longer advancing except in the Peace River country. In fact, land settlement on the northern frontier in Manitoba and Saskatchewan has been at a virtual standstill for some years and in many areas is actually declining.* Land clearing still goes on, however, within the area already occupied.

The pattern of improved land is shown in Figure 7.35. Three areas, Southern Manitoba, Central Saskatchewan, and Central Alberta, all show more than 70 per cent of the farm land to be improved. On the other hand, a large area in the Dry Belt and various other fringe areas show less than half the farm area to consist of improved land. Crop area as per cent of

farm land, as seen in Figure 7.36, varies in much the same way, the Dry Belt and some areas along the northern fringe having less than one-third of the farm land under crop. One reason for the great differences between the areas of improved land and those of crop land is the fact that each year much arable land is given over to summer fallow in preparation for cropping in the following year. Wheat is the most important crop, and its distributional pattern is shown in Figure 7.37. Throughout agricultural Saskatchewan wheat accounts for 60 per cent of the area in crops, while in some special areas it covers more than 75 per cent. Throughout the wheat

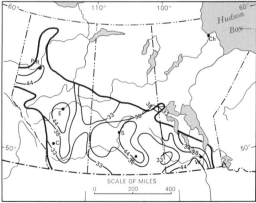

Figure 7.36 Crop Area as Per Cent of Total Farm Land — 1961

The Peace River area, the Edmonton area, the area from Regina to Saskatoon, and the area southwest of Winnipeg, all have more than 44 per cent of the farm land in crops.

* Burke G. Vanderhill. "The Decline of Land Settlement in Manitoba and Saskatchewan". *Economic Geography*. Vol. 38. (1962). pp. 270-277.

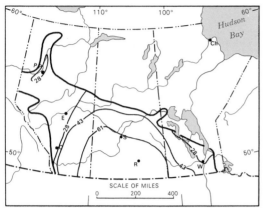

Figure 7.37 Wheat Acreage as Per Cent of Total Crop Land — 1961

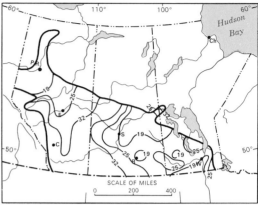

Figure 7.38 Pasture as Per Cent of Total Farm Land — 1961

belt it embraces more than 20 per cent of the total land in farms. Lands near the margin of the agricultural area are, by the same token, marginal for wheat growing.

The importance of pasture as a land use is suggested in Figure 7.38. In dry areas and in areas where the surface is rough, pasture is the land use alternative to grain growing. In both Southwestern and Northwestern Saskatchewan, in Southern Alberta, and in the Rocky Mountain Foothills, grazing is very important both on the farms and on large areas of leased provincial land. In the region around Medicine Hat, for instance, more than 60 per cent of the land is devoted to pasture. On the other hand, the ratio of pasture land is low

in the Peace River country, Eastern Saskatchewan, and the Red River Valley.

The variations in the value of livestock production are shown in Figure 7.39. In the dominantly wheat-growing area of Southern Saskatchewan the values for livestock production are low; they are also low in the Peace River country. On the other hand, they are relatively high in Southern Manitoba and highest of all in an extensive area in Southern and Central Alberta. While these areas are important for cattle feeding, they also contain a large percentage of the hog-raising farms of the Prairie Provinces.

Figure 7.40 indicates that the average size of farm varies from less than 400 acres

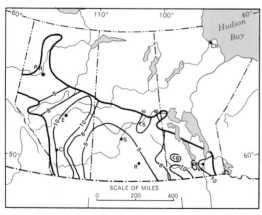

Figure 7.39 Livestock Production in Dollars per Acre of Farm Land — 1961

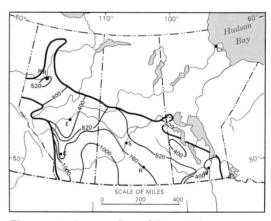

Figure 7.40 Average Size of Farm in Acres — 1961

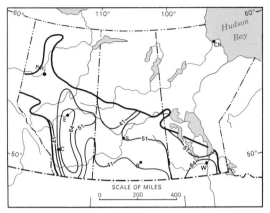

Figure 7.41 Total Farm Capital in Dollars per Acre of Farm Land — 1961

in Southern Manitoba and in the margins of the Peace River country to more than 1,000 acres in the dry lands of Southwestern Saskatchewan and Southeastern Alberta. In fact, in both the Dry Belt and in the Alberta Foothills there are operational units with more than 10,000 acres. Most of the wheat-growing farms in Saskatchewan are larger than 500 acres, and the same is true of the central part of the Peace River country. Even more important than area to the economic health of an agricultural unit is the capital invested in land, buildings, equipment, and livestock. The distribution of farm capital on a per acre basis is shown in Figure 7.41. Two areas stand out — Southern Manitoba and Central Alberta. These areas correspond fairly closely to those which were already noted to excel in value of livestock production. The larger farms of the Saskatchewan wheat belt are not so highly capitalized.

While other census data are also available, the foregoing series of maps provides a relatively good background for a study of the regional differences of agricultural activity in the Prairie Provinces.

Agricultural Zones

Maps of agricultural zones in the Prairie Provinces are based, for the most part, on generalizations from agricultural census data. Consequently, the outlines vary from time to time. Figure 7.42 was drawn on the basis of data from the census of 1961. The central feature of this map, as has been the case for all such maps for decades, is the wheat-farming area of Central and Southeastern Saskatchewan where wheat occupies more than 50 per cent of the crop land, more than 33 per cent of the farm land is in crop, and 60 to 90 per cent of all commercial farms are designated as wheat farms. To the west of this is an area in which less than one-third of the land is cropped and more than one-third is devoted to pasture; the major areas of land not included in the aforementioned land use classes may be largely assigned to summer fallow. Here grain farms and livestock farms are about equal in number, but there are many large tracts devoted strictly to grazing. This constitutes the "Grazing Zone". The adjoining wedge-shaped area in Southern Alberta would be similar in its land use characteristics, were it not for the fact that it contains nearly 1,000,000 acres of land, actually or potentially, under ditch. The presence of irrigation in this area makes for agricultural diversity, with the growth of a number of special crops such as sugar beets, potatoes, vegetables, canning peas, and alfalfa hay.

On the whole, the three areas just described correspond very well with the outlines of Palliser's Triangle. Around them stretches the "Mixed Farming Belt", a crescentic area in which wheat farming, while it exists and is often important, is not dominant over all other types of land use. The "Mixed Farming Belt" is by no means a homogeneous mixture of land uses, but may with reasonable accuracy be divided into subregions, depending upon the chief combinations of land uses. Southeastern Manitoba has so many specialties that it may be designated as a distinct zone. It has a number of dairy farms serving the Winnipeg Metropolitan area, but not enough to create a definite dairy-farming region. Here are also grown a number of commercial crops, including flax, safflower, rape seed, sugar beets, vegetables, and small fruits. In addition, it is noted for the

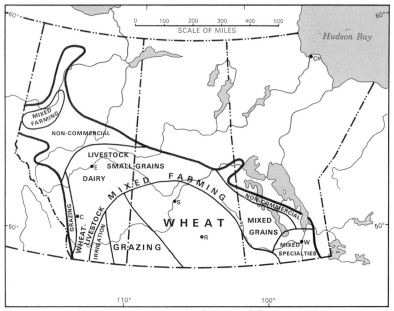

Figure 7.42 Agricultural Zones of the Prairies

production of beef cattle and hogs. Around Edmonton, in Central Alberta, lies another area with a considerable dairy production. Again, the concentration of dairy farmers is not great enough to constitute a dairy-farming region even though this is the area of greatest butter production in the Prairie Provinces as well as the area of milk supply for Edmonton and a number of smaller urban centers. With beef cattle, hogs, small grains, and wheat in evidence not only throughout the district but in the agricultural pattern of a great many individual farms as well, Central Alberta is truly an area of mixed farming. The Peace River country, dominated by a combination of mixed grains, livestock, and wheat, may be considered a northern outlier of the Mixed Farming Zone. The southwestern limit of the crescent is also somewhat of a special case. Much of it, originally short-grass or mixed-grass steppe, is a successful wheat-growing area although wheat growing does not dominate. Calgary and Lethbridge support some fluid-milk enterprises. The chief influence toward mixed farming, however, is the presence of range country both to the east and the west.

This constitutes the source of calves and stockers which may be raised and finished on feeds harvested within the area. The packing plants of Calgary and Edmonton provide markets for beef cattle and hogs from the mixed farms of Alberta although some are also shipped to other areas. The central portion of the crescent has a fairly high concentration of wheat farms although not nearly so great as in the Wheat Belt farther south. The presence of feed grains and livestock also makes this a mixed farming region. Some areas on the northern margins of Manitoba and Alberta have rather poorly developed farms. On many older maps the northern fringe of the agricultural area of the Prairie Provinces is designated as the Pioneer Fringe, a name impressed upon the minds of a whole generation of settlement geographers by Isaiah Bowman.* This undoubtedly was descriptive in the 1920s when Bowman was writing. To a lesser extent it was also true in the 1930s when refugees from the drought areas in the south sought new

---

* Isaiah Bowman. *The Pioneer Fringe.* American Geographical Society. Special Publication No. 13. New York. 1931.

land in the "Mixed Woods". It hardly seems so today when settlement is declining, land is being abandoned, and many farmers are only part-time operators. As in the fringes of Eastern Canada such areas are better designated as *non-commercial*.

FORESTRY

Although the Prairie Provinces have 23 per cent of the total area of forest in Canada, only a relatively small proportion of this resource is utilized. In recent years forests in this region have produced an annual cut of approximately 250 million cubic feet of wood or about 8 per cent of the total for Canada. For specific industries the value is even smaller, for only 2.1 per cent of the total produced from all sawmill products in Canada is derived from the Prairie Provinces. Recent developments suggest that the pulp and paper industry will become more significant as the new mills at Prince Albert and The Pas come into production.

Many factors are involved in the relative lack of importance of the forest industries. Production costs are higher than in the rest of Canada because of the smaller size of tree and the difficulty of access to the timber. In addition, there is the great overland distance from domestic and foreign markets which must be surmounted. These factors create considerable disadvantage for the forest industry of the Prairie Provinces.

In reality, the industry is distributed across the Prairie Provinces in crescentic fashion, from the Winnipeg River and Interlakes region in the east, northward to the vicinity of The Pas, Prince Albert, and the Meadow Lakes District, and westward to Hinton and along the Rocky Mountain Foothills. A small area in the Peace River country forms a separate zone of concentration.

While the lumbering industry is made up mainly of hundreds of small operations, a few larger ones do occur. The Pas was for years one of the chief sawmilling centers. The logs utilized were obtained not only from the immediate district but from the neighboring area in Eastern Saskatchewan. Pulp and paper milling is confined to certain areas where the resource base is adequate. Two mills have operated for some time: one at Hinton, Alberta, the other at Pine Falls, Manitoba. In 1966 other mills were under construction at Prince Albert and The Pas. The new pulp mill at The Pas is to be part of an integrated forest products development. A large sawmill will be one of the first plants to open.

MINING

The mineral wealth of Ontario and Quebec is to be found mainly in their sections of the Canadian Shield. In the Prairie Provinces, despite the development of important mining sites such as Thompson, Lynn Lake, and Flin Flon, the greater part of the mineral production consists of coal, oil, natural gas, and potash from the Great Plains and Rocky Mountain Foothills. The value of the mineral production has increased markedly, from $660,000,000 in 1960 to $1,308,600,000 in 1965, a growth rate of 196 per cent in the five-year period.

In 1965 metal mining, located chiefly in Saskatchewan and Manitoba, produced $102,000,000 in copper, nickel, gold, zinc, and uranium. The value of coal, oil, and natural gas, largely in Alberta and Saskatchewan, was about $859,000,000, while structural materials were worth about $65,-000,000. In 1965 about 25 per cent of all those employed in mining in Canada were located in the Prairie Provinces. Of the 29,000 involved directly, 17 per cent were in Saskatchewan, 19 per cent were in Manitoba, and 64 per cent were in Alberta.

Metals

In 1915 a large ore body containing gold, silver, copper, and zinc was discovered on the Manitoba-Saskatchewan boundary about 100 miles north of The Pas. A railway was built from The Pas, power was obtained from Island Falls on the Churchill River, and a new town, Flin Flon, was built. The mine and smelter, which opened in 1928, are still in operation. Today, custom refining of copper ores from Lynn Lake and from the new mine at Lac La Ronge supplements local resources and supports a city of about 14,000 inhabitants.

Lynn Lake (population 2,300), about 160 miles north of Flin Flon, developed through the wholesale movement of the buildings from the old company town of Sherridon to the new copper mines at Lynn Lake. The move was accomplished during the winters of 1951 to 1953, and the new town was a functional entity in 1954. Concentrates are sent to Fort Saskatchewan, 17 miles northeast of Edmonton, where cheap natural gas, abundant cooling water, and special rail facilities exist.

Uranium is obtained in the Beaverlodge area north of Lake Athabasca. Despite the recent problems in marketing Canadian uranium, the town, Uranium City, is still in operation and serves as a model of government planning.

In 1956 a large nickel-bearing ore body, similar to the deposit at Sudbury, Ontario, was discovered in the Mystery-Moak Lake district of Manitoba. After considerable exploratory drilling the present site of Thompson was selected, and the fully integrated mine and refinery came into operation in 1961. Capable of producing 75,000,000 pounds of nickel annually, it is one of the largest producers in the world. Despite its remoteness, rail service via a spur line from the main Hudson Bay Railway and a new highway both provide ready access. Power needs are met by the Kelsey power project at Grand Rapid on the Nelson River. A modern company town, Thompson is growing rapidly and now has about 9,000 inhabitants.

Coal

While it is estimated that the Cretaceous rocks of the Prairie Provinces contain reserves of more than 72,000,000 tons of coal (77 per cent of Canada's reserves), the region accounted for only 48 per cent of the 11.4 million tons mined in Canada in 1966. Much of the coal in Alberta is bituminous with some anthracite, but lignite deposits predominate in Saskatchewan and Manitoba. Open pit mining of lignite for thermal power generation occurs at Estevan, Saskatchewan, but despite the fact that its mining costs are the lowest for any coal mine in Canada, production is declining. New thermal generating stations in Central Alberta use powdered bituminous coal obtained from the mines near Edmonton. A recent development has been the mining of bituminous coal from Southern Alberta for export to Japan. Distance from domestic markets in Canada, competition with other source areas, and competition with other fuels have retarded development of the industry.

Petroleum and Natural Gas

While petroleum in Canada was first discovered and utilized in Southwestern Ontario, the Prairie Provinces now account for 94 per cent of the oil produced in Canada. Alberta, the national leader, accounted for 63 per cent of the 320 million barrels produced in 1966. Recent developments such as the new Swan Hills and Rainbow Lakes fields north of Edmonton and the Great Canadian Oil Sands project at Fort McMurray to tap the enormous reserves of the Athabasca Tar Sands augur well for the continued primacy of Alberta petroleum.

The first oil well in Western Canada was drilled by Dingman in 1914 in the Turner Valley, 40 miles south of Calgary. Wells such as Royalite 4, which tapped a pool in a Mississippian Dolomite layer 6,000 feet below the surface in 1924, quickly made Turner Valley the second largest field in the British Empire. During the 1930s, 90 per cent of the Canadian output came from Turner Valley, and Calgary profited greatly as the center of the industry and the site of several large oil refineries.

The discovery of the Leduc field in 1947 focused attention further north, in the vicinity of Edmonton. Then in 1953 Pembina, 70 miles southwest of Edmonton, became a major producer. Unlike the Leduc deposit which occurred in a limestone reef

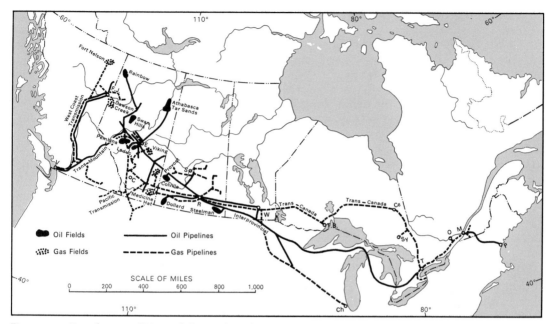

Figure 7.43 Petroleum and Natural Gas in Canada
Marketing the crude oil and natural gas produced in the Prairies requires a complex system of pipelines
to Eastern Canada and the Pacific Coast.

C	Calgary	M	Montreal	Sy	Sudbury
Ce	Cochrane	O	Ottawa	T	Toronto
Ch	Chicago	P	Portland	T.B.	Thunder Bay
E	Edmonton	R	Regina	V	Vancouver
F.J.	Fort St. John	S	Saskatoon	W	Winnipeg

of Devonian age, the Pembina pool occurred in Cardium sandstone of Cretaceous age. As shown by the map, numerous oil fields now produce in Central Alberta, and Edmonton has become the real focal point for the industry. This role is likely to continue for new developments are taking place in the northern Peace River country where the Keg River formation in the Rainbow Lakes area appears to hold even more promise than did the Cardium sandstone a decade previously. Oil production in Saskatchewan and Manitoba has been less spectacular, but through conservation techniques such as water pressurization continued production is assured at fields such as Steelman near Weyburn and the Virden field in Manitoba.

Pipelines carry crude oil from the oilfields of the Prairie Provinces to refineries at the major Prairie cities, to the Pacific Coast, and eastward to the refining complexes of Sarnia and the Toronto-Hamilton Axis. The most important carriers are the Interprovincial pipeline, which extends for 1,928 miles from Edmonton to Port Credit, Ontario, and the Trans-Mountain pipeline, which spans the 718 miles from Edmonton to Vancouver, British Columbia, and Tacoma, Washington. As yet, Canadian crude oil is not competitive in the Quebec and Atlantic markets and dominates Ontario only with the aid of the National Oil Policy.

Natural gas occurs in great abundance in Alberta and is encountered in almost every drilling operation. Large quantities are found in the British Columbia portion of the Peace River area, at Fort Nelson and Fort St. John. Natural gas produced there is transported to the Vancouver and Washington markets via the West Coast Transmission Line. Near Kamloops a junction allows the Inland Natural Gas Company to serve the needs of the smelting complex at Trail.

Alberta leads the rest of Canada in the production of natural gas, producing $144,000,000 worth of natural gas in 1966. Edson, Viking, Provost, Cessford, and Medicine Hat are the major fields. Alberta natural gas is marketed in the western part of the United States and in Eastern Canada. The Alberta Natural Gas Company and Pacific Gas Transmission Company have constructed a 36″ line from Whitecourt, Alberta to San Francisco, California. Eastern Canada is served by the Trans-Canada pipeline which extends for 2,145 miles from the Alberta-Saskatchewan border to Montreal via Winnipeg, Thunder Bay, Cochrane, North Bay, and Toronto. Market growth in Eastern Canada is such that additional facilities will soon be necessary. A logical course would be a loop through the United States if additional markets could be tapped there.

Natural gas, however, must be processed to remove impurities before it can be utilized. Normally, processing must be done near the well for the impurities are injurious to the pipes and pumps. Helium and elemental sulfur are the most frequent contaminants. In Alberta alone 23 sulfur recovery plants are in operation, and in 1966 elemental sulfur production reached 1,900,000 tons.

Other Non-metallic Minerals

Salt occurs in all three Prairie Provinces, in beds 200 to 500 feet in thickness. McMurray and Elk Point in Alberta, Unity in Saskatchewan, and Neepawa in Manitoba are all important producers.

Gypsum is quarried at Gypsumville and Amaranth in the Interlakes region of Manitoba. Building stone such as the famous Tyndall limestone in Manitoba is quarried at various points in Manitoba and Alberta.

Since 1960 potash has become an important mineral in the Prairie Provinces. Concentrated largely in Saskatchewan, the potash resource is believed to exceed 18,000,000,000 tons. Rapid development has taken place; and while 1966 production was a modest 3,200,000 tons, mining facilities are being developed so that mining capacity will exceed 12,000,000 tons in

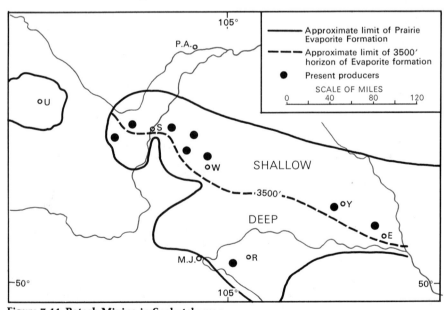

Figure 7.44 Potash Mining in Saskatchewan

E	Esterhazy	R	Regina	W	Watrous
M.J.	Moose Jaw	S	Saskatoon	Y	Yorkton
P.A.	Prince Albert	U	Unity		

1970. It is estimated that in 1970 potash will provide 10 per cent of the rail revenue of Canada, and that nearly 6,000 people will be directly employed by the industry in Saskatchewan alone. On this basis it appears that potash will be the fourth-ranking mineral in Canada and will be exceeded only by nickel, copper, and iron.

As shown by Figure 7.44, potash mines are concentrated near Saskatoon in the area where the mineral occurs less than 3,500 feet below the surface. Of note is the major mine at Esterhazy which was opened in 1962 and by 1966 had produced more than 5,000,000 tons. Only one mining operation occurs in the southern part of the potash zone where the deposit dips below 3,500 feet, namely the Kalium Chemicals Company mine at Belle Plain near Moose Jaw. Here the potash is brought to the surface via the solution method from the 5,300-foot level. Although it is more expensive than shaft mining, this technique produces a higher quality potash that has wide application in the chemical and meat-packing industries.

Water is a problem for the potash industry. Below the surface water is trapped at enormous pressure within the Blairmore formation. Special techniques such as "tubbing" are necessary to penetrate this layer, 200-500 feet thick, and to hold back the water so that the shafts below remain dry. At the surface, however, potash processing requires large amounts of relatively pure water. For example, Kalium Chemicals has installed a 13-mile pipeline from Buffalo Pound Lake to the mine site and has secured permits to use more water from this source than is currently used by the City of Moose Jaw. Near Saskatoon a series of pipelines is being constructed to bring water from the South Saskatchewan River to the potash-processing plants. Extensive surveys are now in progress to ensure that ground water supplies and water from the South Saskatchewan Dam will be available as the industry expands. The concentration of the industry near Saskatoon may soon give that city the title, "Potash Capital of the World".

MANUFACTURING IN THE PRAIRIE PROVINCES

The Prairie Provinces are developing as a significant manufacturing region in Canada for in 1965 the gross value of manufacturing production reached $2,667,613,-000. This amounts to an increase of 26 per cent in the period 1960 to 1965. Thus it now has replaced agriculture as the leading source of income. While growth has occurred in industries which rely on locally available raw materials, secondary industries are developing to serve the rapidly expanding urban population.

Evidences of this trend can be observed in each of the major cities where industrial parks such as Winnipeg's Inkster Park and Calgary's Foothills Industrial Estate are attracting new industries based on secondary manufacturing to meet the needs of the region. However, despite the expansion of steel processing at Regina, heavy machinery at Winnipeg, and chemicals at Edmonton, food processing is still the dominant category of the manufacturing industry. In this respect the industrial structure of the Prairies resembles that of the Great Plains of the United States where food processing and transportation equipment are the most important sectors of the regional industrial structure.

In terms of industrial structure, analysis is often best made by means of employment data. Despite the rapid development of the Prairie Provinces in the last decade, it should be noted that they account for only 6.5 per cent of those employed in manufacturing in Canada. As shown by Table 7.4, the region still relies on a few industries to provide the bulk of the employment, and the industrial structure is not as diversified as that of Central Canada. However, certain of the industries, when analyzed in terms of their location quotient, are quite significant.

According to the location quotient of industrial employment food processing is the most important industrial group. This reflects the agricultural base of the Prairies and the importance of the trade in foodstuffs to markets outside the region.

Table 7.4 **Industrial Structure of the Prairie Provinces:
Production Workers in Major Industrial Groups ***

Major Industrial Groups	Employment in the Prairie Provinces	Employment in Canada	Pr. Prov. Emp. as per cent of Can. Emp.	Prairie Total as per cent of Canada Total	Location Quotient
1. Food and Beverage Industries	18,590	135,110	13.76	6.52	2.11
2. Metal Fabricating Industries	8,056	99,839	8.07	6.52	1.23
3. Clothing Industries	7,853	84,668	9.28	6.52	1.42
4. Wood Industries	5,284	78,389	6.74	6.52	1.03
5. Printing, Publishing, and Allied Industries	4,958	44,746	11.08	6.52	1.70
6. Non-metallic Mineral Products Industries	4,294	38,246	11.23	6.52	1.72
7. Primary Metal Industries	3,772	83,443	4.52	6.52	0.69
8. Transportation Equipment Industries	2,922	99,705	2.93	6.52	0.45
9. Chemical Products Industries	2,624	35,057	5.22	6.52	0.80
10. Machinery Industries	2,543	43,007	5.91	6.52	0.91
11. Paper and Allied Industries	2,422	83,994	2.88	6.52	0.44
12. Furniture and Fixtures Industries	2,382	32,702	7.28	6.52	1.12
13. Others	7,880	256,986			
Total—All Manufacturing Industries	72,786	1,115,892	6.52	6.52	1.00

* Canada Year Book, 1968. pp. 700-711.

Slaughtering and meat packing, one of the most important industries in the group, has expanded rapidly during the last decade in response to the trend to processing the livestock in the region of origin and shipping the finished products to the market regions in Eastern Canada and British Columbia. Thus, concentrations of the industry occur in the main urban centers on the edges of the Prairies, namely, at Winnipeg, Edmonton, and Calgary. Grain milling partially follows this pattern, but is also located in Saskatoon, Regina, Moose Jaw, and Brandon. Butter and cheese manufacture is widely distributed and located largely in Alberta and Manitoba. This reflects both the fact that these two provinces have more dairy cattle than Saskatchewan and that they have a higher market potential for dairy products as well.

The clothing industry as shown by the location quotient is somewhat above the national average, but it is overwhelmingly concentrated in Manitoba. It developed early in Winnipeg and has continued to prosper as the regional market expanded.

Wood industries are widely scattered in response to market potential; the region does not have an extensive production of primary lumber and must rely largely upon British Columbia for its raw materials.

Metal fabrication has developed rapidly during the last decade and should attract new concerns and create expansion in existing ones as demands for materials used in agricultural machinery and heating equipment increase. In the primary metals industry which according to the location quotient is not yet of significance in the Prairie Provinces, there is a trend of rapid growth as shown by steel production at Regina, nickel processing at Thompson, and metal refining at Fort Saskatchewan and Flin Flon.

Similarly, the paper and chemical products sectors of the industrial structure have been underdeveloped in the Prairie Provinces. The increase in processing of natural gas to yield bi-product sulfur in Alberta, the rapid growth of the potash industry in Saskatchewan, and the recent development of new pulp and paper facilities near Prince Albert and The Pas augur well for the future. During the next decade, the significance of the non-metallic mineral products industry will increase, particularly in Saskatchewan, which may surpass the present leading producer, Alberta. Cement manufacture and the ready-mix concrete industry have grown in all three provinces.

Despite the important petroleum resources, petroleum refining has not developed beyond the needs of the local markets. Thus, the industry is well distributed with refineries being located in the vicinity of Edmonton, Calgary, Moose Jaw, Regina, Saskatoon, and Winnipeg.

Despite the rapid population growth of Calgary and Edmonton, Winnipeg remains the most important manufacturing center of the Prairie Provinces. It has had the benefits of an early start and a measure of specialization in certain lines, while the concentration of railway routes on Winnipeg has also proved to be of great advantage. The size of the local market is also an important factor in the encouragement of local industry. In terms of value of shipments in 1965 Alberta provided 47 per cent of the Prairie output, Manitoba 36 per cent, and Saskatchewan 17 per cent. This ranking is in very good agreement with that of the size of urban population in the respective provinces.

The abundance of raw material is significant; in this, Alberta with its resources of petroleum, natural gas, and coal combined with its wealth of grain and livestock, provides a more diversified base for industrial development. On this basis one might predict that Edmonton may soon overtake Winnipeg and become the leading manufacturing center of the Prairies. Saskatchewan may also increase its share of industrial development as the production of potash grows.

PRAIRIE CITIES

For two generations the Prairie Provinces have projected a rural agricultural image to the world, an image which contains little reference to urban development. Yet the census of 1966 recorded the fact that more than 50 per cent of the population was to be found in cities with populations of 10,000 or more. Moreover, the Prairies contain some of the most rapidly growing cities in the country.

Urban development in the Prairie Provinces is relatively recent, and its pattern is clearly related to the development of railway transportation and the service industry structure of large regional areas. Five major cities, Winnipeg, Edmonton, Calgary, Regina, and Saskatoon, ranging in population from 100,000 to somewhat more than 500,000, dominate the pattern. Winnipeg, the oldest and still the largest, traces its origin to the activities of the early fur traders and the founding of Lord Selkirk's Red River settlement in 1811. Edmonton was also the site of fur-traders' posts in the early years of the nineteenth century, while Calgary was founded as a police post in 1875. They remained very small settlements until they became important points in the development of the railway net and regional agricultural settlement. Regina and Saskatoon are even more directly related to railway transportation in their development since both cities began as junction points.

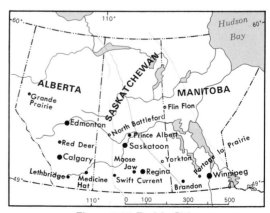

Figure 7.45 Prairie Cities

296 / CANADA: A REGIONAL ANALYSIS

A second rank of cities with populations averaging around 30,000 includes Lethbridge, Moose Jaw, Brandon, Medicine Hat, Prince Albert, and Red Deer, while a third rank with populations from 15,000 down to 10,000 is made up of Swift Current, Portage la Prairie, Yorkton, North Battleford, Grande Prairie, and Flin Flon. Eleven of these cities, all of them being railroad sites, provide subregional service centers for settled agriculture areas. Flin Flon, the last mentioned, is a center of metal extraction in the Canadian Shield and is located on the boundary between Manitoba and Saskatchewan. There are about ten other small cities with populations ranging from 5,000 to 10,000 according to the census of 1966. In addition, there are about 75 towns with populations of 1,500 to 5,000 and several hundred small towns and villages.

The population of the Prairie Provinces has grown slowly since it reached the peak of rural settlement in 1931. Since that time, as we have noted previously, rural population has declined as farms were enlarged and mechanized. Not only were fewer people required on the land but, also, fewer people were required to provide services in small rural railway villages. Many of the villages declined while small hamlets often disappeared. This decline in the population of rural areas and small centers has been more than compensated by the rapid growth of the large cities. Fastest growing have been Edmonton and Calgary which have quadrupled their populations in the past twenty-five years. Winnipeg has grown by 70 per cent while Regina and Saskatoon have more than doubled. The rapid growth of the two Alberta cities must be credited largely to the effects of resource development, particularly petroleum and natural gas, while that of the other three must be interpreted more in the light of regional adjustment of central place functions. It is further evident that Winnipeg is rapidly losing the regional primacy which it had held throughout the period of early settlement. Lethbridge is representative of a group of medium-sized Prairie cities which after a rapid start grew slowly until the end of World War II, but have doubled their populations in the last twenty-five years. Red Deer, on the other hand, remained a small local center for several decades, but since the war it has grown more rapidly than any other Prairie city to provide service functions in an area almost equidistant from Calgary and Edmonton. Dauphin, Manitoba, originally a larger center than Red Deer, has grown much more slowly as befits a city with a rather restricted umland.

Maxwell's system of analysis of the functions of Canadian cities has already been mentioned in CHAPTER 3, and his regional diagram has been reproduced.* It is well to remember that such classifications are for the moment only, and that data from a different decade may place the various cities in quite different positions on such a diagram. The arbitrary inclusion of mining activity while excluding all other primary activities may be severely criticized. Forestry and fishing are important activities in some places and so is agricultural employment. Large excesses in any of these sectors would change the specialization index in just as significant a way as does the mining industry. The closing of coal mines in Lethbridge or the opening of an oil field near Red Deer leads to wide variations in the index of specialization. Indeed it varies so greatly from one census year to another that its geographical value may be questioned. On the other hand, the notion that some activities which are in excess of the minimum requirements provide the basic or propelling forces of the economy leads to an understanding of the function of a city within its umland or surrounding region.

The cities of the Prairies are, for the most part, relatively unspecialized. Most of them have three or more groups of activities comprising more than 10 per cent of the excess employment, while very few have as much as 30 per cent in any one

* J. W. Maxwell. "The Functional Structure of Canadian Cities: A Classification of Cities". *Geographical Bulletin*. Vol. 7, No. 2 (1965). 79-104.

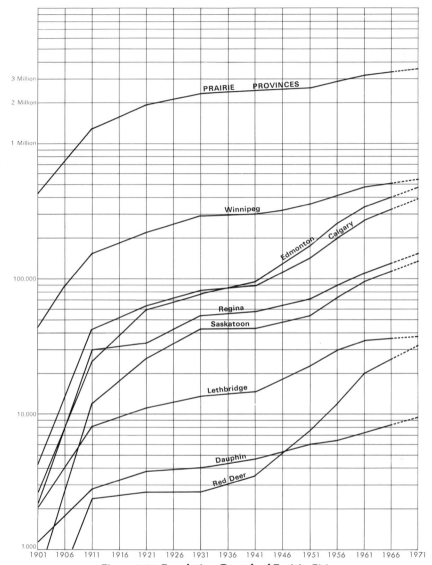

Figure 7.46 Population Growth of Prairie Cities

category. Using Maxwell's minimum requirement values derived from manipulation of 1951 census data and applying them to data for 1961, it becomes evident that the large- and medium-sized cities of the region are even less specialized toward manufacturing than they formerly were, while tending to be dominated by community services, government services, and wholesale trade. In the larger cities wholesale trade is almost twice as important as

retail trade in providing excess employment; on the other hand, retail trade is of slightly greater importance than wholesaling in medium-sized cities, while in small cities retailing is almost twice as important. In third rank cities (10,000-20,000) community services and retail trade usually are of most importance. Transportation and wholesale trade are also significant.

The urban pattern of the Prairie Provinces includes a number of small cities

(10,000 population), towns, villages, and unincorporated trade centers. In recent decades changing conditions have caused many of the smaller places to decline while some have disappeared completely. Nevertheless, some of them have grown into small regional centers. In the context of an interesting study of settlement in the Prairie Provinces, Lenz mapped the change in an area of 14,000 square miles near Hanna in Eastern Alberta.* In 1930 this area had fifteen small trade centers with 334 trade outlets. Eleven of these places had banking facilities. In 1962 the fifteen places were still in existence and had 355 places of business although seven of them had retained only five trade outlets or less, while the four largest now had 275 of the outlets, and were the only ones having banks. During the same three decades the general area had lost about 40 per cent of its total population. Hanna, the only town in the area, had 1,490 people in 1931 while in 1961 it held over 2,600. The average distance between bank centers is about 70 miles and the average population served appears to be about 3,000.

Hodge has given us a comprehensive analysis of trade center viability in Saskatchewan using data for the twenty-year period 1941-61.** In 1941 there were 906

* Karl Lenz. *Die Präirieprovinzen Kanadas*. Marburger Geographische Schriften, Heft 21 (1965). Marburg.
** Gerald Hodge. "The Prediction of Trade Center Viability on the Great Plains". *Regional Science Association Papers*. Vol. XV (1965). pp. 87-115.

trade centers while in 1961 the number was reduced to 779. Hodge found seven types of centers: Primary Wholesale-Retail, Secondary Wholesale-Retail, Complete Shopping Center, Partial Shopping Center, Full Convenience Center, Minimum Convenience Center, and Hamlet. It is perhaps worthwhile to list some of the characteristics of these categories (Table 7.5).

In twenty years the trade centers of the province declined by 14.0 per cent, from 906 in 1941 to 779 in 1961. The two largest cities of Saskatchewan are growing rapidly; no other city is likely to challenge them for some time to come. In twenty years their populations increased by 102 per cent. The secondary centers, however, are not far off the pace, increasing in number by 80 per cent and boasting an average population growth of 85 per cent. There is growth also in the next two ranks. Complete shopping centers have increased in numbers by only 12 per cent, but total population has increased by 84 per cent. Partial shopping centers have increased by 49 per cent. Convenience centers (both ranks) have decreased greatly. While a few have grown to give rise to new shopping centers, more have declined to join the ranks of the hamlets. Finally, although the latter have increased somewhat, almost half of the new hamlets and a similar number of old ones have failed to survive. More than one-third of the current hamlets are former convenience centers in decline.

Table 7.5   Types of Saskatchewan Trade Centers, 1961 *

	Number	Per Cent Change 1941-61	Miles Apart	Median Population	Av. No. of Establish-ments	Av. Sales $000
Primary Wholesale-Retail	2	0.0	144	104,000	1,414.0	120,000
Secondary Wholesale-Retail	9	80.0	68	10,000	232.0	20,000
Complete Shopping	29	11.6	40	1,800	58.5	4,000
Partial Shopping	85	49.2	23	610	26.1	1,400
Full Convenience	100	−41.5	20	360	16.5	520
Minimum Convenience	150	−47.8	14	210	9.9	280
Hamlet	404	12.8	10	50	3.3	80
All Trade Centres	779	−14.0	11	150	17.1	1,000

* From G. Hodge. *op. cit.*

Much of this imbalance seems due to spacing: the full convenience centers are nearly as far apart as the partial shopping centers, while the difference in distance between minimum and full convenience centers is small and becoming smaller. With the improvement of highways, convenience centers tend to lose their customers to the shopping centers; very small hamlets tend to disappear, leaving only one rank of service center at the base of the business pyramid. It is predicted that by 1981, Saskatchewan will be served by a remarkably uniform net of service centers, placed at an average distance of fifteen miles. There is little evidence of the development of Christaller's hexagonal pattern, however, since the original locations of all centers, large or small, was determined by the builders of railways, and not by the demands of those desiring services.* No similar studies have been done for small settlements in Manitoba and Alberta, but the same trend may be seen in some areas there also. In other areas the trend is obscured by the development of petroleum, natural gas, and other resources. It now is in order to look at the characteristics of the larger cities individually.

Calgary

Since World War II Calgary has been one of the most rapidly growing cities in Canada. Situated at the juncture of the Great Plains and the Foothills of the Rocky Mountains, 840 miles west of Winnipeg, 640 miles east of Vancouver, and 185 miles south of Edmonton, it is central to a complex region which includes the southern part of Alberta and a considerable area in the southeastern part of British Columbia as well. The original police post of 1875 was placed on a terrace at the junction of the Elbow and the Bow. Less than ten years later the Canadian Pacific Railway placed its station and other facilities on the alluvial plain of the Bow and the new town developed beside them.

Modern Calgary occupies 150 square miles including the valley floor and alluvial terraces and extends onto the uplands both north and south of the city center. The old city center containing such landmarks as the Palliser Hotel, the Hudson's Bay Company Store, and the Courthouse is now expanding westward with the erection of many tall office buildings. Much of the retail function of the city is now located in large shopping plazas in both the southern and northern areas. To the north also are the airport, the technological institute, and the university which is being planned to accommodate 18,000 students.

Calgary is reputed to be an excellent marketing center with the highest per capita personal disposable income of any city in the province, while standing second in value of retail sales per capita. It ranks with Edmonton as a wholesale center. It is an important cattle market, ranking third in Canada, behind Toronto and Winnipeg. It has good transportation facilities, abundant power and water, but ranks behind Edmonton as a manufacturing center both in terms of employment and in value added by the manufacturing processes. Calgary's most distinctive function, however, derives from the presence of more than 350 administrative offices and operational headquarters of the petroleum and natural gas industries.

Calgary well illustrates the difficulties of using city classification systems. In 1951, according to Maxwell, Calgary was a regional capital with relatively unimportant manufacturing industries, but important employment in extractive industries.* Using Maxwell's minimum requirement standards with 1961 data shows that extractive industries are still dominant and distinctive; government services, wholesale trade, and community services are also highly distinctive. In spite of nominal rates of increase, however, manufacturing no longer provides basic support for the economy of the city. If one adds together basic employment in both wholesale and retail trade,

* G. Hodge, *op. cit.*

* Maxwell, *op. cit.* Figure 5.

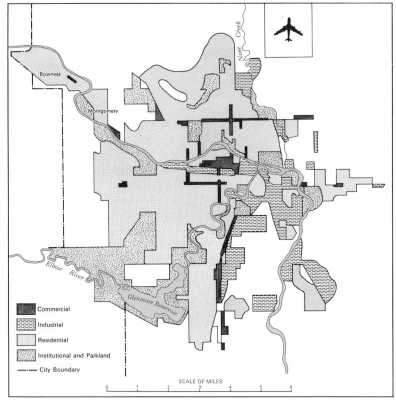

AFTER SMITH

Figure 7.47 Land Use of Calgary — 1961

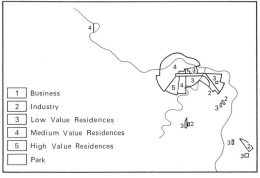

AFTER SMITH

Figure 7.48 Hoyt's Sector Theory Applied to Calgary's Land Use Pattern — 1914

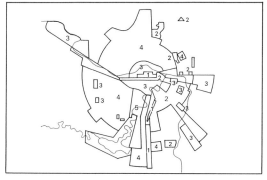

AFTER SMITH

Figure 7.49 Hoyt's Sector Theory Applied to Calgary's Land Use Pattern — 1961
In general terms, the sectors have expanded outwards following transportation routes, but since 1961 the new trends in land use location are weakening the sector pattern which has been so characteristic for Calgary.

then the trade function is dominant. A fairly high complement of government and community services helps to emphasize the central place function.

Calgary is the largest city in Southern Alberta but not the only one. There are three smaller cities: Red Deer to the north, Lethbridge to the south, and Medicine Hat to the southeast. Each of these provides a community service and retail center for a fairly well differentiated subregion. Lethbridge and Medicine Hat have a number of growing industries. Medicine Hat is also the most important greenhouse center of Western Canada.

Edmonton

The capital and largest city of Alberta, Edmonton is located about 185 miles north of Calgary. Fairly central to the whole province, it is the most northerly large city on the continent. It is situated on a fairly flat plain of Pleistocene deposits, deeply trenched by the valley of the North Saskatchewan River.

The fur-trader's post and the early pioneer settlement were on the north side of the river. The first railway, however, came from Calgary to the south, but did not bridge the river. A small independent settlement, later the city of Strathcona, developed at the railhead. Another transcontinental railway, now the Canadian National, gave mainline service to the northern city. In 1912 a high-level bridge was built to carry both rail and road traffic and the two cities were politically amalgamated. Near the bridge and just behind the site of the old fort rises the Alberta Legislative Building flanked by large government office structures. The central service and trading area is on the north bank and is flanked by the two railway stations. The main shopping street is Jasper Avenue, an east-west thoroughfare flanked by numerous high buildings. In the area to the south of the Canadian National Railway station, a rejuvenated city center is taking form. Keyed by the new city hall opened in 1954, it will eventually be a striking collection of hotels, offices, public buildings, and open spaces. While retailing remains solidly based in the central area, there are large up-to-date plazas such as Westmount and Capillano Mall with immense parking spaces in peripheral locations. The south bank of the river is dominated by the university with many large new faculty buildings. Approximately 13,000 students were enrolled in 1967. Edmonton has numerous high-rise apartment buildings but the residential function is mainly taken care of by more than 100 square miles of subdivisions which surround the central city both north and south of the Saskatchewan Valley.

In terms of function, Edmonton is dominated by government services, community services (education, health, and welfare), and trade. Through the city is funneled much of the development of the extractive industries of Central and Northern Alberta and the Northwest Territories even though many central functions remain based in Calgary. Edmonton has considerable manufacturing though not highly developed, especially in suburban areas. Among the important industries are slaughtering and meat packing, petroleum refining, chemicals, metal refining, and building materials.

Even though rivaled in some respects by Calgary, Edmonton is dominant in the central and northern parts of the province where there are hardly any cities of more than 10,000 people. Only Grande Prairie, isolated in the Peace River country, seems to be emerging as a regional center in the north. It is in competition not so much with Edmonton as with Dawson Creek in British Columbia.

Regina

Regina is the typical Prairie city; there are no nearby hills and ridges nor even a deeply dissected river valley to distract attention from the works of man. From any direction the buildings of the central part of the city dominate the horizon. Centrally located with respect to the populated portion of the Prairie Provinces, it lies about 360 miles west of Winnipeg and 460 miles east of Calgary.

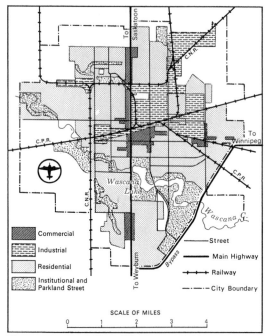

Figure 7.50 Land Use of Regina — 1961
The commercial and industrial zones of the city were once centered about the original railway junction. Recent developments to the south have caused new commercial facilities to develop along Albert Street towards the Bypass.

Wascana Creek which flows through the city was the ancient site of Indian hunting camps. A temporary fur-trading post was located in the vicinity. In 1882 it became the site of a new town on the Canadian Pacific railway. Christened Regina, it was named capital of the Northwest Territories and headquarters of the North West Mounted Police. A branch line was built to Saskatoon, and Regina became an important junction and distribution point. In 1905 with a population of 6,000 it became a city and the capital of the newly formed province of Saskatchewan. Wascana Creek has been dammed to create a picturesque lake flanked on the south by the provincial Legislative Building with its landscaped grounds and on the north by the new Wascana center containing the university, hospitals, the museum, and other public buildings.

The dominant functions of Regina are government services, community services,

and trade. As is the case with other large Prairie cities, despite the actual growth of manufacturing its share of the basic employment continues to decline in favor of the development of tertiary or service industries.

Saskatoon

Saskatoon, second city of Saskatchewan, is located astride the South Saskatchewan River at a point approximately 150 miles northwest of Regina. Founded as a ranching center in 1883, it was connected with Regina by a branch of the Canadian Pacific built in 1890. A few years later it was reached by the main line of the Grand Trunk (now Canadian National), and it began to grow rapidly.

Situated on both banks of the river it is linked together by numerous bridges. A large concrete dam across the river creates a lake several miles in length which adds greatly to the scenic and recreational resources of the city. Along it are located several tree-shaded parks. The business center of the city is located on the west side of the river while the eastern side is dominated by the University of Saskatchewan. The removal of the railway facilities to a new site on the western edge of the city has left space for a major redevelopment of the downtown area.

Saskatoon is not a political capital although it tends heavily to the provision of government services. The dominant function of the city, however, lies in community services, a larger portion of its work force being thus engaged than in any other large Prairie city. Trade is highly important, especially the wholesale sector. Wholesale trade provides Saskatoon with a greater percentage of its basic employment than it does in any of its sister cities, while in transportation and communications it ranks second only to Winnipeg. On the other hand, as with Calgary and Regina, despite impressive actual increases, its manufacturing function continues to fall below the theoretical minimum requirement for a city of its size. Saskatoon is then a primary service center, the importance of which is likely to increase with the development of the potash mining industry in Central Saskatchewan.

Winnipeg

Winnipeg, the oldest, largest, and most complex city of the Prairies, lies on the eastern margin of the region and has long been known as the "Gateway to the West". The junction of the Red and the Assiniboine Rivers early attracted the attention of the fur traders. The "Nor'westers" built Fort Gibraltar in 1806 and the Hudson's Bay Company built Fort Douglas nearby. After a bitter struggle the two companies were merged in 1821. A new and larger post, Fort Garry, was built in 1835. Effective settlement of the area, however, may be dated from 1811 when Lord Selkirk brought the first group of Scottish settlers to make their homes in the Red River Valley.

In 1870 Manitoba entered Confederation and Fort Garry, with its name changed to Winnipeg, became the capital. In 1873 with a population of less than 2,000 it became the first incorporated city on the Prairies. The building of the Canadian Pacific Railway in the early 1880s stimulated Winnipeg to active growth. It became the gateway to settlement not only in Manitoba but in the whole of the northwest. It was the distribution point for all settlers and their effects and for all goods needed during settlement. Shortly it also became the collecting point for agricultural products shipped to distant markets. Its population reached 40,000 by the turn of the century and nearly 150,000 by the beginning of World War I. During the same years a smaller city, St. Boniface, on the east bank of the river took shape as the center of French and Roman Catholic culture and as an industrial suburb of an embryonic metropolitan area.

Today, with more than half a million people metropolitan Winnipeg contains more than half of the population of the province of Manitoba. The central city of Winnipeg has slightly more than half of

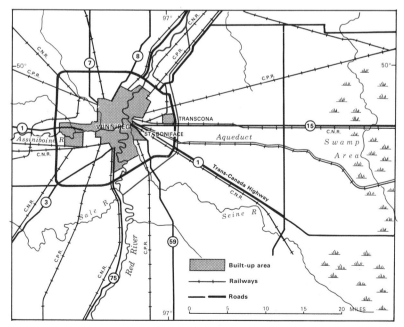

Figure 7.51 Situation of Winnipeg
Highways and railways radiate from Winnipeg. The new perimeter highway around the city has helped the traffic flow considerably.

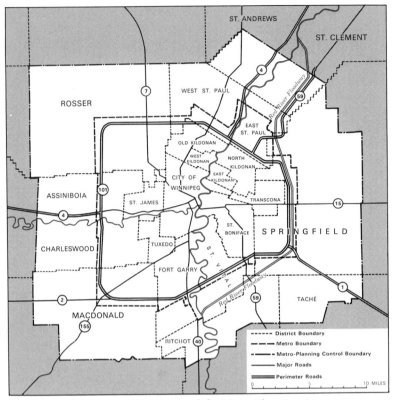

Figure 7.52 Winnipeg and the Metro Planning Area

the metropolitan population while the rest lives in fifteen surrounding municipalities, four of which, St. Boniface, St. James-Assiniboia, East Kildonan, and West Kildonan, are incorporated cities. Among the notable features of the city center are the bridges over the Red and Assiniboine Rivers, the new city hall, and civic center. The Manitoba Legislative building surmounted by the famous "Golden Boy" stands in a spacious park overlooking the Assiniboine River. Nearby are the Law Courts and the Civic Auditorium. St. John's Anglican Cathedral stands in the northern part of the city while across the Red River stands St. Boniface Roman Catholic Cathedral, the largest church building in Western Canada. Notable is the development of a ring-road or peripheral highway to encircle the built-up area of the city. The Winnipeg area is flat and much of it is susceptible to flooding from the converging rivers. As a

protection a capacious floodway has been built on the east side of the city at a cost of many millions of dollars.

The dominant and propelling function of Winnipeg is found in its manufacturing industries which employ more people and produce a greater volume of goods than those of the other four large cities of the Prairie Provinces taken together. Meat packing, clothing, transportation equipment, fabrication of metal products, and printing and publishing are among the largest industries. Winnipeg is the provincial capital with a large number of people employed in government services and educational and medical facilities. It is outstanding also for its activities in wholesale trade, transportation, and finance.

Winnipeg is so completely dominant that few other cities have been able to develop in Manitoba. Portage la Prairie is an important railway center 56 miles west of the metropolis; Brandon is a regional center in Southwestern Manitoba with a number of factories and a university. Northern Manitoba has the mining centers of Flin Flon and Thompson and the port of Churchill on Hudson Bay.

REGIONAL DEVELOPMENT

The Prairie Region is much larger than either Quebec or Ontario, both of which have already been described, but it is divided into three political units, roughly equal in area although differing considerably in natural resources. Differences in population and economic development have already become apparent and are likely to become more rather than less pronounced as time goes on.

By reason of its greater potential for agriculture, Saskatchewan had, by 1911, become the most populous of the three provinces, keeping the lead until surpassed by Alberta in the 1950s and by Manitoba in the 1960s, because of the greater growth of cities in those provinces. Because of its greater development of agriculture Saskatchewan is likely to remain more agrarian in character than either of its near neighbors even though its larger cities may grow to respectable size and eventually come to contain the dominant elements of its population.

One of the more fundamental features of regional development is the migration of population from the rural to the urban environment. Cities grow by means of natural increase, to be sure; but city growth on the Prairies has been much influenced by human migration. As Prairie farms have increased in size and made use of mechanical energy, many displaced farm operators and farm helpers have had to seek a new way of living in the city. And in certain situations people who remain farmers decide to move to the city and to continue to operate their farms from a distance. Reduction of the farm population inevitably leads to the reduction of the rural non-farm population as well. Many of the inhabitants of the small hamlets and convenience centers that used to provide goods and services to the countryside find their incomes so much reduced that they are forced also to join the migration to the cities. For decades there has been a normal migration of excess young adults from the Prairie farms, but more recently the movement has contained large numbers of whole families as well. To a greater degree than ever before the populations of the large Prairie cities are home-grown even though they still contain many people who were born in other parts of Canada or in foreign countries. The out-migration of rural people is by no means all directed toward the nearby cities for substantial numbers of Prairie folk are found in other Canadian provinces while many have gone to the United States.

Subregional differentiation is incomplete in the Prairie Provinces, but this is just another way of stating that development is still going on. It is true that the process of agricultural settlement has all but ceased. Only in local peripheral areas, particularly in the Peace River country, is active land clearing in progress, mainly on farms which already have been occupied for some years. But everywhere agricultural methods are being adopted which are more in harmony with the environment; and in this way the Manitoba Lowland, the Saskatchewan Plains, Central Alberta, and the Dry Belt are becoming more fully differentiated. The growth of cities too reflects regional influences and the development of regional resources. The five major cities themselves are rapidly becoming the dominant nodal centers of their respective subregions and, to a degree, a system of city-centered regions is being developed. Industrial growth is still lagging; only in Winnipeg and Edmonton does the location quotient of industrial employment approach 0.80 on a national scale, whereas in Ontario and Quebec there are a number of cities where it is more than 2.00.

There are, however, chances for industrial development that should be carefully fostered. Chemical industries, clay products, and cement manufacturing are important lines which are being encouraged. Food product industries have long been the outstanding category of manufacturing on the Prairies, and opportunities for expansion exist. This is particularly true of meat products because of the growth of the livestock industry on Prairie farms and the increased market potential of the expanding cities. Opportunities for the production of industrial and mining equipment also exist, and expansion in the production of agricultural machinery and equipment is possible.

Behind all industrial development and all other types of community development as well lies the question of the provision of adequate power supplies, and it is in this direction that the Prairie Region is taking impressive steps. The response to the demand, however, is being met in varying ways. In Alberta it has been largely met through the use of natural gas, but there are also large coal-burning thermal plants. In Saskatchewan the largest generators are powered by burning lignite coal. In both Alberta and Saskatchewan, however, an important although minor part of the requirement is met by hydro-electric developments. On the other hand, the major power supplies of Manitoba are provided by hydro-electric developments. This type of power will be greatly increased in the future when the potentialities of the Nelson River System, perhaps to be augmented by those of the Churchill River as well, are fully harnessed. Much of this power will be devoted to resource development in the north, but there will also be an important contribution to industrial expansion in the south.

BIBLIOGRAPHY

Bentley, C. F. "Soil Management and Fertility — Western Canada". *Resources for Tomorrow Conference. Background Papers.* Vol. 1. Ottawa. 1961. pp. 67-73.

Bowman, Isaiah. *The Pioneer Fringe.* American Geographical Society. Special Publication No. 13. New York. 1931.

Chapman, L. J. and Brown, D. M. *The Climates of Canada for Agriculture.* Canada Land Inventory No. 3. Ottawa. 1966.

Edmunds, F. H. "Recession of the Wisconsin Glacier from Central Saskatchewan". *Saskatchewan Geological Survey Report.* No. 67 (1962).

Hodge, Gerald. "The Prediction of Trade Center Viability on the Great Plains". *Regional Science Association Papers.* Vol. XV (1965). pp. 87-115.

Lenz, Karl. *Die Prärieprovinzen Kanadas.* Marburger Geographische Schriften, Heft 21 (1965). Marburg.

Mackintosh, W. A. *Prairie Provinces: The Geographic Setting.* The Macmillan Company of Canada Limited. Toronto. 1934.

Maxwell, J. W. "The Functional Structure of Canadian Cities: A Classification of Cities". *Geographical Bulletin.* Vol. 7, No. 2 (1965). pp. 79-104.

Putnam, D. F. "Pedogeography of Canada". *Geographical Bulletin.* No. 1 (1951). pp. 57-85.

Sanderson, Marie. "The Climates of Canada According to the New Thornthwaite Classification". *Scientific Agriculture.* Vol. 28 (1948). pp. 501-517.

Smith, P. J. "Calgary — A Study in Urban Patterns". *Economic Geography.* Vol. 38 (1962). pp. 315-329.

Stockwell, G. H. (Editor). *Geology and Economic Minerals of Canada.* Department of Mines and Technical Surveys. Ottawa. 1957.

Szabo, Michael L. "Depopulation of Farms in Relation to the Economic Conditions of Agriculture on the Canadian Prairies". *Geographical Bulletin.* Vol. 8, No. 3-4 (1965). pp. 187-202.

Vanderhill, Burke G. "The Decline of Land Settlement in Manitoba and Saskatchewan". *Economic Geography.* Vol. 38 (1962). pp. 270-277.

Warkentin, John. "Manitoba Settlement Patterns". *Transactions, Historical and Scientific Society of Manitoba.* Series III, No. 16 (1961). pp. 62-77.

———. *The Western Interior of Canada.* The Carleton Library. No. 15. McClelland and Stewart Limited. Toronto. 1964.

Williams, M. Y. "The Physiography of the Southern Plains of Canada". *Transactions, Royal Society of Canada.* 3rd Series. Vol. 23, Section 4 (1929). pp. 61-79.

British Columbia

8 British Columbia is one of the truly unique geographic regions in Canada. Effectively isolated by distance and topography from the remainder of the country it has developed a geographic personality which reflects the enormous variations occurring in the resource base. Currently, (it is the fastest-growing province in Canada, yet more than 75 per cent of the people reside in an area within 90 miles of Vancouver,) an intensively occupied space that is less than 0.5 per cent of the total area of the province. (Over 90 per cent of the region is too high, too steep, or too rocky for farming or close settlement,) and consequently actual size is an economic disadvantage for it increases the costs of administration and has made land communications both difficult and expensive. As somewhat of a compensation, (over 50 per cent of the total area is capable of sustaining commercial forests, and forestry is the leading primary industry in the region.) However, (neither size nor relief deter the mining industry for the geological structure is both varied and complex, and great varieties of minerals are found.)

(A major asset) to the economy of the region (is the Pacific Ocean.) The main body of water and the (innumerable bays and inlets) of the fiord coastline (have abundant marine life, and fishing has become an important industry.) In addition, Western Canada has gained direct access to Asiatic and European markets through the port of Vancouver, and thus foreign trade contributes substantially to the wealth of the region.

With reference to the developed resource base, one can compare British Columbia with the Atlantic Region. Both rely on fishing, forestry, and mining, with agriculture and manufacturing relegated to less important roles. Moreover, both regions are isolated from Central Canada and have developed geographic personalities which are distinctly different. Yet, despite the similarities, the regions strongly differ in economic health.

British Columbia has developed geographic character through the diverse physical and economic environments which are found within its borders. (The varied topography strongly influences the climate.) (The Rocky Mountains block the entry of Polar Continental air from the Prairies, while the Coastal Range creates a very moist windward slope to the Pacific Ocean.) Thus the interior of the region is especially arid. (Rough mountainous terrain and a highly variable climate have combined to greatly influence the location and nature of agriculture and other primary industries and the distribution of population. In essence, topographic relief is the basis of regional character in British Columbia.)

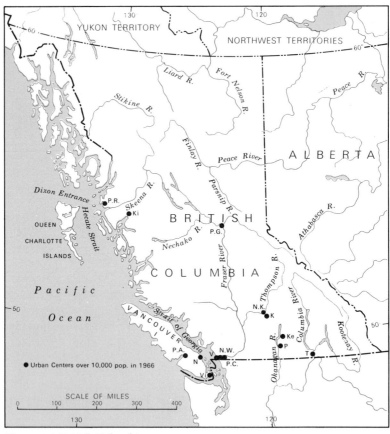

Figure 8.1 British Columbia

K	Kamloops		P.A.	Port Alberni
Ke	Kelowna		P.C.	Port Coquitlam
Ki	Kitimat		P.G.	Prince George
N	Nanaimo		P.R.	Prince Rupert
N.K.	North Kamloops		T	Trail
N.W.	New Westminster		V	Vancouver
P	Penticton		Vi	Victoria

PHYSICAL RESOURCE BASE
Landforms

British Columbia includes two major physiographic divisions of North America: the Cordillera and the Great Plains. The latter occupies less than 10 per cent of the region and is confined to the northeastern corner. The Cordilleran division is broadly divisible into three main systems; the Coast Mountain system on the west, the Interior Uplands, and the Rocky Mountain system on the east. All three trend northwest from the American boundary, but they differ geologically as well as topographically.

The *Western Mountains* are dominated by the Coast Mountains, a high, massive, and rugged wall of granite. Rising abruptly from the Fraser Valley to an elevation of 9,000 feet, the Coast Mountains reach 10,000 feet at latitude 52° then diminish to about 4,000 feet at the Skeena Saddle. Their width likewise varies, from 125 miles in the south to only 40 miles in the north. Although from the air the Coast Mountains appear as a markedly dissected plateau, the numerous icefields and peaks such as Mt. Waddington (13,260 feet) provide much variety. The major rivers, for example, the Fraser and Skeena, flow transversely to the structural trend and provide important corridors for land communication. Numerous fiord valleys occur along the western side of the Coast Mountains, furnishing both well-protected harbor sites and breathtaking scenery of sea and mountains.

West of the Coast Mountains there is the Coastal Trench, and beyond that, the Insular Mountains. The Coastal Trench is a broad rift valley which is part of a complex rift system extending from the Gulf of California to Alaska. Included within the Coastal Trench are the most intensively utilized areas in British Columbia, the Lower Fraser Valley and the eastern lowlands of Vancouver Island. In the Lower Fraser Valley three levels occur: the recent delta below 50 feet, the older delta at 200

feet, and the upper limit at 1,000 feet. The Insular Mountains are a partially submerged range which forms a coastal archipelago. They present a steep face to the Pacific Ocean while on the east numerous fiords are found. Relief is most rugged on Vancouver Island where, in the east-central portion, peaks exceed 7,000 feet, while to the north the Queen Charlotte Islands are lower.

The *Interior Uplands* are, for the most part, underlain by volcanic rocks, with some outcroppings of sedimentaries and metamorphics. Topography is diversified. To the south there is the well-dissected Fraser Plateau, where river valleys are entrenched as much as 4,000 feet below the plateau level of 6,000 feet. While Miocene lavas are responsible for most of the areas of slight relief, glaciation has strongly in-

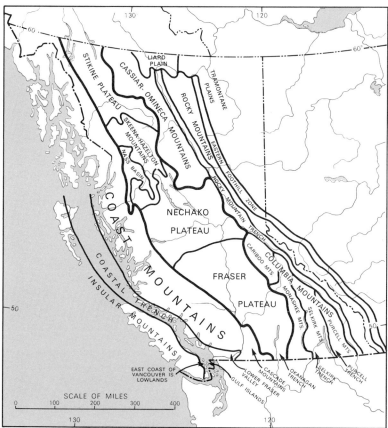

Figure 8.2 Physiographic Regions of British Columbia

fluenced the Fraser Plateau. Till deposits, terraces, morianic hills, and ice-dammed lakes all bear witness to the effects of Pleistocene glaciation. In addition, there is the Okanagan Trench, an area where commercial agriculture is of note.

North of latitude 53°, the relief of the Interior Uplands becomes more subdued, for the major part of the area is a rolling upland at 2,500 feet. This portion is called the Nechako Plateau. Here a thick veneer of fine lacustrine materials was deposited by glacial lakes. The Nechako has, in part, become important as a ranching district in British Columbia. Separated from the Nechako by the Skeena-Hazelton Mountains and the Nass Basin the Stikine Plateau has an average elevation of 4,500 feet. It is composed primarily of lava which has been broken into tablelands by the major streams. Additional relief is afforded by the old volcanic peaks which reach 8,000 feet.

The *Eastern Mountain System* consists of three major mountain groups which trend northwesterly from the 49th parallel. In southeastern British Columbia there is the Columbia Mountain group. As shown by Figure 8.2, the Columbia Mountain group is composed of three main mountain ranges which are separated by trenches and combine to form one mountain mass in the north. Influenced strongly by glaciation the Columbia Mountains are very rugged, and deep U-shaped valleys, cirques, and moraines abound. While the average elevation is 7,000 feet, several peaks exceed 10,000 feet in the Selkirk and Cariboo ranges.

The second mountain group is a complex mass of mountains known as Cassiar-Omineca. Found to the north of the Columbia Mountain group it includes several small ranges: the Finlay, Swannell, and Stikine. While the eastern portions bordering the Rocky Mountain Trench are least rugged, the granite peaks of the Swannell and Stikine ranges surpass 8,000 feet.

The Rocky Mountain Trench and Liard Plain separate the Rocky Mountains from the other two mountain groups. Unusually

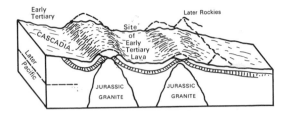

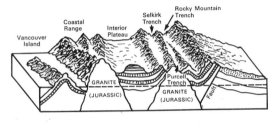

AFTER TAYLOR

Figure 8.3 Evolution of the Mountain Systems in British Columbia

strong compressive forces originating to the west of the Rocky Mountain Trench created a series of thrust faults which forced Precambrian and Palaeozoic materials to override the soft Cretaceous shales of the Great Plains. Subsequent erosion has created in most places a bold east-facing escarpment. The compressive forces also produced a series of folds which gave the Rocky Mountains their characteristic parallel ranges. As the Rocky Mountains form a continuous range with elevations exceeding 10,000 feet in the south and 5,000 feet in the north, the few passes which traverse the range are very important. Crowsnest (4,459 feet), Kicking Horse (5,388 feet), and Yellowhead (3,700 feet) are most significant for land transport in the south, while Pine Pass (3,000 feet) is important in the central portion.

Mt. Robson (12,972 feet) is the highest peak in the Canadian Rockies, and there are many other notable ones. The high ranges of the Rockies have many areas of permanent snow and ice. The most extensive is the Columbia Icefield which lies on the boundary of British Columbia and Alberta. Others are the Reef Icefield, Illecillewaet, Albert, and Revelstoke. The Rocky Mountains form a great tourist

Figure 8.4 The Coast Range
This part of the Coast range is to be found between Prince Rupert and Kitimat.

attractions which brings many people to the area. In addition, mineral deposits are exposed along the mountain flanks giving rise to centers such as Kimberly and other smaller settlements.

Climate

British Columbia has a most diversified climate. The Pacific Coast is the most humid area in Canada; the interior of the province is one of the driest. Subarctic conditions prevail in the north while the southern part of the Okanagan Valley is warm enough to promote the growth of peaches, apricots, and grapes. Mountain slopes and valleys with differences in elevation, exposure to the sun, and prevailing winds give rise to numerous micro-climates within short distances.

The paramount influence upon the climate of British Columbia is its close proximity to the Pacific Ocean. In the winter, mild, moist air is brought onshore by the prevailing westerly winds causing copious orographic precipitation on the windward slopes of the Insular and Coast Mountains. During the summer months the prevailing westerlies are usually interrupted by expansion northwards of the Pacific subtropical high pressure cell. Summer precipitation is thus less frequent and less intense and, in some years, severe drought may occur. Although not severe enough in itself to damage forest growth,

Figure 8.5 The Okanagan Valley
Only where irrigation water is available can the naturally arid Okanagan Valley be transformed into valuable agricultural land.

it frequently creates ideal conditions for forest fires. Fortunately, the rest of the year is wet; there is little danger of forest fire and growth conditions are good.

A complex relationship exists between topographic relief and precipitation. In Figure 8.6, it is seen that each mountain range has a wet western slope and a drier one on the east. Moreover, the wet air mass drops most of its moisture when it encounters the most westerly of the parallel mountain belts and less and less precipitation is received by the mountains of the interior. It is important to note also that adiabatic heating of the descending air masses greatly reduces the precipitation received by such interior valleys as the Okanagan.

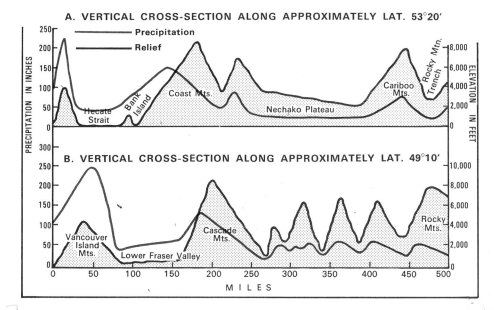

Figure 8.6 **Relationship of Topography to Precipitation in Southern British Columbia**
While each mountain range extracts moisture from the Pacific air masses as they progress
inland, the amount of moisture obtained decreases.

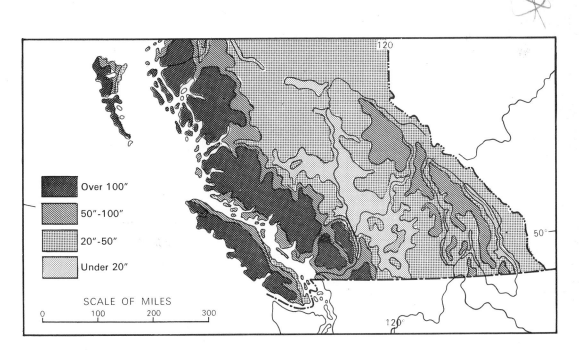

Figure 8.7 **Average Annual Precipitation in Southern British Columbia**

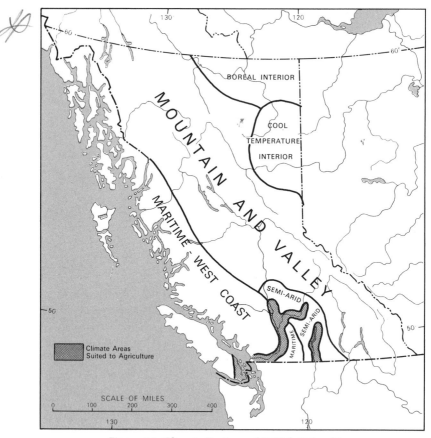

Figure 8.8 Climate Regions of British Columbia

Regional Climates. The climates of Southern British Columbia may be divided into four general regions as summarized in Table 8.1. Their areal distribution is shown in Figure 8.8 which also delimits the areas best suited to agriculture. It is apparent that the area having a true maritime climate is quite limited. On the other hand, there is an extensive area in which extremely continental climates occur. However, a large part of this area has such varied topographical conditions that it can best be labelled "mountain and valley".

The Maritime or *Marine West Coast* type of climate prevails over most of the Pacific coastal region. It is characterized by mild and exceedingly wet winters, cool, moderately wet and foggy summers, relatively high humidities throughout the year, and a relatively narrow annual range of temperature. Except for some snow on high mountain slopes, precipitation is in the form of rain or drizzle, averaging more than 100 inches per annum. One station, Henderson Lake, has an average record of 269 inches over a five-year period. While the frost-free period is extremely long, midsummer temperatures average less than 60°F except in the protected areas of the Fraser Valley where temperatures reach levels more favorable for commercial agriculture. However, the long period in which plant growth is possible and the abundant supply of moisture constitutes conditions ideal for a luxuriant growth of forest vegetation. The higher parts of the Insular, Coast, and Cascade Mountains receive enormous amounts of snow, depths of more than 30 feet hav-

Table 8.1 Characteristics of Climatic Regions *

Region	Jan. Mean Temp.	Jul. Mean Temp.	Frost-free Period (days)	Degree-days above 42°F	PE	Total Ppt.	Percentage Ppt. during Growing Season
Pacific Coast	34°F	61°F	205	2,800	24"	175"	25
Lower Fraser Valley	35°F	64°F	200	3,600	25.5"	60"	25
Interior—South	25°F	70°F	160	3,800	26"	11"	25
Interior—Central	15°F	60°F	70	2,000	19"	25"	50

* After Chapman and Brown.

ing been reported at some stations in the Coast Mountains.

A *Dry Summer Maritime* type of climate is found in the southeastern part of Vancouver Island. Sheltered by the Olympic and the Vancouver Island mountain ranges, this area is cool and dry in summer, and mild and humid in winter. The annual rainfall is less than 40 inches, most of which falls in winter. On the other hand, summer is relatively warm (July mean, 63°F) and dry, with a water deficiency of five to ten inches. Bright sunshine records for Victoria (2,200 hours) are surpassed in Canada only in Southern Alberta and Saskatchewan.

The *Semi-arid* or *Dry Continental* type of climate is found in the rainshadow of the Coast-Cascade Mountains. It occupies most of the Fraser Plateau, all of which has less than 20 inches of precipitation annually. The driest parts are in the southern Okanagan and the middle Thompson Valleys which average less than ten inches. Summers are very warm and sunny with July temperatures averaging 74°F at Oliver in the south, and 63°F at Quesnel in Central British Columbia. Moisture deficiencies in excess of 13 inches are commonly reported. Forest cover is limited and much of the area is a natural grassland. Winters are cold; January temperatures average 26°F at Oliver and 13°F at Quesnel. Sub-zero temperatures are recorded every winter in the northern part of the area. The climate permits grazing throughout the region, dry farming in some areas

which have sufficient rainfall, and irrigated farming in areas with adequate supplementary water supplies.

A *Humid Continental* type of climate occupies large areas in Central and even in Southern British Columbia where the annual precipitation is more than 20 inches per annum. Over much of this area there are great contrasts in elevation above sea level accompanied, of course, by climatic variations, particularly of temperature. These continental climates can perhaps best be grouped as *Mountain and Valley* climates. Summers are relatively warm (July mean, 66°F) in the Kootenay valleys of Southeastern British Columbia, and relatively cool (July mean below 60°F) in the Nechako district. Winters are cold; January in the Kootenay valleys averages about 23°F, while in the Nechako the mean is about 12°F. The Nechako receives more moisture than other parts of the region because the coastal mountains are at their lowest elevation in the Skeena Saddle, permitting greater penetration of damp Pacific air than in regions farther south.

East of the Rocky Mountains, in Northeastern British Columbia, the climate may be considered as an extension of *Cool Temperate Interior* climate of the Prairie Region. Summers are slightly cooler but permit a commercial agriculture based on hardy varieties of cereal crops.

Most of Northern British Columbia has a *Boreal* or *Subarctic* type of climate with short cool summers and long, very cold winters. Precipitation is low (less than 16 inches per annum) and mean annual temperature is just below 32°F; thus, there is little possibility of commercial agriculture in this region.

Natural Vegetation

The natural vegetation of British Columbia is extremely varied and includes a very large number of species and contrasting associations. Trees, principally conifers, predominate and 53 per cent of British Columbia is covered by productive forests. The lofty evergreens of the coast make the resource even more important, and it is currently estimated that British Columbia contains 51 per cent of the volume of standing timber in Canada. However, the resource is not uniform, and in the northeastern interior stunted pines and firs are found. Bunch grasses and drought-resistant bushes have significant distributions in the southern interior valleys and reflect the dryness of those districts. Moreover, approximately one-third of the province is alpine, consisting of bare rock, permanent ice, and patches of meadow scrub.

Five distinctive vegetation regions are usually recognized in British Columbia: the Coast Forest, the Fraser Plateau Forest and Grassland, the Nechako Forest, the Columbia Forest, and the Northern Forest. Within each of these broad regions, however, there is great variation in vegetation in response to the great number of site types. Each site type, of course, is the result of a different combination of factors such as soil material, elevation, slope, exposure, and moisture supply.

The *Coast Forest* is the densest and most luxuriant in Canada. Part of the great

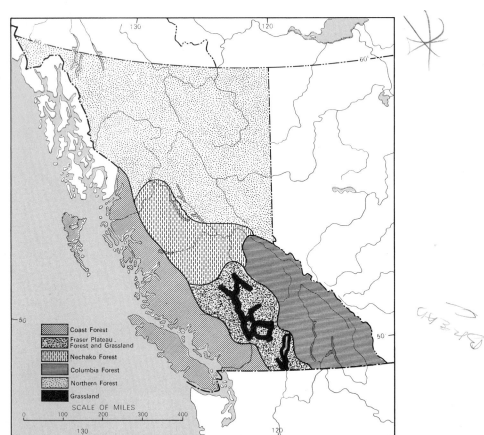

Figure 8.9 Vegetation Regions of British Columbia

coniferous forest belt of the North Pacific slope, it contains few deciduous species except as second growth in logged or burned areas. Western red cedar and western red hemlock are important species, and under ideal conditions attain a height of 150 feet and a diameter of two to five feet. Douglas fir is an even larger tree, and when mature averages 200 feet in height and five feet in diameter. It is intolerant of shade and grows best in southern Vancouver Island and the southern mainland coast where summer drought limits the full development of the cedar-hemlock canopy. Logs derived from mature stands of these species are of great value for lumber and plywood, while much of the young growth timber is used for pulp and paper. The resource is limited for the treeline occurs at an elevation of about 5,000 feet in the south and 4,000 feet in the north.

The *Fraser Plateau Forest and Grassland* region coincides with the zone of semi-arid climate. This forest, often known as the *Montane Forest*, is open and parklike, Ponderosa pine often being the dominant tree. Most drought resistant of the evergreens, this species is often able to invade the grassland where precipitation ranges between 12 and 15 inches per annum. Its greatest distribution is south of latitude 51°, on the south-facing slopes between 1,500 feet and 3,000 feet in elevation. Normally it attains a height of 80 feet and a diameter of 30 inches. Lodgepole pine is also important, particularly as a regrowth species after a forest fire, while Englemann spruce and alpine fir dominate the forest cover between 4,000 feet and the treeline. In the south where precipitation is less than 12 inches annually, the forest is replaced by a natural grassland, and in extremely dry situations xerophytes such as sagebrush, cactus, and antelope bush are common.

The *Nechako Forest* region coincides approximately with the area of the Nechako plateau. Compared to the Fraser plateau, this area receives greater annual precipitation and experiences lower summer temperatures. As a result, the forest

BRITISH COLUMBIA FOREST SERVICE PHOTOGRAPH

Figure 8.10 The Coastal Forest

Figure 8.11 The Montane Forest
In the interior, on the plateau, the Douglas fir forest of the coast gives way to white spruce and alpine fir.

BRITISH COLUMBIA FOREST SERVICE PHOTOGRAPH

cover is more dense and the previously mentioned species grow to a greater height and diameter. Englemann spruce frequently exceed 125 feet in height and two feet in diameter, and recently this forest region has begun to be utilized by the new pulp and paper mills at Prince George.

The *Columbia Forest* is located south of latitude 54° in the eastern Cordillera. It is a heterogeneous association of western red cedar, western hemlock, Ponderosa pine, Douglas fir, grand fir, and western white pine. To the north this association is replaced by Englemann spruce and alpine fir. In general, the forest is less luxuriant than the coastal forest but does possess a dense undergrowth and has potential for the forest industries.

The *Northern Forest* is of limited value to the region. White spruce, Englemann spruce, balsam fir, jack pine, and white birch are all encountered, but more than 50 per cent of the forest consists of scrub trees, and significant portions of the area contain muskeg swamps.

The Peace River country contains an extension of the central Boreal forest where aspen, white birch, white spruce, balsam fir, and jack pine may be found. The Peace River country also has small areas of natural grassland which may be regarded as outliers of the Prairie Grassland formation.

Soils

The soils of British Columbia form a limited resource base because of slope, relief, geological complexity of the parent materials, and the extremes of the climatic influences under which they have been developed. The wet coastal region has Podzolic soils, the dry valleys of the interior have Brown, Dark Brown, and Black soils, while the forested northern areas have Gray Wooded soils like those of Alberta. Above the timberline Alpine Meadow and Tundra soils are found throughout British Columbia.

Brown, Dark Brown, and Black soils are found in the Okanagan Valley and other parts of the southern interior where precipitation is less than 15 inches per annum. Where irrigation water is available as in the Okanagan, these soils are excellent for fruit and vegetable growing. Black and degraded black soils are found in the Peace River region where they are used for cereals and mixed farming.

Brown Podzolic soils are formed under the conditions of heavy rainfall and dense forest cover, which exist along the Pacific Coast. Although quite acid and lacking in basic fertility elements, they are used for agriculture where surface relief permits. Extensive alluvial deposits occur along the major valleys, such as the Lower Fraser, and while drainage is often a problem, the flat surface and natural fertility make the alluvial soils an important part of the resource base of British Columbia.

In effect, however, the soil resource base is very limited, and no additional potentially arable land exists along the Pacific Coast. Inland, there is an extensive acreage of arable land available in the Cordillera (Table 2.3), but much of this is too remote and too far north to be of much value.

CULTURAL RESOURCES

Settlement was only partially sedentary before the coming of the fur traders such as Alexander McKenzie and Simon Fraser. Fairly permanent Indian villages had been established along the coast but not in the interior where a nomadic type of life prevailed. Along the coast, salmon was the basic food, supplemented by berries and starchy roots such as camas, while inland a similar diet prevailed except that game animals became the mainstay. Prior to the coming of the Europeans there was no agriculture in this part of North America. The Indians maintained themselves by a hunting and fishing culture which caused little modification of the natural environment.

The region was one of the last in the world to be charted accurately by European explorers. Vague impressions had been recorded by the Spanish during the 16th and 17th centuries, but it was not until the 18th century that an accurate survey was achieved. Driven by imperialistic glory, Russia, Great Britain, Spain, and the United States became rivals for control of British Columbia. In 1793 Captain George Vancouver completed a survey for Great Britain but little action was taken toward colonization until the fur traders, arriving via overland routes from the east, had established their trading posts.

The discovery of gold in 1858 changed the apparent resource base, and fur-trading posts were replaced by active settlement. British Columbia began to develop roads and trails to the interior, and agricultural settlements had their tenuous beginnings in the Lower Fraser Valley. Shortly afterward the newly arrived miners needed food, and the east coast lowland of Vancouver Island and northern Okanagan Valley became mixed farming regions. Cattle ranching likewise began on the grasslands of the interior valleys.

Although dominant for the first few years, placer mining declined after 1863 as the readily accessible gravel deposits were worked out. The number of miners decreased as new mines developed further north in Alaska and the Yukon. However, other resource industries began to develop, and by 1863 lumber had become a commodity of the export trade from the coast. In addition the salmon fishery commenced to grow although during this period it served mainly local markets.

The two colonies, Vancouver Island and the Mainland, were united in 1866 and joined Canada in 1871. Their joining Confederation was dependent upon the building of a transcontinental railroad within ten years. Various political and financial difficulties plagued this project, and it was not until 1886 that British Columbia was finally connected with Eastern Canada by a "ribbon of steel". Completion of this transportation facility accelerated the growth of the province, but it continued to focus population expansion on the limited area of lowland in the Lower Fraser Valley. However, mining, lumbering, and fishing increased greatly in output and value as

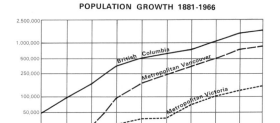

POPULATION GROWTH 1881-1966

Figure 8.12 Population Growth in British Columbia

improved transportation and new techniques engendered continual development.

As shown in Figure 8.12, British Columbia increased rapidly in population until 1911 as the various primary industries began active development. Mining became important in the Kootenay district, and lumbering achieved significance on Vancouver Island. Between 1911 and 1941 population growth continued as the transportation function focused development on Vancouver. Since 1941 growth has been steady, and recently British Columbia has had a very rapid increase in population.

However, population growth has been concentrated in the Victoria and Greater Vancouver areas. Elsewhere, people are distributed along the major valleys such as the Fraser and Okanagan. With the exception of specific settlements such as Kitimat and Prince Rupert, very few people reside along the coast. This pattern was established before 1900 and has continued almost unchanged.

The population distribution pattern of the Pacific Region of Canada contrasts greatly with that of the Atlantic Region where a fairly uniform settlement of the coastal periphery took place. From the early days the Vancouver area developed an overwhelming primacy in trade, industry, and population. This must undoubtedly be credited to the natural advantages of the harbor, the flat alluvial lands of the Lower Fraser, and the corridor to the interior provided by the river.

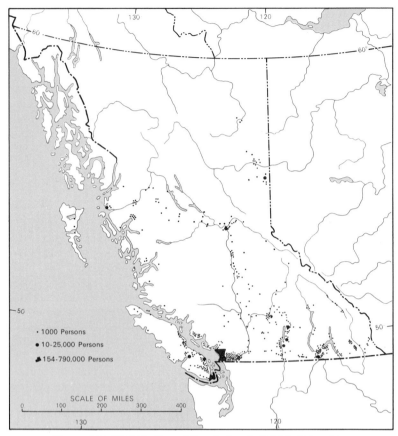

Figure 8.13 Distribution of Population in British Columbia

ECONOMIC ACTIVITIES

Forestry

Forestry is the most important primary industry in British Columbia. The yearly cut averages one and one-half million cubic feet, and the total value produced by the forest industries now reaches one billion dollars in any one year. Over 32,000 people are employed in wood processing alone, and it is estimated that approximately 50 per cent of the population depends directly or indirectly on the forest resources. British Columbia is the third-ranking pulp and paper producing province in Canada and accounts for 20 per cent of the Canadian output. Virtually all of the shingles, veneer, and plywood and nearly 70 per cent of the sawn lumber produced in Canada come from British Columbia.

Since 78 per cent of the output value of British Columbia mills is exported, it is apparent that forestry is the main propelling industry for the regional economy. One measure of its effect is the fact that forest-product industries use 25 per cent of the hydro-electric output.

While the coastal area provides over 55 per cent of the annual cut, sustained yield techniques and government influence have encouraged a dispersion of the industry inland. New pulp and paper mills are being developed in the Prince George area, and forests in the Rocky Mountain area are being allocated to interested companies. However, the threat of overexpansion is likely to restrict further developments in the interior for some time to come.

The extensive softwood forests of the coastal region have long been exploited.

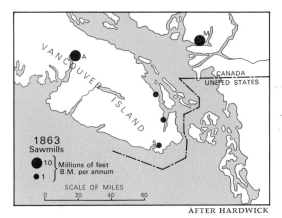

Figure 8.14 Coastal Sawmills in 1863
A Alberni   M Moodyville   S Sooke

Aided by a great coastal waterway, the forest industry tended to concentrate log conversion plants in locations where market accessibility and port facilities coincided. Today, a complex series of linkages exist between the log conversion plants and their sources of raw materials.

Exploitation of the forest resource began during the colonial period of the 1860s when a small commercial mill was erected at Sooke on the southern end of Vancouver Island. The expected market in California failed to materialize; for as the gold rush waned, American concerns in the Puget Sound were better able to compete. Despite this setback other mills were constructed along the southeastern side of the island,

and one on the mainland, at Moodyville on Burrard Inlet. These mills all relied on locally available raw materials.

Completion of the Canadian Pacific railroad provided access to a larger market area and guaranteed permanency to the industry. Mainland mill sites which were adjacent to resources of Douglas fir and to deep water ports grew and prospered, particularly in the Burrard Inlet and New Westminster areas. By 1880 Victoria and Nanaimo were the two major mill locations on Vancouver Island. This pattern continued until the turn of the century, and

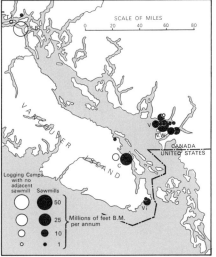

Figure 8.16 Sawmills and Logging Camps in 1900
C   Chemainus   T.I.   Thurlow Island
N.W.   New Westminster   V   Vancouver
R.B.   Rock Bay   Vi   Victoria

the Vancouver area persisted as the dominant processing center. However, as timber resources near the Vancouver mills became depleted, large logging camps more distant from the processing centers became common.

Companies then began to concentrate on sources of supply, and speculators were quick to lease timber rights from the Crown. Many of the investors were Americans who had been successful in the Pacific Coast forests of Washington and Oregon. They brought with them the capital, managerial skills, and American

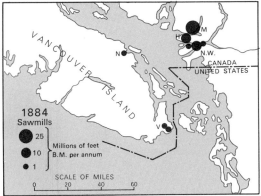

Figure 8.15 Coastal Sawmills in 1884
H Hastings   N Nanaimo   N.W. New
M Moodyville   V Victoria   Westminster

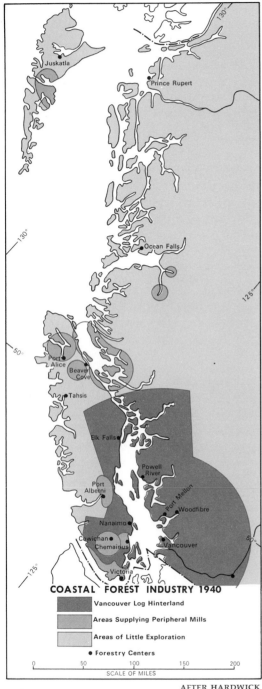

COASTAL FOREST INDUSTRY 1940

■ Vancouver Log Hinterland

Areas Supplying Peripheral Mills

Areas of Little Exploration

● Forestry Centers

0   50   100   150   200
SCALE OF MILES

AFTER HARDWICK

Figure 8.17 The Coastal Forest Industry in 1940
The log hinterland for the Vancouver area in 1940
was restricted to the coast and interior of Southern
British Columbia. The greater area of British
Columbia remained untapped.

market connections necessary for prosperous growth.

As shown by Figure 8.17, the southern
coast between Vancouver Island and the
mainland had developed as the main area
for exploitation. Here abundant supplies of
Douglas fir grew along the lower elevations near Georgia Strait. Relatively protected coastal waters made the use of
simple log booms possible and, as towing
distances increased, the Davis raft was developed to lessen the loss of logs in heavy
seas. It was built log by log on a mat
woven of cables, and the logs were secured
by circumferential lashings. However,
assemblage of the logs and construction of
raft involved considerable time and labor,
and upon delivery breakup was equally
time-consuming. Only companies that had
evolved effective timber cutting and transporting techniques which made possible
the use of valley stands of timber were
able to provide the onshore facilities
needed for the construction of the Davis
rafts.

By 1960 the pattern of logging had
changed radically. Areal dispersion of the
industry took place as sustained yield management and forest administration under
Tree Farm License superceded the laissez-
faire policies which had existed previously.
The decline in the quantity of Douglas fir
caused the loggers to utilize the other
species present, and the manufacturers
were forced to modify their programs to
meet the new species mix. Transportation
techniques were improved, enabling logs to
be transported over longer distances. On
land, the old logging railroads have been
replaced by bush roads and diesel trucks.
Water transportation has been improved
by the introduction of the self-dumping
barge, a craft which is designed specifically
to permit economic haulage of logs from
logging sites along the exposed coast.

Processing of the timber has remained
firmly entrenched in the southern Georgia
Strait area. The early choice of the Vancouver area for sawmilling and the choice
of Vancouver as terminus for the C. P. R.
ensured continued concentration of the in-

Figure 8.19 A Self-dumping Log Barge

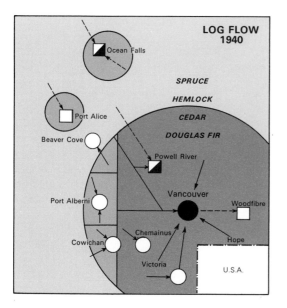

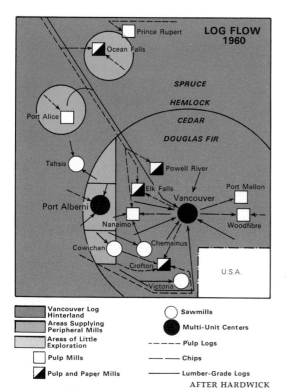

AFTER HARDWICK

Figure 8.18 Log Flow for the Coastal Forest Industry of British Columbia for 1940 and 1960

These schematic diagrams suggest that the sources of supply for the coastal forestry operations expanded considerably during the two decades.

dustry in that area. Within Greater Vancouver, sawmilling is focused on False Creek, New Westminster, and the North Arm of the Fraser River, while mills along Burrard Inlet have ceased to operate. Sawmills were market-oriented and tended to locate where railway and port facilities were readily available.

Pulp and paper mills were established after the issuance of pulpwood leases in 1901. By the end of World War I mills were in operation at Ocean Falls, Swanson Bay, Port Alice, and Powell River. These centers all were at tidewater and had adequate fresh water and hydro-electric power resources. In addition, adequate reserves of hemlock trees existed. After World War II sulphate pulp mills were constructed at Port Alberni, Harmac, Elk Falls, and Crofton. By comparison, pulp and paper mills were far more dispersed than sawmills.

However, all log conversion plants are located along one of the major log flow routes. Frequently there is an integration or grouping of the mills such as the grouped mill complex at Port Alberni where sawmills, pulp mills, and paper mills operate ·together. Technology has improved, and sawmills frequently have gang-mills which can cut small logs into lumber far more efficiently than before. Hemlock can now be used for lumber since drying kilns have been introduced. Government policy has also influenced the industry, for through stumpage charges pressure is applied to encourage the dispersion of lumber mills. Thus the industry

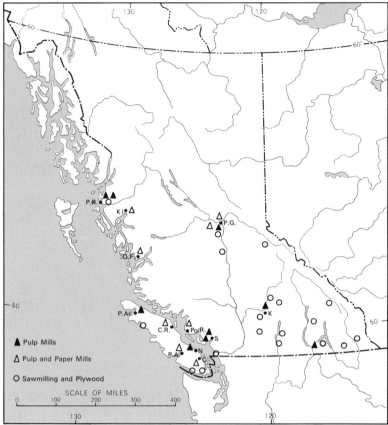

Figure 8.20 Present Distribution of the Forest Processing Industry in British Columbia

C	Chemainus	P.A.	Port Alberni
C.R.	Campbell River	P.Ae.	Port Alice
K	Kamloops	P.G.	Prince George
Ki	Kitimat	P.R.	Prince Rupert
O.F.	Ocean Falls	Po.R.	Powell River
N	Nanaimo	S	Squamish

has evolved a complex distribution in response to a unique series of factors.

Despite a strong coastal development, forestry has also developed in the *Interior*. Under government encouragement pulp and paper mills are now located in the interior where they complement the previously existing pattern of sawmilling. Prince George has become an important forestry center, for rail facilities, hydro power from the Peace River, available water for processing, and forest resources happily coincide. Other forest product industries have been established in the Kootenay area.

Agriculture

Agriculture was not in the historical sense a dominant motif in the settlement of British Columbia; the pioneers were intent upon the exploitation of other natural resources. In the few cases where agriculture developed early, it did so as a service industry, encouraged because of distance from its competitors. Much of the useful agricultural land is located in a few fertile but isolated southern valleys where there was no opportunity for either the extensive production of an export staple as in the Prairie Provinces or the development of the partial-subsistence economy based on a mixed agriculture such as that of the St. Lawrence Lowland. In any case the fur traders, lumbermen, and miners who founded British Columbia did not bring with them an agricultural tradition. Consequently, agriculture is not a particularly important primary industry in the province.

The agricultural areas of British Columbia are small and widely separated, and the industry is greatly varied in its intensity. Of the 4,500,000 acres recorded as farm land in 1966, only 17 per cent is used as crop land while most of the remainder, about 70 per cent, is unimproved and is used mainly as grazing range for cattle and sheep. The most important field crop is hay, grown largely to provide winter feed for grazing livestock. Wheat, which ranks second, is grown almost exclusively on the large farms of the Peace River district.

There are about 20,000 farms in the province, and only about four per cent of the work force is employed in agriculture. However, the area occupied by farms has shown a slight increase in recent years as has also the amount of improved land. The province is by no means self-sufficient in foodstuffs, and with the exception of commercial fruit and poultry products it has little for sale in other parts of Canada.

Surface relief greatly restricts the area of land suitable for agriculture, but climate also profoundly affects the nature of the industry. The valleys of the southern interior have a very low rainfall, and practically all

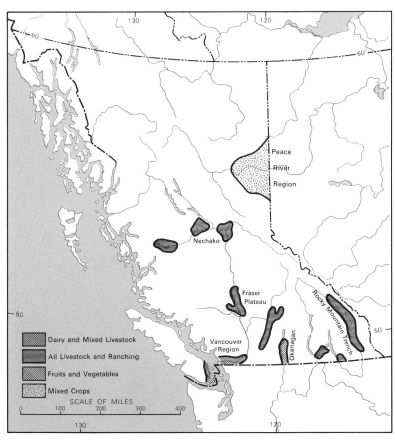

Figure 8.21 Agricultural Regions of British Columbia
Agriculture in British Columbia occurs in small areas which are widely separated.

crops must be grown under irrigation. Fortunately, the growing season here is relatively long while the presence of water bodies provides some protection against unseasonable frosts. Northern valleys also have some areas of favorable relief, but the shortness of the growing season and the great hazard of severe summer frosts limits the northward expansion of crop growing. Other physical limitations, notably stoniness and the deficiency of vital mineral nutrients in the soil, make farming an unprofitable venture even where surface relief and climate are favorable. Above all, the isolation and lack of local markets militate increasingly against the development of prosperous pockets of mixed farming.

The *Vancouver* region is the most important agricultural district in British Columbia, with over 35 per cent of the cultivated land, 70 per cent of the dairy cattle, and 85 per cent of the poultry. It includes the Lower Fraser Valley, a narrow discontinuous plain in the southeastern part of Vancouver Island, and a few scattered tracts of arable land on the other offshore islands. Adjacent to the main market of British Columbia it has developed into an area of intensive agriculture. In addition to dairying, specialty cash crops such as peas, strawberries, and spring flowers are of significance. In recent years experiments have been made in the growing of hops in the Chilliwack area. Despite the importance of the region for agriculture, Crerar states that many of the better endowed portions close to Greater Vancouver are being alienated from agriculture by the spread of urban land uses. Lulu Island and Delta and Surrey districts have all suffered from urban encroachment; and while initially it is the areas of poorer soil which are utilized, urbanization soon spreads to all agricultural land in proximity to the access routes to Vancouver.

The *Okanagan Valley* is the second most important agricultural district. Containing approximately 15 per cent of the land under cultivation and 90 per cent of the orchards, it ranks as a specialty area of paramount significance. Extending north-

ward for over 130 miles from the American border to Shuswap Lake, it averages two miles in width south of Kelowna, but broadens out to include a number of tributary valleys in the north. It is well defined by steep valley walls which rise to over 4,000 feet on the east and west of the rift valley. Most of the valley bottom is occupied by lakes bordered by terraces, the soil texture varying from coarse sands and gravels to fine silts.

Table 8.2   Climatic Characteristics of the Okanagan Valley *

Characteristic	South Okanagan	Okanagan Lake
Temperatures		
Annual Minimum	−5°F	−5°F
January Mean	25°F	26°F
July Mean	70°F	69°F
D-D above 42°F	3,800	3,300
PE	26″	25″
Precipitation	11″	12″
Moisture Deficiency	16″	13″

* After Chapman and Brown.

As shown by the accompanying table, the southern and central portions of the valley are within the climatic requirements of orchard crops and vines if sufficient surface water exists for supplemental irrigation. Most of the orchards and vineyards are located on the lower slopes and terraces of river valleys and along the sides of the lakes. Unfortunately, the valley often acts as a frost-trap when cold air flows down the slopes forming great pools which may reach tens of feet in depth on the valley floor. However, plantings upon the slopes and terraces avoid damage by all but the most severe frosts.

As shown in Figure 8.22, orchards are not found in a continuous belt along the entire length of the valley. In many places relief and soils are not suitable for orchard growing nor is an adequate water supply always available. The best soil is a silt loam which occurs around the southern end of Lake Okanagan. Here almost 8,000 acres are suitable for orchards, and about 5,000 acres are under irrigation for orchards and other special crops. Farms are small, many of them having areas of less than ten acres. Often acquired as retirement sites they produce some income but are too small to be self-sustaining. They have investment value since current land values of $2,000 per acre are more than double the economic limit for agricultural land in the area.

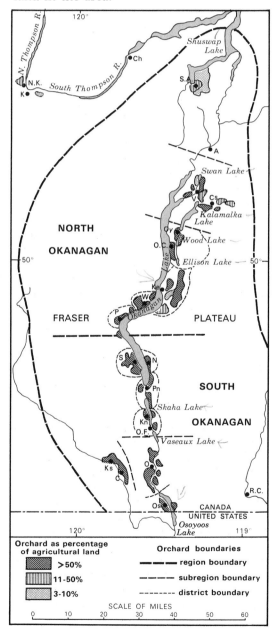

Figure 8.22 The Orchard Regions of British Columbia

AFTER KRUEGER

Most of the orcharding in British Columbia takes place in the Okanagan Valley. It occurs in isolated pockets close to the lakes. Salmon Arm is the northern extreme; Osoyoos, the southern limit.

A	Armstrong	Os	Osoyoos
C	Cawston	Oy	Oyama
Ch	Chase	O.C.	Okanagan Center
Cs	Coldstream	O.F.	Okanagan Falls
K	Kamloops	P	Peachland
Ke	Kelowna	Pn	Penticton
Kn	Kaleden	R.C.	Rock Creek
Ks	Keremeos	S	Summerland
N	Naramata	S.A.	Salmon Arm
N.K.	North Kamloops	V	Vernon
O	Oliver	W	Westbank

The average life of fruit trees in the Okanagan Valley is relatively short. Only in the Penticton area do more than half of the soft fruit trees resist the rigors of the climate for more than ten years. Soft fruit orchards often present a ragged appearance because of many replacements, while much of the land is relatively unproductive. It has become very clear that peaches and apricots face great climatic hazard in the northern part of the Okanagan, and the soft fruit industry is now tending to concentrate in the area around the southern end of Lake Okanagan where about 50 per cent of the orchard area is devoted to soft fruits. The southern end of the Okanagan Valley has also the best conditions for apple orchards. Only here do more than half of the trees last over twenty years. Only here, also, may the tender Delicious varieties be safely grown. Elsewhere and especially in the northern areas the more hardy McIntosh is to be preferred. There are roughly 2.3 million fruit trees in the Okanagan Valley, the number being about equally divided between north and south. The area occupied is somewhat greater in the north because of the wider spacing of the apple trees. Over a number of years Okanagan orchards have yielded an annual average of more than five million bushels of apples and 3.3 million crates of other fruits.

A recent development has been the raising of grapes in the Okanagan Valley. Since 1960 commercial varieties of European grapes have been planted, and the results have been impressive. With irrigation the investment required is high and can amount to more than $250,000 for a producing 80-acre vineyard. The employment needs vary with the season, and many of the part-time pruners and pickers are owners of small orchard or vineyard units. Growing concern is prevalent in the Okanagan Valley about the crop losses resulting from the large numbers of birds now congregating in the area. As yet, no real solution has been found for this problem. Markets appear to be excellent, for government policy concerning the use of domestic grapes for wine produced in British Columbia ensures a market potential which as yet is far in excess of the local supply.

The *Kootenay* valleys comprise a much smaller and more fragmented agricultural region. Parts of it are irrigated and used for the production of tree fruits, small fruits, and vegetables. Wheat is grown on the dyked alluvial lowlands along the Kootenay River near Creston and on the calcareous soils near Cranbrook. Mixed farming featuring dairying is common around the small cities and towns. Throughout the Kootenays cattle and sheep are grazed on the fringes of the cultivated areas.

The *Fraser Plateau* is the principal range area in British Columbia for beef cattle and sheep. The development of the livestock industry followed the gold rush of 1858 when cattle and horses were introduced from the Oregon Country. Grassland areas were eventually overused and ranchers were forced to invade the forest areas. At present, transhumance is successfully practiced in many sections. After summer grazing on alpine pastures many ranchers sell a large part of their herd and keep the remainder as foundation stock on the lowland pastures close to the ranch headquarters. Other areas where livestock are the main source of agricultural income include the Nechako and Rocky Mountain Trench districts. Here as in the Fraser Plateau agriculture is not continuous but is concentrated in ribbonlike fashion along the valley areas where suitable soils, relief, and transportation facilities coincide.

The *Peace River* district is basically an extension of the mixed grains region of Alberta. Wheat, oats, and barley are the main crops and supply 50 per cent of the farm income. However, livestock, particularly beef cattle, form part of the agrarian scene. As in the Fraser Plateau farm sizes are much larger than in the more intensively worked districts such as the Okanagan and Lower Fraser Valley.

In summary, British Columbia has a diversified agriculture. Specialized fruit growing is found in the Okanagan Valley, dairying and truck farming in the southwestern lowlands, and grain farming in the Peace River area. The grazing industry reaches significant proportions on the natural grasslands of the interior. The location and use of agricultural land is greatly influenced by climate and topographic relief. Probably no more than four per cent of the total area will ever be cultivated. Climate and the lack of markets restrict expansion even in topographically suitable areas, yet very gradually the area devoted to agriculture has continued to expand in recent years.

Mining

On the average, mining is the second-ranking primary industry in British Columbia. During the last few years it has averaged three hundred million dollars annually, and contributes about eight per cent of Canada's mineral production. Copper, zinc, lead, and molybdenum are the leading metals. They are found principally along the flanks of the Coast and Columbia Mountains where igneous rocks have been exposed. Oil and natural gas have recently achieved greater importance and have focused new attention on the Peace River country and on the Fort Nelson area. Coal deposits occur in the sedimentary layers of Vancouver Island and in the Rocky Mountains and are currently attracting the attention of Japanese companies who may exploit the resource.

Table 8.3   Mining in British Columbia *

Mineral Group	Production in 1966 in Millions of Dollars	Per Cent of Canadian Production
Metallic Minerals	189.6	9.5
Copper	52.0	11.0
Zinc	42.3	15.0
Lead	29.5	33.0
Molybdenum	25.5	77.0
Iron Ore	20.7	5.1
Tin	1.3	100.0
Non-metallic Minerals	22.8	6.2
Asbestos	15.0	9.0
Sulfur	4.3	10.0
Peat Moss	2.2	30.0
Fuels	63.6	5.1
Crude Oil	36.9	4.5
Natural Gas	17.0	8.5
Coal	6.3	8.7
Structural Materials	39.8	8.5
Total for British Columbia	315.8	7.9

* D.B.S.

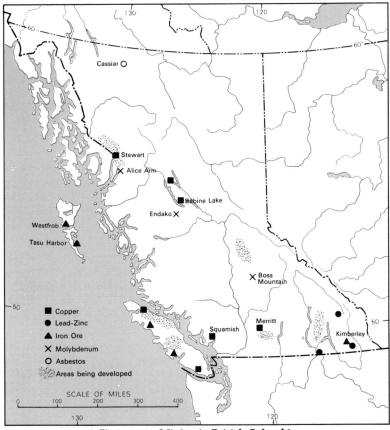

Figure 8.23 Mining in British Columbia

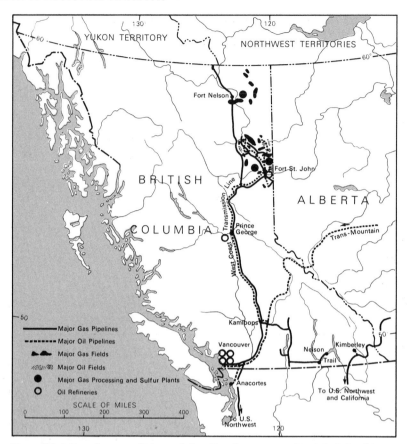

Figure 8.24 Petroleum and Natural Gas Developments in British Columbia
While the deposits are in the Peace River country, the markets are in the
southwest and an extensive system of pipelines has been developed.

As shown by Table 8.3 metallic minerals are the mainstay of mining in the
province. They have received continued
emphasis during the past decade, with new
finds of copper, molybdenum, and iron ore.
Some of the new mines have been developed with the aid of Japanese capital
and their products find a market in Japan.
In this connection an iron ore property on
the Queen Charlotte Islands and a copper
mine at Babine Lake owe their development to Japanese capital and markets. As
shown by Figure 8.23, a linear distribution
is apparent. This follows the "grain of the
country" for rock outcrops and transportation arteries into the interior are controlled
by the linear pattern of the mountain
ranges.

The importance of natural gas and petroleum during the past decade has increased
steadily. While the flow of natural gas
from the Peace River country has increased
consistently during the last few years, for
the time being its value has been surpassed
by crude oil from the new fields in the
Fort St. John area. Processing plants follow
a distribution pattern similar to that noted
in the Prairie Region. Natural gas is treated
and sulfur is removed close to the source,
while crude oil is refined in close proximity
to the major market areas. It appears likely
that existing pipelines will be expanded
and extended to take care of the new petroleum and natural gas deposits which are
being discovered in the area north of Fort
Nelson.

Fisheries

Fishing is less important than other primary industries in the regional economy, but nevertheless its contribution averages slightly more than ninety-seven million dollars each year. British Columbia accounts for 33 per cent of the total value of fish caught in Canada and is the leading province in this field. A great variety of marine life thrives in the North Pacific Ocean. However, the value of fish landed is chiefly in salmon and halibut which account for 63 and 18 per cent respectively.

The salmon fishery is a seasonal industry. Fishing is confined to the summer months when the salmon arrive in the coastal waters prior to ascending the rivers for spawning. Fishermen concentrate in small boats at the mouths of rivers where the salmon converge on their way upstream. Most of the fish are brought to canneries nearby where they are processed. The finished product is shipped to Vancouver for distribution around the world.

Each year the quantity of salmon landed varies, the fluctuation depending upon the number of salmon that were successful in making the arduous journey upstream to spawn some four to six years previously. Water pollution and changes in river flow through power dams and rock falls affect the salmon. It is estimated that only ten per cent of the fry survive to become mature adults. A government experimental program at Babine Lake on the Skeena River has recently proven successful and, if implemented, should improve the quantity of fish available.

Halibut is the second-most important fish resource in the region. It is a large fish, averaging 70 pounds, and it remains off the coast during its entire life. Trawlers are allowed to fish halibut between April and October. Foreign fishing vessels using small mesh nets also catch halibut and are currently causing rapid depletion of the resource. Vancouver and Prince Rupert are the main processing centers for fresh and fast-frozen halibut. Other important species are herring, cod, oysters, clams, and crabs.

Power

British Columbia has long relied on its abundant waterpower for the generation of the electricity necessary to an industrial program. The first large generating station was constructed in 1897 at Bonnington Falls on the Kootenay River to supply the metallurgical industry at Trail. Since then many of the southern rivers of the province have been harnessed, and a beginning has been made in areas farther north. The capacity in 1967 of all generating systems in British Columbia was reported to be 3,627,000 kilowatts, of which almost 90 per cent was derived from waterpower.

Ample power remains to be developed since the waterpower resources of the province are exceeded only by those of Quebec. If the power equivalent of the flow available 50 per cent of the time were to be developed, the province could quadruple its existing generating capacity.

During the past decade there has been a steady increase in demand, much of which has come from industries that rely on great quantities of cheap hydro-electric power. In many instances, industries operate their own generating facilities, particularly the large pulp and paper mills and the Kitimat aluminum smelting complex. In the latter instance, one of the headwaters of the Fraser River System was diverted westward through the mountains to the Kemano generating station, providing a capacity of 812,800 kilowatts.

Forest industries have traditionally been large consumers of electric power. In 1920 one-half of the pulp was produced mechanically by the groundwood process but only one-quarter was produced in this way in 1963. Since the groundwood process requires 1,200 to 1,500 kilowatt hours of electricity per ton of product, the industry relied on coastal locations such as Ocean Falls and Powell River where large amounts of waterpower were available. Technology has changed the power requirements somewhat. The sulfate process of producing pulp is more efficient; lignin is retained and, as "black liquor", can be used as fuel for thermal electric

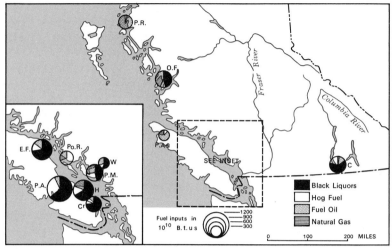

Figure 8.25 Fuel Inputs at British Columbia Pulp and Paper Mills in 1963

C	Castlegar	P.Ae.	Port Alice
Cr	Crofton	P.M.	Port Mellon
E.F.	Elk Falls	P.R.	Prince Rupert
H	Harmac	Po.R.	Powell River
O.F.	Ocean Falls	W	Woodfibre
P.A.	Port Alberni		

generators. In addition, wastes, or "hog", such as bark, chip screen rejects, and sawdust, can be used as fuel. As shown by Figure 8.25, fuel inputs vary from mill to mill, and these reflect the wide range of fuels available. Today the forest industry is linked with provincial power authorities and large blocks of power are purchased. According to Wolforth, purchases accounted for over one-half the electric energy consumed by the industry in 1963, while the development of mills in the in-

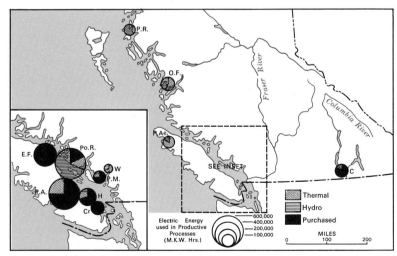

Figure 8.26 Electric Energy Used in Productive Processes at British Columbia Pulp and Paper Mills in 1963

terior since then will increase this considerably (Figure 8.26).*

Thermal power has become important in the Vancouver region where domestic and industrial users have created demands which far exceed the hydro power available from the Bridge River and Lower Fraser generating stations. More than 50 per cent of the thermal generating capacity of British Columbia is concentrated in the three generating stations in this region. The largest is a 600,000 kilowatt station at Burrard Inlet.

Considerable hydro power potential exists in the Columbia, Peace, and Stikine River Systems in locations remote from the

* J. Wolforth. "Comments on the Current Energy Uses of the Pulp and Paper Industry of British Columbia". *Canadian Geographer*. IX, 2 (1965). pp. 104-107.

main area of demand. Construction of the Peace River project at Portage Mountain was begun in 1962. A dam, six hundred feet high and one and a half miles long, stretches across the valley of the Peace River and holds back 62,000,000 acre-feet of water. Partially in service in 1968, the completed power installation will produce nearly 2,300,000 kilowatts of electric energy. The difficulty of transmission over long distances to the market areas has been largely overcome by the use of extra high voltage transmission lines.

The Columbia River is being developed under the terms of the Columbia River Treaty concluded with the United States in 1964. Under these terms three upstream reservoirs are being constructed by Canada, and the accruing downstream power benefits are being sold to the United

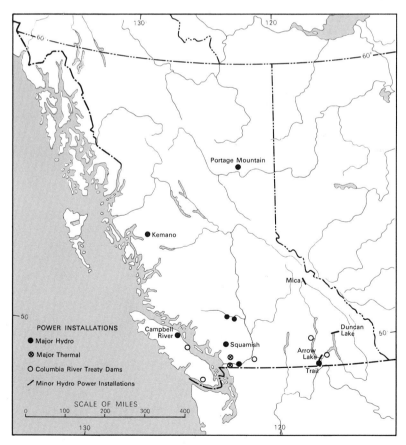

Figure 8.27 **Electric Power Installations in British Columbia**

States. Considerable discord regarding the agreement has clouded the issue, but according to Sewell, the arrangement will be regarded as a precedent in the development of other international rivers in North America.* As a result, British Columbia is now tied into a power system which extends all the way to California.

Manufacturing

Among the provinces of Canada, British Columbia ranks third in value of manufacturing output. The annual average of "value added" during the early 1960s was slightly more than $1,000,000,000, amounting to about one-twelfth of the total Canadian output. At the same time this accounted for about 47 per cent of the value of all commodity production in the province. However, since manufacturing provides about 55 per cent of all commodity production in Canada, British Columbia is slightly below average in this, with a location quotient of about 0.85. It has considerably less intensity of development than Quebec or Ontario. The location quotient calculated on the basis of work force is only 0.75. A comparison of the two location quotients indicates that the average productivity per worker is higher in British Columbia. Wage rates are also higher.

For the most part, the basis of manufacturing is provided by abundant supplies of natural raw materials and available hydro-electric power. Throughout much of the history of the province the forests have been the greatest sources of raw materials. For a long time most of the production came from sawmills, and even today sawmills, planing mills, sash and door factories, and veneer and plywood plants account for about 29 per cent of the value of manufacturing. Following closely in value added and gaining every year are the pulp and paper industries which in 1964 accounted for 21 per cent. Several new mills have since begun production. Veneer

* W. R. D. Sewell. "The Columbia River Treaty: Some Lessons and Implications". *Canadian Geographer*. X, 3 (1966).

and plywood plants, although important industries, have not expanded in recent years because of competition from synthetic wallboard and aluminum building materials. Modern pulp mills may use chips made from sawmill wastes as well as raw pulpwood and may be established as part of an integrated wood-using industrial complex. Thus, in fact, the forests provide the raw materials for half of the manufacturing activity. Also the industries based upon forest raw materials provide jobs for slightly more than half the manufacturing labor force. Sawmilling is the more labor-intensive industry, while the pulp and paper industry requires greater inputs of capital.

Forest-based industries of Canada are concentrated in British Columbia, having a location quotient of 3.50 in terms of either value added or labor force employed. If we look separately at wood industries and pulp and paper mills, we find that the former activity is much more densely concentrated than the latter. But, in any case, there is no denying the overwhelming influence of the forest in the economy of British Columbia.

Within the province wood-using industries have historically been concentrated in coastal regions. Sawmilling began in the southern part of Vancouver Island, on Burrard Inlet, and on the lower part of the Fraser River. Inertia kept them in this small coastal region even when logs had to be transported long distances. Pulp mills were also established in coastal regions where power, wood, and transportation were readily available. In recent years the near exhaustion of virgin forest resources in the coastal areas has led to the establishment of large inland mills such as those at Prince George, Castlegar, and Skookumchuck.

Food and beverage industries employ as many workers as the pulp and paper mills, but the value added by manufacture is only about two-thirds as great. For the most part these industries are organized in small units and are oriented toward British Columbia consumers; the location quotient is

Table 8.4   Industrial Structure of British Columbia, 1964 *

Industrial Category	Canada Production Workers Number	Per Cent	British Columbia Production Workers Number	Per Cent	Location Quotient **
Wood Industries	76,278	7.2	34,231	40.9	5.68
Food and Beverage Industries	131,120	12.4	10,021	12.0	0.96
Paper and Allied Industries	81,397	7.7	9,677	11.6	1.51
Primary Metal Industries	38,275	3.6	5,494	6.6	1.83
Metal Fabricating Industries	89,873	8.5	5,171	6.2	0.72
Transportation Equipment Industries	90,123	8.5	3,745	4.5	0.53
Printing, Publishing, and Allied Industries	43,132	4.1	2,526	3.0	0.73
Machinery Industries	38,275	3.6	1,794	2.1	0.58
Non-metallic Mineral Products Industries	35,598	3.4	1,775	2.1	0.62
Chemical and Chemical Products Industries	33,555	3.2	1,686	2.0	0.62
Clothing Industries	82,945	7.8	1,669	2.0	0.26
Furniture and Fixtures Industries	30,598	2.9	1,657	2.0	0.69
Other Industries	286,333	27.1	4,230	5.1	0.19
Totals	1,057,502	100.0	83,676	100.0	

* Data from Canada Year Book, 1967, p. 681 and p. 695.

** Location Quotient $= \dfrac{\text{Per Cent of B. C. Production Workers in Category}}{\text{Per Cent of Can. Production Workers in Category}}$

about 0.96. However, it should be mentioned that sea-food products, canned salmon in particular, are marketed outside of the province in large quantities.

Primary metal industries rank third in terms both of employment offered and of value added by the manufacturing process. Many of these industries are oriented toward raw materials originating within the province. Most important are the plants at Trail and Kimberley. The aluminum smelter at Kitimat processes imported raw materials and owes its location to the availability of space for plant and port facilities, and the electric energy provided by the installations at Kemano. Markets for most primary metal products lie outside the boundaries of the province. The location quotients for primary metallurgy are about 0.79 in terms of value added and 1.83 in terms of men employed. The province apparently does not possess — or at least has not yet been able to exploit — any great

advantages with respect to this group of industries.

The industries devoted to metal fabricating, machinery, and transportation equipment employ about 13 per cent of the work force and contribute about 11 per cent of the value added by manufacture. By comparison with the rest of Canada, location quotients of 0.72 and 0.53 may be derived, and it may be suspected that these industries are oriented largely toward local demands.

Other groups of industries in the province are small and like the last mentioned oriented largely toward the local market. A few — for example, the chemical fertilizer industries — find their markets outside of the province, but they make up a rather small fraction of the total.

Vancouver. Greater Vancouver is by far the leading manufacturing area in the province. It has, since the beginning, been the focal point of the most active lumbering

Table 8.5   Industrial Structure of Metropolitan Cities of British Columbia *

Industrial Category	Vancouver			Victoria		
	Production Workers Number	Per Cent	Location Quotient **	Production Workers Number	Per Cent	Location Quotient **
Wood Ind.	14,422	25.1	0.61	1,689	28.3	0.69
Food and Beverage Ind.	11,461	19.9	1.66	1,046	17.6	1.46
Paper and Allied Ind.	3,727	6.5	0.56	72	1.2	0.10
Primary Metal Ind.	1,707	3.0	0.45	26	0.4	0.06
Metal Fabricating Ind.	5,181	9.0	1.45	183	3.1	0.50
Transportation Equipment Ind.	2,974	5.2	1.15	1,454	24.3	5.42
Printing, Publishing and Allied Ind.	4,691	8.2	2.73	772	13.0	4.33
Machinery Ind.	1,543	2.7	1.29	28	0.5	0.24
Non-metallic Mineral Products Ind.	1,128	2.0	0.95	97	1.6	0.76
Chemicals and Chemical Products Ind.	1,290	2.2	1.10	252	4.2	2.10
Clothing Ind.	1,690	2.9	1.45	54	0.9	0.45
Furniture and Fixtures Ind.	2,050	3.6	1.80	74	1.2	0.60
Other Ind.	5,621	9.8	1.92	213	3.6	0.71
Totals	57,485	100.0		5,960	100.0	

* Census of Canada, 1961. Bulletin 3.2-2.

** Location Quotient $= \dfrac{\text{Per Cent of City Workers in Category}}{\text{Per Cent of B.C. Workers in Category}}$

and fishing area. Sawmilling began early on Burrard Inlet, False Creek, and the Fraser River near New Westminster. The coming of the railway and the development of the harbor helped attract shipping to the area. As population increased, secondary industries moved in to supply their needs; among these were meat packing, fruit and vegetable processing, dairy products, and printing and publishing. Metal fabricating, machinery, shipbuilding, and boatbuilding also found Vancouver a convenient location from which to supply the demands of the coastal region. Petroleum refining began on Burrard Inlet, making use of imported crude oil. Pipe lines from Edmonton and the Peace River area now supply the industry. The waterside location of the refineries makes possible the distribution of refined products by tanker throughout the coastal regions. Natural gas pipelines from Northeastern British Columbia also contribute to the industrial potential of Vancouver.

Vancouver, however, cannot be considered an outstanding center of manufacturing industries. With a location quotient of almost 4.00 it clearly has dominance in wood industries, and it is above average in employment in foods and beverages, metal fabricating, and printing and publishing. However, its share of other important industries is by Canadian standards quite low; its overall location quotient for employment in manufacturing is 0.93 which may be compared with 1.95 for Hamilton or 1.52 for Greater Montreal. This is undoubtedly due to its geographically isolated position with respect to the chief Canadian markets as well as to the fact that Canada as a whole has not fared very well in competition for a share in the world market for manufactured goods.

Victoria. The Victoria metropolitan area is the second largest manufacturing area in British Columbia. Manufacturing employment, however, is relatively small and rather highly specialized. The wood industries are most important, this area having a historical head start in the sawmilling industry. The biggest single industry, however, is the shipbuilding and repair activity which is largely centered in the Esquimalt dry dock, one of the largest in the world. Third in importance is the printing and publishing industry, a significant part of which may usually be found in any capital city. Food and beverage industries include baking and dairy industries required for the city, breweries, fish processing, soft drink bottling, and distilleries which undoubtedly serve a wider market. No large pulp and paper mills are found in the metropolitan area, but there are a number in the coastal areas tributary to Victoria. In summary, it might be said that, although highly specialized, Victoria is among the least concerned with manufacturing of all the Canadian metropolitan areas.

Special Industrial Areas. Much of British Columbia's industry outside the metropolitan areas is to be found in highly specialized industrial towns, often established by and for a single industry or closely associated group of industries. Two such towns are Trail and Kitimat. Another rapidly growing industrial center is Prince George.

The industrial community of Trail includes the city itself, the adjoining municipalities of Tadanac and Warfield, the nearby city of Rossland, as well as other villages, small communities, and scattered groups of residents in the Columbia Valley. A population of more than 18,000 was recorded in 1966. An early start was gained from the discovery and operation of gold mines at Rossland before the turn of the century. At first the ores were processed at Northport in the State of Washington, a railway having been built to connect the two places. Later under the aegis of the Canadian Pacific Railway Company whose southern line served the mining communities of Southeastern British Columbia, a smelter was built on the Columbia River a few miles from Rossland. A railway spur from Castlegar was built and electricity obtained from a large generating station on the Kootenay a few miles above its conflu-

ence with the Columbia. A number of other power plants have since been built to increase the supply. Greatly enlarged to take care of concentrates from the Sullivan Mine at Kimberley, the Cominco smelter is now one of the largest producers of lead and zinc in the world. Sulfur dioxide produced by the smelter is used to make sulfuric acid which in turn is used in the manufacture of commercial fertilizers at the Warfield plant. Rock phosphate and other ingredients have to be imported. The high degree of specialization in the area is emphasized by the fact that 90 per cent of the workers in manufacturing in the city of Trail find work in these plants; in fact, the plants furnish about 45 per cent of the total employment of Trail.

While there were historical reasons for the location of the plant, it must now be considered as an example of the inertia of capital investment. Practically all the raw materials are brought in, while all the products find distant markets. The benchlands along the Columbia provide the sites while the city of Trail and vicinity provide the labor force. The industrial development appears to be stable, but the population of Trail, Tadanac, Warfield, and Rossland increases at a rate of less than two per cent per decade.

Kitimat is another example of a town with a single large industrial establishment. The Alcan aluminum smelter was located at the head of Douglas Channel because it provided a good port facility on deep, navigable, and protected water, while the alluvial plain of the Kitimat River provided the necessary flat land for the smelter and the town. Moreover, there was a reasonable route to the Canadian National Railway at Terrace. Power was made available by building the Kenny Dam on the Nechako River and turning its flow westward by means of a tunnel through the Coast Mountains to Kemano. Here within a man-made mountain cavern a generating station was installed with a potential of 3,000,000 kilowatts. Another great engineering project was needed to convey the power over the intervening mountains to the smelter at Kitimat. In about fifteen years one of the largest primary metallurgical plants in the world has taken form together with a city which in 1966 was nearing a population of 10,000. The smelter is as yet the only source of industrial employment, but it will soon be joined by pulp and paper plants for which the site and power supply are eminently suitable.

Prince George was not founded as a special industrial site. Since the opening of the transcontinental railway in 1912 it has been a center of forest industry and commercial activity, but until the post-war period its growth was slow. Recently, however, it has been developing very rapidly. Prince George has benefited by the new emphasis upon the forest resources of the interior. The sawmilling industry has expanded, and three new pulp mills have been built. The forest-based industries are being integrated; better use is being made of the various-sized logs while sawmill waste is being utilized as raw material by pulp mills. The position of the city with respect to transportation has also led to the establishment of an oil refinery and a chemical plant. Within ten years the employment doubled, the payroll tripled, and the shipping value of the manufactured products quadrupled.

The Tertiary Industries

According to the census of 1961, tertiary industries provided employment for about 61.5 per cent of the gainfully employed in British Columbia, a figure more than double that for secondary industry. The economic base as well as the economic geography of most urban centers in the province cannot be fully understood without some attention to their trade and service functions.

In much of geographical literature it is indicated that the importance of the "central place" rests in its trade and service functions rather than in its primary and secondary industries. It is therefore in-

structive to look at these functions as exercised by the two metropolitan cities of British Columbia. When one does so, one finds that Vancouver has 67.5 per cent of its work force engaged in tertiary industries while Victoria has 77.5 per cent. Calculated on a total Canadian base the location quotients would be 1.22 and 1.40. However, it must be remembered that the province itself has more than its share of tertiary industries, the location quotient being about 1.11; thus, on the whole, location quotients for tertiary industries in these two cities must be reduced to 1.10 and 1.26 respectively. It has been suggested that a location quotient of 1.20 is strongly indicative of central place functions. From this we might conclude that Victoria was more of a central place than Vancouver in terms of function although not in terms of size.

It may be even more helpful to look at these cities in terms of individual groups of tertiary industries (Table 8.7). Vancouver is seen to have central place status in wholesale trade, insurance and real estate, services to business management, and financial institutions. Health and welfare, communications, and local administration are also above average, but this does not necessarily indicate that the city has extended its services to outlying areas. It more likely indicates that a large city simply requires more people in these services on account of its size. Victoria shows extreme dominance in national defense and provincial administration as well as a clear indication of central place function in federal government services. In one function, health and welfare services, it is exactly on a par with Vancouver. Neither city is an outstanding retail center, nor does either possess that dominance in personal services which indicates outstanding concern for the needs of the traveling public. It may safely be concluded that Vancouver is the commercial capital while Victoria is a political capital and defense headquarters, and there is little overlap in their functions. One strange and unexplained fact is that, despite the presence of universities, neither

Table 8.6   Tertiary Employment Structure in British Columbia, 1961 *

Employment Category	Canada		British Columbia		
	Number	Per Cent	Number	Per Cent	Location Quotient **
Retail Trade	701,606	19.7	67,207	18.9	0.96
Personal Services	437,518	12.3	43,021	12.1	0.98
Transportation	385,031	10.8	41,739	11.8	1.09
Wholesale Trade	289,884	8.1	32,074	9.0	1.12
Health and Welfare	307,433	8.6	31,776	8.9	1.03
Education and Related Services	266,901	7.5	24,044	6.8	0.91
National Defense	173,029	4.9	17,737	5.0	1.02
Communication	130,074	3.6	12,536	3.5	0.97
Insurance and Real Estate	117,969	3.3	11,935	3.4	1.03
Local Administration	123,729	3.5	11,827	3.3	0.94
Services to Business Management	98,987	2.8	10,939	3.1	1.11
Financial Institutions	110,936	3.1	10,707	3.0	0.97
Federal Administration	111,924	3.1	9,672	2.7	0.87
Provincial Administration	68,761	1.9	6,652	1.9	1.00
Other Tertiary Activities	246,186	6.8	22,943	6.4	0.94
Totals	3,569,968	100.0	354,809	100.0	

* Census of Canada, 1961. Bulletin 3.2-1.

** Location Quotient = $\dfrac{\text{Per Cent of B. C. Workers in Category}}{\text{Per Cent of Can. Workers in Category}}$

Table 8.7   Tertiary Employment in Vancouver and Victoria, 1961 *

Categories	Vancouver			Victoria		
	Number	Per Cent	Location Quotient **	Number	Per Cent	Location Quotient **
Retail Trade	37,142	18.7	0.99	7,188	16.8	0.88
Personal Services	22,739	11.4	0.94	4,412	10.3	0.85
Transportation	22,539	11.3	0.96	2,509	5.8	0.51
Wholesale Trade	22,757	11.4	1.27	1,926	4.5	0.50
Health and Welfare	18,828	9.5	1.07	4,087	9.5	1.07
Education and Related Services	12,113	6.1	0.90	2,243	5.2	0.76
National Defense	3,233	1.6	0.32	9,470	22.0	4.40
Communication	7,413	3.7	1.06	829	1.9	0.54
Insurance and Real Estate	8,815	4.4	1.29	1,180	2.8	0.82
Local Administration	7,428	3.7	1.12	1,166	2.7	0.82
Service to Business Management	7,898	4.0	1.29	805	1.9	0.61
Financial Institutions	7,103	3.6	1.20	1,064	2.5	0.83
Federal Administration	4,980	2.5	0.93	1,399	3.3	1.22
Provincial Administration	2,299	1.2	0.63	2,277	5.3	2.80
Other Tertiary Activities	13,728	6.9	1.08	2,411	5.6	0.86
Totals	199,015	100.0		42,966	100.0	

* Census of Canada, 1961. Bulletin 3.2-2.

** Location Quotient = $\dfrac{\text{Per Cent of City Workers in Category}}{\text{Per Cent of B. C. Workers in Category}}$

city exhibits any regional concentration of employment in educational services.

Other cities in British Columbia are smaller, yet their statistics sometimes indicate considerable central place activity. Vernon, Kelowna, and Penticton, for instance, have fairly high rates of employment in wholesale and retail trade and in catering to the traveling public. Vernon, Nelson, Kamloops, and Prince Rupert have administrative functions, while Kamloops, Nelson, and Prince George have some significance as transportation centers.

URBAN DEVELOPMENT IN BRITISH COLUMBIA

To most people British Columbia is a big country with only a few people. With 9.3 per cent of Canada's population living in 9.5 per cent of the total area, this province, more closely than any other, represents the average population distribution in Canada — a little over five persons per square mile. The pattern of distribution, however, is far from average; much less than the Canadian average of the land area is occupied for agriculture, while much more than the average of the population lives in urban places. And, while the area of land occupied by farms is increasing, the proportion of urban dwellers is increasing much more rapidly. In 1961, 72.5 per cent of British Columbia's population lived in urban places, with over 43 per cent living in its two metropolitan areas. By 1966 the urban population had increased to 75.0 per cent while Vancouver and Victoria contained almost 57 per cent of British Columbia's population. The geographical concentration is extremely marked, for both of these large metropolitan cities are tucked away in the southwestern corner of the province while the largest city to be found anywhere else in the province has only 25,000. Not even Ontario which matches British Columbia in urbanization has so great an emphasis upon its metropolitan cities. Moreover, its large cities are more widely scattered.

Behind the metropolitan cities (Vancouver 920,000, and Victoria 180,000), there is no second rank of cities with populations of 30,000 to 100,000 such as one encounters in other regions. The third rank includes Prince George (25,000) and Kamloops together with North Kamloops (23,000). Behind these are eight urban areas with populations between 10,000 and 20,000 including Dawson Creek, Kelowna, Nanaimo, Penticton, Port Alberni, Powell River, Trail, and Vernon. There are approximately ten centers with 5,000 to 10,000 inhabitants, and about 40 centers with 1,000 to 5,000. Not all of these are incorporated. Below the urban threshold of 1,000 population there are about 80 centers with 500 to 1,000 inhabitants and about 500 very small centers with populations of less than 500. It is worth noting that British Columbia has a number of very small incorporated cities while at the same time there are both incorporated and unincorporated villages that are larger than some of these cities. There are also settlements of city size that are not incorporated as urban places at all. Greenwood (pop. 911 in 1961) advertises itself as the smallest city in Canada. However, this doubtful honor must be granted to Dawson in Yukon Territory.

The rate of population increase is very uneven across the province. In five years (1961-1966) the metropolitan population increased by 10.3 per cent; cities of 10,000 to 30,000 increased by 22 per cent as did also the towns and cities of 1,000 to 10,000. Almost all the towns and cities in the province had population increases from 1961 to 1966 although they were minimal in some cases. Among the villages or small centers with populations of 500 to 1,000, about two-thirds registered growth, while one-third stagnated or declined. Hamlets and very small centers showed an even greater degree of stagnation and decline, only about 50 per cent of them indicating significant increase. Nevertheless, maps of British Columbia depict a large number of new centers in this size group of hamlets and small centers.

Figure 8.28 Vancouver, British Columbia
As is typical of a major Canadian city, Vancouver is growing outwards and upwards. The building in the foreground is the H. R. MacMillan Planetarium.

Vancouver

With a population of 900,000 people, Greater Vancouver dominates the province as well as its immediate region. Almost half the population of British Columbia is found within this one rather closely knit urbanized area. The city of Vancouver, itself, with 410,000 people according to the census of 1966, contained only 46 per cent of the total population of the metropolitan area and is year by year steadily falling behind its wide-spreading satellites and suburbs.

Vancouver has a superb location. It is laid out on a gently rolling surface between the flat delta of the Fraser River to the south and Burrard Inlet, its harbor, to the north beyond which rise the slopes of the towering Coast Mountains. The setting and scenery of Vancouver, a combination of sea, lowlands, and mountains, can be matched by few cities in the world.

(Vancouver has become such a complex metropolis that its land use pattern is difficult to describe.] The central business district or downtown area is still confined to

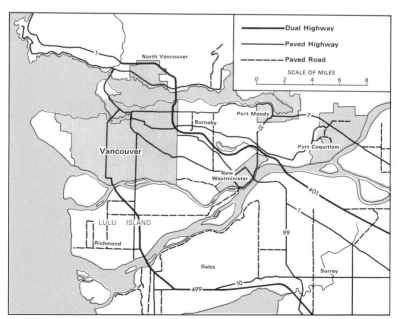

Figure 8.29 Vancouver Metropolitan Area

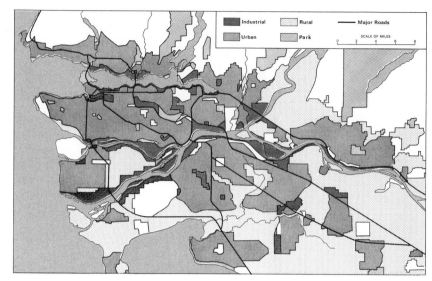

AFTER LOWER MAINLAND PLANNING BOARD

Figure 8.30 The Projected Land Use Pattern for Metropolitan Vancouver

the narrow space between the lower end of the harbor and False Creek which was formerly the site of much sawmill activity. While many old buildings still remain, high-rise office buildings and hotels and modern commercial outlets dominate the scene behind the docks and piers of the waterfront. West of the city center is the English Bay area, noticeably dominated by multi-storey apartment buildings.

Modern thoroughfares and huge bridges over the harbor and False Creek enhance the accessibility of the small downtown area although transportation congestion has not all been eliminated.

Sprawling residential developments have encouraged suburban plazas on the "North Shore", in Burnaby, in Richmond, and recently in Surrey on the south bank of the Fraser. The old shopping center and business district of New Westminster remains restricted to the main street along the waterfront because of sloping land.

Industries are found in the older False Creek and harbor sites. Oil refineries are found at the head of Burrard Inlet. The North Arm of the Fraser from Marpole to Westminster is an area of wood industries. Similar industries are found in Surrey.

Table 8.8   Vancouver Metropolitan Area: Major Municipalities, 1966

Municipality	Population	Per Cent
Vancouver (city)	410,375	46.0
Burnaby (mun.)	112,036	12.5
Coquitlam (mun.)	40,916	4.6
Delta (mun.)	20,664	2.3
New Westminster (city)	38,013	4.2
North Vancouver (city)	26,851	3.0
North Vancouver (mun.)	48,124	5.4
Port Coquitlam (city)	11,121	1.3
Port Moody (city)	7,021	0.8
Richmond (mun.)	50,460	5.6
Surrey (mun.)	81,826	9.2
West Vancouver (mun.)	31,987	3.6
White Rock (city)	7,787	0.9
Other Areas	5,105	0.6
Metropolitan Total	892,286	100.0

Richmond, long the center of the salmon canning industry and since 1930 the site of Vancouver International Airport, has large industries connected with aircraft maintenance, machine shops, and factories producing building materials, chemicals, paper products, and many other goods. The flat land of the delta invites widespread developments.

A final feature of the metropolis must be mentioned — its institutions of learning. The University of British Columbia began to build in Point Grey in the 1920s. It is now a University City with many faculties and departments and more than 18,000 students. Simon Fraser, established in the 1960s on a hilltop in Burnaby, is an architectural monument representative of a new generation of universities in Canada.

Vancouver, however, was not the first center of settlement in the area. This was New Westminster, the port at the head of the Fraser Delta, which was also the capital of mainland British Columbia until the province became united, with its capital located at Victoria. At first Vancouver was simply a small sawmill settlement, and it was not until it was chosen by the Canadian Pacific Railway as its terminal in 1886 that Vancouver began to grow into a transshipment center and even more rapidly into a great city. Lumber for export was its great commodity and despite the label "Gateway to the Orient" only a very small tonnage of imports from that area was received. Moreover, there were other nearby ports which together shipped much more lumber than Vancouver. But Vancouver had its railway and it rapidly became the center of distribution via small coastwise shipping. Between 1890 and 1910 the population grew from 13,000 to 100,000 surpassing both its old rivals, Victoria and New Westminster.

The real boost to port activity came with the opening of the Panama Canal giving a much shorter route to Europe. A small amount of wheat had formerly been shipped from Vancouver, but at the end of World War I this business rapidly increased. Grain from Alberta and much of Western Saskatchewan can reach European markets more cheaply by way of Vancouver than by way of the Great Lakes and the St. Lawrence; and, of course, this is the preferred route for shipment to the Orient. Nine large elevators on Burrard Inlet proclaim the importance of the Vancouver grain trade. By 1964 this outpouring of grain had grown to 6,000,000 tons compared with 13,000,000 tons transshipped at the Lakehead. Most of the latter must be transshipped once, and perhaps twice, again before it takes its ocean voyage. Vancouver still ships wood and wood products, but this tonnage now amounts to less than one-third that of the grain trade. Coal, sulfur, fertilizer, copper ores, and concentrates add considerably to the volume of exports. These are now shipped via the new port at Robert's Bank. But less than 60 per cent of Vancouver's port activity is concerned with international movement of goods; despite the growth of foreign trade, coastwise shipping is still of major importance. New Westminster is still a port in its own right, ranking second in British Columbia and handling about one-fifth the cargo handled by Vancouver. Its major trade is in lumber. If one adds the tonnages of Vancouver and New Westminster and of the small ports on the north arm of the Fraser, the port of Greater Vancouver ranks ahead of all other Canadian ports in volume of cargo handled.

Transportation is undoubtedly the key function of Vancouver, but it ranks below other major categories in terms of total employment. Vancouver has growing manufacturing industries which employ about 20 per cent of the work force. The Vancouver area is the outstanding source of sawmill products, veneers, and plywood; food processing ranks next, including fish, meats, sugar, and carbonated and alcoholic beverages. Metal fabrication, machinery, shipbuilding, paper, printing, petroleum refining, and chemicals are all important industries. Despite the early and continued emphasis on wood processing, Vancouver's manufacturing industries are becoming reasonably well diversified.

Central place functions including trade and services are fundamental to the city's economy. The functions of wholesale and retail trade, finance and insurance, education and health services, all serve to spread the influence of the city to all parts of the province and even beyond its borders while at the same time providing the employment necessary in a large city.

Victoria

Victoria, the capital city of British Columbia, forms the nucleus of the second metropolitan area of the province with a total population of 173,455 in 1966 (Table 8.9). Situated at the southeastern extremity of Vancouver Island it has two deep harbors. Victoria Harbor, around which the old part of the city was built, is the center of port activity, while Esquimalt Bay to the west has a naval yard equipped with one of the largest dry-docks in the world.

The deep ice-free harbor, good water, supply, and the agricultural potential of

Table 8.9   Victoria Metropolitan Area: Major Municipalities, 1966

Municipality	Population	Per Cent
Victoria (city)	57,453	33.2
Esquimalt (mun.)	12,891	7.4
Oak Bay (mun.)	18,123	10.5
Saanich (mun.)	58,845	33.8
Other Areas	26,143	15.1
Greater Victoria	173,455	100.0

the surrounding land encouraged the Hudson's Bay Company to establish Fort Vic-

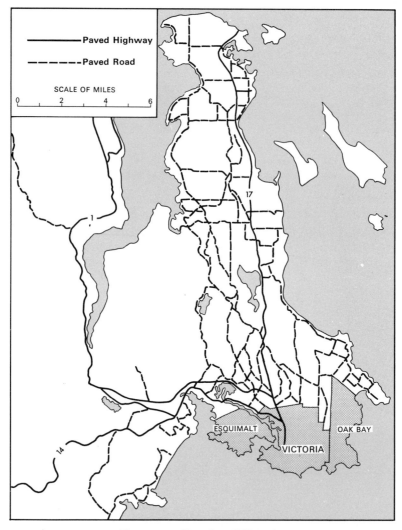

Figure 8.31 Situation of Victoria

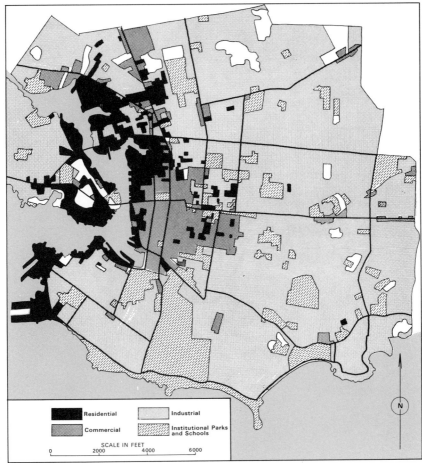

■	Residential	▓	Industrial
▓	Commercial	▨	Institutional Parks and Schools

SCALE IN FEET
0   2000   4000   6000

N

AFTER CAPITAL REGION PLANNING BOARD OF BRITISH COLUMBIA

Figure 8.32 Land Use Pattern of Victoria, 1966

toria in 1843. At first a small settlement, it expanded rapidly in 1858 when gold was discovered in the Cariboo. Being the only accessible port it became the miners' headquarters and commercial center. When British Columbia became a province of Canada, it became the provincial capital. It remained the largest town until the C. P. R. was built with its terminal at Vancouver, which then rapidly outgrew the now somewhat isolated capital.

Victoria is a port and trade center but these functions are far outweighed by the governmental functions, administration and defense. Together, federal, provincial, and local governmental payrolls account for more than 25 per cent of all employment and nearly 50 per cent of the excess over minimum requirements. Victoria is thus a highly specialized administrative center. The service sector, including the university, hospitals, and other institutions, is also well developed. The employment in secondary industries, on the other hand, is little above the minimum. Victoria is sometimes called Canada's English city. English culture and background is proclaimed by such landscape features as carefully tended gardens, narrow winding streets, fine specialty shops, and unmistakably English house types; yet Victoria is essentially a modern Canadian city which moves at only a slightly slower pace than the average North American metropolis.

Other Cities of the Coastal Region

Outside the metropolitan areas the only other city-sized settlements are Nanaimo, Port Alberni, Powell River, and Prince Rupert. All derive their economic support largely from the coastal forests. Nanaimo only might be considered as a subregional center. Kitimat, not yet incorporated as a city although it has nearly 10,000 people, is a one-industry town devoted to aluminum smelting.* It has a good harbor and available industrial sites which will undoubtedly attract other industries. Terrace is a center of forest exploitation, a transportation node, and a regional supply point. Prince Rupert is a port and manufacturing center but appears to be less of a regional service center. Some people see this trio of cities as a complementary system capable of great future development. Chilliwack, a small city located toward the inner end of the Lower Fraser Valley and surrounded by a good agricultural area, is one of the best examples of a *central place* or service center in the whole province.

Cities of the Southern Interior

For our purposes, the southern interior of British Columbia includes the Okanagan, the Kootenay, and the Thompson valleys.

The largest center is Kamloops with a population of about 25,000. The city is divided into two almost equal parts by the river. The older southern section contains most of the business and industry. North Kamloops is mainly suburban and residential. Transportation, manufacturing based on forest products, and diversified service functions provide the foundations for this rapidly growing area.

Three cities, Vernon, Kelowna, and Penticton, are service and trading centers for the Okanagan Valley. In recent years Penticton has developed as a resort and retail area, Kelowna leads in manufacturing and wholesaling, and Vernon with a slightly

smaller population than the first two appears to have significance as a center of accommodation and community services and wholesale and retail trade. It also has a rapidly expanding manufacturing sector. Kelowna and Penticton both occupy attractive sites on the shores of Lake Okanagan. Vernon, although centered inland, extends its suburbs to three lakes. The cities of the Okanagan have well-developed facilities for summer sports.

Trail, on the Columbia River, is the largest and most specialized industrial city in Southeastern British Columbia. Manufacturing employs more than 70 per cent of the work force in excess of the minimum requirements. The smelting and refining of lead, zinc, and silver and the manufacture of commercial fertilizers are the chief industries.

At the outlet of Kootenay Lake, Nelson, once a center for mining and smelting, is now a center of transportation and administration and the site of a university. A few miles to the north, Mt. Kokanee (9,400 feet) dominates the grandeur of Kokanee Glacier Park, a mecca for outdoor recreationists.

Further east are Cranbrook which is engaged largely in transportation and forest industries and Kimberley which is devoted to the mining and processing of ores containing lead, zinc, silver, and iron. Lead-zinc-silver concentrates are sent to Trail for smelting and refining. Chemical fertilizers and a small amount of steel are produced in Kimberley. The surrounding region also has considerable forest industry. Still further east are the small coal-mining centers of Natal and Fernie.

At the confluence of the Kootenay and Columbia Rivers, almost halfway between Nelson and Trail, another somewhat loosely knit urban agglomeration is taking form. It consists of the town of Castlegar and the village of Kinaird on the west bank, together with the smaller settlements of Robson and Brilliant on the east. Since early settlement days a ferry service has been maintained at Castlegar, but with the building of high-level bridges over both

---

* Ira M. Robinson. *New Industrial Towns on Canada's Resource Frontier*. University of Chicago. Department of Geography. Research Paper No. 73. Chicago. 1962. p. 2.

the Columbia and the Kootenay closer contact may be achieved. In this vicinity there are a two-year community college and a large pulp mill. Just upriver is the High Arrow Dam, an important element in the Columbia River development. Nearby are the interesting settlements of the Doukhobor sect, composed of scattered multiple-family residences on community-owned lands.

Cities of the Central Interior

Central British Columbia is a rapidly developing region served by the Canadian National and Pacific Great Eastern railway systems and by the improved provincial highway system.

Prince George, located at the confluence of the Fraser and Nechako Rivers, is the largest city in the interior of British Columbia. It is the junction point of two railway systems and the focus of the highway network. Founded as a fur-trading post in 1807, it became a city in 1915 after the building of the railway. For decades it grew slowly as the distribution center for surrounding farms, ranches, and lumber camps. More recently Prince George has become a significant industrial center with sawmills, three large pulp and paper establishments, an oil refinery, and a chemical products complex. The census of 1966 recorded 25,000 inhabitants in the city with several thousands more in surrounding suburbs.

Quesnel was founded during the Cariboo gold rush of the 1860s and has long been a center of mining activity. More recently it has become the center of an expanding forest products industry. There are also large cattle ranches in the vicinity.

Williams Lake is another settlement on the "Cariboo Trail" which has long been known as the nucleus of a ranching area. More recently it has experienced great expansion of forest-based industries.

Cities of the Peace River Area

The Peace River area of British Columbia is physically an extension of the interior plains of North America and was long effectively cut off from the rest of British Columbia by the difficulties of transportation over mountainous terrain. Early railway and road facilities and, even more, the Alaska highway emphasized its isolation from British Columbia. This was ended by the extension of the Pacific Great Eastern and the building of a new highway from Prince George by way of Pine Pass.

The area has a mixed-farming system similar to that of the adjoining area in Alberta. Productive gas and oil fields have been developed here and in the more distant northeastern corner of the province, and pipelines to the Vancouver market have been provided.

Dawson Creek, long a small pioneer town, has become a regional center with more than 12,000 people in 1966. Transportation, wholesale and retail trade, and construction are its greatest industries.

Located fifty miles northwest of Dawson Creek, on the north bank of the Peace River, the town of Fort St. John (7,000) is the supply point for the neighboring gas and oil fields. Fifty miles westward of this, Hudson Hope has expanded rapidly during the building of the Portage Mountain dam and hydro-electric station on the Peace River.

REGIONAL CONTRASTS

British Columbia is a land of great geographical contrasts. It contains some of Canada's highest mountains as well as some land so low that it must be dyked to protect it from the sea. The severity of the Alpine climate, promoting snowfields, glaciers and extensive areas of permanently frozen ground, contrasts with the mildness of the Pacific Coast. The Pacific slopes unquestionably constitute the wettest areas in Canada while the valleys of the southern interior are among the warmest and driest. Like several other provinces, it has a well-developed, densely settled core area, backed by a huge and only partially developed hinterland. Thus there is the greatest contrast between the metropolitan areas of the southern coastal trench and the scattered, small, urban nuclei in the rest of the province. New developments may, however, be expected in many parts of the province. New industrial centers such as Kitimat will probably arise, while older centers such as Kam-loops, Prince George, and Kimberley will continue their rapid development. But even these will not greatly disturb the geographical pattern of settlement in British Columbia. Because of the abundance of its natural resources it will continue to be one of the wealthiest parts of Canada and yet, seemingly, one of the most sparsely settled.

BIBLIOGRAPHY

Allen, Edward W. "Fishery Geography of the North Pacific Ocean". *Geographical Review.* XLII, 4 (October, 1953). pp. 558-563.

Birch, J. W. "The Expansion of the Canadian Aluminum Industry". *Journal of Geography.* XL, 1 (January, 1955). pp. 52-54.

Crerar, A. D. "Planning in the Lower Mainland Region of British Columbia". *Canadian Geographer.* 4 (1954). pp. 21-26.

Crerar, M. L. and Crerar, A. D. "Land Use Patterns and Land Capabilities in the Lower Fraser Valley". *Occasional Papers in Geography.* No. 3 (1962). pp. 69-79.

Farley, A. L. "Applied Geography in British Columbia". *Canadian Geographer.* 4 (1954). pp. 15-20.

Hardwick, W. G. "Geography of the Forest Industry of Coastal British Columbia". *Occasional Papers in Geography.* No. 5 (1963). pp. 1-89.

———. "The Moran Dam and Availability of Cultivated Land in Interior British Columbia". *Occasional Papers in Geography.* No. 3 (1962). pp. 64-68.

———. "The Persistence of Vancouver as the Focus for Wood Processing in Coastal British Columbia". *Canadian Geographer.* IX, 2 (1965). pp. 92-95.

Jackson, John N. "Geography and Planning in British Columbia". *Canadian Geographer.* VIII, 2 (1964). p. 92.

Kerr, Donald. "The Physical Basis of Agriculture in British Columbia". *Economic Geography.* Vol. 28 (1952). pp. 229-239.

Krueger, Ralph R. "The Geography of the Orchard Industry of Canada". *Geographical Bulletin.* Vol. 7, No. 2 (1965). pp. 27-71.

Mathews; W. H. "Two Self-dumping Ice-dammed Lakes in British Columbia". *Geographical Review.* LV, 1 (January, 1965). pp. 46-52.

McGovern, P. D. "Industrial Development in the Vancouver Area". *Economic Geography.* Vol. 37 (1961). pp. 189-206.

Robinson, Ira M. *New Industrial Towns of Canada's Resource Frontier.* University of Chicago. Department of Geography. Research Paper No. 73. Chicago. 1962.

Robinson, J. Lewis. "Population Trends and Distribution in British Columbia". *Canadian Geographer.* 4 (1954). pp. 27-32.

Sewell, W. R. D. "The Columbia River Treaty: Some Lessons and Implications". *Canadian Geographer.* X, 3 (1966). pp. 145-156.

Wolforth, J. "Comments on the Current Energy Uses of the Pulp and Paper Industry of British Columbia". *Canadian Geographer.* IX, 2 (1965). pp. 104-107.

The Canadian Northland

9 The northland is Canada's largest single region, covering nearly 50 per cent of the country's area. Despite its vast extent, it plays a minor role in Canadian economic development. This is due partly to the fact that less than 0.2 per cent of Canada's people reside within the region.

The northland is by no means a homogeneous region with regard to its physical and cultural features. Probably the only features common to its different parts are a low level of economic development and a harsh climate. Long cold winters prevail, and nowhere does the mean annual temperature exceed 25°F. As a result much of the region is strongly influenced by permafrost conditions. Climate and permafrost combine to make communication by land a problem, while transportation by water is limited by ice. Remote from the ecumene of Canada, the area is further isolated by prohibitive costs of air transportation.

While the Canadian Northland is conceptually easy to define, there is a problem in delimiting the southern boundary. In summary, the region comprises the Yukon, Northwest Territories, Arctic Islands, and the northern part of Labrador and Quebec. Permafrost distribution is probably one of the best natural indicators of the southern limit. As shown by Figure 9.1, there are three possible borders. The middle one, entitled "Southern Limit of Widespread Permafrost" is the one selected here as marking the southern limit of the Canadian Northland. It is of interest that this limit coincides closely with the mean annual isotherm of 25°F.

However, in reality there is a series of Canadian Northlands, for on the basis of physical differences and varying levels of economic growth several subdivisions can be made. In the west there are the forested Yukon and Mackenzie subdivisions. The Yukon is chiefly an area of mountains and linear valleys where the development of a modest road network has encouraged a partial utilization of the mineral resources. The Mackenzie subdivision has the natural advantage of a navigable waterway, and mineral resources along the southern fringe have been tapped with the aid of rail and water transportation facilities. The other subdivisions are part of the Canadian Arctic and include a vast treeless area known as the tundra. While considerable relief does occur on the Queen Elizabeth Islands and on Baffin Island, most of the Arctic is composed of poorly drained plains. Few resources exist in the Arctic, and today only Arctic Char and white fox are actively exploited. Minerals have been discovered, such as the iron ore deposits of Baffin and Belcher Islands and petroleum on Melville Island, but these are too remote from market areas to make utilization economically feasible within the near future. Attempts by the oil tanker Manhattan in 1969 suggest that it will be a long time before the Arctic Ocean can be considered navigable for commercial cargo vessels.

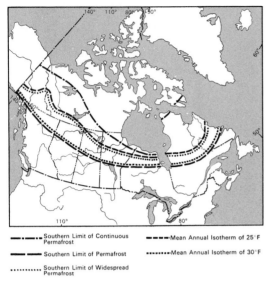

—·—·— Southern Limit of Continuous Permafrost   ■—■—■ Mean Annual Isotherm of 25°F

——— Southern Limit of Permafrost   ···········Mean Annual Isotherm of 30°F

··········· Southern Limit of Widespread Permafrost

Figure 9.1 The Canadian Northland

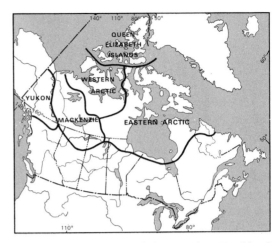

Figure 9.2 Subdivisions of the Canadian Northland

PHYSICAL RESOURCE BASE

Landforms

The *Yukon* is an extension of the Cordilleran physiographic province which extends northwards from British Columbia to encompass the entire Yukon Territory. As is the case with British Columbia, the Yukon can be divided into three: the Coastal Mountain zone, the Interior Plateaux, and the Eastern Mountain zone (Figure 9.3). The rugged barrier of the Coast and St. Elias Ranges effectively isolates the Yukon from the Pacific Ocean and the Alaskan Panhandle. Granitic intrusions with roof pendants of old metamorphic rocks are typical formations for the 7,000-foot coastal range which terminates in the Yukon Territory near Kusawa Lake. The St. Elias Range is the mightiest mountain chain in Canada, and Mt. Logan (19,850 feet) is the second highest peak in North America. Large permanent icefields discharge twisting glaciers down to the fiorded Pacific Coast and also northward into a few valleys draining into the Yukon. In the interior the Yukon Plateau is the main physiographic feature. It is a basin-like dissected plateau averaging 2,500 feet in elevation

and it is rimmed on the southwest, east, and north by mountains. Composed chiefly of crystalline rock broken by younger intrusives and lavas, it has extensive areas where mineralization has occurred, and deposits of gold, silver, and base metals are known to exist. The plateau appears as a rolling upland divided by valleys as deep as 2,000 feet. Glaciation has affected only a limited area for low precipitation during the Pleistocene Epoch did not permit a sufficient accumulation of snow. The other lowland areas are the Porcupine Basin and Liard Basin. Both are separated from the Yukon Plateau by mountains. The Yukon Plateau is effectively isolated from the Mackenzie Lowland and the Shield by the Mackenzie, Selwyn, and Ogilvie Mountains. The Mackenzie Mountains form jagged ridges of barren sedimentary rock and, like the Rocky Mountains to the south, are complexly folded. The Selwyn Mountains on the eastern border of the Yukon are composed of thousands of feet of folded and faulted sedimentary rock.

The *Mackenzie Lowland* is a continuation of the Great Plains physiographic province (Figure 9.4). The Lowland is about 450 miles wide at the southern border of the Northwest Territories and narrows to the northwest between the Mackenzie Mountains and the Canadian Shield. Just west of Great Bear Lake the

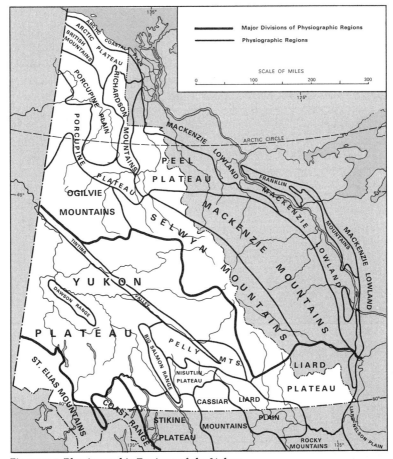

Figure 9.3 Physiographic Regions of the Yukon
As in British Columbia, there is a three-fold division into Coastal Mountain
Zone, Interior Plateaux, and Eastern Mountain Zone.

Franklin Mountains partition the plain into
two sections, the Mackenzie River occupying the western portion. It developed as a
subsequent river between the Western Cordillera and the Shield; thus, its course
below Fort Simpson between the Franklin
and Mackenzie Mountains suggests either
antecedence or superimposition. Evidence of
high-level erosion surfaces in the Mackenzie Mountains indicates that superimposition is not impossible.* The river is
navigable, but navigation is difficult
through the San Sault Rapids at Mile 624
below Norman Wells and the Ramparts at

* J. B. Bird. *Physiography of Arctic Canada.* Johns
Hopkins Press. Baltimore. 1967.

Mile 675 where the narrow channel causes
considerable turbulence. Further downstream at Mile 913 the Delta commences,
and the river disgorges into countless dis-
tributaries and channels.

The Mackenzie is the longest river in
Canada and extends 2,635 miles from the
source of its remotest tributary, the Find-
lay, to the Beaufort Sea. The length from
the outlet of Great Slave Lake to the
mouth, a distance presently considered to
be navigable, is 1,071 miles. Its discharge
may exceed 300,000 cubic feet per second
(cfs) during the summer, with a peak of
over 500,000 cfs at breakup in late May or
early June. The late winter discharge is

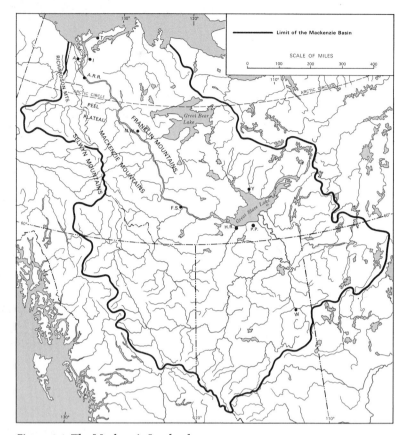

Figure 9.4 The Mackenzie Lowland
A complex drainage pattern occurs in the Lowland, and most of the urban
centers of note are found close to the Mackenzie River.

A	Aklavik	I	Inuvik	W	Waterways
A.R.R.	Arctic Red River	N.W.	Norman Wells	Y	Yellowknife
F.S.	Fort Simpson	P.P.	Pine Point		
H.R.	Hay River	T	Tuktoyaktuk		

below 100,000 cfs.* Flooding occurs during the period of major flow as ice jams
collect in the still frozen delta area. However, while the river is of note and has
been actively studied, much attention has
been focused by geographers on the Delta
region. It is an estuarine delta delimited by
the Richardson Mountains on the west and
the Cariboo Hills to the east. Besides the
myriad lakes and channels which have
been examined, using new quantitative re-

* J. R. MacKay. *The Mackenzie Delta Area,
N.W.T.* Department of Mines and Technical Surveys. Geographical Branch. Memoir VIII. Ottawa.
1963. p. 99.

search techniques, other landforms resulting from freeze-thaw activities and permafrost have been studied intensively.
  Probably the most notable landform is
the *pingo*. It is a large frost mound which
develops from the growth of ice within the
permafrost. Pingos often form conical hills
which are conspicuous features on the
otherwise flat tundra plains. Nearly 1,400
pingos occur on the Pleistocene delta of the
Mackenzie River. Elsewhere in the Canadian Northland they have a limited distribution (Figure 9.7). A few have been discovered in the Great Bear Lake—Copper-
mine area and some are known to exist on

COURTESY DEPT. OF INDIAN AFFAIRS AND NORTHERN DEVELOPMENT

Figure 9.5 The Mackenzie Delta

Figure 9.6 A Pingo

COURTESY NATIONAL RESEARCH COUNCIL OF CANADA

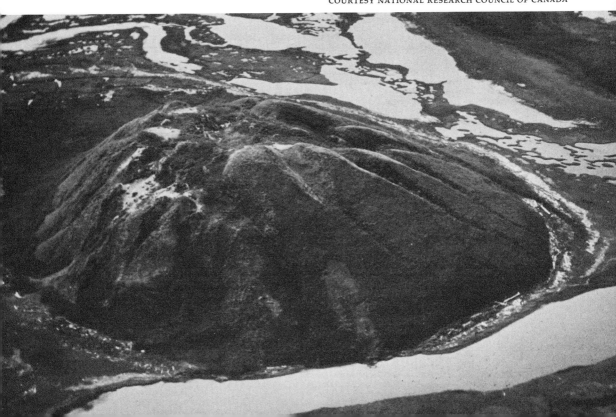

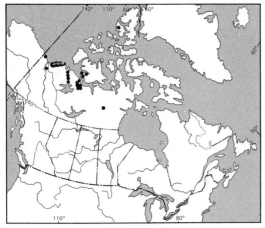

AFTER BIRD

Figure 9.7 Distribution of Pingos in Canada

Victoria Island. However, the world's greatest concentration of pingos occurs within the Mackenzie Delta.

Pingos in the Mackenzie Delta are found in flat areas underlain by sand and are confined to the floors of shallow or recently drained lakes. Layers of peat, sand, and silt cover clear ice. Occasionally some layers are breached at the top and contain a water-filled crater. It is believed that pingos develop as an ice body forms near the surface of a shallow lake bottom which is in the process of being frozen and taken over by permafrost. A closed system results, and as the pore-water changes to permafrost, pressure is exerted on the remaining water which escapes upwards and forms ice beneath the upper permafrost (Figure 9.8). The first evidence of pingo formation is the growth of a low mound within the lake bed. As the mound increases in size the lake becomes ring-shaped and eventually disappears. As the accretion continues, the pingo ruptures at the summit and collapses as the ground ice melts, but this process appears to take thousands of years. A research team lead by Professor Ross MacKay is currently attempting to modify a small lakebed near Tuktoyaktuk so that the development of pingos can be accurately recorded, but it will be several years before the results of the experiment will be known. Pingos are

stable landforms. At Tuktoyaktuk a pingo has been hollowed out for use as an indoor curling rink.

Common features associated with pingos are tundra polygons. These range from about 20 to 100 feet in diameter, their size being dependent on climate, soil characteristics, and stage of growth. Ice wedges which underlie the trenches form as water freezes in the vertical contraction cracks. In the initial stages, the ridges enclose the polygon and give it a saucer shape, but as lateral growth of the ice wedge continues, the central area becomes raised creating a high central polygon. Tundra polygons are

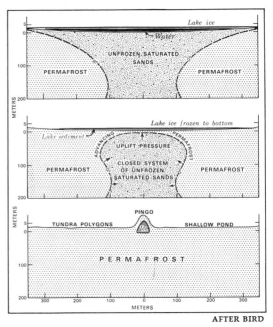

AFTER BIRD

Figure 9.8 Schematic Diagram Illustrating the Origins of a Pingo
A vertical exaggeration of five times has been used for the height above zero in order to show the lake ice and open pool of water. In the top diagram the broad shallow lake has an unfrozen pool of water and no permafrost lies beneath the center of the lake. In the center diagram, continued deposition has made the lake sufficiently shallow to cause freezing right to the bottom and permafrost begins to develop from the lake bottom downward. As this is a closed system, continued freezing causes hydrostatic pressure and the lake bottom begins to dome upward. As shown by the bottom diagram, the pingo has formed as a stable ice core. The old lake bottom is occupied by tundra polygons and shallow ponds.

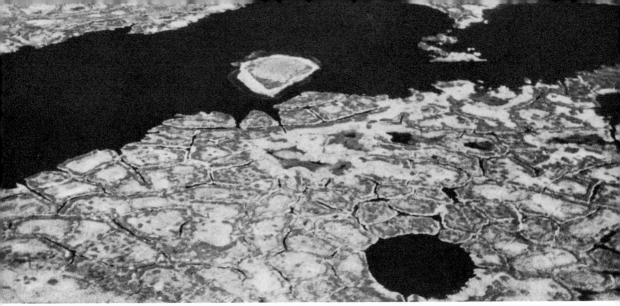

COURTESY NATIONAL RESEARCH COUNCIL OF CANADA

Figure 9.9 Tundra Polygons

most numerous in the southern part of the Delta in the vicinity of Aklavik.

The *Western* and *Eastern Arctic* areas are basically tundra plains, formed on the rocks of the Canadian Shield. While some considerable relief due to folding does occur in the Ungava Peninsula and on Baffin Island, most of the relief features owe their origin to glaciation and the effects of permafrost. In Labrador, "ravines de gelivation" occur where frost shattering along linear fracture zones in the rocks has permitted the removal of materials and the creation of cleft-like valleys which may be 80 feet deep and 300 feet wide. Pleistocene glaciation did much to modify the landscape, particularly in terms of the deposition of glacial drift. Till plains patterned by ice movement, moraine features, waterworked drift in the form of eskers, and crevasse fillings are widespread and obscure the influence of the underlying bedrock. Drumlins, drumlinoids, and long parallel till ridges all give a grain to the landscape and contribute to the derangement of the drainage system. Massive terminal moraines are not common except on Baffin Island, but kame moraines occur north of Great Bear Lake and in northwest Keewatin. Small moraines or "ripple till" occur in many areas, particularly in Labrador, southern Keewatin, and the Thelon River area. Eskers are among the most

prominent landforms in the Arctic. They are found in great numbers on the mainland west of Hudson Bay and in interior Labrador. Many are quite complex and have tributaries which connect with the main trunk. In Keewatin and Mackenzie eskers more than 60 miles in length are common, and heights in excess of 100 feet have been frequently reported.

South of Parry Channel a considerable area (115,000 square miles) is floored by limestone. While some of the area is crystalline and Proterozoic in age, much of it is Ordovician limestone which has been preserved in basins such as the Hudson Bay and Foxe Basin. Solution fissures typical of chemical weathering in more moderate climates are generally missing, while mechanical weathering is far more prevalent. For instance, frost shattering is a prominent process of mechanical weathering and fields of shattered limestone are familiar features. However, above the limit of marine transgressions since the onset of Pleistocene glaciation, a matrix of silt, clay and limestone fragments is typical and is well illustrated by the Putnam Highlands of Baffin Island.

Alpine glaciation is of note along the Labrador coast and on Baffin Island. There, fiorded coastlines are common, while cirques and active glaciers are all part of the terrain.

Permafrost is of great significance in the Canadian Northland. More than 50 per cent of the area of Canada is influenced by permanently frozen ground. Its existence is due to the cold climate which over the ages has caused permafrost to accumulate to depths exceeding 1,000 feet in the Arctic. Permafrost is vitally important to newly discovered mining areas in the Northland for it has a profound influence on open pit mining techniques, and the construction of buildings, roads, and railways. Research on permafrost in Canada began nearly two decades ago, and in 1952 a research station at Norman Wells was established. A decade later this was moved to Inuvik, and in 1965 another field research station was begun at Thompson, Manitoba. Continuous permafrost occurs when the mean annual temperature is below 17°F. Depth varies from 1,000 feet in the Arctic Islands to 200 feet near the southern limit. The surface portion is termed the "active layer" for it thaws in summer to a maximum depth of three feet and then refreezes in winter. In the zone of discontinuous permafrost (Figure 9.1) the type of terrain plays a large role in determining distribution, and the permafrost table is often below the depth reached by the active layer (Figure 9.10). While permafrost does affect vegetation, it is also of direct influence on man's activities in the Canadian Northland. Unthawed it forms an excellent foundation, but melted it supports very little. There are four possibilities when permafrost areas are utilized; disregard the permafrost conditions, preserve the frozen conditions for the life of the structure, remove the permafrost conditions and materials prior to construction, or thaw frozen ground with the expectation of subsequent ground settlement taken into account by foundation design.

Buildings are frequently constructed on pilings so that normal ventilation will keep the permafrost undisturbed. Roads and airstrips use insulation techniques which tend to prevent melting of the permafrost. Provision of services is difficult for sources of year-round water supply are scarce and normal methods of sewage disposal are ineffective because of the impervious nature of the frozen ground. Water mains and sewers in urban communities have to be placed in specially constructed utilidors which are above ground. While technology can overcome the obstacles presented by permafrost, the solutions it offers are expensive.

The *Queen Elizabeth Islands* consist of Cambrian to upper Devonian rocks which were first deformed during the late Silurian Period and again in the late Devonian. Folding was intense and erosion considerable. As as result of these two periods of orogeny and a later one in the Tertiary, the islands are characterized by fold mountains. Research into their structure is still continuing.

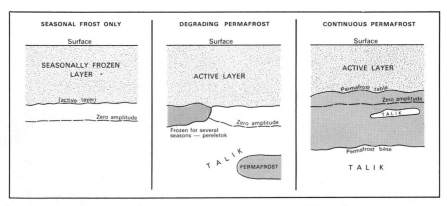

Figure 9.10 Terms Used in the Description of Permafrost
Talik is an unfrozen layer within the permafrost.

Figure 9.11 Trees Affected by Permafrost
Because of the permafrost, the trees do not develop deep roots and are easily blown over when exposed to strong winds.

Figure 9.12 Garage at Hay River
The sag of this building is not due to poor construction but to the melting of the permafrost layer underneath it.

Figure 9.13 Inuvik, N.W.T.
There are several large modern buildings in the town of Inuvik. They are served by aboveground "utilidor lines" which contain the water mains and sewage lines

Figure 9.14 Oil Tank at Inuvik
As the permafrost melts, it poses problems for large structures such as oil storage tanks.

Climate

The Canadian Northland region has a characteristically polar continental climate. Long, dark, dry, and extremely cold winters prevail, while summers are short, cloudy, cool, and wet. The fundamental control of climate in the Arctic is its position or latitude on the earth. North of the Arctic Circle there is a lengthy period when the terrain receives no sunlight yet continues to radiate what little heat it has. During the summer there is continuous daylight, but the angle of the sun is low and temperatures rise slowly. Cold seas filled with melting ice retard the rate of temperature rise in summer and produce cool moist air masses. Another control of the climate is that of *albedo*, the reflection of solar insolation from the earth's surface. According to Larsson, albedo rates are high in the Arctic until the snow cover melts and sea ice begins to puddle. This does not occur until June and by September the higher albedo rates again prevail. This means that much of the sun's energy received during the period of high albedo is lost by reflection back into space without influencing the immediate area.*

* P. Larsson. "The Distribution of Albedo over Arctic Surfaces". *Geographical Review*. LIII, 4 (October, 1963). p. 573.

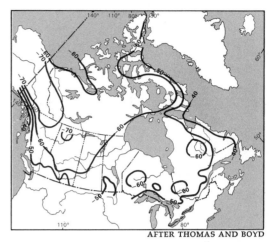
AFTER THOMAS AND BOYD

Figure 9.16 Extreme Lowest Recorded Temperatures for the Period, 1921-1950
The most extreme winter temperatures have been recorded in the Yukon where cold air can accumulate in the valleys, bringing the temperature below −60°F.

Even though winter temperatures are very low, other factors, especially wind chill, need to be considered as a distinct influence on man. Wind chill is basically an index derived from air temperature and wind velocity. It is still one of the best indications we have of "coldness" perceived by the body.* When the mean wind chill factor for the year is calculated, it is apparent that the most severe conditions exist on the Arctic Islands and that Hudson Bay acts to bend the isolines southwards. Thus, the Arctic Islands generally have lower, perceived temperatures than does the Yukon where more extreme, low temperatures have been recorded.

Vegetation

In the Northwest Territories the dominant vegetation is *tundra*, a vegetative ecosystem in which trees are absent although woody bushes are widely distributed. In the Mackenzie Valley, the Yukon, and southern fringe of the Canadian Northland, *taiga* and subarctic vegetation pre-

* M. K. Thomas and D. W. Boyd. "Wind Chill in Northern Canada". *Canadian Geographer*. 10 (1957). pp. 29-39.

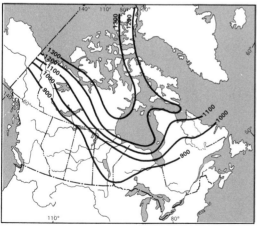
AFTER THOMAS AND BOYD

Figure 9.15 Mean Annual Wind Chill Factor
Expressed in kilogram calories per square meter per hour, the isolines indicate that wind chill is greatest along the Arctic Islands.

vail. The Canadian Northland presents one of the world's harshest environments, and most northern plants have been forced to adapt to it. The growing season is short and is frequently interrupted by frosts, while the presence of permafrost limits the amount of water and soil available for plant growth. In drier locations in the Northland the plants must adapt to severe moisture deficiencies, while in low areas where the active layer of soil is shallow, the plants must adapt to a waterlogged surface.

The Arctic Islands and the uplands of the middle and southern Arctic support lichens and rapidly maturing flowers and are in reality Arctic deserts. Tundras, both wet and dry, form two other vegetative associations. In drier areas lichens such as reindeer moss, heath tundra, and Arctic willow are common, while in wetter locations the wet tundra includes grasses, sedges, and shrubs. As an economic resource the vegetation is extremely limited.

To the south there is a bush or scrub tundra where willows, alder, and birch are common. In the Yukon and Mackenzie areas south of the treeline, a taiga forest complex occurs. While only of limited commercial value, it has served as fuel and as building material. Black spruce, lodgepole pine, and white spruce are representative species within this vegetation zone.

Fauna

In the Arctic portion of the Canadian Northland, the animals form an important part of the resource base. Despite the harsh nature of the environment, land mammals ranging in size from the small Arctic mouse (lemming) to the polar bear, caribou, and muskox manage to live there. Animals have played significant roles in the northern economy as sources of food, clothing, and articles of trade.

The polar bear spends much of its time away from land, on sea ice or in the water itself where it is close to the seal, its main source of food. While the polar bear enters into a torpid state during part of the winter, it is not a true hibernator. Polar

bears are hunted extensively by Eskimos, particularly in the eastern Arctic near Baffin Island and Southampton Island. Bears provide food for sledge dogs and skins for local use or for sale.

Of the small mammals only the ground squirrel is a true hibernator in the Canadian Arctic. For about eight months of the year this squirrel hibernates in a burrow. Unlike the squirrel, lemmings are active all year. Their numbers fluctuate drastically during a four-year cycle, and this affects the numbers of their chief enemy, the Arctic fox. Since the white winter coat of the small eight-pound Arctic fox is commercially valuable, it is trapped by the Eskimo. Thus indirectly the fortunes of the Eskimo trapper depend on the ground squirrel and the lemming. Arctic wolves are also a part of the environment. Their prey includes lemmings, Arctic hares, muskoxen, and caribou.

Muskoxen have been carefully protected from overhunting since 1917, and today there are nearly 10,000 in Canada.* These vegetarian animals graze in herds on the Arctic tundra. The Muskoxen with thick coats of fur are adapted to the rigors of climate. During the long dark winter their eyesight adapts to the twilight conditions so that they can find willow grasses and sedges under the light cover of snow.

One of the most important natural resources of the Canadian Northland is the caribou. It has always been an important year-round source of food and clothing for the northern Indians. Eskimos have relied on the caribou and, traditionally, have hunted it only during the autumn. Gigantic herds of caribou once roamed the Arctic tundra in summer and migrated southwards to winter over in the subarctic forest. As the Eskimos and Indians gained access to the weapons of the fur traders, the whole balance changed in the hunter's favor. Firearms improved the hunting, while fur trapping created a greater de-

* J. S. Tener. "The Animals that are There". *The Unbelievable Land.* Department of Northern Affairs and National Resources. Queen's Printer. Ottawa. 1967. p. 23.

mand for caribou meat for the trappers and their dog teams. Overhunting caused a rapid decline in numbers, and today there are less than 250,000 caribou in Canada.* The migration of caribou takes place in response to environmental conditions. In the Canadian Northland, the fluffy white snow of the coniferous forest of the south in winter makes it easy to obtain lichens, while the treeless tundra of the north in summer provides tender heath, sedges, and lichens. The isolated conditions of the tundra-clad hills of the north are ideal for the raising of fawns and provide some respite from the blackflies and mosquitoes. At present, there is no animal better suited to utilize the lichen forest and tundra, and with wise management the caribou can become an even more significant source of food for people residing in the region.

Of interest too are the 80 different species of birds which congregate in the Arctic. The Mackenzie Delta, Bylot Island, and Hudson Strait are the favorite breeding grounds. Each spring thousands of birds mate and attempt to raise their young to maturity before the rugged conditions of winter return. Because of the short time available for breeding, nests are crude and frequently little more than unlined hollows scraped in the tundra. Most birds migrate southward in the fall, and some travel incredible distances. One species, the Arctic tern, over-winters in the Antarctic. New species of birds are now beginning to appear in the Canadian Northland as thermal conditions continue to improve.

Ice

Two maps (Figures 9.17 and 9.18) show the average annual maximum and minimum extent of ice cover in the Arctic waters of Canada. A line running from northwestern Ellesmere Island to Prince Patrick Island marks the outer boundary of the permanent ice mass. To the south and east, however, many channels remain

---

* A. W. F. Banfield. "Specially the Caribou". The *Unbelievable Land*. The Department of Northern Affairs and National Resources. Queen's Printer. Ottawa. 1967. p. 26.

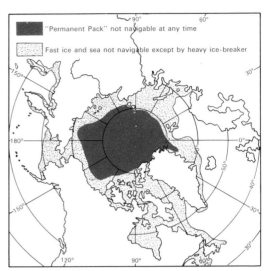

Figure 9.17 **Maximum Extent of Ice Cover, February-March**

clogged even in late summer and can be negotiated only by specially adapted vessels. Ice breakers and cargo carriers whose hulls have been specially strengthened are now able to navigate more freely, using hygrographic charts which have been made available during the past decade. The navigation season is short. Vessels usually operate in the region between June and late September. In September, 1969, the

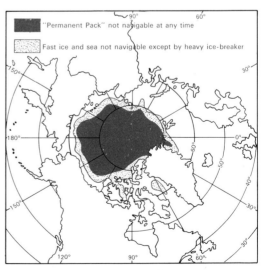

Figure 9.18 **Minimum Extent of Ice Cover, August-September**

tanker Manhattan attempted a trial run across the Arctic. While the voyage was successful, the vessel was trapped by ice in McClure Strait and the hull of the ship damaged.

Prevailing winds dictate when the southern coastal settlements can be reached by boat. Persistent onshore winds drive the loose ice into the bays and inlets and make conditions hazardous for even the most sophisticated vessels. The Arctic Islands are virtually inaccessible until the break-up in late August, and even then pack ice creates difficulties. Many of the weather stations in the high Arctic are now provisioned by aircraft rather than by boat. The prevalence of ice and the need for specially equipped vessels, the short navigation season, and the lack of return loads combine to make water transport costs high.

HUMAN OCCUPANCE OF THE CANADIAN NORTHLAND

The Eskimo

The first evidences of Eskimos in North America are those of the Cape Denbigh Flint complex in northwestern Alaska. These proto-eskimos summered along the Bering Strait and were hunters of seal and caribou. Their artifacts, which date back to 3,000 B.C., were mainly flint tools. These people were adapted to Arctic conditions and by 2,000 B.C. had spread eastward to Hudson Bay and Ungava Peninsula. In Canada, this culture is known as *Pre-Dorset*, and it persisted until 800 B.C. The

Pre-Dorset group lived in small widely scattered, seasonally nomadic bands which used skin tents in summer and lived in small villages of partly underground huts in winter. Harpoons and bows and arrows were used for game such as walrus and caribou. By about 800 B.C. Pre-Dorset had evolved into *Dorset* when more sophisticated tools were employed. Dorset persisted from 800 B.C. to 1,300 A.D., but in many areas it began to give way to the *Thule* culture group by about 900 A.D.

The Thule Eskimo culture also originated in Alaska and moved rapidly eastward. Thule Eskimos were even better adapted to the Arctic and had a full range of gear for hunting the baleen whales. Indeed, whaling is the most distinctive feature of the Thule culture, and most Thule sites have artifacts of baleen and whalebone. Thule people were classic Eskimo in race, language, and culture. Eskimo tools and weapons were utilized, including fur clothing and boots, kayaks, umiaks, sleds, sled dogs, and snow houses. However, their culture was based on the sea and the availability of whales. As the whales became scarce, the Thule Eskimos had to abandon their villages and to become more nomadic. Snow houses and snow house villages on sea ice during the winter became common as the Eskimos began to rely on seal and walrus for food and clothing.

Three factors were responsible for the breakdown of the Thule culture. Colder climate between 1650 and 1850, shallower seas as the earth's crust rebounded isosta-

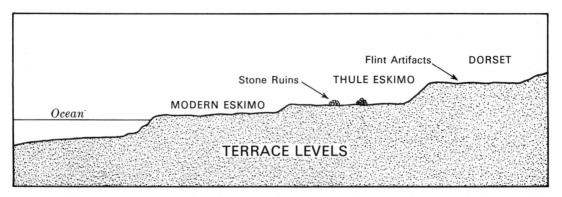

Figure 9.19 Terrace Levels and Native Cultures at Native Point, Southampton Island

tically after glaciation, and the efficiency of European whalers all combined to decrease the numbers of whale and to cause the Thule resource base to collapse. In addition, the arrival of Europeans meant that a new technology was being introduced with a consequent modification of the Thule adaption to the Arctic environment. This was particularly destructive along the coast of the Western Arctic and Mackenzie Delta. Today there are but 12,000 Eskimos in Canada, and most of them live in the East. Traces of these Eskimo cultures have been observed on terraces at Native Point, on Southampton Island.

The Indian

The northern Indians resided primarily within the subarctic life zone where the forests and the caribou are found. Unlike the Eskimos, they settled inland and were nomadic hunters and food gatherers. In the west the Indian tribes spoke dialects of the Athabaskian language, while in the east the language was Algonkian. Their social structure was based on the family unit, and larger groupings occurred only when a large-scale hunt of caribou was intended. Like the Eskimo, the northern Indian suffered a complete change in ways of living when influenced by the European and soon was in imperfect adjustment with the resource base of the subarctic.

European Exploration

Knowledge of the Arctic has been accumulated painstakingly over the centuries since the first attempt to penetrate the region in 1546 by the Cortreil Brothers. In 1576 Frobisher successfully entered the Arctic and landed in the Bay which now bears his name. Other expeditions likewise tried and had varying degrees of success. Radisson and Groseilliers in 1668 entered Hudson Bay, and their experience with fur trading led to the formation of the Hudson's Bay Company. As a result, the search for the Northwest Passage also became a search for new fur territories. Overland expeditions by men such as Samuel Hearne

and Mackenzie expanded knowledge of conditions in the Western Arctic. At the same time the British Navy sponsored a series of expeditions which culminated in the ill-fated trip by Franklin. Under his command two specially constructed vessels were sent to the Arctic in 1845, but their special equipment which included luxuries such as a barrel organ did not include snowshoes or other necessities for overland travel. Arctic ice proved superior, and the Erebus and Terror were never seen again. The search for Franklin touched off a second phase of exploration when in the span of twelve years over forty expeditions penetrated the Arctic. Franklin and his men were never found and thereafter interest in the Northwest Passage languished. By the time it was discovered by Amundsen in 1906, it was no longer of commercial interest. Successful passage in one season was finally accomplished in 1944 by the R. C. M. P. vessel St. Roch.

Interest was also high in the goal to reach the North Pole. The most successful were Peary and Cook, who in 1909 claimed to have lead different expeditions overland to the Pole. Their successes have been disputed by northern experts ever since, and the North Pole still has a strange fascination for man.* Numerous airplane flights have been made over the Pole, and recently the United States has had atomic-powered submarines surface there. Finally, in April, 1968, a team lead by Ralph Plaisted made a bumpy 820 mile dash to the Pole on four 16-horsepower Ski-Doos. Their achievement was the *first* confirmed surface expedition to reach the North Pole.

Scientific exploration can be termed the fourth phase of Arctic exploration. Great impetus was given to scientific study of the region by the Polar Year of 1882-83. Selwyn, Dawson, and McConnell pioneered in British Columbia and the Yukon, while J. B. Tyrell concentrated on the Arctic west of Hudson Bay. Knowledge about interior

---

* R. A. J. Phillips. *Canada's North.* Macmillan Company of Canada Limited. Toronto. 1967. p. 54.

Labrador was improved by A. P. Low who in his traverses accurately identified and mapped the famous iron deposits of the Labrador Trough. Since the findings of these early scientists, work has continued, particularly under the influence of the Geographical Branch and Geological Survey in Ottawa. Researchers such as Mackay, Bird, Lloyd, and Grenier have all made a profound contribution to our knowledge of Canada's Northland, and today it is still a major research frontier.

European Occupance

In the Arctic occupance by Europeans has been at best transitional. Whalers early influenced the indigenous inhabitants by providing them with artifacts such as iron pots, by introducing diseases and alcohol, and by eradicating their source of food, the whale. Fur traders were likewise a negative influence and frequently attempted to break down the existing food resource-population balance. Phillips in his book cites evidence to prove that many of the early fur traders made definite attempts to make the Eskimo and northern Indian de-

Figure 9.20 Fishing for Arctic Char

COURTESY DEPT. OF INDIAN AFFAIRS AND
NORTHERN DEVELOPMENT

pendent upon the fur-trading post.* The Hudson's Bay Company, however, evolved a more positive attitude and attempted to make the fur trade a more reliable source of income for the indigenous inhabitants. However, in recent years the decline in the fur industry has forced the organization to focus more on retail sales. This means that the Eskimo and Indian must have some source of income so that the modern necessities of life to which they have become accustomed can be purchased. This is currently a major problem. Government military bases provide some jobs but are notoriously transitory. Very little mining is carried on. The Rankin Inlet mine was successful in using native labor, but unfortunately it was forced to close when the ore ran out. Recently, attempts have been made to market Arctic Char, and this is providing some employment. In addition certain skills in carving and other art work have been recognized, but competition from foreign-made copies is cutting into the potential market. European occupance in the Arctic has generated many problems for the native residents for it has introduced consumer products with a resulting loss of the old skills of the Eskimo which were in balance with the environment. Eskimos have begun to use motorized toboggans instead of dogs and sleighs. They enjoy condiments such as tea and tobacco. They use rifles and overhunt to be able to purchase these products. The European has introduced the requirement of money which in the past was not necessary in the Eskimo's balanced subsistence economy.

In the Yukon there has been a more permanent settlement of Europeans. This area has developed its mineral resources and possesses a reasonably viable economy. The Yukon has experienced the most colorful history of any area in Canada. Fanned by the aura of gold it burst forth in 1896 as a gold mining area which gripped the imagination of the adventurous around the world. The Klondike became instantly

---

* R. A. J. Phillips. *op. cit.* p. 75.

Figure 9.21 Modern Transportation in the Arctic

famous, and thousands attempted to reach it. Dawson City sprang up as a result of the entrepreneurship of Joseph Leduc, and by January, 1898, it contained 5,000 people. Such was the rush that when the human avalanche reached Dawson on June 8, 1898, the population of the community doubled overnight. It has been estimated that a hundred thousand people set out on the Klondike Trail via the Chilcoot Pass or from Skagway via the White Pass. Both were difficult for each person had to bring one ton of provisions before he could gain entry to the Yukon. Few, however, had the capital or patience to take the long easy water route from St. Micheal at the mouth of the Yukon River, 1,600 miles upstream to Dawson. By 1899 the bubble had burst, and the exodus of prospectors commenced. Dawson was left with its memories. Until recently it was the capital of the region.

Today, the future of the Yukon is still inextricably tied to the fortunes of the mineral industry. Transportation by air, the Alaska Highway, and the Yukon and White Pass Railway makes the region more accessible than in the past, when slow steady growth was recorded only in terms of the mining of minerals that had a high unit value in terms of weight. Gold and silver mining earned two million dollars annually prior to World War II. With the opening of the base metals mine at Keno other mineral resources began to be utilized. Today, the minerals output is more varied and averages 12 million dollars annually. It is expected that this will double in the 1970s as more mines are developed. As shown by Figure 9.22, many minerals are known to exist and have been explored by drilling. Gold is still mined in the Klondike, but each year its significance decreases as gold mines close and the fortunes of Dawson continue to ebb. Mayo to the south is still important as a base metals mining area, but it is much smaller than Whitehorse, the main urban center in the Yukon. Whitehorse enjoys a significant crossroads function and is the regional administrative and service center. It also has experienced growth as nearby copper mines have developed. Nearly half the

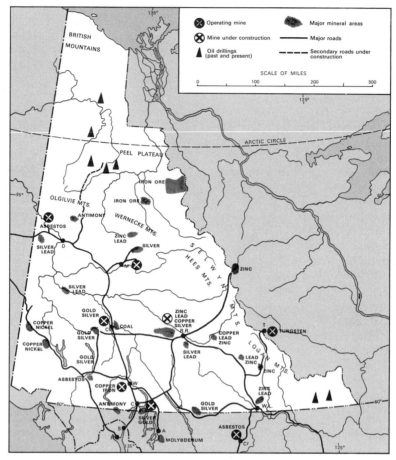

AFTER WHITE PASS & YUKON ROUTE CO.

Figure 9.22 Mineral Resources and Mining in the Yukon

A	Atlin	D	Dawson	S	Skagway
C	Carcross	H	Haines	T	Tungsten
Cr	Cassier	M	Mayo	W	Whitehorse
Cs	Carmacks	R.R.	Ross River	W.L.	Watson Lake

population of the Yukon lives in or near this small community of 4,400. Located at Mile 918 on the Alaska Highway, it boasts radio, television, municipal water and sewers, and two newspapers.

Like all northern towns, it also has a serious problem with squatters congregating around the edge of town on the dangerous portions of the river flats. Unlike southern Canadian cities, where the low income group resides close to the CBD, Whitehorse is typical of the north where low income groups are pushed to the periphery. In a study by Lotz it has been shown that the squatters represent about one-third of the population of Whitehorse.* As they do not pay municipal taxes, and draw heavily on the welfare resources of the community, they do pose a problem for municipal authorities. Yet the lower income groups have little choice other than to become squatters in the face of the temporary nature of the jobs and the high cost of establishing permanent residence in the area.

* J. R. Lotz. "Northern Settlements and the Squatter Problem". *north* XI, 6 (December, 1964). pp. 24-33.

The Mackenzie portion of Canada's Northland has developed quite a stable economy. European occupance commenced with the fur trade after Mackenzie made his traverse to the Delta. Many fur-trading posts were established, but all too frequently these were transient, and only the few which were well situated near water transportation achieved any degree of permanency. Until 1920 the fur trade was virtually the only industry in the region; however, in that year oil was discovered near Fort Norman, and the resource base broadened immediately. Today trapping ranks third in value of production, following minerals and fisheries. Synthetic fur fabrics, lower cash return from trapping, and cyclic fluctuations of animal populations have all worked against the fur industry.*

Inland commercial fishing was established on Great Slave Lake in 1945. The estimated potential is now about 18 million pounds annually, and it is currently the greatest single producer of whitefish and lake trout in Canada. The opening of the all-weather Mackenzie highway has made possible the use of refrigerated trucks, and more markets are now accessible. It is likely that this renewable resource will continue to generate income for the region for some time to come.

Even more significant is the development of the base metals resource at Pine Point. Formerly, only high value, low bulk minerals such as gold from Yellowknife and pitchblende from Port Radium could be mined and transported economically to markets in the ecumene of Canada. The Pine Point deposits form one of Canada's largest known reserves of lead and zinc, the proven reserves exceeding 17 million tons. Although exploration was completed in 1955, the property was not developed fully until satisfactory transportation arrangements had been made. These "satisfactory arrangements" commenced in 1961 when Parliament gave assent to the con-

struction of the Great Slave Lake Railway.* The 400-mile rail line cost more than 66 million dollars and was completed in 1966. The concentrated ore is shipped by rail to Trail, British Columbia, for final processing, and the mining company is committed to ship 215,000 tons of concentrates annually over the Great Slave Lake Railway. To produce this amount, more than 3,000 tons of ore must be mined daily. In addition to rail facilities, an all-weather road to Hay River, a 10 million dollar hydro-electric power plant at Twin Falls, and a new planned community to serve the mine workers all were necessary before mining could begin.

Petroleum was discovered at Norman Wells in 1920 and used to supply local needs. In 1942 the "Canol Project" was initiated to support military activities in the Yukon and Alaska. Sixty wells were drilled, and a pipeline was constructed to Whitehorse where a refinery was built. In 1942-45 almost 2,000,000 barrels of oil were produced. At the end of the war the pipeline was abandoned. Norman Wells continues to supply the needs of the Mackenzie Valley with about 600,000 barrels of oil annually.

PROBLEMS IN DEVELOPING THE CANADIAN NORTHLAND

Population

One of the major difficulties in the Northland is the dearth of people. As shown by Figure 9.23, most of the settlement is confined to isolated pockets in the Yukon and Mackenzie Districts. Elsewhere, few settlements exceed 200 persons; hence, it is difficult for communities to develop viable economic structures. Most of the isolated settlements must rely strictly on the local resource base and infusions of government money.

Agriculture

Food resources in the Canadian Northland are limited. The caribou once func-

---

* W. C. Wonders. "Economic Change in the Mackenzie Valley Area". *Canadian Geographical Journal.* LXIII, 4 (October, 1961). pp. 139-147.

* Consolidated Mining and Smelting Company of Canada. "Mining at Pine Point, N.W.T." *north.* IX, 3 (May-June, 1964). pp. 5-13.

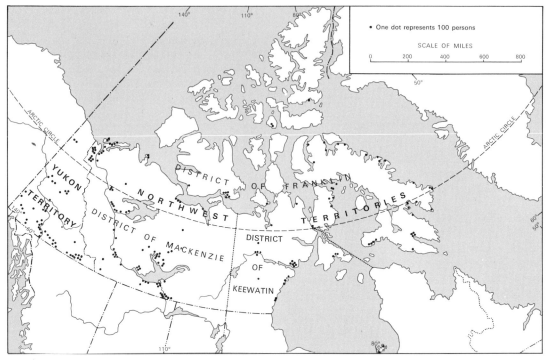

Figure 9.23 Distribution of Population in the Canadian Northland, 1961

tioned as a major source of food, but today they are in limited supply. Commercial agriculture is extremely limited. Vegetables can be grown north of the Arctic Circle, and for years there was a famous vegetable garden at the Aklavik mission. For a time there was even a small dairy herd at Tuktoyaktuk.* Permafrost poses a problem, but once it is thawed so that the active layer extends below four feet, vegetable crops such as peas, potatoes, cabbage, and lettuce do quite well. Plastic-covered green houses are used to start the vegetables from seed in April, and by mid-June the plants can be transplanted into the garden plots. The long days promote rapid growth, and harvest is accomplished in late August.

Research is continuing, and it has recently been discovered that strawberries can be grown successfully in centers such as Inuvik.** However, in areas which can

---

* G. Taylor. *Canada*. Methuen & Company. London. 1947.
** F. S. Nowosad. "Growing Vegetables on Permafrost". *north*. X, 4 (July-August, 1963).

be easily reached, such as the Yukon, the costs of production make competition with foodstuffs imported from the more temperate parts of Canada difficult. As a result, large areas in the Yukon and Mackenzie Districts have not been developed for agriculture despite their potential.

Communications

The physical environment of the Canadian Northland has always made communication a difficult task. Modern technology, particularly the airplane and radio, make penetration much easier but impose certain limitations of cost. During the hostilities of World War II air bases were established, and after that time various communication lines such as the DEW line were put into operation. Both, however, were of limited value in developing the economy of the region.

Communication by land is essential to the growth of the region. This has long been recognized, and in 1960 the federal

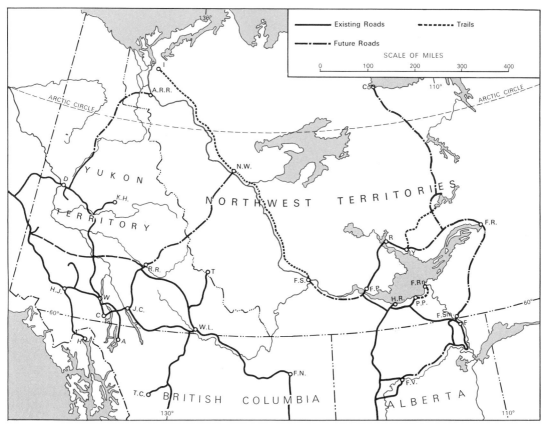

Figure 9.24 Roads in the Canadian Northland

A	Atlin	F.S.	Fort Simpson	P.P.	Pine Point
A.R.R.	Arctic Red River	F.Sm.	Fort Smith	R	Rae
C	Carcross	F.V.	Fort Vermilion	R.R.	Ross River
Co	Coppermine	H	Haines	T	Tungsten
D	Dawson	H.J.	Haines Junction	T.C.	Telegraph Creek
F	Fort Fitzgerald	H.R.	Hay River	W	Whitehorse
F.N.	Fort Nelson	I	Inuvik	W.L.	Watson Lake
F.P.	Fort Providence	J.C.	Johnson's Crossing	Y	Yellowknife
F.R.	Fort Reliance	K.H.	Keno Hill		
F.Rn.	Fort Resolution	N.W.	Norman Wells		

government announced the "Roads to Resources Program". At that time, effort was concentrated upon the improvement of the Mackenzie Highway from Grimshaw, Alberta to Hay River, N. W. T., and on the construction of the Yellowknife Highway. Subsequently, attention was focused on the rail line to Pine Point. In 1965, the Department of Northern Affairs announced a new road-building program. This was to concentrate on the Yukon and Mackenzie Districts and called for an average expenditure of $10,000,000 annually. A new highway to connect Fort Smith with Hay River has been completed, as has an area development road from Ross River to Carmacks in the Yukon. Studies have been made regarding future roads, but it will be a long time before business and commerce cease to rely on the Mackenzie River as the artery of the Northwest Territories. Elsewhere, much of the transportation is by air, and this is not likely to change in the near future.

BIBLIOGRAPHY

Banfield, A. W. F. "Specially the Caribou". *The Unbelievable Land*. Department of Northern Affairs and National Resources. Queen's Printer. Ottawa. 1967.

Bird, J. B. *The Physiography of Arctic Canada*. Johns Hopkins Press. Baltimore. 1967.

Brown, R. J. E. "A Review of Permafrost Investigations in Canada". *Canadian Geographer*. VI, 3-4 (1962). pp. 162-165.

————. "Permafrost Map of Canada". *Canadian Geographical Journal*. LXXVIII, 2 (February, 1968). pp. 56-63.

Cook, Frank A. "Additional Notes on Mud Circles at Resolute Bay, N.W.T.". *Canadian Geographer*. 8 (1956). p. 9.

Fraser, J. Keith. "Physiographic Notes on Features in the Mackenzie Delta Area". *Canadian Geographer*. 8 (1956). p. 18.

Henoch, W. E. S. "Observations of Mackenzie River Discharge". *Canadian Geographer*. 15 (1960). pp. 44-49.

Jenness, D. "Eskimo Art". *Geographical Review* XII, 3 (July, 1922). pp. 161-174.

Jenness, John L. "Erosive Forces in the Physiography of Western Arctic Canada". *Geographical Review*. XLII, 2 (April, 1952). pp. 238-252.

Larsson, P. "The Distribution of Albedo over Arctic Surfaces". *Geographical Review*. LIII, 4 (October, 1963). pp. 572-579.

Lotz, J. R. "Northern Settlements and the Squatter Problem". *north*. XI, 6 (December, 1964). pp. 24-33.

Lloyd, Trevor. "Map of the Distribution of Eskimos and Native Greenlanders in North America". *Canadian Geographer*. 13 (1959). pp. 41-43.

MacKay, J. R. *The Mackenzie Delta Area, N.W.T.* Canada Department of Mines and Technical Surveys. Geographical Branch. Memoir VIII. Ottawa. 1963.

Nowosad, F. S. "Growing Vegetables on Permafrost". *north*. X, 4 (July-August, 1963).

Phillips, R. A. J. *Canada's North*. The Macmillan Company of Canada Limited. Toronto. 1967.

Sanderson, Marie. "Drought in the Canadian Northwest". *Geographical Review*. XXXVIII, 3 (1948). pp. 289-299.

Thomas, M. K. and Boyd, D. W. "Wind Chill in Northern Canada". *Canadian Geographer*. 10 (1957). p. 29.

Stager, K. J. "Progress Report on Analysis of Characteristics of Distribution of Pingos East of Mackenzie Delta". *Canadian Geographer*. 7 (1956). pp. 13-19.

Tener, J. S. "The Animals That Are There". *The Unbelievable Land*. Department of Northern Affairs and National Resources. Queen's Printer. Ottawa. 1967.

Wonders, W. C. "Roads and Winter Roads in the Mackenzie Valley Area". *Occasional Papers in Geography*. No. 3 (1962). pp. 1-18.

————. "Economic Change in the Mackenzie Valley Area". *Canadian Geographical Journal*. LXIII, 4 (October, 1961). pp. 139-147.

Transportation

10 The immense size of Canada has led to a natural division of the country into a series of regions which have achieved regional identity along provincial lines. Recent Federal-Provincial conferences have emphasized these divisions very strongly during the past few years. Transportation has served to bind these regions together into the coherent whole known as Canada. Regions such as the Prairies are linked to the rest of Canada and, for that matter, the world, by means of a sophisticated transportation network. There is no doubt that the economic, social, political, and administrative functions of Canada have in a large measure developed and continue to operate on the basis of adequate transportation services. Other media for communication of data, statements, ideas, and news have developed enormously, especially in the last two decades as telecommunications, micro-wave relay systems, and telephone linkages have become a reality. However, the ability of citizens to circulate, migrate, achieve personal contact, and conduct trade in actual commodities is incontestably dependent upon the existence of transportation facilities.

ECONOMICS

The economics of commodity supply involves three important sectors: the cost of production at the source, transportation to the market, and the facilities for sale and distribution. This is, of course, an extremely simplistic analysis which holds true only in the case of some natural raw materials such as iron ore or wheat. In most cases, however, the process is much more complicated, transportation facilities being brought into play a number of times in the transition from the original producers to the final user or consumer.

Under such a system the final price paid for the commodity includes a great deal of transfer costs; in some cases perhaps such costs constitute the major fraction, especially if great distances have had to be overcome. The natural tendency of the buyer is to seek out the seller with the lowest cost price. Failing any significant differential in original costs, the buyer is liable to choose the nearest producer, or in any event, the producer whose products could be transported as cheaply as possible to the buyer. The producer on his part tries to sell in the nearest market, or the one which may be reached by way of the cheapest transportation facilities, thereby ensuring himself a competitive position and a possibility of profit over production costs.

Such a system can operate only if the buyer and seller can make contact, can in actuality transfer the goods from the possession of one to the other. Such a system is possible only if the value of the transaction is great enough to afford the establishment of the means of transfer. It could be so if the bulk of the commodity were negligible and its value high. A second case could be that of a bulky commodity of low unit value in a transaction which was to continue over a long period of time during which a vast number of commodity units was to be transferred. Special cases may, of course, be demonstrated to have occurred in history and to be present in the modern economy of Canada, and indeed they have their place. The overall development of the Canadian ecumene has required, and has been serviced by, much more general and complicated systems in which the individual commodity, transaction, and even traveler are completely lost from view, being replaced by the statistics of an enormously complicated economic system.

Pure economics, however, does not and never did govern the development of a transportation system. Under an imperial system such as obtained during the early years of settlement in Canada, the Home Government provided for the development of transportation systems for the purposes of defense and administration as well as for the encouragement of economic development. In Canada this meant that the construction of port facilities was even more important than the building of fortifications. Canals such as the Lachine, Rideau, and Welland and, later, those of the St. Lawrence had objectives for both defense and civilian transportation. The early roads, often built largely by military detachments, had an eye to possible movements of troops although they served also to facilitate the influx of settlers to new lands. Later the Colonization Roads reached back into the interior from ports along Lake Ontario in order to exploit the timber resources and to open up the land for settlement. Though started late and never actually completed, the Trent Canal had a similar purpose.

Few of these investments were made under strict business accounting principles which demand that an enterprise produce an adequate income and provide funds for repair and eventual replacement. Even where they purported to be self-supporting, as in the case of the first Welland Canal and the toll roads, they were unable to perpetuate themselves as institutions of free enterprise and were eventually incor-

porated into the public transportation systems. The principle behind these developments was that the provision and maintenance of the route, the establishment of the visible, physical, geographical pattern, was a matter of public enterprise with very important political overtones, while the commercial users, for the most part, remained within the private sector. It would be interesting to speculate upon the pattern that might have emerged had these influences been allowed full play for several decades. Instead, however, a new method of transportation appeared to absorb the attention of both politicians and entrepreneurs. The railway age began.

THE RAILWAYS

The first railway in Canada was opened in 1836 from LaPrairie on the St. Lawrence opposite the city of Montreal, and St. Jean on the Richelieu, thus providing a portage for goods and passengers on the route between Montreal and New York. About the same time a railway was built in Nova Scotia to haul coal from Stellarton to Pictou Harbor. Progress was slow, however, and by 1850 there were only 66 miles of railway in the whole of British North America, whereas in the United States more than 7,300 miles were in operation. This was an effective demonstration that economic wealth and railway development went hand in hand.

Railways at first were not thought of as successful competition for water transportation. Instead they were built as feeders to port areas, as portages where canals could not be built, and as alternative transportation in Canada's cold winters. Such ideas as well as the lack of ready capital probably had much to do with the slow development of railways.

The middle of the nineteenth century marked the beginning of the railway boom in the United States. The early 1850s saw the first of the "trunk lines" operated between the Atlantic ports and the new cities on the Great Lakes and the Ohio River. The later 1850s saw an introduction of the steel rail and heavier rolling stock. Inevitably the enthusiasm for railways spilled over into Canada. Between 1850 and 1860 the Grand Trunk was completed from Sarnia to Rivière-du-Loup, linking Montreal and Toronto as well as many other Canadian cities. An outlet to a winter port on the Atlantic was provided by a line from Montreal to Portland, Maine. The Northern Railway linked Toronto and Collingwood in 1855, thus providing a direct link to the Upper Great Lakes. Confederation gave strong impetus to railway building in Canada. The Intercolonial from Halifax to Rivière-du-Loup was completed in 1876, thus linking the Maritime Provinces with Upper Canada. The link with the West was also forged; the Canadian Pacific, begun in 1874, was completed in 1885. Thus Canada was given railway service from coast to coast only 16 years after such service had been inaugurated in the United States.

Halifax, Saint John, Quebec, Montreal, and Toronto were well-established cities before they obtained railway services, and presumably they would have continued to grow without them. However, it is impossible to think of North Bay, Sudbury, Thunder Bay, Winnipeg, Regina, Saskatoon, Calgary, and Edmonton ever having become cities without the help of railways. The settlement of the western provinces and indeed of Northern Ontario and Quebec is almost completely the product of the railway age.

Railways were overbuilt. Not content with one transcontinental system, two more were initiated in the early part of this century, but they came to serious trouble during World War I and the years which immediately followed. The advantageously placed C. P. R. was able to maintain itself but most of the other lines had to be taken over by the government, becoming the Canadian Government Railways (C. G. R.), and later the Canadian National Railways (C. N. R.). Some mileage was completed during the 1920s, notably the line to Churchill on Hudson Bay. For 25 years thereafter almost no new lines were built in Canada. Indeed many services were curtailed and much track actually abandoned. However, because so many areas were utterly dependent upon the railways it was not feasible to discontinue all non-profitable lines and many of them remain in operation.

Since 1950 a number of short lines in Labrador, Quebec, Northern Ontario, and Manitoba have been built to new mining areas. British Columbia's Pacific Great Eastern has been extended to the Peace River district. Recently a railway has been completed from the Peace River to Pine Point in the Northwest Territories and the Alberta Resources Railway has provided a short cut from the Peace River area to the C. N. R. at Hinton. It is evident that Canadians still believe in railways for access to new sites of resource utilization but they do not necessarily believe in railways as

Table 10.1   Railway Passenger and Freight Service *

	1939	1946	1956	1966
Passengers Carried (000)	20,482	43,405	26,071	23,195
Passenger Miles Traveled (000,000)	1,752	4,649	2,907	2,587
Average Journey (miles)	86	108	112	112
Passenger miles per mile of line	41,053	109,773	64,934	58,619
Freight Carried (000 tons)	84,631	139,256	189,608	206,787
Freight ton-miles (000,000)	31,465	55,310	78,819	95,097
Average Haul (miles)	372	397	420	463
Freight ton-miles per mile of line (000)	737	1,306	1,760	2,154

* Source: Canada Year Book.

moneymaking ventures in themselves. Rather, they regard them strictly as service facilities, carefully controlled with respect to both operations and rate-making when freight services are really significant, and subsidized by the central government when controlled freight rates fail to supply full support.

Railway services are not proportionately as important as they once were. Main line mileage is about 43,000, down slightly from the peak of 44,200 reached in 1959. During the 1950s, however, passenger traffic declined by about one-third, while freight service remained static. Both recorded operational low points in 1961. Since then there has been some improvement. In 1966, 23.2 million passengers were carried 2,587 million miles, an average of 112 miles per journey. About 207 million tons of freight were hauled a total of 95,000 million ton-miles, an average of 460 miles per ton. Freight hauls thus seem to be about four times as long as passenger journeys. Of the commodities carried in 1966, mine products accounted for 40.0 per cent, manufactured goods 32.0, agricultural products 17.1 per cent, forest products 9.7 per cent, animal products 0.7 per cent, and general freight in less than carload lots 0.5 per cent. These proportions have changed little in recent years.

In many respects Canadian railway services appear to have reached an equilibrium with their environment. As population increases and as freight shipments increase because of increased production, railways are able to handle the situation by modernizing their equipment. They are under intense competition, however. Long-haul passengers increasingly take to the air, while both short-haul passengers and short-haul freight are being accommodated on improved highways. Even the building of the St. Lawrence Seaway made a considerable change in the pattern of railway service. Nevertheless, the railway systems of Canada continue to mark out the Canadian ecumene most effectively and their operations continue to serve the purposes of national unity and national prosperity.

For almost a hundred years the railway pattern has received more emphasis than almost any other aspect of Canadian geography.

HIGHWAY TRANSPORTATION

Throughout the history of civilization the highway has been important in the economic and political activities of nations. The Roman Empire was knit together by the famous Roman roads, some of which are still in existence. The Persians and Egyptians also built roads. The Inca empire of South America had a road system. Medieval Europe did little to improve its road system but the rise of new nations, new trade relations, and the improvement of horse-drawn carriages led a renewal of road-building. Toward the end of the eighteenth century a real breakthrough was achieved by McAdam. But shortly thereafter the railway was invented and road-building suffered an eclipse for nearly a century.

Early roads in Canada were merely trails cut through the forest; the surface was the soil with little levelling done and only a few of the stumps removed. Swampy areas were sometimes crossed by corduroy made from cedar poles or small logs laid side by side. The first roads were military roads, colonization roads, and portage roads. Extensive settlement brought with it the attempt at a uniform, geometric road net to give access to all parcels of settled land.

But in the same way that railways were thought at first to be merely feeders for ports and water carriers, so roads in their turn became subordinate to railways. Tiny networks of graded and gravelled roads fanned out from rail terminals and way stations to gather freight and passenger traffic, while between the settled areas were tracts of "backwoods" with almost impassible roads. Winter travel with sleighs on packed snow roads was much easier than summer travel.

With the twentieth century came the automobile, but only in the driest part of the summer could the early Canadian motorist venture to drive from one town or city to another. A journey of a hundred miles might well take a whole day of herculean effort. But as automobiles increased in number and reliability, drivers took up the cry, "lift us out of the mud". Thus was initiated a campaign of highway improvement which is still being waged as more and still more cars take to the roads.

Canadian road patterns vary greatly. In the west the original land surveys provided a regular net of road allowances, oriented north-south and east-west. In most areas a block contains two sections, each a mile square. In general, each square mile has a road allowance on three sides; each block of two square miles has six miles of road which it shares with neighboring blocks. If the province of Saskatchewan were all laid out in this way it would have 330,000 miles of road. Since somewhat less than half of the province is settled and even in settled areas not all of the road allowances have been opened, Saskatchewan has only about 124,000 miles of road; however, this is 28 per cent of all the roads in Canada. The other Prairie Provinces are equally well supplied within their settled areas. It was an accepted principle of economic geography at the time of settlement that no farm should lack a road frontage. It is now an accepted fact that the upkeep of so much road is far too costly, and that only a small part of it can be given a permanent surface.

The road nets of Southern Ontario were also regularly laid out, but a number of patterns were used. Survey blocks were usually rectangular; but in some townships they might contain 1,000 acres, in others there might be 1,200 acres, while in still others only 400 acres per block. Thus Huron county, where most of the blocks have an area of 1,000 acres, has 2,000 miles of road in an area of 1,295 square miles, while Lincoln county has 1,050 miles of road in 332 square miles mainly because it is laid out in blocks of 400 acres. In Northern Ontario two survey systems were used: in one, the blocks have an area of one square mile, while in the other they have an area of 1,800 acres. There are corresponding differences in the length of the road net.

In Quebec the farm lots are characteristically narrow and deep; many farms can thus find frontage on the main road which takes on some of the character of a village street. Even in those areas having townships like those of Ontario, lots are long and narrow so that fewer miles of road are needed.

In the Atlantic Provinces and British Columbia, settlement is often closely correlated with shorelines and river valleys. Main roads usually obey the same physical controls and may have little resemblance to land survey patterns. On the other hand, in some areas regularly spaced road nets are found.

Canada has almost 500,000 miles of highways, rural roads, and urban streets, of which 19 per cent is paved and 55 per cent has gravel surface. In 1939, 3 per cent was paved and 18 per cent gravelled.

The really important statistics, however, are those which pertain to traffic which is

Table 10.2   Motor Vehicle Registration *

Year	Passenger Cars	Commercial Cars, Trucks and other vehicles	Buses	Motorcycles	Total
1939	1,190,021	234,258	2,644	12,322	1,439,245
1946	1,234,006	365,506	5,788	17,163	1,622,463
1957	3,383,419	1,065,096	13,666	34,910	4,497,091
1966	5,499,527	1,395,126	32,674	107,934	7,035,261

* Source: Canada Year Book.

Figure 10.1 A "Spaghetti Junction"
This interchange is part of the 401 complex in Toronto.

increasing very rapidly. Motor vehicle registrations in Canada have been multiplied by five since 1939, numbering more than 7,000,000 in 1966 (Table 10.2). Thus there are at present about 15 motor vehicles for every mile of road, and they are increasing at a rate of about 5 per cent per year. In 1966 roughly 78 per cent was passenger cars and 20 per cent commercial cars and trucks. Despite their smaller number commercial vehicles make the greatest use of the highways. In a study of conditions in 1953 it was estimated that 55.1 per cent of all direct costs of highway use pertained to use by trucks, 36.3 per cent to use by passenger cars, 51.1 per cent to use by taxi cabs, and 3.5 per cent to use by buses.* It

* J. C. Lessard. *Transportation in Canada.* Queen's Printer. Ottawa. 1956.

was surmised that each passenger car averaged 8,000 miles per year and had a life of ten years. It is difficult to estimate the loading of passenger cars but perhaps an average gross of 15,000 ton-miles per year is reasonable. On the other hand, the average truck had a gross of about 45,000 ton-miles, and a transport a gross of 375,-000 ton-miles. Thus each commercial vehicle averaged three times as much use of the highway as a private car, while each truck or transport for hire made about 25 times as much use.

Considerable interest is attached to the idea of competition between railway and highway facilities. In 1958 the total freight carried by common and contract carriers was about 54,000,000 tons, while 154,000,-000 tons were carried by Canadian railways. Highway carriers received $292,-000,000 in freight revenue ($5.40 per ton); railway carriers received $995,325,-000 ($6.45 per ton). In 1966 the highway carriers had a freight revenue of $652,000,-000. Railways carried 207,000,000 tons of freight and received $1,330,000,000 ($6.40 per ton). While statistics are incomplete, it seems fairly obvious that highway carriage of freight has been increasing more rapidly than railway carriage.

There is also competition in passenger traffic. In 1958 highway buses carried almost 69,000,000 passengers and received an average of $0.68 per passenger. Railways carried 21,000,000 passengers, with average receipts of $3.62 per passenger. Rail journeys averaged more than 100 miles, bus journeys hardly 20.

In 1966 the railways carried more than 23,000,000 passengers with average receipts of $2.71 per passenger. Highway buses carried 64,000,000 passengers and received about $1.26 per passenger. The total number of buses has increased from 2,300 in 1958 to 2,750 in 1966, while bus travel has grown from 95,000,000 miles to more than 125,000,000 miles.

One concludes that highway facilities and rail facilities are in competition for certain types of freight and that the highway is winning. In the passenger field there is little competition but bus routes are being increased.

THE ST. LAWRENCE SEAWAY

North America is the only continent that has a navigable fresh-water channel by which vessels of 10,000 tons to 25,000 tons may penetrate deep into the interior, while Canada is the only country where so much of the total economy is closely associated with such a waterway. By means of the Great Lakes—St. Lawrence system ships can travel 2,300 miles into the interior of the continent. In these and other ways as well the waterway is unique among the phenomena of economic geography. But even before its development into a modern transportation facility, in fact, from the

date of its discovery by Europeans, its influence has been significant. The fact that the St. Lawrence flows eastward to the Atlantic instead of northward or southward made it a natural corridor for the exploration, exploitation, and finally the settlement of the interior regions. It is not too much to claim that the existence of the St. Lawrence is itself the prime factor of the environment which led to the formation of the Canadian political unit, just as it remains one of the prime factors in the country's present economic development.

The navigable waterway, however, is international. It was built by the engineering skill of two nations, Canada and the United States. Throughout much of its length it forms the boundary between them. It is also, and very fortunately, a source of power shared by the industries of both nations. From the surface of Lake Superior to sea level the total drop is approximately 600 feet. At four locations, Sault Ste. Marie, Niagara Falls, Cornwall, and Beauharnois, generating stations have been constructed capable of providing more than 7,500,000 kw of electric energy.

Five immense lakes, Superior, Huron, Michigan, Erie, and Ontario, are included in this great water system, as well as the narrow links between them. Between Lake Superior and Lake Huron, St. Marys River drops through a 20-foot rapid thus necessitating a bypassing canal and providing an opportune power site. The great flow of traffic passing this point caused the building of not one but five canals, one on the Canadian side and four on the American side. More than 100,000,000 tons of freight may pass these locks in a single year. Lake Huron and Lake Michigan have the same water level and are joined by a strait rather than a river. Lake Michigan is entirely within the United States so much of its traffic is of little consequence to Canada. However, it is the route to Chicago, one of the ports that contribute significantly to seaway traffic. Between Lake Huron and Lake Erie there is less than ten feet of difference in elevation through the

St. Clair River, Lake St. Clair, and Detroit River, and some channel dredging must be done to maintain a 27-foot depth in the navigation channel.

The St. Lawrence Seaway is not charged with the maintenance of navigation in the Upper Lakes but only with the route from Lake Erie to Montreal Harbor. From Lake Erie to Lake Ontario there is a difference in elevation of 326 feet, including the straight drop of 160 feet at Niagara Falls and the rapids both above and below the cataract. To get around the falls, the first Welland Canal was opened in 1829. Since then the canal has been enlarged a number of times, culminating in 1931 with the present Welland Ship Canal which has eight great locks to take the vessels up and down the Niagara Escarpment. Thus the large grain, ore, and coal carriers of the Upper Lakes were able to ply Lake Ontario.

The waterway from Lake Ontario to Montreal Harbor was a bottleneck. The old

canals had 22 locks, having controlling dimensions of 270 feet in length, 43.6 feet in width, and 14 feet in depth, thus keeping the Great Lakes fleet bottled in while most ocean-going vessels were effectively locked out. On June 26, 1959, the St. Lawrence Seaway was officially opened. It has seven locks, each 766 feet long, 80 feet wide, and 30 feet deep, allowing large ocean vessels to ascend to the lakes and permitting large lake boats to reach Montreal Harbor and the ports of the lower St. Lawrence.

What this means in terms of economic geography only time will tell. The accompanying table, however, shows the trend of traffic on the seaway route over the past thirty years. Through traffic on the St. Lawrence and Welland canals has increased enormously. Great Lakes ports may now receive full cargoes of general freight from overseas ports, while products of the immensely varied industries of

Figure 10.2 Toronto Harbor
This is an aerial view of Toronto, looking east, and it includes Toronto Islands and Island Airport in the foreground and the Toronto Dominion Bank complex in the upper left part (June, 1968).

COURTESY TORONTO HARBOR COMMISSIONERS

Canadian and American cities may find wide outlets in many parts of the world. Iron ore from Quebec and Labrador may be shipped directly to Hamilton and Lake Erie steel mills. Wheat from Lakehead elevators may be taken by lakers to Montreal, Quebec, or Baie Comeau, or by ocean freighters to any port in Europe. The Great Lakes have not become a North American Mediterranean Sea exactly, for there is still the unsolved problem of winter navigation.

Available statistics do not allow us to make a full analysis of regional effects, but Lake Ontario affords a rather striking case. Ever since the opening of the Welland Ship Canal more cargo tonnage has been unloaded at Lake Ontario ports than has been shipped out of them (Table 10.3). Most of this has been from the Upper Lake ports, with a small (and sometimes very small) part from downriver and overseas. In 1966 about 21,000,000 tons of freight moved into the Lake Ontario basin, while 4,400,000 tons moved out of it, a total of over 25,400,000 tons. Almost 22,000,000 tons are handled by the ports in the Toronto-Hamilton area. Half of this is accounted for by iron ore and coal.

While massive and increasing streams of through freight use the locks of the St.

COURTESY IRON ORE COMPANY OF CANADA

Figure 10.3 Sept Iles Ore Docks
Transportation by water is an easy means of shipment for bulky commodities such as iron ore.

Lawrence Seaway, they have very little influence upon the economy of the Ontario basin. By providing access to distant sources of raw materials, however, the Seaway is exerting a profound influence on the local economy.

Table 10.3   Traffic on the St. Lawrence and Welland Ship Canals *

		St. Lawrence and Welland (tons)	Welland only (tons)	St. Lawrence only (tons)	Total Freight (tons)	Lake Ontario Difference (tons)
Upstream	1966	19,394,110	3,050,682	6,214,926	28,659,718	3,164,244
Downstream	1966	22,124,239	14,577,502	1,360,983	38,062,724	13,216,519
Totals	1966	41,518,349	17,628,184	7,575,909	66,722,442	16,380,763
Upstream	1956	3,446,229	1,623,083	2,395,177	7,464,489	772,094
Downstream	1956	3,669,712	14,327,237	3,497,075	21,494,024	10,830,162
Totals	1956	7,115,941	15,950,320	5,892,252	28,958,513	11,602,256
Upstream	1946	748,172	862,777	896,083	2,507,032	33,306
Downstream	1946	1,865,861	8,579,208	2,240,462	12,685,531	6,338,746
Totals	1946	2,614,033	9,441,985	3,136,545	15,192,563	6,372,052
Upstream	1936	1,872,306	833,865	2,323,369	5,029,540	1,489,504
Downstream	1936	2,776,073	4,954,859	1,317,076	9,048,008	3,637,783
Totals	1936	4,648,379	5,788,724	3,640,445	14,077,548	5,127,287

* Source: Canada Year Book.

AIR TRANSPORTATION

Aviation is the newest and most spectacular method of transportation, having in the quarter-century since World War II become the most influential means of maintaining contact between distant parts of the world. Its role in the development of a large country such as Canada is that of timesaver throughout the length of the developed area where regular routes and schedules may be maintained. Aviation is also the chief means whereby pioneer resource exploration and development may be undertaken in the remote and sparsely settled areas of northern Canada.

Man has always had an ambition to fly. He has envied the birds and attempted to emulate them, but even though he might construct a very good wing-apparatus, he could not develop the necessary propelling muscles. The buoyancy of the balloon was discovered and used for some purposes with success, but the problems of propulsion and direction could not be overcome. Even the dirigible, which could be propelled and directed, was not able to overcome all other hazards.

Sustained, reliable, long-distance flight became a reality with the development of a heavier-than-air, streamlined body, powered by a light-weight internal combustion engine.

The first airplane flight was made by the Wright Brothers in 1903. By 1907 France, England, and the United States were adapting airplanes to military use. In 1911 mail pouches were first sent by air although the first regular airmail service was not established until 1918. World War I, of course, caused a rapid development of military aircraft and the abilities of speed, maneuverability, and carrying capacity thus attained were rapidly put to work after the war. While in several countries postal and passenger services were inaugurated, the chief development in Canada was "bush flying", the opening up of the Northland and other remote areas. The enormous numbers of lakes on the Canadian Shield provided an almost ideal habitat for the light plane equipped with pontoons in the summer and skis in the winter.

Air traffic is devoted dominantly to the carriage of passengers and postal matter, but demands are increasing for air-express and air-freight services for light-weight commodities of high intrinsic value and for commodities that are wanted in a hurry. Thus even heavy machinery and all sorts of ordinary supplies may sometime be transported long distances in "flying boxcars". High-pedigreed cattle and race horses are often flown across the continent or the Atlantic or from North America to South America. Continued reduction in passenger rates combined with speed and safety have given the airlines much of the transcontinental and transoceanic passenger service. Even the shorter routes which are just a little too long for travel by private automobile also tend to be serviced by plane flights. Yet it is obvious that personnel carriage will not all take to the air, just as it is certain that most of the heavy, bulky commodities such as coal, iron ore, grain, lumber, and pulpwood will continue to move by surface transportation.

Regular air services in densely populated regions require good ground facilities for take-off and landing, but the building, maintenance, and regulation of airports costs a great deal of money. Therefore, as in the development of other forms of transportation, public money has been involved. As early as 1927 the federal government began to construct a series of airfields which would make continuous service possible across Canada. The scheme proceeded slowly during the 1930s but was forced to a rapid conclusion in 1940 after the outbreak of World War II. Since the war a greatly improved network of airports has been maintained by the federal Department of Transport. The increase in air traffic year by year, the increase in size of aircraft, and the change to jet propulsion have all presented great problems to the operations of major airports.

Public money also had to be provided to set up a transcontinental flight service in Canada. Early in 1936 the government of

Canada tried to get private airline operators to set up a transcontinental service but was unsuccessful. In 1937 the government established Trans-Canada Air Lines as a subsidiary of the Canadian National Railways. By and large, it has given good service and has become one of the more successful airlines of the world. As well as operating across Canada it has established routes to United States centers, Britain, and the continent of Europe. In recent years the name has been changed to Air Canada.

By refusing to co-operate in forming Trans-Canada Air Lines in 1936, the Canadian Pacific Railway Company had by no means renounced its ambition for long-distance air service. It already had a number of interests in short-distance and regional services. In 1942 these interests were amalgamated to form Canadian Pacific Airlines. However, for some years its business was confined to regional services. In 1958 it began to operate daily from Vancouver to Toronto and Montreal, and in 1967 these services were increased. Meanwhile transpacific services were inaugurated as well as services to Mediterranean countries. Canadian Pacific recently abandoned its regional role in order to concentrate on long-distance competition with Air Canada and the large airlines of other nations.

International competition is a very real factor in both the economics and the geographical pattern of air service operations. For reasons of prestige even very small and newly emergent nations have set up national airlines and, as was done in Canada for the first airline, provided the capital from national treasuries. The rights to terminal facilities within national territories are highly valued, closely controlled, and subject to hard bargaining. For every right to terminal facilities in another nation Canada must be prepared to offer equivalent facilities in Canada; hence the designation, *International Airport*, applied to airports at centers such as Montreal, Toronto, Vancouver, and a number of others. Anomalies are bound to occur in these arrangements. Most transatlantic airlines are permitted to establish terminal facilities only at Montreal, whereas the larger volume of overseas traffic originates in Toronto. In dealing with the United States, Canada is sometimes required to allow more effective and direct competition in major traffic sources than is permitted in return. There are also cases where Canadian airlines would like to establish services where there is no potential for reciprocal services. At the beginning of 1968, twenty-six foreign airlines were licensed to operate scheduled commercial air services into Canada.

In addition to the two major Canadian air services, Air Canada and Canadian Pacific, four independent air lines offer scheduled air services in Canada. These are: Eastern Provincial Airways serving the Atlantic Provinces, Eastern Quebec, and Labrador; Quebecair, with services in Quebec and Labrador; TransAir based in Winnipeg and offering services in Manitoba, Saskatchewan, Ontario, and the Northwest Territories; and Pacific Western Airlines with headquarters in Vancouver, serving British Columbia, Alberta, Saskatchewan, Yukon, and Northwest Territories.

The role of the air carrier is expanding rapidly in Canada, but it is difficult to give a simple picture of this growth. All averages are, of course, weighted by the fact that the six scheduled carriers already mentioned perform the bulk of the services. They carry about 90 per cent of all revenue paying passengers and about 70 per cent of the total freight tonnage. With these qualifications, Table 10.4 presents a summary of Canadian Civil Aviation Statistics.

The rate of growth in five years is indeed impressive. In percentage terms, the number of flights has increased by 33 per cent, flying time by 45 per cent, total mileage by 38 per cent, number of passengers by 50 per cent, and passenger miles by about 72 per cent. The amount of air freight has also grown by 55 per cent. It should be noted, too, that the role of foreign air services, while small, is growing. In 1960 they had about 4.5 per cent of the mileage and 14 per cent of the passengers; in 1966

Table 10.4   Summary of Canadian Civil Aviation Statistics *

	1961	1966
Departures	464,406	620,935
Hours flown	646,465	940,434
Average flight	1 hr. 23.5 min.	1 hr. 30 min.
Miles flown	97,577,514	135,058,819
Average flight (miles)	210	218
Passengers carried	4,950,897	7,461,687
Passengers per flight	10.7	12.0
Passenger miles	3,500,000,000	6,000,212,600
Average passenger journey (miles)	708	805
Goods carried (tons)	114,538	178,520
Goods ton-miles	———	8,649,711

* Source: Canada Year Book, 1966 and 1968.

they had 5.6 per cent of the mileage and 17 per cent of the passengers.

In geographical terms the great bulk of all air service is performed in and for the more densely populated band of territory along the southern border of the country including, of course, the connecting of this area with economically important areas in other countries. Nevertheless, it must not be forgotten that service to out-of-the-way places had a great bearing upon the beginnings of air services in Canada, and it is still required in the development of resource industries.

THE SIGNIFICANCE OF TRANSPORTATION

Modern societies and modern economies emphasize mobility of people and carriage of goods. This emphasis becomes very great indeed in countries with large areas such as Canada, especially if at the same time population is small and areas of economic enterprise are widely separated. Nevertheless, it comes as somewhat of a surprise when we consider the proportion of total wealth which is devoted to the costs of transportation. A study of this sort was made for the Gordon Commission on Canada's Economic Prospects.*

In 1953 transportation required 29 cents out of every dollar collectively spent by

* J. C. Lessard. *Transportation in Canada.* Queen's Printer. Ottawa. 1956.

the nation; by far the greater part of this was spent by the users of transportation services and only a small part by government. However, this small part had mainly to do with the provision of facilities for which costs cannot easily be apportioned. Highway services were by far the most costly, amounting to 75 per cent of the grand total, while the railways absorbed 15 per cent. At that time the costs of both railway and water transportation were declining in proportion to the total, while highway and air service costs were rising. Even considering the building of the Seaway and the construction of railways to northern resource areas in recent years, this is still the dominant trend.

Transportation problems are deeply embedded in the politics of the Canadian nation, as indeed they are in the politics of most nations. In Canada, from the very first, transportation facilities were considered to be essential in the formation and development of the national territory. Political problems are often dependent upon economic differences, and it is quite apparent that transportation costs lie at the roots of many of Canada's economic problems. At the core of these problems is the question of space relations and propinquity. And this points to the need for more intensive investigations of Canada's regional economic geography, both in itself and in the context of the commercial systems of the world.

Index

Pine Falls, Man., 289
Pine Pass, 310, 347
Pine Point, N.W.T., 367, 369
pingo, 352-354
pioneer fringe, 43, 285, 288
Plantagenet Sand Plain, 188
Podzol Soils, 266
Podzol-Tundra Soils, 266
Pointe Noire, P.Q., 148
population: Atlantic Provinces, 86-88;
    Canada, 55-62; gross population den-
    sities, Prairie Provinces, (map), 267;
    Mississaga urban and rural populations,
    232; population change in province of
    Quebec, 162; population distribution in
    British Columbia (map), 320; population
    distribution in Canadian Northland,
    (map), 368; population growth in British
    Columbia (graph), 319; population
    growth in Ontario, (table), 223; Prairie
    Provinces, 266-267; Quebec, 136, 137;
    rural population density, Prairie Prov-
    inces, (map), 267
Porcupine, Ont., 53, 181
Porcupine Basin, 350
Port Alberni, B.C., 323, 340
Port Alice, B.C., 323
Port Cartier, P.Q., 163
Port Colborne, Ont., 200
Port Hawkesbury, Ont., 106
Port Radium, N.W.T., 367
Portage la Prairie, Man., 296
Portage Mountain Dam, B.C., 347
potash, 255, 289, 292-293
potential evapotranspiration, 28, 129
Powell River, B.C., 323, 331, 340
Prairie Farm Assistance Act, 274
Prairie Farm Rehabilitation Act, 274, 282
Prairie Provinces, 7, 8, 251-306; agricul-
    tural gradients, 284; agricultural zones,
    287-289; agriculture, 273-289; changes
    in land use on Prairie farms, 276; cities,
    295-305; climate, 256-260; climatic divi-
    sions, 260-261; degree-days above 42°F
    (map), 259; exploration, 268; fallow land,
    276; farm operations, 277; forestry, 289;
    fur trade, 267-268; gross population
    densities, (map), 267; Indian settlement,
    267; industrial structure, 294; irrigation,
    280-284; January isotherms, 257; July
    isotherms, 258; land survey system, 270-
    271; landform and geology, 251-256;
    manufacturing, 293-295; mean annual
    precipitation (map), 259; mean annual
    water deficiency (map), 260; mining,
    289-293; population, 266-267; popula-
    tion distribution in 1886 (map), 51; rail-
    way pattern, 271-273; regional develop-
    ment, 305-306; rural population density,
    (map), 267; the Selkirk settlement, 269;
    settlement, 50; settlement patterns, 267-
    271; soils, 261-266; transportation, 271-
    273; vegetation, 261-266
Prairie Region (vegetation), 35

primate city, 64, 164
Prince Albert, Sask., 261, 271, 289, 296
Prince Edward Island, 1, 86-102. See Atlan-
    tic Provinces.
Prince George, B.C., 52, 334, 337, 338, 340,
    347, 348
Prince Rupert, B.C., 52, 319, 331, 346
Pugwash, N.S., 104
pulp and paper, 105-107, 142-143, 214-
    216, 323-324, 331-332, 338
Putnam Highlands, 355

QU'APPELLE RIVER, 255
Quebec, P.Q., 44, 45, 46, 48, 132, 141, 159,
    161, 162, 173-175, 373; manufacturing,
    174; settled areas in 1760 (map), 44;
    tertiary employment, 175; zones, 173
Quebec, province of, 1, 7, 8, 123-179, 243;
    agriculture, 153-158; cities, 162-177;
    climate, 127-129; economic develop-
    ment, 131-161; electric power, 151-153;
    forestry, 142-143; Gulf Shore, 178; land-
    forms, 123-127; manufacturing, 138-
    142; mining and mineral industries, 143-
    151; population change, 162; population
    distribution in 1961 (map), 136; recrea-
    tion, 159-161; regional entities, 177;
    roads, 375; sequent occupance, 131-137;
    soils, 130; tourism, 159-161; vegetation,
    129-130. See also New Quebec and
    Western Quebec.
Quebec Cartier Mining Company, 148
Queen Charlotte Islands, 309
Queen Elizabeth Islands, 356
Queenston, Ont., 221
Quesnel, B.C., 347

RAINBOW LAKES REGION, 291
Rainy River, Ont., 214
Rankin Inlet, N.W.T., 364
Reciprocity Treaty, 46, 49
Recreation, 113-114, 159-161
Red Deer, Alta., 296, 301
Red Fife Wheat, 274
Red Lake, Ont., 201, 220, 247
Red River, Man., 268, 303; settlement,
    273; Valley, 253
Regina, Sask., 65, 257, 267, 271, 293, 294,
    295, 296, 300-302, (map), 302, 373
Regina Plains, 255, 264
regions, geographic, 4; natural, 3; nodal,
    4; single-factor, 3
resource frontier, 43
Riding Mountain, Man., 255
Rimouski, P.Q., 142
Robert's Bank, 343
Rocky Mountains, 20, 251, 255, 257, 308,
    310
Rocky Mountain, Foothills, 251, 255, 278,
    286, 289; Forest, 35; Trench, 310
Rouyn, P.Q., 144, 162

This book is set in 10/11 pt. Palatino, with chapter titles in 24 pt. Perpetua Italics. The paper is 60 lb. Belvedere Opaque Litho.
1 2 3 4 5 6 7 8 9 10 McC 79 78 77 76 75 74 73 72 71 70